AF544865

Fundamentals of Computer Science

Contents

Contents

Contents

Contents

To the Student

Computer Science Fundamentals is your introduction to the fascinating field of computer science. It uses a language-independent approach to teach you programming concepts and problem-solving skills, without assuming any previous programming experience. By using easy-to-understand pseudocode, flowcharts, and other tools, you learn how to design the logic of programs without the complication of language syntax. As you build your understanding, you have opportunities to design and create code using your choice of programming tools.

Fundamental topics such as data types, variables, input, output, control structures, modules, functions, arrays, and files are covered as well as object-oriented concepts, GUI development, and event-driven programming.

In addition to learning essential computer concepts, you will learn the problem-solving and reasoning skills that are the foundation of computer science careers. You will prepare for your next steps in computer science through the selection of appropriate technology, synthesizing data, creating solutions, and evaluating results. You will also learn about positive digital citizenship by researching current laws and regulations and by practicing integrity and respect.

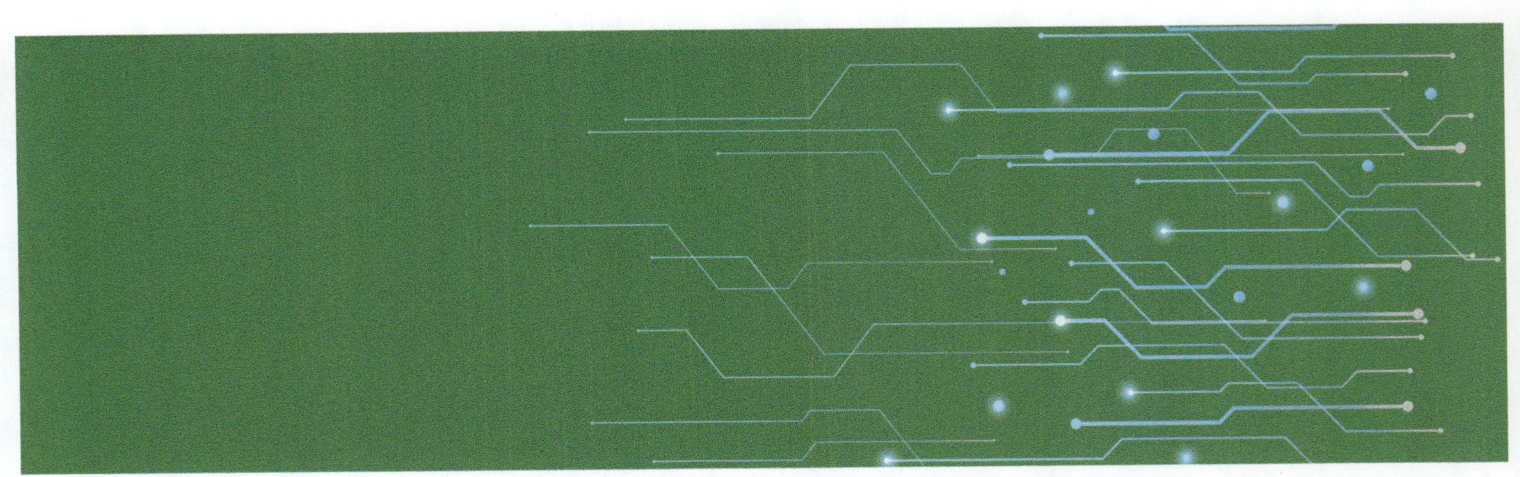

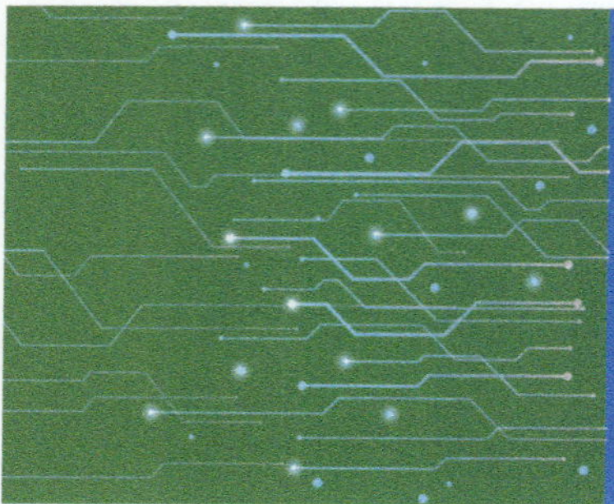

Chapter Overviews

Chapter 1 Getting Started with Computer Systems

Chapter 1 covers basic computer concepts, including hardware, software, programming tools, and using an operating system for file management.

Chapter 2 Understanding Data Processing

Chapter 2 introduces the binary system. You will learn to convert binary to decimal and decimal to binary. You will also learn to represent data using ASCII or Unicode.

Chapter 3 Introduction to Programming Languages

How does a computer know what to do? In Chapter 3, you will learn how a computer can process program code. You will learn about machine code and high-level languages as well as the purpose of interpreters and compilers. You will explore the differences and similarities of common programming languages, and learn how to use a problem-solving process to create algorithms.

Chapter 4 Getting Started with HTML and CSS

HTML and CSS are the fundamental languages for web development, and you don't need any special hardware or software to get started. In Chapter 4 you design and create web pages and websites using HTML and CSS.

Chapter 5 Programming Basics

In Chapter 5 you learn how to design and create programs using pseudocode and flowcharts. You explore input and output, variables, and data types.

Chapter 6 Introduction to Calculations

Chapter 6 introductions mathematical operations You learn how to use math operators and how to convert math formulas to programming statements. You explore common algorithms, and practice designing a program that uses calculations.

Chapter 7 Introduction to Boolean Logic and Decision Statements

In this chapter, you learn the importance of Boolean logic in programming. You use conditional statements, logical operators, Boolean variables, and decision structures to design and build algorithms and programs.

Chapter 8 Getting Started with Loop Statements

In Chapter 8, you learn about repetitive structures in the form of loop statements. Loops help you incorporate repetition into a program without having to write the same code over and over. You learn about condition-controlled loops, like while, and do-while, as well as count-controlled loops and the for statement.

Chapter 9 Introduction to Modules and Functions

In this chapter you explore modules and functions. You learn how to use local variables and global variables and constants. You put this information to work by designing a program to generate random numbers.

Chapter Overviews

Chapter 10 Understanding Input Validation

A program's output is only as good as the input it receives. In Chapter 10, you learn the importance of valid input for security and quality. You also learn how to design an input validation loop to control the input users can enter.

Chapter 11 Arrays

Chapter 11 covers arrays, which are called lists in some programs. You learn the basics of working wit arrays, including how to search an array and how to process the contents of an array.

Chapter 12 Testing and Debugging Your Code

In this chapter you learn about common coding errors, including logic, runtime, and syntax. You learn how to find errors and fix them, and how to avoid them. You also learn about exception handling.

Chapter 13 Getting Started with Object-Oriented Programming

In this chapter you learn the difference between procedural and object-oriented programming. You also learn how to use classes and instances in object-oriented programming, as well as the concepts of inheritance and polymorphism

Chapter 14 Getting Started with GUI Applications

Chapter 14 introduces you to graphical user interfaces and how to design a GUI for an application. You also learn some key differences between designing apps for mobile devices.

Chapter 15 Preparing for a Career in Computer Science

In this chapter you will explore computer science careers. You will learn how to plan for a computer science career while in school and how to develop the skills you will need to succeed in your chosen career.

Chapter 16 Digital Citizenship

In Chapter 16, you learn how technology can pose legal and ethical challenges to individuals and to society. You learn how you can prevent cybercrime and maintain digital privacy, and what role you have in making sure technology is safe and accessible to all.

Chapter 17 Focus on Python

While the concepts are the same, there are differences in how to apply them in each programming language. In Chapter 17, you explore concepts and terminology for working with Python.

Chapter 18 Focus on Java

In Chapter 18, you learn how to apply the programming concepts you have learned while working with the Java programming language.

Chapter 19 Focus on C++

In Chapter 19, you learn how to apply the programming concepts you have learned while working with C++.

Chapter Overviews

Appendix A ASCII Character Set with Decimal and Binary Codes

Appendix A lists the decimal and binary codes for the ASCII character set for easy reference.

Appendix B Flowchart Symbols

Appendix B identifies the flowchart symbols used in this text.

Appendix C Pseudocode Reference

Appendix C provides a reference to the pseudocode conventions used in this text.

Appendix D Keywords for Python, C++, and Java

Appendix D provides a list of the words that are reserved and cannot be used as a variable name, function name, or an identifier in a Python, Java, or C++ program.

Appendix E Installing Python or OpenJDK

In order to work with programs in Python or Java, you must download and install the required software. Appendix E provides instructions for downloading and installing Python or OpenJDK for Java on your computer system. It also provides installation instructions for NetBeans, an IDE for Java programming.

Appendix F Introduction to IDLE

Appendix F introduces the IDLE integrated development environment that comes with Python. You will learn how to start IDLE and then create, save, and run a program. You will also learn about some of the benefits of using IDLE.

Appendix G Common Colors, Tags, and Properties for HTML5 and CSS

Appendix G lists more than 100 common HTML tags, over four pages of CSS properties, and a web safe color palette for web page design.

Using Your Text

The text is organized into 19 chapters and seven appendices. Each chapter is organized into sections. Within the text you will find the following features.

Keypoint Each major section of the text starts with a concept statement that summarizes the main point of the section.

Program 1-1 **Programs** Within each chapter, concepts and coding skills are illustrated with complete and partial example programs, each designed to highlight the current topic. Pseudocode, flowcharts, and other design tools are used in the example programs.

Chapter Overviews

Program Files This icon means that a Java or Python code file for the program is available for download.

In the Spotlight *In the Spotlight* case studies provide detailed, step-by-step analysis of problems. These case studies provide the opportunity for you to test your knowledge and skills by working through the problem on your own or with a partner, before viewing the solution provided in the text.

VideoNotes A VideoNotes icons indicates a video about the current topic is available for download.

Notes Notes appear throughout the text. They are short explanations of interesting or often misunderstood points relevant to the current topic.

Tips Tips advise you on the best techniques for approaching different programming problems.

Warnings Warnings caution you about programming techniques or practices that can lead to malfunctioning programs or lost data.

Checkpoints Checkpoints are questions at the end of each main section in each chapter. They are designed to reinforce concepts from the section.

Chapter Review Each chapter includes a set of review questions and exercises. They include Multiple Choice, True/ False, and Short Answer.

Exercises Each chapter offers a pool of exercises designed to reinforce your knowledge of the chapter topics. Some exercises let you work alone or with others to research and report on related topics, while Programming Exercises give you the opportunity to practice your coding skills. Many chapters also include Algorithm Workbench and Debugging exercises, for using algorithms and problem-solving to analyze and solve programming problems.

Getting Started with Computer Systems

TOPICS

Introduction to Computer Science

Computer science is the study of computers and computing.

A computer is a machine that processes information. Computers come in all shapes and sizes, from massive computational mainframes to small devices like smartphones and tablets. The physical parts of a computer are called **hardware**. Hardware includes the screen, mouse, and keyboard, as well as the processing and storage devices.

How do people use computers? Students write papers, conduct research, and participate in online classes. At work, people analyze data, make presentations, conduct business transactions, communicate with customers and coworkers, control machines in manufacturing facilities, and much more. At home, people pay bills, shop online, communicate with friends and family, and play games. And don't forget all the smart devices that connect to the internet, like televisions, audio speakers, lights, automobiles, and doorbells.

Computers can perform such a wide variety of tasks because they can be programmed. This means that computers are not designed to do just one job, but to do any job that their programs tell them to do. A **program** is a set of instructions that a computer follows to perform a task. For example, Figure 1-1 shows screens using Microsoft Word and PowerPoint, two commonly used programs.

Programs are **software**. Software is essential because it controls everything the computer does. All of the software that we use to make our computers useful is created by individuals working in the field of computer science as programmers or software developers. A **programmer**, or **software developer**, is a person with the training and skills necessary to design, create, and test computer programs.

Figure 1-1 A word processing program and a presentation program

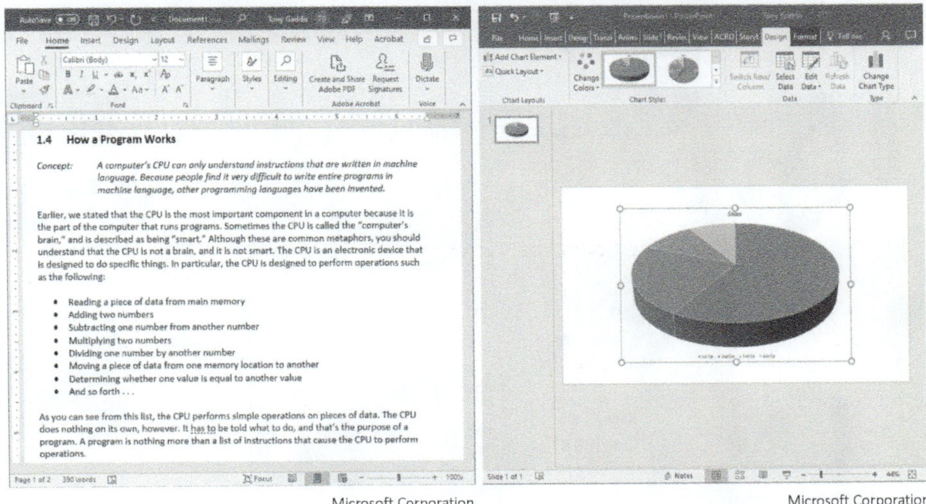

Microsoft Corporation Microsoft Corporation

Computer science is the study of computers and computing. It covers a wide range of topics including how computer hardware works to how networks enable devices to connect and communicate. By studying computer science, you can learn how to design, create, improve, repair, and use computer systems. This book introduces you to the fundamental concepts of computer science with a focus on computer programming.

Before we begin exploring the concepts of programming, you need to understand a few basic things about computers and how they work. This chapter will build a solid foundation of knowledge that you will continually rely on as you study computer science. First, we will discuss the physical components that computers are commonly made of. Next, we will look at how computers store data and execute programs. Finally, we will discuss the major types of software that computers use.

1.2 Hardware Basics

The physical devices of which a computer is made are referred to as the computer's hardware.

Hardware

The term hardware refers to all of the physical devices, or **components**, of which a computer is made. A computer is not one single device, but a system of devices that all work together. Like the different instruments in a symphony orchestra, each device in a computer plays its own part.

If you have ever shopped for a computer, you've probably seen sales literature listing components such as microprocessors, random-access memory, and graphics cards, which are found inside the case. It might also list **peripheral** devices, such as video displays, keyboards, and printers, which are found outside the case. As shown in Figure 1-2, a typical computer system consists of the following major components:

- The central processing unit (CPU)
- Primary memory

Figure 1-2 Typical components of a computer system

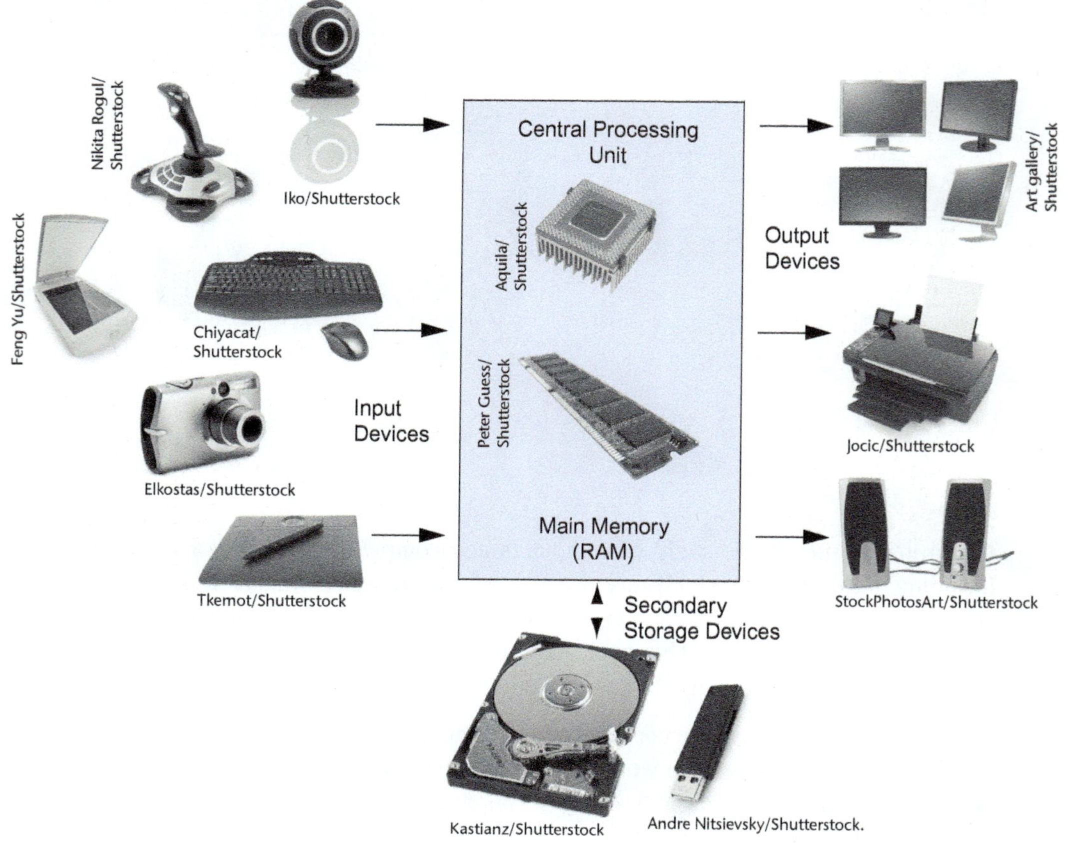

- Secondary memory (storage devices)
- Input devices
- Output devices

Let's take a closer look at each of these components.

The CPU

When a computer is **processing**, or performing the tasks that a program tells it to do, we say that the computer is **running** or **executing** the program. The **central processing unit (CPU)**, is the part of a computer that actually runs programs. The CPU is the most important component in a computer because without it, the computer could not run software.

In the earliest computers, CPUs were huge devices made of electrical and mechanical components such as vacuum tubes and switches. Figure 1-3 shows such a device. The two people in the photo are working with the historic ENIAC computer. The ENIAC, which is considered by many to be the world's first programmable electronic computer, was built in 1945 to calculate artillery ballistic tables for the U.S. Army. This machine, which was primarily one big CPU, was 8 feet tall, 100 feet long, and weighed 30 tons.

Figure 1-3 The ENIAC computer

US Army Center of Military History

Figure 1-4 A lab technician holds a microprocessor

Creativa/Shutterstock

Today, CPUs are small chips known as **microprocessors**. Figure 1-4 shows a photo of a lab technician holding a modern microprocessor. In addition to being much smaller than the old electromechanical CPUs in early computers, microprocessors are also much more powerful.

Primary Memory

Primary memory, or **main memory**, is the computer's work area. It is also called primary storage. This is where the computer stores a program while the program is running, as well as the data that the program is working with. For example, suppose you are using a word processing program to write an essay for one of your classes. While you do this, both the word processing program and the essay are stored in main memory.

One type of primary memory is called **random-access memory (RAM)**. It is called this because the CPU is able to quickly access data stored at any random location in RAM. RAM is usually a **volatile** type of memory that is used only for temporary storage while a program is running.

Figure 1-5 Memory chips

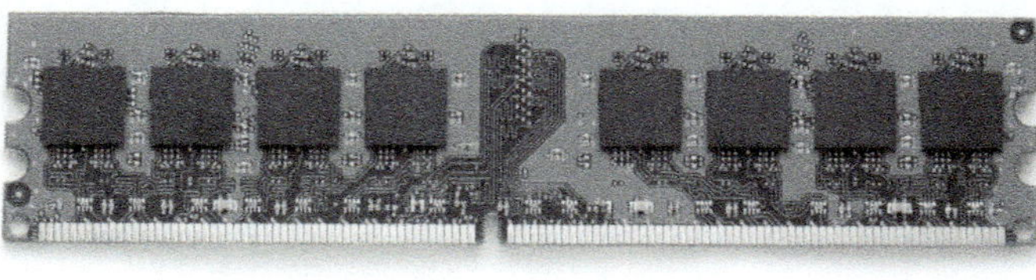

Garsya/Shutterstock

When the computer is turned off, the contents of RAM are erased. Inside your computer, RAM is stored in chips, similar to the ones shown in Figure 1-5.

Another type of primary memory is called **read-only memory (ROM)**. ROM chips store instructions for starting the computer. ROM is **nonvolatile** memory. It stores data permanently, even when the power to the computer is off.

Secondary Memory

Secondary memory is a type of memory that can hold data for long periods of time, even when there is no power to the computer. Secondary memory is what most people think of as **storage**, or **secondary storage**. Programs are normally stored in secondary memory and loaded into main memory as needed. Important data, such as word processing documents, payroll data, and inventory records, is saved to secondary storage, as well.

The most common type of secondary storage device is the **disk drive**. A traditional disk drive stores data by magnetically encoding it onto a spinning circular disk. **Solid-state drives** store data in solid-state memory. A solid-state drive has no moving parts and operates faster than a traditional disk drive. Most computers have some sort of secondary storage device, either a traditional disk drive or a solid-state drive, mounted inside their case. Even cell phones have internal storage, and can perform as external storage devices, as well. External storage devices, which connect to one of the computer's communication ports, can be used to create backup copies of important data or to move data to another computer.

In addition to external storage devices, many types of devices have been created for copying data and for moving it to other computers. For example, **USB drives** are small devices that plug into the computer's USB (universal serial bus) port and appear to the system as a disk drive. These drives do not actually contain a disk, however. They store data in a special type of memory known as **flash memory**. USB drives, which are also known as **memory sticks** and **flash drives**, are inexpensive, reliable, and small enough to be carried in your pocket.

Cloud storage, or **online storage**, is storage space on a network **server** at a remote location. You use a software application program to upload and download files to the server over a network. Examples of cloud storage are Google Drive, Microsoft OneDrive, and Apple iCloud.

Input Devices

Input is any data the computer collects from people and from other devices. The component, or peripheral device, that collects the data and sends it to the computer is called an **input device**. You use common input devices such as a keyboard, mouse, touchscreen, scanner, microphone, and digital camera. Disk drives and optical drives can also be considered input devices, because programs and data are retrieved from them and loaded into the computer's memory.

Output Devices

Output is any data the computer produces for people or for other devices. It might be a sales report, a list of names, or a graphic image. The data is sent to a peripheral **output device**, which formats and presents it. You use common output devices such as video displays and printers. Disk drives can also be considered output devices because the system sends data to them in order to be saved.

Checkpoint

1.1 What is a program?

1.2 What is hardware?

1.3 Identify the five major components of a computer system and their functions.

1.4 What part of the computer actually runs programs?

1.5 What type of memory serves as a work area to store a program and its data while the program is running?

1.6 What type of memory holds data even when there is no power to the computer?

1.7 What type of peripheral device collects data from people and from other devices?

1.8 What type of peripheral device formats and presents data for people or other devices?

1.3 Software Basics

The programs that run on a computer are referred to as software.

For a computer to function, it needs software. Everything a computer does, from the time you turn the power switch on until you shut the system down, is under the control of software. There are two general categories of software: **system software**, which are the programs that control and manage the basic operations of the computer, and **application software**, which are the programs that make a computer useful for everyday tasks. Most computer programs clearly fit into one of these two categories. Let's take a closer look at each.

System Software

System software typically includes the operating system, utility programs, and software development tools.

Operating Systems

An **operating system** is the most fundamental set of programs on a computer. The operating system provides the instructions that control the internal operations of the computer's hardware. It manages all of the devices connected to the computer, allows data to be saved to and retrieved from storage devices, and allows other programs to run on the computer.

Popular operating systems for laptop and desktop computers include Windows, macOS, and Linux. Some version of macOS runs all Apple Macintosh computers. Microsoft Windows runs on most non-Apple personal computers. Linux is an open-source operating system, which means the source code used to create it is available to the public. Google's Chrome OS is based on Linux. Popular operating systems for mobile devices include Android and iOS. iOS is used exclusively on Apple mobile devies. Android runs on devices manufactured by many companies. Android is considered to be more open and customizable.

Utility Programs

A **utility program** performs a specialized task that enhances the computer's operation or safeguards data. Examples of utility programs are virus scanners, file compression programs, and data backup programs.

Probably the most important utilities are file managers, which let you work with data stored on your computer. The operating system, programs, and data are all stored in files, each with a name. Files can be grouped together into folders. Folders are also called directories. A folder can be divided into subfolders.

Software Development Tools

Software development tools are the programs that programmers use to create, modify, and test software. These programs may be called **software development applications.** Along with the hardware they run on, they are referred to as a **development environment.** Assemblers, compilers, interpreters, code editors, and debuggers are examples of software development applications.

An **integrated software development environment (IDE)** is a group, or suite, of software development applications that have a common user interface and are designed to work together. Examples of IDEs for progamming include Visual Studio, NetBeans, PyCharm, Replit, and Eclipse.

There are two basic categories of programming and programming tools: procedural and object-oriented. **Procedural programming** uses step-by-step instructions to tell a computer what to do. Procedural programming languages include C, Fortran, Pascal, and Basic. **Object-oriented programming** provides rules for creating and managing **objects**, which are items that include both data and how to process the data. Object-oriented programming languages include Python, Java, Alice, and VBScript. Some programming combines the two. C++ is an example of a **programming language** that uses both procedural and object-oriented programming.

Special programs called **compilers** translate the source code into binary form using only 0s and 1s. The result, called **object code**, can be read and acted on by a computer. Sometimes programs called **interpreters** are used to translate the source code directly into actions, bypassing the need for a compiler. Interpreters are able to immediately follow the instructions in the binary code while compilers must first wait and translate the binary. Even though the compilers take longer to get started, they are able to complete tasks much faster than interpreters.

Some programming languages require the programmer to assign a **data type** to variable data. Some basic, or **primitive**, data types include **string**, which is a sequence of characters that does not contain numbers used for calculations; **numeric**, which is numbers or amounts that are used in calculations; **character**, which is text; **integer** which represents whole numbers; **real**, which is used for numbers with decimal points; and **date**, which is the method of coding dates.

Application Software

Programs that make a computer useful for everyday tasks are known as **application software**. These are the programs that people normally spend most of their time running on their computers. Figure 1-1, at the beginning of this chapter, shows screens from two commonly used applications: Microsoft Word, a word processing program, and PowerPoint, a presentation program. Some other examples of application software are spreadsheet programs, email programs, web browsers, and game programs. **App** is an abbreviation for the term **application**. The term app is usually used for programs developed specifically for smartphones, tablet computers, and other handheld devices.

In the past, applications were written to run on a specific operating system. Now, most applications can be used on many operating systems. For example, versions of Microsoft Office applications are available for PCs running Windows, Macs running macOS, mobile devices running iOS, Chromebooks running Chrome OS, and mobile devices running Android OS. In addition, most programs include a Save As command that lets you save files in different formats and an Open command that lets you open files saved in a different format. There are also utility programs that can translate files that previously may have been unreadable so they can be used on devices running a different OS.

Checkpoint

1.9 What fundamental set of programs control the internal operations of the computer's hardware?

1.10 What operating system runs on all Apple Macintosh computers?

1.11 What operating system has a source code that is available to the public?

1.12 What do you call a program that performs a specialized task, such as a virus scanner, a file compression program, or a data backup program?

1.13 Python is an example of what type of programming language?

1.14 Word processing programs, spreadsheet programs, email programs, web browsers, and game programs belong to what category of software?

1.4 File Management Basics

Operating systems have a file manager system utility that you use to manage data stored in files on a computer.

Among the most important system utilities is the file manager, called File Explorer in Windows, Files in Chrome OS, and Finder in macOS. This utility allows you to organize, view, copy, move, rename, and delete files.

Directories and Folders

Most operating systems manage file storage using a multilevel, or **hierarchical**, filing system called a **directory**. At the top is the main storage location, called the **root directory**. Root directories are labeled with letters followed by a colon. On most Windows computers, the root directory is C:, and external hard drives may be D:, E:, and so on. Within the root are subdirectories called folders, which may contain subfolders and files. Figure 1-6 shows an example of hierarchical file system.

Navigating the File System

You navigate through the file system by expanding and collapsing folders to show or hide their contents. You use a **path** to identify the specific location of a folder or file. The path lists each location in the directory hierarchy beginning with the root. Each specific location is separated by a \ character. So, the path C:\Documents\Schoolwork\Report.doc is the storage location for a document file named Report, stored in the Schoolwork subfolder, stored in the Documents folder, in the root directory C:.

Figure 1-6 A hierarchical file system is like the roots of a tree extending out into folders, subfolders, and files.

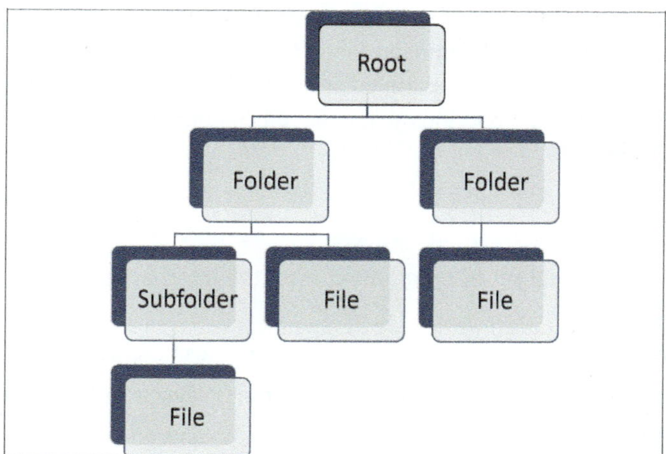

Most operating systems come with some folders already set up. Windows comes with folders set up for each user, including folders for Documents, Pictures, and Downloads. Android devices have a Files or My Files folder with subfolders for Images, Downloads, Audio, Video, and so on.

Use your file manager to identify and change the default storage locations. For example, to find the default Downloads storage location in Windows, open File Explorer, right-click the Downloads folder in the navigation pane on the left of the window, select Properties, and then select the Location tab. The path to the folder displays. For example, the default Downloads storage location for a user named Sam might be C:\Users\Sam\Downloads. The default Documents storage location for the same user might be C:\Users\Sam\Documents.

Naming Files and Folders

When you create a new file or folder, you give it a **file name**. Using descriptive names helps you identify the contents and keep your data organized. For example, the name *Second Semester Grades* is more descriptive than *Grades*. It also helps keep you from accidentally deleting or overwriting files and folders that have the same name. Most operating systems have specific file and folder naming conventions. They usually let you use file and folder names with up to 255 characters, including spaces and punctuation. You cannot use <, >, :, ", /, \, |, ?, or *.

File Type

Operating systems add a period and a file extension to file names. A **file extension** is a short series of letters that indicate the application used to create the file and the **file format**, or **file type**. For example, a Microsoft Word document has the extension .doc or .docx. You can set options to display file types when you view a file list, as shown in Figure 1-7. By default, the operating system uses the program associated with the file type to open the file. So, a file with an .xlsx extension opens in Microsoft Excel and a file with a .pdf extension opens in Adobe Reader or Acrobat.

Cross-Platform Compatibility

Cross-platform compatibility is the ability to use a file on any device no matter what operating system is in use. This is possible because the OS associates files with specific programs, not with an OS. So, a word processing document created with a word processor on a macOS system can be opened on any device running the same word processing application, such as a Windows notebook, iOS tablet, or Android OS phone.

File and Folder Management

You use the file manager in your operating system to create, view, copy, move, rename, and delete files, folders, and subfolders. For example, you can open a file simply by double-clicking it in the file manager window. The operating system stores a lot of information called **metadata** with a file so it can find the file when you need it. For most users, the most important piece of information for identifying files and folders is the name. If you want to remember what a folder contains and what file you need, you should use logical, recognizable names that describe the contents.

Figure 1-7 You can display file types when viewing files with Windows

Desktop › Work in Progress

Name	Type	Size
Current Projects	File folder	
Book Report Compressed.zip	Compressed (zipped) Folder	4,770 KB
IMG_1519.JPG	JPG File	3,888 KB
Data.xlsx	Microsoft Excel Worksheet	7 KB
Book Report Presentation.pptx	Microsoft PowerPoint Presentation	893 KB
New Microsoft Publisher Document.pub	Microsoft Publisher Document	59 KB
Book Report.docx	Microsoft Word Document	14 KB
Book Report Video.mp4	MP4 File	3,760 KB
audiobook.png	PNG File	12 KB

Checkpoint

1.15 What is the file manager called in Chrome OS?

1.16 What is the main storage location in a hierarchical filing system?

1.17 What is the maximum number of characters allowed for a file name in most operating systems?

1.18 What type of file usually has a .docx extension?

1.19 What is metadata?

Chapter Review

Multiple Choice

1. A(n) __________ is a set of instructions that a computer follows to perform a task.
    a. compiler
    b. program
    c. interpreter
    d. programming language

2. The physical devices that a computer is made of are referred to as __________.
    a. hardware
    b. software
    c. the operating system
    d. tools

3. The part of a computer that runs programs is called __________.
    a. RAM
    b. secondary storage
    c. main memory
    d. the CPU

4. Today, CPUs are small chips known as __________.
    a. ENIACs
    b. microprocessors
    c. memory chips
    d. operating systems

5. The computer stores a program while the program is running, as well as the data that the program is working with, in __________.
    a. secondary memory
    b. the CPU
    c. main memory
    d. the microprocessor

6. This is a volatile type of memory that is used only for temporary storage while a program is running.
    a. RAM
    b. secondary storage
    c. the disk drive
    d. the USB drive

7. A type of memory that can hold data for long periods of time, even when there is no power to the computer, is called __________.
   a. RAM
   b. secondary memory
   c. secondary storage
   d. CPU storage

8. A peripheral that collects data from people or other devices and sends it to the computer is called __________.
   a. an output device
   b. an input device
   c. a secondary storage device
   d. main memory

9. A video display is a(n) __________ device.
   a. output
   b. input
   c. secondary storage
   d. main memory

10. A __________ is a secondary storage device with no moving parts.
   a. solid-state drive
   b. magnetic disk drive
   c. CD drive
   d. DVD drive

11. __________ is nonvolatile primary memory.
   a. RAM
   b. CPU
   c. compiler
   d. ROM

12. __________ is secondary storage on a network server.
   a. Flash storage
   b. Cloud storage
   c. Peripheral storage
   d. RAM

13. __________ is an operating system for mobile devices.
   a. iOS
   b. Windows
   c. Linux
   d. MacOS

14. __________ is an operating system based on Linux.
    a. Windows
    b. Chrome
    c. iOS
    d. MacOs

15. An example of a system utility is __________.
    a. word processing
    b. spreadsheet
    c. procedural
    d. antivirus program

16. The type of programming that uses step-by-step instructions to tell a computer what to do is __________.
    a. object-oriented
    b. procedural
    c. VBScript
    d. Python

17. Programs used for every day tasks are called __________.
    a. utilities
    b. debuggers
    c. applications
    d. viruses

18. Spreadsheet programs, email programs, web browsers, and game programs are examples of __________.
    a. utilities
    b. file managers
    c. operating systems
    d. applications

19. The term __________ is usually used for programs developed specifically for smartphones, tablet computers, and other handheld devices.
    a. files
    b. apps
    c. macs
    d. docs

20. The system utility that lets you copy a file from one storage device to another is called a __________.
    a. scanner
    b. copier
    c. file manager
    d. decoder

21. The file manager in macOS is called __________.
    a. Mac Explorer
    b. Finder
    c. File Explorer
    d. Files

22. On Windows computers, the root directory is usually called __________.
    a. A:
    b. B:
    c. C:
    d. D:

23. You cannot use the character __________ in a file name.
    a. 2
    b. c
    c. /
    d. -

24. The file extension for an Adobe Reader file is __________.
    a. pdf
    b. xlsx
    c. pptx
    d. pdfx

25. A file with a .doc file extension will probably open in a(n)__________ application.
    a. spreadsheet
    b. slide manager
    c. word processor
    d. image editing

True or False

1. Today, CPUs are huge devices made of electrical and mechanical components such as vacuum tubes and switches.
2. Volatile primary memory is called RAM.
3. A flash drive is volatile primary memory.
4. A peripheral device is connected inside the computer case.
5. A mouse is an output device.
6. A printer is an output device.
7. An antivirus program is an example of an application.
8. You use a system utility to copy or move files and folders.
9. Microsoft PowerPoint is an example of a software development application.
10. Word processing programs, spreadsheet programs, email programs, web browsers, and games are all examples of utility programs.

Short Answer

1. Identify the function of a CPU.
2. What is the difference between primary and secondary memory?
3. Compare three different operating systems.
4. What is the difference between an operating system and an application program?
5. Choose two input devices and explain how to use them.
6. Choose two output devices and explain how to use them.
7. What is RAM?
8. What is a software development application? Give two examples.
9. Analyze and explain the concept of a primitive variable.

Exercises

1. Working alone or with a partner or small team, examine a computer system to identify the major internal and external hardware components. Look at how the different components are connected. Create a five-column chart to record your observations. In the first column, list all the hardware components that you can identify, including primary and secondary memory, storage, the CPU, and peripheral devices. Include the components you think are inside the computer box. In the remaining columns, state the function of each item and whether it is used for inputting, processing, outputting, or storage. With your teacher's permission, unplug and replug all of the computer components, including external drives, a printer, mouse, keyboard, monitor, projector, and the power supply. Start the system. Use the operating system to locate the system specifications and add them to your column chart. Discuss your findings as a class.

2. Working alone or with a partner or small team, write a one-page report that explains the desktop on your computer to someone who has never used a computer before. Describe each icon, and explain what happens when you click, double-click, or right-click it. Identify files or programs that are represented on the desktop, and explain what they are used for, and what file formats they use. Finally, explain how the desktop helps you manage your work on the computer. Share your report with others.

3. Open a word-processing program. Name and save the new, blank file. Use the keyboard to input the definition of five terms you learned in this chapter. Save the changes to the file and close it. Use the file manager to make a copy of the file on a different storage device, and then delete the original file. Rename the copied file. Discuss the process with a partner, or with the class.

4. With your teacher's permission, use the internet to research two or three computer operating systems. As you work, take notes and keep track of your sources. Evaluate the information you find and only use it if it is accurate, relevant, and valid. Create a column chart comparing and contrasting the operating systems. Share the chart with a partner or with the class.

5. With your teacher's permission, use the internet to research two or three software development applications. As you work, take notes and keep track of your sources. Evaluate the information you find and only use it if it is accurate, relevant, and valid. To demonstrate your knowledge, create a column chart comparing and contrasting types of software development applications. Present the chart to a partner or to the class.

6. With a partner, prepare a demonstration on how to use a computer including input, output, and processing devices, as well as primary and secondary storage. Seek and respond to feedback from peers and your teacher as you develop the demonstration. Practice your demonstration, and when it is ready, deliver it to your class, or to a different class. If possible, make a video of the demonstration, and publish it online.

CHAPTER 2

Understanding Data Processing

TOPICS

2.1 How Computers Store Data

All data that is stored in a computer is converted to sequences of 0s and 1s.

A computer's memory is divided into tiny storage locations known as **bytes**. One byte is only enough memory to store a letter of the alphabet or a small number. In order to do anything meaningful, a computer has to have lots of bytes. Most computers today have millions, or even billions, of bytes of memory.

Each byte is divided into eight smaller storage locations known as bits. The term **bit** stands for **binary digit**. Computer scientists usually think of bits as tiny switches that can be either on or off. Bits aren't actual "switches," however, at least not in the conventional sense. In most computer systems, bits are tiny electrical components that can hold either a positive or a negative charge. Computer scientists think of a positive charge as a switch in the *on* position, and a negative charge as a switch in the off position. Figure 2-1 shows the way that a computer scientist might think of a byte of memory: as a collection of switches that are each flipped to either the on or off position.

Figure 2-1 Think of a byte as eight switches

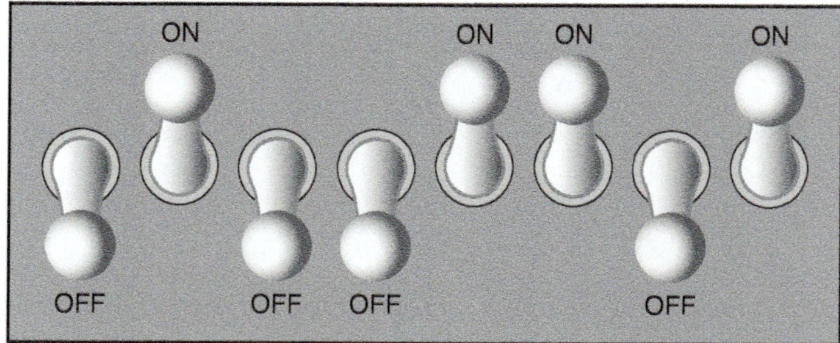

When a piece of data is stored in a byte, the computer sets the eight bits to an on/off pattern that represents the data. For example, the pattern on the left in Figure 2-2 shows how the number 77 would be stored in a byte, and the pattern on the right shows how the letter A would be stored in a byte.

Figure 2-2 Bit patterns for the number 77 and the letter A

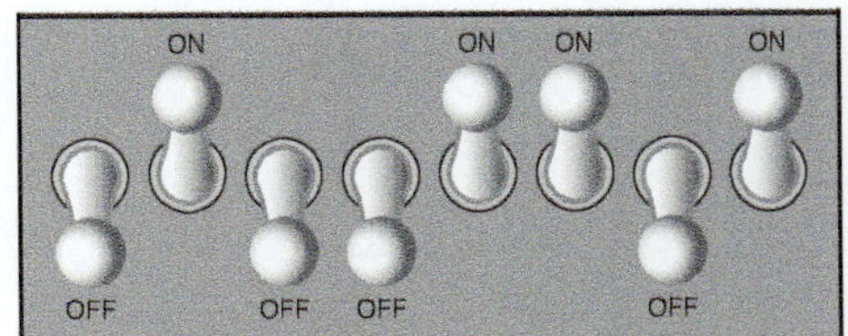

The number 77 stored in a byte.

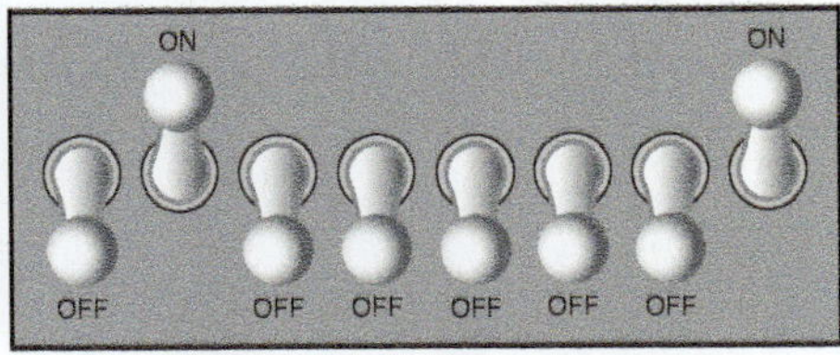

The letter A stored in a byte.

Storing Numbers

A bit can be used in a very limited way to represent numbers. Depending on whether the bit is turned on or off, it can represent one of two different values. In computer systems, a bit that is turned off represents the number 0, and a bit that is turned on represents the number 1. This corresponds perfectly to the **binary numbering system**. In the binary numbering system (or **binary**, as it is usually called), all numeric values are written as sequences of 0s and 1s. Here is an example of a number that is written in binary:

10011101

The position of each digit in a binary number has a value assigned to it. Starting with the rightmost digit and moving left, the position values are 2^0, 2^1, 2^2, 2^3, and so forth, as shown in Figure 2-3. Figure 2-4 shows the same diagram with the position values calculated. Starting with the rightmost digit and moving left, the position values are 1, 2, 4, 8, and so forth.

Figure 2-3 The values of binary digits as powers of 2

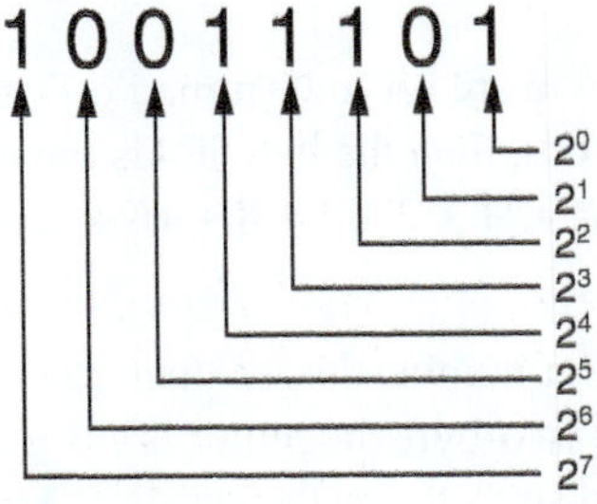

Figure 2-4 The values of binary digits

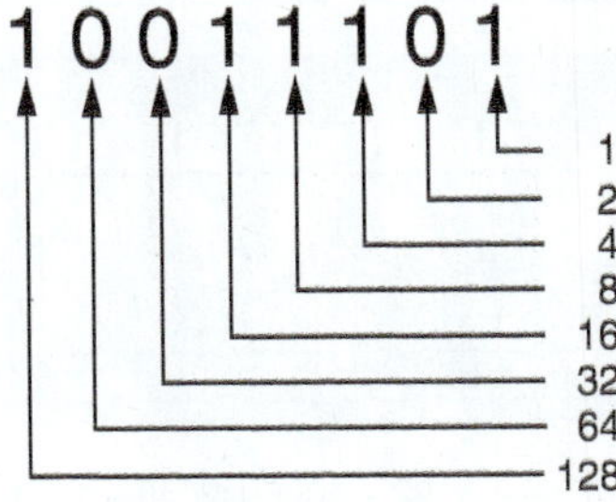

To determine the value of a binary number, you simply add up the position values of all the 1s. For example, in the binary number 10011101, the position values of the 1s are 1, 4, 8, 16, and 128. This is shown in Figure 2-5. The sum of all of these position values is 157. So, the value of the binary number 10011101 is 157.

Figure 2-5 Determining the value of 10011101

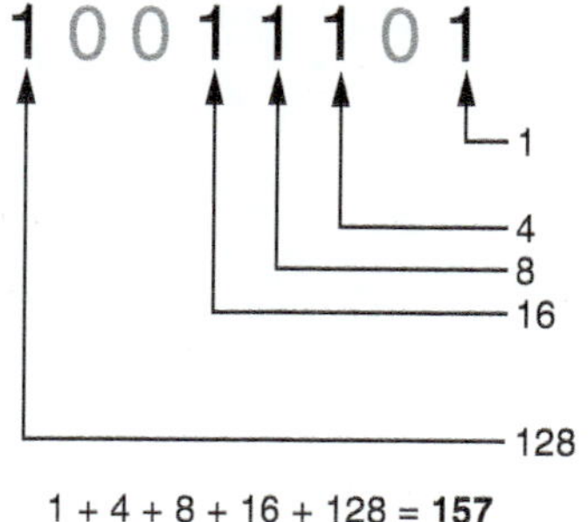

Figure 2-6 shows how you can picture the number 157 stored in a byte of memory. Each 1 is represented by a bit in the on position, and each 0 is represented by a bit in the off position.

Figure 2-6 The bit pattern for 157

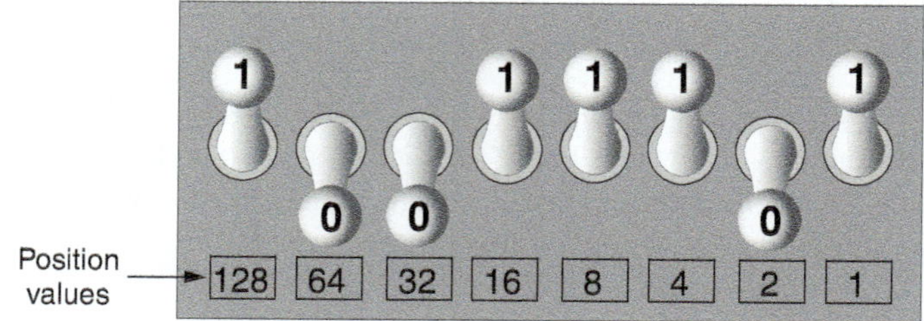

When all of the bits in a byte are set to 0 (turned off), then the value of the byte is 0. When all of the bits in a byte are set to 1 (turned on), then the byte holds the largest value that can be stored in it. The largest value that can be stored in a byte is 1 + 2 + 4 + 8 + 16 + 32 + 64 + 128 = 255. This limit exists because there are only eight bits in a byte.

What if you need to store a number larger than 255? The answer is simple: use more than one byte. For example, suppose we put two bytes together. That gives us 16 bits. The position values of those 16 bits would be 2^0, 2^1, 2^2, 2^3, and so forth, up through 2^{15}. As shown in Figure 2-7, the maximum value that can be stored in two bytes is 65,535. If you need to store a number larger than this, then more bytes are necessary.

Figure 2-7 Two bytes used for a large number

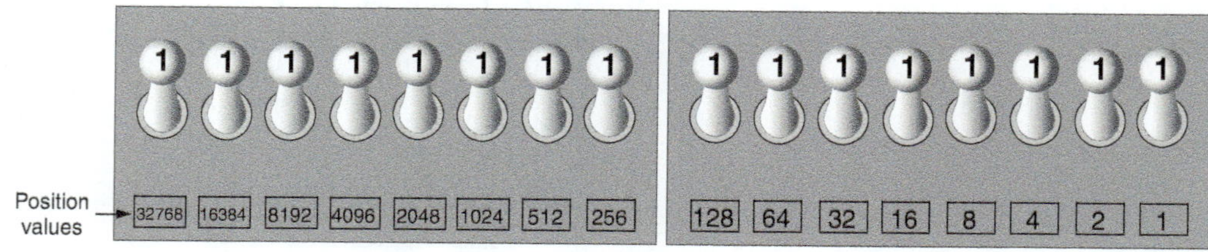

TIP: In case you're feeling overwhelmed by all this, relax! You will not have to actually convert numbers to binary while programming. Knowing that this process is taking place inside the computer will help you as you learn, and in the long term, this knowledge will make you a better programmer.

Storing Characters

Any piece of data that is stored in a computer's memory must be stored as a binary number. That includes nonnumeric characters, such as letters and punctuation marks. When a character is stored in memory, it is first converted to a numeric code. The numeric code is then stored in memory as a binary number.

Over the years, different coding schemes have been developed to represent characters in computer memory. Historically, the most important of these coding schemes is **ASCII**, which stands for the **American Standard Code for Information Interchange**. ASCII is a set of 128 numeric codes that represent the English letters, various punctuation marks, and other characters. For example, the ASCII code for the uppercase letter A is 65. When you type an uppercase A on your computer keyboard, the number 65 is stored in memory (as a binary number, of course). This is shown in Figure 2-8.

Figure 2-8 The letter A is stored in memory as the number 65

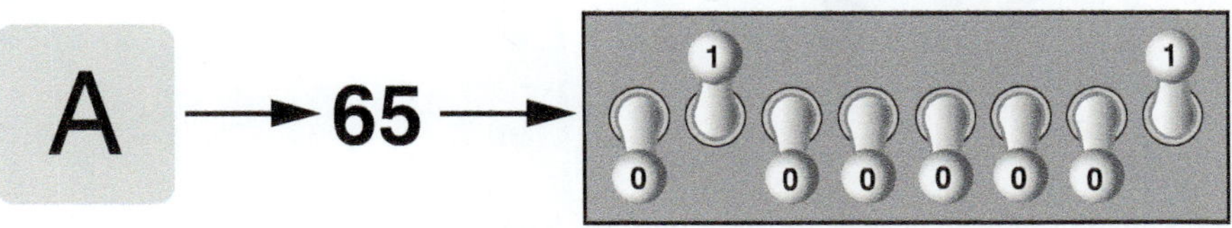

TIP: The acronym ASCII is pronounced "askee."

The ASCII character set was developed in the early 1960s and was eventually adopted by almost all computer manufacturers. ASCII is limited, however, because it defines codes for only 128 characters. To remedy this, the Unicode character set was developed in the early 1990s. **Unicode** is an extensive encoding scheme that is compatible with ASCII, but can also represent characters for many of the languages in the world. Today, Unicode is quickly becoming the standard character set used in the computer industry. Section 2.4 provides more information on working with ASCII and Unicode.

Advanced Number Storage

Earlier, you read about numbers and how they are stored in memory. While reading that section, perhaps it occurred to you that the binary numbering system can be used to represent only integer numbers, beginning with 0. Negative numbers and real numbers (such as 3.14159) cannot be represented using the simple binary numbering technique we discussed.

Computers are able to store negative numbers and real numbers in memory, but to do so, they use encoding schemes along with the binary numbering system. Negative numbers are encoded using a technique known as **two's complement**, and real numbers are encoded in **floating-point notation**. You don't need to know how these encoding schemes work, only that they are used to convert negative numbers and real numbers to binary format.

Other Types of Data

Computers are often referred to as digital devices. The term **digital** can be used to describe anything that uses binary numbers. **Digital data** is data that is stored in binary format, and a **digital device** is any device that works with binary data. In this section, we have discussed how numbers and characters are stored in binary, but computers also work with many other types of digital data.

For example, consider the pictures that you take with your digital camera or mobile phone. These images are composed of tiny dots of color known as **pixels**. (The term pixel stands for **picture element**.) As shown in Figure 2-9, each pixel in an image is converted to a numeric code that represents the pixel's color. The numeric code is stored in memory as a binary number.

Figure 2-9 A digital image is stored in binary format

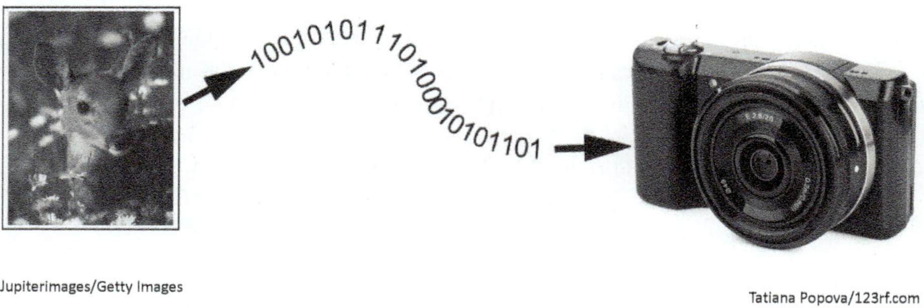

Jupiterimages/Getty Images

Tatiana Popova/123rf.com

The music that you stream or download is also digital. A digital song is broken into small pieces known as samples. Each sample is converted to a binary number, which can be stored in memory. The more samples that a song is divided into, the more it sounds like the original music when it is played back.

NOTE: In programming, data type refers to the way data is classified for use with variables and operations. You learn more about variables and data types in Chapter 5.

Checkpoint

2.1 What amount of memory is enough to store a letter of the alphabet or a small number?

2.2 What do you call a tiny "switch" that can be set to either on or off?

2.3 In what numbering system are all numeric values written as sequences of 0s and 1s?

2.4 What is the purpose of ASCII?

2.5 What encoding scheme is extensive enough to represent the characters of many of the languages in the world?

2.6 What do the terms "digital data" and "digital device" mean?

2.2 Converting Decimal Numbers to Binary

Knowing how to convert from decimal to binary will help you understand the difference between the two numbering systems.

Binary vs. Decimal

While the binary numbering system is base 2, using just 0 and 1, the decimal numbering system is base ten. That means it uses ten digits: 0, 1, 2, 3, 4, 5, 6, 7, 8, and 9. It is easier for people to use decimal numbers, because you need fewer digits to represent a number. For example, 500 in binary is 111110100. A computer does not care how many digits there are in a number; it just needs simple, logical rules, like a two base numbering system where a switch can be either on or off.

As a programmer, when you write a number such as 40 in a program, the computer assumes it is a decimal number. Internally, computer software converts between decimal and binary numbers.

Counting in Binary

How do you count when you only have 1s and 0s? In a decimal system, when you reach 9, you add a place and start again. In binary, you start again when you reach 1. So, starting at zero and counting to 10 in binary looks like this: 0, 1, 10, 11, 100, 101, 110, 111, 1000, 1001, 1010.

Converting from Decimal to Binary

You can convert a decimal number to binary by drawing a simple chart, and then performing repeated subtraction. The following steps show how to convert the decimal number 162 to binary.

1. Make a two-row chart. The top row should list all of the numbers that are powers of two, up to but not greater than the number you are trying to convert. (Powers of two are $2^0 = 1$, $2^1 = 2$, $2^2 = 4$, $2^3 = 8$, and so forth.) The numbers should be listed from right to left.

   To convert the decimal number 162 to binary, you would make the following chart. (The chart stops at 128 because the next power of two would be 256, which is greater than the number we are trying to convert.)

128	64	32	16	8	4	2	1

2. Find the greatest number in the chart (in this case it is 128), and write a 1 below it in the second row. Then, subtract the greatest number in the chart from the number you are trying to convert. In this problem, the result is 34. This is your new number. Your workspace should look something like this:

128	64	32	16	8	4	2	1
1							

$$\begin{array}{r} 162 \\ -\underline{128} \\ 34 \end{array}$$

3. Find the greatest number in the chart that is not greater than the new number you calculated in Step 2. In this problem, we are looking for the greatest number that is not greater than 34. The number we are looking for is 32. Write a 1 below that number in the second row. Then, subtract this new "greatest number" from the number you are currently working with. In this problem, the result is 2. This is your new number. Your workspace should look something like this:

128	64	32	16	8	4	2	1
1		1					

$$\begin{array}{r} 162 \\ -\underline{128} \\ 34 \\ -\underline{32} \\ 2 \end{array}$$

4. Find the greatest number in the chart that is not greater than the new number you calculated in Step 3. In this problem, we are looking for the greatest number that is not greater than 2. The number we are looking for is 2. Write a 1 below that number in the second row. Then, subtract this new "greatest number" from the number you are currently working with. In this problem, the result is 0. This is your new number. Your workspace should look something like this:

128	64	32	16	8	4	2	1
1		1				1	

$$\begin{array}{r} 162 \\ -\underline{128} \\ 34 \\ -\underline{32} \\ 2 \\ -\underline{2} \\ 0 \end{array}$$

5. When you reach 0 as your new value, you have converted the number. Go back to the chart and write a 0 in each empty slot in the second row. Your chart should look like this:

128	64	32	16	8	4	2	1
1	0	1	0	0	0	1	0

The second row now shows the binary number that is equivalent to 162: 10100010

Checkpoint

2.6 What base is the binary numbering system?

2.7 What base is the decimal numbering system?

2.8 What mathematical operation do you use to convert decimal numbers to binary?

2.3 Converting Binary Numbers to Decimal

To easily read large binary numbers, convert them to decimal.

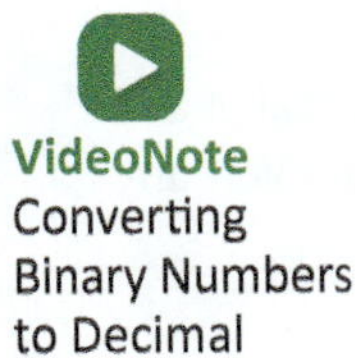

VideoNote
Converting Binary Numbers to Decimal

Now that you understand how to convert a decimal number to binary, you can reverse the process and convert a binary number to a decimal number. This might come in handy if you encounter a large binary number. It will be much easier to read if you convert it to decimal.

The following steps show how to convert the binary number 1011 to its equivalent decimal number.

1. Draw a two-row, eight-column chart similar to the one you used in the previous section. For very large binary numbers, you will need more columns, but eight columns is a good place to start. Place the binary number you want to convert in the bottom row, listed from right to left.

   To convert the binary number 1011, your chart should look like this:

				1	0	1	1

2. In the top row, place the decimals numbers that are powers of two of the numbers you are going to convert. Begin by placing the first number in the top-right block, then work from right to left. As a reminder, the powers of two are: $2^0 = 1$, $2^1 = 2$, $2^2 = 4$, $2^3 = 8$, $2^4 = 16$, $2^5 = 32$, and so on.

   Your chart should look like this:

				8	4	2	1
				1	0	1	1

3. To determine the equivalent decimal number, add together all the top row numbers that have a 1 in the row below them.

   $8 + 2 + 1 = 11$

4. The total is the equivalent decimal number:
   The binary number 1011 = the decimal number 11

Checkpoint

2.9 Why might you need to convert a binary number to decimal?

2.10 What do you place in the top row of your conversion chart?

2.11 What numbers do you add in the top row to get the equivalent decimal number of the binary number in the bottom row?

2.4 Representing Data using ASCII or Unicode

For a computer to understand alphanumeric characters, it converts ASCII or Unicode to binary.

Using the ASCII Standard

The ASCII standard is an arbitrary decimal numeric code assigned to each letter in the English alphabet and to other symbols, such as punctuation marks. Once you have the ASCII decimal code, you can convert any alphanumeric character to a binary representation.

The table below is a list of standard ASCII codes that represent a corresponding character.

Character	Code	Character	Code	Character	Code
!	33	A	65	a	97
"	34	B	66	b	98
#	35	C	67	c	99
$	36	D	68	d	100
%	37	E	69	e	101
&	38	F	70	f	102
'	39	G	71	g	103
(	40	H	72	h	104
)	41	I	73	i	105
*	42	J	74	j	106
+	43	K	75	k	107
,	44	L	76	l	108
-	45	M	77	m	109
.	46	N	78	n	110
/	47	O	79	o	111
0	48	P	80	p	112
1	49	Q	81	q	113
2	50	R	82	r	114
3	51	S	83	s	115
4	52	T	84	t	116
5	53	U	85	u	117
6	54	V	86	v	118
7	55	W	87	w	119
8	56	X	88	x	120
9	57	Y	89	y	121
:	58	Z	90	z	122
;	59	[	91	{	123
<	60	\	92	|	124
=	61	]	93	}	125
>	62	^	94	~	126
?	63	_	95	DEL	127
@	64	`	96		

Because the ASCII codes are decimal, you can convert them to binary. The table below adds a column to the ASCII table to show the corresponding binary value. The binary value is what the computer will ultimately understand.

Character	Decimal Code	Binary Code	Character	Decimal Code	Binary Code	Character	Decimal Code	Binary Code
!	33	100001	A	65	1000001	a	97	1100001
"	34	100010	B	66	1000010	b	98	1100010
#	35	100011	C	67	1000011	c	99	1100011
$	36	100100	D	68	1000100	d	100	1100100
%	37	100101	E	69	1000101	e	101	1100101
&	38	100110	F	70	1000110	f	102	1100110
'	39	100111	G	71	1000111	g	103	1100111
(	40	101000	H	72	1001000	h	104	1101000
)	41	101001	I	73	1001001	i	105	1101001
*	42	101010	J	74	1001010	j	106	1101010
+	43	101011	K	75	1001011	k	107	1101011
,	44	101100	L	76	1001100	l	108	1101100
-	45	101101	M	77	1001101	m	109	1101101
.	46	101110	N	78	1001110	n	110	1101110
/	47	101111	O	79	1001111	o	111	1101111
0	48	110000	P	80	1010000	p	112	1110000
1	49	110001	Q	81	1010001	q	113	1110001
2	50	110010	R	82	1010010	r	114	1110010
3	51	110011	S	83	1010011	s	115	1110011
4	52	110100	T	84	1010100	t	116	1110100
5	53	110101	U	85	1010101	u	117	1110101
6	54	110110	V	86	1010110	v	118	1110110
7	55	110111	W	87	1010111	w	119	1110111
8	56	111000	X	88	1011000	x	120	1111000
9	57	111001	Y	89	1011001	y	121	1111001
:	58	111010	Z	90	1011010	z	122	1111010
;	59	111011	[	91	1011011	{	123	1111011
<	60	111100	\	92	1011100	|	124	1111100
=	61	111101	]	93	1011101	}	125	1111101
>	62	111110	^	94	1011110	~	126	1111110
?	63	111111	_	95	1011111	DEL	127	1111111
@	64	1000000	`	96	1100000			

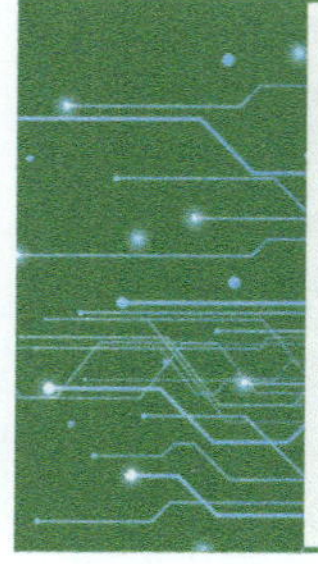

In the Spotlight:

Using a code to represent something else is actually a practice you do all the time. Consider the symbol '4.' If you have a shopping list that says 4 apples, you know to put four apples in your shopping cart. You recognize that the symbol '4' represents four items. The symbol itself has no meaning, but it is a standard symbol that represents four items in our counting system.

TIP: While it is not necessary to memorize the ASCII table, it is helpful to notice the sequential numeric pattern. For instance, the letter A = 65, followed by B = 66, C = 67, and so on. The lowercase letters also have a sequential pattern of ASCII code values beginning with a = 97, b = 98, c = 99, and so on.

Using the Unicode Standard

ASCII represents 128 different alphanumeric characters of the English language. Unicode is a newer encoding standard developed in 1991. Like ASCII, Unicode assigns a unique decimal value to each character. The decimal value can then be converted to binary.

Unicode includes the 128 characters in the ASCII character set, as well as letters and symbols for other major languages such as Greek, Arabic, Urdu, and Hindu. It also includes emojis and math symbols. In Unicode version 15.0, there are nearly 150,000 unique symbols and codes. Unicode continues to evolve, adding new characters with each release.

Appendix A includes a table with ASCII codes, which align with the first 128 Unicode symbols. You can search online for a Unicode table to learn more about the Unicode standard.

Checkpoint

2.12 How many characters are represented by the ASCII standard?

2.13 Identify the ASCII code for a lowercase k character.

2.14 What is the difference between ASCII and Unicode?

2.15 Identify the binary equivalent of the Unicode code for an uppercase Q character.

Chapter Review

Multiple Choice

1. Each byte is divided into eight smaller storage locations known as __________.
   a. bots
   b. bats
   c. bits
   d. bets

2. Computer scientists think of a positive charge as a switch in the ___________ position.
   a. on
   b. off
   c. go
   d. stop

3. Computer scientists think of a negative charge as a switch in the ___________ position.
   a. on
   b. off
   c. go
   d. stop

4. In computer systems, a bit that is turned off represents the number 0, and a bit that is turned on represents the number ______________.
   a. 1
   b. 10
   c. 100
   d. 1,000

5. The rightmost digit in a binary number has a position value of__________.
   a. 2^3
   b. 2^0
   c. 21
   d. 22

6. What is the value of a byte when all of the bits are set to 0?
   a. 0
   b. 1
   c. 8
   d. 10

7. What is the largest value that can be stored in a byte?
   a. 1
   b. 8
   c. 155
   d. 255

8. ASCII defines codes for how many characters?
   a. 78
   b. 128
   c. 278
   d. 328

9. Computers encode negative numbers using a technique known as ___________.
   a. ten's complement
   b. one's complement
   c. five's complement
   d. two's complement

10. Each pixel in an image is converted to a numeric code that represents its ________.
   a. size
   b. color
   c. position
   d. name

True or False

1. 12002001 is an example of a binary number.
2. Any piece of data that is stored in a computer's memory must be stored as a binary number.
3. The binary number system is base 2.
4. The decimal numbering system is base ten.
5. The binary system uses fewer digits to represent a number than the decimal system.
6. Unicode has the same number of codes as ASCII.
7. ASCII codes are binary.
8. ASCII includes codes for punctuation marks.

Short Answer

1. Explain the relationship between bits and bytes.
2. Why do computer scientists think of bits as switches that can be off or on?
3. Compare a binary numbering system with a decimal numbering system.
4. Explain what you would do if you need a to store a number larger than 255 while using a binary numbering system.
5. Explain the difference between ASCII and Unicode?
6. What is 20 in the binary numbering system?

Exercises

1. Convert binary number 1011101 to its decimal equivalent.
    1. Create a chart with two rows and eight columns.
    2. Working from right to left, place the binary number in the bottom row.
    3. Working from right to left, place the decimal numbers that are powers of two in the top row.
    4. Add the values of the top row that have a 1 in the row below it.
    5. Your solution should look like this:

	64	32	16	8	4	2	1
	1	0	1	1	1	0	1

2. Convert the decimal number 54 to its binary equivalent.
    1. Create a chart with two rows and eight columns.
    2. Working from right to left, place the decimal numbers that are a power of two in the top row. (1, 2, 4, 8, 16, 32, 64, 128)
    3. Perform the steps to fill in the 1's in the bottom row.
    4. When your remainder is 0, you are finished identifying the 1's.
    5. Fill in all empty blocks on the bottom row with a 0.

    Your workspace to find the solution should look similar to the following

128	64	32	16	8	4	2	1
0	0	1	1	0	1	1	0

Start here → 54 − 32 = 22 → 22 − 16 = 6 → 8> 6 so skip → 6 − 4 = 2 → 2 − 2 = 0

3. Using the ASCII table, identify the ASCII code assigned to the uppercase letter A.
4. Using the ASCII table, identify the binary code for an exclamation point.
5. With a partner or a small team, write a sentence in ASCII. Exchange coded sentences with another team. Decode the other team's sentence.
6. Try writing a two- or three-word phrase in binary. Then, exchange your work with a partner, and see if you can convert it so you can read what it says.
7. With a partner, make a chart counting from 1 to 50 in decimal and in binary.

3 Introduction to Programming Languages

TOPICS

3.1 Communicating with a Machine

No matter how complex a computer's tasks might be, they are all based on instructions made up of 1s and 0s.

The computers widely used today are digital machines. Each piece of information used in the computer is identified by a distinct number. As a result, the computer acts on each piece of data by comparing its value to the value of other data or by performing a mathematical operation on it.

How does a computer know what to do with data? Software gives it the instructions it needs. Experts called **programmers** write the instructions that become software. Programmers write these instructions, called **source code**, using a programming language.

Recall that computers break data into pieces called bits and give each bit a value of either 0 or 1. A byte is a group of bits—usually 8. Using 8 bits in different combinations, each byte can represent a different value. For example, one byte might be 00000000, another might be 01010101, and another might be 00110011.

Earlier, we stated that the CPU is the most important component in a computer because it is the part of the computer that runs programs. Sometimes the CPU is called the "computer's brain" and is described as being "smart." Although these are common metaphors, you should understand that the CPU is not a brain, and it is not smart. The CPU is an electronic device that is designed to do specific things. In particular, the CPU is designed to perform operations such as the following:

- Reading a piece of data from main memory
- Adding two numbers
- Subtracting one number from another number
- Multiplying two numbers
- Dividing one number by another number
- Moving a piece of data from one memory location to another
- Determining whether one value is equal to another value

As you can see from this list, the CPU performs simple operations on pieces of data. The CPU does nothing on its own, however. It has to be told what to do, and that's the purpose of a program. A program is nothing more than a list of instructions that cause the CPU to perform operations.

Each instruction in a program is a command that tells the CPU to perform a specific operation. Here's an example of an instruction that might appear in a program:

```
10110000
```

To you and me, this is only a series of 0s and 1s. To a CPU, however, this is an instruction to perform an operation. It is written in 0s and 1s because CPUs only understand instructions that are written in **machine language**, and machine language instructions always have an underlying binary structure.

A machine language instruction exists for each operation that a CPU is capable of performing. For example, there is an instruction for adding numbers, there is an instruction for subtracting one number from another, and so forth. The entire set of instructions that a CPU can execute is known as the CPU's **instruction set.**

The machine language instruction `10110000` is an example of only one instruction. It takes a lot more than one instruction, however, for the computer to do anything meaningful. Because the operations that a CPU knows how to perform are so basic in nature, a meaningful task can be accomplished only if the CPU performs many operations. For example, if you want your computer to calculate how many hours you must babysit to earn enough money to buy a new pair of shoes, the CPU will have to perform a large number of instructions, carried out in the proper sequence. It is not unusual for a program to contain thousands or even millions of machine language instructions.

Checkpoint

3.1 How does a computer know what to do with a piece of data?

3.2 What does binary mean?

3.3 What is a program?

3.4 a CPU understands instructions that are written only in what language?

3.2 How a Program Works

Because people find it very difficult to write entire programs in machine language, other programming languages have been invented.

Programs may be stored on a secondary storage device such as a disk drive, or they may be stored on a network server. When you install a program on your computer, the program is typically downloaded from a website or installed from an online app store.

Although a program can be stored on a secondary storage device or on a server, it has to be copied into main memory, or RAM, each time the CPU executes it. For example, suppose you have a word processing program on your computer's disk. To execute the program, you use the mouse to double-click the program's icon. This causes the program to be copied from the disk into main memory. Then, the computer's CPU executes the copy of the program that is in main memory. This process is illustrated in Figure 3-1.

Figure 3-1 A program is copied into main memory and then executed

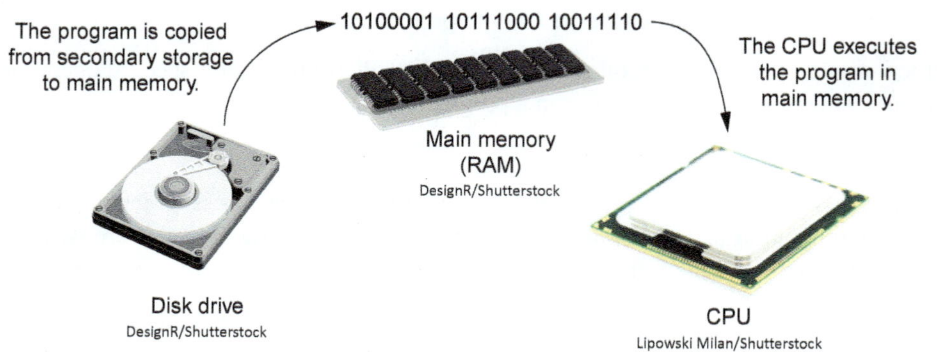

When a CPU executes the instructions in a program, it is engaged in a process that is known as the **fetch-decode-execute cycle**. This cycle, which consists of three steps, is repeated for each instruction in the program. The steps are:

1. **Fetch.** A program is a long sequence of machine language instructions. The first step of the cycle is to fetch, or read, the next instruction from memory into the CPU.
2. **Decode.** A machine language instruction is a binary number that represents a command that tells the CPU to perform an operation. In this step, the CPU decodes the instruction that was just fetched from memory, to determine which operation it should perform.
3. **Execute.** The last step in the cycle is to execute, or perform, the operation.

Figure 3-2 illustrates these steps.

Figure 3-2 The fetch-decode-execute cycle

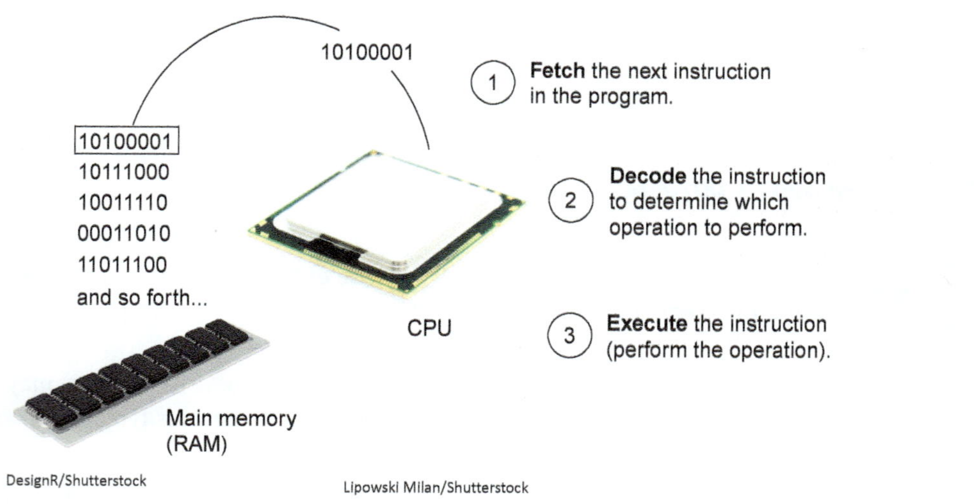

From Machine Language to Assembly Language

Computers can only execute programs that are written in machine language. As previously mentioned, a program can have thousands or even millions of binary instructions, and writing such a program would be very tedious and time consuming. Programming in machine language would also be very difficult, because putting a 0 or a 1 in the wrong place will cause an error.

Although a computer's CPU only understands machine language, it is impractical for people to write programs in machine language. For this reason, **assembly language** was created in the early days of computing as an alternative to machine language. Instead of using binary numbers for instructions, assembly language uses short words that are known as **mnemonics**. For example, in assembly language, the mnemonic `add` typically means to add numbers, `mul` typically means to multiply numbers, and `mov` typically means to move a value to a location in memory. When a programmer uses assembly language to write a program, he or she can write short mnemonics instead of binary numbers.

NOTE: There are many different versions of assembly language. It was mentioned earlier that each brand of CPU has its own machine language instruction set. Each brand of CPU typically has its own assembly language, as well.

Assembly language programs cannot be executed by the CPU, however. The CPU only understands machine language, so a special program known as an **assembler** is used to translate an assembly language program to a machine language program. This process is shown in Figure 3-3. The machine language program that is created by the assembler can then be executed by the CPU.

Figure 3-3 An assembler translates an assembly language program to a machine language program

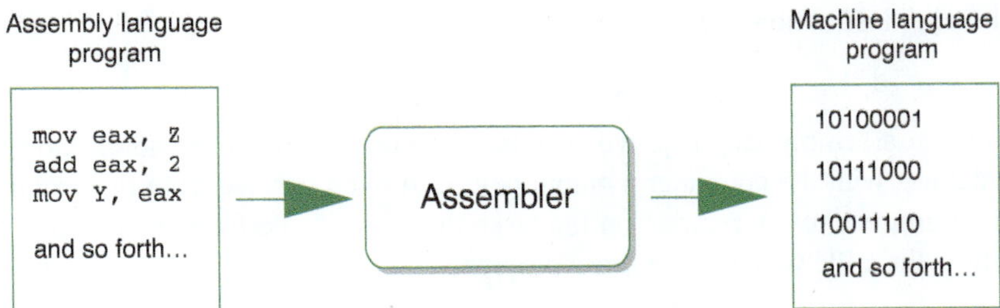

Checkpoint

3.5 A program has to be copied into what type of memory each time the CPU executes it?

3.6 What happens in the Decode step of the fetch-decode-execute cycle?

3.7 What is assembly language?

3.8 Give an example of an assembly language mnemonic word.

3.3 High Level Languages

High-level languages make it faster and easier to write programs without an extensive knowledge of machine language.

Assembly language makes it unnecessary to write binary machine language instructions, but it is still complex. Assembly language is primarily a direct substitute for machine language, and like machine language, it requires that you know a lot about the CPU. Assembly language also requires that you write a large number of instructions for even the simplest program. Because assembly language is so close in nature to machine language, it is referred to as a **low-level language.**

In the 1950s, a new generation of programming languages known as **high-level languages** began to appear. A high-level language allows you to create powerful and complex programs without knowing how the CPU works and without writing large numbers of low-level instructions. In addition, most high-level languages use words that are easy to understand. For example, if a programmer were using COBOL (which was one of the early high-level languages created in the 1950s), they would write the following instruction to display the message ***Hello world*** on the computer screen:

```
DISPLAY "Hello world"
```

Python is a modern, high-level programming language. In Python, you would display the message ***Hello world*** with the following instruction:

```
print('Hello world')
```

Doing the same thing in assembly language would require several instructions and an intimate knowledge of how the CPU interacts with the computer's output device. As you can see from this example, high-level languages allow programmers to concentrate on the tasks they want to perform with their programs, rather than the details of how the CPU will execute those programs.

Keywords, Operators, and Syntax: An Overview

Each high-level language has its own set of predefined words that the programmer must use to write a program. The words that make up a high-level programming language are known as **keywords** or **reserved words.** Each keyword has a specific meaning and cannot be used for any other purpose. Appendix D lists keywords for the Python, Java, and C++ programming languages.

Programming languages have **operators** that perform various operations on data. For example, all programming languages have math operators that perform arithmetic. In most languages, the + sign is an operator that adds two numbers. The following adds 12 and 75:

```
12 + 75
```

Each language also has its own **syntax,** which is a set of rules that must be strictly followed when writing a program. The syntax rules dictate how keywords, operators, and various punctuation characters must be used in a program. When you are learning a programming language, you must learn the syntax rules for that particular language.

The individual instructions that you use to write a program in a high-level programming language are called **statements.** A programming statement can consist of keywords, operators, punctuation, and other allowable programming elements, arranged in the proper sequence to perform an operation.

NOTE: Chapter 17 provides basic information specific to the Python language, including keywords, operators, and syntax. Chapter 18 provides the information for Java, and Chapter 19 provides it for C++.

VideoNote Compiling and Executing a Program

Compilers and Interpreters

Because the CPU understands only machine language instructions, programs that are written in a high-level language must be translated into machine language. Depending on the language in which a program has been written, the programmer will use either a compiler or an interpreter to make the translation.

A **compiler** is a program that translates a high-level language program into a separate machine language program. The machine language program can then be executed any time it is needed. This is shown in Figure 3-4. As shown in the figure, compiling and executing are two different processes.

Figure 3-4 Compiling a high-level program and executing it

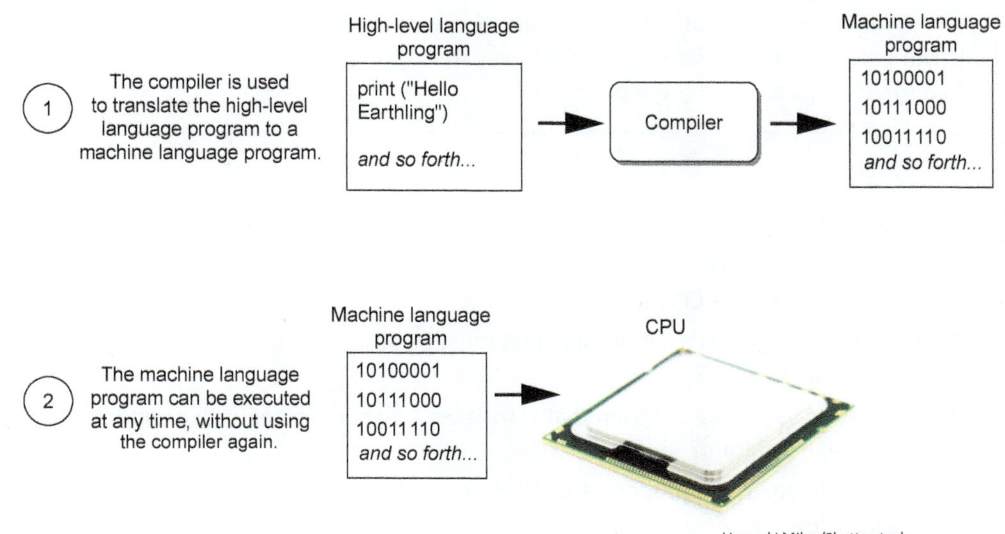

Lipowski Milan/Shutterstock

Python is an example of a language that uses an **interpreter**, which is a program that both translates and executes the instructions in a high-level language program. As the interpreter reads the program, it converts each individual instruction to machine language and immediately executes it. This process repeats for every instruction in the program. This process is illustrated in Figure 3-5. Because interpreters combine translation and execution, they typically do not create separate machine language programs.

Figure 3-5 Executing a high-level program with an interpreter

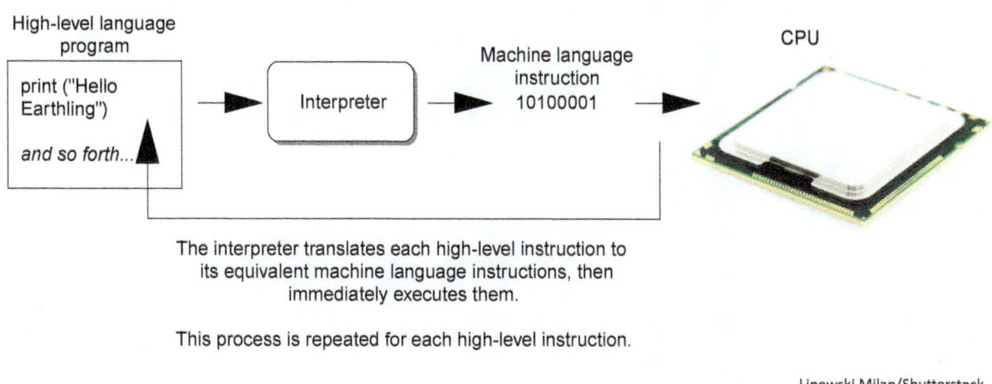

Lipowski Milan/Shutterstock

The statements that a programmer writes in a high-level language are called **source code**, or simply **code**. Typically, the programmer types a program's code into a text editor, then saves the code in a file on the computer's disk. Next, the programmer uses a compiler to translate the code into a machine language program, or an interpreter to translate and execute the code. If the code contains a syntax error, however, it cannot be translated. A **syntax error** is a mistake such as a misspelled keyword, a missing punctuation character, or the incorrect use of an operator. When this happens, the compiler or interpreter displays an error message indicating that the program contains a syntax error. The programmer corrects the error, then attempts once again to translate the program.

NOTE: Human languages also have syntax rules. Do you remember when you took your first English class, and you learned all those rules about commas, apostrophes, capitalization, and so forth? You were learning the syntax of the English language.

Although people commonly violate the syntax rules of their native language when speaking and writing, other people usually understand what they mean. Unfortunately, compilers and interpreters do not have this ability. If even a single syntax error appears in a program, the program cannot be compiled or executed. When an interpreter encounters a syntax error, it stops executing the program.

Checkpoint

3.9 What type of programming language allows you to create powerful and complex programs without knowing how the CPU works?

3.10 Each language has a set of rules that must be strictly followed when writing a program. What is this set of rules called?

3.11 What do you call a program that translates a high-level language program into a separate machine language program?

3.12 What do you call a program that both translates and executes the instructions in a high-level language program?

3.13 What type of mistake is usually caused by a misspelled keyword, a missing punctuation character, or the incorrect use of an operator?

3.4 Comparing Programming Languages

If you learn the fundamentals of coding in one language, it is easier to learn additional languages later.

Similarities and Differences between Languages

There are hundreds of different high-level programming languages, and they are constantly evolving. It is helpful to understand the similarities and differences between languages. Below is a comparison of code in the popular languages of C, C#, Java, Python, and JavaScript. All code segments accomplish the same task of printing "Hello World!" to the screen.

As you compare the code, notice that the syntax is different across the languages. For instance, some languages encase segments of code in brackets { } , while others do not. The method name used to print to the screen is different across languages. For instance, JavaScript uses console.log() and Python uses print(). Note that each code segment includes comments that begin with either '//' or '#'. Despite these differences, all the code results in the same output.

C Code:

```
// C program to display Hello World!

// include an external file
#include <stdio.h>

// main function -
int main()
{

     // prints hello world!
     printf("Hello World!");

     return 0;
}
```

C# Code:

```
// C# program to display Hello World!

using System;

// namespace declaration
namespace HelloWorldApp {

// Class declaration
class HelloWorld
     // Main Method
     static void Main(string[] args)
     {

             // prints Hello World!
             Console.WriteLine("Hello World!");

             // To prevent the program from
             // from closing
             Console.ReadKey();
     }
}
}
```

Java Code:

```
// Java program to display Hello World!
class HelloWorld {

     public static void main(
             String args[])
     {
             System.out.println("Hello World!");
     }
}
```

Python Code:

```
# Python program to display Hello World!
print("Hello World!")
```

JavaScript Code:

```
// JavaScript program to display Hello World!
<script>
  console.log('Hello World!');
</script>
```

Output for all Code Segments:

```
Hello World!
```

Which Language is Right for You?

With over 600 programming languages and more being introduced all the time, how do you know which one is right for you? While you might start by learning a simple high-level language such as Python, that does not mean you cannot learn other languages as you progress. In fact, if you continue in the field of computer science, you are almost certain to learn how to code in more than one language. Some languages are used to develop specific types of applications. Others, such as Python and Java, are general-purpose languages used for a variety of applications. In these cases, the decision on which language to use may be a personal preference. Your school or company policy can also influence the language you will use. In any case, you will find a language that allows you to create programs, stories, games, and animations so you can demonstrate your coding proficiency.

Table 3-1 lists several well-known languages, a brief history, and their typical uses.

Table 3-1 Programming languages

Language	Description
Ada	Ada was created in the 1970s, primarily for applications used by the U.S. Department of Defense. The language is named in honor of Countess Ada Lovelace, an influential and historic figure in the field of computing.
BASIC	**B**eginners **A**ll-purpose **S**ymbolic **I**nstruction **C**ode is a general-purpose language that was originally designed in the early 1960s to be simple enough for beginners to learn. Today, there are many different versions of BASIC.
FORTRAN	**FOR**mula **TRAN**slator was the first high-level programming language. It was designed in the 1950s for performing complex mathematical calculations. It is used in science and engineering. Other languages are more popular today, but there are many legacy applications that still require updates using FORTRAN.
COBOL	**CO**mmon **B**usiness-**O**riented **L**anguage was created in the 1950s and was designed for business applications.
Pascal	Pascal was created in 1970 and was originally designed for teaching programming. The language was named in honor of the mathematician, physicist, and philosopher Blaise Pascal.
C and C++	C and C++ (pronounced "c plus plus") are powerful, general-purpose languages developed at Bell Laboratories. The C language was created in 1972, and the C++ language was created in 1983. These languages are often used to create operating systems, graphical user interfaces, and functionality for embedded devices such as smart watches, thermostats, or traffic lights.

Table 3-1 Programming languages *(continued)*

Language	Description
C#	Pronounced "c sharp." This language was created by Microsoft around the year 2000 for developing applications based on the Microsoft .NET platform.
Java	Java was created by Sun Microsystems in the early 1990s. It can be used to develop programs that run on a single computer or over the internet from a web server. It is a popular multi-purpose language widely used to create business applications.
JavaScript	JavaScript, created in the 1990s, can be used in web pages. Despite its name, JavaScript is not related to Java. It is a very popular language to create interactive websites and mobile applications.
Python	Python is a general-purpose language created in the early 1990s. It is a very popular language used in business applications, artificial intelligence, and data science. Several social media sites such as Instagram are written in Python. It is often used to teach programming because the syntax is easy to understand.
Ruby	Ruby is a general-purpose language that was created in the 1990s. It is increasingly becoming a popular language for programs that run on web servers.

Strongly-Typed versus Loosely-Typed Languages

One trait that differentiates languages from one another is whether the language is strongly typed or loosely typed. **Strongly-typed languages**, which may be called strong or typed, require you to explicitly declare the type of data you plan to store in a variable. Examples of data types are integers, strings, and floating-point numbers. Once declared, that variable can only store the designated type of data. An error occurs if the rule is violated.

Loosely-typed languages, which may be called weak or untyped, are more flexible. They allow you to store data in variables without explicitly declaring what type of data you plan to store.

There are pros and cons to both approaches. A loosely-typed language gives you more flexibility to code and make changes more quickly. JavaScript is an example of a loosely-typed language. A strongly-typed language provides more structure and prevents you from inadvertently storing the wrong type of data, which can potentially cause unforeseen errors in your application. It is an excellent choice if you are collaborating with a team of programmers as it forces everyone to use the intended data type. Java and C++ are examples of strongly-typed languages.

Python is generally considered a strongly-typed language, because the interpreter keeps track of variable types and will only perform operations on the variable that are suitable for that type. It is also considered a loosely-typed language because in Python, a variable is a value attached to a name. The value has a data type, but the variable does not. That gives the programmer flexibility to change the variable in the future by assigning a different data type.

The following is a Java code example to explicitly declare a variable:

Java Code:

```
//declare a variable called num of an integer data type
int number;

//assign the value of 100 to a variable named number
number = 100;
```

The following is a Python code example to implicitly declare a variable:

Python Code:

```
#assign the numeric value of 100 to a variable named number
number = 100

#easily change the value to a string
number = 'hello'
```

Checkpoint

3.14 What method name does JavaScript use to print to the screen?

3.15 What does BASIC stand for?

3.16 What powerful languages are often used to create operating systems, graphical user interfaces, and functionality for embedded devices such as smart watches, thermostats, or traffic lights?

3.17 Why is Python often used to teach programming?

3.18 What is a strongly-typed programming language?

3.5 Algorithms and the Problem-Solving Process

You can use a six-step process to identify and solve problems.

A **problem**, or challenge, is something that gets between you and a **goal**. People make decisions every day to solve problems that affect their lives. The problems may be as unimportant as what to eat for breakfast or as important as choosing where to go to college. If they make a good decision, they will overcome the problem and achieve their goal. If they make a bad decision, they waste time and resources and might never achieve their goal

To solve a problem, you must identify the problem's description, purpose, and goals. There are six steps you can follow to solve a problem. If you complete all six steps, you should come up with an effective solution. If any of the six steps are not completed well, you are unlikely to solve the problem. You can use these steps to solve your own problems, or as part of your work as a computer scientist. In computer science, solving problems is key to meeting the needs of clients and producing effective programming.

Six Steps of Problem-Solving

These six steps are:

1. **Identify the problem.** This includes identifying the problem's description, purpose, and the goal the problem is interfering with. If you don't know what the problem is, you cannot solve it.
2. **Understand the problem.** This includes understanding how the problem is interfering with the goal. It also means understanding the **knowledge base** of the person or machine for whom you are solving the problem.
    - When you are setting up a solution for a person—yourself or a client—then you must know what that person knows. You will want to customize the solution based on this knowledge base. For example, you would use a more detailed set of instructions to tell someone how to find a restaurant in your city if they have a limited knowledge of the city than if they know the city well.
    - When you are working with a computer, its knowledge base is the limited instructions the computer can understand in the particular language or application you are using to solve the problem. Knowing the knowledge base is very important since you cannot use any instructions outside this base.
    - You also must know your own knowledge base. You cannot solve a problem if you do not know the subject. For example, to solve a problem involving accounting, you must know accounting. Knowing your knowledge base lets you communicate with your client and understand how to solve the problem.
3. **Identify ways to solve the problem.** Make a list of all possible solutions. This list should be as complete as possible. Do not stop thinking of solutions until you run out of ideas. You can even talk to other people such as co-workers, teammates, and professionals in related fields to find solutions you did not think of. All solutions must be reasonable and acceptable ways to solve the problem without creating new problems. For example, you could travel from Denver to Los Angeles by way of New York, but this would probably not be an acceptable solution to your travel needs.
4. **Select the best solution from your list.** Set criteria for your solutions. For example, you may want the fastest solution or the least expensive solution. Evaluate the pros and cons of each possible solution based on the criteria, and then select the best solution. Keep in mind that the solution should fall within the knowledge base set in step 2.
5. **Write an action plan for putting the solution into effect.** This means listing complete instructions in a logical sequence of steps that enable you to solve the problem using the selected solution. These

numbered, step-by-step instructions must fall within the knowledge base set in step 2. That means that no instruction can be used unless the individual or the machine can understand it. This can be very limiting, especially when working with computers.

6. **Evaluate the solution.** To evaluate or test a solution means to check its result to see if it satisfies the needs of the person(s) with the problem. If the result is either incorrect or unsatisfactory, then the problem solver must review the list of instructions to see if they are correct or start the process all over again.

Problem-Solving in Action

People solve problems daily at home, or work, or wherever they go. Problems at home include such things as what to cook for dinner, what to do on family night, which car to buy, or how to sell the house. At work, the problems might involve dealing with fellow employees, work policies, management, or customers. The better the decisions an employee can make, the more valuable that person will be to the company. In each case, the six steps in problem-solving can be followed. Most people use them without even knowing it. Here is an example:

1. **Identify the problem.** Describe the problem, its purpose, and goals. What to do on family night?
2. **Understand the problem.** With this simple problem, also, the knowledge base of the participants must be considered. The only solutions that should be selected are ones that everyone involved would know how to do. You probably would not select playing a game of chess as a possible solution if only one person in the family knows how to play.
3. **Identify alternatives.** The alternatives might include: a. Watch television. b. Play a board game. c. Play video games. d. Go to the movies. e. Go to play miniature golf. f. Go to the amusement park. g. Go visit a relative. The list is complete only when you can think of no more alternatives.
4. **Select the best way to solve the problem.** Set criteria and evaluate the solutions. This step often involves seeking and responding to advice or feedback from peers, teachers, or professionals who understand the problem and goals, and can help you evaluate the problem solutions. Criteria might be what costs the least or how long would it take to get someplace. Based on your criteria, identify the pros and cons of each alternative. For example, going to the movies is expensive but close by. Miniature golf is less expensive and nearby. Based on the pros and cons, select the best solution.
5. **Prepare an action plan for achieving the solution.** For example, if you select miniature golf, the action plan might include the time you will meet, the location you will meet, and who will drive.
6. **Evaluate the solution.** Is it correct and satisfactory? In this case, does it meet the needs of everyone in the family, and will everyone have a good time? If not, review the criteria you used to select a solution and the action plan to see if you should have made a different choice.

What is an Algorithm?

Some problems, such as baking a cake, have a pretty straight-forward solution. They can be solved with a series of actions called an **algorithm**. These solutions are called **algorithmic solutions.** You can diagram an algorithmic solution as a flowchart, like the one in Figure 3-6 which shows an algorithm for baking a cake. You follow the steps to an acceptable and satisfying solution. A story, game, video, or animation can also be an algorithm that you diagram with a flowchart. For example, a very simple story about a hidden prize might include this series of actions: A character is facing a door. They open the door, walk through and find a box. They open the box and find a prize.

Of course, to make the story more interesting and fun, the series of actions would be longer and involve more variation and choice. But, it would still be an algorithm leading to an acceptable and satisfying solution.

NOTE: In later chapters, you learn about the tools programming languages provide for using algorithms to make programs more interesting and fun, such as variables, sequences, conditional statements, and iteration.

Figure 3-6 A flowchart illustrating an algorithm for baking a cake

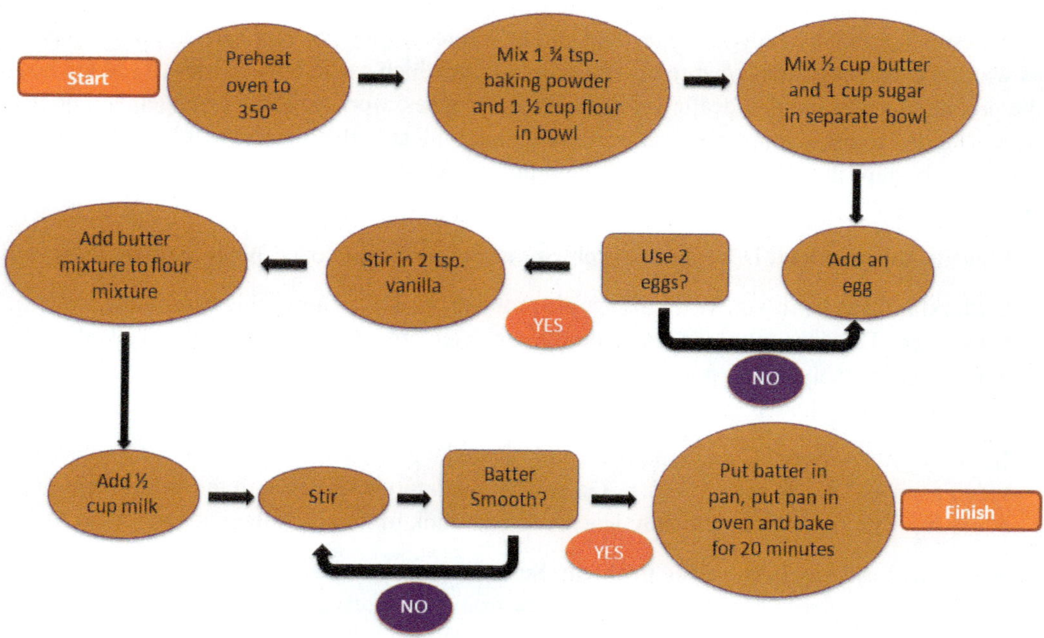

The solutions for some problems, such as what elective to take next semester, are not so straightforward. These solutions require reasoning built on knowledge and experience, and a process of trial and error. Solutions that cannot be reached through a direct set of steps are called **heuristic solutions**.

As a problem solver, you can use the six step process for both algorithmic and heuristic solutions. However, in step 6, evaluating the solution, the correctness and appropriateness of heuristic solutions are far less certain. It's easy to tell pretty quickly if your completed cake or a computer program you wrote is correct and satisfactory, but it might take a long time to know if you chose the elective best for you. With heuristic solutions, the problem solver will often need to follow the six steps more than once, carefully evaluating each possible solution before deciding which is best.

Furthermore, the same solution you choose may not be correct and satisfactory at another time, or for a different client. For example, you might decide a course on coding with Python is the best option, but it might not fit into your schedule next semester. In that case, you may have to reevaluate and resolve the same problem later. Most problems require a combination of the two kinds of solutions

Problem Solving with Computers

A computer program is basically a problem-solving algorithm. The challenge for the programmer is breaking a task into steps that that the computer can understand. Take the task of deciding which number is the largest from a group of three numbers. Almost any person can immediately tell which is the largest, but many cannot explain the steps they followed to arrive at it. Most people will say, "I can't explain how I know, I just know it!" This explanation is not good enough for the computer. The computer is a tool that will perform only tasks that the user can explain.

The computer has a specific system of communication that programmers and users must learn. This system demands that no step in the solution to a problem be skipped and that all steps be in the proper order. You must assume the computer knows nothing except what you tell it. You must think of it as an ignorant but efficient aid to problem solving. Computers are built to deal with algorithmic solutions, which are often difficult or very time consuming for humans. People are better than computers at developing heuristic solutions. Solving a complicated calculus problem or alphabetizing 10,000 names is an easy task for the computer, but the problem of how to throw a ball or how to speak English is not.

How can problems such as how to throw a ball or speak English be solved in a set of steps that a computer can understand? The field of computers that deals with heuristic types of problems is called **artificial intelligence.** Artificial intelligence enables a computer to do things like build its own knowledge bank and speak in a human language. Using artificial intelligence, the computer's problem-solving abilities are similar to those of a human being.

Artificial intelligence is an expanding computer field, especially with the increased use of robotics. However, until computers can be built to think like humans, people will process mostly heuristic solutions and computers will process mostly algorithmic solutions. Heuristic problem solving can help determine alternative solutions. However, for computer use, they must be transformed into an algorithmic format.

Difficulties with Problem Solving

People have many problems with problem solving. Some people have never been taught how to solve problems. Others are afraid to make a decision for fear it will be the wrong one.

Often, when people go through the problem-solving process, they complete one or more of the steps inadequately. They may not define the problem correctly or may not generate a sufficient list of alternatives. When choosing the best alternative, they may eliminate good alternatives or list the pros and cons too hastily. They may not use a logical sequence of steps in their action plan, or they may focus on details before the framework for the solution is in place. Finally, they may incorrectly or haphazardly evaluate the solution. The problem-solving process is not easy. It takes practice and time to perfect, but in the long run the process proves to be of great benefit.

3.19 How many steps are in the problem-solving process?

3.20 What is an algorithmic solution?

3.21 What is a heuristic solution?

3.22 What are two things that could go wrong with the problem-solving process?

Chapter Review

Multiple Choice

1. If you were to look at a machine language program, you would see __________.
   a. Python code
   b. a stream of binary numbers
   c. English words
   d. circuits

2. In the __________ part of the fetch-decode-execute cycle, the CPU determines which operation it should perform.
   a. fetch
   b. decode
   c. execute
   d. deconstruct

3. Computers can only execute programs that are written in __________.
   a. Java
   b. assembly language
   c. machine language
   d. Python

4. The __________ translates an assembly language program to a machine language program.
   a. assembler
   b. compiler
   c. translator
   d. interpreter

5. The words that make up a high-level programming language are called __________.
   a. binary instructions
   b. mnemonics
   c. commands
   d. keywords

6. The rules that must be followed when writing a program are called __________.
   a. syntax
   b. punctuation
   c. keywords
   d. operators

7. A(n) __________ program translates a high-level language program into a separate machine language program.
   a. assembler
   b. compiler
   c. translator
   d. utility

8. What method name does Python use to print to the screen?
   a. console.log()
   b. print()
   c. console.log{}
   d. print {}

9. What was the first high-level programming language?
   a. Python
   b. BASIC
   c. FORTRAN
   d. Ruby

10. What is an example of a loosely-typed programming language?
    a. JavaScript
    b. BASIC
    c. C++
    d. COBOL

True or False

1. Machine language is the only language that a CPU understands.
2. Assembly language is considered a high-level language.
3. An interpreter is a program that both translates and executes the instructions in a high-level language program.
4. A syntax error does not prevent a program from being compiled and executed.
5. C++ is considered a loosely-typed programming language.
6. There is only one algorithm for solving any given problem.
7. A recipe is an example of an algorithm.

Short Answer

1. What are the words that make up a high-level programming language called?
2. What are the short words that are used in assembly language called?
3. What is the difference between a compiler and an interpreter?
4. Differentiate between Python, JavaScript, and C++. Discuss the general purpose of each.
5. Compare the pros and cons of a strongly-typed language and a loosely-typed language, giving examples of each.
6. What are the six steps of problem solving?
7. Name three current challenges in your life that you could solve using an algorithmic process. Identify each problem's description, purpose, and goals. Explain why each of these problems is algorithmic in nature.

Exercises

1. Choose a high-level compiled programming language and an interpreted language. With your teacher's permission, research the two languages online. Make a two-column chart differentiating between the two. Share your chart with a partner or with the class.

2. On your own or with a partner, create a flowchart or process diagram that illustrates the fetch - decode - execute process. Explain your illustration to a partner or to the class.

3. Select one of the following tasks (challenges). Working alone or with a partner, use the problem-solving process to write a set of numbered, step-by-step instructions (a solution) that another person could follow to perform the task without asking questions. Define the knowledge base of this person by listing what you expect the person to know in order to follow your directions. For example, for task "a" (below), make a cup of cocoa, the knowledge base might include such things as knowledge of milk or water, a refrigerator, pan, spoon, cocoa, cup, range top or microwave, and so forth.

    a. Make a cup of cocoa.

    b. Sharpen a pencil.

    c. Walk from the classroom to the cafeteria.

    d. Get a glass of water from your kitchen.

    f. Start your computer.

4. Test your solution for Exercise 3 by giving your instructions to a classmate to see whether they can accomplish the task without your help. If they can't, seek feedback from the class or your teacher on why the solution did not work. Then, respond to the feedback by modifying your solution so that the person can accomplish the task. Check the solution again by giving the instructions to another person.

5. With your teacher's permission, use the internet to look for job listings for software programmers. You might look on a site such as Indeed.com or LinkedIn or you might look on a company's website for programming careers. Take notes on the types of programming projects and the languages they list. Do you notice any trends? Is there one language mentioned more often than others? Share your findings with a partner or with the class.

6. Working alone or with a partner, write an algorithm to define the steps for a short, simple story, game, video, or animation. After listing the steps, try diagramming it with a flowchart. Write a paragraph explaining how you might expand the algorithm to make it more interesting and fun. Seek feedback from the class or your teacher on how to improve the algorithm, and then respond to the feedback by making improvements.

Getting Started with HTML and CSS

TOPICS

4.1 Introduction to HTML

HTML is the foundational programming language for web page development.

HTML (Hypertext Markup Language) is a web-based programming language, which means it is used to develop pages that will display on the world wide web. It is not the only web-based language; others include CSS, JavaScript, Python, and Java. **Markup languages** consist of sets of directions that tell software that retrieves and renders web content, such as web browsers, how to display and manage static and interactive web documents..

HTML is the set of markup symbols or codes placed in a file that is intended for display on a web page. The World Wide Web Consortium (W3C) sets the standards for HTML and its related languages. HTML5 is the latest version of HTML.

HTML markup symbols and codes identify structural elements such as paragraphs, headings, and lists. HTML can also be used to place media such as graphics, video, and audio, on a web page, and to add interactivity with features such as hyperlinks or fill-in forms. The web browser interprets the markup code and renders the page. With HTML, no matter what type of computer a web page was created on, any web browser running on any operating system can display the page.

HTML Tags

Each individual markup code is referred to as an **element** or a **tag**. Tags are enclosed in angle brackets, the < and > symbols. Most tags come in pairs: an **opening tag** (also called a **start tag**) and a **closing tag** (also called an **end tag**). These tags act as containers and are sometimes referred to as container tags. For example, when an HTML document is displayed by a web browser, the text that appears between the `<title>` and `</title>` tags would be displayed in the title bar on the browser window. Note the slash in the closing tag. All closing tags have a slash to the left of the tag name, enclosed in the angle brackets.

Some tags are used alone and are not part of a pair. For example, a `<hr>` tag that displays a horizontal line on a web page is a **stand-alone tag** (also called a **self-contained tag**) and does not have a closing tag. You will become familiar with these as you use them. Most tags can be modified with **attributes** that further describe their purpose.

Document Type Definition

Because multiple versions and types of HTML exist, the W3C recommends identifying the markup language used in a web page document with a **Document Type Definition (DTD)**. The DTD identifies the version of HTML in the document. Web browsers and HTML code validators use the information in the DTD when processing the web page. The DTD statement, commonly called a **DOCTYPE** statement, is the first line of a web page document. The DTD for HTML5 is:

```
<!DOCTYPE html>
```

Web Page Template

Every single web page you create will include the html, head, title, meta, and body elements. We will follow the coding style to use lowercase letters and place quotes around attribute values. A basic HTML5 web page template is:

```
<!DOCTYPE html>
<html lang="en">
<head>
<title>Page Title Goes Here</title>
<meta charset="utf-8">
</head>
<body>
. . . body text and more HTML tags go here . . .
</body>
</html>
```

With the exception of the specific page title, the first seven lines will usually be the same on every web page that you create. Review the code above and notice the DTD statement has its own formatting, but that the HTML tags all use lowercase letters. Next, let's explore the purpose of the html, head, title, meta, and body elements.

HTML Element

The purpose of the **html element** is to indicate that the document is HTML formatted. The html element tells the web browser how to interpret the document. The opening <html> tag is placed on a line below the DTD. The closing `</html>` tag indicates the end of the web page and is placed after all other HTML elements in the document.

The html element also needs to indicate the spoken language, such as English, of the text in the document. This additional information is added to the `<html>` tag in the form of an attribute, which modifies or further describes the function of an element. The lang attribute specifies the spoken language of the document. For example, `lang="en"` indicates the English language. Search engines and screen readers may access this attribute.

The html element contains the two sections of a web page: the head and the body. The **head section** contains information that describes the web page document. The **body section** contains the tags, text, images, and other objects that are displayed by the web browser as a web page.

Head Section

Elements that are located in the head section include the title of the web page, meta tags that describe the document (such as the character encoding used and information that may be accessed by search engines), and references to scripts and styles. Many of these do not show directly on the web page.

Head Element. The head element contains the head section, which begins with the <head> tag and ends with the `</head>` tag. You'll always code at least two other elements in the head section: a title element and a meta element.

Title Element. The first element in the head section, the title element, configures the text that will appear in the title bar of the browser window. The text between the `<title>` and `</title>` tags is called the title of the web page. This title text is accessed when web pages are bookmarked and printed. Popular search engines, such as Google, use the title text to help determine keyword relevance and even display the title text on the results page of a search. A descriptive title that includes the website or organization name is a crucial component for establishing a brand or presence on the Web.

Meta Element. The meta element describes a characteristic of a web page, such as the character encoding. Character encoding is the internal representation of letters, numbers, and symbols in a file, such as a web page or other file, that is stored on a computer and may be transmitted over the internet. There are many different character-encoding sets. A form of Unicode called utf-8 character encoding is typically used for web pages. The meta tag is not used as a pair of opening and closing tags. It is a stand-alone selfcontained tag (referred to as a void element in HTML5). The meta tag uses the charset attribute to indicate the character encoding. An example meta tag is: <meta charset=”utf-8”>

Body Section

The body section contains text and elements that display directly on the web page within the browser window, also referred to as the browser viewport. The purpose of the body section is to configure the contents of the web page.

Body Element. The body element contains the body section, which begins with the <body> tag and ends with the `</body>` tag. You will spend most of your time writing code in the body of a web page. Text and elements typed between the opening and closing body tags will be displayed on the web page in the browser viewport.

Web Development Tools

There are several methods of using a web-based language such as HTML.

Text editing programs like Notepad and TextEdit are simple tools you can use to enter both text and HTML tags by typing. Using these programs can be tedious, though. If you want your web page to include a menu, for example, you have to write the HTML code for each detail of that menu.

HTML editors such as Notepad++ and BBEdit feature text editing and an easier way to add HTML tags, but you still have to do most or all of the HTML coding manually. You can also use a word-processing program to create a web page. However, it must be a program such as Microsoft Word that allows you to save your work as an .htm or .html file.

Graphical authoring tools are the sophisticated editing programs that let you create a web page without entering tags yourself. Sometimes called **WYSIWYG (What You See Is What You Get)** editors, they are almost as easy to use as a word processor and feature many of the same editing and formatting tools. The difference is that these programs automatically apply the HTML coding for you. You set up the page to look the way you want, including graphics or hyperlinks, and the program adds the HTML codes. Adobe® Dreamweaver® is an example of a program that automates the process of formatting documents for the web.

You may also use other programming languages, like JavaScript or Python, to write scripts which you can embed in a web page.

In the Spotlight:

Creating A Web Page

As mentioned, you don't need any special software to create a web page document—all you need is a text editor. The Notepad text editor is included with Microsoft Windows. TextEdit is distributed with the Mac OS operating system. An alternative to using a simple text editor or word processor is to use a commercial web authoring tool, such as Adobe Dreamweaver. There are also many free or shareware editors available, including Notepad++, Brackets, Visual Studio Code, and BBEdit. Your instructor may ask you to use a specific web development tool, or you may use one of your choice. The examples here use Notepad.

Now that you're familiar with the basic elements used on every web page, it's your turn to create your first web page, shown in Figure 4-1.

Figure 4-1 Your first web page

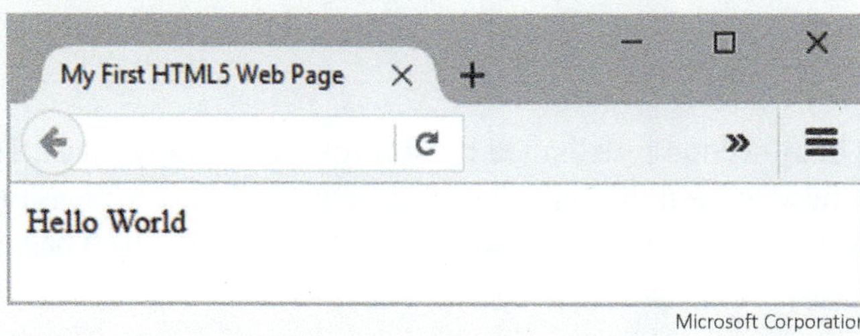

Microsoft Corporation

Create a Folder

Organizing web pages in folders is an important part of website development. Websites are stored in folders on web servers. Getting into the habit of using folders now will make it easier for you to follow best practices in the future. Use your operating system to create a new folder named chapter1 on your hard storage device.

To create a new folder on a Mac:

1. In the Finder, go to the location where you'd like to create the new folder.
2. Choose File > New Folder. An untitled folder is created.
3. To rename the folder with a new name: select the folder and click on the current name. Type a name for the folder and press the Return key.

To create a new folder with Windows:

1. Right-click on the Start Button and select File Explorer. Then, navigate to the location where you'd like to create the new folder, such as Documents, your C: drive, or an external USB drive.
2. Select the Home tab. Select New folder.
3. To rename the new folder: right-click on it, select Rename from the context-sensitive menu, type the new name, and press the Enter key. Now, you are ready to create your first web page. Launch Notepad or any web development tool.

Type in the following code.

```
<!DOCTYPE html>
<html lang="en">
<head>
<title>My First HTML5 Web Page</title>
<meta charset="utf-8">
</head>
<body>
Hello World
</body>
</html>
```

Notice that the first line in the file contains the DTD. The HTML code begins with an opening `<html>` tag and ends with a closing `</html>` tag. The purpose of these tags is to indicate that the content between the tags makes up a web page.

The head section is delimited by `<head>` and `</head>` tags and contains a pair of title tags with the words "My First HTML5 Web Page" in between along with a `<meta>` tag to indicate the character encoding.

The body section is delimited by `<body>` and `</body>` tags. The words "Hello World" are typed on a line between the body tags. See Figure 4-2 for a screenshot of the code as it would appear in Notepad. You have just created the source code for a web page document.

Figure 4-2 Your web page source code displayed in Notepad

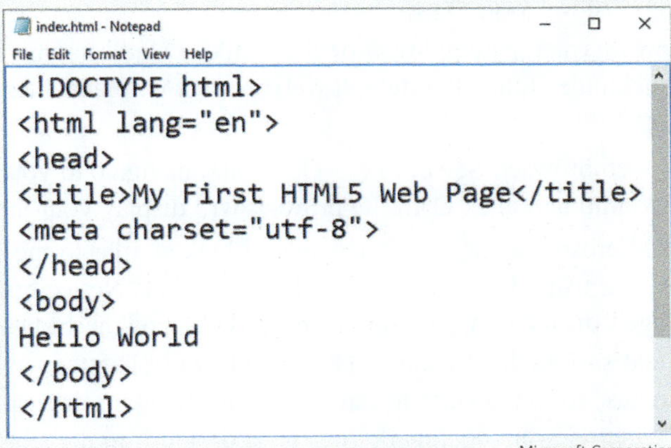

Microsoft Corporation

TIP: You do not have to start each tag on a separate line. A web browser can display a page even if all the tags follow each other on one line with no spaces. However, you will find it easier to write and read web page code if line breaks and indentation are used.

Save Your File

Web pages use either an .htm or .html file extension. A common file name for the home page of a website is index.html or index.htm. The web pages in this book use the .html file extension.

You will save your file with the name of index.html.

1. Display your file in Notepad or another text editor.
2. Select File from the menu bar, and then select Save As.
3. The Save As dialog box appears. Using Figure 4-3 as an example, type the file name.
4. Click the Save button.

Figure 4-3 Save and name your file

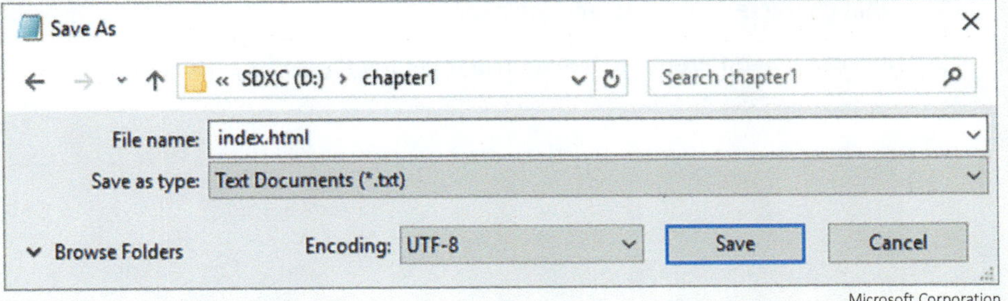

Microsoft Corporation

TIP: Ask your instructor for information on how to access the files available for use with this chapter.

Test Your Page

There are two ways to test your page:

1. In Windows Explorer (Windows) or the Finder (Mac), navigate to your index.html file. Double-click index.html. The default web browser will launch and will display your index.html page.
2. Launch a web browser. Select File > Open, and navigate to your index.html file. Double-click index.html and click OK. The browser will display your index.html page.

If you are using Microsoft Edge, your page should look similar to the one shown in Figure 4-4. A display of the page using Firefox is shown in Figure 1.11. Notice how the title text, "My First HTML5 Web Page" displays in the tab and the title bar of the browser window. Some search engines use the text surrounded by the `<title>` and `</title>` tags to help determine relevance of keyword searches, so make certain that your pages contain descriptive titles. The `<title>` tag is also used when viewers bookmark your page or add it to their Favorites. An engaging and descriptive page title may entice a visitor to revisit your page. If your web page is for a company or an organization, it's a good idea to include the name of the company or organization in the title.

Figure 4-4 Web page displayed by Microsoft Edge

Microsoft Corporation

Checkpoint

4.1 Discuss methods of using a web-based language such as HTML.

4.2 What character is used to enclose a tag?

4.3 How can you differentiate between an opening tag and a closing tag?

4.2 HTML Basics

HTML tags let you configure the structure and formatting of a web page.

Heading element

Heading elements are organized into six levels: h1 through h6. The text within a heading element is rendered as a block of text called a **block display** by the browser and appears with empty space called **white space** or **negative space** above and below. The size of the text is largest for the heading 1 tag <h1> and smallest for the heading 6 tag <h6>. Depending on the **font** being used, the text within <h4>, <h5>, and <h6> tags may be displayed smaller than the default text size. All text within heading tags is displayed with bold font weight.

In the Spotlight:

Using Heading Tags

To create a web page with headings, launch your web development tool and open the template.html file from the chapter04 folder. Modify the title element and add heading tags to the body section as indicated by the following code:

```
<!DOCTYPE html>
<html lang="en">
<head>
<title>Heading Example</title>
<meta charset="utf-8">
</head>
<body>
<h1>Heading Level 1</h1>
<h2>Heading Level 2</h2>
<h3>Heading Level 3</h3>
<h4>Heading Level 4</h4>
<h5>Heading Level 5</h5>
<h6>Heading Level 6</h6>
</body>
</html>
```

Save the document as heading.html. Launch a browser to test your page. It should look similar to the page shown in Figure 4-5.

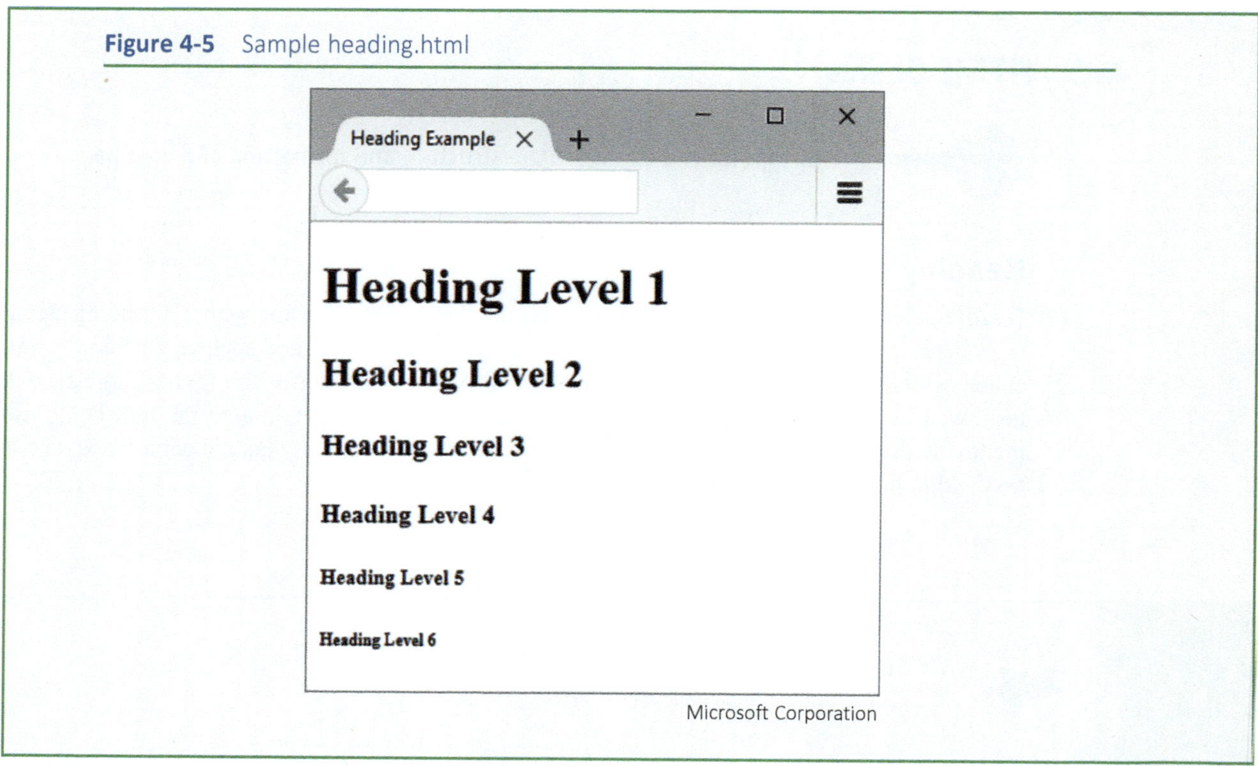

Figure 4-5 Sample heading.html

Microsoft Corporation

Paragraph element

A **paragraph element** groups sentences and sections of text together. Text within <p> and </p> tags is rendered as block display with empty space above and below. Figure 4-6 shows a web page document containing a paragraph after the first heading.

Figure 4-6 Web page using headings and a paragraph

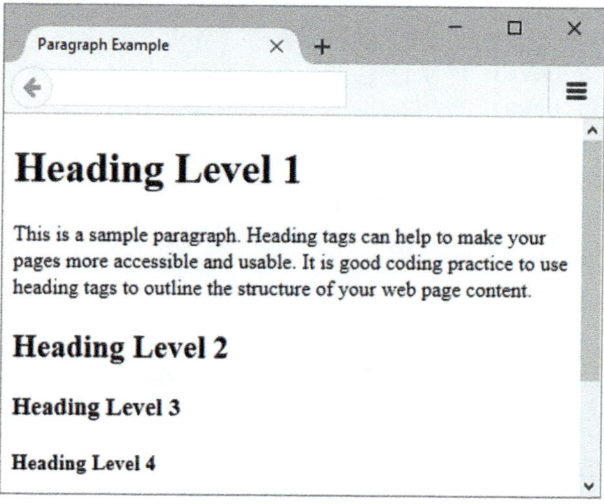

Microsoft Corporation

In the Spotlight:

Using a Paragraph Element

To create a web page with headings and a paragraph, launch your web development tool and open the heading.html file from the chapter04 folder. Modify the page title and add a paragraph of text to your page below the line with the <h1> tags and above the line with the <h2> tags:

```
<!DOCTYPE html>
<html lang="en">
<head>
<title>Paragraph Example</title>
<meta charset="utf-8">
</head>
<body>
<h1>Heading Level 1</h1>
<p>This is a sample paragraph. Heading tags can help to make your
pages more accessible and usable. It is good coding practice to use
heading tags to outline the structure of your web page content.
</p>
<h2>Heading Level 2</h2>
<h3>Heading Level 3</h3>
<h4>Heading Level 4</h4>
<h5>Heading Level 5</h5>
<h6>Heading Level 6</h6>
</body>
</html>
```

Save the document as paragraph.html. Launch a browser to open and test your page. It should look similar to the page shown in Figure 4-6. Notice how the text in the paragraph wraps automatically as you resize your browser window.

NOTE: As you test your web pages, you may notice that the headings and text begin near the left margin. This is called left alignment, and it is the default alignment for web pages. You'll learn techniques to change alignment with Cascading Style Sheets (CSS) later in this chapter.

TIP: When writing for the Web, avoid long paragraphs. People tend to skim web pages rather than reading them word for word. Use heading tags to outline the page content along with short paragraphs (about three to five sentences each) and lists (which you'll learn about later in this chapter).

The Line Break Element

The **line break element** causes the browser to advance to the next line before displaying the next element or text on a web page. The line break tag is not coded as a pair of opening and closing tags. It is a void element and is coded as `<br>`. Figure 4-7 shows a web page document with a line break after the first sentence in the paragraph.

Figure 4-7 Notice the line break after the first sentence

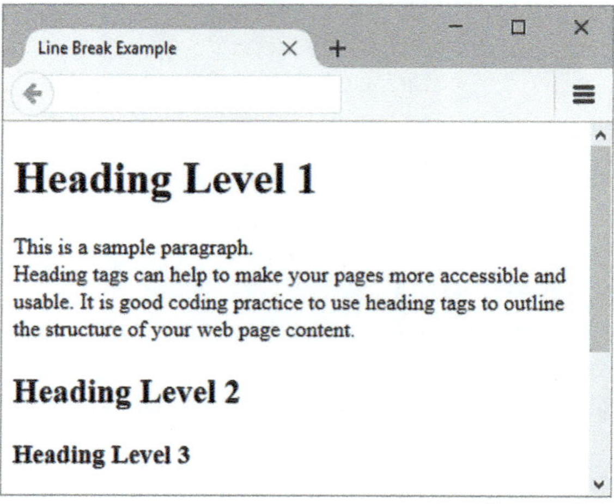

Microsoft Corporation

The Horizontal Rule Element

Web designers often use visual elements such as lines and borders to separate or define areas on web pages. The **horizontal rule element,** `<hr>`, configures a horizontal line across a web page. Since the horizontal rule element does not contain any text, it is coded as a void element and not in a pair of opening and closing tags. The horizontal rule element has an additional purpose in HTML5, it can be used to indicate a thematic break or change in the content. Figure 4-8 shows a web page document with a horizontal rule after the paragraph.

Figure 4-8 The horizontal line is below the paragraph

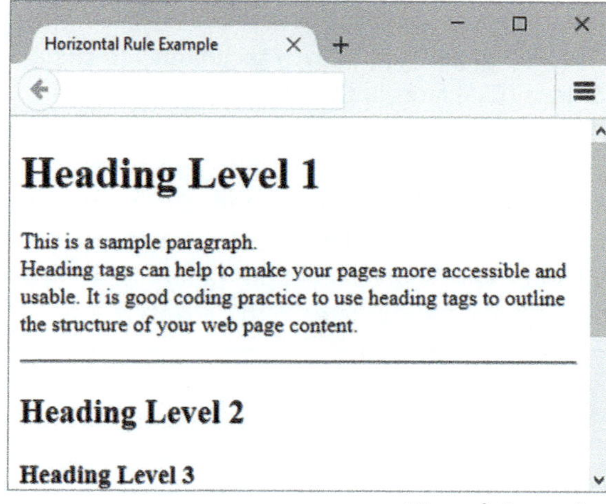

Microsoft Corporation

TIP: When you are tempted to use a horizontal rule on a web page, consider whether it is really needed. Usually, just leaving extra blank space on the page will serve to separate the content.

Ordered List

An **ordered list,** displays a numbering or lettering system to sequence the information in the list. An ordered list can be organized using numerals (the default), uppercase letters, lowercase letters, uppercase Roman numerals, and lowercase Roman numerals.

Ordered lists begin with an `<ol>` tag and end with an `</ol>` tag. Each list item begins with an `<li>` tag and ends with an `</li>` tag. The code to configure the heading and ordered list shown in Figure 4-8 follows:

```
<h1>My Favorite Colors</h1>
<ol>
<li>Blue</li>
<li>Teal</li>
<li>Red</li>
</ol>
```

The `type`, `start`, and `reversed` Attributes

The type attribute configures the symbol used for ordering the list. For example, to create an ordered list organized by uppercase letters, use `<ol type="A">`. Table 4-1 documents the type attribute and its values for ordered lists.

Table 4-1 The type Attribute for Ordered Lists

Value	Symbol
1	Numerals (the default)
A	Uppercase letters
a	Lowercase letters
I	Roman numerals
i	Lowercase Roman numerals

Another handy attribute that can be used with ordered lists is the start attribute, with which you can specify the start value for the list (for example, `start="10"`). Use the reversed attribute (`reversed="reversed"`) to indicate that a list is in descending order.

Unordered List

An **unordered list** displays a bullet, or list marker, before each list entry. The default list marker is determined by the browser but is typically a disc, which is a filled-in circle. See Figure 4-9 for a sample unordered list.

Figure 4-9 An unordered list

My Favorite Colors

- Blue
- Teal
- Red

Unordered lists begin with a `<ul>` tag and end with a `</ul>` tag. The ul element is a block display element and is rendered with empty space above and below. Each list item begins with an `<li>` tag and ends with an `</li>` tag. The code to configure the heading and unordered list shown in Figure 4-9 is as follows:

```
<h1>My Favorite Colors</h1>
<ul>
<li>Blue</li>
<li>Teal</li>
<li>Red</li>
</ul>
```

Special Entity Characters

When you want to include certain characters such as quotation marks, the greater than sign (>), the less than sign (<), and the copyright symbol (©) in your web page document, you need to identify them as special characters, sometimes called entity characters. To do this, you do not use an HTML tag; instead, you use a special character code. For example, if you want to include a copyright line on your page as follows:

© Copyright 2024 My Company. All rights reserved.

you need to use the special character code `©` to display the copyright symbol, as shown below:

```
&copy; Copyright 2024 My Company. All rights reserved.
```

Another useful special character is ` `, which stands for nonbreaking space. You may have noticed that web browsers treat multiple spaces as a single space. If you want multiple spaces to be displayed in your text, you can use   multiple times to indicate multiple blank spaces. This is acceptable if you simply need to tweak the position of an element a little. If you find that your web pages contain many ` ` special characters in a row, you should use a different method to align elements, such as configuring the margin or padding with Cascading Style Sheets.

See Table 4-2 for a description of commonly used special characters and their codes.

Table 4-2 The type Attribute for Ordered Lists

Character	Entity Name	Code
"	Quotation mark	"
©	Copyright symbol	©
&	Ampersand	&
Empty space	Nonbreaking space	
'	Apostrophe	'
–	Long dash	—
		Vertical bar		
<	Less than sign	<
>	Greater than sign	>

HTML Syntax Validation

The W3C has a free Markup Validation Service available at http://validator.w3.org that will check your code for syntax errors and validate your web pages. **HTML validation** provides you with quick self-assessment—you can prove that your code uses correct syntax. In the working world, HTML validation serves as a quality assurance tool. Invalid code may cause browsers to render the pages slower than otherwise.

NOTE: Some HTLM editors and graphical authoring tools include HTML validation features.

TIP: In addition to the W3C validation service, there are other tools that you can use to check the syntax of your code. Try out the validators at the following websites:

- **Validator.nu: https://html5.validator.nu**
- **Freeformatter.com: https://www.freeformatter.com/html-validator.html**

Structural Elements

The div element has been used for many years to configure a generic structural area or "division" on a web page as a block display with empty space above and below. A div element begins with a `<div>` tag and ends with a `</div>` tag. Use a div element when you need to format an area of a web page that may contain other block display elements such as headings, paragraphs, unordered lists, and even other div elements. You'll use Cascading Style Sheets (CSS) later in this chapter to style and configure the color, font, and layout of HTML elements using generally accepted design standards.

HTML5 includes the header, nav, main, and footer structure elements that can be used along with the generic div element to configure specific areas on a web page. Figure 4-10 shows a diagram of a page (called a **wireframe**) that indicates how the structure of a web page could be configured with the header, nav, main, div, and footer elements.

Figure 4-10 Structural elements

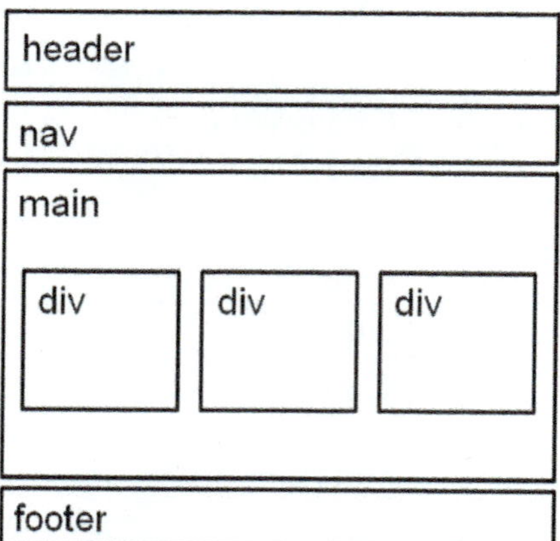

The Header Element. The purpose the HTML5 header element, discussed earlier in this chapter, is to is to contain the headings of either a web page document or an area within the document such as a section or an article. The header element begins with the `<header>` tag and ends with the `</header>` tag. The header element is block display and typically contains one or more heading level elements (h1 through h6).

The Nav Element. The purpose of the HTML5 nav element is to contain a section of navigation links. The block display nav element begins with the `<nav>` tag and ends with the `</nav>` tag.

The Main Element. The purpose of the HTML5 main element is to contain the main content of a web page document. The block display main element begins with the `<main>` tag and ends with the `</main>` tag.

The Footer Element. The purpose of the HTML5 footer element is to contain the footer content of a web page or section of a web page. The block display footer element begins with the `<footer>` tag and ends with the `</footer>` tag.

Checkpoint

4.4 How many HTML heading levels are there?

4.5 What tags do you use to set up a paragraph in HTML?

4.6 What is the difference between an ordered list and an unordered list?

4.7 Give an example of a special entity character.

4.3 Working with Hyperlinks

Without hyperlinks, a web page is just a document.

Well-designed web pages usually are not crammed with information. Designers generally break the information into shorter sections and use hyperlinks to let users navigate from one section to another, from one web page to another, and even to pages on different websites. A web page must have a user interface with logical, working hyperlinks to engage users and provide all necessary information.

Use the a element (commonly called the anchor element) to specify a **hyperlink**, often referred to as a link, to another web page or file that you want to display. Each anchor element begins with an <a> tag and ends with an </a> tag. The opening and closing anchor tags surround the text that the user can click to perform the hyperlink. Use the href attribute to configure the hyperlink reference, which identifies the name and location of the file to access.

Figure 4-11 shows a web page document with an anchor tag that configures a hyperlink to the website, http://webdevbasics.net.

The code for the anchor tag in Figure 4-11 is as follows:

```
<a href="http://webdevbasics.net">Basics of Web Design Textbook
Companion</a>
```

Notice that the href value is the URL for the website and will display the home page. The text that is typed between the two anchor tags displays on the web page as a hyperlink and is underlined by most browsers. When you move the mouse over a hyperlink, the cursor changes to a pointing hand, as shown in Figure 4-11.

Figure 4-11 Sample hyperlink

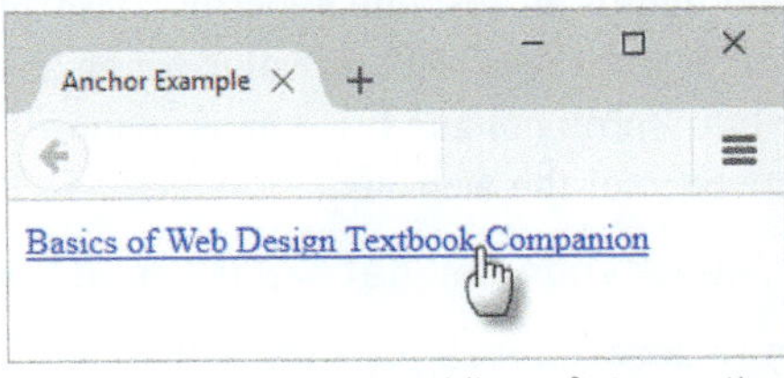

Microsoft Corporation

In the Spotlight:

Insert a Hyperlink on a Web Page

To create the web page shown in Figure 4-11, launch your web development tool and open the template.html file from the chapter04 folder. Modify the title element and add an anchor tag to the body section as indicated by the following code:

```
<!DOCTYPE html>
<html lang="en">
<head>
<title>Anchor Example</title>
<meta charset="utf-8">
</head>
<body>
<a href="http://webdevbasics.net">Basics of Web
Design Textbook Companion</a>
</body>
</html>
```

Save the document as anchor.html on your hard drive or flash drive. Launch a browser and test your page. It should look similar to the page shown in Figure 4-11.

Targeting Hyperlinks

By default, when a visitor clicks a hyperlink, the new web page automatically opens in the same browser window. You can configure the target attribute on an anchor tag with `target="_blank"` to open a hyperlink in a new browser window or browser tab. Note that you cannot control whether the web page opens in a new window or opens in a new tab—that is dependent on your visitor's browser configuration.

Absolute Hyperlink

An **absolute hyperlink** indicates the absolute location of a resource on the Web. The hyperlink the previous In the Spotlight is an absolute hyperlink. Use an absolute hyperlink when you need to link to resources on other websites. The href value for an absolute hyperlink to the home page of a website includes the http://protocol and the domain name. The following hyperlink is an absolute hyperlink to the home page of the website:

```
<a href="http://webdevbasics.net">Basics of Web Design</a>
```

Note that if we want to access a web page other than the home page on the book's website, we can also include a specific folder name and file name. For example, the following anchor tag configures an absolute hyperlink for a file named chapter1.html located in a folder named 6e on the website:

```
<a href="http://webdevbasics.net/6e/chapter1.html">Chapter 1</a>
```

Relative Hyperlink

When you need to link to web pages within your site, use a **relative hyperlink.** The href value for a relative hyperlink does not begin with http:// and does not include a domain name. For a relative hyperlink, the href value will contain only the file name (or folder and file name) of the web page you want to display. The hyperlink location is relative to the page currently being displayed. For example, if you are coding a home page (index.html) for a website and want to link to a page named contact.html located in the same folder as index.html, you can configure a relative hyperlink as shown in the following code sample:

```
<a href="contact.html">Contact Us</a>
```

Block Anchor

It's typical to use anchor tags to configure phrases or even just a single word as a hyperlink. HTML5 provides a new function for the anchor tag—the block anchor. A block anchor can configure one or more entire elements (even those that display as a block, such as a div, h1, or paragraph) as a hyperlink.

E-Mail Hyperlinks

The anchor tag can also be used to create e-mail hyperlinks. An e-mail hyperlink will automatically launch the default mail program configured for the browser. It is similar to an external hyperlink with the following two exceptions:

- It uses `mailto:` instead of `http://`.
- It launches the default e-mail application for the visitor's browser with your e-mail address as the recipient.

For example, to create an e-mail hyperlink to the e-mail address help@webdevbasics.net, code the following:

```
<a href="mailto:help@webdevbasics.net">help@webdevbasics.net</a>
```

It is good practice to place the e-mail address both on the web page and within the anchor tag. Not everyone has an e-mail program configured with his or her browser. By placing the e-mail address in both places, you increase usability for all of your visitors.

In the Spotlight:

Inserting an Email Hyperlink on a Web Page

Working on your own or with a partner, launch your web development tool and open the contact.html file in the chapter04 folder.

Configure the e-mail address in the content area as an e-mail hyperlink as given below:

```
<li>E-mail:
<a href="mailto:contact@trilliummediadesign.com">contact@
trilliummediadesign.com</a>
</li>
```

Save and test the page in a browser. The browser display should look similar to the page shown in Figure 4-12.

Figure 4-12 An e-mail hyperlink has been configured on the Contact page

Microsoft Corporation

Checkpoint

4.8 Explain the purpose of the href attribute.

4.9 What attribute should you configure if you want a hyperlink to open in a new browser tab?

4.10 Explain the difference between an absolute hyperlink and a relative hyperlink.

4.4 Using Cascading Style Sheets

Cascading style sheets are the programming tools for formatting consistent, user-friendly web pages.

Have you ever applied a heading style to format text text in a word processing program? **Cascading Style Sheets (CSS)** provides this same functionality for web designers. CSS allows web designers to apply typographical styles such as font size, color, and page layout instructions to a web page.

CSS is a flexible, cross-platform, standards-based language developed by the W3C.

Advantages of Cascading Style Sheets

There are several advantages to using CSS (see Figure 4-13).

- **Typography and page layout can be better controlled.** These features include fonts, spacing, color schemes, indents, margins, and element positioning.
- **Style is separate from structure.** The format of the text and colors used on the page can be configured and stored separately from the body section of the web page document.
- **Styles can be stored.** You can store styles in a separate document and associate them with the web page. When the styles are modified, the web page code remains intact. This means that if your client decides to change the background color from red to white, you only need to change one file that contains the styles, instead of each web page document.
- **Documents are potentially smaller.** The formatting is separate from the document; therefore, the actual documents should be smaller.
- **Site maintenance is easier.** Again, if the styles need to be changed, it's possible to complete the modifications by changing only the style sheet file.

Figure 4-13 The power of a single CSS file

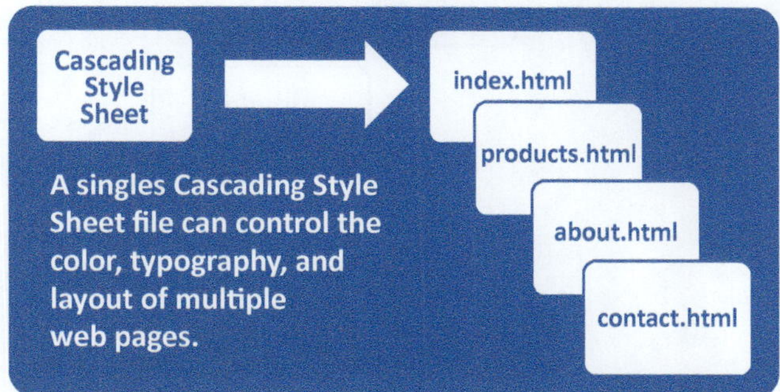

Methods of Configuring Cascading Style Sheets

Web designers use four methods to incorporate CSS technology in a website: inline, embedded, external, and imported.

Inline styles are coded in the body of the web page as an attribute of an HTML tag. The style only applies to the specific element that contains it as an attribute.

Embedded styles are defined in the head section of a web page. These style instructions apply to the entire web page document.

External styles are coded in a separate text file, called an **external style sheet**. This text file is associated with a web page by coding a link element in the head section.

Imported styles are similar to external styles in that they can connect styles coded in a separate text file with a web page document. An external style sheet can be imported into embedded styles or into another external style sheet by using the @import directive.

The "Cascade" in Cascading Style Sheets

The term cascade means waterfall. Figure 4-14 shows the cascade that applies the styles in order of precedence from the top external styles to the bottom inline styles. This allows the sitewide styles to be configured with an external style sheet file but overridden when needed by more pagespecific styles such as embedded or inline styles. The order the styles are coded in the web page matters. If styles are conflicting or apply to the same element, the last style rendered by the browser overrides earlier styles.

Figure 4-14 The "cascade" of Cascading Style Sheets

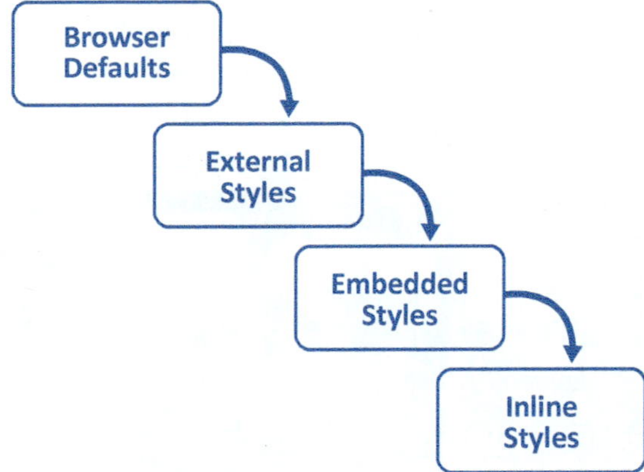

Style Rule Basics

Style sheets are made up of rules that describe the styling you want to apply. Each rule has two parts: a **selector** and a **declaration**.

- **CSS Style Ruler Selector.** The selector comes first. It tells the browser what HTML elements to select so the rule can be applied to them.
- **CSS Style Rule Declaration.** The declaration indicates the CSS **property** you are setting and the value you are assigning to the property. For example, the CSS rule shown in Figure 4-15 would set the color of the body text on a web page to blue. The selector represents the body element, and the declaration sets the color property to the value of blue.

Figure 4-15 Using CSS to set the text color to blue

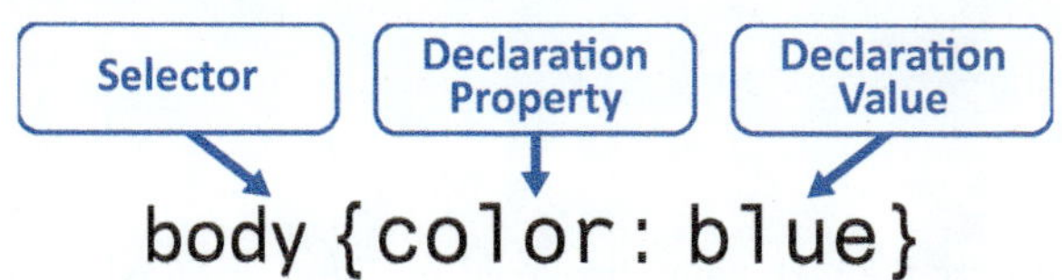

The background-color Property

The purpose of the CSS background-color property is to configure the background color of an element. The following style rule will configure the background color of a web page to be yellow:

```
body { background-color: yellow }
```

Notice how the declaration is enclosed within braces and how the colon symbol (:) separates the declaration property and the declaration value.

The color Property

The CSS property to configure the text color of an element is color. The following CSS style rule will configure the text color of a web page to be blue:

```
body { color: blue }
```

Configure Background and Text Color

To configure more than one property for a selector, use a semicolon (;) to separate the declarations The following CSS style rule configures a web page with white text and an orchid background:

```
body { color: white; background-color: orchid; }
```

See Appendix G for a list of CSS properties, including those for configuring color.

CSS Syntax for Color Values

For more flexibility and control, over colors on a web page, use a numerical color value, such as the **hexadecimal color values** listed in Appendix G. Hexadecimal color values are 6-digit codes where the first two digits represent the intensity of red, the second two are green, and the last two are blue.

Figure 4-16 A web page with light aqua background color and dark blue text color

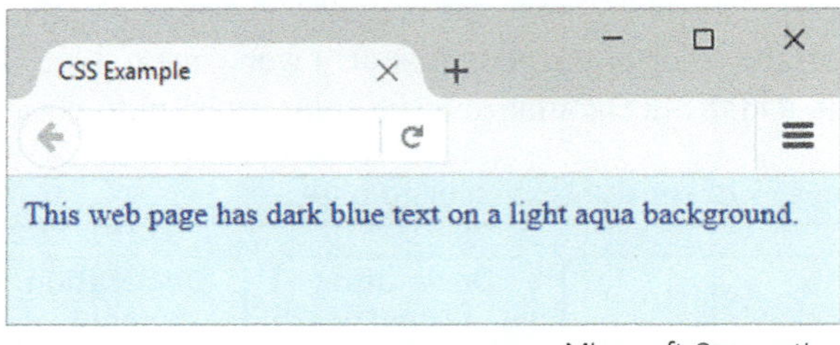

Microsoft Corporation

A style rule to configure the web page displayed in Figure 4-16 with dark blue text (hexadecimal #000066) on a light aqua background (hexadecimal #CCFFFF) is

```
body { color: #000066; background-color: #CCFFFF; }
```

The spaces in these declarations are optional. The ending semicolon (;) is also optional but useful in case you need to add additional style rules at a later time. The following alternative versions of the code above are also valid:

EXAMPLE 1:

```
body {color:#000066;background-color:#CCFFFF}
```

EXAMPLE 2:

```
body { background-color:#000066; color:#CCFFFF; }
```

EXAMPLE 3:

```
body {
color: #000066;
background-color: #CCFFFF;
}
```

EXAMPLE 4:

```
body { color: #000066;
background-color: #CCFFFF;
}
```

Configure Inline CSS

Inline styles are coded as an attribute on an HTML tag using the style attribute. The value of the style attribute is set to the style rule declaration that you need to configure. Recall that a declaration consists of a property and a value. Each property is separated from its value with a colon (:). The following code will set the text color of an <h1> tag to a shade of red:

```
<h1 style="color:#cc0000">This is displayed as a red heading</h1>
```

If there is more than one property, each is separated by a semicolon (;). The following code configures the heading with a red text color and a gray background color:

```
<h1 style="color:#cc0000;background-color:#cccccc;">
This is displayed as a red heading on a gray background</h1>
```

Configure Embedded CSS with the Style Element

The opening `<style>` tag begins the area with embedded style rules, and the closing `</style>` tag ends the area containing embedded style rules. Embedded styles apply to the entire document and are typically placed within a style element located in the head section of a web page. Note that while HTML 5.2 also allows the style element in the body section, we'll always code the style element in the head section.

Figure 4-17 Web page using embedded styles

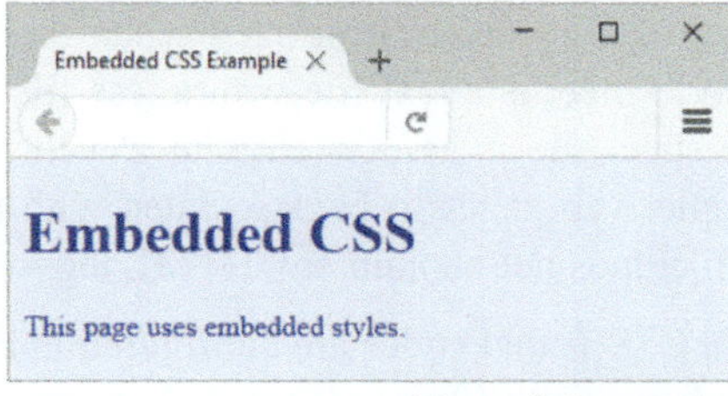

Microsoft Corporation

The web page in Figure 4-17 uses embedded styles to set the text color and background color of the web page document with the body element selector. See the example file provided, chapter04/embed.html.

```
<!DOCTYPE html>
<html lang="en">
<head>
<title>Embedded CSS Example</title>
<meta charset="utf-8">
<style>
body { background-color: #E6E6FA;
       color: #191970;
}
</style>
</head>
<body>
  <h1>Embedded CSS</h1>
  <p>This page uses embedded styles.</p>
</body>
</html>
```

Notice the way the style rules were coded with each rule on its own line. This makes the styles more readable and easier to maintain than one long row of text. The styles are in effect for the entire web page document because they were applied to the `<body>` tag using the body element selector.

Configure External CSS

The flexibility and power of CSS are best utilized when the CSS is external to the web page document. An external style sheet is a text file with a .css file extension that contains CSS style rules. The external style sheet file is associated with a web page using the link element. This provides a way for multiple web pages to be associated with the same external style sheet file. The external style sheet file does not contain any HTML tags—it only contains CSS style rules.

The advantage of external CSS is that styles are configured in a single file. This means that when styles need to be modified, only one file needs to be changed, instead of multiple web pages. On large sites, this can save a web developer much time and increase productivity. Let's get some practice with this useful technique.

In the Spotlight:

Using External Styles

To practice using external styles, first create an external style sheet. Then you'll configure a web page to be associated with the external style sheet. You may work on your own, or with a partner.

Create an External Style Sheet. Launch a text editor and type style rules to set the background color of a page to blue and the text color to white. Save the file as color.css. The code follows:

```
body { background-color: #0000FF;
       color: #FFFFFF; }
```

Figure 4-18 shows the external color.css style sheet displayed in Notepad. Notice that there is no HTML in this file. HTML tags are not coded within an external style sheet. Only CSS rules (selectors, properties, and values) are coded in an external style sheet.

Figure 4-18 The external style sheet color.css

color.css - Notepad

File Edit Format View Help

```
body { background-color: #0000FF;
       color: #FFFFFF;
}
```

Microsoft Corporation

Configure the Web Page. To create the web page shown in Figure 4-19, launch a text editor and open the template.html file from the chapter04 folder. Modify the title element, add a link tag to the head section, and add a paragraph to the body section as indicated by the following code:

```
<!DOCTYPE html>
<html lang="en">
<head>
<title>External Styles</title>
<meta charset="utf-8">
<link rel="stylesheet" href="color.css">
</head>
<body>
<p>This web page uses an external style sheet.</p>
</body>
</html>
```

Save your file as external.html in the same folder as your color.css file. Launch a browser and test your page. It should look similar to the page shown in Figure 4-19.

Figure 4-19 This page is associated with an external style sheet

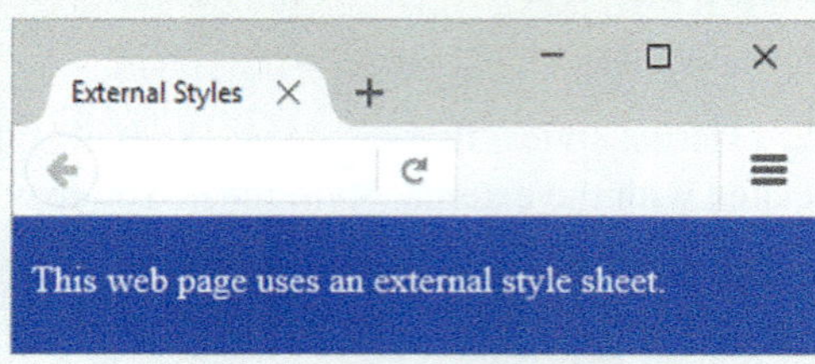

Microsoft Corporation

The color.css style sheet can be associated with any number of web pages. If you ever need to change the style of formatting, you only need to change a single file (color.css) instead of multiple files (all of the web pages). As mentioned earlier, this technique can boost productivity on a large site. This is a simple example, but the advantage of having only a single file to update is significant for both small and large websites.

The Cascade

Figure 4-20 shows the "cascade" (order of precedence) that applies the styles from outermost (external styles) to innermost (inline styles).

This set of rules allows the site-wide styles to be configured but overridden when needed by more granular page-specific styles (such as embedded or inline styles).

Figure 4-20 The cascade

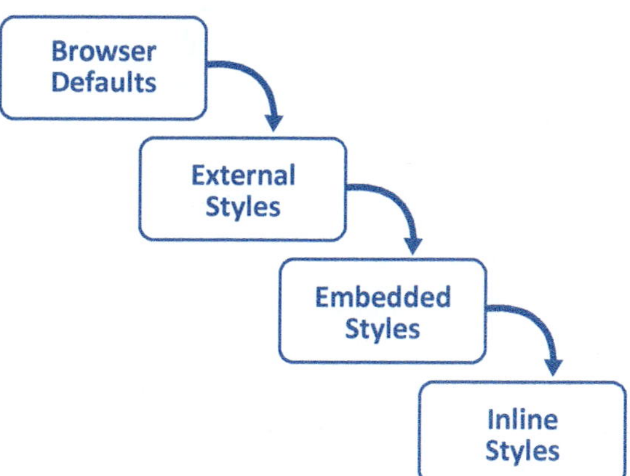

External styles can apply to multiple pages. The order the styles are coded in the web page matters. When using both external and embedded styles, it is a typical practice to code the link element (for external styles) before the style element (for embedded styles). So, when a web page contains both an association with an external style sheet and embedded styles, the external styles will be applied first, and then the embedded styles will be applied. This approach allows a web developer to override global external styles on selected pages.

If a web page also contains inline styles, any external and embedded styles are applied first as just described, and then the inline styles are applied. This approach allows a web developer to override page-wide styles for particular HTML tags or classes.

Note that an HTML tag or attribute will override styles. For example, a `<strong>` tag will override corresponding font-related styles configured for an element. If no attribute or style is applied to an element, the browser's default is applied. However, the appearance of the browser's default may vary by browser, and you might be disappointed with the result. Use CSS to specify the properties of your text and web page elements. Avoid depending on the browser's default.

In addition to the general cascade of CSS types described previously, the style rules themselves follow an order of precedence. Style rules applied to more local elements (such as a paragraph) take precedence over those applied to more global elements (such as a `<div>` that contains the paragraph).

Figure 4-21 Inheritance in action

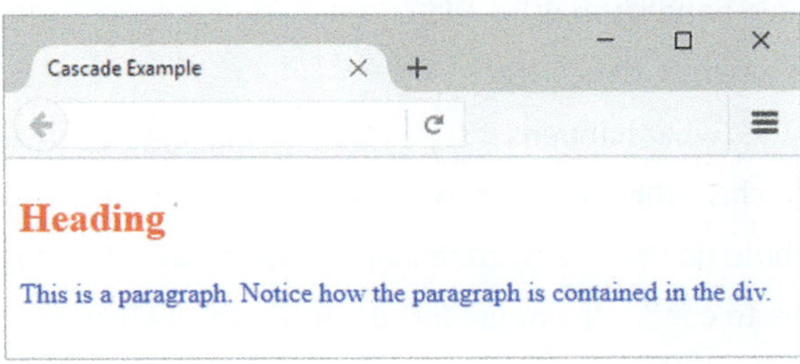

Microsoft Corporation

Let's look at the code for the page shown in Figure 4-21.

```
.special { color: red; }
p { color: blue; }
```

The CSS has two style rules: a rule creating a class named `special` that configures red text and a rule configuring all paragraphs to display blue text.

The HTML on the page contains a `<div>` with multiple elements, such as headings and paragraphs, as shown in the following code:

```
<div class="special">
<h2>Heading</h2>
<p>This is a paragraph. Notice how the paragraph is contained in the div.</p>
</div>
```

Here is how the browser would render the code:

1. The text within the heading is displayed using the color red because it is part of the `<div>` assigned to the special class. It inherits the properties from its parent (`<div>`) class. This is an example of inheritance, in which certain CSS properties are passed down to elements nested within a container element, such as a `<div>` or `<body>` element.
2. The text within the paragraph is displayed using the color blue because the browser applies the styles associated with the most local element (the paragraph). Even though the paragraph is within (and is considered a child of) the special class, the local paragraph style rules take precedence and are applied by the browser.

CSS Syntax Validation

The W3C has a free Markup Validation Service (http://jigsaw.w3.org/css-validator) that will validate your CSS code and check it for syntax errors. CSS validation provides students with quick self-assessment—you can prove that your code uses correct syntax. In the working world, CSS validation serves as a quality assurance tool. Invalid code may cause browsers to render the pages slower than otherwise or not render the page at all.

Checkpoint

4.11 What are five benefits to using CSS?

4.12 What is an external style sheet?

4.13 If you use CSS, what happens if styles are conflicting or apply to the same element?

4.14 Explain and show the CSS rule to set the color of text on a web page to green.

4.15 What attribute do you use to code inline styles on an HTML tag?

4.16 Explain how to configure embedded styles for an HTML page.

4.17 What element do you use to associate an external style sheet with a web page?

4.5 Graphics Basics

Properly adding graphics to a web page makes it more engaging and informative.

Graphics can make web pages compelling and engaging. GIF, JPEG, and PNG formatted images are well-supported on the Web. GIFs are best suited for line art or clip art. JPEGs are best suited for photographs. PNGs can be used for either purpose, so you may want to consider the file size and quality of the images when you make your decision. A newer format developed by Google is WebP. Not all browsers support it. Table 4-3 lists characteristics of these file types.

Table 4-3 Overview of Common Web Graphic File Formats

Image Type	File Extension	Compression	Transparency	Animation	Colors	Progressive Display
GIF	.gif	Lossless	Yes	Yes	256	Interlacing
JPEG	.jpg or .jpeg	Lossy	No	No	Millions	Progressive
PNG	.png	Lossless	Yes	No	Millions	Interlacing
WebP	.webp	Lossy and Lossless	Yes	Yes	Millions	None

Img Element

The img element (often referred to as the image element) configures graphics on a web page, such as photographs, banners, company logos, and navigation buttons. The img element is a void element and is not coded as a pair of opening and closing tags. The following code example configures an image named logo.gif, which is located in the same folder as the web page:

```
<img src="logo.gif" height="200" width="500" alt="My Company Name">
```

The src attribute specifies the file name of the image. The alt attribute provides a text replacement, typically a text description, of the image. The browser reserves the correct amount of space for your image if you use the height and width attributes with values either equal to or approximately the size of the image. Table 4-4 lists some common img element attributes and their values.

Table 4-4 Attributes of the Img Element

Attribute	Value
`alt`	Text phrase that describes the image; required
`height`	Height of image in pixels or percentage
`id`	Text name, alphanumeric, beginning with a letter, no spaces—the value must be unique and not used for other id values on the same web page document
`src`	The URL or file name of the image; required
`usemap`	Value corresponding to the name and id of an associated map element
`width`	Width of image in pixels or percentage

When naming image files for use on a web page, use all lowercase letters. Avoid punctuation symbols and spaces. Use hyphens to separate words. Do not change file extensions. Keep your file names short, but descriptive. For example: myphotowithmydogonmybirthday.jpg is too long, d1.jpg is probably too short, birthday-dog.jpg may be just about right.

Image Hyperlinks

Writing the HTML code to make an image function as a hyperlink is very straightforward. To create an **image link**, all you need to do is surround your `<img>` tag with anchor tags. For example, to place a link around an image called home.gif, use the following code:

```
<a href="index.html"><img src="home.gif" height="19" width="85"
alt="Home"></a>
```

A thumbnail image link is a small image configured as an image link with an href attribute value that points to another image file instead of to a web page. For example,

```
<a href="sunset.jpg"><img src="thumb.jpg" height="100" width="100"
alt="view a larger sunset"></a>
```

To see this in action, launch a browser and view chapter04/thumb.html, provided.

Fonts with CSS

The font-family property configures font typefaces. A web browser displays text with the fonts that have been installed on the user's computer. When a font that is not installed on your web visitor's computer is specified, the default font is substituted. Times New Roman is the default font displayed by most web browsers. Figure 4-22 shows font family categories and some common font typefaces.

Figure 4-22 Common Fonts

Font Family Category	Font Family Description	Font Typeface Examples
serif	Serif fonts have small embellishments on the end of letter strokes; often used for headings.	Times New Roman, Georgia, Palatino
sans-serif	Sans-serif fonts do not have serifs; often used for web page text.	Arial, Tahoma, Helvetica, Verdana
monospace	Fixed-width font; often used for code samples.	Courier New, Lucida Console
cursive	Hand-written style; use with caution; may be difficult to read on a web page.	Lucida Handwriting, Brush Script, Comic Sans MS
fantasy	Exaggerated style; use with caution; sometimes used for headings; may be difficult to read on a web page.	Jokerman, Impact, Papyrus

The Verdana, Tahoma, and Georgia font typefaces were specifically designed to display well on computer monitors. A common practice is to use a serif font (such as Georgia or Times New Roman) for headings and a sans-serif font (such as Verdana or Arial) for detailed text content. Not every computer has the same fonts installed. Create a built-in backup plan by listing multiple fonts and categories for the value of the `font-family` property. The browser will attempt to use the fonts in the order listed. The following CSS configures the p element selector to display text in Verdana (if installed) or Arial (if installed) or the default installed sans-serif font.

```
p { font-family: Verdana, Arial, sans-serif; }
```

CSS Text Properties

Typography can be described as the style or arrangement of text. You will use CSS to configure the text on your web pages. In this section, you'll explore the `font-size`, `font-weight`, `font-style`, `line-height`, `textalign`, `text-decoration`, `text-indent`, `text-transform`, and `letter-spacing` properties.

The `font-size` Property

The font-size property sets the size of the font. Table 4-5 lists several categories of font size values, characteristics, and recommended usage.

Table 4-5 Configuring Font Size

Value	Category	Values Notes
Text Value	`xx-small`, `x-small`, `small`, `medium` (default), `large`, `x-large`, `xx-large`	Scales well when text is resized; limited options for text size
Pixel Unit (px)	Numeric value with unit, such as `10px`	Pixel-perfect display depends on screen resolution; may not scale in every browser when text is resized
Point Unit (pt)	Numeric value with unit, such as `10pt`	Use to configure print version of web page (see Chapter 8); may not scale in every browser when text is resized
Em Unit (em)	Numeric value with unit, such as `.75em`	Recommended by W3C; scales well when text is resized in browser; many options for text size
Percentage Value	Numeric value with percentage, such as 75%	Recommended by W3C; scales well when text is resized in browser; many options for text size

The **em unit** is a relative font unit that has its roots in the print industry back in the day when printers set type manually with blocks of characters. An em unit is the width of a square block of type (typically the uppercase M) for a particular font and type size. On web pages, an em unit corresponds to the width of the font and size used in the parent element (typically the body element).

The `font-weight` Property

The font-weight property configures the boldness of the text. The CSS `font-weight: bold;` declaration has an effect similar to the `<b>` or `<strong>` HTML element. Sample CSS to configure bold text in the nav:

```
nav { font-weight: bold; }
```

The `font-style` Property

The font-style property is used to configure text displayed in italics. Valid values are `normal` (the default), `italic`, and `oblique`. The CSS `font- style: italic;` declaration has the same visual effect in the browser as an `<i>` or `<em>` HTML element. Sample CSS to configure italic text in the footer:

```
footer { font-style: italic; }
```

The `line-height` Property

The line-height property modifies the default height of a line of text and is often configured using a percentage value. Sample CSS to configure a paragraph with double-spaced lines:

```
p { line-height: 200%; }
```

The `text-align` Property

HTML elements are left-aligned by default—they begin at the left margin. The CSS text-align property configures the alignment of text and inline elements within block elements such as headings, paragraphs, and divs. The `left` (default), `center`, `right`, and `justify` values are valid. Sample CSS to configure centered text within an h1 element:

```
h1 { text-align: center; }
```

The `text-decoration` Property

The purpose of the CSS text-decoration property is to modify the display of text. Commonly used values include `none`, `underline`, `overline`, and `line-through`. Although hyperlinks are underlined by default, you can remove the underline with the text- decoration property. Sample CSS to remove the underline on a hyperlink:

```
a { text-decoration: none; }
```

The `text-indent` Property

The CSS text-indent property configures the indentation of the first line of text within an element. The value can be numeric (with a px, pt, or em unit) or a percentage. Sample CSS to configure a 5em indent for the first line of a paragraph:

```
p { text-indent: 5em; }
```

The `text-transform` Property

The text-transform property configures the capitalization of text. Valid values are `none` (default), `capitalize`, `uppercase`, or `lowercase`. Sample CSS to configure uppercase text within an h3 element:

```
h3 { text-transform: uppercase; }
```

The `letter-spacing` Property

The letter-spacing property configures the space between text characters. Valid values are normal (default) and a numeric pixel or em unit. Sample CSS to configure extra spacing within an h3 element:

```
h3 { letter-spacing: 3px; }
```

In the Spotlight:

Configuring Text and Graphics

You will apply your new skills with configuring images and text while you create the web page shown in Figure 4-23. You may work alone or with a partner.

Figure 4-23 A Home page

Microsoft Corporation; Images courtesy of Terri Ann Morris

Create a folder named kayakpractice.

Copy the starter.html file from the chapter04 folder into your kayakpractice folder.

Copy the following files from the chapter04 folder into your kayakpractice folder: hero.jpg, background.jpg, and headerbackblue.jpg.

Launch your web development tool, open the starter.html file, and save the file as index.html. Edit the code as follows:

1. Locate the style tags in the head section and code embedded CSS to style the following:
   a. Configure the body element selector to display background.jpg as the page background and set Verdana, Arial, or the default sans-serif font as the global font typeface.

   ```
   body { background-image:
           url(background.jpg);
           font-family: Verdana,
           Arial, sans-serif; }
   ```

   b. Configure the header element selector with a #000033 background color and to display the headerbackblue. jpg image in the background. Configure this image to display on the right and to not repeat. Also configure #FFFF99 text color, 400% line height, and a 1em text indent.

   ```
   header { background-color: #000033;
            background-image: url(headerbackblue.jpg);
            background-position: right;
            background-repeat: no-repeat;
            color: #FFFF99;
            line-height: 400%;
            text-indent: 1em;}
   ```

   c. Configure the h1, h2, and h3 element selectors with Georgia, Times New Roman, or the default serif font.

   ```
   h1, h2, h3 { font-family: Georgia, "Times New Roman", serif; }
   ```

   d. Configure the nav element selector with bold font that is 1.5em in size.

   ```
   nav { font-weight: bold;
         font-size: 1.5em; }
   ```

   e. Configure navigation anchor elements to not display an underline. Use a descendant selector.

   ```
   nav a { text-decoration: none; }
   ```

   f. Configure paragraph elements to be indented 2em units.

   ```
   p { text-indent: 2em; }
   ```

   g. Configure the footer element selector to be centered with italic font that is .80em in size.

   ```
   footer { text-align: center;
            font-style: italic;
            font-size: .80em; }
   ```

2. Remove the small and i tags from the page footer area.

3. Code an img element after the h2 element to display the hero.jpg image. Set appropriate values forthe alt, width, and height attributes.

```
<img src="hero.jpg" alt="tour guide paddling a kayak" width="500"
height="350">
```

Save your file. Test your page in a browser. It should look similar to Figure 4-23.

Configure List Markers with CSS

The default display for an unordered list is to show a disc marker (often referred to as a bullet) in front of each list item. The default display for an ordered list is to show a decimal number in front of each list item. Use the `list-style-type` property to configure the marker for an unordered or ordered list. See Table 4-6 for common property values.

Table 4-6 CSS Properties for Ordered and Unordered List Markers

Property	Description	Value	List Marker Display

`list-style-type`	Configures the style of the list marker	`none`
		`disc`
		`circle`
		`square`
		`decimal`
		`upper-alpha`
		`lower-alpha`
		`lower-roman`
			No list markers display
			Circle ("bullet")
			Open circle
			Square
			Decimal numbers
			Uppercase letters
			Lowercase letters
			Lowercase Roman numerals

`list-style-image`	Image replacement for the list marker	The `url` keyword with parentheses surrounding the file name or path for the image	The image displays in front of each list item
`list-style-position`	Configures placement of markers	`inside`	Markers are indented, text wraps under the markers
		`outside` (default)	Markers have default placement

The property `list-style-type: none` prevents the browser from displaying the list markers. Figure 4-24 shows an unordered list configured with square markers using the following CSS:

```
ul { list-style-type: square; }
```

Figure 4-25 shows an ordered list configured with uppercase letter markers using the following CSS:

```
ol { list-style-type: upper-alpha; }
```

Configure an Image as a List Marker

Use the `list-style-image` property to configure an image as the marker in an unordered or ordered list. In Figure 4-26, an image named marker.gif was configured to replace the list markers using the following CSS:

```
ul {list-style-image: url(marker.gif); }
```

Figure 4-24 The unordered list markers are square

- Specialty Coffee and Tea
- Gluten-free Pastries
- Organic Salads

Figure 4-25 The ordered list markers use uppercase letters

A. Specialty Coffee and Tea
B. Gluten-free Pastries
C. Organic Salads

Figure 4-26 The list markers are replaced with an image

Specialty Coffee and Tea
Gluten-free Pastries
Organic Salads

In the Spotlight:

Customizing List Markers

In this exercise, you'll replace the list markers on a web page with an image file named marker.gif. You will use your files from a previous exercise as a starting point. You may work alone or with a partner.

1. Launch your web development tool and open index.html from the chapter04 folder. Add the following style rule to the embedded CSS in the head section to configure the ul element selector with the `list-style-image` property:

```
ul { list-style-image: url(marker.gif); }
```

2. Save your page as index.html. Launch in a browser and test your page. You should see a small coffee cup before each item in the unordered list.

Checkpoint

4.18 What are JPEG images best suited for?

4.19 What HTML element configures graphics on a web page?

4.20 Explain the src attribute.

4.21 What do you have to do to turn an image already placed on a web site into a hyperlink?

4.22 What is the purpose of the text-transform property?

4.6 Adding Multimedia to a Web Page

Add multimedia and interactive elements to a web page using HTML and CSS.

The easiest way to give your website visitors access to an audio or a video file is to create a simple hyperlink to the file. For example, the code to hyperlink to a sound file named WDFpodcast.mp3 follows:

```
<a href="WDFpodcast.mp3">Podcast Episode 1</a> (MP3)
```

When your website visitor clicks the link, the player for .mp3 files that is installed on the device will typically display embedded in a new browser window or tab. Your web page visitor can then play the sound. If your website visitor right-clicks on the hyperlink, the media file can be downloaded and saved.

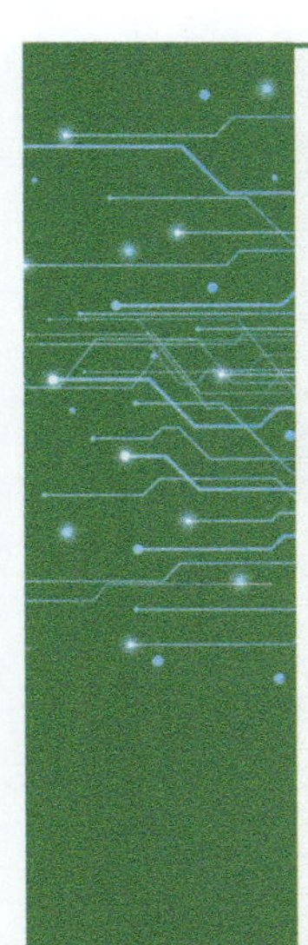

In the Spotlight:

Link to Audio from a Web Page

In this exercise, use a hyperlink to an MP3 file so that visitors can link to a podcast. The web page will also provide a hyperlink to a text transcript of that file to provide for accessibility. It can be useful to your web page visitors if you indicate the type of file (such as an MP3) and, optionally, the size of the file to be accessed. You may work alone or with a partner.

Copy the podcast.mp3 and podcast.txt files from the chapter04 folder and save them to a folder named podcast. Use the chapter04/template.html file as a starting point and create a web page containing a page title of Podcast, an h1 element with the text Web Design Podcast, a hyperlink to the MP3 file, and a hyperlink to the text transcript. Save your page as podcast.html. Display the file in a browser. Try to test your page in different browsers and browser versions. When you click on the MP3 hyperlink, an audio player (whichever player is configured on the device) will display in a new browser window or tab. When you click on the hyperlink for the text transcript, the text will display in the browser.

Containers and Codecs

When working with native HTML5 video and audio, it's useful to be aware of the container and the codec. The **container** is designated by the file extension, such as .mpa or .aac. The **codec** is the algorithm used to compress and decompress the media, such as the Advanced Audio Coding (AAC) codec.

Explore Tables 4-7 and 4-8, which list common media file extensions, including a description with codec information (if applicable for HTML5) and the **MIME type**. MIME, or multipurpose internet mail extensions, identifies the file format. Note that there is not always a one-to-one correspondence between file extensions and codecs. In some cases, multiple codecs may use the same files extension as their container.

Table 4-7 Commonly Used Audio File Types

File Extension	Description	MIME Type
.aac, .mp4	MPEG-4 Audio; audio-only MPEG-4 format that uses the Advanced Audio Coding (AAC) codec	audio/mp4
.mp3	MPEG-1 Audio Layer-3	audio/mpeg
.ogg	Open-source audio file format; Vorbis and Opus codecs	audio/ogg
.wav	Waveform Audio File Format	audio/wav

Table 4-8 Commonly Used Video File Types

File Extension	Description	MIME Type
.av1, .mp4	Open-source, royalty-free AV1 video codec; Alliance for Open Media	video/avi
.m4v, .mp4	MPEG-4 (MP4) codec; H.264 codec	video/mp4
.mov	Developed by Apple; originally indicated a video with a MPEG-4 codec used in Apple's Quicktime application	video/ quicktime
.mov, .mp4, .hevc	Newer High-efficiency Video Coding HEVC codec (also called H.265 codec); Apple has begun using the .mov file extension for HEVC video	video/mp4
.ogv, .ogg	Open-source video file format; Theora codec	video/ogg
.webm	Open media file format; VP8 and VP9 video codecs	video/ webm

NOTE: For the most current information about browser support for HTML video and codecs, visit https://caniuse.com.

The Audio Element

The audio element supports native play of audio files in the browser—without the need for plug-ins or players. The audio element begins with the `<audio>` tag and ends with the `</audio>` tag. Table 4-9 lists the attributes of the audio element.

Table 4-9 Audio Element Attributes

Attribute	Value	Description
`src`	file name	Optional; audio file name
`type`	MIME Type	Optional; the MIME type of the audio file, such as audio/mpeg or audio/ogg
`autoplay`		Optional; boolean attribute; if present, indicates whether audio should start playing automatically; use with caution
`controls`		Optional; boolean attribute; if present, indicates whether controls should be displayed; recommended
`loop`		Optional; boolean attribute; if present, indicates whether audio should be played over and over
`preload`	`none`, `auto`, `metadata`	Optional; values: none (no preload), `metadata` (only download media file metadata), and `auto` (download the media file)
`title`		Optional; specifies a brief text description that may be displayed by browsers or assistive technologies

You'll need to supply multiple versions of the audio due to browser support of different codecs. Plan to supply audio files in at least two different containers, including ogg and mp3. It is typical to omit the `src` and `type` attributes from the audio tag and, instead, configure multiple versions of the audio file with the source element.

The Source Element

The source element is a self-contained, or void, tag that specifies a multimedia file and a MIME type. The `src` attribute identifies the file name of the media file. The `type` attribute indicates the MIME type of the file. Code `type="audio/mpeg"` for an MP3 file. Code `type="audio/ogg"` for audio files using the Vorbis codec. Configure a source element for each version of the audio file. Place the source elements before the closing audio tag.

The following code sample configures the web page shown in Figure 4-27 to display a controller for an audio file:

Figure 4-27 The Firefox browser supports the HTML5 audio element

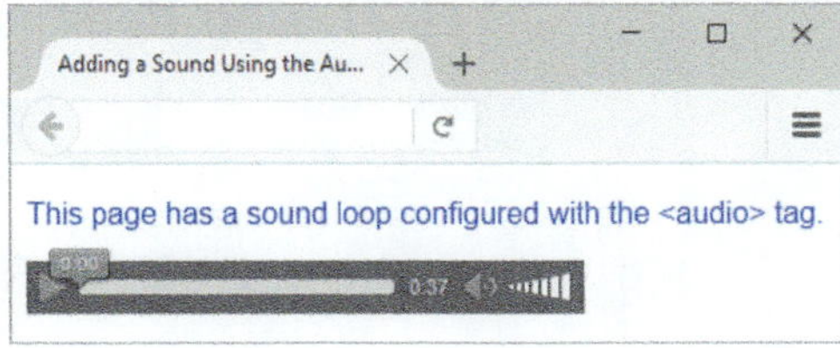

Microsoft Corporation

```
<audio controls>
  <source src="soundloop.mp3" type="audio/mpeg">
  <source src="soundloop.ogg" type="audio/ogg">
  <a href="soundloop.mp3">Download the Audio File</a> (MP3)
</audio>
```

Current versions of modern browsers support the HTML5 audio element. The controls displayed by each browser are different. Review the code sample just given and note the hyperlink placed between the second source element and the closing audio tag. Any HTML elements or text placed in this area is rendered by browsers that do not support the HTML5 audio element. This is referred to as fallback content—if the audio element is not supported, the MP3 version of the file is made available for download.

In the Spotlight:

Configuring an Audio Control on a Web Page

In this exercise, you will launch your web development tools and create a web page (see Figure 4-28) that displays an audio control to play a podcast. You may work alone or with a partner.

Copy the podcast.mp3, podcast.ogg, and podcast.txt files from the chapter04 folder and save them to a folder named audio. Use the chapter04/template.html file as a starting point and create a web page containing a page title and an h1 element with the text Web Design Podcast, an audio control (use the audio element and two source elements), and a hyperlink to the text transcript. Configure a hyperlink to the MP3 file as the fallback content. The code for the audio element follows:

```
<audio controls>
  <source src="podcast.mp3" type="audio/mpeg">
  <source src="podcast.ogg" type="audio/ogg"><br>
  <a href="podcast.mp3">Download the Podcast</a> (MP3)
</audio>
```

Save your page as index.html in the audio folder. Display the file in a browser. Try to test your page in different browsers and browser versions. When you click on the hyperlink for the text transcript, the text will display in the browser.

Figure 4-28 Using the audio element to provide access to a podcast

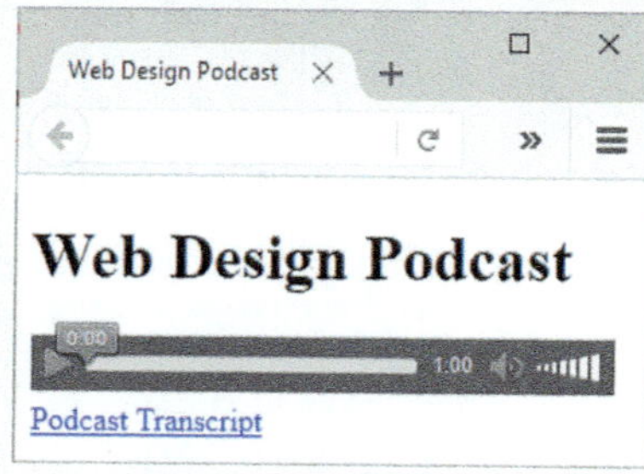

Microsoft Corporation

The Video Element

VideoNote
HTML5 Video

The video element supports native play of video files in the browser—without the need for plug-ins or players. The video element begins with the `<video>` tag and ends with the `</video>` tag. Table 4-10 lists the attributes of the video element.

Table 4-10 Video Element Attributes

Attribute	Value	Description
`src`	file name	Optional; video file name
`type`	MIME Type	Optional; the MIME type of the video file, such as video/mp4 or video/ogg
`autoplay`		Optional; boolean attribute; if present, indicates whether video should start playing automatically; use with caution
`controls`		Optional; boolean attribute; if present, indicates whether controls should be displayed
`height`	number	Optional; video height in pixels
`loop`		Optional; boolean attribute; if present, indicates whether video plays continuously
`poster`	file name	Optional; specifies an image to display while the video is downloading and before the browser plays the video
`preload`	`none`, `metadata`, `auto`	Optional; values: none (no preload), `metadata` (only download media file metadata), and `auto` (download the media file)
`title`		Optional; specifies a brief text description that may be displayed by browsers or assistive technologies
`width`	number	Optional; video width in pixels

Due to browser support of different codecs, plan to supply video files in at least two different containers, including mp4 and ogg (or ogv). It is typical to omit the `src` and `type` attributes from the video tag and, instead, configure multiple versions of the audio file with the source element.

The Source Element

The source element is a self-contained, or void, tag that specifies a multimedia file and a MIME type. The `src` attribute identifies the file name of the media file. The `type` attribute indicates the MIME type of the file. Code `type="video/mp4"` for video files using the MP4 codec. Code `type="video/ogg"` for video files using the Theora codec. Configure a source element for each version of the video file. Place the source elements before the closing video tag.

The following code sample configures the web page shown in Figure 4-29 (see the file chapter04/sparky.html) with the native HTML5 browser controls to display and play a video. Most current versions of modern browsers support the HTML5 video element.

```
<video controls poster="sparky.jpg"
       width="160" height="150">
  <source src="sparky.m4v" type="video/mp4">
  <source src="sparky.ogv" type="video/ogg">
  <a href="sparky.mov">Sparky the Dog</a> (.mov)
</video>
```

Figure 4-29 Video on a web page

Microsoft Corporation; Image courtesy of Terri Ann Morris

Review the code sample just given and note the anchor element placed between the second source element and the closing video tag. Any HTML elements or text placed in this area is rendered by browsers that do not support the HTML5 video element. This is referred to as fallback content. In this case, a hyperlink to a .mov version of the file is supplied for the user to download.

In the Spotlight:

Configuring Video on a Web Page

In this exercise, you will launch your web development tool and create the web page in Figure 4-30, which displays a video control to play a movie. You may work alone or with a partner. Copy the sedona.m4v, sedona.ogv, sedona.mov, and sedona.jpg files from the chapter04 folder and save them to a new folder named video.

Figure 4-30 Video element

Microsoft Corporation; Image courtesy of Terri Ann Morris

Open the chapter04/template.html file in your web development tool. Save the file with the name index.html in the video folder. Edit the index.html file:

1. Modify the title element and configure the h1 element with the text: Sedona Scenes.
2. Configure a video control (use the video element and two source elements) to display the video.
   a. Configure a hyperlink for the sedona.mov file as fallback content.
   b. Configure the sedona.jpg file as a poster image, which will display as the video downloads and before the browser plays the video.
   c. The code for the video element follows:

```
<video controls poster="sedona.jpg">
  <source src="sedona.m4v" type="video/mp4">
  <source src="sedona.ogv" type="video/ogg">
  <a href="sedona.mov">Photos of Sedona, Arizona</a> (.mov)
</video>
```

3. Notice that the video element does not contain `height` and `width` attributes. You can configure the HTML5 video to be flexible with CSS. Place your cursor in the head section and code a style element. Configure the following style rule to set 100% width, auto height, and a maximum width of 1280 pixels (which is the actual width of the video).

```
video { width: 100%; height: auto; max-width: 1280px; }
```

   Save your page as index.html in the video folder. Display the file in a browser. Try to test in different browsers and browser versions.

WARNING: Be careful to use only imedia that you have personally created or have obtained the rights or license to use. If another individual has created an image, sound, video, or document that you think would be useful on your own website, ask permission to use the material instead of simply taking it.

Configuring a Details and Summary Widget

A **widget** is a small program or component, written in a language such as JavaScript, that can be embedded as an element on a web page. The widget runs independently from the page. An example might be a countdown clock or a slideshow. Many graphical authoring tools come with libraries of widgets that you can use and you may be able to find others for free online.

You can use the details element and summary element together to configure an interactive widget that will hide and show information.

Details Element

The purpose of the details element is to configure the browser to render an interactive widget, which contains one summary element and detailed information (which can be a combination of text and HTML tags). The details element begins with the `<details>` tag and ends with the `</details>` tag.

Summary Element

The summary element is coded within the details element. The purpose of the summary element is to contain the text summary (typically some type of term or heading) shown in the interactive widget. The summary element begins with the <summary> tag and ends with the </summary> tag.

Details and Summary Widget

Figures 4-31 and 4-32 show the details and summary elements in action using the Chrome browser. Figure 4-31 shows the initial display of the web page with each summary item (in this case the terms Repetition, Contrast, Proximity, and Alignment) visible and displayed next to a triangle rendered automatically by the Chrome browser.

In Figure 4-32, the visitor has selected the first summary item (Repetition), which caused browser to display the detailed information for that item. The visitor can select the same summary item again to hide the details or can select another summary item to also show its corresponding detailed information.

Figure 4-31 Initial browser display

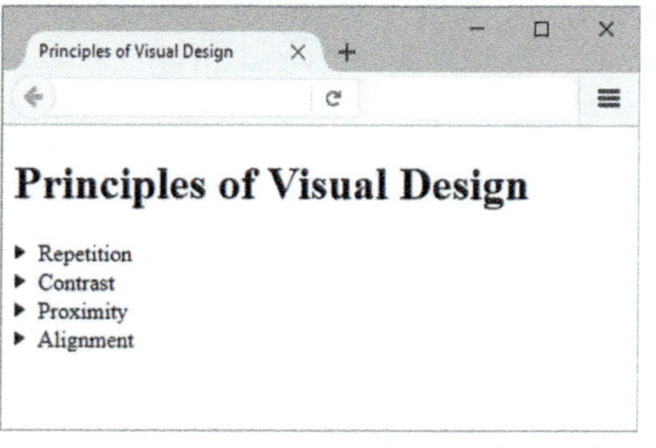

Microsoft Corporation

Figure 4-32 Detailed information displays

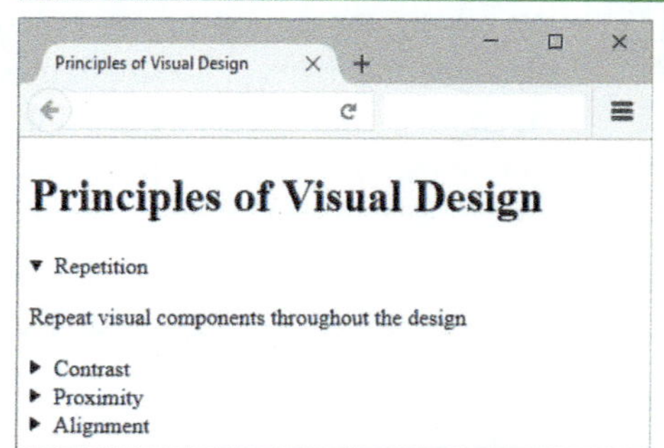

Microsoft Corporation

Current versions of modern browsers support the details and summary elements. Browsers that do not support the details and summary elements display all the information immediately and do not provide interactivity.

In the Spotlight:

Configuring an Interactive Widget

In this exercise, you will configure an interactive widget with the details and summary elements as you create a web page. Create a new folder named ch04details. Launch your web development tool and open the template file located at chapter04/template.html. Save the file as index.html in your ch04details folder. Modify the file to configure a web page as indicated:

1. Configure the text, Principles of Visual Design, within an h1 element and within the title element.
2. Code the following in the body of the web page:

```
<details>
   <summary>Repetition</summary>
   <p>Repeat visual components throughout the design</p>
</details>
<details>
   <summary>Contrast</summary>
   <p>Add visual excitement and draw attention</p>
</details>
<details>
   <summary>Proximity</summary>
   <p>Group related items</p>
</details>
<details>
   <summary>Alignment</summary>
   <p>Align elements to create visual unity</p>
</details>
```

Save your file and test your page in a browser. Try selecting or clicking on each of the terms or arrows to display the information you coded within the details element.

JavaScript

Although some interactivity on web pages can be achieved with CSS, JavaScript powers much of the interactivity on the Web. **JavaScript**, developed initially by Brendan Eich at Netscape, is an object-based, client-side scripting language interpreted by a web browser. JavaScript is considered to be object-based because it's used to work with the objects associated with a web page document: the browser window, the document itself, and elements such as forms, images, and hyperlinks.

JavaScript statements can be placed in a separate file (with a .js extension) that is accessed by a web browser or within an HTML script element. The purpose of the script element is to either contain scripting statements or indicate a file that contains scripting statements. Some JavaScript also can be coded within the HTML. In all cases, the web browser interprets the JavaScript statements. Because JavaScript is interpreted by a browser, it is considered to be a client-side scripting language.

JavaScript can be used to respond to events such as moving the mouse, clicking a button, and loading a web page. This technology is also often utilized to edit and verify information on HTML form controls such as text boxes, check boxes, and radio buttons. Other uses for JavaScript include pop-up windows, image slideshows, animation, date manipulation, and calculations. The following code uses JavaScript to determine and display the current date. The JavaScript statements are enclosed within an HTML script element and coded directly in the .html file.

```
<h2>Today is
<script>
var myDate = new Date()
var month = myDate.getMonth() + 1
var day = myDate.getDate()
var year = myDate.getFullYear()
document.write(month + "/" + day + "/" + year)
</script>
</h2>
```

jQuery

Web developers often need to configure the same type of common interactive features (such as slideshows,vform validation, and animation) on web pages. One approach is to write one's own JavaScript code andvtest it in a wide variety of browsers and operating systems. As you might guess, this can become quitevtime-consuming. The free, open-source jQuery JavaScript library was developed by John Resig in 2006 to simplify client-side scripting. The jQuery Foundation is a volunteer organization that contributes to the continued development of jQuery and provides jQuery documentation at https://api.jquery.com.

An application programming interface (API) is a protocol that allows software components to communicate—interacting and sharing data. The jQuery API can be used to configure many interactive features, including the following:

- image slideshows
- ianimation (moving, hiding, and fading)
- ievent handling (mouse movements and mouse clicking)
- idocument manipulation

Many web developers and designers have found that jQuery is easier to learn and work with than writing their own JavaScript, although a basic understanding of JavaScript is needed to be efficient when using jQuery. An advantage of the jQuery library is its compatibility with all current browsers.

jQuery is often used on popular websites, such as Amazon and Twitter. Because jQuery is an open-source library, anyone can extend the jQuery library by writing a new jQuery plugin that provides a new or enhanced interactive feature. For example, the jQuery Cycle plugin18 supports a variety of transition effects. Figure 4-33 (see https://webdevfoundations.net/jquery) shows an example of using jQuery and the Cycle plugin to create an image slideshow. There are many jQuery plugins available, providing interactions and functionality such as slideshows, tooltips, and form validation.

Figure 4-33 jQuery plugin slideshow

Microsoft Corporation; Image courtesy of Terri Ann Morris

Checkpoint

4.23 What element supports playing audio files in a browser without a plug-in or player?

4.24 What element supports playing video files in a browser without a plug-in or player?

4.25 What is a widget?

4.26 Why is JavaScript considered object-based?

4.7 Web Publishing Basics

Designing a web page is just the beginning; in order to share it with others, you must publish it.

File Organization

An unorganized website often contains a long list of files, which can become difficult to maintain over time. It's common practice to create a separate folder for images on a website. It's also a good idea to organize your web pages into folders by purpose or subject. This section introduces you to coding relative hyperlinks for a website with multiple folders.

Recall that a relative hyperlink is used to link to web pages within your site. You've been coding relative links to display web pages that are all inside the same folder. Let's consider a website for a bed and breakfast that features rooms and events. The folder and file listing is shown in Figure 4-34. The main folder for this website is called casita, and the web developer has created separate subfolders—named images, rooms, and events—to organize the site.

Figure 4-34 The web page files are organized in folders

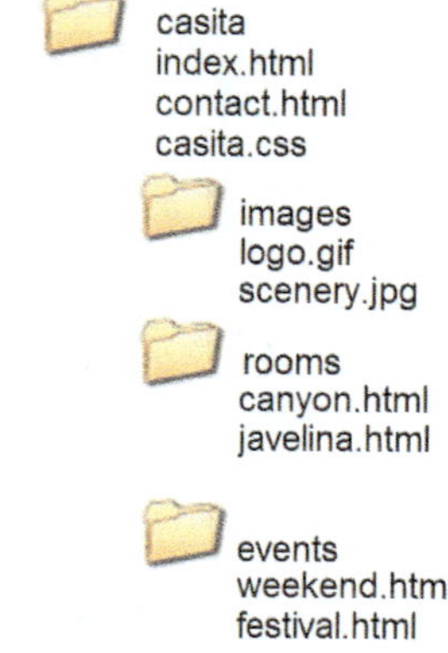

Register a Domain Name

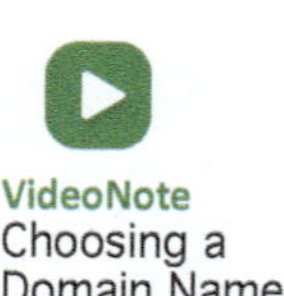

VideoNote
Choosing a Domain Name

A crucial part of establishing an effective web presence is choosing a **domain name**; it serves to locate your website on the internet (Figure 4-35). If your business or organization is brand new, then it's often convenient to select a domain name while you are deciding on a company name. If your organization is well established, you should choose a domain name that relates to your existing business presence. Although many domain names have already been purchased, there are still many options available.

Figure 4-35 The web page files are organized in folders

Microsoft Corporation

Describe Your Business. Although there is a long-standing trend to use "fun" words as domain names (such as yahoo.com, google.com, bing.com, woofoo.com, and so on), think carefully before doing so. Domain names for traditional businesses and organizations are the foundation of the organization's web presence and should include the business name or purpose.

Be Brief, If Possible. Although most people find new websites with search engines, some of your visitors will type your domain name in a browser. A shorter domain name is preferable to a longer one—it's easier for your web visitors to remember.

Avoid Hyphens in Your Domain Name. Using the hyphen character (commonly called a dash) in a domain name makes it difficult to pronounce the name. Also, someone typing your domain name may forget the dash and end up at a competitor's site! If you can, avoid the use of dashes in a domain name.

There's More Than .com. While the .com top-level domain name (TLD) is still the most popular for commercial and personal websites, consider also registering your domain name with other TLDs, such as .biz, .net, .us, and so on. Commercial businesses should avoid the .org TLD, which is the first choice for nonprofit organizations. You don't have to create a website for each domain name that you register. You can arrange with your domain name registrar for the "extra" domain names to point visitors to the domain name where your website is located. This is called **domain name redirection.**

Brainstorm Potential Keywords. Think about words that a potential visitor might type into a search engine when looking for your type of business or organization. This is the starting point for your list of keywords. If possible, work one or more keywords into your domain name (but still keep it as short as possible).

Avoid Trademarked Words or Phrases. The U.S. Patent and Trademark Office (USPTO)1 defines a trademark as a word, phrase, symbol, or design, or a combination of words, phrases, symbols, or designs, that identifies and distinguishes the source of the goods of one party from those of others. A starting point in researching trademarks is the USPTO Trademark Electronic Search System (TESS) at http://tess2.uspto.gov.

Know the Territory. Explore the way your potential domain name and keywords are already used on the Web. It's a good idea to type your potential domain names (and related words) into a search engine to see what may already exist.

Verify Availability. Check with one of the many domain name registrars to determine whether your domain name choices are available. A few of the many sites that offer domain name registration services are as follows:

- https://register.com
- https://networksolutions.com
- https://godaddy.com

Each of these sites offers a search feature that provides a way to determine whether a potential domain name is available and, if it is owned, who owns it. Often the domain name is already taken. If that's the case, the sites listed here will provide alternate suggestions that may be appropriate. Don't give up; a domain name is out there waiting for your business.

Registering a Domain Name

Once you've found your perfect domain name, don't waste any time in registering it. The cost of registering a domain name varies but is quite reasonable. It's perfectly OK to register a domain name even if you are not ready to publish your website immediately. Some web hosting services offer discounted domain name registration, but you will have the most control over your domain name if you register it directly with a domain name registrar. When you register a domain name, your contact information (such as name, phone number, mailing address, and e-mail address) will be entered into the WHOIS database and available to anyone unless you choose the option for private registration. While there is usually a small annual fee for private registration, it shields your personal information from unwanted spam and curiosity seekers.

Obtaining a domain name is just one part of establishing a web presence—you also need to host your website somewhere. The next section introduces you to factors involved in choosing a web host.

Choose a Web Host

A **web host provider** is an organization that offers storage for your website files along with the service of making them available on the internet. Your domain name, such as webdevbasics.net, is associated with an IP address that points to your website on the web server at the web host provider.

It is common for web host providers to charge a setup fee in addition to the monthly hosting fee. Hosting fees vary widely. The cheapest hosting company is not necessarily the one to use. Never consider using a "free" web host provider for a business website. These free sites are great for kids, college students, and hobbyists, but they are unprofessional. The last thing you or your client wants is to be perceived as unprofessional or not serious about the business at hand. As you consider different web host providers, try contacting their support phone numbers and e-mail addresses to determine just how responsive they really are. Word of mouth, web searches, and online directories are all resources in your quest for the perfect web host provider.

Types of Web Hosting

- **Virtual Hosting,** or shared hosting, is a popular choice for small websites. The web host provider's physical web server is divided into a number of virtual domains, and multiple websites are setup on the same computer. You have the authority to update files in your own website space, while the web host provider maintains the web server computer and internet connectivity.
- **Dedicated Hosting** is the rental and exclusive use of a computer and connection to the internet that is housed on the web hosting company's premises. A dedicated server is usually needed for a website that could have a considerable amount of traffic, such as tens of millions of hits a day. The server can usually be configured and operated remotely from the client company, or you can pay the web host provider to administer it for you.
- **Colocated Hosting** uses a computer that your organization has purchased and configured. Your web server is housed and connected to the internet at the web host's physical location, but your organization administers this computer.
- **Cloud Hosting** is different from other types of hosting in that your website is stored on multiple web servers, usually in different physical locations. A major benefit of cloud hosting is reliability. Instead of depending on a single web server, there are multiple servers that can serve your website resources at any time. Cloud hosting is also scalable and can flexibly handle unexpected increases in website traffic more easily than a website hosted on a single web sever.

Secure Sockets Layer (SSL)

Secure Sockets Layer (SSL) is a protocol that allows data to be privately exchanged over public networks. It was initially developed by Netscape in 1994 to encrypt data sent between a client (usually a web browser) and a web server.

Transport Layer Security (TLS) was later developed and implemented as an improvement and replacement for Secure Sockets Layer. However, the acronym SSL is commonly used to indicate encrypted secure communication between a web browser and a web server.

SSL provides secure communication between a client and a server by using the following:

- Server and (optionally) client digital certificates for authentication
- Symmetric-key cryptography with a "session key" for bulk encryption
- Public-key cryptography for transfer of the session key
- Message digests (hash functions) to verify the integrity of the transmission.

You can tell that a website is using SSL by the protocol in the web browser address text box—it shows https instead of http. When a URL begins with https://, it indicates that the browser is using HTTPS, which stands for Hypertext Transfer Protocol Secure. HTTPS combines HTTP with SSL. In addition to displaying the https protocol, browsers typically display a lock icon or other indicator of SSL, as shown in Figure 4-36.

Figure 4-36 The browser indicates that SSL is being used

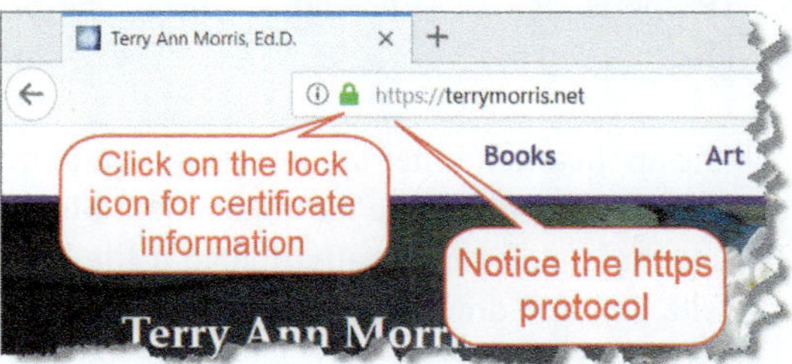

Microsoft Corporation

Publish with File Transfer Protocol

Once you obtain your web hosting, you'll need to upload your files. While your web host may offer a web-based file manager application for client use, a common method of transferring files is to use **File Transfer Protocol (FTP)**. A **protocol** is a convention or standard that enables computers to speak to one another. FTP is used to copy and manage files and folders over the internet. FTP uses two ports to communicate over a network— one for the data (typically port 20) and one for control commands (typically port 21).

There are many FTP applications available for download or purchase on the Web; several are listed in Table 4-11.

Table 4-11 FTP Applications

Application	Platform	URL	Cost
FileZilla	Windows, Mac, Linux	https://filezilla-project.org	Free download
SmartFTP	Windows	https://www.smartftp.com	Free download
CuteFTP	Windows, Mac	https://www.cuteftp.com	Free trial download, academic pricing available
WS_FTP	Windows	https://www.ipswitch.com	Free trial download

Your web host will provide you with the following information for connecting to your FTP server, along with any other specifications, such as whether the FTP server requires the use of active mode or passive mode:

```
FTP Host: ftp://yourhostaddress
Username: your_account_username
Password: your_account_password
```

After you download an FTP application of your choice, install the program on your computer using the instructions provided.

Launch and Login. Launch the application. Enter the information required by your web host (such as FTP host, username, and password) and initiate the connection. Most ftp hosts work in a similar way to a file manager. For example, you can usually upload a file by dragging the file from the local site list to the remote site list, and download a file by dragging from the remote site list to the local site list.

Search Engine Optimization

If you have followed recommended web design practices, you've already designed your website so that the pages are appealing and compelling to your target audience. How can you also make your site work well with search engines? Here are some suggestions and hints on designing your pages for optimal ranking by search engines—a process called **Search Engine Optimization (SEO).**

- Include keywords (terms or phrases that describe your website) that people may use when searching for your site.
- Use descriptive page titles. Search engines often display the page title's text in search results, and browsers save the page title by default when a visitor bookmarks your site.
- Use structural tags such as <h1>, <h2>, and so on to organize your page content. Some search engines will give a higher list position if keywords are included in a page title or headings.
- Configure an engaging description for your web page by coding a meta tag in the page header area. Some search engines display your description in search results. For example, the description meta tag for a website about a web development consulting firm called Acme

Design could be configured as follows: <meta name="description" content="Acme Design, a web consulting group that specializes in e-commerce, website design, development, and redesign.">

- Verify that all hyperlinks are working and not broken, with descriptive text and keywords as appropriate.
- Use file names that contain readable words, and consider separating the words with hyphens.
- If possible, select a web host that will provide HTTPS for your website. Google considers the HTTPS protocol in its page rank algorithm to prioritize internet security.
- Configure meaningful alternate text for images, including relevant keywords.
- Ensure that your code is valid and well-structured, so search engine robots can process it more easily.
- Publish high-quality, well-organized content that is of value to your visitors.

Web Accessibility Standards

The accessibility recommendations presented in this text are intended to satisfy Section 508 of the Rehabilitation Act and the W3C's Web Content Accessibility Guidelines.

Section 508 of the Rehabilitation Act. Section 508 requires electronic and information technology, including web pages, that are used by federal agencies to be accessible to people with disabilities. The U.S. Access Board released a Section 508 Refresh in 2017 that updated the standard to harmonize with WCAG 2.0 Success Criteria.

Web Content Accessibility Guidelines (WCAG 2.1). WCAG 2.1 considers an accessible web page to be perceivable, operable, and understandable for people with a wide range of abilities. The page should be robust to work with a variety of browsers and other user agents, such as screen readers and mobile devices. WCAG 2.1 includes and extends WCAG 2.0 accessibility Success Criteria. The guiding principles of WCAG 2.0 and WCAG 2.1 are as follows:

1. Content must be Perceivable.
2. Interface components in the content must be Operable.
3. Content and controls must be Understandable.
4. Content should be Robust enough to work with current and future user agents, including **assistive technologies.**

Reference the following tips to meet web accessibility standards for screen readers, phones, and a wide range of web browsers:

- Use heading tags to outline the structure of your web page content.
- Create hyperlinks with helpful, descriptive labels. For example, a link that says "Sign in" is more useful than a hyperlink that simply says "Click here."
- Use the alt attribute to provide a text description of any images on your website. If using images for navigation, your text description should match the image's exact wording (for example, code alt="Home" in the <img> tag for the Home button).
- Include a list of plain text navigation hyperlinks in the page footer.
- Provide alternate content for the audio and video files on your website, such as captions or a transcript PDF.

Testing for Accessibility Compliance

No single testing tool can automatically test for all web standards. The first step in testing the accessibility of a web page is to verify that it is coded according to W3C standards with the Markup Validation Service (https://validator.w3.org) and the CSS Validation Service (https://jigsaw.w3.org/css-validator).

Automated Accessibility Testing. An automated accessibility evaluation tool is no substitute for your own manual evaluation but can be useful to quickly identify potential issues with a web page. WebAim Wave and ATRC AChecker are two popular free online accessibility evaluation tools. The online applications typically require the URL of a web page and reply with an accessibility report. The Web Developer Extension is a browser toolbar that can be used to assess accessibility. The Web Developer Extension is multifunctional, with options to validate HTML, validate CSS, disable images, view alt text, outline block-level elements, resize the browser viewport, disable styles, and more.

Manual Accessibility Testing. It's important not to rely completely on automated tests—you'll want to review the pages yourself. For example, while an automated test can check for the presence of an alt attribute, it takes a human to critically think and decide whether the text of the alt attribute is an appropriate description for a person who cannot view the image.

Usability Testing

In addition to accessibility, another aspect of universal design is the usability of the website. **Usability** is how easy, efficient, and pleasant it is for visitors to interact with your website. Usability.gov describes factors that affect the user's experience:

- **Intuitive Design** – How easy is it for a new visitor to understand the organization of the site? Is the navigation intuitive for a new user?
- **Ease of Learning** – How easy is it to learn to use the website? Do new visitors consider it easy to learn to perform basic tasks on the website or are they frustrated?
- **Efficiency of Use** – How do experienced users perceive the website? Once they are comfortable, are they able to complete tasks efficiently and quickly or are they frustrated?
- **Memorability** – When visitors returns to a website, do they remember enough to use it productively or is the visitor back at the beginning of the learning curve (and frustrated)?
- **Error Frequency and Severity** – Do website visitors make errors when navigating or filling in forms on the website? Are they serious errors? Is it easy to recover from errors or are visitors frustrated?
- **Subjective Satisfaction** – Do users "like" using the website? Are they satisfied? Why or why not?

Checkpoint

4.27 What is a domain name?

4.28 What is the name of the database where all domain names are recorded and stored?

4.29 What is a web host provider?

4.30 What does it mean when a URL begins with https://?

4.31 Explain universal design and give an example of how you can use it when designing a web page.

Chapter Review

Multiple Choice

1.. What symbol to the left of a tag name .identifies a closing tag?
   a. #
   b. *
   c. /
   d. !

2. What is the document type definition for HTML5?
   a. <!DOCTYPE html>
   b. <!HTML5: doc>
   c. <!HTML:5>
   d. <!DOCTYPE:5>

3. Which tag is used to hyperlink web pages to each other?
   a.
   b. <hyperlink>Review and Apply
   c. <a>
   d. <link>

4. Which tag pair configures the largest heading?
   a. <h1> </h1>
   b. <h9> </h9>
   c. <h type="largest"> </h>
   d. <h6> </h6>

5. Which tag configures the following text or element to display on a new line?
   a. <new line>
   b. <nl>
   c.
   d. <line>

6. Which tag pair configures a paragraph?
   a. <para> </para>
   b. <paragraph> </paragraph>
   c. <p> </p>
   d. <body> </body>

7. Which type of CSS is coded in the body of the web page as an attribute of an HTML tag?
   a. embedded
   b. inline
   c. external
   d. imported

8. Which of the following can be a CSS selector?
   a. an HTML element name
   b. a class name
   c. an id name
   d. all of the above

9. Which of the following is the CSS property used to set the background color of a web page?
   a. bgcolor
   b. color
   c. bcolor
   d. background-color

10. Which of the following associates a web page with an external style sheet?
    a. <style rel="external" href="style.css">
    b. <style src="style.css">
    c. <link rel="stylesheet" href="style.css">
    d. <link rel="stylesheet" src="style.css">

11. Where do you place the code to associate a web page with an external style sheet?
    a. in the external style sheet
    b. in the DOCTYPE of the web page document
    c. in the body section of the web page document
    d. in the head section of the web page document

12. Which of the following configures a background color of #FFF8DC for a web page using CSS?
    a. body { background-color: #FFF8DC; }
    b. document { background: #FFF8DC; }
    c. body {bgcolor: #FFF8DC;}
    d. body { color: #FFF8DC; }

13. Which attribute specifies text that is available to browsers and other user agents that do not support graphics?
    a. alt
    b. text
    c. src
    d. accessibility

14. Which of the following creates an image link to the index.html page when the home.gif graphic is clicked?
    a. <a href="index.html" src="home.gif" alt="Home"></a>
    b. <a href="index.html"><img src="home.gif" alt="Home"></a>
    c. <img src="home.gif" href="index.html" alt="Home">
    d. <a src="home.gif"><img src="home.gif" alt="Home"></a>

15. Which CSS property will configure the font typeface?
    a. font-face
    b. font-style
    c. font-family
    d. typeface
16. Which of the following is an open-source video codec?
    a. Theora
    b. MP3
    c. Vorbis
    d. API
17. Which of the following is an object-based, client-side scripting language?
    a. HTML
    b. CSS
    c. JavaScript
    d. API
18. Which HTML elements can be used to configure an interactive widget?
    a. hide and show
    b. details and summary
    c. display and hidden
    d. title and summary
19. Which of the following should you do to provide for usability and accessibility?
    a. Use video and sound whenever possible.
    b. Supply text descriptions of audio files and caption video files that appear in your web pages.
    c. Never use audio and video files.
    d. None of the above.
20. Which of the following is a protocol commonly used to transfer files over the internet?
    a. HTML
    b. HTTP
    c. FTP
    d. SMTP
21. Which web hosting option is appropriate for the initial web presence of an organization?
    a. dedicated hosting
    b. free web hosting
    c. virtual hosting
    d. colocated hosting

True or False

1. Markup languages contain sets of directions that tell web browser software how to display and manage a web document.
2. The title of the web page is displayed by the meta element.
3. All HTML codes must have both an opening and a closing tag.
4. The only web development tool you need to create a web page document is a text editor.
5. By default, each line in an ordered list begins with a bullet.
6. Use a CSS class selector when you want to apply a style to one or more than one area on a web page.
7. JPEG images are best suited for line art.
8. When a font that is not installed on your web visitor's computer is specified on the web page, it automatically downloads to the visitor's device.
9. The font-weight property configures the boldness of the text.
10. The easiest way to give your website visitors access to an audio or a video file is to create a simple hyperlink to the file.
11. You can get a domain name for free.
12. It is common for web host providers to charge a setup fee in addition to the monthly hosting fee.

Short Answer

1. Explain the difference between a text editor, an HTML editor, and a graphic authoring tool. Give an example of each.
2. Give an example of when you might use an ordered list on a web page and when you might use an unordered list.
3. Explain why CSS is like a cascade.
4. List and explain the four methods of using CSS in a website.
5. Explain the use of the alt attribute for configuring an image.
6. What is a widget? Give an example
7. Explain why some websites display https:// instead of http://.

Programming Exercises

1. Write the markup language code to display your name in the largest-size heading element.
2. Write the markup language code for an unordered list to display the days of the week.
3. Write the markup language code for an ordered list that uses uppercase letters to order the items. This ordered list will display the following: Spring, Summer, Fall, and Winter.
4. Write the code to create an absolute hyperlink to your school's website.
5. Write the CSS code for an external style sheet file named mystyle.css that configures the text to be brown, 1.2em in size, and in Arial, Verdana, or a sans-serif font.
6. Write the HTML and CSS code for an embedded style sheet that configures a class called priority, which has bold and italic text.
7. Write the code to place an image called primelogo.gif on a web page. The image is 100 pixels high by 650 pixels wide.
8. Write the HTML for a hyperlink to a video called sparky.mov on a web page.
9. Write the HTML to embed an audio file called soundloop.mp3 on a web page that can be controlled by the visitor.
10. Write the HTML to display a video on a web page. Use video files named prime.m4v, prime.webm, and prime.ogv. The width is 213 pixels. The height is 163 pixels. The poster image is prime.jpg.
11. Create a web page that includes a widget that will show the summary and detail information for at least three items.
12. Working in small teams, create a website with at least two pages for a musical group. The group can be real, or it can be one you make up. The website should include the following:
    - Images.
    - Links to other pages and to external content such as other websites, audio, or video files.
    - An email contact link.
    - One ordered and one unordered list.
    - An interactive widget or a script.
    - An email contact link in the page footer area.
    - An external style sheet.

    Start by assigning team roles. Then, brainstorm what you will include on the website and how you will organize and configure the information.

    Some things you might consider including or linking to are the name of the band and profiles of the band members; a hyperlink to an actual band's website; a list of songs; a concert schedule; pictures; audio or video clips; reviews; and gossip.

Brainstorm the formatting you will use for the website. Using generally accepted standards for design, plan the fonts, color scheme, and spacing that will make your website interface attractive and engaging. You might want to draw the web pages and map out the links. Plan to use an external style sheet to make sure the formatting is consistent for all pages in the site.

For images, look online for some you can use legally. Some websites have a link to their copyright policy. Most websites will give permission for you to use an image in a school assignment. If there is no available policy, email the site's contact person and request permission to use the photo. If you are unable to obtain permission, you may substitute with a picture you take yourself, clip art, or an image from a free site instead. Throughout the process, seek and respond to feedback from your teammates and teacher. If possible reach out to a web development professional for feedback, as well.

When you are ready, use your chosen web authoring tool to develop the website. Save files with descriptive, appropriate names, using an organized file and folder system. Create and apply the external style sheet for the website, and link the pages to it. Remember to test your work as you go to make sure it displays and functions the way you want. When it is complete, publish the website.

CHAPTER

5 Programming Basics

TOPICS

5.1 Introduction to Program Design

Programs must be carefully designed before they are written.

Recall that programmers typically use high-level languages to write programs. However, all professional programmers will tell you that a program should be carefully designed before the code is actually written. When programmers begin a new project, they never jump right in and start writing code as the first step. They begin by creating a design of the program.

After designing the program, the programmer begins writing code in a high-level language. Recall that each language has its own rules, known as syntax, that must be followed when writing a program. A language's syntax rules dictate things such as how key words, operators, and punctuation characters can be used. A syntax error occurs if the programmer violates any of these rules.

If the program contains a syntax error, or even a simple mistake such as a misspelled keyword, the compiler or interpreter displays an error message indicating what the error is. Virtually all code contains syntax errors when it is first written, so the programmer will typically spend some time correcting these. Once all of the syntax errors and simple typing mistakes have been corrected, the program can be compiled and translated into a machine language program, or executed by an interpreter, depending on the language being used.

Once the code is in an executable form, it is tested to determine whether any logic errors exist. A **logic error** is a mistake that does not prevent the program from running, but causes it to produce incorrect results. For example, mathematical mistakes are common causes of logic errors.

If there are logic errors, the programmer **debugs** the code. This means that the programmer finds and corrects the code that is causing the error. Sometimes during this process, the programmer discovers that the original design must be changed. This entire process, which is known as the **program development cycle**, is repeated until no errors can be found in the program. Figure 5-1 shows the steps in the process.

Figure 5-1 The program development cycle

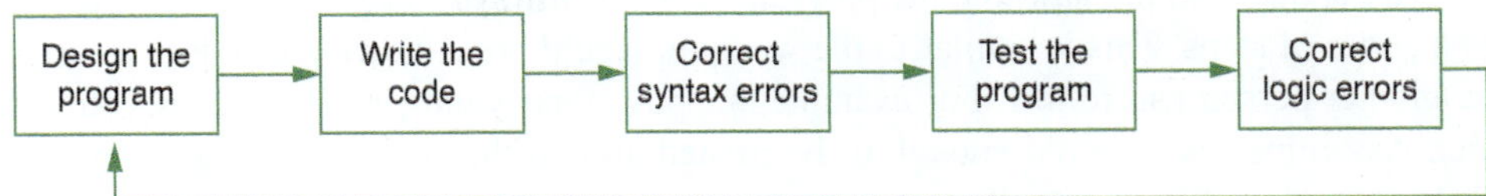

This text focuses primarily on the first step of the program development cycle: designing the program. The process of designing a program may be the most important part of the cycle. You can think of a program's design as its foundation. If you build a house on a poorly constructed foundation, eventually you will find yourself doing a lot of work to fix the house! If your program is designed poorly, eventually you will find yourself doing a lot of work to fix the program.

Designing a Program

The process of designing a program is similar to solving a problem. You must start by identifying the problem's description, purpose, and goals. It can be summarized in the following two steps:

1. Understand the task that the program is to perform.
2. Determine the steps that must be taken to perform the task.

Let's take a closer look at each of these steps.

Understand the Task That the Program Is to Perform

Just like when solving a problem, it is essential that you understand what a program is supposed to do before you can determine the steps that the program will perform. Typically, a professional programmer gains this understanding by working directly with the customer. We use the term **customer** to describe the person, group, or organization that is asking you to write a program. This could be a customer in the traditional sense of the word, meaning someone who is paying you to write a program. It could also be your boss, or the manager of a department within your company. Regardless of who it is, the customer will be relying on your program to perform an important task.

To get a sense of what a program is supposed to do, the programmer usually interviews the customer. During the interview, the customer will describe the task that the program should perform, and the programmer will ask questions to uncover as many details as possible about the task. A follow-up interview is usually needed because customers rarely mention everything they want during the initial meeting, and programmers often think of additional questions.

The programmer studies the information that was gathered from the customer during the interviews and creates a list of different software requirements. A **software requirement** is a single function that the program must perform in order to satisfy the customer. Once the customer agrees that the list of requirements is complete, the programmer can move to the next phase.

TIP: If you choose to become a professional software developer, your customer will be anyone who asks you to write programs as part of your job. As long as you are a student, however, your customer is your instructor! In every programming class that you will take, it's practically guaranteed that your instructor will assign programming problems for you to complete. For your academic success, make sure that you understand your instructor's requirements for those assignments and write your programs accordingly.

Determine the Steps That Must Be Taken to Perform the Task

Once you understand the task that the program will perform, you begin by breaking down the task into a series of steps. This is similar to the way you would break down a task into a series of steps that another person can follow. For example, suppose your younger sibling asks you how to boil water. Assuming they are old enough to be trusted around the stove, you might break down that task into a series of steps as follows:

1. Pour the desired amount of water into a pot.
2. Put the pot on a stove burner.
3. Turn the burner to high.
4. Watch the water until you see large bubbles rapidly rising. When this happens, the water is boiling.

Recall from the problem-solving process that this is an example of an algorithm. Notice that the steps in this algorithm are sequentially ordered. Step 1 should be performed before Step 2, and so on. If someone follows these steps exactly as they appear, and in the correct order, they should be able to boil water successfully.

A programmer breaks down the task that a program must perform in a similar way. They create an algorithm which lists all of the logical steps that must be taken. For example, suppose you have been asked to write a program to calculate and display the gross pay for an hourly paid employee. Here are the steps that you would take:

1. Get the number of hours worked.
2. Get the hourly pay rate.
3. Multiply the number of hours worked by the hourly pay rate.
4. Display the result of the calculation that was performed in Step 3.

Checkpoint

5.1 What is a syntax error?

5.2 What is a logic error?

5.3 Who is a programmer's customer?

5.4 What is a software requirement?

5.2 Using Pseudocode and Flowcharts

Pseudocode and flowcharts are tools programmers use to create models of programs.

Before an algorithm can be executed by a computer, the steps have to be translated into code. Programmers commonly use two tools to start this process: pseudocode and flowcharts. These tools are vital for designing a program. Let's look at each of these in more detail.

Pseudocode

Recall that each programming language has strict rules, known as syntax, that the programmer must follow when writing a program. If the programmer writes code that violates these rules, a syntax error will result and the program cannot be compiled or executed. When this happens, the programmer has to locate the error and correct it.

Because small mistakes like misspelled words and forgotten punctuation characters can cause syntax errors, programmers have to be mindful of every detail when writing code. For this reason, programmers find it helpful to write their programs in **pseudocode** (pronounced "sue doe code") before they write it in the actual code of a programming language.

The word pseudo means fake, so pseudocode is fake code. It is an informal language that has no syntax rules, and is not meant to be compiled or executed. Instead, programmers use pseudocode to create models, or "mock-ups" of programs. Because programmers don't have to worry about syntax errors while writing pseudocode, they can focus all of their attention on the program's design. Once they create a satisfactory design with pseudocode, the pseudocode can be translated directly to actual code.

Here is an example of how you might write pseudocode for the pay calculating program that we discussed earlier:

```
Display "Enter the number of hours the employee worked."
Input hours
Display "Enter the employee's hourly pay rate."
Input payRate
Set grossPay = hours * payRate
Display "The employee's gross pay is $", grossPay
```

Each statement in the pseudocode represents an operation that can be performed in any high-level language. For example, all languages provide a way to display messages on the screen, read input that is typed on the keyboard, and perform mathematical calculations.

NOTE: As you read the examples in this book, keep in mind that pseudocode is not an actual programming language. It is a generic way to write the statements of an algorithm, without worrying about syntax rules. If you mistakenly write pseudocode into an editor for an actual programming language, such as Python or Visual Basic, errors will result.

Flowcharts

Flowcharting is another tool that programmers use to design programs. A **flowchart** is a diagram that graphically shows the steps that take place in a program. Figure 5-2 shows how you might create a flowchart for the pay calculating program.

Figure 5-2 Flowchart for the pay calculating program

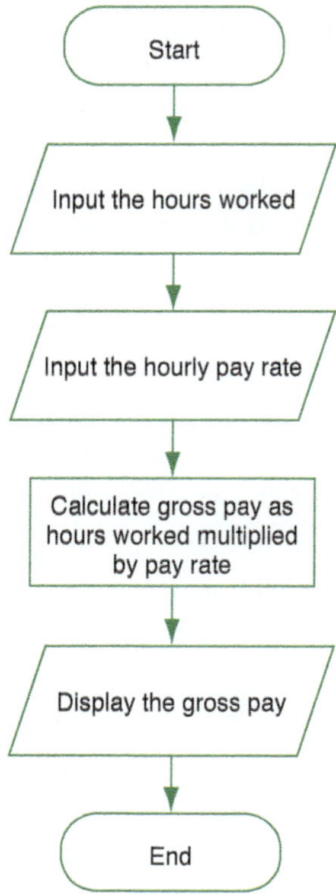

Notice that there are three types of symbols in the flowchart: ovals, parallelograms, and rectangles. The ovals, which appear at the top and bottom of the flowchart, are called **terminal symbols**. The Start terminal symbol marks the program's starting point and the End terminal symbol marks the program's ending point.

Between the terminal symbols are parallelograms, which are used for both **input symbols** and **output symbols**, and rectangles, which are called **processing symbols**. Each of these symbols represents a step in the program.

The symbols are connected by arrows that represent the "flow" of the program. To step through the symbols in the proper order, you begin at the Start terminal and follow the arrows until you reach the End terminal. Throughout this chapter we will look at each of these symbols in greater detail. For your reference, Appendix B summarizes all of the flowchart symbols that we use in this book.

There are a number of different ways that you can draw flowcharts, and your instructor will most likely give you instructions that are specific for your class. Perhaps the simplest and least expensive way is to sketch the flowchart by hand with pencil and paper. If you need to make your hand-drawn flowcharts look more professional, you can purchase a flowchart template, which is a small plastic sheet that has the flowchart symbols cut into it. You can use the template to trace the symbols onto a piece of paper.

The disadvantage of drawing flowcharts by hand is that you have to manually erase mistakes, and in many cases, redraw the entire page. A more efficient and professional way to create flowcharts is to use software. Many productivity applications, such as the Microsoft Office suite, include tools for inserting diagrams. (In Office it is called SmartArt.) Flowcharts are usually included in the list of available diagrams. There are also specialized software packages that you can use to create flowcharts.

Flowchart Connector Symbols

Often, a flowchart for a program design is too long to fit on a page. Sometimes you can remedy this by breaking the flowchart into two or more smaller flowcharts, and placing them side-by-side on the page. When you do this, you use a **connector symbol** to connect the pieces of the flowchart. A connector symbol is a small circle with a letter or number written inside it. Figure 5-3 shows an example of a flowchart with an (A) connector symbol.

Figure 5-3 Flowchart with a connector symbol

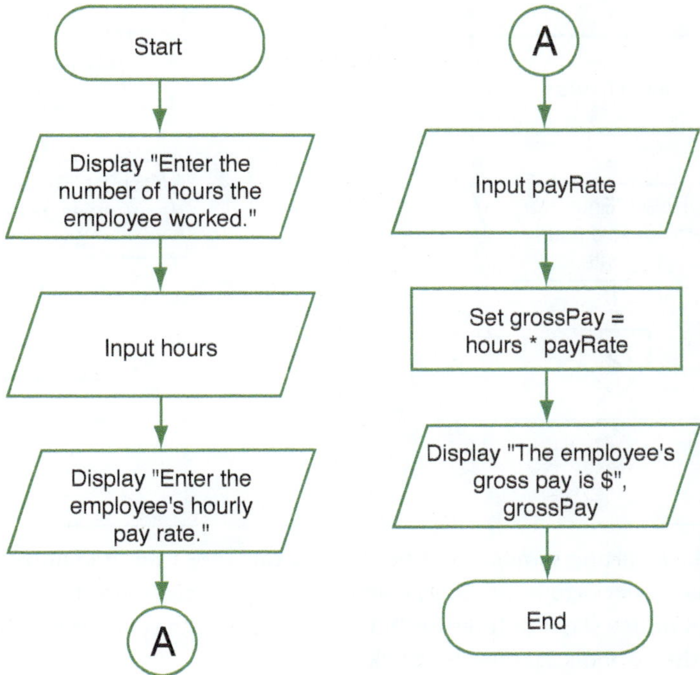

In Figure 5-3, the (A) connector symbol indicates that the second flowchart segment begins where the first flowchart segment ends.

When a flowchart is simply too large to fit on a single page, even when you split it as in Figure 5-3, you can break the flowchart into parts, and place the parts on separate pages. You then use the **off-page connector symbol** to connect the pieces of the flowchart. The off-page connector symbol is the "home plate" shape, with a page number shown inside it. If the connector is at an exit point in the flowchart, the number indicates the page where the next part of the flowchart is located. If the connector is at an entry point in the flowchart, it indicates the page where the previous part of the flowchart is located.

Figure 5-4 shows an example. In the figure, the flowchart on the left is on page 1. At the bottom of the flowchart is an off-page connector. In the flowchart on the right (which is page 2), the off-page connector at the top indicates that the previous part of the flowchart is on page 1.

Figure 5-4 Flowchart with an off-page connector

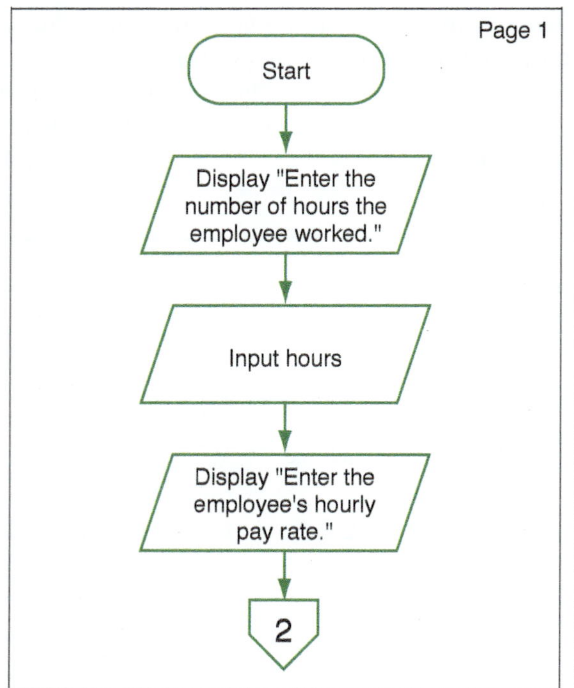

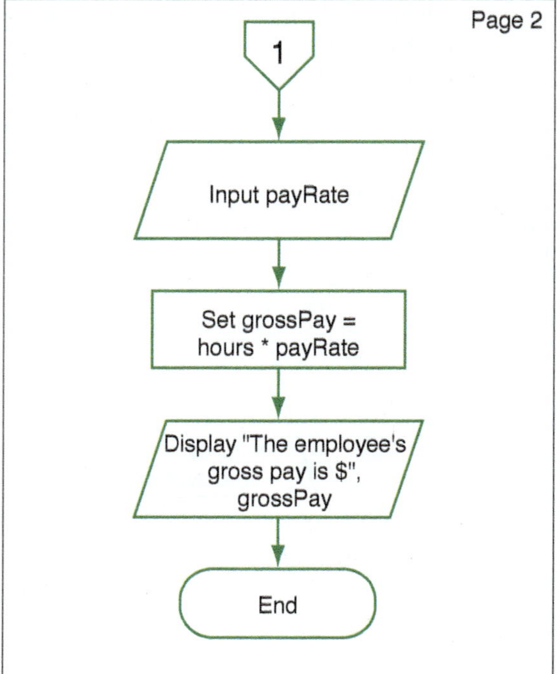

NOTE: Flowcharting symbols and techniques can vary from one book to another, or from one software package to another. If you are using specialized software to draw flowcharts, you might notice slight differences between some of the symbols that it uses, compared to some of the symbols used in this book .

Checkpoint

5.5 What is pseudocode?

5.6 What is a flowchart?

5.7 Explain how each of the following symbols is used n a flowchart:

- Oval
- Parallelogram
- Rectangle

5.3 Output, Input, and Variables

Output is data that is generated and displayed by the program. Input is data that the program receives. When a program receives data, it stores it in variables, which are named storage locations in memory

Computer programs typically perform the following three-step process:

1. Input is received.
2. Some process is performed on the input.
3. Output is produced.

Input is any data that the program receives while it is running. One common form of input is data that you type on the keyboard. Once input is received, some process, such as a mathematical calculation, is usually performed on it. The results of the process are then sent out of the program as output.

Figure 5-5 illustrates these three steps in the pay calculating program that we discussed earlier. The number of hours worked and the hourly pay rate are provided as input

Figure 5-5 The input, processing, and output of the pay calculating program

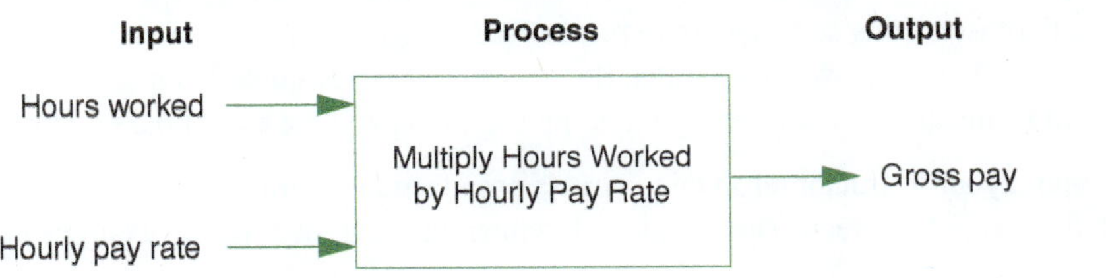

The program processes this data by multiplying the hours worked by the hourly pay rate. The results of the calculation are then displayed on the screen as output.

IPO Charts

An IPO chart is a simple but effective tool that programmers commonly use while designing programs. IPO stands for *input, processing,* and *output*, and an **IPO chart** describes the input, processing, and output of a program. These items are usually laid out in columns. The input column shows a description of the data that is required as input. The processing column shows a description of the process, or processes, that the program performs. The output column describes the output that is produced by the program. Figure 5-6 shows an IPO chart for the pay calculating program.

In the remainder of this section, you will look at some simple programs that perform output and input. In the next section, you will explore how a computer processes data.

Figure 5-6 IPO chart for the pay calculating program

IPO Chart for the Pay Calculating Program		
Input	Processing	Output
Number of hours worked Hourly pay rate	Multiply the number of hours worked by the hourly pay rate. The result is the gross pay.	Gross pay

Displaying Screen Output

Perhaps the most fundamental thing that you can do in a program is to display a message on the computer screen. As previously mentioned, all high-level languages provide a way to display screen output. In this book, we use the word `Display` to write pseudocode statements for displaying output on the screen. Here is an example:

```
Display "Hello world"
```

The purpose of this statement is to display the message *Hello world* on the screen. Notice that after the word `Display`, we have written `Hello world` inside quotation marks. The quotation marks are not to be displayed. They simply mark the beginning and the end of the text that we want to display.

Suppose your instructor tells you to write a pseudocode program that displays your name and address on the computer screen. The pseudocode shown in Program 5-1 is an example of such a program.

Program 5-1: 

```
Display "Kate Austen"
Display "1234 Walnut Street"
Display "Asheville, NC 28899"
```

It is important for you to understand that the statements in this program execute in the order that they appear, from the top of the program to the bottom. This is shown in Figure 5-7. If you translate this pseudocode into an actual program and run it, the first statement would execute, followed by the second statement, and followed by the third statement. If you try to visualize the way this program's output would appear on the screen, you should imagine something like that shown in Figure 5-8. Each Display statement produces a line of output.

NOTE: Although this text uses the word `Display` for an instruction that displays screen output, some programmers use other words for this purpose. For example, some programmers use the word `Print`, and others use the word `Write`. Pseudocode has no rules that dictate the words that you may or may not use.

Figure 5-7 The statements execute in order

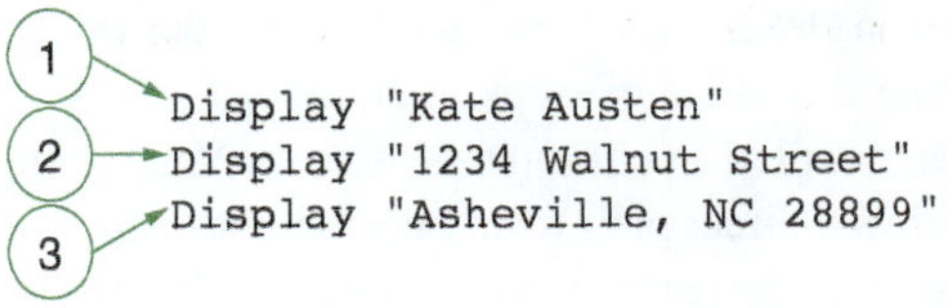

1
2
3
Display "Kate Austen"
Display "1234 Walnut Street"
Display "Asheville, NC 28899"

Figure 5-8 Output of Program 5-1

Command Prompt
Kate Austen
1234 Walnut Street
Asheville, NC 28899

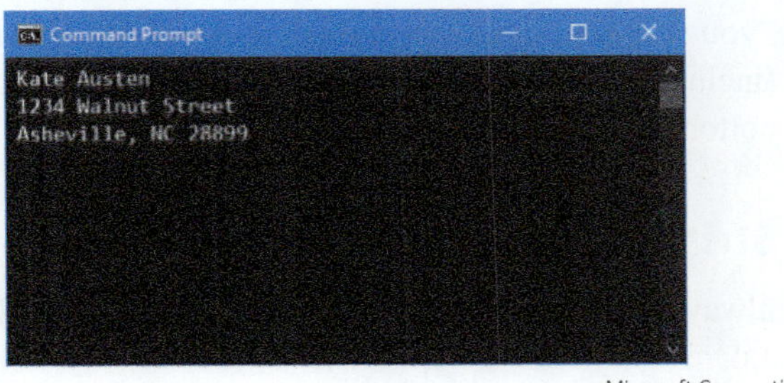

Microsoft Corporation

Figure 5-9 shows the way you would draw a flowchart for this program. Notice that between the *Start* and *End* terminal symbols there are three parallelograms. A parallelogram can be either an output symbol or an input symbol. In this program, all three parallelograms are output symbols. There is one for each of the `Display` statements.

Figure 5-9 Flowchart for Program 5-1

Start
Display "Kate Austen"
Display "1234 Walnut Street"
Display "Asheville, NC 28899"
End

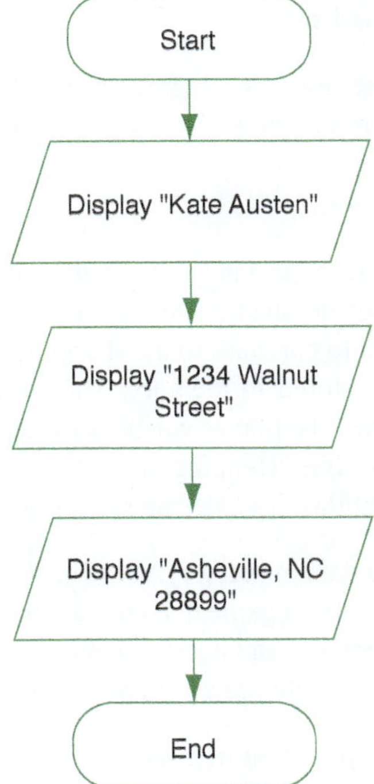

Sequence Structures

Recall that the statements in Program 5-1 execute in the order that they appear, from the top of the program to the bottom like the series of steps in an algorithm.. A set of statements that execute in the order that they appear is called a **sequence structure**. You would use a sequence structure for a simple program that follows a direct path from beginning to end. For example, recall the algorithm for the simple story about a hidden prize from Chapter 3. That story uses a sequence structure. All of the programs that you will see in this chapter are sequence structures.

A **structure**, also called a **control structure**, is a logical design that controls the order in which a set of statements executes. A sequence structure is the simplest structure used in programming. Later in this text, you will learn about decision structures and repetition structures, which let you design programs (including stories, games, and animations) that do not simply progress in a straight path from top to bottom.

Strings and String Literals

Programs almost always work with data of some type. For example, Program 5-1 uses the following three pieces of data:

```
"Kate Austen"
"1234 Walnut Street"
"Asheville, NC 28899"
```

These pieces of data are sequences of characters. In programming terms, a sequence of characters that is used as data is called a string. When a **string** appears in the actual code of a program (or in pseudocode, as it does in Program 5-1) it is called a **string literal**. In program code, or pseudocode, a string literal is usually enclosed in quotation marks. As mentioned earlier, the quotation marks show where the string begins and ends.

In this text, we will always enclose string literals in double quote marks ("). Most programming languages use this same convention, but a few use single quote marks (').

VideoNote
Variables and Input

Variables and Input

Quite often a program needs to store data in the computer's memory so it can perform operations on that data later. For example, consider the typical online shopping experience: You browse a website and add the items that you want to purchase to the shopping cart. As you add items to the shopping cart, data about those items is stored in memory. Then, when you click the checkout button, a program running on the website's computer calculates the total of all the items you have in your shopping cart, applicable sales taxes, shipping costs, and the total of all these charges. When the program performs these calculations, it stores the results in the computer's memory.

Programs use variables to store data in memory. A **variable** is a storage location in memory that is represented by a name. For example, a game that only allows three tries might use a variable named `tries` to hold that value in memory. And a story or animation with a character practicing to jump high enough to dunk a basketball might use a variable named `height` to hold that value in memory.

When a program reads data that you input from the keyboard, usually it stores that data in a variable so it can use it later. In pseudocode we will read data from the keyboard with the `Input` statement. As an example, look at the following statement, which appeared earlier in the pay calculating program:

```
Input hours
```

The word `Input` is an instruction to read a piece of data from the keyboard. The word `hours` is the name of the variable in which that data will be stored. When this statement executes, two things happen:

- The program pauses and waits for the user to type something on the keyboard, and then press the [Enter] key.
- When the [Enter] key is pressed, the data that was typed is stored in the hours variable.

Program 5-2 is a simple pseudocode program that demonstrates the Input statement. Before we examine the program, we should mention a couple of things. First, you will notice that each line in the program is numbered. The line numbers are not part of the pseudocode. We will refer to the line numbers later to point out specific parts of the program. Second, the program's output is shown immediately following the pseudocode. From now on, all pseudocode programs in this text will be shown this way.

Program 5-2:

```
1 Display "What is your age?"
2 Input age
3 Display "Here is the value that you entered:"
4 Display age
```

Program Output (with Input Shown in Bold)

```
What is your age?
24 [Enter]
Here is the value that you entered:
24
```

The statement in line 1 displays the string "`What is your age?`" Then, the statement in line 2 waits for the user to type a value on the keyboard and press [Enter]. The value that is typed will be stored in the `age` variable. In the example execution of the program, the user has entered 24. The statement in line 3 displays the string "`Here is the value that you entered:`" and the statement in line 4 displays the value that is stored in the `age` variable.

Notice that in line 4 there are no quotation marks around age. If quotation marks were placed around `age`, it would have indicated that we want to display the word `age` instead of the contents of the `age` variable. In other words, the following statement is an instruction to display the contents of the `age` variable:

```
Display age
```

This statement, however, is an instruction to display the word *age*:

```
Display "age"
```

NOTE: In this section, we have mentioned the user. The *user* is simply any hypothetical person that is using a program and providing input for it. The user is sometimes called the *end user*.

Figure 5-10 Flowchart for Program 5-2

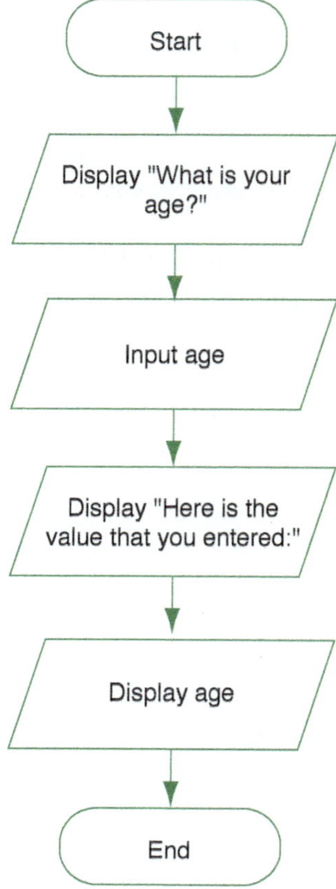

Figure 5-10 shows a flowchart for Program 5-2. Notice that the Input operation is also represented by a parallelogram.

Variable Names

All high-level programming languages allow you to make up your own names for the variables that you use in a program. You don't have complete freedom in naming variables, however. Every language has its own set of rules that you must abide by when creating variable names.

Although the rules for naming variables differ slightly from one language to another, there are some common restrictions:

- Variable names must be one word. They cannot contain spaces.
- In most languages, punctuation characters cannot be used in variable names. It is usually a good idea to use only alphabetic letters and numbers in variable names.
- In most languages, the first character of a variable name cannot be a number.

In addition to following the programming language rules, you should always choose descriptive names for your variables that give an indication of what they are used for. For example, a variable that holds the temperature might be named `temperature`, and a variable that holds a car's speed might be named `speed`. You may be tempted to give variables names like `x` and `b2`, but names like these give no clue as to what the variable's purpose is.

Because a variable's name should reflect the variable's purpose, programmers often find themselves creating names that are made of multiple words. For example, consider the following variable names:

```
grosspay
payrate
hotdogssoldtoday
```

Unfortunately, these names are not easily read by the human eye because the words aren't separated. Because we can't have spaces in variable names, we need to find another way to separate the words in a multiword variable name, and make it more readable to the human eye.

One way to do this is to use the underscore character to represent a space. For example, the following variable names are easier to read than those previously shown:

```
gross_pay
pay_rate
hot_dogs_sold_today
```

Another way to address this problem is to use the **camelCase** naming convention. camelCase names are written in the following manner:

- You begin writing the variable name with lowercase letters.
- The first character of the second and subsequent words is written in uppercase.

For example, the following variable names are written in camelCase:

```
grossPay
payRate
hotDogsSoldToday
```

Because the camelCase convention is very popular with programmers, we will use it from this point forward. In fact, you have already seen programs that use camelCase variable names. The pay calculating program shown at the beginning of the chapter uses the variable name payRate.

NOTE: This style of naming is called camelCase because the uppercase characters that appear in a name are sometimes reminiscent of a camel's humps.

Displaying Multiple Items with One Display Statement

If you refer to Program 5-2 you will see that we used the following two `Display` statements in lines 3 and 4:

```
Display "Here is the value that you entered:"
Display age
```

We used two `Display` statements because we needed to display two pieces of data. Line 3 displays the string literal `"Here is the value that you entered:"` and line 4 displays the contents of the `age` variable.

Most programming languages provide a way to display multiple pieces of data with one statement. Because this is a common feature of programming languages, frequently we will write `Display` statements in our pseudocode that display multiple items. We will simply separate the items with a comma, as shown in line 3 of Program 5-3.

Program 5-3:

```
1 Display "What is your age?"
2 Input age
3 Display "Here is the value that you entered: ", age
```

Program Output (with Input Shown in Bold)

```
What is your age?
24 [Enter]
Here is the value that you entered: 24
```

Take a closer look at line 3 of Program 2-3:

```
Display "Here is the value that you entered: ", age
```

Notice the space.

Notice that the string literal "`Here is the value that you entered: `" ends with a space. That is because in the program output, we want a space to appear after the colon, as shown here:

```
Here is the value that you entered: 24
```

Notice the space.

In most cases, when you are displaying multiple items on the screen, you want to separate those items with spaces between them. Most programming languages do not automatically print spaces between multiple items that are displayed on the screen. For example, look at the following pseudocode statement:

```
Display "January", "February", "March"
```

In most programming languages, such as statement would produce the following output:

```
JanuaryFebruaryMarch
```

To separate the strings with spaces in the output, the Display statement should be written as:

```
Display "January ", "February ", "March"
```

String Input

Programs 5-2 and 5-3 read numbers from the keyboard, which were stored in variables by `Input` statements. Programs can also read string input. For example, the pseudocode in Program 5-4 uses two `Input` statements: one to read a string and one to read a number.

Program 5-4: 

```
1 Display "Enter your name."
2 Input name
3 Display "Enter your age."
4 Input age
5 Display "Hello ", name
6 Display "You are ", age, " years old."
```

Program Output (with Input Shown in Bold)

```
Enter your name.
Andrea [Enter]
Enter your age.
24 [Enter]
Hello Andrea
You are 24 years old.
```

The `Input` statement in line 2 reads input from the keyboard and stores it in the name variable. In the example execution of the program, the user entered Andrea. The `Input` statement in line 4 reads input from the keyboard and stores it in the `age` variable. In the example execution of the program, the user entered 24.

Prompting the User

Getting keyboard input from the user is normally a two-step process:

1. Display a prompt on the screen.
2. Read a value from the keyboard.

A **prompt** is a message that tells (or asks) the user to enter a specific value. For example, the pseudocode in Program 5-3 gets the user to enter their age with the following statements:

```
Display "What is your age?"
Input age
```

In most programming languages, the statement that reads keyboard input does not display instructions on the screen. It simply causes the program to pause and wait for the user to type something on the keyboard. For this reason, whenever you write a statement that reads keyboard input, you should also write a statement just before it that tells the user what to enter. Otherwise, the user will not know what they are expected to do. For example, suppose we remove line 1 from Program 5-3, as follows:

```
Input age
Display "Here is the value that you entered: ", age
```

If this were an actual program, can you see what would happen when it is executed? The screen would appear blank because the `Input` statement would cause the program to wait for something to be typed on the keyboard. The user would probably think the computer was malfunctioning. The term **user-friendly** is commonly used in the software business to describe programs that are easy to use. Programs that do not display adequate or correct instructions are frustrating to use, and are not considered user-friendly. One of the simplest things that you can do to increase a program's user-friendliness is to make sure that it displays clear, understandable prompts prior to each statement that reads keyboard input.

TIP: When designing a program, remember that the typical user knows nothing about the program's inner workings. To avoid input mistakes, your programs should provide clear instructions for the user

Checkpoint

5.8 What are the three operations that programs typically perform?

5.9 What is an IPO chart?

5.10 What is a sequence structure?

5.11 What is a string? What is a string literal?

5.12 A string literal is usually enclosed inside a set of what characters?

5.13 What is a variable?

5.14 Summarize three common rules for naming variables.

5.15 What variable naming convention do we follow in this text?

5.16 Look at the following pseudocode statement:

```
Input temperature
```

What happens when this statement executes?

5.17 Who is the user?

5.18 What is a prompt?

5.19 What two steps usually take place when a program prompts the user for input?

5.20 What does the term *user-friendly* mean?

5.4 Introduction to Variables

You can store a value in a variable with an assignment statement. The value can be the result of a calculation, which is created with math operators.

Variable Assignment

In the previous section, you saw how the `Input` statement gets a value typed on the keyboard and stores it in a variable. You can also write statements that store specific values in variables. The following is an example, in pseudocode:

```
Set price = 20
```

This is called an assignment statement. An **assignment statement** sets a variable to a specified value. In this case, the variable `price` is set to the value 20. When we write an assignment statement in pseudocode, we will write the word Set, followed by the name of the variable, followed by an equal sign (=), followed by the value we want to store in the variable. The pseudocode in Program 5-5 shows another example.

Program 5-5:

```
1 Set dollars = 2.75
2 Display "I have ", dollars, " in my account."
```

Program Output

```
I have 2.75 in my account.
```

In line 1, the value 2.75 is stored in the `dollars` variable. Line 2 displays the message "I have 2.75 in my account." Just to make sure you understand how the `Display` statement in line 2 is working, let's walk through it.

The word `Display` is followed by three pieces of data, so that means it will display three things. The first thing it displays is the string literal `"I have"`. Next, it displays the contents of the `dollars` variable, which is 2.75. Last, it displays the string literal `"in my account."`

Variables are called "variable" because they can hold different values while a program is running. Once you set a variable to a value, that value will remain in the variable until you store a different value in the variable. For example, look at the pseudocode in Program 5-6.

Program 5-6:

```
Set dollars = 2.75
Display "I have ", dollars, " in my account."
Set dollars = 99.95
Display "But now I have ", dollars, " in my account!"
```

Program Output

```
I have 2.75 in my account.
But now I have 99.95 in my account!
```

Line 1 sets the `dollars` variable to 2.75, so when the statement in line 2 executes, it displays "I have 2.75 in my account." Then, the statement in line 3 sets the `dollars` variable to 99.95. As a result, the value 99.95 replaces the value 2.75 that was previously stored in the variable. When line 4 executes, it displays "But now I have 99.95 in my account!" This program illustrates two important characteristics of variables:

- A variable holds only one value at a time.
- When you store a value in a variable, that value replaces the previous value that was in the variable.

NOTE: When writing an assignment statement, all programming languages require that you write the name of the variable that is receiving the value on the left side of the = operator. For example, the following statement is incorrect:

```
Set 99.95 = dollars   ← This is an error!
```

A statement such as this would be considered a syntax error.

NOTE: In this text, we have chosen to start variable assignment statements with the word `Set` because it makes it clear that we are setting a variable to a value. In most programming languages, however, assignment statements do not start with the word `Set`. In most languages, an assignment statement looks similar to the following:

```
dollars = 99.95
```

If your instructor allows it, it is permissible to write assignment statements without the word `Set` in your pseudocode. Just be sure to write the name of the variable that is receiving the value on the left side of the equal sign.

In flowcharts, an assignment statement appears in a processing symbol, which is a rectangle. Figure 5-11 shows a flowchart for Program 5-6.

Figure 5-11 Flowchart for Program 5-6

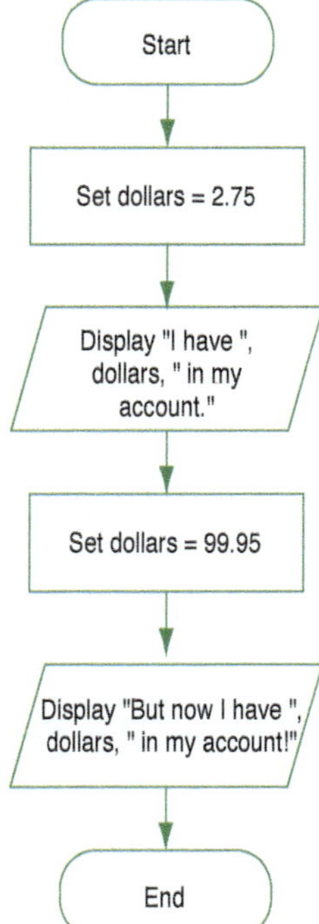

Checkpoint

5.21 What is an assignment statement?

5.22 When you assign a value to a variable, what happens to any value that is already stored in the variable?

5.23 In the following statement, what value is assigned to what variable?

```
Set dollars = 5.50
```

5.24 In a flowchart, what symbol is used to contain an assignment statement?

5.5 Data Types and Variable Declarations

Most languages require that variables be declared before they are used in a program. When a variable is declared, it can optionally be initialized with a value. Using an uninitialized variable is the source of many errors in programming.

Most programming languages require that you **declare** all of the variables that you intend to use in a program. A **variable declaration** is a statement that typically specifies two things about a variable:

- The variable's name
- The variable's data type

A variable's **data type** is the type of data that the variable will hold. It assigns the data to a category or classification so a compiler or interpreter knows how to process the data. Once you declare a variable, it can be used to store values of only the specified data type. In most languages, an error occurs if you try to store values of other types in the variable.

The data types that you are allowed to use depend on the programming language. For example, the Java language provides four data types for integer numbers, two data types for real numbers, one data type for strings, and others.

So far, we haven't declared any of the variables that we have used in our example pseudocode programs. We have simply used the variables without first declaring them. This is allowed with short pseudocode programs, but as programs grow in length and complexity, it makes sense to declare them. When you declare variables in a pseudocode program, it will make the job of translating the pseudocode to actual code easier.

Simple data types, which are also called *primitive* or *basic*, represent a single value. Integer is an example of a simple data type. Complex data types may represent more than one value or data type in a nested data structure. An **array** is an example of a complex data type. You use array to store a set of variables of the same data type (such as Integer) in consecutive order.

In most of the programs in this text, we use these three data types when we declare variables: Integer, Real, and String. Here is a summary of each:

- A variable of the `Integer` data type can hold whole numbers. For example, an `Integer` variable can hold values such as 42, 0, and −99. An `Integer` variable cannot hold numbers with a fractional part, such as 22.1 or −4.9.

- A variable of the `Real` data type can hold either whole numbers or numbers with a fractional part. For example, a `Real` variable can hold values such as 3.5, −87.95, and 3.0.
- A variable of the `String` data type can hold any string of characters, such as someone's name, address, password, and so on.

Other complex data types include **list**, **enumeration**, and **object**. Some other common, simple data types are listed in Table 5-1.

Table 5-1 Common Data Types

Data Type	Used For	Examples
char	a single character	a, 5, *, ?
Boolean	logical true or false	true, false or 1, 0
date	calendar dates including the year, month, and day	2024-10-31
time	clock times including the hour, minute, and seconds	11:32:59
float	32-bit representation of a real number (up to 7 decimal digits)	2.4567234
double	64-bit representation of a real number (up to 15 decimal digits)	2.456789123456789

In this text, we will begin variable declarations with the word Declare, followed by a data type, followed by the variable's name. Here is an example:

```
Declare Integer length
```

This statement declares a variable named length, of the `Integer` data type. Here is another example:

```
Declare Real grossPay
```

This statement declares a variable named grossPay, of the `Real` data type. Here is one more example:

```
Declare String name
```

This statement declares a variable named name, of the `String` data type.

If we need to declare more than one variable of the same data type, we can use one declaration statement. For example, suppose we want to declare three variables, length, width, and height, all of the `Integer` data type. We can declare all three with one statement, as shown here:

```
Declare Integer length, width, height
```

NOTE: In addition to a `String` data type, many programming languages also provide a `Character` data type. The difference between a `String` variable and a `Character` variable is that a String variable can hold a sequence of characters of virtually any length, and a `Character` variable can hold only one character. In this text, we will keep things simple. We will use `String` variables to hold all character data.

Declaring Variables Before Using Them

The purpose of a variable declaration statement is to tell the compiler or interpreter that you plan to use a particular variable in the program. A variable declaration statement typically causes the variable to be created in memory. For this reason, you have to write a variable's declaration statement *before* any other statements in the program that use the variable. This makes perfect sense because you cannot store a value in a variable if the variable has not been created in memory.

For example, look at the following pseudocode. If this code were converted to actual code in a language like Java or C++, it would cause an error because the `Input` statement uses the age variable before the variable has been declared.

```
Display "What is your age?"
Input age
Declare Integer age
```

This pseudocode has an error!

Program 5-7 shows the correct way to declare a variable. Notice that the declaration statement for the age variable appears before any other statements that use the variable.

Program 5-7:

```
Declare Integer age
Display "What is your age?"
Input age
Display "Here is the value that you entered:"
Display age
```

Program Output (with Input Shown in Bold)

```
What is your age?
24 [Enter]
Here is the value that you entered:
24
```

Program 5-8 shows another example. This program declares a total of four variables: three to hold test scores and another to hold the average of those test scores.

Program 5-8:

```
Declare Real test1
Declare Real test2
Declare Real test3
Declare Real average

Set test1 = 88.0
Set test2 = 92.5
Set test3 = 97.0
Set average = (test1 + test2 + test3) / 3
Display "Your average test score is ", average
```

Program Output

```
Your average test score is 92.5
```

Using Style Conventions

This program shows a common technique for declaring variables: they are all declared at the beginning of the program, before any other statements. This is one way of making sure that all variables are declared before they are used.

Notice that line 5 in this program is blank. This blank line does not affect the way the program works because most compilers and interpreters ignore blank lines. For the human reader, however, this blank line visually separates the variable declarations from the other statements. This makes the program appear more organized and easier for people to read.

Programmers commonly use blank lines and indentations in their code to create a sense of organization visually. This is similar to the way that authors visually arrange the text on the pages of a book. Instead of writing each chapter as one long series of sentences, they break it into paragraphs. This does not change the information in the book; it only makes it easier to read.

Although you are generally allowed to place blank lines and indentations anywhere in your code, you should follow certain conventions. For example, you have just learned that one convention is to use a blank line to separate a group of variable declaration statements from the rest of the statements in a program. These conventions are known as **programming style**.

Variable Initialization

When you declare a variable, you can optionally assign a value to it in the declaration statement. This is known as **initialization**. For example, the following statement declares a variable named price and assigns the value 49.95 to it:

```
Declare Real price = 49.95
```

We would say that this statement *initializes* the price variable with the value 49.95. The following statement shows another example:

```
Declare Integer length = 2, width = 4, height = 8
```

This statement declares and initializes three variables. The length variable is initialized with the value 2, width is initialized with the value 4, and height is initialized with the value 8.

Uninitialized Variables

An **uninitialized variable** is a variable that has been declared, but has not been initialized or assigned a value. Uninitialized variables are a common cause of logic errors in programs. For example, look at the following pseudocode:

```
Declare Real dollars
Display "I have ", dollars, " in my account."
```

In this pseudocode, we have declared the `dollars` variable, but we have not initialized it or assigned a value to it. Therefore, we do not know what value the variable holds. Nevertheless, we have used the variable in a `Display` statement.

You might wonder what a program like this would display. An honest answer would be "I don't know." This is because each language has its own way of handling uninitialized variables. Some languages assign a default value such as 0 to uninitialized variables. In many languages, however, uninitialized variables hold unpredictable values. This is because those languages set aside a place in memory for the variable, but do not alter the contents of that place in memory. As a result, an uninitialized variable holds the value that happens to be stored in its memory location. Programmers typically refer to unpredictable values such as this as "garbage."

Uninitialized variables can cause logic errors that are hard to find in a program. This is especially true when an uninitialized variable is used in a calculation. For example, look at the following pseudocode, which is a modified version of Program 5-9. Can you spot the error?

Program 5-9:

```
1 Declare Real test1
2 Declare Real test2
3 Declare Real test3
4 Declare Real average
5
6 Set test1 = 88.0
7 Set test2 = 92.5
8 Set average = (test1 + test2 + test3) / 3
9 Display "Your average test score is ", average
```

This pseudocode has an error!

This program will not work properly because the test3 variable is never assigned a value. The test3 variable will contain garbage when it is used in the calculation in line 8. This means that the calculation will result in an unpredictable value, which will be assigned to the average variable. A beginning programmer might have trouble finding this error because it would initially be assumed that something is wrong with the math in line 8.

In the next section, we will discuss a debugging technique that will help uncover errors such as the one in the modified version of Program 5-9. However, as a rule you should always make sure that your variables either (1) are initialized with the correct value when you declare them, or (2) receive the correct value from an assignment statement or an Input statement before they are used for any other purpose.

Numeric Literals and Data Type Compatibility

Many of the programs that you have seen so far have numbers written into their pseudocode. For example, the following statement, which appears in Program 5-6, has the number 2.75 written into it.

```
Set dollars = 2.75
```

And, the following statement, which appears in Program 5-7, has the number 100 written into it.

```
Set price = 100
```

A number that is written into a program's code is called a **numeric literal**. In most programming languages, if a numeric literal is written with a decimal point, such as 2.75, that numeric literal will be stored in the computer's memory as a Real and it will be treated as a Real when the program runs. If a numeric literal does not have a decimal point, such as 100, that numeric literal will be stored in the computer's memory as an Integer and it will be treated as an Integer when the program runs.

This is important to know when you are writing assignment statements or initializing variables. In many languages, an error will occur if you try to store a value of one data type in a variable of another data type. For example, look at the following pseudocode:

```
Declare Integer i
Set i = 3.7      ← This is an error!
```

The assignment statement will cause an error because it attempts to assign a real number, 3.7, in an Integer variable. The following pseudocode will also cause an error.

```
Declare Integer i
Set i = 3.0   ←—— This is an error!
```

> **NOTE: Most languages do not allow you to assign real numbers to `Integer` variables because `Integer` variables cannot hold fractional amounts. In many languages, however, you are allowed to assign an integer value to a `Real` variable without causing an error. Here is an example:**
>
> ```
> Declare Real r
> Set r = 77
> ```
>
> **Even though the numeric literal 77 is treated as an Integer, it can be assigned to a `Real` variable without the loss of data.**

Even though the numeric literal 3.0 does not have a fractional value (it is mathematically the same as the integer 3), it is still treated as a real number by the computer because it is written with a decimal point.

Integer Division

Be careful when dividing an integer by another integer. In many programming languages, when an integer is divided by an integer the result will also be an integer. This behavior is known as **integer division**. For example, look at the following pseudocode:

```
Set number = 3 / 2
```

This statement divides 3 by 2 and stores the result in the `number` variable. What will be stored in number? You might think that 1.5 would be stored in number because that's the result your calculator shows when you divide 3 by 2. However, that's not what will happen in many programming languages. Because the numbers 3 and 2 are both treated as integers, the programming language that you are using might throw away the fractional part of the answer. (Throwing away the fractional part of a number is called **truncation**.) As a result, the statement will store 1 in the `number` variable, not 1.5.

If you are using a language that behaves this way and you want to make sure that a division operation yields a real number, at least one of the operands must be a real number or a `Real` variable.

> **NOTE: In Java, C++, and C, the / operator throws away the fractional part of the result when both operands are integers. In these languages the result of the expression `3/2` would be 1. In Visual Basic, the / operator does not throw away the fractional part of the answer. In Visual Basic, the result of the expression `3/2` would be 1.5.**

Checkpoint

5.26 What two items do you usually specify with a variable declaration?

5.27 Does it matter where you write the variable declarations in a program?

5.28 What is variable initialization?

5.29 Do uninitialized variables pose any danger in a program?

5.30 What is an uninitialized variable?

5.6 Introduction to Named Constants

A named constant represents a value that cannot be changed during the program's execution.

Assume that the following statement appears in a banking program that calculates data pertaining to loans:

```
Set amount = balance * 0.069
```

In such a program, two potential problems arise. First, it is not clear to anyone other than the original programmer what 0.069 is. It appears to be an interest rate, but in some situations there are fees associated with loan payments. How can the purpose of this statement be determined without painstakingly checking the rest of the program?

The second problem occurs if this number is used in other calculations throughout the program and must be changed periodically. Assuming the number is an interest rate, what if the rate changes from 6.9 percent to 7.2 percent? The programmer would have to search through the source code for every occurrence of the number. (It is not advisable to use an editor's global search and replace feature to change values in a program. You might change an unintended value in the program, and inadvertently cause a logic error.)

Both of these problems can be addressed by using named constants. A **named constant** is a name that represents a value that cannot be changed during the program's execution. The following is an example of how we will declare named constants in our pseudocode:

```
Constant Real INTEREST_RATE = 0.069
```

This creates a constant named `INTEREST_RATE`. The constant's value is the `Real` number 0.069. Notice that the declaration looks a lot like a variable declaration, except that we use the word Constant instead of Declare. Also, notice that the name of the constant is written in all uppercase letters. This is a standard practice in most programming languages because it makes named constants easily distinguishable from regular variable names. An initialization value must be given when declaring a named constant.

An advantage of using named constants is that they make programs more self-explanatory. The following statement:

```
Set amount = balance * 0.069
```

can be changed to read

```
Set amount = balance * INTEREST_RATE
```

A new programmer can read the second statement and know what is happening. It is evident that `balance` is being multiplied by the interest rate. Another advantage to this approach is that widespread changes can easily be made to the program. Let's say the interest rate appears in a dozen different statements throughout the program. When the rate changes, the initialization value in the declaration of the named constant is the only value that needs to be modified. If the rate increases to 7.2 percent, the declaration can be changed to the following:

```
Constant Real INTEREST_RATE = 0.072
```

The new value of 0.072 will then be used in each statement that uses the `INTEREST_RATE` constant.

NOTE: A named constant cannot be assigned a value with a `Set` statement. If a statement in a program attempts to change the value of a named constant, an error will occur.

Checkpoint

5.31 What is a named constant?

5.32 Why is it good practice to write the name of a constant in all uppercase letters?

5.33 What are two advantages of using named constants?

5.7 Hand Tracing a Program

Hand tracing is a simple debugging process for locating hard-to-find errors in a program.

Hand tracing is a debugging process where you imagine that you are the computer executing a program. (This process is also known as **desk checking**.) You can use it to test program solutions by investigating the intended outcomes. You step through each of the program's statements one by one. As you carefully look at a statement, you record the contents that each variable will have after the statement executes. This process is often helpful in finding mathematical mistakes and other logic errors.

To hand trace a program, you construct a chart that has a column for each variable, and a row for each line in the program. For example, Figure 5-12 shows how we would construct a hand trace chart for the program for averaging test scores. The chart has a column for each of the four variables: `test1`, `test2`, `test3`, and `average`. The chart also has nine rows, one for each line in the program.

Figure 5-12 A program with a hand trace chart

```
Declare Real test1
Declare Real test2
Declare Real test3
Declare Real average

Set test1 = 88.0
Set test2 = 92.5
Set average = (test1 + test2 + test3) / 3
Display "Your average test score is ", average
```

	test1	test2	test3	average
1				
2				
3				
4				
5				
6				
7				
8				
9				

To hand trace this program, you step through each statement, observing the operation that is taking place, and then record the value that each variable will hold after the statement executes. When the process is complete, the chart will appear as shown in Figure 5-13. We have written question marks in the chart to indicate that a variable is uninitialized.

Figure 5-13 Program with the hand trace chart completed

```
Declare Real test1
Declare Real test2
Declare Real test3
Declare Real average

Set test1 = 88.0
Set test2 = 92.5
Set average = (test1 + test2 + test3) / 3
Display "Your average test score is ", average
```

	test1	test2	test3	average
1	?	?	?	?
2	?	?	?	?
3	?	?	?	?
4	?	?	?	?
5	?	?	?	?
6	88	?	?	?
7	88	92.5	?	?
8	88	92.5	?	undefined
9	88	92.5	?	undefined

When we get to line 8 we will carefully do the math. This means we look at the values of each variable in the expression. At that point we discover that one of the variables, `test3`, is uninitialized. Because it is uninitialized, we have no way of knowing the value that it contains. Consequently, the result of the calculation will be undefined. After making this discovery, we can correct the problem by adding a line that assigns a value to `test3`.

Hand tracing is a simple process that focuses your attention on each statement in a program. Often this helps you locate errors that are not obvious

Checkpoint

5.34 What is hand tracing?

5.35 How many columns and rows do you have in a hand trace chart?

5.36 Explain the process of using a hand trace chart.

5.8 Introduction to Comments

Comments are internal documentation for the programmer, that explain how parts of the program work.

A program's documentation explains various things about the program. There are usually two types of program documentation: external and internal. **External documentation** is typically designed for the user. It consists of documents such as a reference guide that describes the program's features, and tutorials that teach the user how to operate the program.

Sometimes the programmer is responsible for writing all or part of a program's external documentation. This might be the case in a small organization, or in a company that has a relatively small programming staff. Some organizations, particularly large companies, will employ a staff of technical writers whose job is to produce external documentation. These documents might be in printed manuals, or in files that can be viewed on the computer. In recent years it has become common for software companies to provide all of a program's external documentation in PDF (Portable Document Format) files.

Internal documentation appears as **comments** in a program's code. Comments are short notes placed in different parts of a program, explaining how those parts of the program work. Although comments are a critical part of a program, they are ignored by the compiler or interpreter. Comments are intended for human readers of a program's code, not the computer.

Programming languages provide special symbols or words for writing comments. In several languages, including Java, C, and C++, you begin a comment with two forward slashes (//). Everything that you write on the same line, after the slashes, is ignored by the compiler. Here is an example of a comment in any of those languages:

```
// Get the number of hours worked.
```

Some languages use symbols other than the two forward slashes to indicate the beginning of a comment. For example, Visual Basic uses an apostrophe ('), and Python uses the # symbol. In this text, we will use two forward slashes (//) in pseudocode.

Block Comments and Line Comments

Programmers generally write two types of comments in a program: block comments and line comments. **Block comments** take up several lines and are used when lengthy explanations are required. For example, a block comment often appears at the beginning of a program, explaining what the program does, listing the name of the author, giving the date that the program was last modified, and any other necessary information. The following is an example of a block comment:

```
// This program calculates an employee's gross pay.
// Written by Kiran Sharma.
// Last modified on 12/14/2021
```

NOTE: Some programming languages provide special symbols to mark the beginning and ending of a block comment.

Line comments are comments that occupy a single line, and explain a short section of the program. The following statements show an example:

```
// Calculate the interest.
Set interest = balance * interest_Rate
// Add the interest to the balance.
Set balance = balance + interest
```

A line comment does not have to occupy an entire line. Anything appearing after the // symbol, to the end of the line, is ignored, so a comment can appear after an executable statement. Here is an example:

```
Input age // Get the user's age.
```

As a beginning programmer, you might be resistant to the idea of liberally writing comments in your programs. After all, it's a lot more fun to write code that actually does something! It is crucial that you take the extra time to write comments, however. They will almost certainly save you time in the future when you have to modify or debug the program. Even large and complex programs can be made easy to read and understand if they are properly commented.

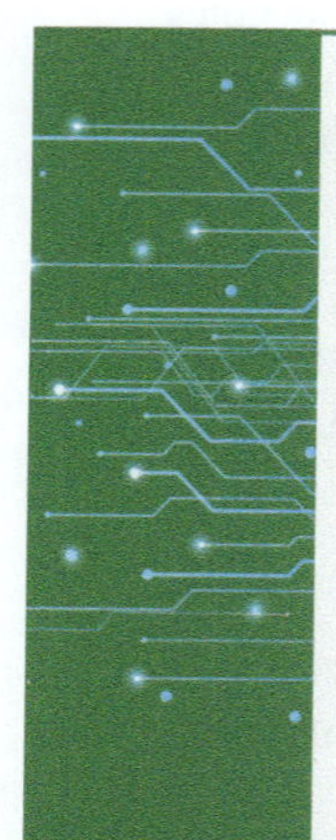

In the Spotlight:

Using Named Constants, Style Conventions, and Comments

Suppose we have been given the following programming problem: Scientists have determined that the world's ocean levels are currently rising at about 1.5 millimeters per year. Write a program to display the following:

- The number of millimeters that the oceans will rise in five years
- The number of millimeters that the oceans will rise in seven years
- The number of millimeters that the oceans will rise in ten years

On Your Own: Working alone or with a partner, write the algorithm steps, draw a flowchart, and write the pseudocode. Then, read on to see how you did. Remember, your solution does not have to be exactly the same as the one in the text in order to come up with the same result.

Here is the algorithm:

1. Calculate the amount that the oceans will rise in five years.
2. Display the result of the calculation in Step 1.
3. Calculate the amount that the oceans will rise in seven years.
4. Display the result of the calculation in Step 3.
5. Calculate the amount that the oceans will rise in ten years.
6. Display the result of the calculation in Step 5.

This program is straightforward. It performs three calculations and displays the results of each. The calculations should give the amount the oceans will rise in five, seven, and ten years. Each of these values can be calculated with the following formula:

Amount of yearly rise × Number of years

The amount of yearly rise is the same for each calculation, so we will create a constant to represent that value. Program 5-9 shows the pseudocode for the program

Program 5-9:

```
// Declare the variables
Declare Real fiveYears
Declare Real sevenYears
Declare Real tenYears

// Create a constant for the yearly rise
Constant Real YEARLY_RISE = 1.5

// Display the amount of rise in five years
Set fiveYears = YEARLY_RISE * 5
Display “The ocean levels will rise “, fiveYears,
        “ millimeters in five years.”

// Display the amount of rise in seven years
Set sevenYears = YEARLY_RISE * 7
Display “The ocean levels will rise “, sevenYears,
        “ millimeters in seven years.”

// Display the amount of rise in ten years
Set tenYears = YEARLY_RISE * 10
Display “The ocean levels will rise “, tenYears,
        “ millimeters in ten years.”
```

Program Output

```
The ocean levels will rise 7.5 millimeters in five years.
The ocean levels will rise 10.5 millimeters in seven years.
The ocean levels will rise 15 millimeters in ten years.
```

Three variables, `fiveYears`, `sevenYears`, and `tenYears`, are declared in lines 2 through 4. These variables will hold the amount that the ocean levels will rise in five, seven, and ten years.

Line 7 creates a constant, `YEARLY_RISE`, which is set to the value 1.5. This is the amount that the oceans rise per year. This constant will be used in each of the program's calculations.

Lines 10 through 12 calculate and display the amount that the oceans will rise in five years. The same values for seven years and ten years are calculated and displayed in lines 15 through 17 and 20 through 22.

This program illustrates the following programming style conventions:

- Several blank lines appear throughout the program (see lines 5, 8, 13, and 18). These blank lines do not affect the way the program works, but make the pseudocode easier to read.
- Line comments are used in various places to explain what the program is doing.
- Notice that each of the `Display` statements is too long to fit on one line. (See lines 11 and 12, 16 and 17, 21 and 22.) Most programming languages allow you to write long statements across several lines. When we do this in pseudocode, we will indent the second and subsequent lines. This will give a visual indication that the statement spans more than one line.

Figure 5-14 shows a flowchart for the program.

Figure 5-14 Flowchart for Program 5-9

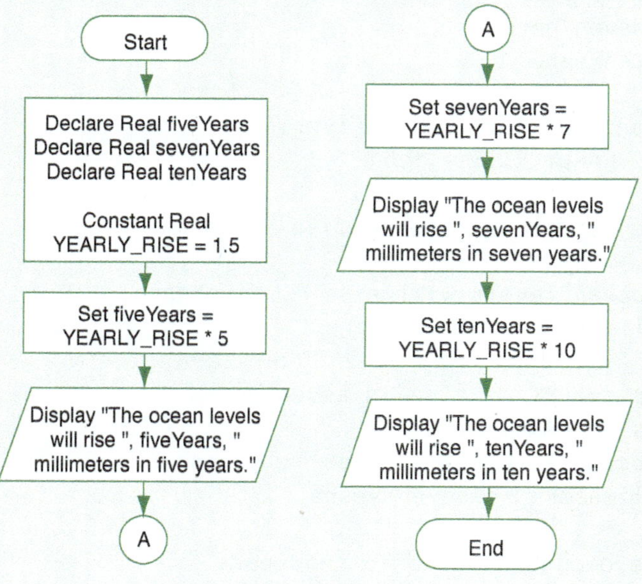

Checkpoint

5.37 What is a comment?

5.38 In Java, what character(s) do you use to begin a comment?

5.39 What is the difference between a block comment and a line comment?

Chapter Review

Multiple Choice

1. A __________ error does not prevent the program from running, but causes it to produce incorrect results.
   a. syntax
   b. hardware
   c. logic
   d. fatal

2. A __________ is a single function that the program must perform in order to satisfy the customer.
   a. task
   b. software requirement
   c. prerequisite
   d. predicate

3. A(n) __________ is a set of well-defined logical steps that must be taken to perform a task.
   a. logarithm
   b. plan of action
   c. logic schedule
   d. algorithm

4. An informal language that has no syntax rules, and is not meant to be compiled or executed is called __________.
   a. faux code
   b. pseudocode
   c. Java
   d. a flowchart

5. A __________ is a diagram that graphically depicts the steps that take place in a program.
   a. flowchart
   b. step chart
   c. code graph
   d. program graph

6. A(n) __________ is a set of statements that execute in the order that they appear.
   a. serial program
   b. sorted code
   c. sequence structure
   d. ordered structure

7. A __________ is a sequence of characters that is used as data.
   a. sequence structure
   b. character collection
   c. string
   d. text block

8. A __________ is a storage location in memory that is represented by a name.
   a. variable
   b. register
   c. RAM slot
   d. byte

9. A __________ is any hypothetical person that is using a program and providing input for it.
   a. designer
   b. user
   c. guinea pig
   d. test subject

10. A(n) __________ is a message that tells (or asks) the user to enter a specific value.
    a. inquiry
    b. input statement
    c. directive
    d. prompt

11. A(n) __________ sets a variable to a specified value.
    a. variable declaration
    b. assignment statement
    c. math expression
    d. string literal

12. A(n) __________ specifies a variable's name and data type.
    a. assignment
    b. variable specification
    c. variable certification
    d. variable declaration

13. Assigning a value to a variable in a declaration statement is called __________.
    a. allocation
    b. initialization
    c. certification
    d. programming style

14. A(n) __________ variable is one that has been declared, but has not been initialized or assigned a value.
    a. undefined
    b. uninitialized
    c. empty
    d. default

15. A(n) __________ is a variable whose content has a value that is read only and cannot be changed during the program's execution.
    a. static variable
    b. uninitialized variable
    c. named constant
    d. locked variable

16. A debugging process in which you imagine that you are the computer executing a program is called __________.
    a. imaginative computing
    b. role playing
    c. mental simulation
    d. hand tracing

17. Short notes placed in different parts of a program, explaining how those parts of the program work, are called __________.
    a. comments
    b. reference manuals
    c. tutorials
    d. external documentation

True or False

1. Programmers must be careful not to make syntax errors when writing pseudocode programs.
2. Variable names can have spaces in them.
3. In most languages, the first character of a variable name cannot be a number.
4. The name gross_pay is written in the camelCase convention.
5. In languages that require variable declarations, a variable's declaration must appear before any other statements that use the variable.
6. Uninitialized variables are a common cause of errors.
7. The value of a named constant cannot be changed during the program's execution.
8. Hand tracing is the process of translating a pseudocode program into machine language by hand.
9. Internal documentation refers to books and manuals that document a program, and are intended for use within a company's programming department..

Short Answer

1. What data type should you use if variable values will be whole numbers?
2. What is pseudocode?
3. Computer programs typically perform what three steps?
4. What does the term *user-friendly* mean?
5. Explain how to use a sequence structure in a program for a story, game, or animation.
6. Explain how to use a variable in a program for a story, game, or animation.
7. What two things must you normally specify in a variable declaration?
8. What value is stored in uninitialized variables?

Algorithm Workbench

1. Design an algorithm that prompts the user to enter the temperature and stores the user's input in a variable named `temperature`.
2. Design an algorithm that prompts the user to enter their favorite color and stores the user's input in a variable named `color`.
3. Write a pseudocode statement that declares the variable cost so it can hold real numbers.
4. Write a pseudocode statement that declares the variable total so it can hold integers. Initialize the variable with the value 0.

Debugging Exercises

1. If the following pseudocode were an actual program, why would it not display the output that the programmer expects?

```
Declare String favoriteFood

Display "What is the name of your favorite food?"
Input favoriteFood

Display "Your favorite food is "
Display "favoriteFood"
```

2. If the programmer translates the following pseudocode to an actual programming language, a syntax error is likely to occur. Can you find the error?

```
Declare String 1stPrize

Display "Enter the award for first prize."
Input 1stPrize

Display "The first prize winner will receive ", 1stPrize
```

4. Find the error in the following pseudocode.

```
Display "Enter the length of the room."
Input length
Declare Integer length
```

Programming Exercises

1. Personal Information

Design a program that displays the following information:

- Your name
- Your address, with city, state, and ZIP
- Your telephone number
- Your college major

2. Reward Prediction

In a story, a character is rewarded with 23 percent of total coins collected. Design a program with a sequential structure that asks the user to enter the projected amount of total coins, and then displays the number of coins the character will receive based on the user input. Write the code for the program and use hand tracing to test your solution.

Hint: Use the value 0.23 to represent 23 percent.

3. Land Calculation

One acre of land is equivalent to 43,560 square feet. Design a program that asks the user to enter the total square feet in a tract of land and calculates the number of acres in the tract.

Hint: Divide the amount entered by 43,560 to get the number of acres.

4. Total Purchase

A customer in a store is purchasing five items. Design a program that asks for the price of each item, and then displays the subtotal of the sale, the amount of sales tax, and the total. Assume the sales tax is 6 percent.

5. Distance Traveled

Assuming there are no accidents or delays, the distance that a car travels down the interstate can be calculated with the following formula:

$$Distance = Speed \times Time$$

A car is traveling at a constant 60 miles per hour. Design a program that displays the following:

- The distance the car will travel in 5 hours
- The distance the car will travel in 8 hours
- The distance the car will travel in 12 hours

6. Miles-per-Gallon

A car's miles-per-gallon (MPG) can be calculated with the following formula:

MPG = Miles driven Gallons of gas used

Design a program that asks the user for the number of miles driven and the gallons of gas used. It should calculate the car's miles-per-gallon and display the result on the screen.

7. Leftover Pizza

You're planning a pizza party and you plan to give each person three slices of pizza. Design a program that displays the number of slices that will be leftover. The program should ask for the following input:

- The number of pizzas you will have
- The number of slices that each pizza is cut into
- The number of people that will be attending

The program should display the number of slices that will be left over.

CHAPTER 6 Introduction to Calculations

TOPICS

6.1 Getting Started with Calculations

Understanding calculations is a vital part of creating clean, effective code in any programming language.

Most real-world algorithms require calculations. A programmer's tools for performing calculations are **math operators**. Programming languages commonly provide the operators shown in Table 6-1.

Table 6-1 Common math operators

Symbol	Operator	Description
+	Addition	Adds two numbers
–	Subtraction	Subtracts one number from another
*	Multiplication	Multiplies one number by another
/	Division	Divides one number by another and gives the quotient
MOD	Modulus	Divides one number by another and gives the remainder
^	Exponent	Raises a number to a power

NOTE: In some programming languages, the % character is used as the modulus operator, and sometimes the ** characters are used as the exponent operator.

Programmers use the operators shown in Table 6-1 to create math expressions. A **math expression** performs a calculation and gives a value. The following is an example of a simple math expression:

```
12 + 2
```

The values on the right and left of the + operator are called **operands**. These are values that the + operator adds together. The value that is given by this expression is 14.

Variables may also be used in a math expression. For example, suppose we have two variables named hours and payRate. The following math expression uses the * operator to multiply the value in the hours variable by the value in the payRate variable:

```
hours * payRate
```

When we use a math expression to calculate a value, normally we want to save that value in memory so we can use it again in the program. We do this with an assignment statement. Recall that an assignment statement sets a variable to a specified value. Program 6-1 shows an example.

Program 6-1:

```
1 Set price = 100
2 Set discount = 20
3 Set sale = price - discount
4 Display "The total cost is $", sale
```

Program Output

```
The total cost is $80
```

Line 1 sets the price variable to 100, and line 2 sets the discount variable to 20. Line 3 sets the sale variable to the result of the expression price – discount. As you can see from the program output, the sale variable holds the value 80.

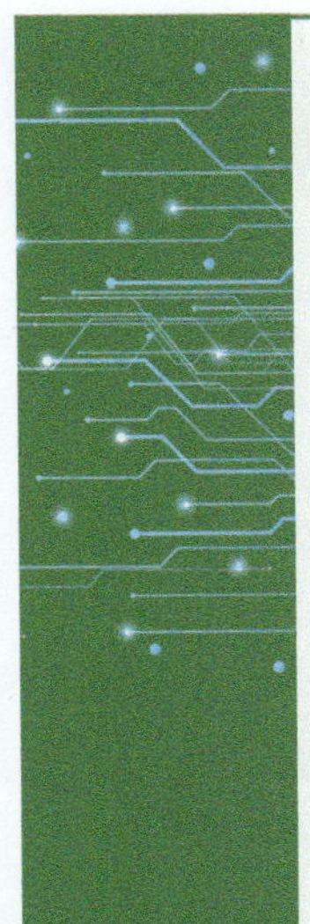

In the Spotlight:

Calculating Cell Phone Overage Fees

Suppose your cell phone calling plan allows you to use 700 minutes per month. If you use more than this limit in a month, you are charged an overage fee of 35 cents for each excess minute. Your phone shows you the number of excess minutes that you have used in the current month, but it does not show you how much your overage fee currently is. Until now, you've been doing the math the old-fashioned way (with pencil and paper, or with a calculator), but you would like to design a program that will simplify the task. You would like to be able to enter the number of excess minutes, and have the program perform the calculation for you.

First, you want to make sure that you understand the steps that the program must perform. It will be helpful if you closely look at the way you've been solving this problem, using only paper and pencil, or calculator.

On Your Own: Before reading on, give this program a try. Working alone or with a partner, make a list of the steps you would take to manually calculate the overage fee. When the list is complete, continuing reading to see if your list matches the one in the text.

Manual Algorithm (Using pencil and paper, or calculator)

1. You get the number of excess minutes that you have used.
2. You multiply the number of excess minutes by 0.35.
3. The result of the calculation is your current overage fee.

Ask yourself the following questions about this algorithm:

Question: What input do I need to perform this algorithm?
Answer: I need the number of excess minutes.

Question: What must I do with the input?
Answer: I must multiply the input (the number of excess minutes) by 0.35. The result of that calculation is the overage fee.

Question: What output must I produce?
Answer: The overage fee.

Now that you have identified the input, the process that must be performed, and the output, you can write the general steps of the program's algorithm:

On Your Own: Pause here to try writing the algorithm in steps, creating a flowchart for it, and then writing it in pseudocode. When you have it complete, continue reading to see how you did. Don't worry if your solution is not exactly the same as the one in the text; there is usually more than one way to design a program!

Computer Algorithm

1. Get the number of excess minutes as input.
2. Calculate the overage fee by multiplying the number of excess minutes by 0.35.
3. Display the overage fee.

In Step 1 of the computer algorithm, the program gets the number of excess minutes from the user. Any time a program needs the user to enter a piece of data, it does two things: (1) it displays a message prompting the user for the piece of data, and (2) it reads the data that the user enters on the keyboard, and stores that data in a variable. In pseudocode, Step 1 of the algorithm will look like this:

```
Display "Enter the number of excess minutes."
Input excessMinutes
```

Notice that the `Input` statement stores the value entered by the user in a variable named `excessMinutes`.

In Step 2 of the computer algorithm, the program calculates the overage fee by multiplying the number of excess minutes by 0.35. The following pseudocode statement performs this calculation, and stores the result in a variable named overageFee:

```
Set overageFee = excessMinutes * 0.35
```

In Step 3 of the computer algorithm, the program displays the overage fee. Because the overage fee is stored in the overageFee variable, the program will display a message that shows the value of the overageFee variable. In pseudocode we will use the following statement:

```
Display "Your current overage fee is $", overageFee
```

Program 6-2 shows the entire pseudocode program, with example output. Figure 6-1 shows the flowchart for this program.

Program 6-2:

```
Display "Enter the number of excess minutes."
Input excessMinutes
Set overageFee = excessMinutes * 0.35
Display "Your current overage fee is $", overageFee
```

Program Output (with Input Shown in Bold)

```
Enter the number of excess minutes.
100 [Enter]
Your current overage fee is $35
```

Figure 6-1 Flowchart for Program 6-2

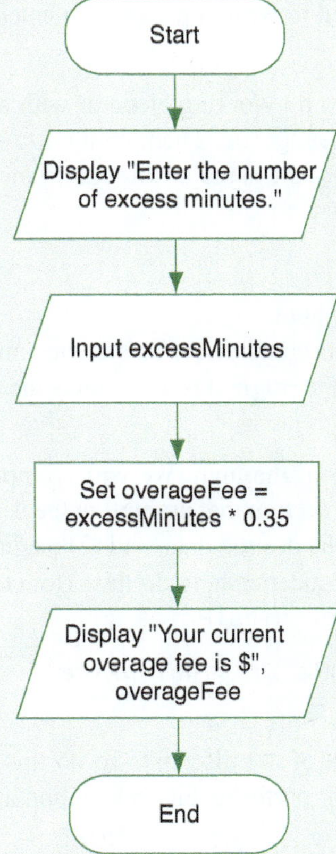

Calculating a Percentage

Determining percentages is a common calculation in computer programming. In mathematics, the % symbol is used to indicate a percentage, but most programming languages don't use the % symbol for this purpose. In a program, you usually have to convert a percentage to a decimal number. To convert a percentage to a decimal, you divide the percentage by 100. For example, 50 percent would be 0.5 and 2 percent would be written as 0.02.

In the Spotlight:

20% Off Sale

Suppose a retail business is planning to have a storewide sale where the prices of all items will be 20 percent off. We have been asked to write a program to calculate the sale price of an item after the discount is subtracted.

On Your Own: How would you do it? Working alone or with a partner, write the algorithm steps, draw a flowchart, and write the pseudocode. Then, read on to see how you did. Remember, your solution does not have to be exactly the same as the one in the text in order to come up with the same result.

Here is the algorithm:

1. Get the original price of the item.
2. Calculate 20 percent of the original price. This is the amount of the discount.
3. Subtract the discount from the original price. This is the sale price.
4. Display the sale price.

In Step 1 we get the original price of the item. We will prompt the user to enter this data on the keyboard. Recall from the previous section that prompting the user is a two-step process: (1) display a message telling the user to enter the desired data, and (2) reading that data from the keyboard. We will use the following pseudocode statements to do this. Notice that the value entered by the user will be stored in a variable named `originalPrice`.

```
Display "Enter the item's original price."
Input originalPrice
```

In Step 2, we calculate the amount of the discount. To do this we multiply the original price by 20 percent. The following statement performs this calculation and stores the result in the discount variable.

```
Set discount = originalPrice * 0.2
```

In Step 3, we subtract the discount from the original price. The following statement does this calculation and stores the result in the salePrice variable.

```
Set salePrice = originalPrice – discount
```

Last, in Step 4, we will use the following statement to display the sale price:

```
Display "The sale price is $", salePrice
```

Program 6-3 shows the entire pseudocode program, with example output. Figure 6-2 shows the flowchart for this program.

Program 6-3:

```
Display "Enter the item's original price."
Input originalPrice
Set discount = originalPrice * 0.2
Set salePrice = originalPrice - discount
Display "The sale price is $", salePrice
```

Program Output (with Input Shown in Bold)

```
Enter the item's original price.
100 [Enter]
The sale price is $80
```

Figure 6-2 Flowchart for Program 6-3

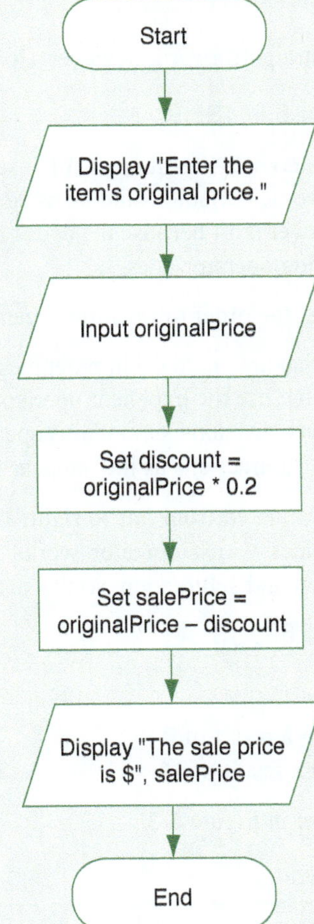

Checkpoint

6.1 What math operator does the symbol * represent?

6.2 What is the purpose of the exponent operator?

6.3 What is the purpose of a math expression in programming?

6.4 In the math expression below, what are the operands?

```
12 / 3
```

6.2 Using the Order of Operations

A computer processes calculations based on the standard order of operations. If you get the order wrong, the output will be wrong, too.

You can build mathematical expressions with several operators. The following statement assigns the sum of 17, the variable x, 21, and the variable y to the variable answer.

```
Set answer = 17 + x + 21 + y
```

Some expressions are not that straightforward, however. Consider the following statement:

```
Set outcome = 12 + 6 / 3
```

What value will be stored in outcome? The number 6 is used as an operand for both the addition and division operators. The outcome variable could be assigned either 6 or 14, depending on when the division takes place. The answer is 14 because the **order of operations** dictates that the division operator works before the addition operator does.

In most programming languages, the order of operations can be summarized as follows:

1. Perform any operations that are enclosed in parentheses.
2. Perform any operations that use the exponent operator to raise a number to a power.
3. Perform any multiplications, divisions, or modulus operations as they appear from left to right.
4. Perform any additions or subtractions as they appear from left to right.

Mathematical expressions are evaluated from left to right. When two operators share an operand, the order of operations determines which operator works first. Multiplication and division are always performed before addition and subtraction, so the statement

```
Set outcome = 12 + 6 / 3
```

works like this:

1. 6 is divided by 3, yielding a result of 2
2. 12 is added to 2, yielding a result of 14

It could be diagrammed as shown in Figure 6-3.

Figure 6-3 The order of operations at work

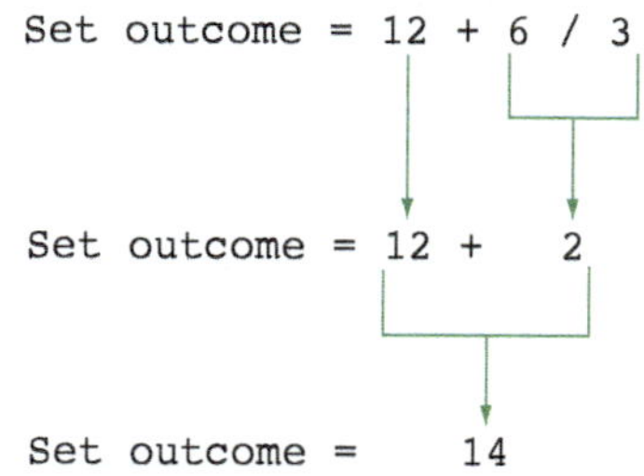

Table 6-2 shows some other sample expressions with their values.

Table 6-2 Some expressions and their values

Expression	Value
5 + 2 * 4	13
10 / 2 – 3	2
8 + 12 * 2 – 4	28
6 – 3 * 2 + 7 – 1	6

Grouping with Parentheses

Parts of a mathematical expression may be grouped with parentheses to force some operations to be performed before others. In the following statement, the variables a and b are added together, and their sum is divided by 4:

```
Set result = (a + b) / 4
```

Without the parentheses, however, b would be divided by 4 and the result added to a.

Table 6-3 shows more expressions and their values.

Table 6-3 More expressions and their values

Expression	Value
(5 + 2) * 4 2	8
10 / (5 – 3)	5
8 + 12 * (6 – 2)	56
(6 – 3) * (2 + 7) / 3	9

NOTE: Parentheses can be used to enhance the clarity of a math expression, even when they are unnecessary to get the correct result. For example, look at the following statement:

```
Set fahrenheit = celsius * 1.8 + 32
```

Even when it is unnecessary to get the correct result, we can insert parentheses to clearly show that `celsius * 1.8` happens first in the math expression:

```
Set fahrenheit = (celsius * 1.8) + 32
```

In the Spotlight:

Calculating an Average

Determining the average of a group of values is a simple calculation: You add all of the values and then divide the sum by the number of values. Although this is a straightforward calculation, it is easy to make a mistake when writing a program that calculates an average. For example, let's assume that the variables a, b, and c each hold a value and we want to calculate the average of those values. If we are careless, we might write a statement such as the following to perform the calculation:

```
Set average = a + b + c / 3
```

Can you see the error in this statement? When it executes, the division will take place first. The value in c will be divided by 3, and then the result will be added to `a + b`. That is not the correct way to calculate an average. To correct this error we need to put parentheses around `a + b + c`, as shown here:

```
Set average = (a + b + c) / 3
```

Let's step through the process of writing a program that calculates an average. Suppose you have taken three tests in your computer science class, and you want to write a program that will display the average of the test scores

On Your Own: Working alone or with a partner, write the algorithm steps, draw a flowchart, and write the pseudocode. Then, read on to see how you did. Remember, your solution does not have to be exactly the same as the one in the text in order to come up with the same result.

Here is the algorithm:

1. Get the first test score.
2. Get the second test score.
3. Get the third test score.
4. Calculate the average by adding the three test scores and dividing the sum by 3.
5. Display the average.

In Steps 1, 2, and 3 we will prompt the user to enter the three test scores. We will store those test scores in the variables `test1`, `test2`, and `test3`. In Step 4 we will calculate the average of the three test scores. We will use the following statement to perform the calculation and store the result in the average variable:

```
Set average = (test1 + test2 + test3) / 3
```

Last, in Step 5, we display the average. Program 6-4 shows the pseudocode for this program, and Figure 6-4 shows the flowchart.

Program 6-4:

```
Display "Enter the first test score."
Input test1
Display "Enter the second test score."
Input test2
Display "Enter the third test score."
Input test3
Set average = (test1 + test2 + test3) / 3
Display "The average score is ", average
```

Program Output (with Input Shown in Bold)

```
Enter the first test score.
90 [Enter]
Enter the second test score.
80 [Enter]
Enter the third test score.
100 [Enter]
The average score is 90
```

Figure 6-4 Flowchart for Program 6-4

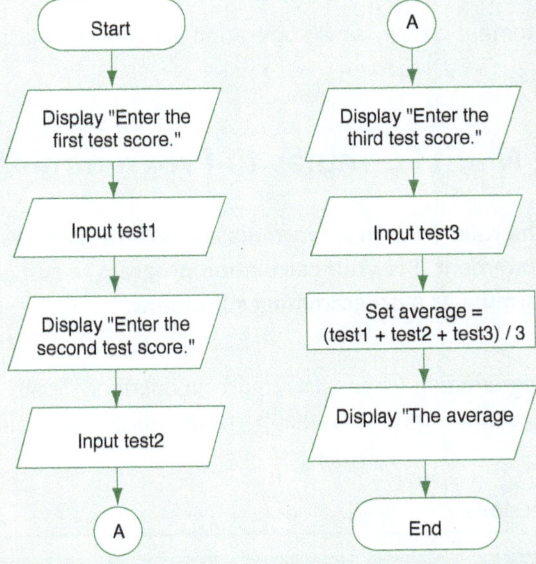

Advanced Arithmetic Operators: Exponent and Modulus

In addition to the basic math operators for addition, subtraction, multiplication, and division, many languages provide an exponent operator and a modulus operator. The ^ symbol is commonly used as the exponent operator, and its purpose it to raise a number to a power. For example, the following pseudocode statement raises the `length` variable to the power of 2 and stores the result in the `area` variable:

```
Set area = length^2
```

The word `MOD` is used in many languages as the modulus operator. (Some languages use the % symbol for the same purpose.) The modulus operator performs division, but instead of returning the quotient, it returns the remainder. The following statement assigns 2 to `leftover`:

```
Set leftover = 17 MOD 3
```

This statement assigns 2 to `leftover` because 17 divided by 3 is 5 with a remainder of 2. You will not use the modulus operator frequently, but it is useful in some situations. It is commonly used in calculations that detect odd or even numbers, determine the day of the week, measure the passage of time, and other specialized operations

Checkpoint

6.5 Summarize the mathematical order of operations, as it works in most programming languages.

6.6 In the statement below, which operation is performed first?

```
Set outcome = 10 + 25 / 5
```

6.7 In the statement below, which operation is performed last?

```
Set result = (a + b) * 2
```

6.3 Converting Math Formulas to Programming Statements

The rules for a math formula are not the same as for a programming statement. For your calculation program to run correctly, you must code the formula as a programming statement.

Unlike algebra, programming languages require an operator for any mathematical operation. Table 6-4 shows some algebraic expressions that perform multiplication and the equivalent programming expressions.

Table 6-4 Algebraic expressions

Algebraic Expression	Operation Being Performed	Programming Expression
6B	6 times B	6 * B
(3)(12)	3 times 12	3 * 12
4xy	4 times x times y	4 * x * y

When converting some algebraic expressions to programming expressions, you may have to insert parentheses that do not appear in the algebraic expression. For example, look at the following formula:

$$x = \frac{a + b}{c}$$

To convert this to a programming statement, $a + b$ will have to be enclosed in parentheses:

```
Set x = (a + b) / c
```

Table 6-5 shows additional algebraic expressions and their pseudocode equivalents.

Table 6-5 Algebraic expressions and pseudocode statements

Algebraic Expression	Pseudocode Statement
$y = 3\frac{x}{2}$	`Set y = x / 2 * 3`
$z = 3bc + 4$	`Set z = 3 * b * c + 4`
$a = \frac{x + 2}{a - 1}$	`Set a = (x + 2) / (a - 1)`

In the Spotlight:

Converting a Math Formula to a Programming Statement

Suppose you want to deposit a certain amount of money into a savings account, and then leave it alone to draw interest for the next 10 years. At the end of 10 years you would like to have $10,000 in the account. How much do you need to deposit today to make that happen? You can use the following formula to find out:

$$P = \frac{F}{(1 + r)^n}$$

The terms in the formula are as follows:

- P is the present value, or the amount that you need to deposit today.
- F is the future value that you want in the account. (In this case, F is $10,000.)
- r is the annual interest rate.
- n is the number of years that you plan to let the money sit in the account.

It would be nice to write a computer program to perform the calculation, because then we can experiment with different values for the terms

On Your Own: Working alone or with a partner, write the algorithm steps, draw a flowchart, and write the pseudocode. Then, read on to see how you did. Remember, your solution does not have to be exactly the same as the one in the text in order to come up with the same result.

Here is an algorithm that we can use:

1. Get the desired future value.
2. Get the annual interest rate.
3. Get the number of years that the money will sit in the account.
4. Calculate the amount that will have to be deposited.
5. Display the result of the calculation in Step 4.

In Steps 1 through 3, we will prompt the user to enter the specified values. We will store the desired future value in a variable named `futureValue`, the annual interest rate in a variable named `rate`, and the number of years in a variable named years.

In Step 4, we calculate the present value, which is the amount of money that we will have to deposit. We will convert the formula previously shown to the following pseudocode statement. The statement stores the result of the calculation in the `presentValue` variable.

```
Set presentValue = futureValue / (1 + rate)^years
```

In Step 5, we display the value in the `presentValue` variable. Program 6-5 shows the pseudocode for this program, and Figure 6-5 shows the flowchart.

Program 6-5:

```
Display "Enter the desired future value."
Input futureValue
Display "Enter the annual interest rate."
Input rate
Display "How many years will you let the money grow?"
Input years
Set presentValue = futureValue / (1 + rate)^years
Display "You will need to deposit $", presentValue
```

Program Output (with Input Shown in Bold)

```
Enter the desired future value.
10000 [Enter]
Enter the annual interest rate.
0.05 [Enter]
How many years will you let the money grow?
10 [Enter]
You will need to deposit $6139
```

Figure 6-5 Flowchart for Program 6-5

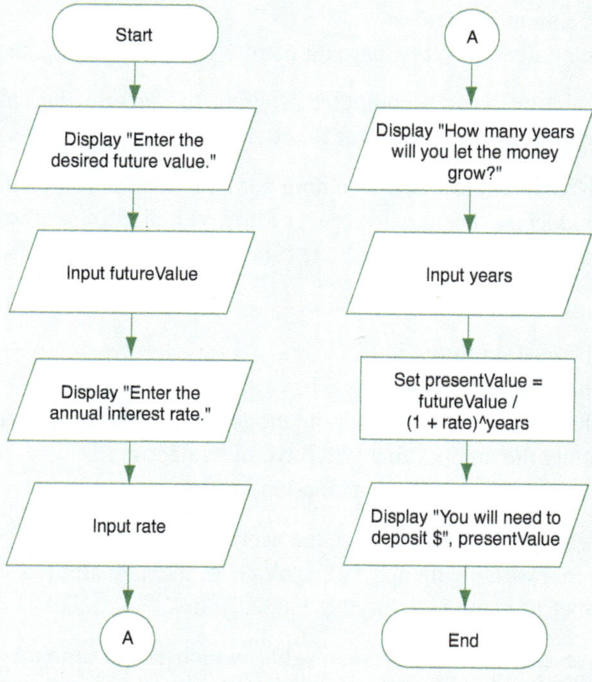

Checkpoint

6.8 What is the programming expression for the algebraic expression below?

5x

6.9 Explain why you might need to insert parentheses when converting a math expression to a programming expression.

6.10 What is the pseudocode statement for the math expression below?

$$x = \frac{a+2}{x-2}$$

6.4 Exploring Common Algorithms

There are common algorithms used often in programming that you can learn and save for future use.

Many calculations are commonly used in programming. You can save time and write clean code by learning the algorithms for these calculations so you can use them whenever you need them.

In this section, you will examine these three common algorithms:

- Finding the greatest common divisor
- Finding the largest of three values
- Finding a prime number

As you read this section, practice creating and testing the algorithms. You may work on your own, or with a partner or small group. Save your practice solutions. They will be a good reference as you continue to design programs and write code. Your instructor may provide time to discuss your solutions with others, receive feedback, and implement any changes to your solution based on the feedback.

Finding the Greatest Common Divisor

In math, the **greatest common divisor** (GCD) of two integers is the largest number that can divide both. It is sometimes called the greatest common factor.

For example

- The greatest common divisor of the two integers **4** and **2** is **2.**
- The greatest common divisor of the two integers **16** and **24** is **8.**

How would you write a program to find the greatest common divisor? Would you immediately begin to write the code? No. It is important to th*ink before you code.* Thinking enables you to generate a logical solution for the problem without concern about how to write the code.

Give it a try.

Step 1. Let the two input integers be **a** and **b.**

Step 2. You know that number **1** is a common divisor, but it may not be the greatest common divisor. So, you can check whether **k** (where **k** is **2**, then **3**, then **4**, and so on) is a common divisor for **a** and **b**.

Step 3. Keep incrementing **k** by **1** number until **k** is greater than **a** or **b**.

Step 4. Store the common divisor in a variable named **gcd**.

Initially, **gcd** is **1**. Whenever a new common divisor is found, it becomes the new gcd. When you have checked all the possible common divisors from **2** up to **a** or **b**, the value in variable **gcd** is the greatest common divisor.

Finding the Largest of Three Values

Suppose you have a list of three numbers, and you need to determine which of the three numbers is the largest, then print the largest number to the screen.

Start by writing out the steps on paper. You will discover that there is usually more than one right answer to writing an algorithm.

Your steps may look like Example 1:

```
Example 1
Step 1: Compare number1 to number2
Step 2: If number1 > number2, then number1 = largestNumber
Step 3: if number2 > number1, then number2 = largestNumber
Step 4: If number3 > largestNumber, then number3 = largestNumber
Step 5: Print largestNumber
```

Or your steps may look like Exampe 2:

```
Example 2
Step 1: Store the values in x,y,z
Step 2: If x > y and x > z, print x
Step 3: Otherwise, if y > z and y > x, print y
Step 4: Otherwise, print z
```

Both solutions provide the correct answer. More advanced topics of computer science discuss how some algorithms are more efficient than others. For now, we will focus on developing an accurate solution and understanding that your solution may look slightly different from other solutions.

It is helpful to test your algorithm by plugging in actual values, stepping through the algorithm, and evaluating the results. Perform the following steps to test the accuracy of Example 1:

1. Replace the words number1, number2, and number3 with the numbers 2, 4, and 6.
2. Step through the algorithm. Is the output correct?
   (*Hint*: The output should be: 6.)
3. Change the order of the numbers and test again. Is the output correct?
4. Try an entirely different set of numbers, such as 54, 120, 18. Is the output correct?
5. Your testing should confirm that the solution works for any set of three numbers.

Repeat the process for Example 2. Are both solutions accurate?

Finding a Prime Number

A prime number is any whole number greater than 1 that is only divisible by 1 or itself. For example, 2, 3, 5, and 7 are prime numbers. The numbers 4, 6, 8, and 9 are not prime numbers.

Creating the Algorithm

Write the steps to find the first 10 prime numbers then display them to the screen. They should each be displayed on a separate line.

Example Solution

Step 1: For numbers 2, 3, 4, 5, 6, 7 …. And so on, test each number to see if it is prime.

Step 2: Count the number of prime numbers found. When you reach 10, stop testing.

Step 3: Print a prime number, then go to the next line.

Step 4: Repeat step 3 until all 10 prime numbers are displayed to the screen.

Remember, this is an example of a possible solution. Your solution may look different than the solution given in this book or the solutions of classmates.

Checkpoint

6.11 What are two benefits of learning common algorithms?

6.12 What is a greatest common divisor?

6.13 What is a prime number?

6.14 Explain how you can test an algorithm.

6.5 Designing a Program with Calculations

KEY POINT **No matter what language you are using, the basics of program design are the same.**

Whenever you are faced with a new programming problem, it is a good idea to review the basics of program design. In this section we will present a simple problem, go through the process of analyzing the program's requirements, and design the algorithm in pseudocode and a flowchart. You may work through the problem as you read the section, or, try working it out on your own or with a partner first. Remember, there are usually multiple ways to solve a programming problem and arrive at the same result. Here is the programming problem:

You are working on a game that will determine the MVP of a baseball team based on batting average. You use the following formula to calculate a player's batting average:

$$\textit{Batting Average} = \textit{Hits} \div \textit{Times at Bat}$$

In the formula, *Hits* is the number of successful hits made by the player, and Times at Bat is the number of times the player was at bat. For example, if a player is at bat 500 times during a season, and gets 150 hits, that player's batting average is .300. Design a program using a sequence structure to calculate any player's batting average.

Recall that a program's actions can typically be divided into the following three phases:

1. Input is received.
2. Some process (such as a calculation) is performed on the input.
3. Output is produced.

Your first step is to determine what is required in each phase. Usually these requirements are not stated directly in the problem description. For example, the previously shown batting average problem explains what a batting average is, and merely instructs you to design a program to calculate any player's batting average. It is up to you to brainstorm the problem and determine the requirements of each phase. Let's take a closer look at each phase of the batting average problem.

1. Input is received.

To determine a program's input requirements, you must determine the pieces of data that are required for the program to complete its task. If we look at the batting average formula, we see that two values are needed to perform the calculation:

- The number of hits
- The number of times at bat

Because these values are unknown, the program will have to prompt the user to enter them.

Each piece of input will be stored in a variable. You will have to declare those variables when you design the program, so it is helpful in this phase to think about each variable's name and data type. In the batting average program we will use the name `hits` for the variable that stores the number of hits, and the name `atBat` for the variable that holds the number of times at bat. Both of these values will be whole numbers, so the data type for these variables will be declared as Integers.

2. Some process (such as a calculation) is performed on the input.

Once the program has gathered the required input, it can proceed to use that input in any necessary calculations, or other operations. The batting average program will divide the number of hits by the number of times at bat. The result of the calculation is the player's batting average.

Keep in mind that when a mathematical calculation is performed, you typically want to store the result of that calculation in a variable. So, you should think about the names and data types of any variables that are needed in this phase. In this example, we will use the name battingAverage for the variable that stores the player's batting average. Because this variable will store the result of a division, we will declare the data type as a `Real`.

3. Output is produced.

A program's output will typically be the result of the process or processes that it has performed. The output of the batting average program will be the result of the calculation, which is stored in a variable named `battingAverage`. The program will display this number in a message that explains what it is.

Now that we have identified the input, processing, and output requirements, we can create the pseudocode and/or flowcharts. First, we will write the pseudocode variable declarations:

```
Declare Integer hits
Declare Integer atBat
Declare Real battingAverage
```

Next we will write the pseudocode for gathering input. Recall that a program typically does two things when it needs the user to enter a piece of input on the keyboard: (1) it displays a message prompting the user for the piece of data, and (2) it reads the user's input and stores that data in a variable. Here is the pseudocode for reading the two pieces of input required by the batting average program:

```
Display "Enter the player's number of hits."
Input hits

Display "Enter the player's number of times at bat."
Input atBat
```

Next we will write the pseudocode for calculating the batting average:

```
Set battingAverage = hits / atBat
```

And finally, we write the pseudocode for displaying the output:

```
Display "The player's batting average is ", battingAverage
```

Now we can put all of these pieces together to form a complete program. Program 6-6 shows a pseudocode program with comments, and Figure 6-6 shows the flowchart.

Program 6-6:

```
// Declare the necessary variables.
Declare Integer hits
Declare Integer atBat
Declare Real battingAverage

// Get the number of hits.
Display "Enter the player's number of hits."
Input hits

// Get the number of times at bat.
Display "Enter the player's number of times at bat."
Input atBat

// Calculate the batting average.
Set battingAverage = hits / atBat

// Display the batting average.
Display "The player's batting average is ", battingAverage
```

Program Output (with Input Shown in Bold)

```
Enter the player's number of hits.
150 [Enter]
Enter the player's number of times at bat.
500 [Enter]
The player's batting average is 0.3
```

Figure 6-6 Flowchart for Program 6-6

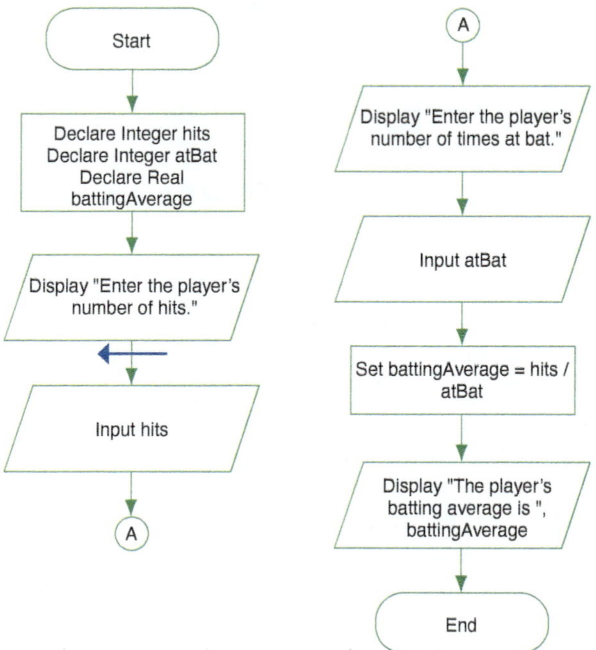

Summary

Whenever you have trouble getting started with a program design, determine the program's requirements as follows:

1. **Input:** Carefully study the problem and identify the pieces of data that the program needs to read as input. Once you know what data is needed as input, decide the names of the variables for those pieces of data, and their data types.

2. **Process:** What must the program do with the input that it will read? Determine the calculations and/or other processes that must be performed. At this time, decide the names and data types of any variables needed to hold the results of calculations.

3. **Output:** What output must the program produce? In most cases, it will be the results of the program's calculations and/or other processes.

Once you have determined these requirements, you will have an understanding of what the program must do. You will also have a list of variables and their data types. The next step is writing the algorithm in pseudocode, or drawing it as a flowchart.

Chapter Review

Multiple Choice

1. In the expression 12 + 7, the values on the right and left of the + symbol are called ________.
   a. operands
   b. operators
   c. arguments
   d. math expressions

2. A(n) __________ operator raises a number to a power.
   a. modulus
   b. multiplication
   c. exponent
   d. operand

3. A(n) __________ operator performs division, but instead of returning the quotient it returns the remainder.
   a. modulus
   b. multiplication
   c. exponent
   d. operand

4. What is the symbol for the operator that divides one number by another and gives the quotient?
   a. *
   b. /
   c. #
   d. ^

5. What kind of statement do you use to save a value in memory for future use?
   a. operand
   b. expressive
   c. assignment
   d. variable

6. What is the first order of operation in most programming languages?
   a. multiplication operations
   b. operations enclosed in parentheses
   c. additions on the left
   d. operations that use an exponent

7. What is the term for the largest number that can divide two integers?
   a. greatest common integer
   b. biggest dividing number
   c. greatest common divisor
   d. ten

8. What is typically the first phase of a program's action?
    a. calculation
    b. output
    c. prompt
    d. input

9. In the statement Set answer = 5 + (4 * 2) what operation is performed first?
    a. multiplying 4 times 2
    b. adding 4 plus 5
    c. adding 4 plus 2
    d. multiplying 5 times 2

10. What symbol do some programming languages use as the modulus operator?
    a. >
    b. #
    c. %
    d. <

True or False

1. The common math operator for multiplication is x.
2. In a math expression, multiplication and division take place before addition and subtraction.
3. The exponent operator raises a number to a power.
4. Operands are the values on the left and right of an operator.
5. To force an operation to be performed before others, enclose it in curly brackets.
6. Programming languages require an operator for all mathematical operation.
7. There is only one right way to write an algorithm.

Short Answer

1. Give an example of how a programmer might use math operators.
2. Write a math expression that calculates the number of hours in a week.
3. Explain the exponent operator.
4. What is one change you might have to make to convert a math expression to a programming expression?
5. Explain why it is important to think before you write an algorithm.

Algorithm Workbench

1. With a partner or a small group, create an algorithm for finding the average of a series of numbers. Write the steps on paper and then test them. Share your solution with another team or with the class, and make changes to your solution based on feedback.
2. Another common algorithm is called "Making Change." It solves the problem: What is the minimum number of coins I need to make a specific total? With a partner or small group, create an algorithm for making change. Write the steps on paper and then test them. For example, your friend owes you $9.35 and gives you a $10 bill. What is the minimum number of coins you need to pay them back? Share your solution with another team or with the class, and make changes to your solution based on the feedback you receive.
3. Write a pseudocode statement that assigns the sum of 10 and 14 to the variable `total`.
4. Write a pseudocode statement that subtracts the variable `downPayment` from the variable `total` and assigns the result to the variable `due`.
5. Write a pseudocode statement that multiplies the variable `subtotal` by 0.15 and assigns the result to the variable `totalFee`.
6. If the following pseudocode were an actual program, what would it display?

```
Declare Integer a = 5
Declare Integer b = 2
Declare Integer c = 3
Declare Integer result
Set result = a + b * c
Display result
```

Debugging Exercises

1. Find the error in the following pseudocode.

```
Declare Integer value1, value2, value3, sum
Set sum = value1 + value2 + value3

Display "Enter the first value."
Input value1

Display "Enter the second value."
Input value2

Display "Enter the third value."
Input value3

Display "The sum of numbers is ", sum
```

2. Find the error in the following pseudocode.

```
Declare Real pi
Set 3.14159265 = pi
Display "The value of pi is ", pi
```

3. Find the error in the following pseudocode.

```
Constant Real GRAVITY = 9.81
Display "Rates of acceleration of an object in free fall:"
Display "Earth: ", GRAVITY, " meters per second every second."
Set GRAVITY = 1.63
Display "Moon: ", GRAVITY, " meters per second every second."
```

Programming Exercises

1. Sales Tax

Design a program that will ask the user to enter the amount of a purchase. The program should then compute the state and county sales tax. Assume the state sales tax is 4 percent and the county sales tax is 2 percent. The program should display the amount of the purchase, the state sales tax, the county sales tax, the total sales tax, and the total of the sale (which is the sum of the amount of purchase plus the total sales tax).

Hint: Use the value 0.02 to represent 2 percent, and 0.04 to represent 4 percent.

VideoNote The Tip, Tax, and Total Problem

2. Tip, Tax, and Total

Design a program that calculates the total amount of a meal purchased at a restaurant. The program should ask the user to enter the charge for the food, and then calculate the amount of a 15 percent tip and 7 percent sales tax. Display each of these amounts and the total.

3. Celsius to Fahrenheit Temperature Converter

Design a program that converts Celsius temperatures to Fahrenheit temperatures. The formula is as follows:

$$F = \frac{9}{5} C + 32$$

The program should ask the user to enter a temperature in Celsius, and then display the temperature converted to Fahrenheit.

4. Major and Nonmajor Percentages

The computer science department at a college offers a programming course that is required for all computer science majors. The course is also popular with students who are not computer science majors. Design a program that asks the user to enter the number of computer science majors that are registered in the class, and the number of nonmajor students that are registered in the class. The program should display the percentages of computer science majors and nonmajor students that are registered in the class.

Hint: Suppose there are 12 computer science majors and 8 nonmajor students in the class. There are 20 students in the class. The percentage of computer science majors can be calculated as $12 \div 20 = 0.6$, or 60%. The percentage of nonmajors can be calculated as $8 \div 20 = 0.4$, or 40%.

5. Ingredient Adjuster

A cookie recipe calls for the following ingredients:

- 1.5 cups of sugar
- 1 cup of butter
- 2.75 cups of flour

The recipe produces 48 cookies with these amounts of the ingredients. Design a program that asks the user how many cookies they want to make, and then displays the number of cups of each ingredient needed for the specified number of cookies.

Introduction to Boolean Logic and Decision Structures

TOPICS

7.1 Using Boolean Logic and If Statements

A decision, or selection structure, allows a program to perform actions only under certain conditions.

VideoNote
The Single Alternative Decision Structure

A control structure is a logical design that controls the order in which a set of statements executes. So far in this book we have used only the simplest type of control structure: the **sequence structure**. Recall that programs follow the same linear sequence of actions every time they run. For example, if a program is solving the equation 2(x + 1), it always adds 1 then multiplies by 2. If it performs the operations in a different order—say, multiplies by 2 and then adds 1—the answer would not be correct. This is a sequence structure: a set of statements that execute in the order that they appear. For example, the following pseudocode is a sequence structure because the statements execute from top to bottom.

```
Declare Integer age
Display "What is your age?"
Input age
Display "Here is the value that you entered:"
Display age
```

Although the sequence structure is heavily used in programming, it cannot handle every type of task. Some problems simply cannot be solved by performing a set of ordered steps, one after the other. Or, in the case of a game, story, or animation, a program with a sequence structure is not as compelling or fun as one that offers a choice.

Recall the simple story about a character opening a door and finding a box in which there is a prize. What if there are two doors? A program could determine that if the character opens the door on the right, they find the box and the prize. But, if the character opens the door on the left, they find another door.

Another example is a pay calculating program that determines whether an employee has worked overtime. If the employee has worked more than 40 hours, they are paid extra for all the hours over 40. Otherwise, the overtime calculation should be skipped.

Programs like this require a different type of control structure: one that can execute a set of statements only under certain circumstances. This can be accomplished with a **decision structure**. Decision structures are also known as **selection structures**.

In a decision structure's simplest form, a specific action is performed only if a certain condition exists, or is True. If the condition does not exist, or is False, the action is not performed. The decisions are determined with **IF statements**. An IF statement defines conditions that must be met for the program to move to the next step. For example, *IF* you have finished adding the ingredients to the cake batter, *then* you can put the cake in the oven. Sometimes an action is repeated in a *loop*, or iteration, until a desired result occurs. (Loops are covered in Chapter 8.)

The flowchart shown in Figure 7-1 shows how the logic of an everyday decision can be diagrammed as a decision structure. The diamond symbol represents a true/false condition. If the condition is true, we follow one path, which leads to an action being performed. If the condition is false, we follow another path, which skips the action.

Figure 7-1 A simple decision structure for an everyday task

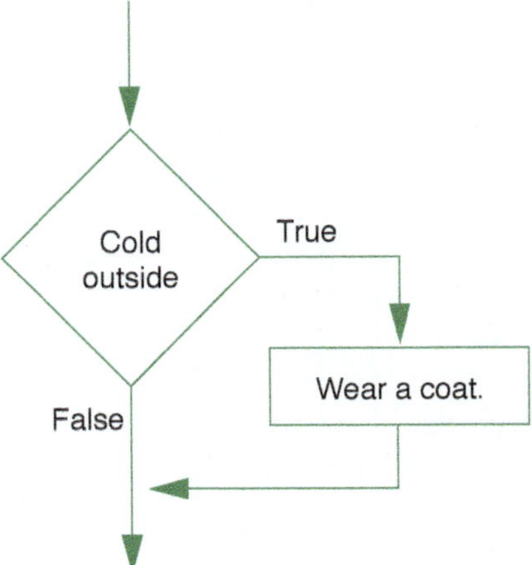

In the flowchart, the diamond symbol indicates the condition that must be tested. In this case, we are determining whether the condition *Cold outside* is true or false. If this condition is true, the action *Wear a coat* is performed. If the condition is false, the action is skipped. The action is **conditionally executed** because it is performed only when a certain condition is true.

Programmers call the type of decision structure shown in Figure 7-1 a **single alternative decision structure**. This is because it provides only one alternative path of execution. If the condition in the diamond symbol is true, we take the alternative path. Otherwise, we exit the structure.

Combining Structures

You cannot use decision structures alone to create a complete program. You use a decision structure to handle any part of a program that needs to test a condition and conditionally execute an action depending on the outcome of the condition. For other parts of a program you need to use other structures. For example, Figure 7-2 shows a complete flowchart that combines a decision structure with two sequence structures. (Figure 7-2 is not a flowchart of a computer algorithm, but of a human action.)

The flowchart in the figure starts with a sequence structure. Assuming you have an outdoor thermometer in your window, the first step is *Go to the window*, and the next step is *Read thermometer*. A decision structure appears next, testing the condition *Cold outside*. If this is true, the action Wear a coat is performed. Another sequence structure appears next. The step *Open the door* is performed, followed by *Go outside*.

Quite often, structures must be **nested** inside of other structures. For example, look at the partial flowchart in Figure 7-3. It shows a decision structure with a sequence structure nested inside it. (Once again, this is a flowchart showing human actions, not program statements.) The decision structure tests the condition *Cold outside*. If that condition is true, the steps in the sequence structure are executed.

Figure 7-2 Combining sequence structures with a decision structure

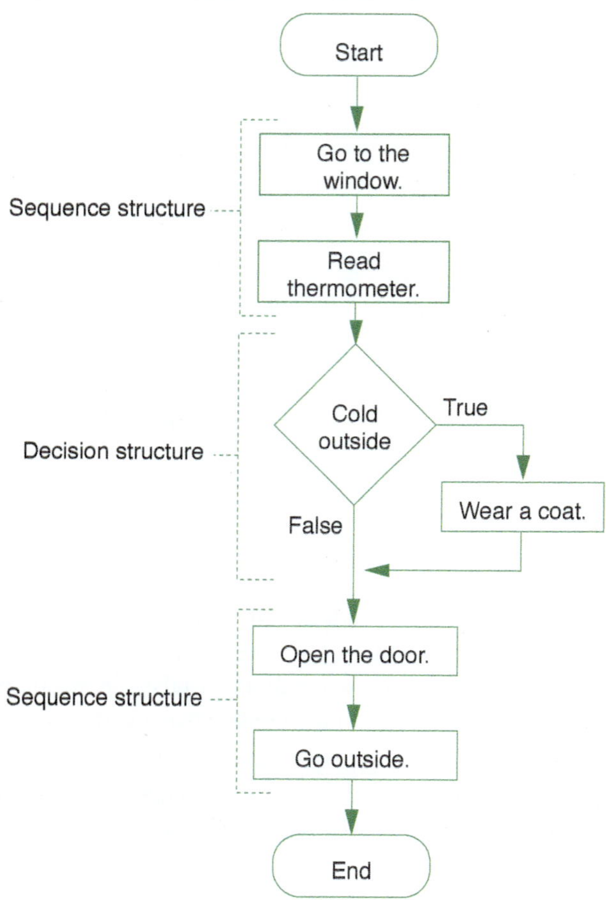

Figure 7-3 A sequence structure nested inside a decision structure

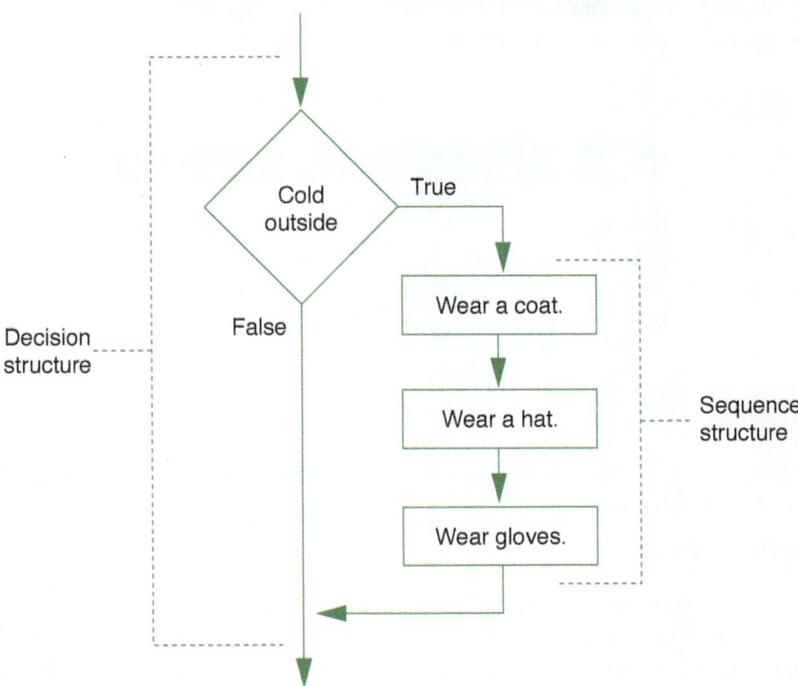

Writing a Decision Structure in Pseudocode

In pseudocode we use the `If-Then` statement to write a single alternative decision structure. Here is the general format of the `If-Then` statement:

```
If condition Then
statement
statement
etc.
End If
```

These statements are conditionally executed.

In this text, the line that begins with the word `If` is called the *If clause*, and to the line that reads `End If` is the *End If clause*. In the general format, the condition is any expression that can be evaluated as either true or false. When the `If-Then` statement executes, the *condition* is tested. If it is true, the statements that appear between the `If` clause and the `End If` clause are executed. The `End If` clause marks the end of the `If-Then` statement.

Boolean Expressions and Relational Operators

All programming languages allow you to create expressions that can be evaluated as either true or false. These are called **Boolean expressions**, named in honor of the English mathematician George Boole. In the 1800s Boole invented a system of mathematics in which the abstract concepts of true and false can be used in computations. The condition that is tested by an If-Then statement must be a Boolean expression.

Typically, the Boolean expression that is tested by an If-Then statement is formed with a relational operator. A **relational operator** determines whether a specific relationship exists between two values. For example, the greater than operator (>) determines whether one value is greater than another. The equal to operator (==) determines whether two values are equal. Table 7-1 lists the relational operators that are commonly available in most programming languages.

Table 7-1 Relational operators

Operator	Meaning
>	Greater than
<	Less than
>=	Greater than or equal to
<=	Less than or equal to
==	Equal to
!=	Not equal to

The following is an example of an expression that uses the greater than (>) operator to compare two variables, `length` and `width`:

```
length > width
```

This expression determines whether the value of `length` is greater than the value of width. If `length` is greater than width, the value of the expression is true. Otherwise, the value of the expression is false. Because the expression can be only true or false, it is a Boolean expression. The following expression uses the less than operator to determine whether length is less than width:

```
length < width
```

Table 7-2 shows examples of several Boolean expressions that compare the variables x and y.

Table 7-2 Boolean expressions using relational operators

Expression	Meaning
x > y	Is x greater than y?
x < y	Is x less than y?
x >= y	Is x greater than or equal to y?
x <= y	Is x less than or equal to y?
x == y	Is x equal to y?
x != y	Is x not equal to y?

The >= and <= Operators

Two of the relational operators, >= and <=, test for more than one relationship. The >= operator determines whether the operand on its left is greater than or equal to the operand on its right. For example, assuming that a is 4, b is 6, and c is 4, both of the expressions `b >= a` and `a >= c` are true, and the expression `a >= 5` is false.

The <= operator determines whether the operand on its left is less than or equal to the operand on its right. Once again, assuming that a is 4, b is 6, and c is 4, both `a <= c` and `b <= 10` are true, but `b <= a` is false.

The == Operator

The == relational operator determines whether the operand on its left is equal to the operand on its right. If both operands have the same value, the expression is true. Assuming that a is 4, the expression `a == 4` is true and the expression `a == 2` is false.

In this text, we use two = characters as the equal to operator to avoid confusion with the assignment operator, which is one = character. Several programming languages, most notably Java, Python, C, and C++, also follow this practice.

WARNING! When programming in a language that uses = = as the equal to operator, take care not to confuse this operator with the assignment operator, which is one = sign. In languages such as Java, Python, C, and C++ the = = operator determines whether a variable is equal to another value, but the = operator assigns the value to a variable.

The != Operator

The != relational operator is the not equal to operator. It determines whether the operand on its left is not equal to the operand on its right, which is the opposite of the == operator. As before, assuming a is 4, b is 6, and c is 4, both `a != b` and `b != c` are true because a is not equal to b and b is not equal to c. However, `a != c` is false because a is equal to c.

Note that != is the same character sequence used by several languages for the not equal to operator, including Java, C, and C++. Some languages, such as Visual Basic, use <> as the not equal to operator.

Putting It All Together

Let's look at the following example of the `If-Then` statement in pseudocode:

```
If sales > 50000 Then
   Set bonus = 500.0
End If
```

This statement uses the > operator to determine whether `sales` is greater than 50,000. If the expression `sales > 50000` is true, the variable `bonus` is assigned 500.0. If the expression is false, however, the assignment statement is skipped. Figure 7-4 shows a flowchart for this section of code.

The following example conditionally executes a set of statements. Figure 7-5 shows a flowchart for this section of code.

```
If sales > 50000 Then
   Set bonus = 500.0
   Set commissionRate = 0.12
   Display "You've met your sales quota!"
End If
```

Figure 7-4 Example decision structure

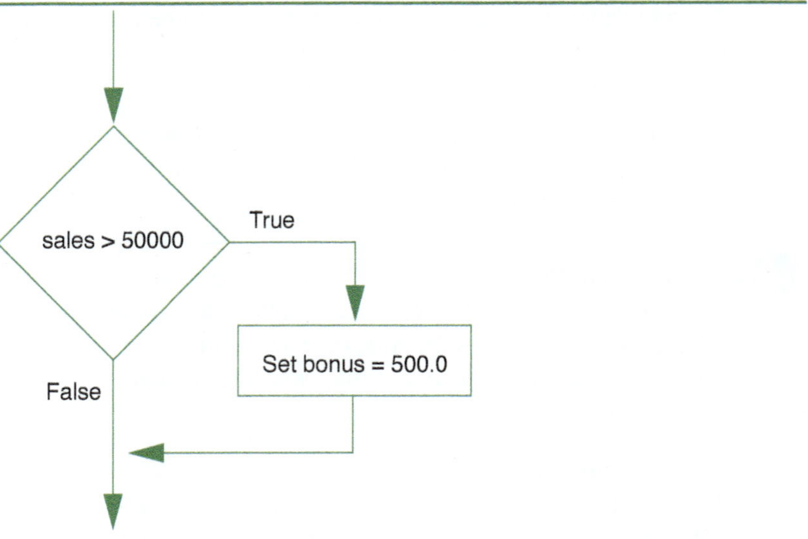

Figure 7-5 Example decision structure

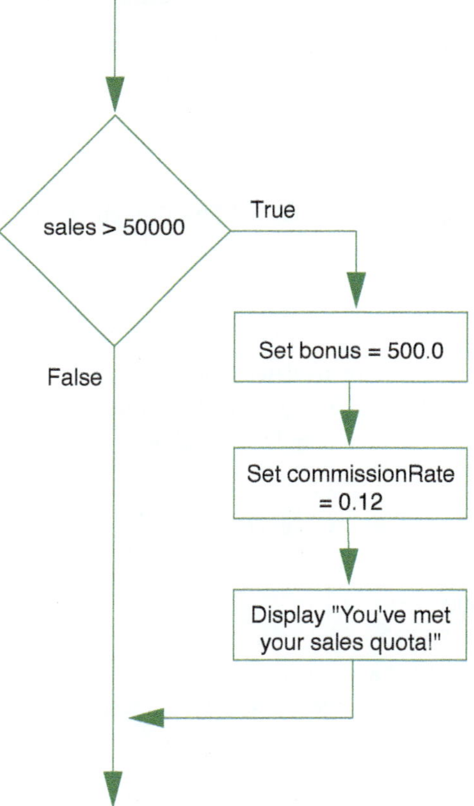

The following pseudocode uses the `==` operator to determine whether two values are equal. The expression `balance == 0` will be true if the `balance` variable is set to `0`. Otherwise the expression will be false.

```
If balance == 0 Then
   // Statements appearing here will
   // be executed only if balance is
   // equal to 0.
End If
```

The following pseudocode uses the `!=` operator to determine whether two values are *not* equal. The expression `choice != 5` will be true if the `choice` variable is not set to 5. Otherwise the expression will be false.

```
If choice != 5 Then
   // Statements appearing here will
   // be executed only if choice is
   // not equal to 5.
End If
```

Programming Style and the `If-Then` Statement

As shown in Figure 7-6, you should use the following programming style conventions when you write an `If-Then` statement:

- Make sure the `If` clause and the `End If` clause are aligned.
- Indent the conditionally executed statements that appear between the `If` clause and the `End If` clause.

By indenting the conditionally executed statements you visually set them apart from the surrounding code. This makes your program easier to read and debug. Most programmers use this style of writing `If-Then` statements in both pseudocode and actual code.

Figure 7-6 Programming style with an `If-Then` statement

Align the `If` and `End If` clauses.

```
If sales > 50000 Then
   Set bonus = 500.0
   Set commissionRate = 0.12
   Display "You've met your sales quota!"
End If
```

Indent the conditionally executed statements.

In the Spotlight:

Using the If-Then Statement

Martina teaches a science class and her students are required to take three tests. She wants to write a program that her students can use to calculate their average test score. She also wants the program to congratulate the student enthusiastically if the average is greater than 95.

On Your Own: Working alone or with a partner, write the algorithm steps, draw a flowchart, and write the pseudocode. Then, read on to see how you did. Remember, your solution does not have to be exactly the same as the one in the text in order to come up with the same result.

Here is an algorithm:

1. Get the first test score.
2. Get the second test score.
3. Get the third test score.
4. Calculate the average.
5. Display the average.
6. If the average is greater than 95, congratulate the user.

Program 7-1 shows the pseudocode, and Figure 7-7 shows a flowchart for the program.

Program 7-1:

```
// Declare variables
Declare Real test1, test2, test3, average

// Get test 1
Display "Enter the score for test #1."
Input test1

// Get test 2
Display "Enter the score for test #2."
Input test2

// Get test 3
Display "Enter the score for test #3."
Input test3

// Calculate the average score.
Set average = (test1 + test2 + test3) / 3

// Display the average.
Display "The average is ", average

// If the average is greater than 95
// congratulate the user.
If average > 95 Then
   Display "Congratulations! Great average!"
End If
```

Program Output (with Input Shown in Bold)

```
Enter the score for test #1.
82 [Enter]
Enter the score for test #2.
76 [Enter]
Enter the score for test #3.
91 [Enter]
The average is 83
```

Program 7-1: *(continued)*

Program Output (with Input Shown in Bold)

```
Enter the score for test #1.
93 [Enter]
Enter the score for test #2.
99 [Enter]
Enter the score for test #3.
96 [Enter]
The average is 96
Congratulations! Great average!.
```

Figure 7-7 Flowchart for Program 7-1

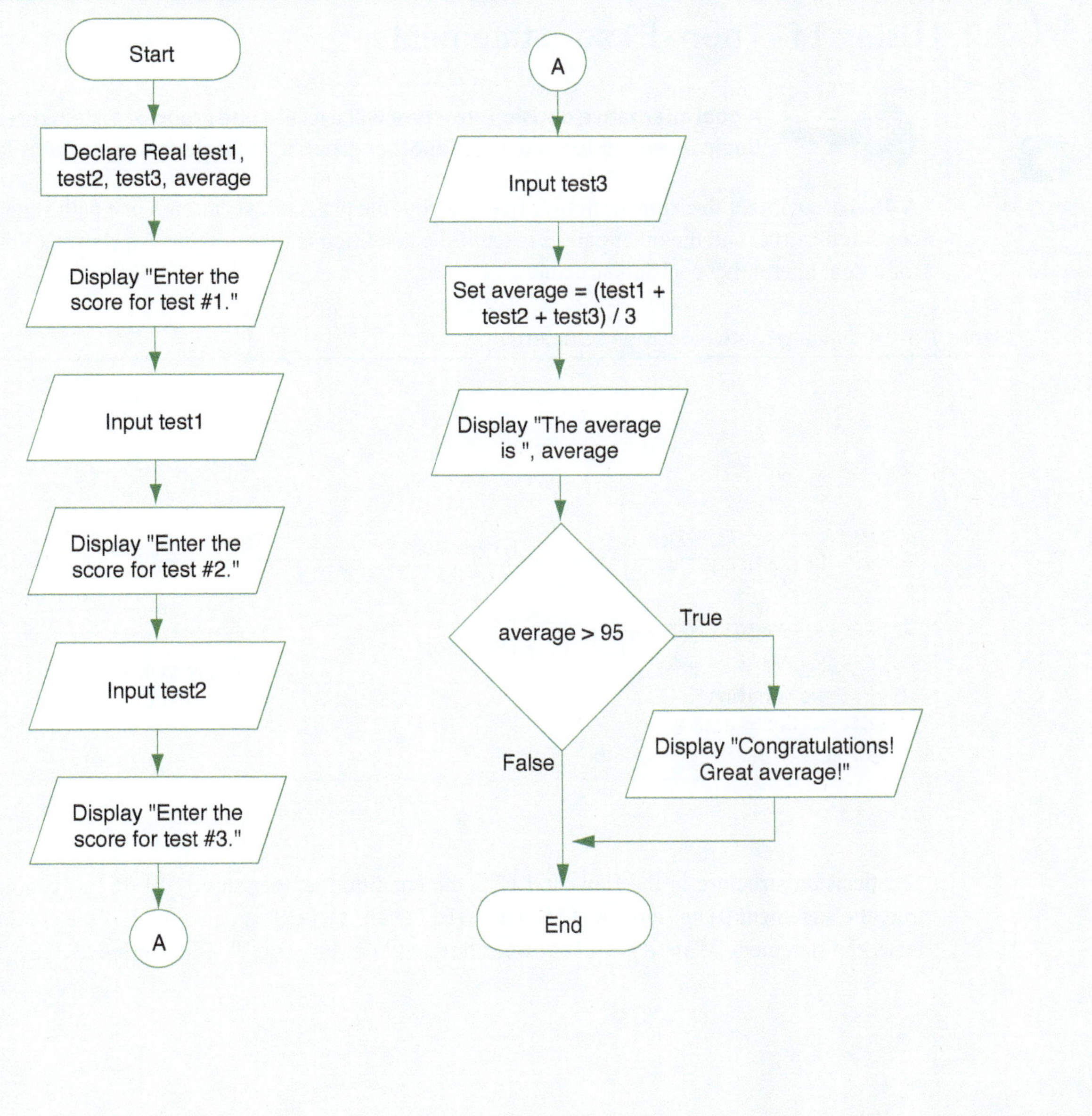

Checkpoint

7.1 What is a control structure?

7.2 What is a decision structure?

7.3 What is a single alternative decision structure?

7.4 What is a Boolean expression?

7.5 What types of relationships between values can you test with relational operators?

7.6 Write a pseudocode If-Then statement that assigns 0 to x if y is equal to 20.

7.7 Write a pseudocode If-Then statement that assigns 0.2 to commission if sales is greater than or equal to 10,000.

7.2 Using `If-Then-Else` Statements

A dual alternative decision structure will execute one group of statements if its Boolean expression is true, or another group if its Boolean expression is false.

VideoNote The Dual Alternative Decision Structure

A **dual alternative decision structure** has two possible paths of execution—one path is taken if a condition is true, and the other path is taken if the condition is false. Figure 7-8 shows a flowchart for a dual alternative decision structure.

Figure 7-8 A dual alternative decision structure

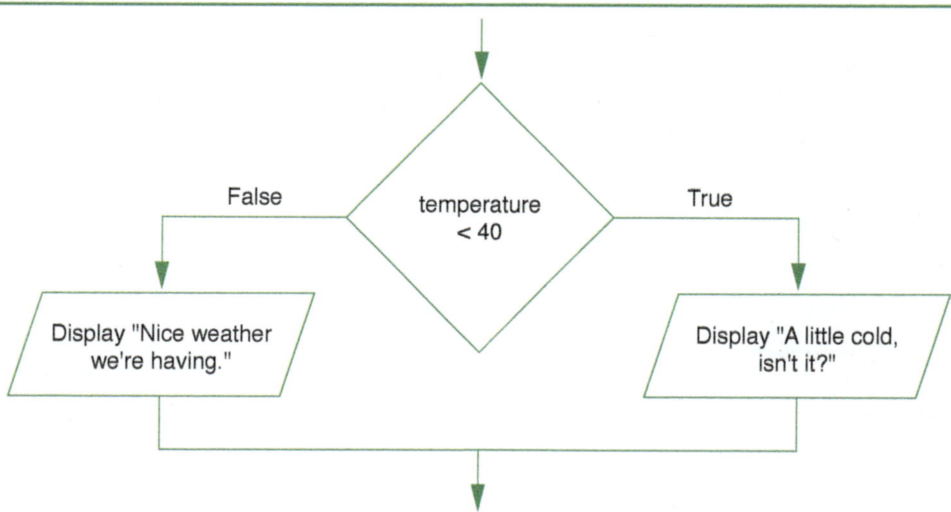

The decision structure in the flowchart tests the condition temperature < 40. If this condition is true, the statement `Display "A little cold, isn't it?"` is performed. If the condition is false, the statement `Display "Nice weather we're having."` is performed.

In pseudocode, we write a dual alternative decision structure as an `If-Then-Else` statement. Here is the general format of the `If-Then-Else` statement:

```
If condition Then
    statement
    statement        } These statements are executed if the condition is true.
    etc.
Else
    statement
    statement        } These statements are executed if the condition is true.
    etc.
End If
```

In the general format, the condition is any Boolean expression. If the expression is true, the statements that appear next are executed, up to the line that reads Else. If the expression is false, the statements that appear between `Else` and `End If` are executed. The line that reads `End If` marks the end of the `If-Then-Else` statement.

The following pseudocode shows an example of an `If-Then-Else` statement. This pseudocode matches the flowchart that was shown in Figure 7-8.

```
If temperature < 40 Then
   Display "A little cold, isn't it?"
Else
   Display "Nice weather we're having."
End If
```

We will refer to the line that reads `Else` as the **Else clause.** When you write an `If-Then-Else` statement, use the following programming style conventions:

- Make sure the `If` clause, the `Else` clause, and the `End If` clause are aligned.
- Indent the conditionally executed statements that appear between the `If` clause and the `Else` clause, and between the `Else` clause and the `End If` clause.

This is shown in Figure 7-9.

Figure 7-9 Programming style with an `If-Then` statement

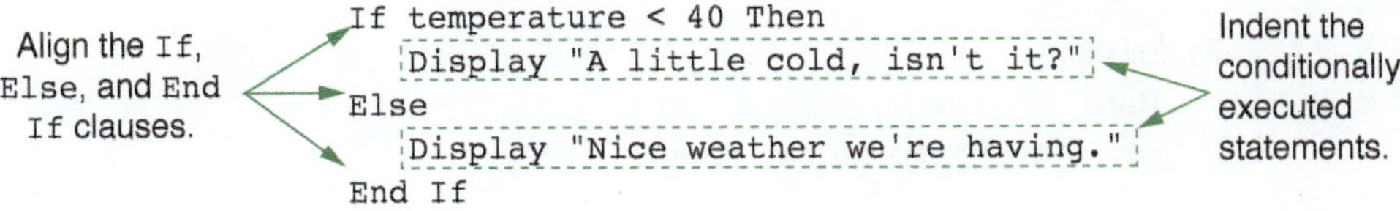

In the Spotlight:

Using the If-Then Statement

Kris owns an auto repair business and has several employees. If an employee works more than 40 hours in a week, Kris pays that employee 1.5 times their regular hourly pay rate for all hours over 40. For example, suppose an employee's regular hourly pay rate is \$20, and that employee works 45 hours in a week. Kris will pay the employee \$20 per hour for the first 40 hours, plus \$30 per hour for the 5 hours of overtime work. Here is a summary of the calculation:

Regular pay for the first 40 hours:	40 × \$20 = \$800
Overtime pay for 5 hours:	5 × \$30 = \$150
Total Pay:	\$800 + \$150 = \$950

Kris has asked you to design a simple payroll program that calculates an employee's gross pay, including any overtime wages.

On Your Own: Working alone or with a partner, write the algorithm steps, draw a flowchart, and write the pseudocode. Then, read on to see how you did. Remember, your solution does not have to be exactly the same as the one in the text in order to come up with the same result.

You could design the following algorithm:

1. Get the number of hours worked.
2. Get the hourly pay rate.
3. If the employee worked more than 40 hours, calculate the gross pay with overtime. Otherwise, calculate the gross pay as usual.
4. Display the gross pay.

The pseudocode for the program is shown in Program 7-2, and Figure 7-10 shows a flowchart for the program.

Program 7-2:

```
// Constants
Constant Integer BASE_HOURS = 40
Constant Real OT_MULTIPLIER = 1.5

// Variables
Declare Real hoursWorked, payRate, grossPay,
             overtimeHours, overtimePay

// Get the number of hours worked.
Display "Enter the number of hours worked."
Input hoursWorked

// Get the hourly pay rate.
Display "Enter the hourly pay rate."
Input payRate
```

Program 7-2: *(continued)*

```
16
17 // Calculate the gross pay.
18 If hoursWorked > BASE_HOURS Then
19      // Calculate the number of overtime hours.
20      Set overtimeHours = hoursWorked - BASE_HOURS
21
22      // Calculate the overtime pay.
23      Set overtimePay = overtimeHours * payRate * OT_MULTIPLIER
24
25      // Calculate the gross pay.
26      Set grossPay = BASE_HOURS * payRate + overtimePay
27 Else
28      Set grossPay = hoursWorked * payRate
29 End If
30
31 // Display the gross pay.
32 Display "The gross pay is $", grossPay
```

Program Output (with Input Shown in Bold)

```
Enter the number of hours worked.
40 [Enter]
Enter the hourly pay rate.
20 [Enter]
The gross pay is $800
```

Program Output (with Input Shown in Bold)

```
Enter the number of hours worked.
50 [Enter]
Enter the hourly pay rate.
20 [Enter]
The gross pay is $1100
```

Let's take a closer look at the pseudocode. Two named constants are declared in lines 2 and 3. The `BASE_HOURS` constant is set to 40, which is the number of hours an employee can work in a week without getting paid overtime. The `OT_MULTIPLIER` constant is set to 1.5, which is the pay rate multiplier for overtime hours. This means that the employee's hourly pay rate is multiplied by 1.5 for all overtime hours.

The variables that are declared in lines 6 and 7 are used for the following purposes:

- The `hoursWorked` variable will hold the number of hours worked by the employee. This value will be entered as input.
- The `payRate` variable will hold the employee's hourly payrate. This value will also be entered as input.
- The `grossPay` variable will hold the employee's gross pay. This value will be calculated.
- The `overtimeHours` variable will hold the number of hours over 40 worked by the employee. This value will be calculated.
- The `overtimePay` variable will hold the amount of pay the employee earned for overtime hours. This value will be calculated.

Line 10 prompts the user to enter the number of hours the employee worked, and line 11 reads that value, assigning it to the `hoursWorked` variable.

Line 14 prompts the user to enter the employee's hourly payrate, and line 15 reads that value, assigning it to the `payRate` variable.

The If statement in line 18 determines whether `hoursWorked` is greater than 40. If this is true, it means the employee has worked overtime hours and the program executes the statements in lines 19–26. Those statements perform the following actions:

- Line 20 calculates the number of overtime hours worked, which is the number of hours over 40. The result is assigned to the `overtimeHours` variable.
- Line 23 calculates the amount of pay for the overtime hours. The result is assigned to the overtimePay variable.
- Line 26 calculates the employee's gross pay. This is the amount of pay for 40 hours worked at the regular payrate, plus the overtime pay. The result is assigned to the `grossPay` variable.

When the `If` statement in line 18 executes, if `hoursWorked` is not greater than 40, it means the employee has not worked more than 40 hours. In this case, the program will branch to the `Else` clause in line 27. This causes the statement line 28 to execute. This statement calculates the gross pay by multiplying the number of hours worked by the hourly payrate. The result is assigned to the `grossPay` variable.

Last, the statement in line 32 displays the employee's gross pay.

Figure 7-10 Flowchart for Program 7-2

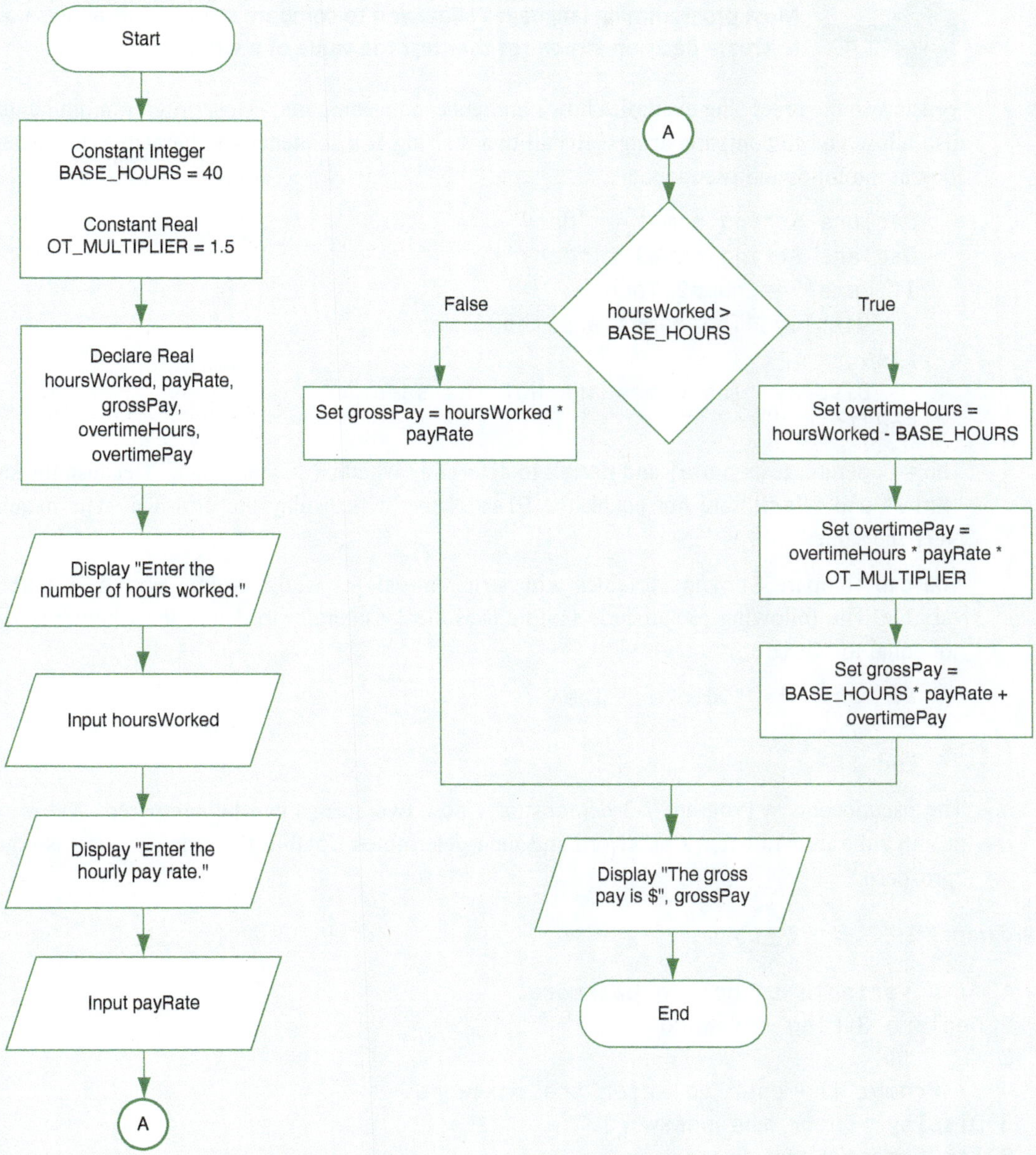

Start

Constant Integer BASE_HOURS = 40

Constant Real OT_MULTIPLIER = 1.5

Declare Real hoursWorked, payRate, grossPay, overtimeHours, overtimePay

Display "Enter the number of hours worked."

Input hoursWorked

Display "Enter the hourly pay rate."

Input payRate

A

A

hoursWorked > BASE_HOURS

False

Set grossPay = hoursWorked * payRate

True

Set overtimeHours = hoursWorked - BASE_HOURS

Set overtimePay = overtimeHours * payRate * OT_MULTIPLIER

Set grossPay = BASE_HOURS * payRate + overtimePay

Display "The gross pay is $", grossPay

End

Checkpoint

7.8 How does a dual alternative decision structure work?

7.9 What statement do you use in pseudocode to write a dual alternative decision structure?

7.10 Explain how you might use a conditional statement to program a story, game, or animation.

7.3 Comparing Strings

Most programming languages allow you to compare strings. This allows you to create decision structures that test the value of a string.

You saw in the preceding examples how numbers can be compared. Most programming languages also allow you to compare strings. Recall that a string is a sequence of characters. For example, look at the following pseudocode:

```
Declare String name1 = "Mary"
Declare String name2 = "Mark"
If name1 == name2 Then
   Display "The names are the same."
Else
   Display "The names are NOT the same."
End If
```

The == operator tests `name1` and `name2` to determine whether they are equal. Because the strings `"Mary"` and `"Mark"` are not equal, the `Else` clause will display the message "The names are NOT the same."

You can compare `String` variables with string literals as well. Assume `month` is a `String` variable. The following pseudocode sample uses the `!=` operator to determine whether `month` is not equal to `"October"`.

```
If month != "October" Then
   statement
End If
```

The pseudocode in Program 7-3 demonstrates how two strings can be compared. The program prompts the user to enter a password and then determines whether the string entered is equal to "prospero."

Program 7-3:

```
// A variable to hold a password.
Declare String password

// Prompt the user to enter the password.
Display "Enter the password."
Input password

// Determine whether the correct password
// was entered.
If password == "prospero" Then
   Display "Password accepted."
Else
   Display "Sorry, that is not the correct password."
End If
```

Program 7-3: *(continued)*

Program Output (with Input Shown in Bold) *(continued)*

```
Enter the password.
ferdinand [Enter]
Sorry, that is not the correct password.
```

Program Output (with Input Shown in Bold)

```
Enter the password.
prospero [Enter]
Password accepted.
```

NOTE: In most languages, string comparisons are case sensitive. For example, the strings `"saturday"` **and** `"Saturday"` **are not equal because the "s" is lowercase in the first string, but uppercase in the second string.**

Other String Comparisons

In addition to determining whether strings are equal or not equal, many languages allow you to determine whether one string is greater than or less than another string. This is a useful capability because programmers commonly need to design programs that sort strings in some order.

Recall that computers do not actually store characters, such as A, B, C, and so on, in memory. Instead, they store numeric codes that represent the characters. ASCII (the American Standard Code for Information Interchange) is the most commonly used character coding system. You can see the set of ASCII codes in Appendix A, but here are some facts about it:

- The uppercase characters "A" through "Z" are represented by the numbers 65 through 90.
- The lowercase characters "a" through "z" are represented by the numbers 97 through 122.
- When the digits "0" through "9" are stored in memory as characters, they are represented by the numbers 48 through 57. (For example, the string `"abc123"` would be stored in memory as the codes 97, 98, 99, 49, 50, and 51.)
- A blank space is represented by the number 32.

In addition to establishing a set of numeric codes to represent characters in memory, ASCII also establishes an order for characters. The character "A" comes before the character "B," which comes before the character "C," and so on.

When a program compares characters, it actually compares the codes for the characters. For example, look at the following pseudocode:

```
If "a" < "b" Then
   Display "The letter a is less than the letter b."
End If
```

This `If` statement determines whether the ASCII code for the character "a" is less than the ASCII code for the character "b." The expression `"a" < "b"` is true because the code for "a" is less than the code for "b." So, if this were part of an actual program it would display the message "The letter a is less than the letter b."

Let's look at how strings containing more than one character are typically compared. Suppose we have the strings "Mary" and "Mark" stored in memory, as follows:

```
Declare String name1 = "Mary"
Declare String name2 = "Mark"
```

Figure 7-11 shows how the strings "Mary" and "Mark" would actually be stored in memory, using ASCII codes.

Figure 7-11 Character codes for the strings "Mary" and "Mark"

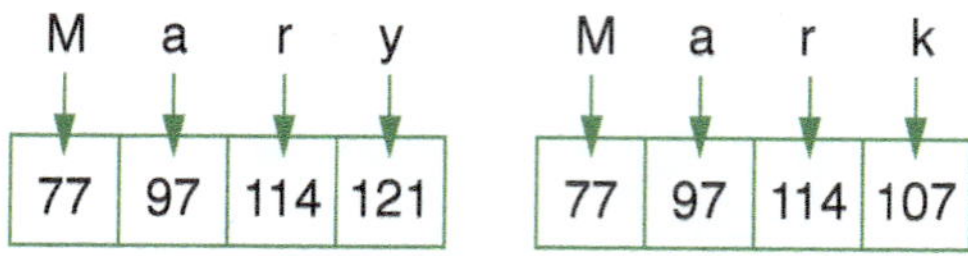

When you use relational operators to compare these strings, they are compared character-by-character. For example, look at the following pseudocode:

```
Declare String name1 = "Mary"
Declare String name2 = "Mark"
If name1 > name2 Then
   Display "Mary is greater than Mark."
Else
   Display "Mary is not greater than Mark."
End If
```

The > operator compares each character in the strings "Mary" and "Mark," beginning with the first, or leftmost, characters. This is shown in Figure 7-12.

Figure 7-12 Comparing each character in a string

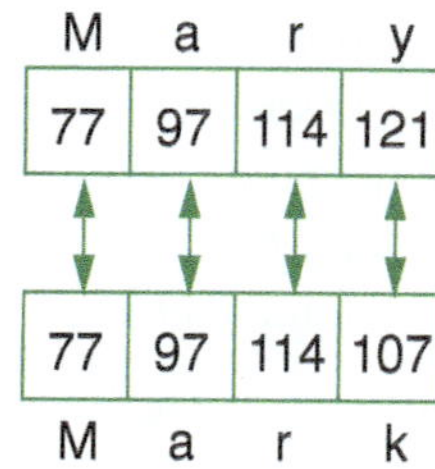

Here is how the comparison typically takes place:

1. The "M" in "Mary" is compared with the "M" in "Mark." Because these are the same, the next characters are compared.
2. The "a" in "Mary" is compared with the "a" in "Mark." Because these are the same, the next characters are compared.
3. The "r" in "Mary" is compared with the "r" in "Mark." Because these are thensame, the next characters are compared.
4. The "y" in "Mary" is compared with the "k" in "Mark." Because these are not the same, the two strings are not equal. The character "y" has a higher ASCII code (121) than "k" (107), so it is determined that the string "Mary" is greater than the string "Mark."

If one of the strings in a comparison is shorter than the other, many languages compare only the corresponding characters. If the corresponding characters are identical, then the shorter string is considered less than the longer string. For example, suppose the strings "`High`" and "`Hi`" were being compared. The string "`Hi`" would be considered less than "`High`" because it is shorter.

The pseudocode in Program 7-4 shows a simple demonstration of how two strings can be compared with the < operator. The user is prompted to enter two names and the program displays those two names in alphabetical order.

Program 7-4:

```
// Declare variables to hold two names.
Declare String name1
Declare String name2

// Prompt the user for two names.
Display "Enter a name (last name first)."
Input name1
Display "Enter another name (last name first)."
Input name2

// Display the names in alphabetical order.
Display "Here are the names, listed alphabetically:"
If name1 < name2 Then
   Display name1
   Display name2
Else
   Display name2
   Display name1
End If
```

Program Output (with Input Shown in Bold)

```
Enter a name (last name first).
Sharma, Kiran [Enter]
Enter another name (last name first).
Costa, Joan [Enter]
Here are the names, listed alphabetically:
Costa, Joan
Sharma, Kiran
```

7.11 If the following pseudocode were an actual program, what would it display?

```
If "z" < "a" Then
   Display "z is less than a."
Else
   Display "z is not less than a."
End If
```

7.12 If the following pseudocode were an actual program, what would it display?

```
Declare String s1 = "New York"
Declare String s2 = "Boston"
If s1 > s2 Then
   Display s2
   Display s1
Else
   Display s1
   Display s2
End If
```

7.4 Nested Decision Structures

To test more than one condition, a decision structure can be nested inside another decision structure.

In Section 7.1, we mentioned that programs are usually designed as combinations of different control structures. In that section you saw an example of a sequence structure nested inside a decision structure (see Figure 7-3). You can also nest decision structures inside of other decision structures. In fact, this is a common requirement in programs that need to test more than one condition. For example, to move up a level in a game, a player might have to meet two conditions: (1) the player must collect 100 tokens, and (2) the player must unlock a door in less than 2 minutes.

Here is another example. Consider a program that determines whether a bank customer qualifies for a loan. To qualify, two conditions must exist: (1) the customer must earn at least $30,000 per year, and (2) the customer must have been employed at their current job for at least two years. Figure 7-13 shows a flowchart for an algorithm that could be used in such a program. Assume that the `salary` variable contains the customer's annual salary, and the `yearsOnJob` variable contains the number of years that the customer has worked at their current job.

If we follow the flow of execution, we see that the condition `salary >= 30000` is tested. If this condition is false, there is no need to perform further tests; we know that the customer does not qualify for the loan. If the condition is true, however, we need to test the second condition. This is done with a nested decision structure that tests the condition `yearsOnJob >= 2`. If this condition is true, then the customer qualifies for the loan. If this condition is false, then the customer does not qualify. Program 7-5 shows the pseudocode for the complete program.

Figure 7-13 A nested decision structure

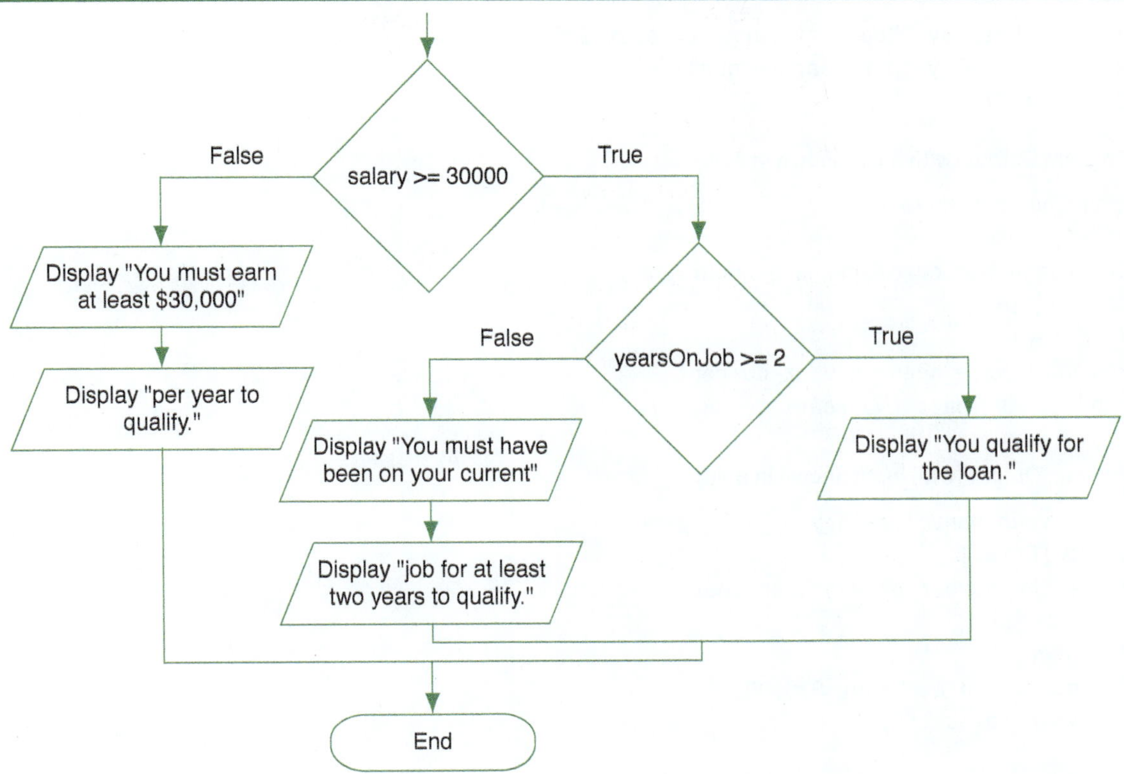

Program 7-5:

```
// Declare variables
Declare Real salary, yearsOnJob

// Get the annual salary.
Display "Enter your annual salary."
Input salary

// Get the number of years on the current job.
Display "Enter the number of years on your"
Display "current job."
Input yearsOnJob

// Determine whether the user qualifies.
If salary >= 30000 Then
  If yearsOnJob >= 2 Then
     Display "You qualify for the loan."
  Else
     Display "You must have been on your current"
     Display "job for at least two years to qualify."
  End If
  Else
```

Program 7-5: *(continued)*

```
22       Display "You must earn at least $30,000"
23       Display "per year to qualify."
24    End If
```

Program Output (with Input Shown in Bold)

```
Enter your annual salary.
35000 [Enter]
Enter the number of years on your
current job.
1 [Enter]
You must have been on your current
job for at least two years to qualify.
```

Program Output (with Input Shown in Bold)

```
Enter your annual salary.
25000 [Enter]
Enter the number of years on your
current job.
5 [Enter]
You must earn at least $30,000
per year to qualify.
```

Program Output (with Input Shown in Bold)

```
Enter your annual salary.
35000 [Enter]
Enter the number of years on your
current job.
5 [Enter]
You qualify for the loan.
```

Look at the `If-Then-Else` statement that begins in line 14. It tests the condition salary >= 30000. If this condition is true, the `If-Then-Else` statement that begins in line 15 is executed. Otherwise the program jumps to the `Else` clause in line 21 and executes the two `Display` statements in lines 22 and 23. The program then leaves the decision structure and the program ends.

Programming Style and Nested Decision Structures

For debugging purposes, it's important to use proper alignment and indentation in a nested decision structure. Using standard programming style conventions makes it easier to see which actions are performed by each part of the structure. For example, in most languages the following pseudocode is functionally equivalent to lines 14 through 24 in Program 7-5. Although this pseudocode is logically correct, it would be very difficult to debug because it is not properly indented.

```
If salary >= 30000 Then
If yearsOnJob >= 2 Then
Display "You qualify for the loan."
Else
Display "You must have been on your current"
Display "job for at least two years to qualify."
End If
Else
Display "You must earn at least $30,000"
Display "per year to qualify.
End If
```

Proper indentation and alignment conventions also make it easier to see which `If`, `Else`, and `End If` clauses belong together, as shown in Figure 7-14.

Figure 7-14 Alignment of `If`, `Else`, and `End If` clauses

```
If salary >= 30000 Then
    If yearsOnJob >= 2 then
        Display "You qualify for the loan."
    Else
        Display "You must have been on your current"
        Display "job for at least two years to qualify."
    End If
Else
    Display "You must earn at least $30,000"
    Display "per year to qualify.
End If
```

This If, Else, and End If go together.

This If, Else, and End If go together.

Testing a Series of Conditions

In the previous example you saw how a program can use nested decision structures to test more than one condition. It is not uncommon for a program to have a series of conditions to test, and then perform an action depending on which condition is true. One way to accomplish this is to have a decision structure with numerous other decision structures nested inside it. For example, consider the program presented in the following *In the Spotlight* section.

In the Spotlight:

Multiple Nested Decision Structures

Dr. Suarez teaches a literature class and uses the following 10 point grading scale for all of his exams:

Test Score	Grade
90 and above	A
80–89	B
70–79	C
60–69	D
Below 60	F

He has asked you to write a program that will allow a student to enter a test score and then display the grade for that score.

On Our Own: Working alone or with a partner, write the algorithm steps, draw a flowchart, and write the pseudocode. Then, read on to see how you did. Remember, your solution does not have to be exactly the same as the one in the text in order to come up with the same result.

Here is an algorithm that you could use:

1. Ask the user to enter a test score.
2. Determine the grade in the following manner:

If the score is less than 60, then the grade is "F."
  Otherwise, if the score is less than 70, then the grade is "D."
    Otherwise, if the score is less than 80, then the grade is "C."
      Otherwise, if the score is less than 90, then the grade is "B."
        Otherwise, the grade is "A."

You decide that the process of determining the grade will require several nested decision structures, as shown in Figure 7-15. Program 7-6 shows the pseudocode for the complete program. The code for the nested decision structures is in lines 9 through 25.

Figure 7-15 Nested decision structure to determine a grade

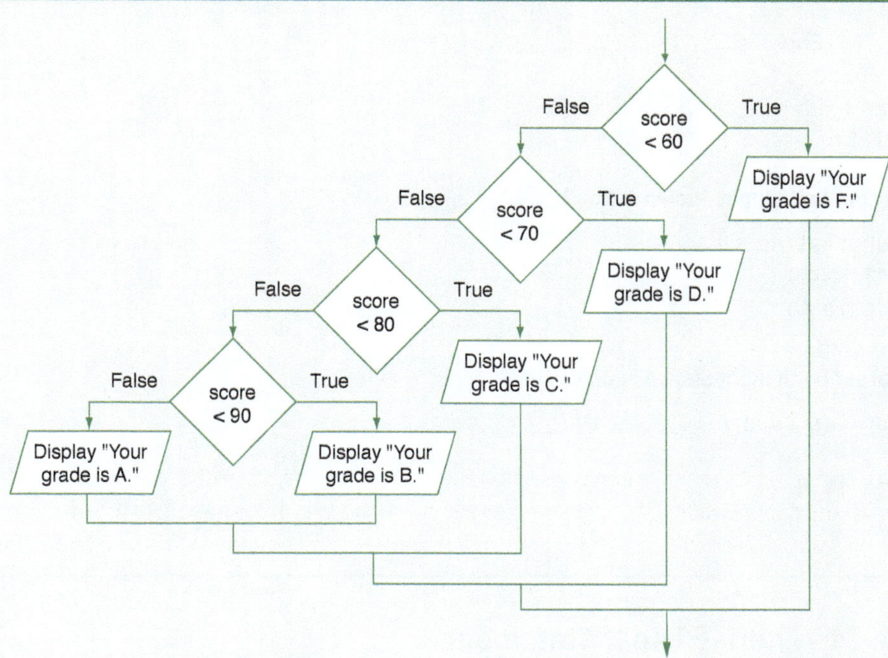

Program 7-6:

```
// Variable to hold the test score
Declare Real score

// Get the test score.
Display "Enter your test score."
Input score

// Determine the grade.
If score < 60 Then
   Display "Your grade is F."
Else
   If score < 70 Then
      Display "Your grade is D."
   Else
      If score < 80 Then
        Display "Your grade is C."
      Else
        If score < 90 Then
          Display "Your grade is B."
        Else
          Display "Your grade is A."
```

Program 7-6: *(continued)*

```
            End If
         End If
      End If
   End If
```

Program Output (with Input Shown in Bold)

```
Enter your test score.
78 [Enter]
Your grade is C.
```

Program Output (with Input Shown in Bold)

```
Enter your test score.
84 [Enter]
Your grade is B.
```

The `If-Then-Else If` Statement

Even though Program 7-6 is a simple example, the logic of the nested decision structure is fairly complex. Most languages provide a special version of the decision structure known as the `If-Then-Else If` statement, which makes this type of logic simpler to write. In pseudocode we will write the `If-Then-Else If` statement using the following general format:

```
If condition_1 Then
   statement      } If condition_1 is true these statements are executed,
   statement      } and the rest of the structure is ignored.
   etc.
Else If condition_2 Then
   statement      } If condition_2 is true these statements are executed,
   statement      } and the rest of the structure is ignored.
   etc.
Insert as many Else If clauses as necessary
Else
   statement      } These statements are executed if none of the
   statement      } conditions above are true.
   etc.
End If
```

When the statement executes, *condition_1* is tested. If *condition_1* is true, the statements that immediately follow are executed, up to the `Else If` clause. The rest of the structure is ignored. If *condition_1* is false, however, the program jumps to the very next `Else If` clause and tests *condition_2*. If it is true, the statements that immediately follow are executed, up to the next `Else If` clause. The rest of the structure is then ignored. This process continues until a condition is found to be true, or no more `Else If` clauses are left. If none of the conditions are true, the statements following the `Else` clause are executed.

The pseudocode in Program 7-7 shows an example of the `If-Then-Else If` statement. This program works the same as Program 7-6. Instead of using a nested decision structure, this program uses the If-Then-Else If statement in lines 9 through 19.

Program 7-7:

```
1  // Variable to hold the test score
2  Declare Real score
3
4  // Get the test score.
5  Display "Enter your test score."
6  Input score
7
8  // Determine the grade.
9  If score < 60 Then
10      Display "Your grade is F."
11 Else If score < 70 Then
12      Display "Your grade is D."
13 Else If score < 80 Then
14      Display "Your grade is C."
15 Else If score < 90 Then
16      Display "Your grade is B."
17 Else
18      Display "Your grade is A."
19 End If
```

Program Output (with Input Shown in Bold)

`Enter your test score.`
`78 [Enter]`
`Your grade is C.`

Program Output (with Input Shown in Bold)

`Enter your test score.`
`84 [Enter]`
`Your grade is B.`

Notice the alignment and indentation that are used with the `If-Then-Else If` statement: The `If`, `Else If`, `Else`, and `End If` clauses are all aligned, and the conditionally executed statements are indented.

You never have to use the `If-Then-Else If` statement because its logic can be coded with nested `If-Then-Else` statements. However, a long series of nested `If-Then-Else` statements has two particular disadvantages when you are debugging code:

- The code can grow complex and become difficult to understand.
- Because indenting is important in nested statements, a long series of nested `If`-Then-Else statements can become too long to be displayed on the computer screen without horizontal scrolling. Also, long statements tend to "wrap around" when printed on paper, making the code even more difficult to read.

The logic of an `If-Then-Else If` statement is usually easier to follow than a long series of nested `If-Then-Else` statements. And, because all of the clauses are aligned in an `If-Then-Else If` statement, the lengths of the lines in the statement tend to be shorter.

Checkpoint

7.13 Explain or diagram the flow of execution for a programmed game in which a player must meet two conditions to move up a level.

7.14 Why is it important to use proper alignment and indentation when writing a nested decision structure?

7.15 What is one way to write a program that tests a series of conditions and then performs an action depending on which condition is true?

7.16 What is the purpose of an `If-Then-Else If` statement?

7.5 Using Logical Operators

The logical AND operator and the logical OR operator allow you to connect multiple Boolean expressions to create a compound expression. The logical NOT operator reverses the truth of a Boolean expression.

Programming languages provide a set of operators known as **logical operators**, which you can use to create complex Boolean expressions. Table 7-3 describes these operators. Table 7-4 shows examples of several **compound Boolean expressions** that use logical operators.

Table 7-3 Logical operators

Operator	Meaning
AND	The AND operator connects two Boolean expressions into one compound expression. Both subexpressions must be true for the compound expression to be true.
OR	The OR operator connects two Boolean expressions into one compound expression. One or both subexpressions must be true for the compound expression to be true. It is only necessary for one of the subexpressions to be true, and it does not matter which.
NOT	The NOT operator is a unary operator, meaning it works with only one operand. The operand must be a Boolean expression. The NOT operator reverses the truth of its operand. If it is applied to an expression that is true, the operator returns false. If it is applied to an expression that is false, the operator returns true.

Table 7-4 Compound Boolean expressions using logical operators

Expression	Meaning
`x > y AND a < b`	Is x greater than y AND is a less than b?
`x == y OR x == z`	Is x equal to y OR is x equal to z?
`NOT (x > y)`	Is the expression x > y NOT true?

NOTE: In many languages, most notably C, C++, and Java, the AND operator is written as &&, the OR operator is written as | |, and the NOT operator is written as !.

The AND Operator

The AND operator takes two Boolean expressions as operands and creates a compound Boolean expression that is true only when both subexpressions are true. The following is an example of an If-Then statement that uses the AND operator:

```
If temperature < 20 AND minutes > 12 Then
    Display "The temperature is in the danger zone."
End If
```

In this statement, the two Boolean expressions temperature < 20 and minutes > 12 are combined into a compound expression. The Display statement will be executed only if temperature is less than 20 AND minutes is greater than 12. If either of the Boolean subexpressions is false, the compound expression is false and the message is not displayed.

You can use a **truth table** to diagram the outcomes of all possible true or false values in an expression. Table 7-5 shows a truth table for the AND operator. It lists expressions showing all the possible combinations of true and false connected with the AND operator. The resulting values of the expressions are also shown.

Table 7-5 Truth table for the AND operator

Expression	Value of the Expression
true AND false	false
false AND true	false
false AND false	false
true AND true	true

As Table 7-5 shows, both sides of the AND operator must be true for the operator to return a true value.

The OR Operator

The OR operator takes two Boolean expressions as operands and creates a compound Boolean expression that is true when either of the subexpressions is true. The following is an example of an If-Then statement that uses the OR operator:

```
If temperature < 20 OR temperature > 100 Then
   Display "The temperature is in the danger zone."
End If
```

The Display statement will execute only if temperature is less than 20 OR temperature is greater than 100. If either subexpression is true, the compound expression is true. Table 7-6 shows a truth table for the OR operator.

Table 7-6 Truth table for the OR operator

Expression	Value of the Expression
true OR false	true
false OR true	true
false OR false	false
true OR true	true

All it takes for an OR expression to be true is for one side of the OR operator to be true. It doesn't matter if the other side is false or true.

Short-Circuit Evaluation

In many languages both the AND and OR operators perform short-circuit evaluation. Here's how it works with the AND operator: If the expression on the left side of the AND operator is false, the expression on the right side will not be checked. Because the compound expression will be false if only one of the subexpressions is false, it would waste CPU time to check the remaining expression. So, when the AND operator finds that the expression on its left is false, it short-circuits and does not evaluate the expression on its right.

Here's how short-circuit evaluation works with the OR operator: If the expression on the left side of the OR operator is true, the expression on the right side will not be checked. Because it is only necessary for one of the expressions to be true, it would waste CPU time to check the remaining expression.

TIP: If you are using a programming language that performs short-circuit evaluation, you should put some thought into the order in which you write the subexpressions in a compound Boolean expression. If you know which of the subexpressions is most likely to be true, you can improve the efficiency of the code.

For example, when writing an expression that uses the OR operator, you can improve the code's efficiency by writing the subexpression that is most likely to be true on the left side of the OR operator. If the left subexpression is true most of the time, that means the right subexpression will not be tested as many times, and the code will execute faster.

When writing an expression that uses the AND operator, you can improve the code's efficiency by writing the subexpression that is least likely to be true on the left side of the AND operator. If the left subexpression is false most of the time, that means the right subexpression will not be tested as many times, and the code will execute faster.

The NOT Operator

The NOT operator is a unary, or single, operator that takes a Boolean expression as its operand and reverses its logical value. In other words, if the expression is true, the NOT operator returns false, and if the expression is false, the NOT operator returns true. The following is an If-Then statement using the NOT operator:

```
If NOT(temperature > 100) Then
   Display "This is below the maximum temperature."
End If
```

First, the expression (temperature > 100) is tested and a value of either true or false is the result. Then the NOT operator is applied to that value. If the expression (temperature > 100) is true, the NOT operator returns false. If the expression (temperature > 100) is false, the NOT operator returns true. The previous code is equivalent to asking: "Is the temperature not greater than 100?".

NOTE: In this example, we have put parentheses around the expression temperature > 100. The reason for this is that, in many languages, the NOT operator has higher precedence than the relational operators. Suppose we wrote the expression as follows:

```
NOT temperature > 100
```

In many languages this expression would not work correctly because the NOT operator would be applied to the temperature variable, not the expression temperature > 100. To make sure that the operator is applied to the expression, we enclose it in parentheses.

Table 7-7 shows a truth table for the NOT operator.

Table 7-7 Truth table for the NOT operator

Expression	Value of the Expression
NOT true	false
NOT false	true

Checking Numeric Ranges with Logical Operators

Sometimes you will need to design an algorithm that determines whether a numeric value is within a specific range of values or outside a specific range of values. When determining whether a number is inside a range, it is best to use the AND operator. For example, the following If-Then statement checks the value in x to determine whether it is in the range of 20 through 40:

```
If x >= 20 AND x <= 40 Then
   Display "The value is in the acceptable range."
End If
```

The compound Boolean expression being tested by this statement will be true only when x is greater than or equal to 20 AND less than or equal to 40. The value in x must be within the range of 20 through 40 for this compound expression to be true.

When determining whether a number is outside a range, it is best to use the OR operator. The following statement determines whether x is outside the range of 20 through 40:

```
If x < 20 OR x > 40 Then
   Display "The value is outside the acceptable range."
End If
```

It is important not to get the logic of the logical operators confused when testing for a range of numbers. For example, the compound Boolean expression in the following pseudocode would never test true:

```
// This is an error!
If x < 20 AND x > 40 Then
   Display "The value is outside the acceptable range."
End If
```

Obviously, x cannot be less than 20 and at the same time be greater than 40

Checkpoint

7.17 What is a compound Boolean expression?

7.18 The following truth table shows various combinations of the values true and false connected by a logical operator. Complete the table by circling T or F to indicate whether the result of such a combination is true or false.

Logical Expression	Result (choose T or F)	
True AND False	T	F
True AND True	T	F
False AND True	T	F
False AND False	T	F
True OR False	T	F
True OR True	T	F
False OR True	T	F
False OR False	T	F
NOT True	T	F
NOT False	T	F

7.19 Assume the variables a = 2, b = 4, and c = 6. Circle the T or F for each of the following conditions to indicate whether its value is true or false.

a == 4 OR b > 2	T	F
6 <= c AND a > 3	T	F
1 != b AND c != 3	T	F
a >= -1 OR a <= b	T	F
NOT (a > 2)	T	F

7.20 Explain how short-circuit evaluation works with the AND and OR operators.

7.21 Write an `If-Then` statement that displays the message "The number is valid" if the variable speed is within the range 0 through 200.

7.22 Write an `If-Then` statement that displays the message "The number is not valid" if the variable speed is outside the range 0 through 200.

7.5 Using Boolean Variables

A Boolean variable can hold one of two values: true or false. Boolean variables are commonly used to indicate whether specific conditions exist.

In addition to numeric and string data types, most programming languages provide a `Boolean` data type. The **`Boolean` data type** allows you to create variables that may hold one of two possible values: `True` or `False`. Here is an example of the way we declare `Boolean` variables in this text:

```
Declare Boolean isHungry
```

Most programming languages have key words such as `True` and `False` that can be assigned to Boolean variables. Here are examples of how we assign values to a Boolean variable:

```
Set isHungry = True
Set isHungry = False
```

Boolean variables are most commonly used as flags. A **flag** is a variable that signals when some condition exists in the program. When the flag variable is set to `False`, it indicates the condition does not exist. When the flag variable is set to `True`, it means the condition does exist.

For example, suppose a salesperson has a quota of $50,000. Assuming the `sales` variable holds the amount that the salesperson has sold, the following pseudocode determines whether the quota has been met:

```
If sales >= 50000 Then
   Set salesQuotaMet = True
Else
   Set salesQuotaMet = False
End If
```

As a result of this code, the `salesQuotaMet` variable can be used as a flag to indicate whether the sales quota has been met. Later in the program we might test the flag in the following way:

```
If salesQuotaMet Then
   Display "You have met your sales quota!"
End If
```

This code displays the message "You have met your sales quota!" if the Boolean variable `salesQuotaMet` equals True. Notice that we did not have to use the == operator to explicitly compare the `salesQuotaMet` variable with the value `True`. This code is equivalent to the following:

```
If salesQuotaMet == True Then
   Display "You have met your sales quota!"
End If
```

Checkpoint

7.23 What values can you store in a Boolean variable?

7.24 What is a flag variable?

7.25 What does it mean when a Boolean variable flag is set to True?

Chapter Review

Multiple Choice

1. A _____ structure can execute a set of statements only under certain circumstances.
   a. sequence
   b. circumstantial
   c. decision
   d. Boolean

2. A _____ structure provides one alternative path of execution.
   a. sequence
   b. single alternative decision
   c. one path alternative
   d. single execution decision

3. In pseudocode, the `If-Then` statement is an example of a _____.
   a. sequence structure
   b. decision structure
   c. pathway structure
   d. class structure

4. A(n) _____ expression has a value of either true or false.
   a. binary
   b. decision
   c. unconditional
   d. Boolean

5. The symbols >, <, and == are all _____ operators.
   a. relational
   b. logical
   c. conditional
   d. ternary

6. A(n) _____ structure tests a condition and then takes one path if the condition is true, or another path if the condition is false.
   a. `If-Then` statement
   b. single alternative decision
   c. dual alternative decision
   d. sequence

7. You use a(n) _____ statement in pseudocode to write a single alternative decision structure.
   a. `Test-Jump`
   b. `If-Then`
   c. `If-Then-Else`
   d. `If-Call`

8. You use a(n) _____ statement in pseudocode to write a dual alternative decision structure.
   a. Test-Jump
   b. If-Then
   c. If-Then-Else
   d. If-Call

9. AND, OR, and NOT are _____ operators.
   a. relational
   b. logical
   c. conditional
   d. ternary

10. A compound Boolean expression created with the _____ operator is true only if both of its subexpressions are true.
   a. AND
   b. OR
   c. NOT
   d. BOTH

11. A compound Boolean expression created with the _____ operator is true if either of its subexpressions is true.
   a. AND
   b. OR
   c. NOT
   d. EITHER

12. The _____ operator takes a Boolean expression as its operand and reverses its logical value.
   a. AND
   b. OR
   c. NOT
   d. EITHER

15. A _____ is a Boolean variable that signals when some condition exists in the program.
   a. flag
   b. signal
   c. sentinel
   d. siren

True or False

1. You can write any program using only sequence structures.
2. A program can be made of only one type of control structure. You cannot combine structures.
3. A single alternative decision structure tests a condition and then takes one path if the condition is true, or another path if the condition is false.
4. A decision structure can be nested inside another decision structure.
5. A compound Boolean expression created with the AND operator is true only when both subexpressions are true.

Short Answer

1. Explain what is meant by the term *conditionally* executed.
2. You need to test a condition and then execute one set of statements if the condition is true. If the condition is false, you need to execute a different set of statements. What structure will you use?
3. If you need to test the value of a variable and use that value to determine which statement or set of statements to execute, which structure would be the most straightforward to use?
4. Briefly describe how the AND operator works.
5. Briefly describe how the OR operator works.
6. When determining whether a number is inside a range, which logical operator is it best to use?
7. What is a flag and how does it work?

Algorithm Workbench

1. Design an `If-Then` statement (or a flowchart with a single alternative decision structure) that assigns 20 to the variable y and assigns 40 to the variable z if the variable x is greater than 100.
2. Design an `If-Then` statement (or a flowchart with a single alternative decision structure) that assigns 0 to the variable b and assigns 1 to the variable c if the variable a is less than 10.
3. Design an `If-Then-Else` statement (or a flowchart with a dual alternative decision structure) that assigns 0 to the variable b if the variable a is less than 10. Otherwise, it should assign 99 to the variable b.

4. The following pseudocode contains several nested `If-Then-Else` statements. Unfortunately, it was written without proper alignment and indentation. Rewrite the code and use the proper conventions of alignment and indentation.

```
If score < 60 Then
Display "Your grade is F."
Else
If score < 70 Then
Display "Your grade is D."
Else
If score < 80 Then
Display "Your grade is C."
Else
If score < 90 Then
Display "Your grade is B."
Else
Display "Your grade is A."
End If
End If
End If
End If
```

5. Design nested decision structures that perform the following: If `amount1` is greater than 10 and `amount2` is less than 100, display the greater of `amount1` and `amount2`.
6. Design an `If-Then-Else` statement (or a flowchart with a dual alternative decision structure) that displays "Speed is normal" if the `speed` variable is within the range of 24 to 56. If `speed` holds a value outside this range, display "Speed is abnormal."
7. Design an `If-Then-Else` statement (or a flowchart with a dual alternative decision structure) that determines whether the `points` variable is outside the range of 9 to 51. If the variable holds a value outside this range it should display "Invalid points." Otherwise, it should display "Valid points."
8. Write an `If-Then` statement that sets the variable `hours` to 10 when the flag variable `minimum` is set.

Debugging Exercises

1. Part of the following pseudocode is incompatible with the Java, Python, C, and C++ languages. Identify the problem. How would you fix the problem if you were to translate this pseudocode into one of the aforementioned languages?

```
If num1 = num2 Then
    Display "The values are equal."
Else
    Display "The values are NOT equal."
End If
```

2. The intended purpose of the following pseudocode is to set the temp variable to the value 32.0 if it is not already equal to 32.0. This will not work as the programmer expects, however. Find the problem.

```
If NOT temp == 32.0 Then
   Set temp = 32.0
End If
```

3. The intended purpose of the following pseudocode is to determine whether the value variable is within a specified range. The logic will not work, however. Find the problem.

```
If value < lower AND value > upper Then
   Display "The value is outside the range."
Else
   Display "The value is within the range."
End If
```

Programming Exercises

1. Roman Numerals

Design a program that prompts the user to enter a number within the range of 1 through 10. The program should display the Roman numeral version of that number. If the number is outside the range of 1 through 10, the program should display an error message

2. Areas of Rectangles

VideoNote The Areas of Rectangles Problem

The area of a rectangle is the rectangle's length times its width. Design a program that asks for the length and width of two rectangles. The program should tell the user which rectangle has the greater area, or whether the areas are the same.

3. Mass and Weight

Scientists measure an object's mass in kilograms and its weight in Newtons. If you know the amount of mass of an object, you can calculate its weight, in Newtons, with the following formula:

$$Weight = Mass \times 9.8$$

Design a program that asks the user to enter an object's mass, and then calculates its weight. If the object weighs more than 1,000 Newtons, display a message indicating that it is too heavy. If the object weighs less than 10 Newtons, display a message indicating that it is too light.

4. Magic Dates

The date June 10, 1960, is special because when it is written in the following format, the month times the day equals the year:

6/10/60

Design a program that asks the user to enter a month (in numeric form), a day, and a two-digit year. The program should then determine whether the month times the day equals the year. If so, it should display a message saying the date is magic. Otherwise, it should display a message saying the date is not magic.

5. Color Mixer

The colors red, blue, and yellow are known as the primary colors because they cannot be made by mixing other colors. When you mix two primary colors, you get a secondary color, as shown here:

- When you mix red and blue, you get purple.
- When you mix red and yellow, you get orange.
- When you mix blue and yellow, you get green.

Design a program that prompts the user to enter the names of two primary colors to mix. If the user enters anything other than "red," "blue," or "yellow," the program should display an error message. Otherwise, the program should display the name of the secondary color that results.

6. Book Club Points

Serendipity Booksellers has a book club that awards points to its customers based on the number of books purchased each month. The points are awarded as follows:

- If a customer purchases 0 books, 0 points are awarded.
- If a customer purchases 1 book, 5 points are awarded.
- If a customer purchases 2 books, 15 points are awarded.
- If a customer purchases 3 books, 30 points are awarded.
- If a customer purchases 4 or more books, 60 points are awarded.

Design a program that asks the user to enter the number of books they have purchased this month and displays the number of points awarded.

7. Software Sales

A software company sells a package that retails for $99. Quantity discounts are given according to the following table:

Quantity	Discount
1 0–19	20%
20–49	30%
50–99	40%
100 or more	50%

Design a program that asks the user to enter the number of packages purchased. The program should then display the amount of the discount (if any) and the total amount of the purchase after the discount.

8. Change for a Dollar Game

Design a change-counting game that gets the user to enter the number of coins required to make exactly one dollar. The program should ask the user to enter the number of pennies, nickels, dimes, and quarters. If the total value of the coins entered is equal to one dollar, the program should congratulate the user for winning the game. Otherwise, the program should display a message indicating whether the amount entered was more than or less than one dollar.

9. Shipping Charges

The Fast Freight Shipping Company charges the following rates:

Weight of Package	Rate per Pound
2 pounds or less	$1.10
Over 2 pounds but not more than 6 pounds	$2.20
Over 6 pounds but not more than 10 pounds	$3.70
Over 10 pounds $	3.80

Design a program that asks the user to enter the weight of a package and then displays the shipping charges.

10. Time Calculator

Design a program that asks the user to enter a number of seconds, and works as follows:

- There are 60 seconds in a minute. If the number of seconds entered by the user is greater than or equal to 60, the program should display the number of minutes in that many seconds.
- There are 3,600 seconds in an hour. If the number of seconds entered by the user is greater than or equal to 3,600, the program should display the number of hours in that many seconds.
- There are 86,400 seconds in a day. If the number of seconds entered by the user is greater than or equal to 86,400, the program should display the number of days in that many seconds.

11. Leap Year Detector

Design a program that asks the user to enter a year, and then displays a message indicating whether that year is a leap year or not. Use the following logic to develop your algorithm:

- If the year is evenly divisible by 100 and is also evenly divisible by 400, then it is a leap year. For example, 2000 is a leap year but 2026 is not.
- If the year is not evenly divisible by 100, but it is evenly divisible by 4, it is a leap year. For example, 2024 is a leap year but 2025 is not.

Getting Started with Loop Statements

TOPICS

8.1 Introduction to Loops

A repetition structure causes a statement or set of statements to execute repeatedly.

Programmers commonly have to write code that performs the same task over and over. For example, suppose you have been asked to write a program that calculates a 10 percent sales commission for several salespeople. Although it would not be a good design, one approach would be to write the code to calculate one salesperson's commission, and then repeat that code for each salesperson. For example, look at the following pseudocode:

```
// Variables for sales and commission.
Declare Real sales, commission

// Constant for the commission rate.
Constant Real COMMISSION_RATE = 0.10

// Get the amount of sales.
Display "Enter the amount of sales."
Input sales

// Calculate the commission.
Set commission = sales * COMMISSION_RATE

// Display the commission
Display "The commission is $", commission
```

This calculates the first salesperson's commission.

```
// Get the amount of sales.
Display "Enter the amount of sales."
Input sales

// Calculate the commission.
Set commission = sales * COMMISSION_RATE

// Display the commission
Display "The commission is $", commission
```

This calculates the second salesperson's commission.

. . . and this code goes on and on . . .

As you can see, this is one long sequence structure containing a lot of duplicated code. There are several disadvantages to this approach, including the following:

- The duplicated code makes the program large.
- Writing a long sequence of statements can be time consuming.
- If part of the duplicated code has to be corrected or changed, then the correction or change has to be done many times.

Instead of writing the same sequence of statements over and over, a better way to repeatedly perform an operation is to write the code for the operation once, and then place that code in a structure that makes the computer repeat it as many times as necessary. This can be done with a **repetition structure**, which is more commonly known as iteration or a **loop**.

There are two broad categories of loops: condition-controlled and count-controlled. A **condition-controlled loop** uses a true/false condition to control the number of times that it repeats. A **count-controlled loop** repeats a specific number of times.

Checkpoint

8.1 What is a repetition structure?

8.2 What is a condition-controlled loop?

8.3 What is a count-controlled loop?

8.2 Introduction to Condition-Controlled Loops: `While`, `Do-While`, and `Do-Until`s

Both the `While` and `Do-While` loops cause a statement or set of statements to repeat as long as a condition is true. The `Do-Until` loop causes a statement or set of statements to repeat until a condition is true.

The While Loop

VideoNote
The While Loop

The While loop gets its name from the way it works: *While a condition is true, do some task.* The loop has two parts: (1) a condition that is tested for a true or false value, and (2) a statement or set of statements that is repeated as long as the condition is true. Figure 8-1 shows the logic of a While loop

Figure 8-1 The logic of a While loop

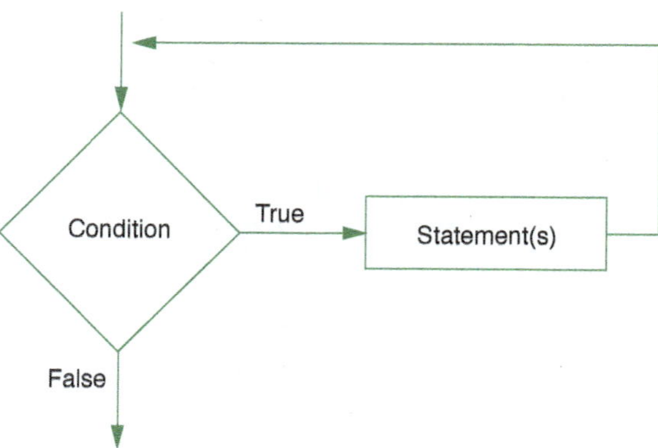

The diamond symbol in the flowchart represents the condition that is tested. Notice what happens if the condition is true: one or more statements are executed and the program's execution flows back to the point just above the diamond symbol. The condition is tested again, and if it is true, the process repeats. If the condition is false, the program exits the loop. In a flowchart, you will always recognize a loop when you see a flow line going back to a previous part of the flowchart.

Writing a While Loop in Pseudocode

In pseudocode, we will use the While statement to write a While loop. Here is the general format of the While statement:

```
While condition
      statement    }  These statements are the body of the loop.
      statement    }  They are repeated while the condition is true.
      etc.         }
End While
```

In the general format, the *condition* is a Boolean expression, and the statements that appear on the lines between the While and the End While clauses are called the *body of the loop*. When the loop executes, the *condition* is tested. If it is true, the statements that appear in the body of the loop are executed, and then the loop starts over. If the *condition* is false, the program exits the loop.

As shown in the general format, you should use the following programming style conventions when you write a While statement:

- Make sure the While clause and the End While clause are aligned.
- Indent the statements in the body of the loop.

By indenting the statements in the body of the loop you visually set them apart from the surrounding code. This makes your program easier to read and debug. Also, this is similar to the style that most programmers follow when writing loops in actual code.

Program 8-1 shows how we might use a `While` loop to write the commission calculating program that was described at the beginning of this chapter.

Program 8-1:

```
// Variable declarations
Declare Real sales, commission
Declare String keepGoing = "y"

// Constant for the commission rate
Constant Real COMMISSION_RATE = 0.10

While keepGoing == "y"
    // Get the amount of sales.
    Display "Enter the amount of sales."
    Input sales

    // Calculate the commission.
    Set commission = sales * COMMISSION_RATE

    // Display the commission
    Display "The commission is $", commission

    Display "Do you want to calculate another"
    Display "commission? (Enter y for yes.)"
    Input keepGoing
End While
```

Program Output (with Input Shown in Bold)

```
Enter the amount of sales.
10000.00 [Enter]
The commission is $1000
Do you want to calculate another
commission? (Enter y for yes.)
y [Enter]
Enter the amount of sales.
5000.00 [Enter]
The commission is $500
Do you want to calculate another
commission? (Enter y for yes.)
y [Enter]
Enter the amount of sales.
12000.00 [Enter]
The commission is $1200
Do you want to calculate another
commission? (Enter y for yes.)
n [Enter]
```

In line 2, we declare the sales variable, which will hold the amount of sales, and the commission variable, which will hold the amount of commission. Then, in line 3 we declare a String variable named keepGoing. Notice that the variable is initialized with the value "y." This initialization value is important, and in a moment you will see why. In line 6 we declare a constant, COMMISSION_RATE, which is initialized with the value 0.10. This is the commission rate that we will use in our calculation.

Line 8 is the beginning of a While loop, which starts like this:

```
While keepGoing == "y"
```

Notice the condition that is being tested: keepGoing == "y". The loop tests this condition, and if it is true, the statements in the body of the loop (lines 9 through 21) are executed. Then, the loop starts over at line 8. It tests the expression keepGoing == "y" and if it is true, the statements in the body of the loop are executed again. This cycle repeats until the expression keepGoing == "y" is tested in line 8 and found to be false. When that happens, the program exits the loop. This is illustrated in Figure 8-2.

In order for this loop to stop executing, something has to happen inside the loop to make the expression keepGoing == "y" false. The statements in lines 19 through 21 take care of this. Lines 19 and 20 display a message asking "Do you want to calculate another commission? (Enter y for yes.)" Then, the Input statement in line 21 reads the user's input and stores it in the keepGoing variable. If the user enters y (and it must be a lowercase y), then the expression keepGoing == "y" will be true when the loop starts over. This will cause the statements in the body of the loop to execute again. But, if the user enters anything other than lowercase y, the expression will be false when the loop starts over, and the program will exit the loop.

Figure 8-2 The While Loop

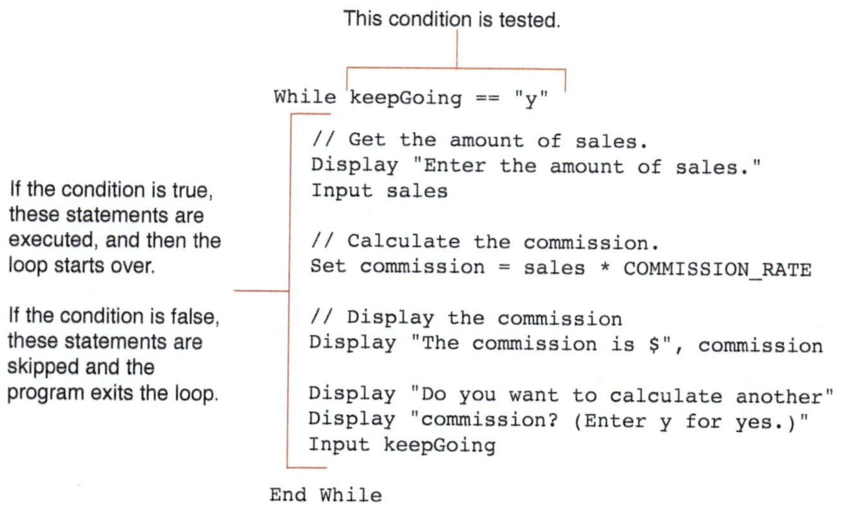

This condition is tested.

If the condition is true, these statements are executed, and then the loop starts over.

If the condition is false, these statements are skipped and the program exits the loop.

```
While keepGoing == "y"
    // Get the amount of sales.
    Display "Enter the amount of sales."
    Input sales

    // Calculate the commission.
    Set commission = sales * COMMISSION_RATE

    // Display the commission
    Display "The commission is $", commission

    Display "Do you want to calculate another"
    Display "commission? (Enter y for yes.)"
    Input keepGoing
End While
```

Now that you have examined the pseudocode, look at the program output in the sample run. First, the program prompted the user to enter the amount of sales. The user entered 10000.00, and then the program displayed the commission for that amount, which is $1000.00. Then, the user is prompted "Do you want to calculate another commission? (Enter y for yes.)" The user entered y, and the loop started the steps over. In the sample run, the user went through this process three times. Each execution of the body of a loop is known as an **iteration**. In the sample run, the loop iterated three times.

Figure 8-3 shows a flowchart for Program 8-1. By looking at this flowchart you can see that we have a repetition structure (the `While` loop) with a sequence structure (the body of the loop) nested inside it. The fundamental structure of the `While` loop is still present, however. A condition is tested, and if it is true one or more statements are executed and the flow of execution returns to the point just above the conditional test.

Figure 8-3 Flowchart for Program 8.1

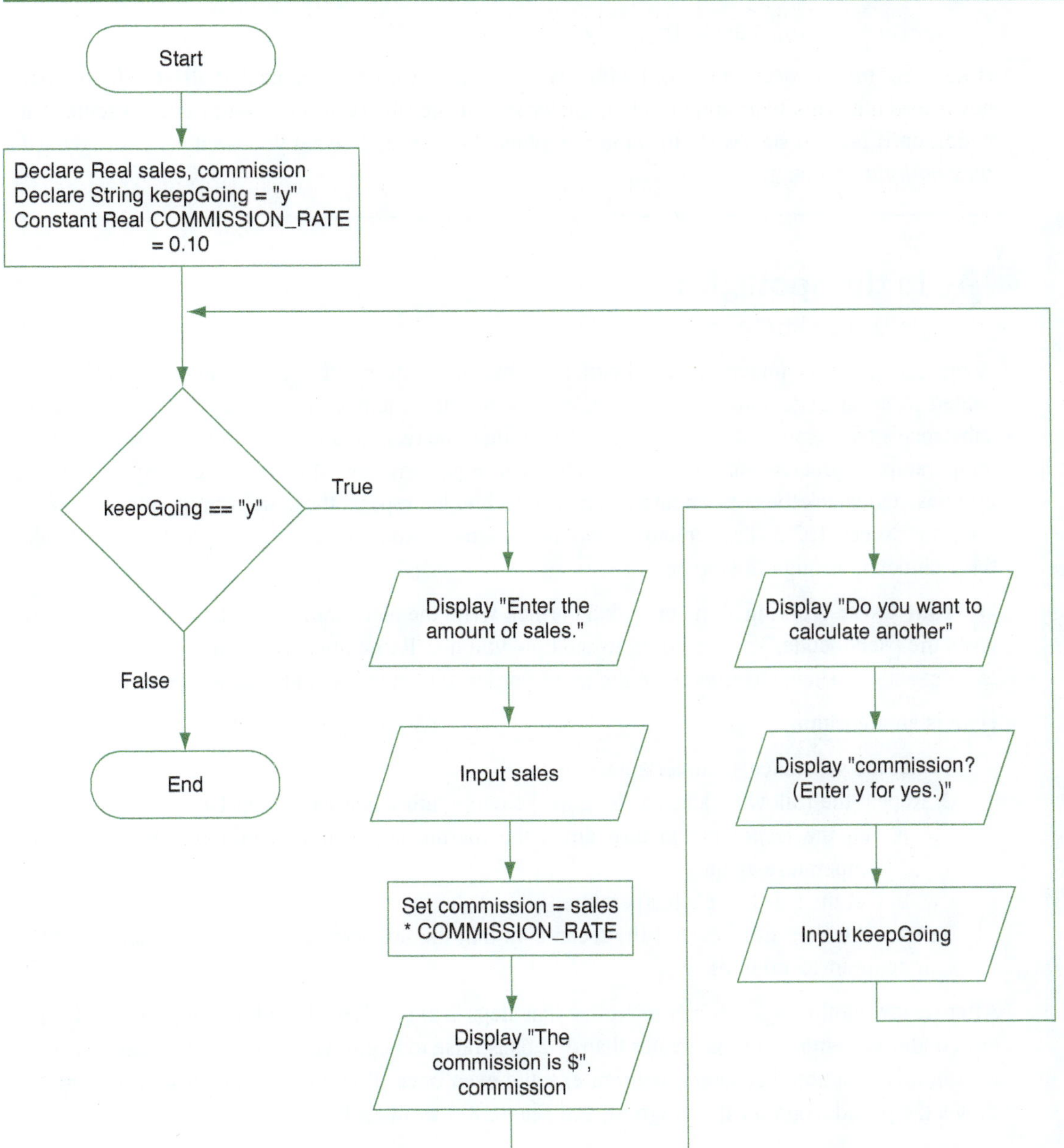

The While Loop is a Pretest Loop

The While loop is known as a **pretest** loop, which means it tests its condition *before* performing an iteration. Because the test is done at the beginning of the loop, you usually have to perform some steps prior to the loop to make sure that the loop executes at least once. For example, the loop in Program 8-1 starts like this:

```
While keepGoing == "y"
```

The loop will perform an iteration only if the expression `keepGoing == "y"` is true. To make sure the expression is true the first time that the loop executes, we declared and initialized the keepGoing variable in line 3 as follows:

```
Declare String keepGoing = "y"
```

If keepGoing had been initialized with any other value (or not initialized at all), the loop would never execute. This is an important characteristic of the While loop: it will never execute if its condition is false to start with. In some programs, this is exactly what you want. The following *In the Spotlight* section gives an example.

In the Spotlight:

Designing a While Loop

A project currently underway at Chemical Labs, Inc. requires that a substance be continually heated in a vat. A technician must check the substance's temperature every 15 minutes. If the substance's temperature does not exceed 102.5, then the technician does nothing. However, if the temperature is greater than 102.5, the technician must turn down the vat's thermostat, wait five minutes, and check the temperature again. The technician repeats these steps until the temperature does not exceed 102.5. The director of engineering has asked you to design a program that guides the technician through this process

On Your Own: Working alone or with a partner, write the algorithm steps, draw a flowchart, and write the pseudocode. Then, read on to see how you did. Remember, your solution does not have to be exactly the same as the one in the text in order to come up with the same result.

Here is an algorithm:

1. Get the substance's temperature.
2. Repeat the following steps as long as the temperature is greater than 102.5:
   a. Tell the technician to turn down the thermostat, wait five minutes, and check the temperature again.
   b. Get the substance's temperature.
3. After the loop finishes, tell the technician that the temperature is acceptable and to check it again in 15 minutes.

After reviewing this algorithm, you realize that steps 2(a) and 2(b) should not be performed if the test condition (temperature is greater than 102.5) is false to begin with. The While loop will work well in this situation, because it will not execute even once if its condition is false. Program 8-2 shows the pseudocode for the program, and Figure 8-4 shows a flowchart.

Program 8-2:

```
// Variable to hold the temperature
Declare Real temperature

// Constant for the maximum temperature
Constant Real MAX_TEMP = 102.5

// Get the substance's temperature.
Display "Enter the substance's temperature."
Input temperature

// If necessary, adjust the thermostat.
While temperature > MAX_TEMP
   Display "The temperature is too high."
   Display "Turn the thermostat down and wait"
   Display "five minutes. Take the temperature"
   Display "again and enter it here."
   Input temperature
End While

// Remind the user to check the temperature
// again in 15 minutes.
Display "The temperature is acceptable."
Display "Check it again in 15 minutes."
```

Program Output (with Input Shown in Bold)

```
Enter the substance's temperature.
104.7 [Enter]
The temperature is too high.
Turn the thermostat down and wait
five minutes. Take the temperature
again and enter it here.
103.2 [Enter]
The temperature is too high.
Turn the thermostat down and wait
five minutes. Take the temperature
again and enter it here.
102.1 [Enter]
The temperature is acceptable.
Check it again in 15 minutes.
```

Program Output (with Input Shown in Bold)

```
Enter the substance's temperature.
102.1 [Enter]
The temperature is acceptable.
Check it again in 15 minutes.
```

Figure 8-4 Flowchart for Program 8.2

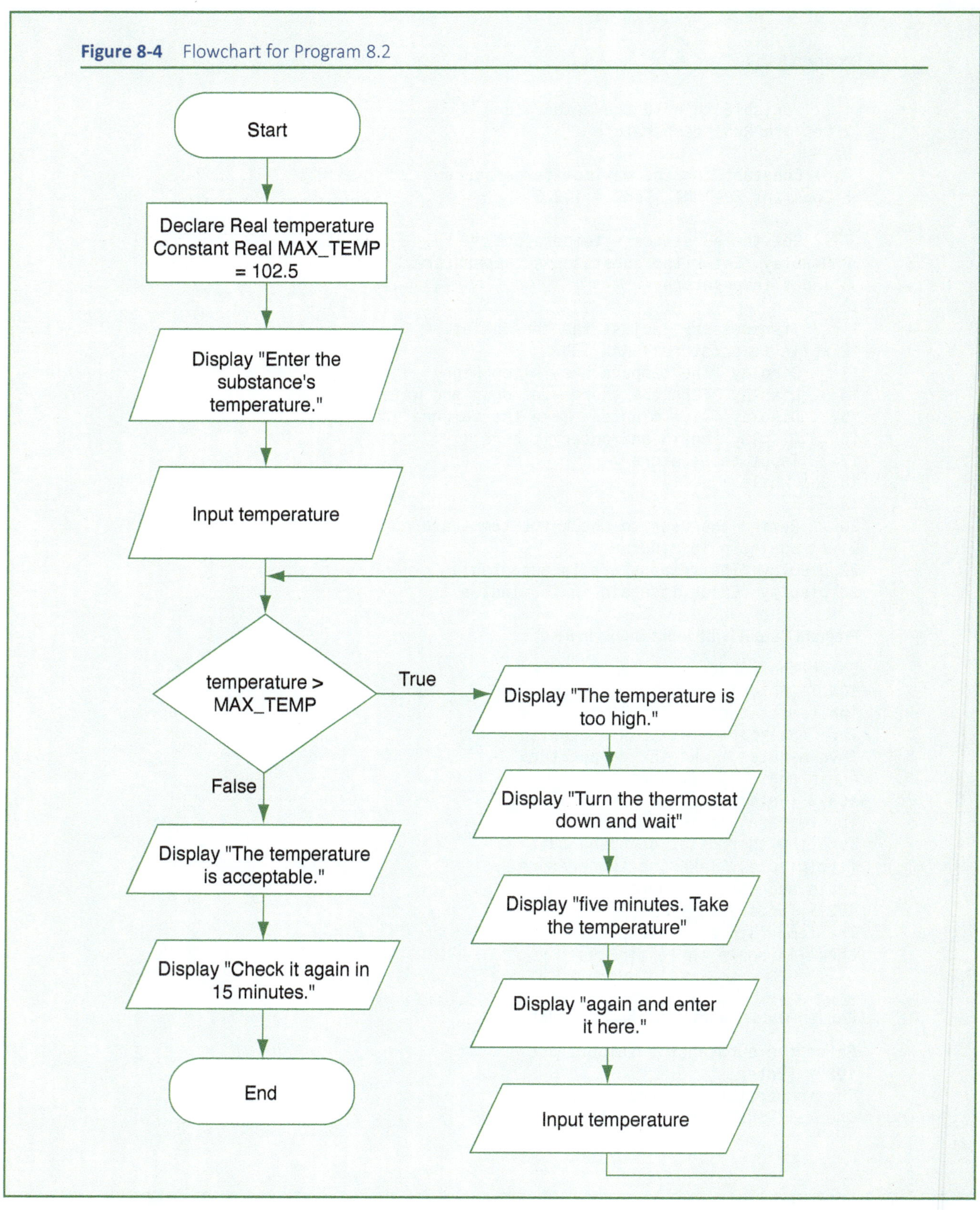

Infinite Loops

In all but rare cases, loops must contain within themselves a way to terminate. This means that something inside the loop must eventually make the test condition false. The loop in Program 8-1 stops when the expression `keepGoing == "y"` is false. If a loop does not have a way of stopping, it is called an **infinite loop**. An infinite loop continues to repeat until the program is interrupted. Infinite loops usually occur when the programmer forgets to write code inside the loop that makes the test condition false. In most circumstances you should avoid writing infinite loops.

The pseudocode in Program 8-3 demonstrates an infinite loop. This is a modified version of the commission calculating program. In this version, we have removed the code that modifies the `keepGoing` variable in the body of the loop. Each time the expression `keepGoing == "y"` is tested in line 9, `keepGoing` will contain the string `"y"`. As a consequence, the loop has no way of stopping.

Program 8-3:

```
1  // Variable declarations
2  Declare Real sales, commission
3  Declare String keepGoing = "y"
4
5  // Constant for the commission rate
6  Constant Real COMMISSION_RATE = 0.10
7
8  // Warning! Infinite loop!
9  While keepGoing == "y"
10     // Get the amount of sales.
11     Display "Enter the amount of sales."
12     Input sales
13
14     // Calculate the commission.
15     Set commission = sales * COMMISSION_RATE
16
17     // Display the commission
18     Display "The commission is $", commission
19 End While
```

The Do-While Loop

VideoNote
The Do-While Loop

You have learned that the `While` loop is a pretest loop, which means it tests its condition before performing an iteration. The `Do-While` loop is a **posttest** loop. This means it tests its condition after performing an iteration. As a result, the `Do-While` loop always performs at least one iteration, even if its condition is false to begin with. The logic of a `Do-While` loop is shown in Figure 8-5.

Figure 8-5 The logic of a Do-While loop

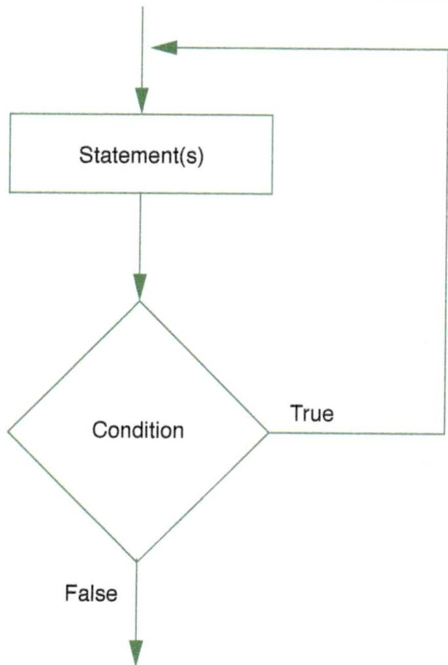

In the flowchart, one or more statements are executed, and then a condition is tested. If the condition is true, the program's execution flows back to the point just above the first statement in the body of the loop, and this process repeats. If the condition is false, the program exits the loop.

Writing a Do-While Loop in Pseudocode

In pseudocode, we will use the `Do-While` statement to write a `Do-While` loop. Here is the general format of the `Do-While` statement:

```
Do
   statement     ⎫ These statements are the body of the loop.
   statement     ⎬ They are always performed once, and then
   etc.          ⎭ repeated while the condition is true.
While   condition
```

In the general format, the statements that appear in the lines between the `Do` and the `While` clauses are the body of the loop. The *condition* that appears after the `While` clause is a Boolean expression. When the loop executes, the statements in the body of the loop are executed, and then the *condition* is tested. If the *condition* is true, the loop starts over and the statements in the body are executed again. If the condition is false, however, the program exits the loop. For example, in a programmed story, game, or animation, a token might drop in front of a character. If the character picks it up, a door unlocks. If the character does not pick up the token, the program flows back and the coin drops again.

As shown in the general format, you should use the following conventions when you write a `Do-While` statement:

- Make sure the `Do` clause and the `While` clause are aligned.
- Indent the statements in the body of the loop.

As shown in Program 8-4, the commission calculating program can be easily modified to use a `Do-While` loop instead of a `While` loop. Notice that in this version of the program, in line 3, we do not initialize the `keepGoing` variable with the string "`y`". It isn't necessary because the `Do-While` loop, in lines 7 through 15, will always execute at least once. This means that the Input statement in line 14 will read a value into the `keepGoing` variable before the condition is ever tested in line 15.

Figure 8-6 shows a flowchart for the program.

Program 8-4:

```
1  // Variable declarations
2  Declare Real sales, commission
3  Declare String keepGoing = "y"
4
5  // Constant for the commission rate
6  Constant Real COMMISSION_RATE = 0.10
7
8  Do
9     // Get the amount of sales.
10    Display "Enter the amount of sales."
11    Input sales
12
13    // Calculate the commission.
14    Set commission = sales * COMMISSION_RATE
15
16    // Display the commission
17    Display "The commission is $", commission
18
19    // Do it again?
20    Display "Do you want to calculate another"
21    Display "commission? (Enter y for yes.)"
22    Input keepGoing
23 While keepGoing == "y"
```

Program Output (with Input Shown in Bold)

```
Enter the amount of sales.
10000.00 [Enter]
The commission is $1000
Do you want to calculate another
commission? (Enter y for yes.)
y [Enter]
Enter the amount of sales.
5000.00 [Enter]
The commission is $500
Do you want to calculate another
commission? (Enter y for yes.)
y [Enter]
Enter the amount of sales.
12000.00 [Enter]
The commission is $1200
Do you want to calculate another
commission? (Enter y for yes.)
n [Enter]
```

Figure 8-6 Flowchart for Program 8-4

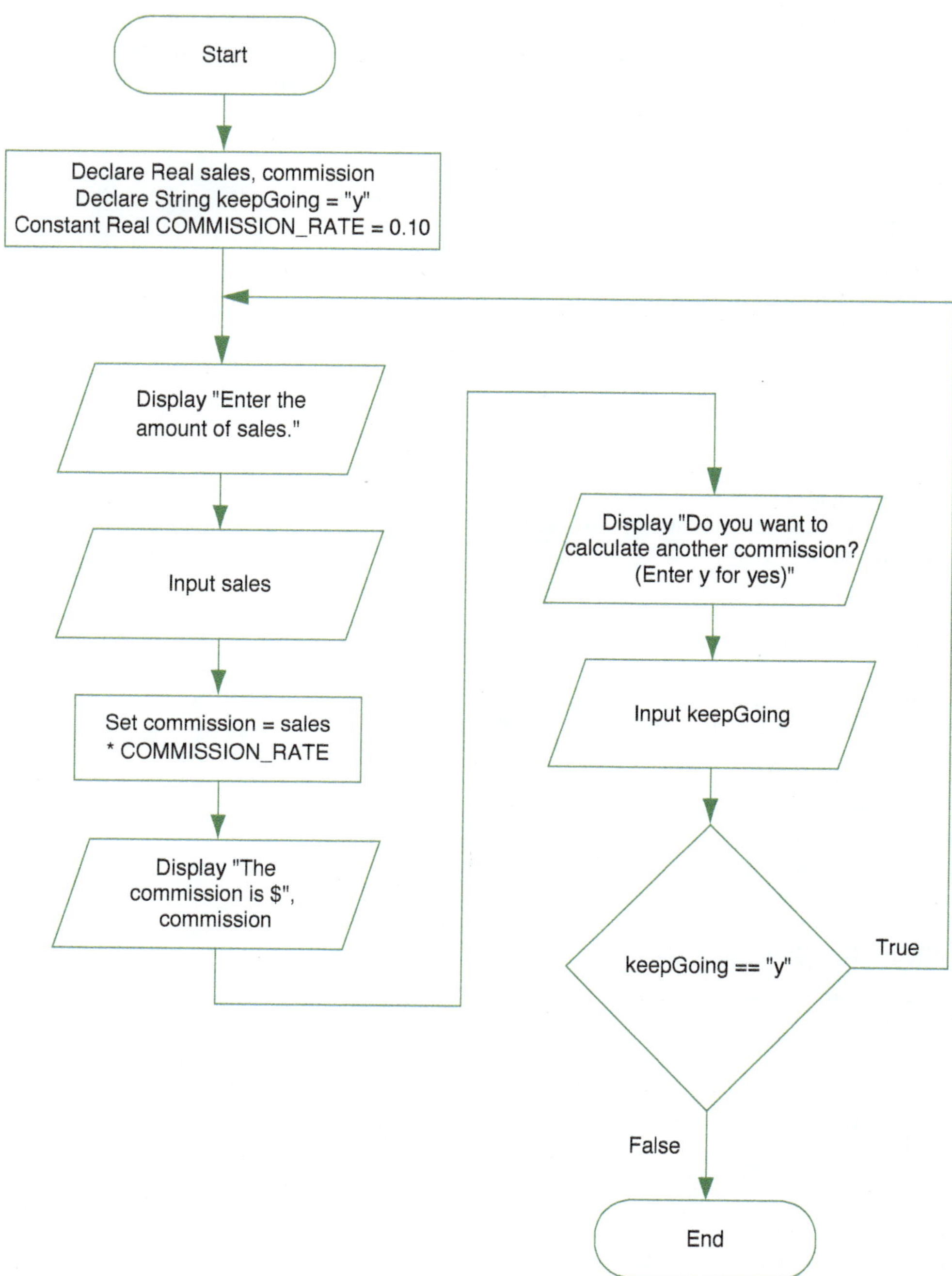

Although the `Do-While` loop is convenient to use in some circumstances, it is never required. Any loop that can be written as a `Do-While` loop can also be written as a `While` loop. As previously mentioned, some circumstances require that you initialize data prior to executing a `While` loop, to ensure that it executes at least once.

In the Spotlight:

Designing a `Do-While` Loop

Samantha owns an import business and she calculates the retail prices of her products with the following formula:

$$\textit{Retail Price} = \textit{Wholesale Cost} \times 2.5$$

She has asked you to design a program to do this calculation for each item that she receives in a shipment. You learn that each shipment contains various numbers of items, so you decide to use a loop that calculates the price for one item, and then asks her whether she has another item. The loop will iterate as long as she indicates that she has another item.

On Your Own: Working alone or with a partner, draw a flowchart, and write the pseudocode. Then, read on to see how you did. Remember, your solution does not have to be exactly the same as the one in the text in order to come up with the same result.

Program 8-5 shows pseudocode for the program, and Figure 8-7 shows the flowchart.

Program 8-5:

```
// Variable declarations
Declare Real wholesale, retail
Declare String doAnother

// Constant for the markup percentage
Constant Real MARKUP = 2.50

Do
   // Get the wholesale cost.
   Display "Enter an item's wholesale cost."
   Input wholesale

   // Calculate the retail price.
   Set retail = wholesale * MARKUP

   // Display the retail price.
   Display "The retail price is $", retail

   // Do this again?
   Display "Do you have another item? (Enter y for yes.)"
   Input doAnother
While doAnother == "y" OR doAnother == "Y"
```

Program Output (with Input Shown in Bold)

```
Enter an item's wholesale cost.
10.00 [Enter]
The retail price is $25
Do you have another item? (Enter y for yes.)
y [Enter]
```

Program Output (with Input Shown in Bold) *(continued)*
```
Enter an item's wholesale cost.
15.00 [Enter]
The retail price is $37.50
Do you have another item? (Enter y for yes.)
y [Enter]
Enter an item's wholesale cost.
12.50 [Enter]
The retail price is $31.25
Do you have another item? (Enter y for yes.)
n [Enter]
```

Figure 8-7 Flowchart for Program 8-5

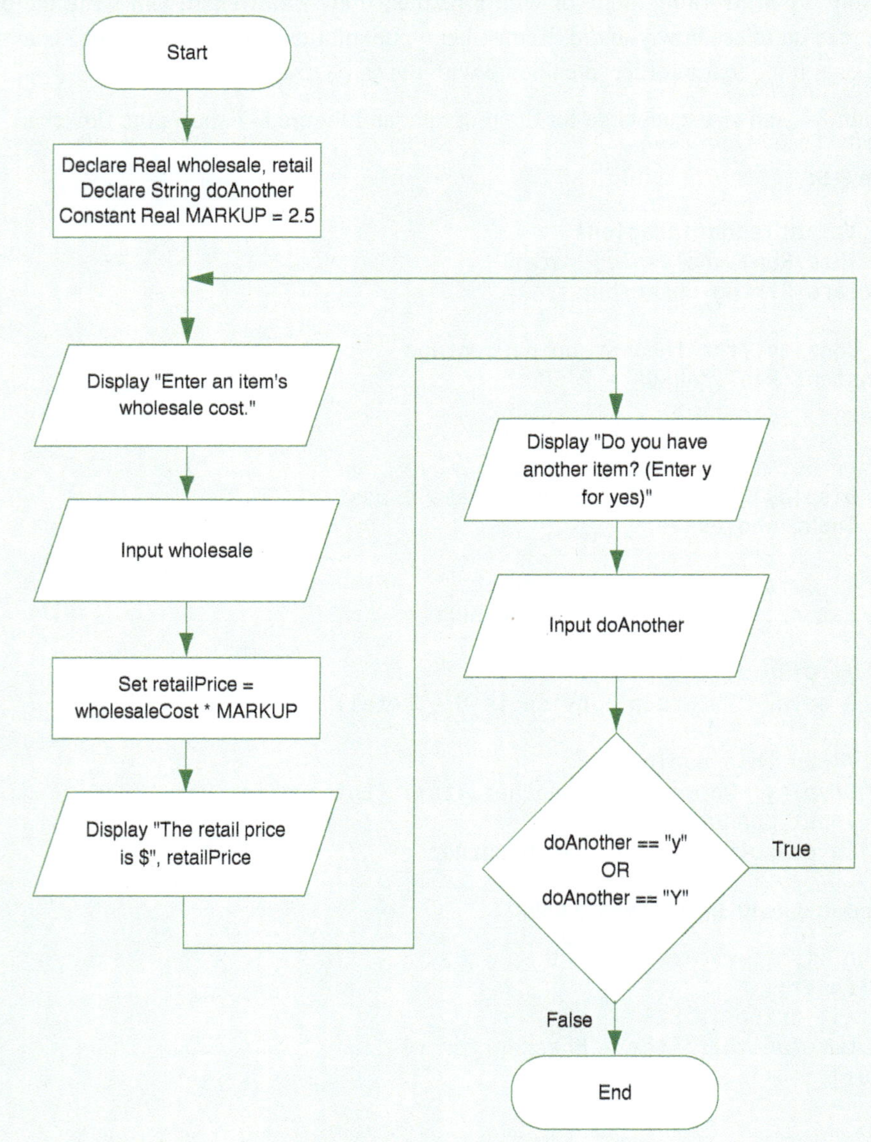

In the pseudocode, a `Do-While` loop appears in lines 8 through 22. Inside the loop, lines 10 through 11 get an item's wholesale cost, line 14 calculates the item's retail price, and line 17 displays the item's retail price. Then, in line 20, the user is prompted "Do you have another item? (Enter y for yes.)" In line 21, the user's input is stored in the `doAnother` variable. In line 22, the following statement is the end of the `Do-While` loop:

```
While doAnother == "y" OR doAnother == "Y"
```

Notice that we are using the logical OR operator to test a compound Boolean expression. The expression on the left side of the OR operator will be true if `doAnother` is equal to lowercase `"y"`. The expression on the right side of the OR operator will be true if `doAnother` is equal to uppercase `"Y"`. If either of these subexpressions is true, the loop will iterate. This is a simple way to make a case insensitive comparison, which means that it does not matter whether the user enters uppercase or lowercase letters.

The `Do-Until` Loop

Both the `While` and the `Do-While` loops iterate as long as a condition is true. Sometimes, however, it is more convenient to write a loop that iterates until a condition is true—that is, a loop that iterates as long as a condition is false, and then stops when the condition becomes true.

For example, consider a machine in an automobile factory that paints cars as they move down the assembly line. When there are no more cars to paint, the machine stops. If you were programming such a machine, you would want to design a loop that causes the machine to paint cars until there are no more cars on the assembly line.

A loop that iterates until a condition is true is known as a `Do-Until` loop. Figure 8-8 shows the general logic of a `Do-Until` loop.

Figure 8-8 The logic of a `Do-Until` loop

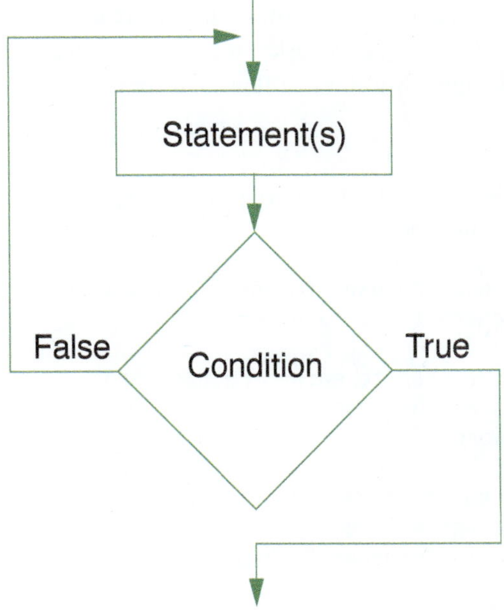

Notice that the Do-Until loop is a posttest loop. First, one or more statements are executed, and then a condition is tested. If the condition is false, the program's execution flows back to the point just above the first statement in the body of the loop, and this process repeats. If the condition is true, the program exits the loop.

NOTE: Because the Do-Until loop is a posttest loop, it will always iterate at least one time.

Writing a Do-Until Loop in Pseudocode

In pseudocode, we will use the Do-Until statement to write a Do-Until loop. Here is the general format of the Do-Until statement:

```
Do
   statement
   statement
   etc.
Until   condition
```

These statements are the body of the loop. They are always performed once, and then repeated until the condition is true.

In the general format, the statements that appear in the lines between the Do and the Until clauses are the body of the loop. The *condition* that appears after the While clause is a Boolean expression. When the loop executes, the statements in the body of the loop are executed, and then the *condition* is tested. If the *condition* is true, the program exits the loop. If the *condition* is false, the loop starts over and the statements in the body are executed again.

As shown in the general format, you should use the following conventions when you write a Do–Until statement:

- Make sure the Do clause and the Until clause are aligned.
- Indent the statements in the body of the loop.

The pseudocode in Program 8-6 shows an example of the Do-Until loop. The loop in lines 6 through 16 repeatedly asks the user to enter a password until the string "prospero" is entered. Figure 8-9 shows a flowchart for the program.

Program 8-6:

```
1  // Declare a variable to hold the password.
2  Declare String password
3
4  // Repeatedly ask the user to enter a password
5  // until the correct one is entered.
6  Do
7     // Prompt the user to enter the password.
8     Display "Enter the password."
9     Input password
10
11    // Display an error message if the wrong
12    // password was entered.
13    If password != "prospero" Then
```

Program 8-6: *(continued)*

```
        Display "Sorry, try again."
     End If
  Until password == "prospero"

  // Indicate that the password is confirmed.
  Display "Password confirmed."
```

Program Output (with Input Shown in Bold)

Enter the password.
ariel [Enter]
Sorry, try again.
Enter the password.
caliban [Enter]
Sorry, try again.
Enter the password.
prospero [Enter]
Password confirmed.

Figure 8-9 Flowchart for Program 8.6

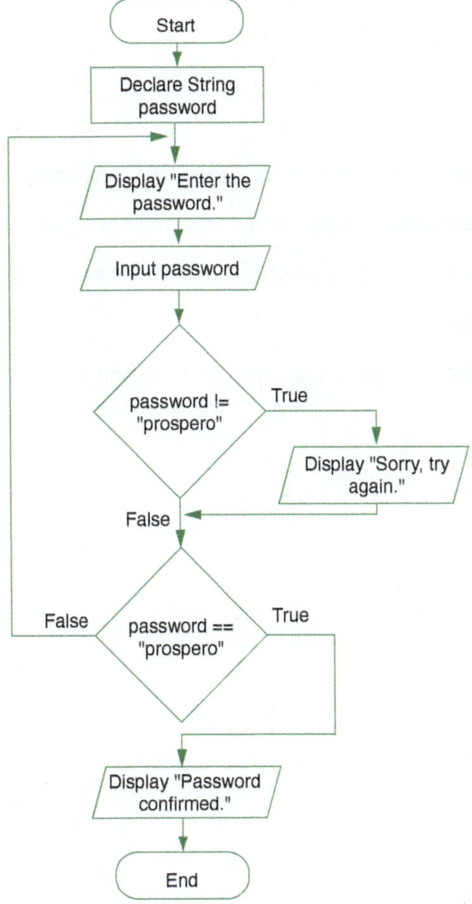

NOTE: Not all programming languages provide a Do-Until loop because you can write a Do-While loop that is logically equivalent to any Do-Until loop.

Deciding Which Loop to Use

In this section, we have introduced three different types of condition-controlled loop: the While loop, the Do-While loop, and the Do-Until loop. When you write a program that requires a condition-controlled loop, you will have to decide which loop to use.

You want to use the While loop to repeat a task as long as a condition is true. The While loop is a pretest loop, so it is ideal in situations where the condition might be false to start with, and in such cases you do not want the loop to iterate at all. The pseudocode that you saw in Program 8-2 is a good example.

The Do-While loop is also a candidate in situations where a task must be repeated as long as a condition is true. It is a posttest loop, so it is the best choice when you always want the task to be performed at least once, regardless of whether the condition is true or false to start with.

The Do-Until loop is also a posttest loop, so it performs a task at least once. It is the best choice when you want to perform a task until a condition is true. The Do-Until loop will repeat as long as its condition is false. When the condition is true, the Do-Until loop stops.

Checkpoint

8.4 What is a loop iteration?

8.5 What is the difference between a pretest loop and a posttest loop?

8.6 Does the While loop test its condition before or after it performs an iteration?

8.7 Does the Do-While loop test its condition before or after it performs an iteration?

8.8 What is an infinite loop?

8.9 What is the difference between a Do-While loop and a Do-Until loop?

8.3 Count-Controlled Loops and the For Statement

A count-controlled loop iterates a specific number of times. Although you can write the logic of a condition-controlled loop so it iterates a specific number of times, most languages provide a loop known as the For loop, which is specifically designed as a count-controlled loop.

A count-controlled loop iterates a specific number of times. For example, suppose a business is open six days per week, and you are going to write a program that calculates the total sales for a week. You will need a loop that iterates exactly six times. Each time the loop iterates, it will prompt the user to enter the sales for one day.

The way that a count-controlled loop works is simple: the loop keeps a count of the number of times that it iterates, and when the count reaches a specified amount, the loop stops. A count-controlled loop uses a variable known as a **counter variable**, or simply **counter**, to store the number of iterations that it has performed. Using the counter variable, the loop typically performs the following three actions: initialization, test, and increment:

1. **Initialization**: Before the loop begins, the counter variable is initialized to a starting value. The starting value that is used will depend on the situation.
2. **Test**: The loop tests the counter variable by comparing it to a maximum value. If the counter variable is less than or equal to the maximum value, the loop iterates. If the counter is greater than the maximum value, the program exits the loop.
3. **Increment**: To **increment** a variable means to increase its value. During each iteration, the loop increments the counter variable by adding 1 to it.

Figure 8-10 shows the general logic of a count-controlled loop. The initialization, test, and increment operations are indicated with the 1, 2, and 3 callouts.

Figure 8-10 Logic of a count-controlled loop

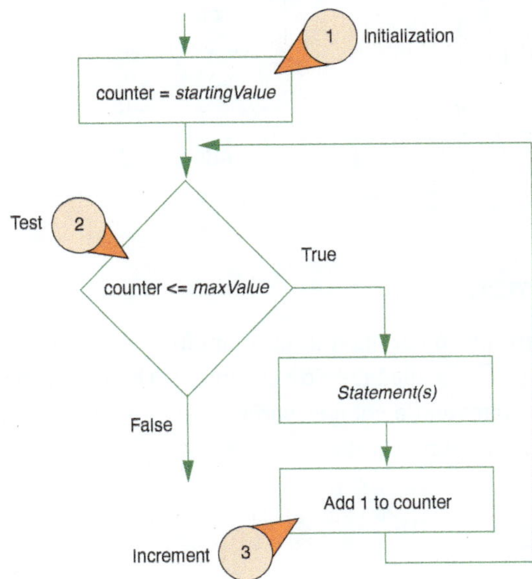

In the flowchart, assume that counter is an Integer variable. The first step is to set counter to the appropriate starting value. Then, determine whether counter is less than or equal to the maximum value. If this is true, the body of the loop executes. Otherwise, the program exits the loop. Notice that in the body of the loop one or more statements are executed, and then 1 is added to counter.

For example, look at the flowchart in Figure 8-11. First, an Integer variable named counter is declared and initialized with the starting value 1. Then, the expression counter <= 5 is tested. If this expression is true the message "Hello world" is displayed and 1 is added to counter. Otherwise, the program exits the loop. If you follow the logic of this program you will see that the loop will iterate five times.

Figure 8-11 A count-controlled loop

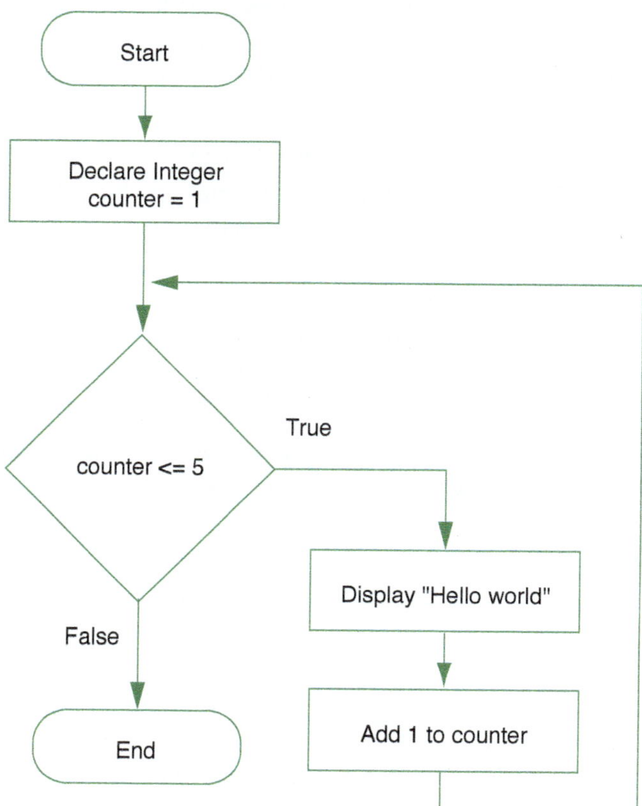

The For Statement

VideoNote
The For Statement

Count-controlled loops are so common in programming that most languages provide a statement just for them. This is usually called the For statement. The For statement is specifically designed to initialize, test, and increment a counter variable. Here is the general format that we will use to write the For statement in pseudocode:

```
For counterVariable = startingValue To maxValue
    statement
    statement
    statement
    etc.
End For
```

These statements are the body of the loop.

In the general format, *counterVariable* is the name of a variable that is used as a counter, *startingValue* is the value that the counter will be initially set to, and *maxValue* is the maximum value that the counter can contain. When the loop executes, the following actions are performed:

1. The *counterVariable* is set to the *startingValue*.
2. The *counterVariable* is compared to the *maxValue*. If the *counterVariable* is greater than *maxValue*, the loop stops. Otherwise:
   a. The statements that appear in the body of the loop are executed.
   b. The *counterVariable* is incremented.
   c. The loop starts over again at Step 2.

An actual `For` loop is easy to understand, so let's look at one. The pseudocode in Program 8-7 uses a `For` loop to display "Hello world" five times. The flowchart in Figure 8-12 shows the logic of the program.

Program 8-7: 

```
1 Declare Integer counter
2 Constant Integer MAX_VALUE = 5
3
4 For counter = 1 To MAX_VALUE
5    Display "Hello world"
6 End For
```

Program Output

```
Hello world
Hello world
Hello world
Hello world
Hello world
```

Line 1 declares an `Integer` variable that will be used as the counter variable. You do not have to name the variable `counter` (you are free to name it anything you wish), but in many cases that is an appropriate name. Line 2 declares a constant named `MAX_VALUE` that will be used as the counter's maximum value. The `For` loop begins in line 4 with the statement `For counter = 1 To MAX_VALUE`. This specifies that the `counter` variable will start with the value 1 and will end with the value 5. At the end of each loop iteration, the `counter` variable will be incremented by 1, so this loop will iterate five times. Each time it iterates, it displays "Hello world."

Notice that the loop does not contain a statement to increment the `counter` variable. This happens automatically in a `For` loop, at the end of each iteration. For that reason, you should be careful not to place a statement that modifies the `counter` variable inside the body of a `For` loop. Doing so will usually disrupt the way the `For` loop works.

Figure 8-12 Flowchart for Program 8-7

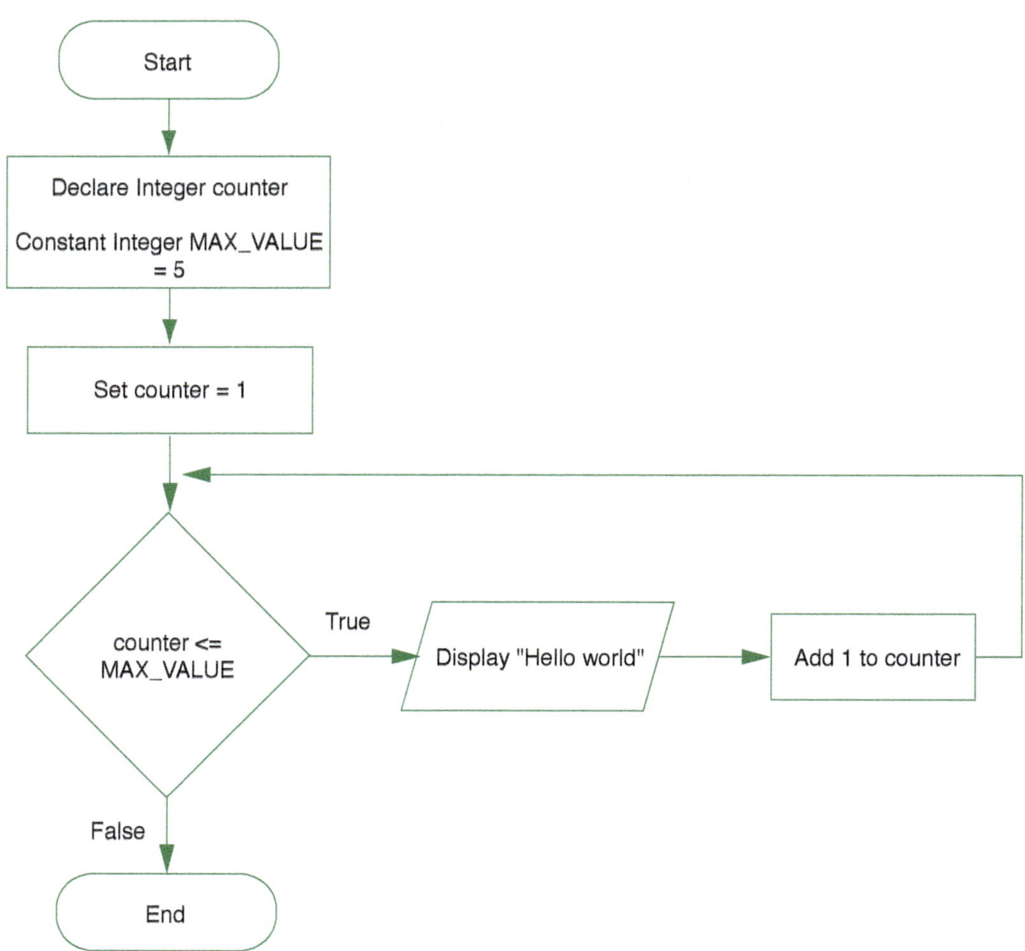

TIP: Program 8-7 has a constant, MAX_VALUE, that represents the counter variable's maximum value. The first line of the loop could have been written as follows, to achieve the same result:

```
For counter = 1 To 5
```

Although creating the named constant is not necessary for this simple program, creating named constants to represent important values is a good habit. Named constants make a program easier to read and easier to maintain.

Flowcharting the For Statement

The flowchart in Figure 8-12 shows some statements that do not appear in the pseudocode shown in Program 8-7. Specifically, the flowchart shows a statement that initializes the counter variable, and a statement that increments the counter variable. Figure 8-13 shows the flowchart again, pointing out where these operations appear.

Figure 8-13 The counter variable's initialization and increment

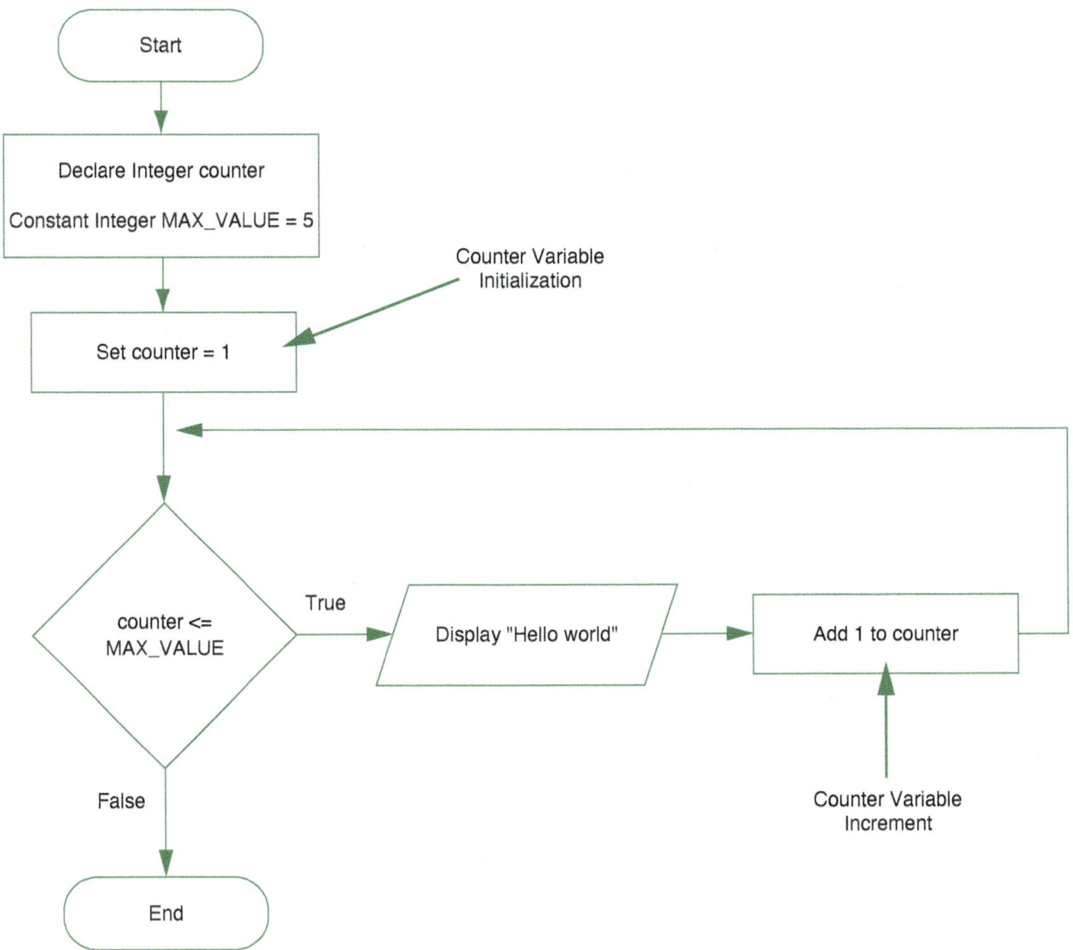

These statements do not appear in the pseudocode because they are implied by the `For` statement. When we read the pseudocode statement `For counter = 1 To MAX_VALUE`, we understand that `counter` is initialized with the value 1, and that `counter` is incremented each time the loop iterates.

To make the flowchart match the pseudocode, we introduce a new symbol to represent the For statement. The new symbol is a hexagon, as shown in Figure 8-14.

Figure 8-14 Flowcharting symbol for the For statement

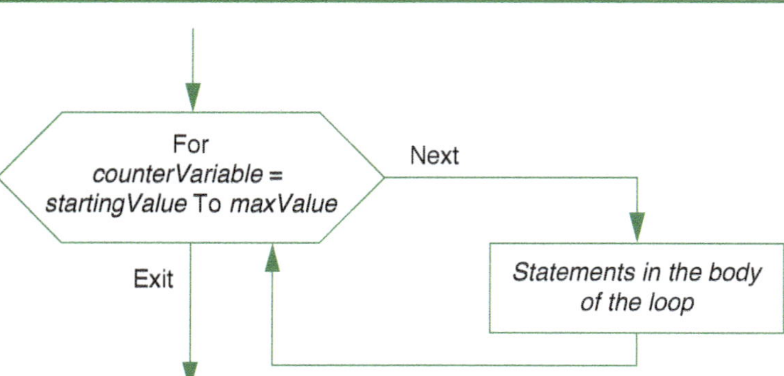

Inside the hexagon, we write the For statement that shows the name of the counter variable, the counter variable's starting value, and the counter variable's maximum value. Notice that the hexagon has two branches: *Next* and *Exit*. Each time the loop iterates, the program follows the *Next* branch to execute the statements inside the body of the loop. When the loop has finished, the program follows the *Exit* branch. When we use this symbol in our flowcharts, we do not have to show the steps for initializing the counter variable and incrementing the counter variable. It is understood that these steps happen as part of the For statement. Figure 8-15 shows a flowchart for Program 8-7 using this new symbol for the For statement.

Figure 8-15 Another flowchart for Program 8-7

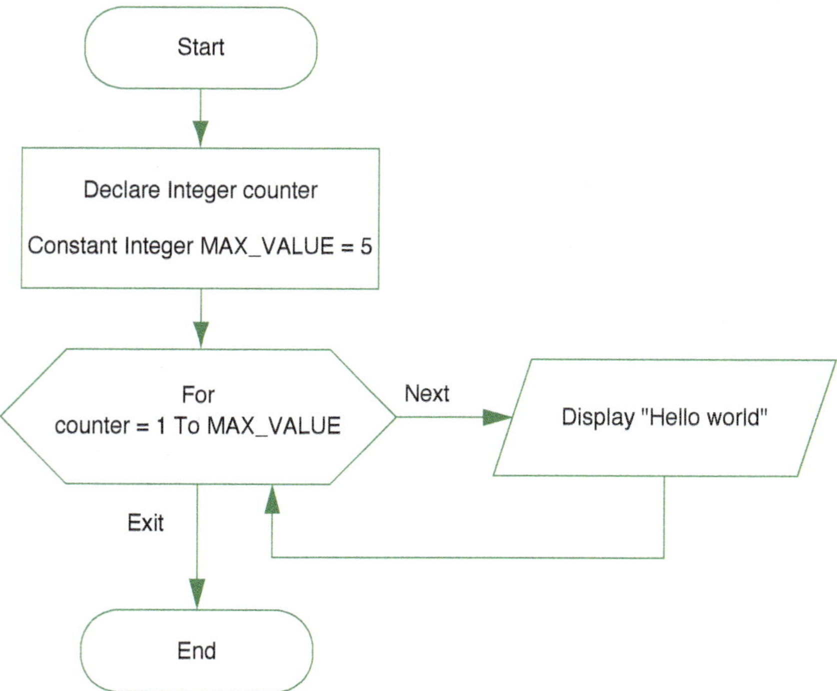

Using the Counter Variable in the Body of the Loop

In a count-controlled loop, the primary purpose of the counter variable is to store the number of times that the loop has iterated. In some situations, it is also helpful to use the counter variable in a calculation or other task within the body of the loop. For example, suppose you need to write a program that displays the numbers 1 through 10 and their squares, in a table similar to the following:

Number	Square
1	1
2	4
3	9
4	16
5	25
6	36
7	49
8	64
9	81
10	100

This can be accomplished by writing a count-controlled loop that iterates 10 times. During the first iteration, the counter variable will be set to 1, during the second iteration it will be set to 2, and so forth. Because the counter variable will take on the values 1 through 10 during the loop's execution, you can use it in the calculation inside the loop.

The flowchart in Figure 8-16 shows the logic of such a program. Notice that in the body of the loop, the counter variable is used in the following calculation:

```
Set square = counter^2
```

This assigns the result of `counter^2` to the square variable. After performing this calculation, the contents of the `counter` variable and the `square` variable are displayed. Then, 1 is added to `counter` and the loop starts over again.

Program 8-8 shows the pseudocode for the program. Notice that the word `Tab` is used in the `Display` statements in lines 8 and 18. This is simply a way of indicating in pseudocode that we are indenting the screen output. For example, look at the following statement, which appears in line 18:

```
Display counter, Tab, square
```

This statement displays the contents of the `counter` variable, indents (or "tabs over"), and then displays the contents of the `square` variable. As a result, the numbers that are displayed will be aligned in two columns. Most programming languages provide a way to indent, or tab, screen output.

Figure 8-16 Displaying the numbers 1 through 10 and their squares

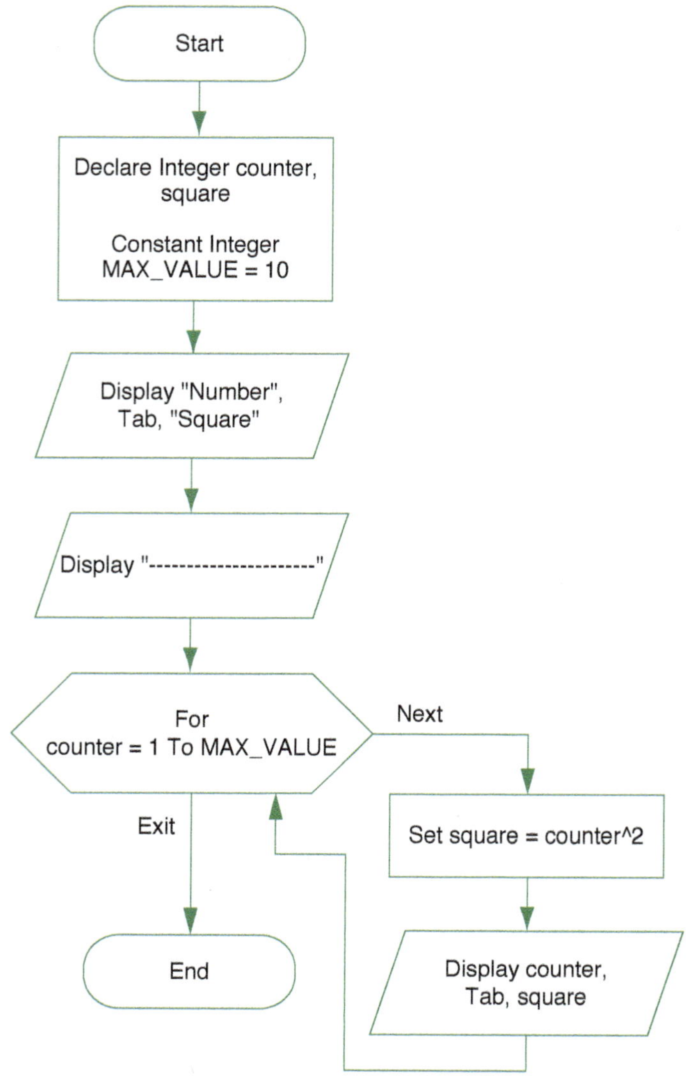

Program 8-8:

```
// Variables
Declare Integer counter, square
// Constant for the maximum value
Constant Integer MAX_VALUE = 10
// Display table headings.
Display "Number", Tab, "Square"
Display "----------------------"
// Display the numbers 1 through 10 and
```

Program 8-8: *(continued)*

```
// their squares.
For counter = 1 To MAX_VALUE
   // Calculate number squared.
   Set square = counter^2

   // Display number and number squared.
   Display counter, Tab, square
End For
```

Program Output

```
Number          Square
--------------------------
   1               1
   2               4
   3               9
   4              16
   5              25
   6              36
   7              49
   8              64
   9              81
  10             100
```

Incrementing by Values Other Than 1

The amount by which the counter variable is incremented in a `For` loop is known as the **step amount**. By default, the step amount is 1. Most languages provide a way to change the step amount. This gives you the ability to increment the counter variable by any value you wish.

In pseudocode, we will use the optional `Step` clause to specify a step value in a `For` loop. For example, look at the following pseudocode:

```
For counter = 0 To 100 Step 10
   Display counter
End For
```

In this loop, the starting value of the `counter` variable is 0, and its ending value is 100. The `Step` clause specifies a step value of 10, which means that 10 is added to the `counter` variable at the end of each iteration. During the first iteration, `counter` is 0, during the second iteration, `counter` is 10, during the third iteration, `counter` is 20, and so forth.

The pseudocode in Program 8-9 gives another demonstration. The program displays all of the odd numbers from 1 through 11. Figure 8-17 shows a flowchart for the program. Notice that the step value is shown in the hexagon symbol for the `For` statement.

Program 8-9: 

```
// Declare a counter variable
Declare Integer counter

// Constant for the maximum value
Constant Integer MAX_VALUE = 11
```

Program 8-9: *(continued)*

```

// Display the odd numbers from 1 through 11.
For counter = 1 To MAX_VALUE Step 2
   Display counter
End For
```

Program Output

```
1
3
5
7
9
```

Figure 8-17 Flowchart for Program 8-9

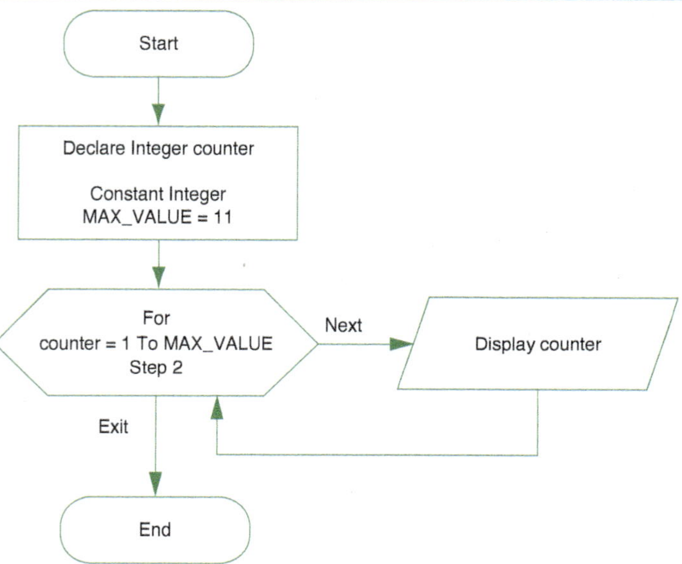

In the Spotlight:

Designing a Count-Controlled Loop with the For Statement

Amanda just inherited a European sports car from her uncle. Amanda lives in the United States, and she is afraid she will get a speeding ticket because the car's speedometer works in kilometers per hour. She has asked you to write a program that displays a table of speeds in kilometers per hour with their values converted to miles per hour. The formula for converting kilometers per hour to miles per hour is:

$$MPH = KPH \times 0.6214$$

In the formula, *MPH* is the speed in miles per hour and *KPH* is the speed in kilometers per hour.

The table that your program displays should show speeds from 60 kilometers per hour through 130 kilometers per hour, in increments of 10, along with their values converted to miles per hour. The table should look something like this:

KPH	MPH
60	37.284
70	43.498
80	49.712
etc. . . .	
130	80.782

On Your Own: Working alone or with a partner draw a flowchart, and write the pseudocode. Then, read on to see how you did. Remember, your solution does not have to be exactly the same as the one in the text in order to come up with the same result.

You can write a For loop that uses a counter variable to hold the kilometer-per-hour speeds. The counter's starting value will be 60, its ending value will be 130, and a step value of 10 will be used. Inside the loop you will use the counter variable to calculate a speed in miles-per-hour. Program 8-10 shows the pseudocode for the program, and Figure 8-18 shows a flowchart.

Program 8-10:

```
// Declare variables to hold speeds in MPH and KPH.
Declare Real mph
Declare Integer kph

// Display the table headings.
Display "KPH", Tab, "MPH"
Display "----------------------"

// Display the speeds.
For kph = 60 To 130 Step 10
   // Calculate the miles-per-hour.
   Set mph = kph * 0.6214

   // Display KPH and MPH.
   Display kph, Tab, mph
End For
```

Program Output

```
KPH            MPH
------------------------
60             37.284
70             43.498
80             49.712
90             55.926
100            62.14
110            68.354
120            74.568
130            80.782
```

Notice that a variable named kph is used as the counter. Until now we have used the name counter for our counter variables. In this program, however, kph is a better name for the counter because it will hold speeds in kilometers-per-hour.

Figure 8-18 Flowchart for Program 8-10

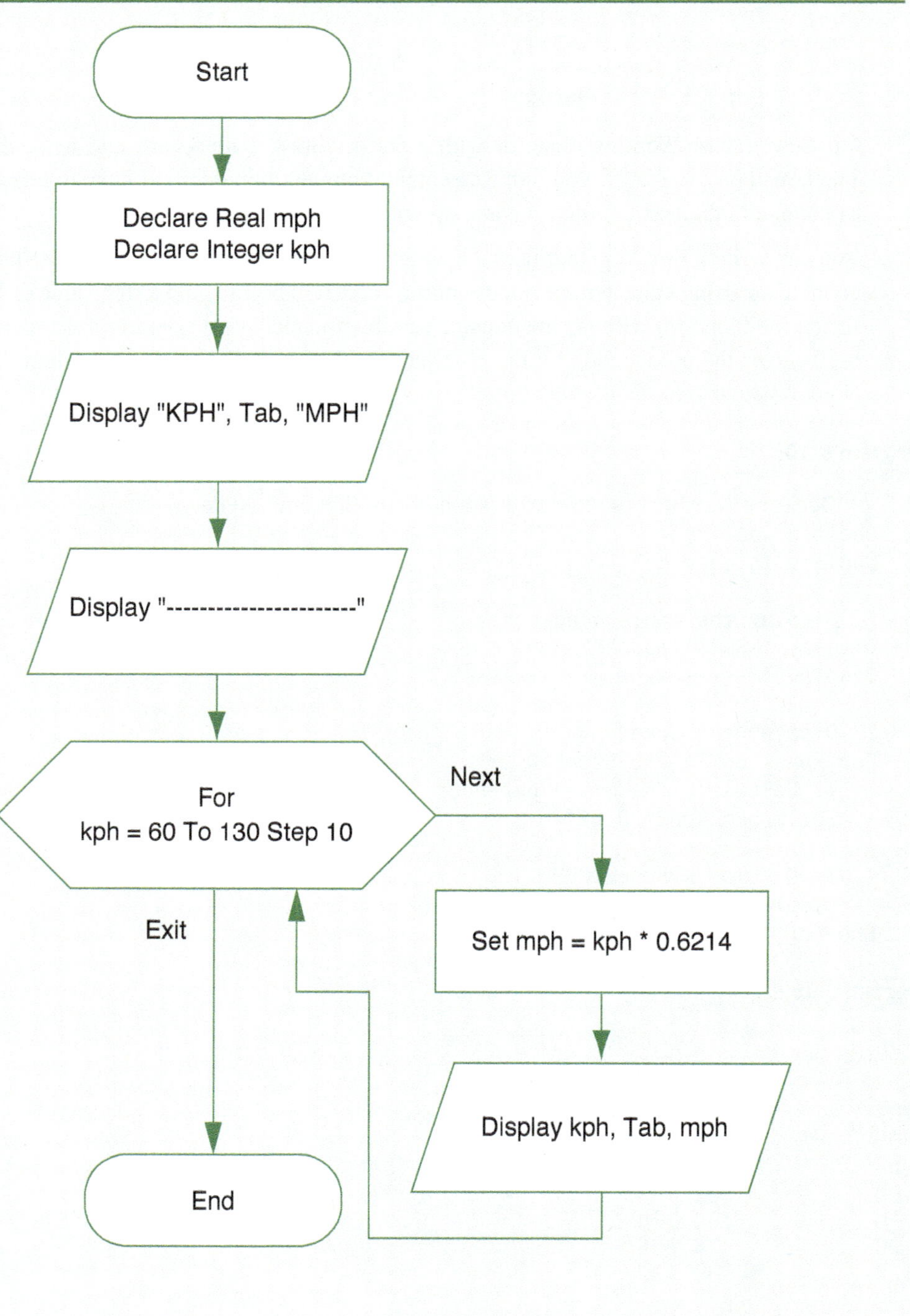

Counting Backward by Decrementing the Counter Variable

Although the counter variable is usually incremented in a count-controlled loop, you can alternatively decrement the counter variable. To **decrement** a variable means to decrease its value. In a For statement, you specify a negative step value to decrement the counter variable. For example, look at the following loop:

```
For counter = 10 To 1 Step -1
   Display counter
End For
```

In this loop, the starting value of the counter variable is 10, and its ending value is 1. The step value is -1, which means that 1 is subtracted from counter at the end of each iteration. During the first iteration, counter is 10; during the second iteration, counter is 9; and so forth. If this were an actual program, it would display the numbers 10, 9, 8, and so forth, down to 1.

Letting the User Control the Number of Iterations

In many cases, the programmer knows the exact number of iterations that a loop must perform. For example, recall Program 8-8, which displays a table showing the numbers 1 through 10 and their squares. When the pseudocode was written, the programmer knew that the loop had to iterate 10 times. A constant named MAX_VALUE was initialized with the value 10, and the loop was written as follows:

```
For counter = 1 To MAX_VALUE
```

As a result, the loop iterates exactly 10 times. Sometimes, however, the programmer needs to let the user decide the number of times that a loop should iterate. For example, what if you want Program 8-8 to be a bit more versatile by allowing the user to specify the maximum value displayed by the loop? The pseudocode in Program 8-11 shows how you can accomplish this.

Program 8-11:

```
// Variables
Declare Integer counter, square, upperLimit

// Get the upper limit.
Display "This program displays numbers, starting at 1,"
Display "and their squares. How high should I go?"
Input upperLimit

// Display table headings.
Display "Number", Tab, "Square"
Display "--------------------"

// Display the numbers and their squares.
For counter = 1 To upperLimit
   // Calculate number squared.
   Set square = counter^2

   // Display number and number squared.
   Display counter, Tab, square
End For
```

Program 8-11: *(continued)*

Program Output (with Input Shown in Bold)

```
This program displays numbers, starting at 1,and their squares. How high should I go?
5 [Enter]

     Number        Square
---------------------------------
1                    1
2                    4
3                    9
4                   16
5                   25
```

Lines 5 and 6 ask the user how high the numbers in the table should go, and the statement in line 7 stores the user's input in the `upperLimit` variable. Then, the `For` loop uses the `upperLimit` variable as the counter's ending value:

```
For counter = 1 To upperLimit
```

As a result, the `counter` variable starts with 1, and ends with the value in upperLimit. In addition to specifying the counter's ending value, you can also specify its starting value. The pseudocode in Program 8-12 shows an example. In this program, the user specifies both the starting value and the ending value of the numbers displayed in the table. Notice that in line 20 the `For` loop uses variables to specify both the starting and ending values of the `counter` variable..

Program 8-12:

```
1 // Variables
2 Declare Integer counter, square,
3                 lowerLimit, upperLimit
4
5 // Get the lower limit.
6 Display "This program displays numbers and"
7 Display "their squares. What number should"
8 Display "I start with?"
9 Input lowerLimit
10
11 // Get the upper limit.
12 Display "What number should I end with?"
13 Input upperLimit
14
15 // Display table headings.
16 Display "Number", Tab, "Square"
17 Display "-----------------------"
18
19 // Display the numbers and their squares.
20 For counter = lowerLimit To upperLimit
21     // Calculate number squared.
22     Set square = counter^2
23
24     // Display number and number squared.
25     Display counter, Tab, square
26 End For
```

Program 8-12: *(continued)*

Program Output (with Input Shown in Bold)

```
This program displays numbers and
their squares. What number should
I start with?
3 [Enter]
What number should I end with?
7 [Enter]

    Number      Square
  ---------------------------
      3            9
      4           16
      5           25
      6           36
      7           49
```

Designing a Count-Controlled `While` Loop

In most situations, it is best to use the `For` statement to write a count-controlled loop. Most languages, however, make it possible to use any looping mechanism to create a count-controlled loop. For example, you can create a count-controlled `While` loop, a count-controlled `Do-While` loop, or a count-controlled `Do-Until` loop. Regardless of the type of mechanism that you use, all count-controlled loops perform an initialization, test, and increment operation on a counter variable.

In pseudocode, you can use the following general format to write a count-controlled `While` loop:

```
Declare Integer counter = startingValue   ← 1. Initialize a counter variable to the starting value.

While counter <= maxValue                 ← 2. Compare the counter to the maximum value.
    statement
    statement
    statement
    Set counter = counter + 1             ← 3. Add 1 to the counter variable during each iteration.
End While
```

The 1, 2, and 3 callouts show where the initialization, test, and increment actions are performed.

1 shows the declaration of an `Integer` variable that will be used as the counter. The variable is initialized with the appropriate starting value.

2 shows where the `While` loop tests the expression counter `<=` *`maxValue`*. In this general format, *`maxValue`* is the maximum value that the counter variable can be set to.

3 shows where 1 is added to the `counter` variable. In a `While` loop, the counter variable will not automatically be incremented. You have to explicitly write a statement that performs this action. It's important that you understand how this statement works, so let's take a closer look at it:

```
Set counter = counter + 1
```

This is how the statement would be executed by the computer: First, the computer would get the value of the expression on the right side of the `=` operator which is `counter + 1`. Then, that value would be assigned to the `counter` variable. The effect of the statement is that 1 is added to the counter variable.

WARNING! If you forget to increment the counter variable in a count-controlled While loop, the loop will iterate an infinite number of times.

The pseudocode in Program 8-13 shows an example of a count-controlled `While` loop. This program follows the same logic that you previously saw in Figure 8-11, and displays "Hello world" five times. Figure 8-19 points out where the counter variable's initialization, test, and increment occur in the pseudocode.

Program 8-13:

```
// Declare and initialize a counter variable.
Declare Integer counter = 1

// Constant for the maximum value
Constant Integer MAX_VALUE = 5

While counter <= MAX_VALUE
   Display "Hello world"
   Set counter = counter + 1
End While
```

Program Output

```
Hello world
Hello world
Hello world
Hello world
Hello world
```

Figure 8-19 The initialization, test, and increment of the counter variable

```
                      // Declare and initialize a counter variable.
Initialization (1) -->Declare Integer counter = 1

                      // Constant for the maximum value
                      Constant Integer MAX_VALUE = 5

                      While counter <= MAX_VALUE <-- (2) Test
                         Display "Hello world"
Increment (3) -->        Set counter = counter + 1
                      End While
```

The pseudocode in Program 8-14 shows another example. This program produces the same output that was produced by Program 8-8: the numbers 1 through 10 and their squares. The flowchart that you previously saw in Figure 8-16 shows the logic of this program.

Program 8-14:

```
// Variables
Declare Integer counter = 1
Declare Integer square

// Constant for the maximum value
Constant Integer MAX_VALUE = 10

// Display table headings.
Display "Number", Tab, "Square"
Display "--------------------"

// Display the numbers 1 through 10 and
// their squares.
While counter <= MAX_VALUE
   // Calculate the square of a number.
   Set square = counter^2

   // Display the number and its square.
   Display counter, Tab, square

   // Increment counter.
   Set counter = counter + 1
End While
```

Program Output

```
Number      Square
--------------------
1           1
2           4
3           9
4           16
5           25
6           36
7           49
8           64
9           81
10          100
```

Incrementing by Values Other Than 1

In Programs 8-13 and 8-14 the counter variable is incremented by 1 during each loop iteration, with a statement such as this:

```
Set counter = counter + 1
```

This statement can be easily modified to increment the counter variable by values other than 1. For example, you could add 2 to the counter variable with the following statement:

```
Set counter = counter + 2
```

The pseudocode in Program 8-15 demonstrates how you can use this statement in a count-controlled `While` loop. The program displays all of the odd numbers from 1 through 11.

Program 8-15:

```
// Declare a counter variable
Declare Integer counter = 1

// Constant for the maximum value
Constant Integer MAX_VALUE = 11

// Display the odd numbers from 1
// through 11.
While counter <= MAX_VALUE
   Display counter
   Set counter = counter + 2
End While
```

Program Output

```
1
3
5
7
9
11
```

Counting Backward by Decrementing

Previously you saw how a negative step value can be used to decrement the counter variable in a `For` statement. In a count-controlled `While` loop, you decrement the counter variable with a statement such as the following:

```
Set counter = counter - 1
```

This statement subtracts 1 from the `counter` variable. If the `counter` variable is set to the value 5 before this statement executes, it will be set to 4 after the statement executes. The pseudocode in Program 8-16 demonstrates how you can use this statement in a `While` loop. The program counts backward from 10 down to 1.

Program 8-16:

```
// Declare a counter variable
Declare Integer counter = 10

// Constant for the minimum value
Constant Integer MIN_VALUE = 1

// Display a count-down.
Display "And the countdown begins..."
While counter >= MIN_VALUE
   Display counter
   Set counter = counter - 1
End While
Display "Blast off!"
```

Program 8-16: *(continued)*

Program Output

```
And the countdown begins...
10
 9
 8
 7
 6
 5
 4
 3
 2
 1
Blast off!
```

Let's take a closer look at this program. Notice that line 11 subtracts 1 from the `counter` variable. Because we are counting backward, we have to reverse many parts of the logic. For example, in line 2 the `counter` variable must be initialized with the value 10 instead of 1. This is because 10 is the counter's starting value in this program. Also, in line 5 we create a constant to represent the counter's minimum value (which is 1) instead of the maximum value. Because we are counting down, we want the loop to stop when it reaches 1. Finally, notice that we are using the `>=` relational operator in line 9. In this program we want the loop to iterate as long as the counter is greater than or equal to 1. When the counter becomes less than 1, the loop should stop.

Checkpoint

8.10 What is a counter variable?

8.11 What three actions do count-controlled loops typically perform using the counter variable?

8.12 When you increment a variable, what are you doing? When you decrement a variable, what are you doing?

8.13 Look at the following pseudocode. If it were a real program, what would it display?

```
Declare Integer number = 5
Set number = number + 1
Display number
```

8.14 Look at the following pseudocode. If it were a real program, what would it display?

```
Declare Integer counter
For counter = 1 To 5
   Display counter
End For
```

8.15 Look at the following pseudocode. If it were a real program, what would it display?

```
Declare Integer counter
For counter = 0 To 500 Step 100
  Display counter
End For
```

8.16 Look at the following pseudocode. If it were a real program, what would it display?

```
Declare Integer counter = 1
Constant Integer MAX = 8
While counter <= MAX
   Display counter
   Set counter = counter + 1
End While
```

8.17 Look at the following pseudocode. If it were a real program, what would it display?

```
Declare Integer counter = 1
Constant Integer MAX = 7
While counter <= MAX
   Display counter
   Set counter = counter + 2
End While
```

8.18 Look at the following pseudocode. If it were a real program, what would it display?

```
Declare Integer counter
Constant Integer MIN = 1
For counter = 5 To MIN Step -1
   Display counter
End For
```

8.4 Calculating a Running Total

A running total is a sum of numbers that accumulates with each iteration of a loop. The variable used to keep the running total is called an accumulator.

Many programming tasks require you to calculate the total of a series of numbers. For example, suppose you are writing a program for a game that calculates the total number of tokens a player collects in all levels. The program would read the number of tokens for each level as input and calculate the total of those numbers.

Programs that calculate the total of a series of numbers typically use two elements:

- A loop that reads each number in the series.
- A variable that accumulates the total of the numbers as they are read.

The variable that is used to accumulate the total of the numbers is called an **accumulator**. It is often said that the loop keeps a **running total** because it accumulates the total as it reads each number in the series. Figure 8-20 shows the general logic of a loop that calculates a running total.

Figure 8-20 General logic for calculating a running total

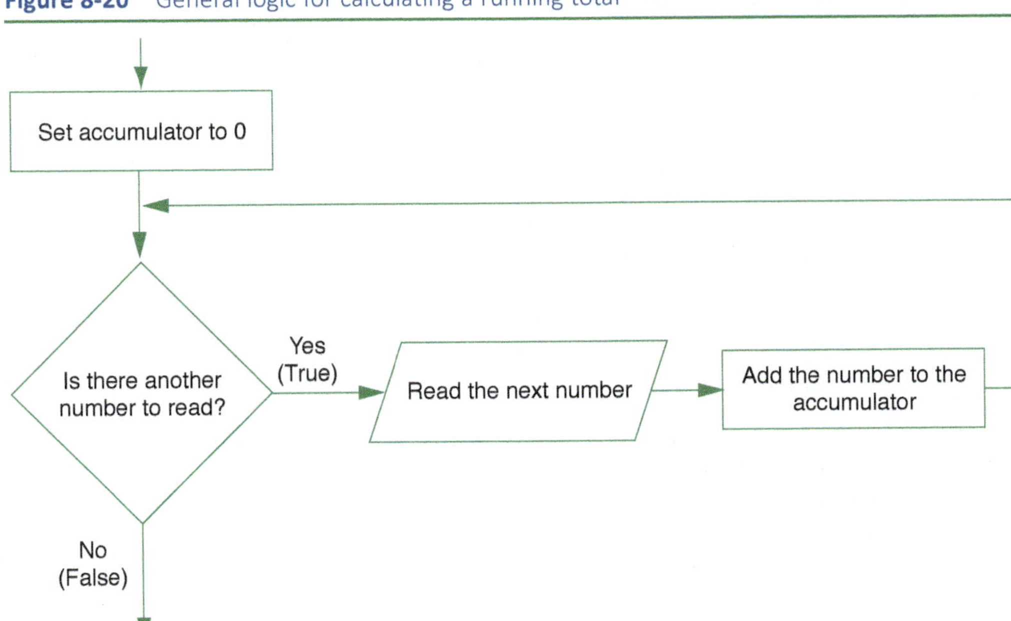

When the loop finishes, the accumulator will contain the total of the numbers that were read by the loop. Notice that the first step in the flowchart is to set the accumulator variable to 0. This is a critical step. Each time the loop reads a number, it adds it to the accumulator. If the accumulator starts with any value other than 0, it will not contain the correct total when the loop finishes.

Let's look at the design of a program that calculates a running total. The pseudocode shown in Program 8-17 allows the user to enter five numbers, and it displays the total of the numbers entered.

Program 8-17: 

```
// Declare a variable to hold each number
// entered by the user.
Declare Integer number

// Declare an accumulator variable,
// initialized with 0.
Declare Integer total = 0

// Declare a counter variable for the loop.
Declare Integer counter

// Explain what we are doing.
Display "This program calculates the"
Display "total of five numbers."

// Get five numbers and accumulate them.
For counter = 1 To 5
    Display "Enter a number."
```

Program 8-17: *(continued)*

```
19        Input number
20        Set total = total + number
21     End For
22
23     // Display the total of the numbers.
24     Display "The total is ", total
```

Program Output (with Input Shown in Bold)

```
This program calculates the
total of five numbers.
Enter a number.
2 [Enter]
Enter a number.
4 [Enter]
Enter a number.
6 [Enter]
Enter a number.
8 [Enter]
Enter a number.
10 [Enter]
The total is 30
```

First, let's look at the variable declarations. The `number` variable, declared in line 3, will be used to hold a number entered by the user. The `total` variable, declared in line 7, is the accumulator. Notice that it is initialized with the value 0. The `counter` variable, declared in line 10, will be used as a counter by the loop.

The `For` loop, in lines 17 through 21, does the work of getting the numbers from the user and calculating their total. Line 18 prompts the user to enter a number, and line 19 gets the user's input and stores it in the `number` variable. Then, the following statement in line 20 adds `number` to total:

```
Set total = total + number
```

After this statement executes, the value in the `number` variable will be added to the value in the `total` variable. When the loop finishes, the `total` variable will hold the sum of all the numbers that were added to it. This value is displayed in line 24. Figure 8-21 shows a flowchart for the Program 8-17.

Figure 8-21 Flowchart for Program 8-17

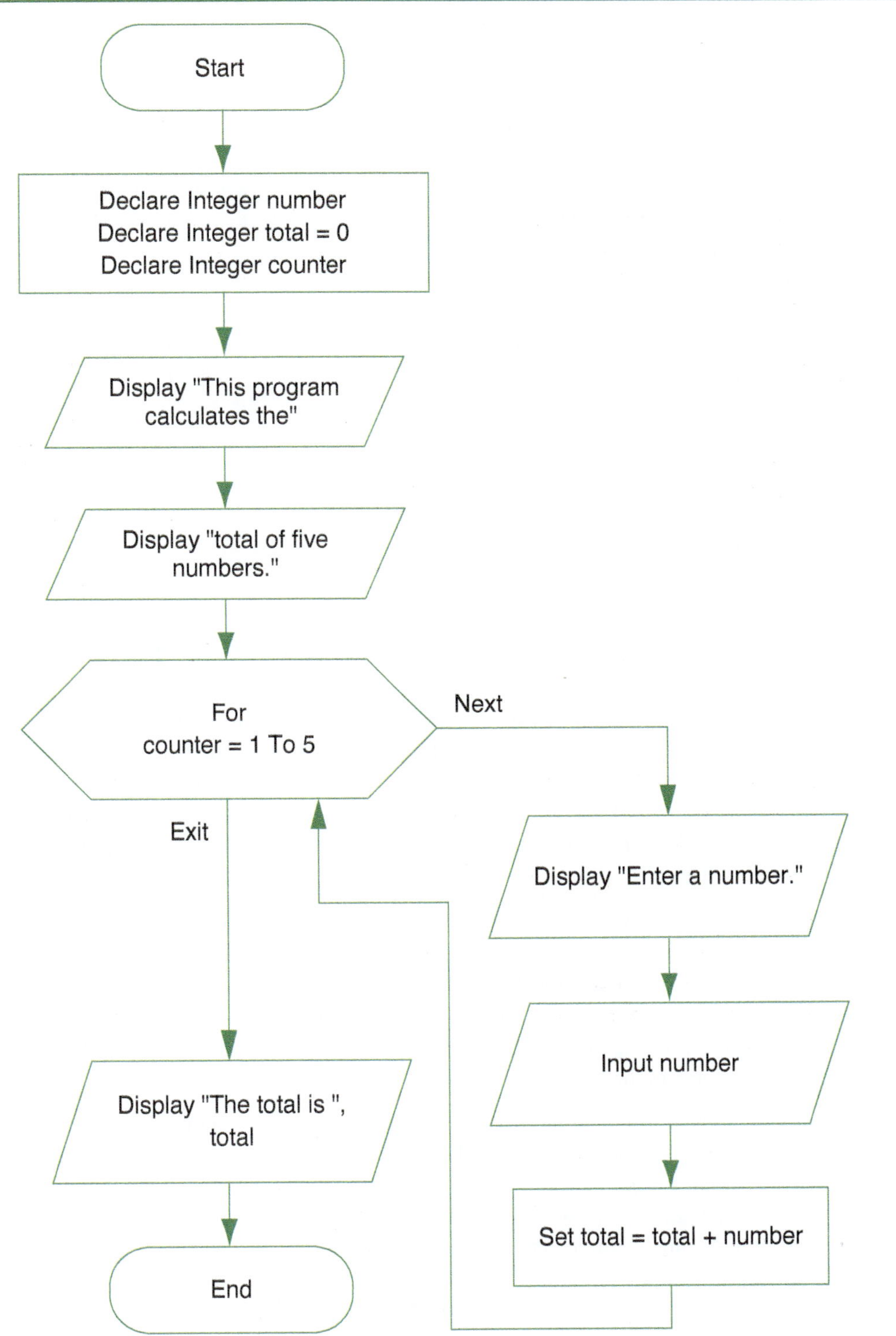

Checkpoint

8.19 A program that calculates the total of a series of numbers typically has what two elements?

8.20 What is an accumulator?

8.21 Should an accumulator be initialized to any specific value? Why or why not?

8.22 Look at the following pseudocode. If it were a real program, what would it display?

```
Declare Integer number1 = 10, number2 = 5
Set number1 = number1 + number2
Display number1
Display number2
```

8.23 Look at the following pseudocode. If it were a real program, what would it display?

```
Declare Integer counter, total = 0
For counter = 1 To 5
Set total = total + counter
End For
Display total
```

8.5 Sentinels

A sentinel is a special value that marks the end of a list of values.

Consider the following scenario: You are designing a program that will use a loop to process a long list of values. At the time you are designing the program, you do not know the number of values that will be in the list. In fact, the number of values in the list could be different each time the program is executed. What is the best way to design such a loop? Here are some techniques that you have seen already in this chapter, along with the disadvantages of using them when processing a long list of values:

- Ask the user, at the end of each loop iteration, whether there is another value to process. If the list of values is long, however, asking this question at the end of each loop iteration might make the program cumbersome for the user.
- Ask the user at the beginning of the program how many items the list contains. This might also inconvenience the user, however. If the list is very long, and the user does not know the number of items in the list, it will require the user to count them.

When processing a long list of values with a loop, perhaps a better technique is to use a sentinel. A **sentinel** is a special value that marks the end of a list of items. When a program reads the sentinel value, it knows it has reached the end of the list, so the loop terminates. For example, suppose a doctor wants a program to calculate the average weight of patients. The program might work like this: A loop prompts the user to enter either a patient's weight, or 0 if there are no more weights. When the program reads 0 as a weight, it interprets this as a signal that there are no more weights. The loop ends and the program displays the average weight.

A sentinel value must be unique enough that it will not be mistaken as a regular value in the list. In the example cited above, the doctor (or their medical assistant) enters 0 to signal the end of the list of weights. Because no patient's weight will be 0, this is a good value to use as a sentinel.

In the Spotlight:

Using a Sentinel

The county tax office calculates the annual taxes on property using the following formula:

$$\textit{Property Tax} = \textit{Property Value} \times 0.0065$$

Every day, a clerk in the tax office gets a list of properties and has to calculate the tax for each property on the list. You have been asked to design a program that the clerk can use to perform these calculations.

On Your Own: Working alone or with a partner, write the algorithm steps, draw a flowchart, and write the pseudocode. Then, read on to see how you did. Remember, your solution does not have to be exactly the same as the one in the text in order to come up with the same result.

In your interview with the tax clerk, you learn that each property is assigned a lot number, and all lot numbers are 1 or greater. You decide to write a loop that uses the number 0 as a sentinel value. During each loop iteration, the program will ask the clerk to enter either a property's lot number, or 0 to end. Program 8-18 shows the pseudocode for the program, and Figure 8-22 shows a flowchart.

Program 8-18:

```
// Declare variables.
Declare Real propertyValue, tax
Declare Integer lotNumber

// Constant for the tax factor.
Constant Real TAX_FACTOR = 0.0065

// Get the first lot number.
Display "Enter the property's lot number"
Display "(or enter 0 to end)."
Input lotNumber

// Continue processing as long as the user
// does not enter lot number 0.
While lotNumber != 0
   // Get the property's value.
   Display "Enter the property's value."
   Input propertyValue

   // Calculate the property's tax.
   Set tax = propertyValue * TAX_FACTOR

   // Display the tax.
   Display "The property's tax is $", tax

   // Get the next lot number.
   Display "Enter the lot number for the"
   Display "next property (or 0 to end)."
   Input lotNumber
End While
```

Program 8-18: *(continued)*

Program Output (with Input Shown in Bold)

```
Enter the property's lot number
(or enter 0 to end).
417 [Enter]
Enter the property's value.
100000 [Enter]
The property's tax is $650
Enter the lot number for the
next property (or 0 to end).
692 [Enter]
Enter the property's value.
60000 [Enter]
The property's tax is $390
Enter the lot number for the
next property (or 0 to end).
0 [Enter]
```

Figure 8-22 Flowchart for Program 4-18

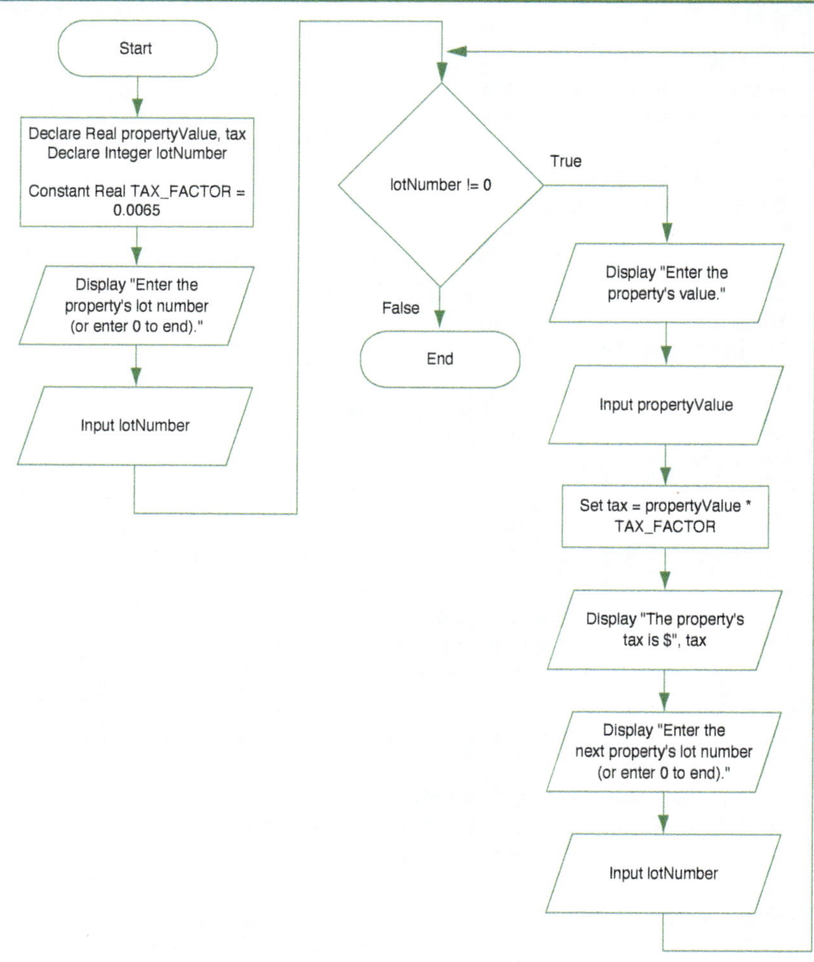

9.24 What is a sentinel?

9.25 Why should you take care to choose a unique value as a sentinel?

8.6 Nested Loops

A loop that is inside another loop is called a nested loop.

A **nested loop** is a loop that is inside another loop. A clock is a good example of something that works like a nested loop. The second hand, minute hand, and hour hand all spin around the face of the clock. The hour hand, however, only makes 1 revolution for every 12 of the minute hand's revolutions. And it takes 60 revolutions of the second hand for the minute hand to make 1 revolution. This means that for every complete revolution of the hour hand, the second hand has revolved 720 times. Here is pseudocode with a loop that partially simulates a digital clock. It displays the seconds from 0 to 59:

```
Declare Integer seconds
For seconds = 0 To 59
   Display seconds
End For
```

We can add a minutes variable and nest the loop above inside another loop that cycles through 60 minutes:

```
Declare Integer minutes, seconds
For minutes = 0 To 59
   For seconds = 0 To 59
      Display minutes, ":", seconds
   End For
End For
```

To make the simulated clock complete, another variable and loop can be added to count the hours:

```
Declare Integer hours, minutes, seconds
For hours = 0 To 23
   For minutes = 0 To 59
      For seconds = 0 To 59
         Display hours, ":", minutes, ":", seconds
      End For
   End For
End For
```

If this were a real program, its output would be:

```
0:0:0
0:0:1
0:0:2
```

(The program will count through each second of 24 hours.)

```
23:59:59
```

The innermost loop will iterate 60 times for each iteration of the middle loop. The middle loop will iterate 60 times for each iteration of the outermost loop. When the outermost loop has iterated 24 times, the middle loop will have iterated 1,440 times and the innermost loop will have iterated 86,400 times! Figure 8-23 shows a flowchart for the complete clock simulation program previously shown.

Figure 8-23 Flowchart for a clock simulator

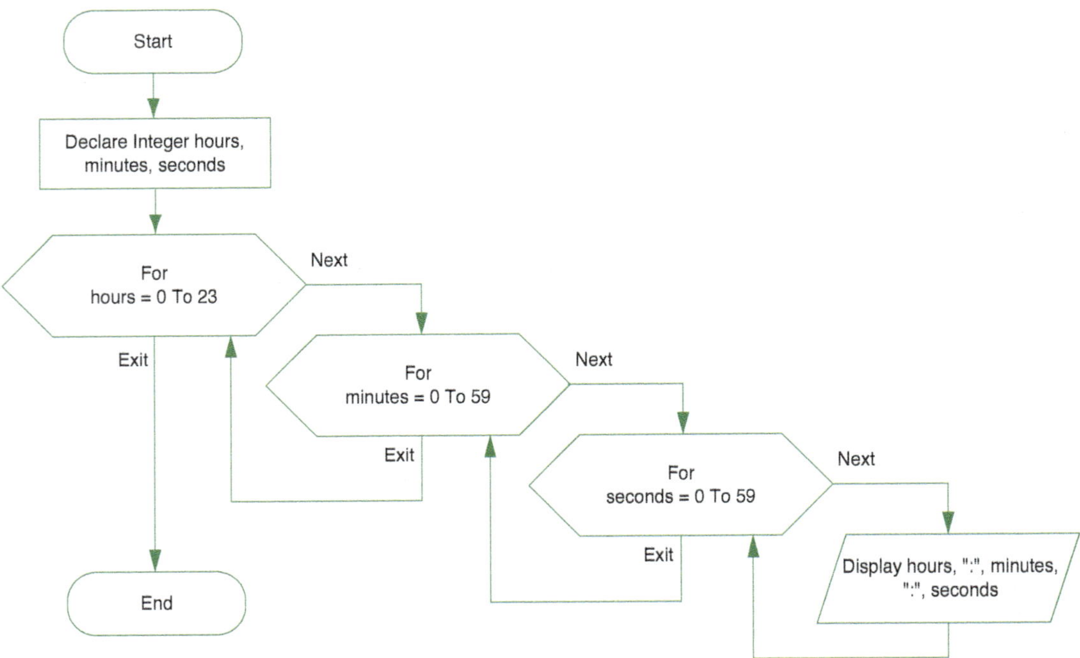

The simulated clock example brings up a few points about nested loops:

- An inner loop goes through all of its iterations for every single iteration of an outer loop.
- Inner loops complete their iterations faster than outer loops.
- To get the total number of iterations of a nested loop, multiply the number of iterations of all the loops.

Program 8-19 shows another example in pseudocode. It is a program that a teacher might use to get the average of each student's test scores. The statement in line 13 gets the number of students, and the statement in line 17 gets the number of test scores per student. The `For` loop that begins in line 20 iterates once for each student. The nested inner loop, in lines 27 through 31, iterates once for each test score.

Program 8-19:

```
// This program averages test scores. It asks the user for the
// number of students and the number of test scores per student.
Declare Integer numStudents
Declare Integer numTestScores
Declare Integer total
Declare Integer student
Declare Integer testNum
Declare Real score
Declare Real average

// Get the number of students.
Display "How many students do you have?"
Input numStudents

// Get the number of test scores per student.
Display "How many test scores per student?"
Input numTestScores

// Determine each student's average test score.
For student = 1 To numStudents
    // Initialize an accumulator for test scores.
    Set total = 0

    // Get a student's test scores.
    Display "Student number ", student
    Display "-----------------"
    For testNum = 1 To numTestScores
        Display "Enter test number ", testNum, ":"
        Input score
        Set total = total + score
    End For

    // Calculate the average test score for this student.
    Set average = total / numTestScores

    // Display the average.
    Display "The average for student ", student, " is ", average
    Display
End For
```

Program Output (with Input Shown in Bold)

How many students do you have?
3 [Enter]
How many test scores per student?
3 [Enter]
Student number 1

Enter test number 1:
100 [Enter]
Enter test number 2:
95 [Enter]

Program Output (with Input Shown in Bold) *(continued)*

```
Enter test number 3:
90 [Enter]
The average for student number 1 is 95.0

Student number 2
-----------------
Enter test number 1:
80 [Enter]
Enter test number 2:
81 [Enter]
Enter test number 3:
82 [Enter]
The average for student number 2 is 81.0

Student number 3
-----------------
Enter test number 1:
75 [Enter]
Enter test number 2:
85 [Enter]
Enter test number 3:
80 [Enter]
The average for student number 3 is 80.0
```

Chapter Review

Multiple Choice

1. A _____-controlled loop uses a true/false condition to control the number of times that it repeats.
   a. Boolean
   b. condition
   c. decision
   d. count

2. A _____-controlled loop repeats a specific number of times.
   a. Boolean
   b. condition
   c. decision
   d. count

3. Each repetition of a loop is known as a(n) _____.
   a. cycle
   b. revolution
   c. orbit
   d. iteration

4. The `While` loop is a _____ type of loop.
   a. pretest
   b. posttest
   c. prequalified
   d. post iterative

5. The `Do-While` loop is a _____ type of loop.
   a. pretest
   b. posttest
   c. prequalified
   d. post iterative

6. The `For` loop is a _____ type of loop.
   a. pretest
   b. posttest
   c. prequalified
   d. post iterative

7. A(n) _____ loop has no way of ending and repeats until the program is interrupted.
   a. indeterminate
   b. interminable
   c. infinite
   d. timeless

8. A _____ loop always executes at least once.
   a. pretest
   b. posttest
   c. condition-controlled
   d. count-controlled

9. A(n) _____ variable keeps a running total.
   a. sentinel
   b. sum
   c. total
   d. accumulator

10. A(n) _____ is a special value that signals when there are no more items from a list of items to be processed. This value cannot be mistaken as an item from the list.
    a. sentinel
    b. flag
    c. signal
    d. accumulator

True or False

1. A condition-controlled loop always repeats a specific number of times.
2. The `While` loop is a pretest loop.
3. The `Do-While` loop is a pretest loop.
4. You should not write code that modifies the contents of the counter variable in the body of a `For` loop.
5. You cannot display the contents of the counter variable in the body of a loop.
6. It is not possible to increment a counter variable by any value other than 1.
7. The following statement decrements the variable `x`: `Set x = x - 1`.
8. It is not necessary to initialize accumulator variables.
9. In a nested loop, the inner loop goes through all of its iterations for every single iteration of the outer loop.
10. To calculate the total number of iterations of a nested loop, add the number of iterations of all the loops.

Short Answer

1. Why should you indent the statements in the body of a loop?
2. Describe the difference between pretest loops and posttest loops.
3. What is a condition-controlled loop?
4. What is a count-controlled loop?
5. What three actions do count-controlled loops typically perform using the counter variable?
6. What is an infinite loop? Write the code for an infinite loop.
7. A For loop looks like what other loop in a flowchart?
8. Why is it critical that accumulator variables are properly initialized?
9. What is the advantage of using a sentinel?
10. Explain how you can use loops (iteration) within a programmed story, game, or animation.

Algorithm Workbench

1. Design a While loop that lets the user enter a number. The number should be multiplied by 10, and the result stored in a variable named product. The loop should iterate as long as product contains a value less than 100.
2. Design a Do-While loop that asks the user to enter two numbers. The numbers should be added and the sum displayed. The loop should ask the user whether they wish to perform the operation again. If so, the loop should repeat; otherwise it should terminate.
3. Design a For loop that displays the following set of numbers:
   0, 10, 20, 30, 40, 50, . . . , 1000
4. Design a loop that asks the user to enter a number. The loop should iterate 10 times and keep a running total of the numbers entered.
5. Design a For loop that calculates the total of the following series of numbers:
   $$\frac{1}{30} + \frac{2}{29} + \frac{2}{28} + \ldots + \frac{30}{1}$$
6. Design a nested loop that displays 10 rows of # characters. There should be 15 # characters in each row.
7. Convert the While loop in the following code to a Do-While loop:

```
Declare Integer x = 1
While x > 0
    Display "Enter a number."
    Input x
End While
```

8. Convert the Do-While loop in the following code to a While loop:

```
Declare String sure
Do
    Display "Are you sure you want to quit?"
    Input sure
While sure != "Y" AND sure != "y"
```

9. Convert the following While loop to a For loop:

```
Declare Integer count = 0
While count < 50
    Display "The count is ", count
    Set count = count + 1
End While
```

10. Convert the following For loop to a While loop:

```
Declare Integer count
    For count = 1 To 50
    Display count
End For
```

Debugging Exercises

1. Find the error in the following pseudocode.

```
Declare Boolean finished = False
Declare Integer value, cube

While NOT finished
    Display "Enter a value to be cubed."
    Input value;
    Set cube = value^3
    Display value, " cubed is ", cube
End While
```

2. The programmer intended the following pseudocode to display the numbers 1 through 60, and then display the message "Time's up!" It will not function as intended, however. Find the error.

```
Declare Integer counter = 1
Const Integer TIME_LIMIT = 60
    While counter < TIME_LIMIT
    Display counter
    Set counter = counter + 1
End While
Display "Time's up!"
```

3. The programmer intended the following pseudocode to get five sets of two numbers each, calculate the sum of each set, and calculate the sum of all the numbers entered. It will not function as intended, however. Find the error.

```
// This program calculates the sum of five sets of two numbers.
Declare Integer number, sum, total
Declare Integer sets, numbers

Constant Integer MAX_SETS = 5
Constant Integer MAX_NUMBERS = 2

Set sum = 0;
Set total = 0;

For sets = 1 To MAX_NUMBERS
    For numbers = 1 To MAX_SETS
        Display "Enter number ", numbers, " of set ", sets, "."
        Input number;
        Set sum = sum + number
    End For
    Display "The sum of set ", sets, " is ", sum, "."
    Set total = total + sum
    Set sum = 0
End For
Display "The total of all the sets is ", total, "."
```

Programming Exercises

VideoNote The Bug Collector Problem

1. Bug Collector Game

In a game, players compete to see which bug collector can collect the most bugs in seven days. Design a program that keeps a running total of the number of bugs collected for one player during the seven days. The loop should ask for the number of bugs collected for each day, and when the loop is finished, the program should display the total number of bugs collected. With a partner, create the program and run it. As an extra challenge, design a program that will calculate the total for two players, and display which player collected the most bugs.

2. Candy Factory

A machine at a candy factory can produce 80 chocolate bars per minute. Design a program that uses a loop to display the number of chocolate bars the machine can produce in 10, 15, 20, 25, and 30 minutes.

3. Budget Analysis

Design a program that asks the user to enter the amount they have to spend for a month. A loop should then prompt the user to enter each expense for the month, and keep a running total. When the loop finishes, the program should display the amount that the user is over or under budget.

4. Sum of Numbers

Design a program with a loop that asks the user to enter a series of positive numbers. The user should enter a negative number to signal the end of the series. After all the positive numbers have been entered, the program should display their sum.

5. Tuition Increase

At one college, the tuition for a full-time student is $6,000 per semester. It has been announced that the tuition will increase by 2 percent each year for the next five years. Design a program with a loop that displays the projected semester tuition amount for the next five years.

6. Distance Traveled

The distance a vehicle travels can be calculated as follows:

$$\textit{Distance} = \textit{Speed} \times \textit{Time}$$

For example, if a train travels 40 miles per hour for three hours, the distance traveled is 120 miles. Design a program that asks the user for the speed of a vehicle (in miles per hour) and how many hours it has traveled. It should then use a loop to display the distance the vehicle has traveled for each hour of that time period.

Here is an example of the output:

```
What is the speed of the vehicle in mph? 40 [Enter]
How many hours has it traveled? 3 [Enter]

     Hour        Distance Traveled
--------------------------------------------
       1                1
       2                4
       3                9
```

7. Average Rainfall

Design a program that uses nested loops to collect data and calculate the average rainfall over a period of years. The program should first ask for the number of years. The outer loop will iterate once for each year. The inner loop will iterate twelve times, once for each month. Each iteration of the inner loop will ask the user for the inches of rainfall for that month. After all iterations, the program should display the number of months, the total inches of rainfall, and the average rainfall per month for the entire period.

8. Celsius to Fahrenheit Table

Design a program that displays a table of the Celsius temperatures 0 through 20 and their Fahrenheit equivalents. The formula for converting a temperature from Celsius to Fahrenheit is

$$F = \frac{9}{5}C + 32$$

where F is the Fahrenheit temperature and C is the Celsius temperature. Your program must use a loop to display the table.

9. Pennies for Pay

Design a program that calculates the amount of money a person would earn over a period of time if their salary is one penny the first day, two pennies the second day, and continues to double each day. The program should ask the user for the number of days. Display a table showing what the salary was for each day, and then show the total pay at the end of the period. The output should be displayed in a dollar amount, not the number of pennies.

10. Largest and Smallest

Design a program with a loop that lets the user enter a series of numbers. The user should enter −99 to signal the end of the series. After all the numbers have been entered, the program should display the largest and smallest numbers entered.

11. First and Last

Design a program that asks the user for a series of names (in no particular order). After the final person's name has been entered, the program should display the name that is first alphabetically and the name that is last alphabetically. For example, if the user enters the names Kumiko, Joel, Adam, Samara, Zeb, and Darius, the program would display Adam and Zeb.

12. Multiplication Table

Design a program that uses nested loops to display a multiplication table for the numbers 1 through 12. The program's output should look like this:

```
1 * 0 = 0
1 * 1 = 1
1 * 2 = 2
1 * 3 = 3
```

and so forth...

```
12 * 9 = 108
12 * 10 = 120
12 * 11 = 132
12 * 12 = 144
```

Introduction to Modules and Functions

TOPICS

9.1 Introduction to Modules

A module is a group of statements that exist for the purpose of performing a specific task within a program.

Recall the simple program that performs the task of calculating an employee's pay. That program multiplied the number of hours that the employee worked by the employee's hourly pay rate. A more realistic payroll program, however, would do much more than this. In a real-world application, the overall task of calculating an employee's pay would consist of several **subtasks**, such as the following:

- Getting the employee's hourly pay rate
- Getting the number of hours worked
- Calculating the employee's gross pay
- Calculating overtime pay
- Calculating withholdings for taxes and benefits
- Calculating the net pay
- Printing the paycheck

Most programs perform tasks that are large enough to be broken down into several subtasks. For this reason, programmers usually break down their programs into modules. A **module** is a group of statements that exist within a program for the purpose of performing one specific task. Instead of writing a large program as one long sequence of statements, it can be written as several small modules, each one performing a specific part of the task. These small modules can then be executed in the desired order to perform the overall task.

This approach is sometimes called **divide and conquer** because a large task is divided into several smaller tasks that are easily performed. Figure 9-1 illustrates this idea by comparing two programs: one that uses a long, complex sequence of statements to perform a task, and another that divides a task into smaller tasks, each of which is performed by a separate module.

Figure 9-1 Using modules to divide and conquer a large task

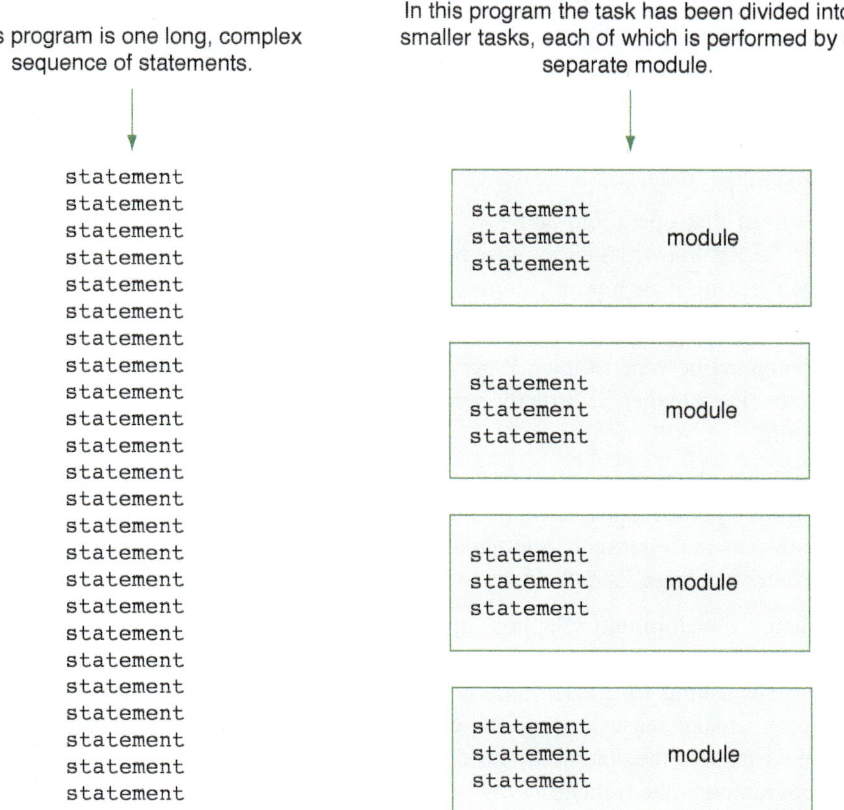

When using modules in a program, you generally isolate each task within the program in its own module. For example, a realistic pay calculating program might have the following modules:

- A module that gets the employee's hourly pay rate
- A module that gets the number of hours worked
- A module that calculates the employee's gross pay
- A module that calculates the overtime pay
- A module that calculates the withholdings for taxes and benefits
- A module that calculates the net pay
- A module that prints the paycheck

Although every modern programming language allows you to create modules, they are not always called modules. Modules may be called **procedures**, **subroutines**, **subprograms**, **methods**, and **functions**. (A function is a special type of module discussed later in this chapter.)

Benefits of Using Modules

A program benefits in the following ways when it is modularized:

- **Simpler code.** A program's code tends to be simpler and easier to understand when it is modularized. Several small modules are much easier to read than one long sequence of statements.
- **Code reuse.** Modules also reduce the duplication of code within a program. If a specific operation is performed in several places in a program, a module can be written once to perform that operation, and then be executed any time it is needed. This benefit of using modules is known as **code reuse** because you are writing the code to perform a task once and then reusing it each time you need to perform the task.
- **Better testing.** When each task within a program is contained in its own module, testing and debugging become simpler. Programmers can test each module in a program individually, to determine whether it correctly performs its operation. This makes it easier to isolate and fix errors.
- **Easier maintenance.** Most programs must be periodically modified to correct logic errors, improve performance, and provide a better experience for the user. Such modifications are known as **maintenance**. A modularized program is easier to maintain than an unmodularized program because its code tends to be simpler, smaller, and easier to understand
- **Faster development.** Suppose a programmer or a team of programmers is developing multiple programs. They discover that each of the programs performs several common tasks, such as asking for a username and a password, displaying the current time, and so on. It doesn't make sense to write the code for these tasks multiple times. Instead, modules can be written for the commonly needed tasks, and those modules can be incorporated into each program that needs them.
- **Efficient teamwork.** Modules also make it easier for programmers to work in teams. When a program is developed as a set of modules that each perform an individual task, then different programmers can be assigned the job of writing different modules.

Checkpoint

9.1 What is a module?

9.2 What is meant by the phrase "divide and conquer"?

9.3 How do modules help you reuse code in a program?

9.4 How can modules make the development of multiple programs faster?

9.5 How can modules make it easier for programs to be developed by teams of programmers?

9.2 Defining and Calling a Module

To execute a module, you write a statement that calls it.

Module Names

Before we discuss the process of creating and using modules, we should mention a few things about module names. Just as you name the variables that you use in a program, you also name the modules. A module's name should be descriptive enough so that anyone reading your code can reasonably guess what the module does.

Because modules perform actions, most programmers prefer to use verbs in module names. For example, a module that calculates gross pay might be named `calculateGrossPay`. This name would make it evident to anyone reading the code that the module calculates gross pay. Other examples of good module names would be `getHours`, `getPayRate`, `calculateOvertime`, `printCheck`, and so on. Each module name describes what the module does.

When naming a module, most languages require that you follow the same rules that you follow when naming variables. This means that module names cannot contain spaces, cannot typically contain punctuation characters, and usually cannot begin with a number. These are only general rules, however. The specific rules for naming a module depend on the programming language.

Defining and Calling a Module

VideoNote Defining and Calling a Module

To create a module you write its definition. In most languages, a **module definition** has two parts: a header and a body. The header indicates the starting point of the module, and the body is a list of statements that belong to the module. Here is the general format that we will follow when we write a module definition in pseudocode:

```
Module name()
  statement  ┐
  statement  ├ These statements are the body of the module.
  etc.       ┘
End Module
```

The first line is the module header. In our pseudocode the header begins with the word `Module`, followed by the name of the module, followed by a set of parentheses. It is a common practice in most programming languages to put a set of parentheses after a module name.

Beginning at the line after the module header, one or more statements will appear. These statements are the module's body, and are performed any time the module is executed. The last line of the definition, after the body, reads `End Module`. This line marks the end of the module definition.

Let's look at an example. Keep in mind that this is not a complete program.

```
Module showMessage()
   Display "Hello world."
End Module
```

This pseudocode defines a module named `showMessage`. As its name implies, the purpose of this module is to show a message on the screen. The body of the `showMessage` module contains one statement: a `Display` statement that displays the message "Hello world."

Notice in the previous example that the statement in the body of the module is indented. Unless you are using Python, indenting the statements in the body of a module is not usually required, but it makes your code much easier to read. By indenting the statements inside a module, you visually set them apart. As a result, you can tell at a glance which statements are inside the module. This practice is a programming style convention that virtually all programmers follow.

NOTE: The Python language requires you to indent the statements inside a function. In Python, a function is the same as a module as described in this chapter.

Calling a Module

A module definition specifies what a module does, but it does not cause the module to execute. To execute a module, we must **call** it. In pseudocode we will use the word `Call` to call a module. This is how we would call the `showMessage` module:

```
Call showMessage()
```

When a module is called, the computer jumps to that module and executes the statements in the module's body. Then, when the end of the module is reached, the computer jumps back to the part of the program that called the module, and the program resumes execution at that point.

To fully demonstrate how module calling works, we will look at Program 9-1.

Program 9-1:

```
1 Module main()
2    Display "I have a message for you."
3    Call showMessage()
4    Display "That's all, folks!"
5 End Module
6
7 Module showMessage()
8    Display "Hello world"
9 End Module
```

Program Output

```
I have a message for you.
Hello world
That's all, folks!
```

First, notice that Program 9-1 has two modules: a module named `main` appears in lines 1 through 5, and the `showMessage` module appears in lines 7 through 9. Many programming languages require that programs have a **`main` module**. The `main` module is the program's starting point, and it generally calls other modules. When the end of the `main` module is reached, the program stops executing. In this book, any time you see a pseudocode program with a module named `main`, we are using that module as the program's starting point. Likewise, when the end of the `main` module is reached, the program will stop executing. This is shown in Figure 9-2.

Figure 9-2 The `main` module

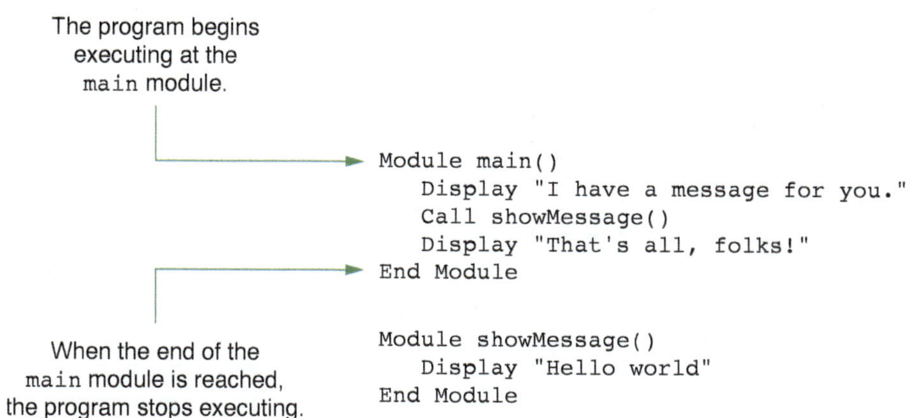

NOTE: Many languages, including Java, C, and C++, require that the `main` module actually be named `main`, as we have shown in Program 9-1.

Let's step through the program. When the program runs, the `main` module starts and the statement in line 2 displays "I have a message for you." Then, line 3 calls the `showMessage` module. As shown in Figure 9-3, the computer jumps to the `showMessage` module and executes the statements in its body. There is only one statement in the body of the `showMessage` module: the `Display` statement in line 8. This statement displays "Hello world" and then the module ends. As shown in Figure 9-4, the computer jumps back to the part of the program that called `showMessage`, and resumes execution from that point. In this case, the program resumes execution at line 4, which displays "That's all, folks!" The `main` module ends at line 5, so the program stops executing.

Figure 9-3 Calling the `showMessage` module

```
Module main()
   Display "I have a message for you."
   Call showMessage()
   Display "That's all, folks!"
End Module

Module showMessage()
   Display "Hello world"
End Module
```

The computer jumps to the `showMessage` module and executes the statements in its body.

Figure 9-4 The showMessage module return

When the `showMessage` module ends, the computer jumps back to the part of the program that called it, and resumes execution from that point.

```
Module main()
   Display "I have a message for you."
   Call showMessage()
   Display "That's all, folks!"
End Module

Module showMessage()
   Display "Hello world"
End Module
```

When the computer encounters a module call, such as the one in line 3 of Program 9-1, it has to perform some operations "behind the scenes" so it will know where to return after the module ends. First, the computer saves the memory address of the location that it should return to. This is typically the statement that appears immediately after the module call. This memory location is known as the **return point**. Then, the computer jumps to the module and executes the statements in its body. When the module ends, the computer jumps back to the return point and resumes execution.

NOTE: When a program calls a module, programmers commonly say that the *control* of the program transfers to that module. This simply means that the module takes control of the program's execution.

Modules may be called by statements in control structures, such as loops and `If` statements. For example, Program 9-2 uses a `For` loop to repeatedly call the `showMessage` module.

Program 9-2:

```
Module main()
   // Declare a counter variable.
   Declare Integer counter

   // Constant for the counter's maximum value
   Constant Integer MAX_VALUE = 5

   // Call the showMessage module 5 times.
   Display "I have some messages for you."
   For counter = 1 To MAX_VALUE
      Call showMessage()
   End For
   Display "That's all, folks!"
End Module

Module showMessage()
   Display "Hello world"
End Module
```

Program 9-2: *(continued)*

Program Output

```
I have some messages for you.
Hello world
Hello world
Hello world
Hello world
Hello world
That's all, folks!
```

Program 9-3 shows another example. It asks the user to enter a test score. The program then determines whether the user passed or failed the test. One of two modules, pass or fail, is called to display a message.

Program 9-3:

```
Module main()
   // Variable to hold a test score.
   Declare Real testScore

   // Get the user's test score.
   Display "Enter your test score."
   Input testScore

   // Determine whether the user passed the test.
   If testScore >= 60 Then
      Call pass()
   Else
      Call fail()
   End If
End Module

Module pass()
   Display "You passed the test."
End Module

Module fail()
   Display "You did not pass the test."
End Module
```

Program Output (with Input Shown in Bold)

```
Enter your test score.
75 [Enter]
You passed the test.
Enter your test score.
50 [Enter]
You did not pass the test.
```

Flowcharting a Program with Modules

In a flowchart, a module call is shown with a rectangle that has vertical bars at each side, as shown in Figure 9-5. The name of the module that is being called is written on the symbol. The example shown in Figure 9-5 shows how we would represent a call to the `showMessage` module.

Figure 9-5 Module call symbol

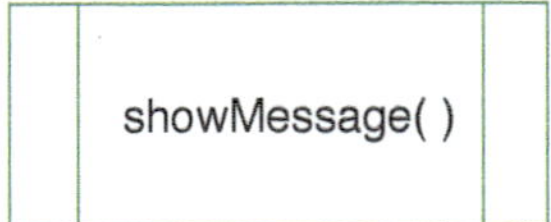

Programmers typically draw a separate flowchart for each module in a program. For example, Figure 9-6 shows how Program 9-1 would be flowcharted. Notice that the figure shows two flowcharts: one for the `main` module (left) and another for the `showMessage` module (right).

Figure 9-6 Flowchart for Program 9-1

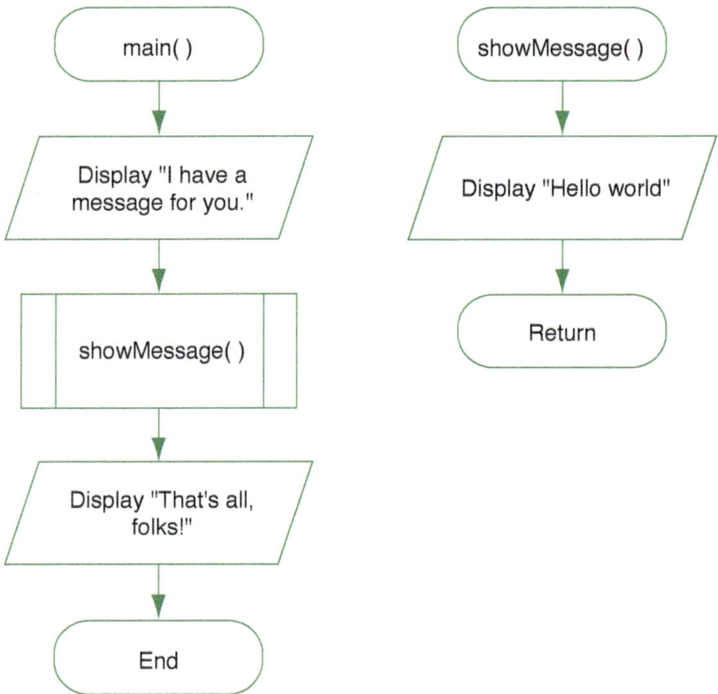

When drawing a flowchart for a module, the starting terminal symbol usually shows the name of the module. The ending terminal symbol in the `main` module reads `End` because it marks the end of the program's execution. The ending terminal symbol for all other modules reads `Return` because it marks the point where the computer returns to the part of the program that called the module. Figure 9-7 shows a flowchart for Program 9-2, and Figure 9-8 shows a flowchart for Program 9-3.

Figure 9-7 Flowchart for Program 9-2

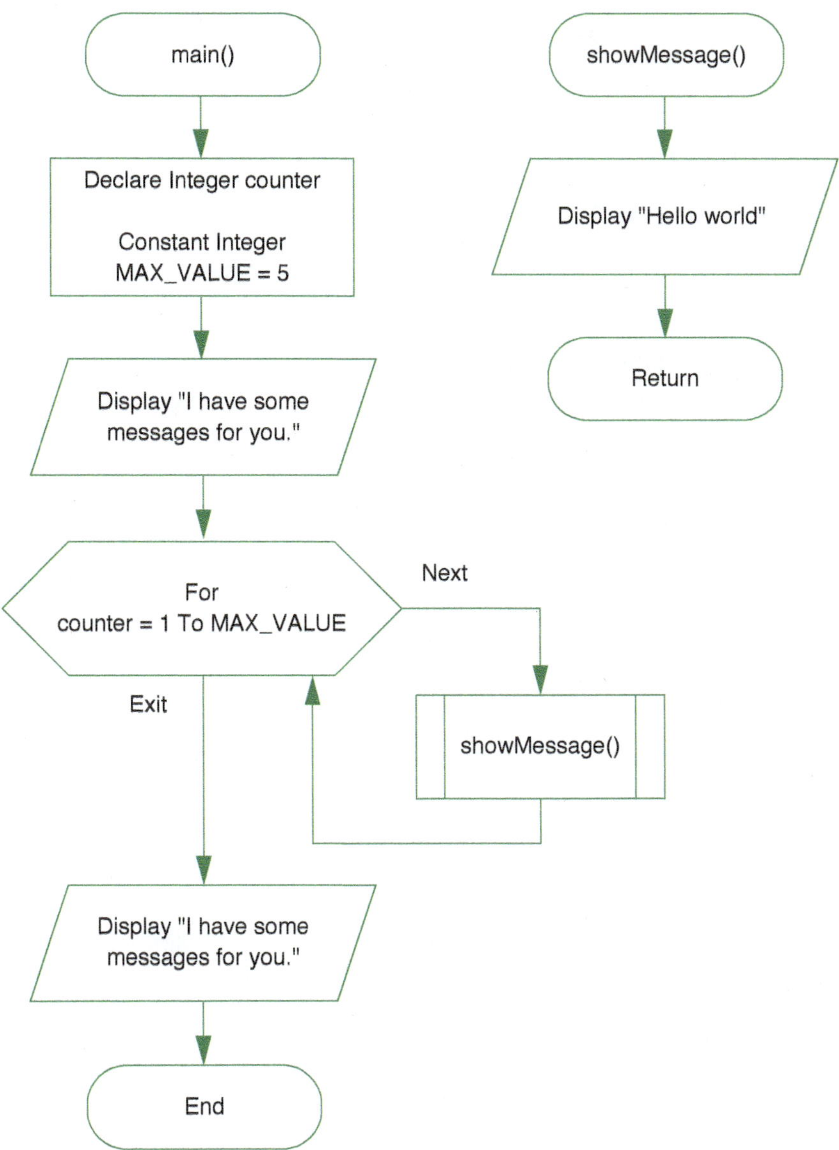

Figure 9-8 Flowchart for Program 9-3

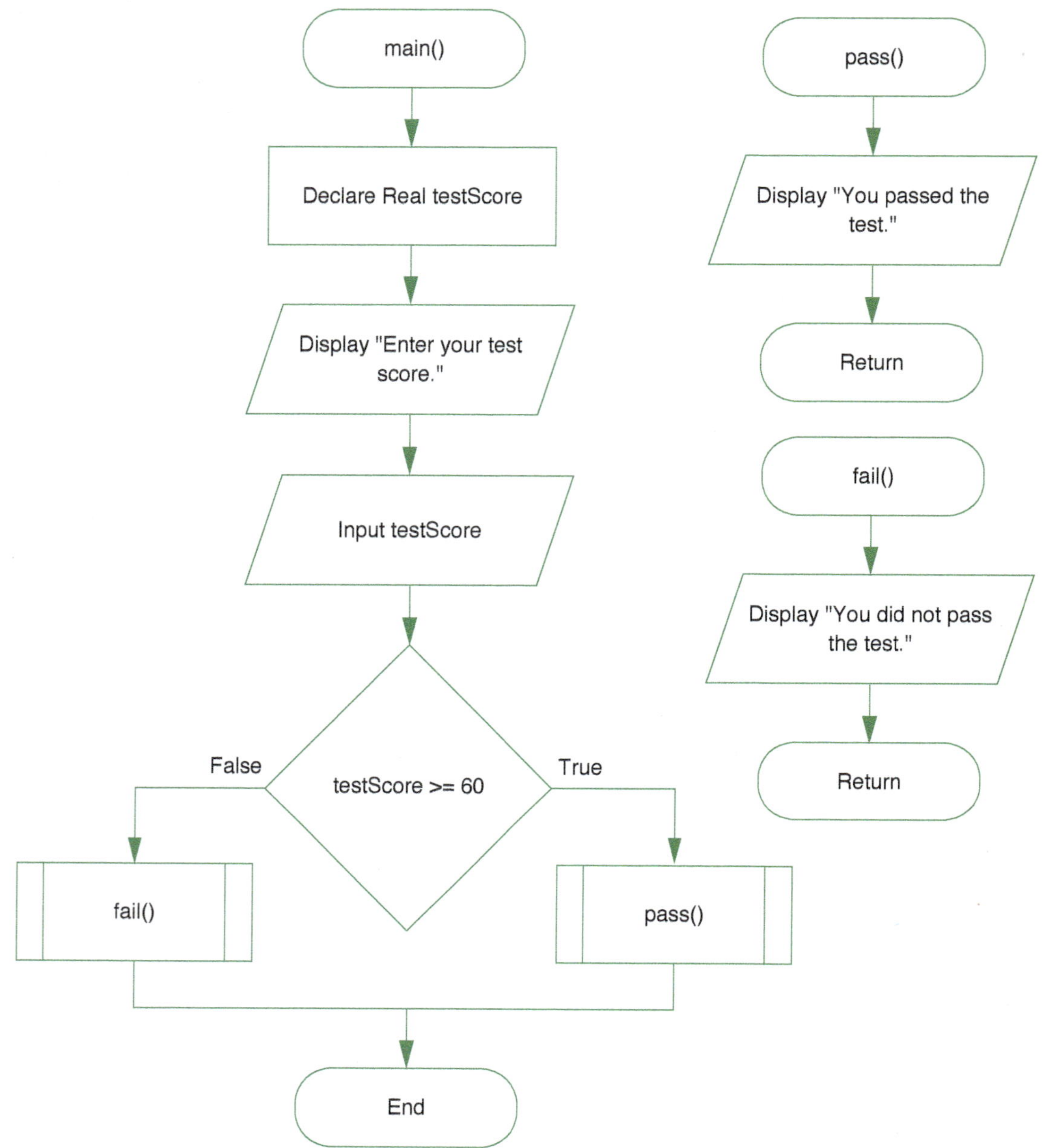

Top-Down Design

In this section, we have discussed and demonstrated how modules work. You've seen how the computer jumps to a module when it is called, and returns to the part of the program that called the module when the module ends. It is important that you understand these mechanical aspects of modules. Just as important as understanding how modules work is understanding how to design a modularized program. Programmers commonly use a technique known as **top-down design** to break down an algorithm into modules. The process of top-down design is performed in the following manner:

- The overall task that the program is to perform is broken down into a series of subtasks.
- Each of the subtasks is examined to determine whether it can be further broken down into more subtasks. This step is repeated until no more subtasks can be identified.
- Once all of the subtasks have been identified, they are written in code.

This process is called top-down design because the programmer begins by looking at the topmost level of tasks that must be performed, and then breaks down those tasks into lower levels of subtasks.

NOTE: The top-down design process is sometimes called *stepwise refinement.*

Hierarchy Charts

Flowcharts are good tools for graphically depicting the flow of logic inside a module, but they do not give a visual representation of the relationships between modules. Programmers commonly use **hierarchy charts** for this purpose. A hierarchy chart, which is also known as a **structure chart**, shows boxes that represent each module in a program. The boxes are connected in a way that illustrates their relationship to one another. Figure 9-9 shows an example of a hierarchy chart for a pay calculating program.

Figure 9-9 A hierarchy chart

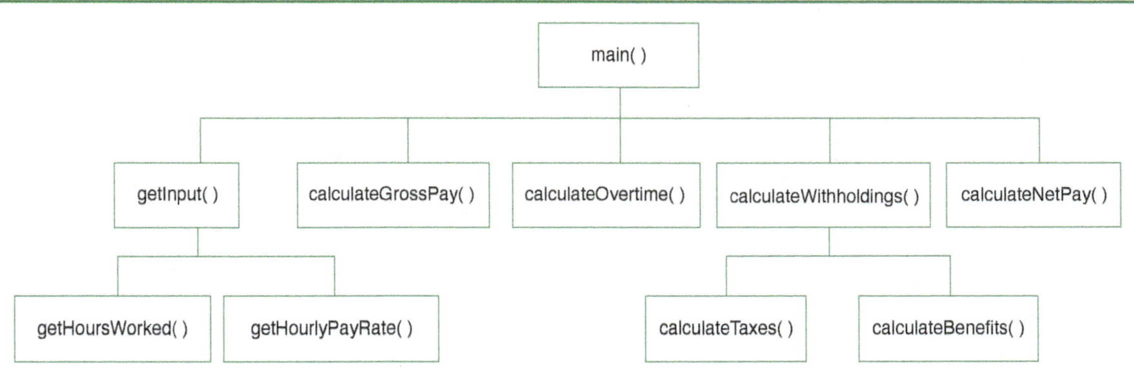

The chart shown in Figure 9-9 shows the `main` module as the topmost module in the hierarchy. The `main` module calls five other modules: `getInput`, `calculateGrossPay`, `calculateOvertime`, `calculateWithholdings`, and `calculateNetPay`. The `getInput` module calls two additional modules: `getHoursWorked` and `getHourlyPayRate`. The `calculateWithholdings` module also calls two modules: `calculateTaxes` and `calculateBenefits`.

Notice that the hierarchy chart does not show the steps that are taken inside a module. Because hierarchy charts do not reveal any details about how modules work, they do not replace flowcharts or pseudocode. They are a separate tool you can use to illustrate the relationship between modules.

In the Spotlight:

Defining and Calling Modules

Professional Appliance Service, Inc. offers maintenance and repair services for household appliances. The owner wants to give each of the company's service technicians a small handheld computer that displays step-by-step instructions for many of the repairs that they perform. To see how this might work, the owner has asked you to develop a program that displays the following instructions for disassembling an ACME laundry dryer:

Step 1. Unplug the dryer and move it away from the wall.
Step 2. Remove the six screws from the back of the dryer.
Step 3. Remove the dryer's back panel.
Step 4. Pull the top of the dryer straight up.

During your interview with the owner, you determine that the program should display the steps one at a time. You decide that after each step is displayed, the user will be asked to press a key to see the next step.

On Your Own: Working alone or with a partner, write the algorithm steps, draw a hierarchy chart, draw a flowchart, and write the pseudocode. Then, read on to see how you did. Remember, your solution does not have to be exactly the same as the one in the text in order to come up with the same result.

Here is an algorithm for the program:

1. Display a starting message, explaining what the program does.
2. Ask the user to press a key to see Step 1.
3. Display the instructions for Step 1.
4. Ask the user to press a key to see the next step.
5. Display the instructions for Step 2.
6. Ask the user to press a key to see the next step.
7. Display the instructions for Step 3.
8. Ask the user to press a key to see the next step.
9. Display the instructions for Step 4.

This algorithm lists the top level of tasks that the program needs to perform, and becomes the basis of the program's main module. Figure 9-10 shows the program's structure in a hierarchy chart.

Figure 9-10 Hierarchy chart for the program

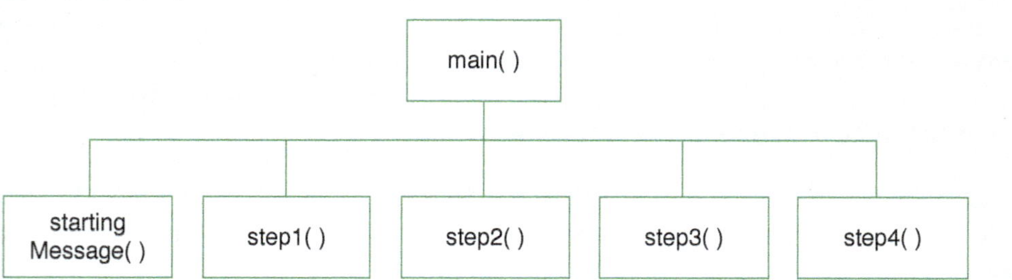

As you can see from the hierarchy chart, the `main` module will call several other modules.

Here are summaries of those modules:

- startingMessage—This module will display the starting message that tells the technician what the program does.
- step1—This module will display the instructions for Step 1.
- step2—This module will display the instructions for Step 2.
- step3—This module will display the instructions for Step 3.
- step4—This module will display the instructions for Step 4.

Between calls to these modules, the `main` module will instruct the user to press a key to see the next step in the instructions. Program 9-4 shows the pseudocode for the program. Figure 9-11 shows the flowchart for the `main` module, and Figure 9-12 shows the flowcharts for the `startingMessage`, `step1`, `step2`, `step3`, and `step4`

Program 9-4:

```
Module main()
   // Display the starting message.
   Call startingMessage()
   Display "Press a key to see Step 1."
   Input

   // Display Step 1.
   Call step1()
   Display "Press a key to see Step 2."
   Input

   // Display Step 2.
   Call step2()
   Display "Press a key to see Step 3."
   Input

   // Display Step 3.
   Call step3()
   Display "Press a key to see Step 4."
   Input

   // Display Step 4.
   Call step4()
End Module

// The startingMessage module displays
// the program's starting message.
Module startingMessage()
   Display "This program tells you how to"
   Display "disassemble an ACME laundry dryer."
   Display "There are 4 steps in the process."
End Module
```

Program 9-4: *(continued)*

```
// The step1 module displays the instructions
// for Step 1.
Module step1()
   Display "Step 1: Unplug the dryer and"
   Display "move it away from the wall."
End Module

// The step2 module displays the instructions
// for Step 2.
Module step2()
   Display "Step 2: Remove the six screws"
   Display "from the back of the dryer."
End Module

// The step3 module displays the instructions
// for Step 3.
Module step3()
   Display "Step 3: Remove the dryer's"
   Display "back panel."
End Module

// The step4 module displays the instructions
// for Step 4.
Module step4()
   Display "Step 4: Pull the top of the"
   Display "dryer straight up."
End Module
```

Program Output (with Input Shown in Bold)

```
This program tells you how to
disassemble an ACME laundry dryer.
There are 4 steps in the process.
Press a key to see Step 1.
[Enter]
Step 1: Unplug the dryer and
move it away from the wall.
Press a key to see Step 2.
[Enter]
Step 2: Remove the six screws
from the back of the dryer.
Press a key to see Step 3.
[Enter]
Step 3: Remove the dryer's
back panel.
Press a key to see Step 4.
[Enter]
Step 4: Pull the top of the
dryer straight up.
```

NOTE: Lines 5, 10, 15, and 20 show an `Input` statement with no variable specified. In our pseudocode, this is the way we will read a keystroke from the keyboard without saving the character that was pressed. Most programming languages provide a way to do this.

Figure 9-11 Flowchart for the `main` module in Program 9-4

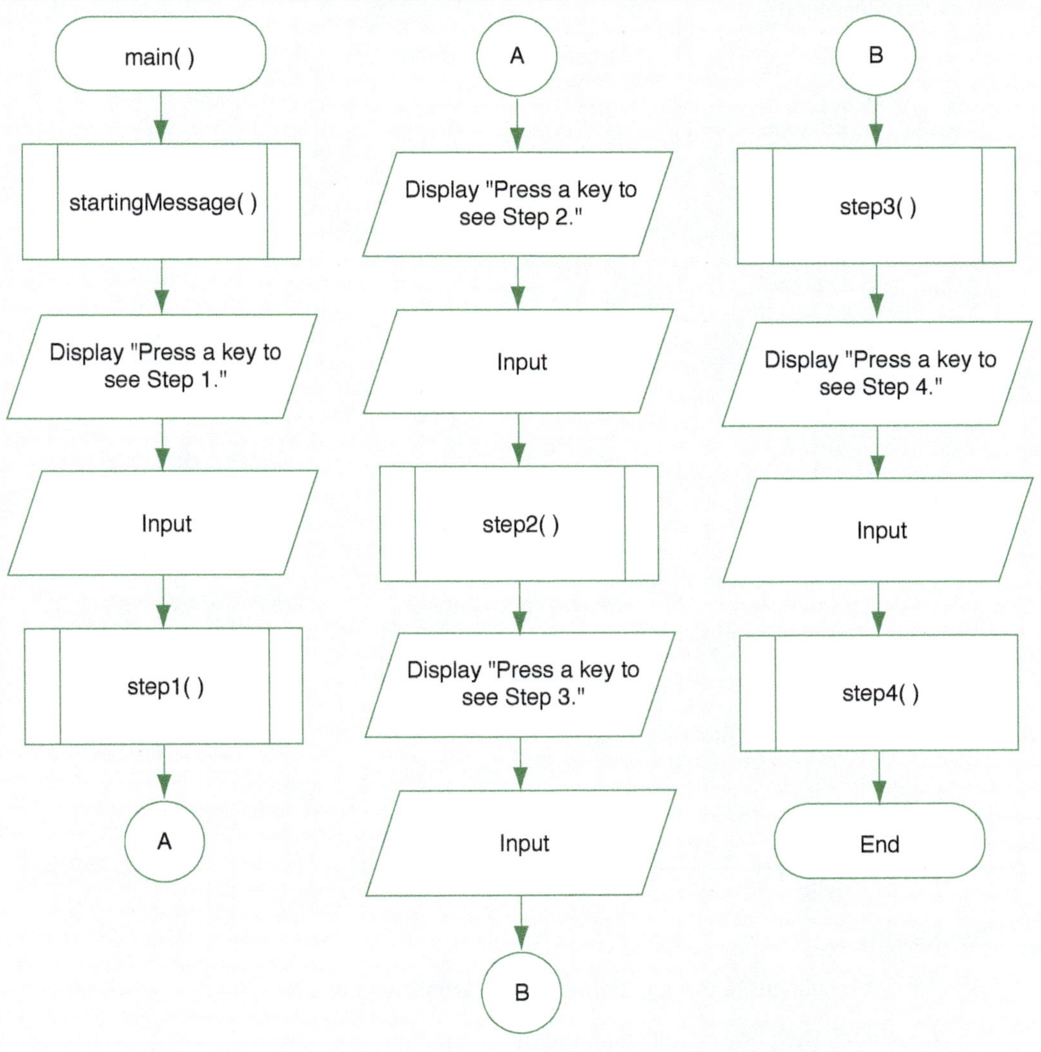

Figure 9-12 Flowchart for the other modules in Program 9-4

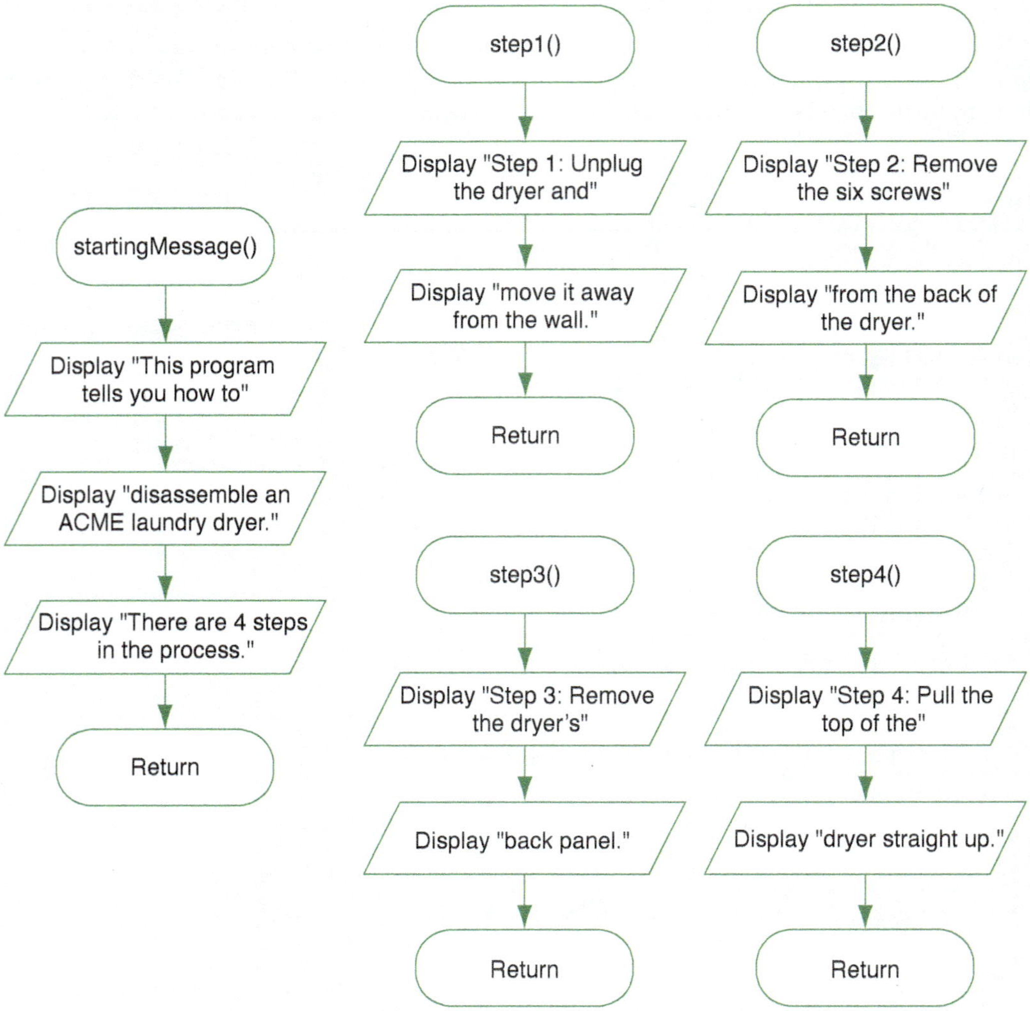

startingMessage()
Display "This program tells you how to"
Display "disassemble an ACME laundry dryer."
Display "There are 4 steps in the process."
Return

step1()
Display "Step 1: Unplug the dryer and"
Display "move it away from the wall."
Return

step2()
Display "Step 2: Remove the six screws"
Display "from the back of the dryer."
Return

step3()
Display "Step 3: Remove the dryer's"
Display "back panel."
Return

step4()
Display "Step 4: Pull the top of the"
Display "dryer straight up."
Return

Checkpoint

9.6 In most languages, a module definition has what two parts?

9.7 What does the phrase "calling a module" mean?

9.8 When a module is executing, what happens when the end of the module is reached?

9.9 Describe the steps involved in the top-down design process.

9.3 Local Variables

A local variable is declared inside a module or function and cannot be accessed by statements that are outside the module. Different modules can have local variables with the same names because the modules cannot see each other's local variables.

In most programming languages, a variable that is declared inside a module or function is called a **local variable**. A local variable belongs to the module or function in which it is declared, and only statements inside that module or function can access the variable. (In this section, we look at local variables in modules; we will use them in functions later in this chapter.) An error will occur if a statement in one module tries to access a local variable that belongs to another module. For example, look at the pseudocode in Program 9-5.

Program 9-5:

```
 1 Module main()
 2    Call getName()
 3    Display "Hello ", name        ◄──── This will cause an error!
 4 End Module
 5
 6 Module getName()
 7    Declare String name           ◄──── This is a local variable
 8    Display "Enter your name."
 9    Input name
10 End Module
```

The `name` variable is declared in line 7, inside the `getName` module. Because it is declared inside the `getName` module, it is a local variable belonging to that module. Line 8 prompts the user to enter their name, and the `Input` statement in line 9 stores the user's input in the `name` variable.

The `main` module calls the `getName` module in line 2. Then, the `Display` statement in line 3 tries to access the `name` variable. This results in an error because the `name` variable is local to the `getName` module, and statements in the `main` module cannot access it.

Scope and Local Variables

Programmers commonly use the term **scope** to describe the part of a program in which a variable may be accessed. A variable is visible only to statements inside the variable's scope.

A local variable's scope usually begins at the variable's declaration and ends at the end of the module in which the variable is declared. The variable cannot be accessed by statements that are outside this region. This means that a local variable cannot be accessed by code that is outside the module, or inside the module but before the variable's declaration. For example, look at the following code. It has an error because the `Input` statement tries to store a value in the `name` variable, but the statement is outside the variable's scope. Moving the variable declaration to a line before the `Input` statement will fix this error.

```
Module getName()
   Display "Enter your name."
   Input name
   Declare String name
End Module
```

This statement will cause an error because the name variable has not been declared yet.

Duplicate Variable Names

In most programming languages, you cannot have two variables with the same name in the same scope. For example, look at the following module:

```
Module getTwoAges()
   Declare Integer age
   Display "Enter your age."
   Input age
   Declare Integer age
   Display "Enter your pet's age."
   Input age
End Module
```

This will cause an error! A variable named age has already been declared.

This module declares two local variables named age. The second variable declaration will cause an error because a variable named `age` has already been declared in the module. Renaming one of the variables will fix this error.

TIP: You cannot have two variables with the same name in the same module because the compiler or interpreter would not know which variable to use when a statement tries to access one of them. All variables that exist within the same scope must have unique names.

Although you cannot have two local variables with the same name in the same module, it is usually okay for a local variable in one module to have the same name as a local variable in a different module. For example, look at Program 9-6.

Program 9-6:

```
Module main()
   Call showSquare()
   Call showHalf()
End Module

Module showSquare()
   Declare Real number
   Declare Real square

   Display "Enter a number."
   Input number
   Set square = number^2
   Display "The square of that number is ", square
End Module
```

Program 9-6: *(continued)*

```
15
16 Module showHalf()
17     Declare Real number
18     Declare Real half
19
20     Display "Enter a number."
21     Input number
22     Set half = number / 2
23     Display "Half of that number is ", half
24 End Module
```

Program Output (with Input Shown in Bold)

```
Enter a number.
5 [Enter]
The square of that number is 25
Enter a number.
20 [Enter]
Half of that number is 10
```

Program 9-6 has three modules: `main`, `showSquare`, and `showHalf`. Notice that the `showSquare` module has a local variable named `number` (declared in line 7) and the `showHalf` module also has a local variable named `number` (declared in line 17). It is legal for the two modules to have a local variable with the same name because the variables are not in the same scope. The scope of the two `number` variables is shown in Figure 9-13.

Figure 9-13 Scope of the two number variables

```
Module main()
   Call showSquare()
   Call showHalf()
End Module

Module showSquare()
   Declare Real number
   Declare Real square

   Display "Enter a number."
   Input number
   Set square = number^2
   Display "The square of that number is ", square
End Module

Module showHalf()
   Declare Real number
   Declare Real half

   Display "Enter a number."
   Input number
   Set half = number / 2
   Display "Half of that number is ", half
End Module
```

Scope of the `number` variable in the `showSquare` module.

Scope of the `number` variable in the `showHalf` module.

Checkpoint

9.10 What is a local variable? How is access to a local variable restricted?

9.11 What is a variable's scope?

9.12 Is it usually permissible to have more than one variable with the same name in the same scope? Why or why not?

9.13 Is it usually permissible for a local variable in one module to have the same name as a local variable in a different module?

9.4 Passing Arguments to Modules

An argument is any piece of data that is passed into a module when the module is called. A parameter is a variable that receives an argument that is passed into a module

Sometimes it is useful not only to call a module, but also to send one or more pieces of data into the module. Pieces of data that are sent into a module are known as **arguments**. The module can use its arguments in calculations or other operations.

If you want a module to receive arguments when it is called, you must equip the module with one or more parameter variables. A **parameter variable**, often simply called a **parameter**, is a special variable that receives an argument when a module is called. Here is an example of a pseudocode module that has a parameter variable:

```
Module doubleNumber(Integer value)
    Declare Integer result
    Set result = value * 2
    Display result
End Module
```

This module's name is `doubleNumber`. Its purpose is to accept an integer number as an argument and display the value of that number doubled. Look at the module header and notice the words `Integer value` that appear inside the parentheses. This is the declaration of a parameter variable. The parameter variable's name is `value` and its data type is Integer. The purpose of this variable is to receive an `Integer` argument when the module is called. Program 9-7 demonstrates the module in a complete program

Program 9-7:

```
Module main()
    Call doubleNumber(4)
End Module

Module doubleNumber(Integer value)
    Declare Integer result
    Set result = value * 2
    Display result
End Module
```

Program Output

```
8
```

When this program runs, the `main` module will begin executing. The statement in line 2 calls the `doubleNumber` module. Notice that the number 4 appears inside the parentheses. This is an argument that is being passed to the `doubleNumber` module. When this statement executes, the `doubleNumber` module will be called with the number 4 copied into the `value` parameter variable. This is shown in Figure 9-14.

Figure 9-14 The argument 4 is copied into the `value` parameter variable

```
Module main()
   Call doubleNumber(4)
End Module

Module doubleNumber(Integer value)
   Declare Integer result
   Set result = value * 2
   Display result
End Module
```

The argument 4 is copied into the `value` parameter variable.

Let's step through the `doubleNumber` module. As we do, remember that the value parameter variable will contain the number that was passed into it as an argument. In this program, that number is 4.

Line 6 declares a local `Integer` variable named result. Then, line 7 assigns the value of the expression `value * 2` to result. Because the `value` variable contains 4, this line assigns 8 to result. Line 8 displays the contents of the `result` variable. The module ends at line 9.

```
For example, if we had called the module as follows:
  Call doubleNumber(5)
the module would have displayed 10.
```

We can also pass the contents of a variable as an argument. For example, look at Program 9-8. The `main` module declares an `Integer` variable named `number` in line 2. Lines 3 and 4 prompt the user to enter a number, and line 5 reads the user's input into the `number` variable. Notice that in line 6 `number` is passed as an argument to the `doubleNumber` module, which causes the number variable's contents to be copied into the `value` parameter variable. This is shown in Figure 9-15.

Program 9-8: 

```
1 Module main()
2    Declare Integer number
3    Display "Enter a number and I will display"
4    Display "that number doubled."
5    Input number
6    Call doubleNumber(number)
7 End Module
8
9 Module doubleNumber(Integer value)
10    Declare Integer result
11    Set result = value * 2
12    Display result
13 End Module
```

Program 9-8: *(continued)*

Program Output (with Input Shown in Bold)

```
Enter a number and I will display
that number doubled.
20 [Enter]
40
```

Figure 9-15 The contents of the number variable passed as an argument

```
Module main()
   Declare Integer number
   Display "Enter a number and I will display"
   Display "that number doubled."
   Input number
   Call doubleNumber(number)
End Module
                                    20

Module doubleNumber(Integer value)
   Declare Integer result
   Set result = value * 2
   Display result
End Module
```

The contents of the `number` variable are copied into the `value` parameter variable.

Argument and Parameter Compatibility

When you pass an argument to a module, most programming languages require that the argument and the receiving parameter variable be of the same data type. If you try to pass an argument of one type into a parameter variable of another type, an error usually occurs. For example, Figure 9-16 shows that you cannot pass a real number or a `Real` variable into an `Integer` parameter.

Figure 9-16 Arguments and parameter variables must be of the same type

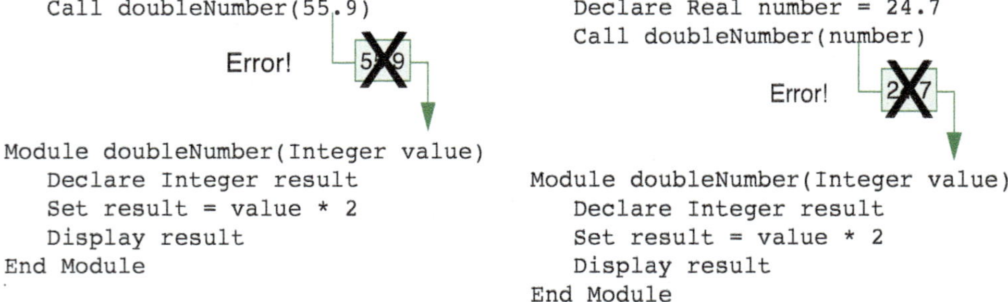

NOTE: Some languages allow you to pass an argument into a parameter variable of a different type as long as no data will be lost. For example, some languages allow you to pass integer arguments into real parameters because real variables can hold whole numbers. If you pass a real argument, such as 24.7, into an integer parameter, the fractional part of the number would be lost.

Parameter Variable Scope

Earlier in this chapter, you learned that a variable's scope is the part of the program in which the variable may be accessed. A variable is visible only to statements inside the variable's scope. A parameter variable's scope is usually the entire module in which the parameter is declared. No statement outside the module can access the parameter variable.

Passing Multiple Arguments

Most languages allow you to write modules that accept multiple arguments. Program 9-9 shows a pseudocode module named `showSum` that accepts two `Integer` arguments. The module adds the two arguments and displays their sum.

Program 9-9:

```
 1 Module main()
 2    Display "The sum of 12 and 45 is:"
 3    Call showSum(12, 45)
 4 End Module
 5
 6 Module showSum(Integer num1, Integer num2)
 7    Declare Integer result
 8    Set result = num1 + num2
 9    Display result
10 End Module
```

Program Output

```
The sum of 12 and 45 is:
57
```

Notice that two parameter variables, `num1` and `num2`, are declared inside the parentheses in the module header. This is often referred to as a **parameter list**. Also, notice that a comma separates the declarations.

The statement in line 3 calls the `showSum` module and passes two arguments: 12 and 45. The arguments are passed into the parameter variables in the order that they appear in the module call. In other words, the first argument is passed into the first parameter variable, and the second argument is passed into the second parameter variable. So, this statement causes 12 to be passed into the `num1` parameter and 45 to be passed into the `num2` parameter, as shown in Figure 9-17.

Figure 9-17 Two arguments passed into two parameters

```
Module main()
   Display "The sum of 12 and 45 is:"
   Call showSum(12, 45)
End Module


Module showSum(Integer num1, Integer num2)
   Declare Integer result
   Set result = num1 + num2
   Display result
End Module
```

Suppose we were to reverse the order in which the arguments are listed in the module call, as shown here:

```
Call showSum(45, 12)
```

This would cause 45 to be passed into the `num1` parameter and 12 to be passed into the `num2` parameter. The following pseudocode code shows one more example. This time we are passing variables as arguments.

```
Declare Integer value1 = 2
Declare Integer value2 = 3
Call showSum(value1, value2)
```

When the `showSum` method executes as a result of this code, the `num1` parameter will contain 2 and the `num2` parameter will contain 3.

In the Spotlight:

Passing an Argument to a Module

Your friend Michael runs a catering company. Some of the ingredients that his recipes require are measured in cups. When he goes to the grocery store to buy those ingredients, however, they are sold only by the fluid ounce. He has asked you to write a simple program that converts cups to fluid ounces.

On Your Own: Working alone or with a partner, write the algorithm steps, draw a hierarchy chart and a flowchart, and write the pseudocode. Then, read on to see how you did. Remember, your solution does not have to be exactly the same as the one in the text in order to come up with the same result.

You could design the following algorithm:

1. Display an introductory screen that explains what the program does.
2. Get the number of cups.
3. Convert the number of cups to fluid ounces and display the result.

This algorithm lists the top level of tasks that the program needs to perform, and becomes the basis of the program's main module. Figure 9-18 shows the program's structure in a hierarchy chart.

Figure 9-18 Hierarchy chart for the program

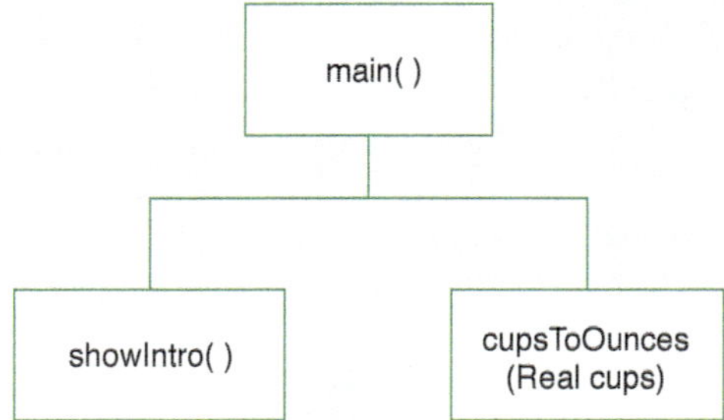

As shown in the hierarchy chart, the `main` module will call two other modules. Here are summaries of those modules:

- `showIntro`—This module will display a message on the screen that explains what the program does.
- `cupsToOunces`—This module will accept the number of cups as an argument and calculate and display the equivalent number of fluid ounces.

In addition to calling these modules, the `main` module will ask the user to enter the number of cups. This value will be passed to the `cupsToOunces` module. Program 9-10 shows the pseudocode for the program, and Figure 9-19 shows a flowchart.

Program 9-10:

```
Module main()
   // Declare a variable for the
   // number of cups needed.
   Declare Real cupsNeeded

   // Display an intro message.
   Call showIntro()

   // Get the number of cups.
   Display "Enter the number of cups."
   Input cupsNeeded

   // Convert cups to ounces.
   Call cupsToOunces(cupsNeeded)
End Module

// The showIntro module displays an
// introductory screen.
Module showIntro()
   Display "This program converts measurements"
   Display "in cups to fluid ounces. For your"
   Display "reference the formula is:"
   Display " 1 cup = 8 fluid ounces."
End Module

// The cupsToOunces module accepts a number
// of cups and displays the equivalent number
// of ounces.
Module cupsToOunces(Real cups)
   // Declare variables.
   Declare Real ounces

   // Convert cups to ounces.
   Set ounces = cups * 8

   // Display the result.
   Display "That converts to ",
   ounces, " ounces."
End Module
```

Program 9-10: *(continued)*

Program Output (with Input Shown in Bold)

```
This program converts measurements
in cups to fluid ounces. For your
reference the formula is:
1 cup = 8 fluid ounces.
Enter the number of cups.
2 [Enter]
That converts to 16 ounces.
```

Figure 9-19 Flowchart for Program 9-10

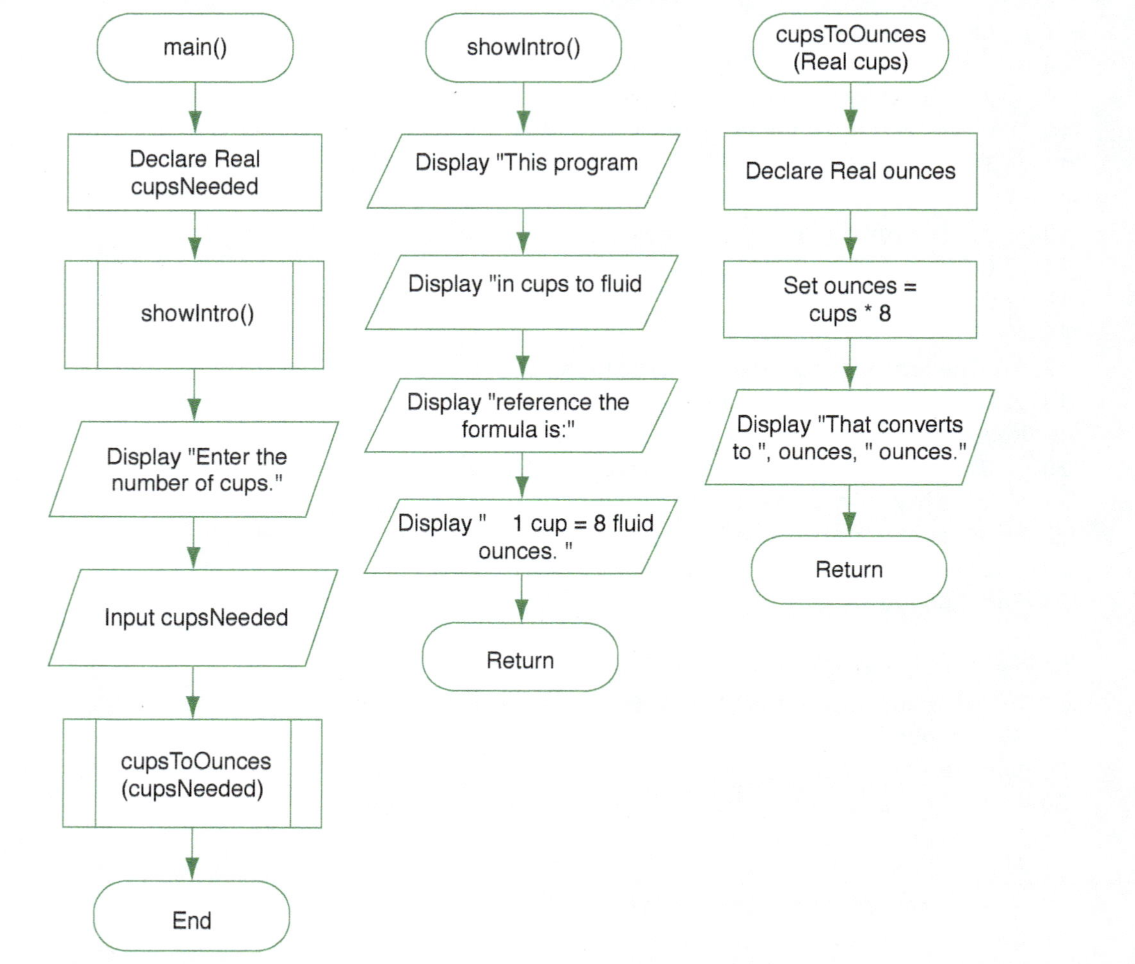

Checkpoint

9.14 What are the pieces of data that are passed into a module called?

9.15 What are the variables that receive pieces of data in a module called?

9.16 Does it usually matter whether an argument's data type is different from the data type of the parameter that it is being passed to?

9.17 Typically, what is a parameter variable's scope?

9.5 Global Variables and Global Constants

A global variable is accessible to all the modules in a program.

Global Variables

A **global variable** is a variable that is visible to every module in the program. A global variable's scope is the entire program, so all of the modules in the program can access a global variable. In most programming languages, you create a global variable by writing its declaration statement outside of all the modules, usually at the top of the program. Program 9-11 shows how you can declare a global variable in pseudocode

Program 9-11:

```
 1 // The following declares a global Integer variable.
 2 Declare Integer number
 3
 4 // The main module
 5 Module main()
 6     // Get a number from the user and store it
 7     // in the global variable number.
 8     Display "Enter a number."
 9     Input number
10
11     // Call the showNumber module.
12     Call showNumber()
13 End Module
14
15 // The showNumber module displays the contents
16 // of the global variable number.
17 Module showNumber()
18     Display "The number you entered is ", number
19 End Module
```

Program Output (with Input Shown in Bold)

```
Enter a number.
22 [Enter]
The number you entered is 22
```

Line 2 declares an `Integer` variable named number. Because the declaration does not appear inside a module, the number variable is a global variable. All of the modules that are defined in the program have access to the variable. When the `Input` statement in line 9 (inside the `main` module) executes, the value entered by the user is stored in the global variable number. When the `Display` statement in line 18 (inside the showNumber module) executes, it is the value of the same global variable that is displayed.

Most programmers agree that you should restrict the use of global variables, or not use them at all. The reasons are as follows:

- Global variables make debugging difficult. Any statement in a program can change the value of a global variable. If you find that the wrong value is being stored in a global variable, you have to track down every statement that accesses it to determine where the bad value is coming from. In a program with thousands of lines of code, this can be difficult.
- Modules that use global variables are usually dependent on those variables. If you want to use such a module in a different program, most likely you will have to redesign it so it does not rely on the global variable.
- Global variables make a program hard to understand. A global variable can be modified by any statement in the program. If you are to understand any part of the program that uses a global variable, you have to be aware of all the other parts of the program that access the global variable.

In most cases, you should declare variables locally and pass them as arguments to the modules that need to access them.

Global Constants

Although you should try to avoid the use of global variables, it is permissible to use global constants in a program. A **global constant** is a named constant that is available to every module in the program. Because a global constant's value cannot be changed during the program's execution, you do not have to worry about many of the potential hazards that are associated with the use of global variables.

Global constants are typically used to represent unchanging values that are needed throughout a program. For example, suppose a banking program uses a named constant to represent an interest rate. If the interest rate is used in several modules, it is easier to create a global constant, rather than a local named constant in each module. This also simplifies maintenance. If the interest rate changes, only the declaration of the global constant has to be changed, instead of several local declarations.

Checkpoint

9.18 What is the scope of a global variable?

9.19 Give one good reason that you should not use global variables in a program.

9.20 What is a global constant? Is it permissible to use global constants in a program?

9.6 Introduction to Functions: Generating Random Numbers

A function is a module that returns a value back to the part of the program that called it. Most programming languages provide a library of prewritten functions that perform commonly needed tasks. In these libraries you typically find a function that generates random numbers.

A **function** is a special type of module. It is like a regular module in the following ways:

- A function is a group of statements that perform a specific task.
- When you want to execute a function, you call it.

When a function finishes, however, it returns a value back to the statement that called it. The value that is returned from a function can be used like any other value: it can be assigned to a variable, displayed on the screen, used in a mathematical expression (if it is a number), and so on.

NOTE: In our pseudocode, you use the `Call` statement to call a module. You do not use the Call statement to call a function, however. Function calls are usually inserted into statements that perform some operation with the value that is returned from the function. For example, a function call might be inserted into a `Set` statement that assigns the value that is returned from the function to a variable. A function call might also be inserted into a `Display` statement that displays the value that is returned from the function.

Library Functions

Most programming languages come with a library of functions that have already been written. These functions, known as **library functions**, are built into the programming language, and you can call them any time you need them. Library functions make a programmer's job easier because they perform many of the tasks that programmers commonly need to perform. For example, there are library functions to manipulate numbers and perform various math operations, to convert data from one type to another, and to manipulate strings.

The code for a language's library functions is usually stored in special files. These files are normally placed on your computer when you install a compiler or interpreter. When you call a library function in one of your programs, the compiler or interpreter automatically causes the function to execute, without requiring the function's code to appear in your program. This way, you never have to see the code for a library function—you only need to know the purpose of the library function, the arguments that you must pass to it, and what type of data it returns.

Because you do not see the internal workings of library functions, many programmers think of them as black boxes. The term **black box** is used to describe any mechanism that accepts input, performs some operation that cannot be seen on the input, and produces output. Figure 9-20 illustrates this idea.

Figure 9-20 A library function viewed as a black box

This section demonstrates how functions work by looking at a library function that generates random numbers. Most programming languages provide such a function, and we will look at some interesting programs that can be written with it. In the following section you will learn to write your own functions.

Using the `random` Function

Most programming languages provide a library function that generates random numbers. This chapter uses the `random` function for this purpose in the pseudocode. Random numbers are useful for lots of different programming tasks. The following are just a few examples:

- Random numbers are commonly used in programmed games. For example, computer games that let the player roll dice use random numbers to represent the values of the dice. Programs that show cards being drawn from a shuffled deck use random numbers to represent the face values of the cards.
- Random numbers are useful in programmed simulations, animations, and stories. In some programs, the computer must randomly decide how a person, animal, insect, or other living being will behave. Formulas can be constructed in which a random number is used to determine various actions and events that take place in the program.
- Random numbers are useful in statistical programs that must randomly select data for analysis.
- Random numbers are commonly used in computer security to encrypt sensitive data.

The following pseudocode statement shows an example of how you might call the `random` function. Assume that `number` is an `Integer` variable.

```
Set number = random(1, 100)
```

The part of the statement that reads `random(1, 100)` is a call to the `random` function. Notice that two arguments appear inside the parentheses: 1 and 100. These arguments tell the function to give a random number in the range of 1 through 100. Figure 9-21 illustrates this part of the statement.

Notice that the call to the `random` function appears on the right side of an = operator. When the function is called, it will generate a random number in the range of 1 through 100 and then return that number. The number that is returned will be assigned to the `number` variable, as shown in Figure 9-22.

Figure 9-21 A statement that calls the `random` function

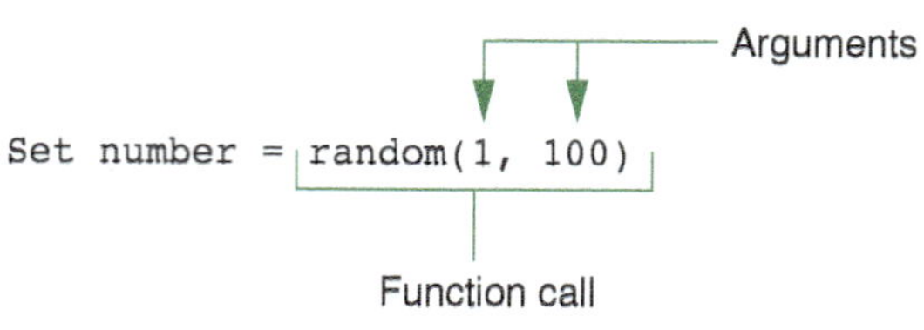

Figure 9-22 The `random` function returns a value

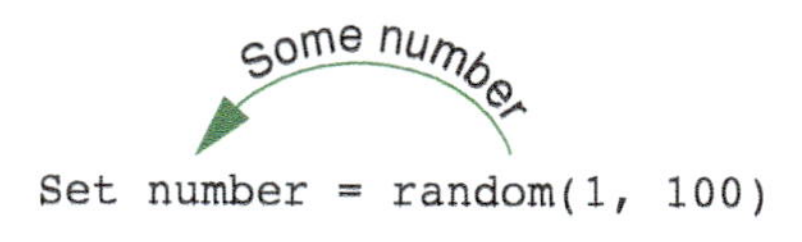

A random number in the range of 1 through 100 will be assigned to the `number` variable.

Program 9-12 shows the pseudocode for a complete program that uses the `random` function. The statement in line 2 generates a random number in the range of 1 through 10 and assigns it to the `number` variable. (The program output shows that the number 7 was generated, but this value is arbitrary. If this were an actual program, it could display any number between 1 and 10.)

Program 9-12:

```
1 Declare Integer number
2 Set number = random(1, 10)
3 Display number
```

Program Output

```
7
```

NOTE: The way that you set up a program to work with library functions differs among programming languages. In some languages you don't have to do anything special to call library functions. That's the approach we take in our pseudocode. In other languages, however, you may have to write a statement near the top of a program indicating that it will access a particular library function.

The pseudocode in Program 9-13 shows another example. This program uses a `For` loop that iterates five times. Inside the loop, the statement in line 9 calls the `random` function to generate a random number in the range of 1 through 100.

Program 9-13: 

```
 1 // Declare variables
 2 Declare Integer number, counter
 3
 4 // The following loop displays
 5 // five random numbers.
 6 For counter = 1 To 5
 7    // Get a random number in the range of
 8    // 1 through 100 and assign it to number.
 9    Set number = random(1, 100)
10
11    // Display the number.
12    Display number
13 End For
```

Program Output

```
89
7
16
41
12
```

The pseudocode in both Programs 9-12 and 9-13 calls the random function and assigns its return value to the `number` variable. If you just want to display a random number, it is not necessary to assign the random number to a variable. You can send the `random` function's return value directly to the `Display` statement, as shown here:

```
Display random(1, 10)
```

When this statement executes, the `random` function is called. The function generates a random number in the range of 1 through 10. That value is returned and then sent to the `Display` statement. As a result, a random number in the range of 1 through 10 will be displayed. Figure 9-23 illustrates this.

The pseudocode in Program 9-14 shows how you could simplify Program 9-13. This program also displays five random numbers, but this program does not use a variable to hold those numbers. The `random` function's return value is sent directly to the `Display` statement in line 4.

Figure 9-23 Displaying a random number

A random number in the range of
1 through 10 will be displayed.

Program 9-14:

```
1 // Counter variable
2 Declare Integer counter
3
4 // This loop displays five random numbers.
5 For counter = 1 To 5
6    Display random(1, 100)
7 End For
```

Program Output

```
32
79
6
12
98
```

In the Spotlight:

Using Random Numbers

Dr. Kimura teaches an introductory statistics class, and has asked you to write a program to use in class to simulate the rolling of dice. The program should randomly generate two numbers in the range of 1 through 6 and display them. In your interview with Dr. Kimura, you learn that the program should simulate several rolls of the dice, one after the other. You decide to write a loop that simulates one roll of the dice, and then asks the user whether another roll should be performed. As long as the user answers "y" for yes, the loop will repeat.

On Your Own: Working alone or with a partner, write the algorithm steps, draw a flowchart, and write the pseudocode. Then, read on to see how you did. Remember, your solution does not have to be exactly the same as the one in the text in order to come up with the same result.

Program 9-15 shows pseudocode for the program, and Figure 9-24 shows the flowchart.

Program 9-15:

```
// Declare a variable to control the
// loop iterations.
Declare String again

Do
    // Roll the dice.
    Display "Rolling the dice..."
    Display "Their values are:"
    Display random(1, 6)
    Display random(1, 6)

    // Do this again?
    Display "Want to roll them again? (y = yes)"
    Input again
While again == "y" OR again == "Y"
```

Program Output (with Input Shown in Bold)

```
Rolling the dice...
Their values are:
2
6
Want to roll them again? (y = yes)
y [Enter]
Rolling the dice...
Their values are:
4
1
Want to roll them again? (y = yes)
y [Enter]
Rolling the dice...
Their values are:
3
3
Want to roll them again? (y = yes)
n [Enter]
```

Figure 9-24 Flowchart for Program 9-15

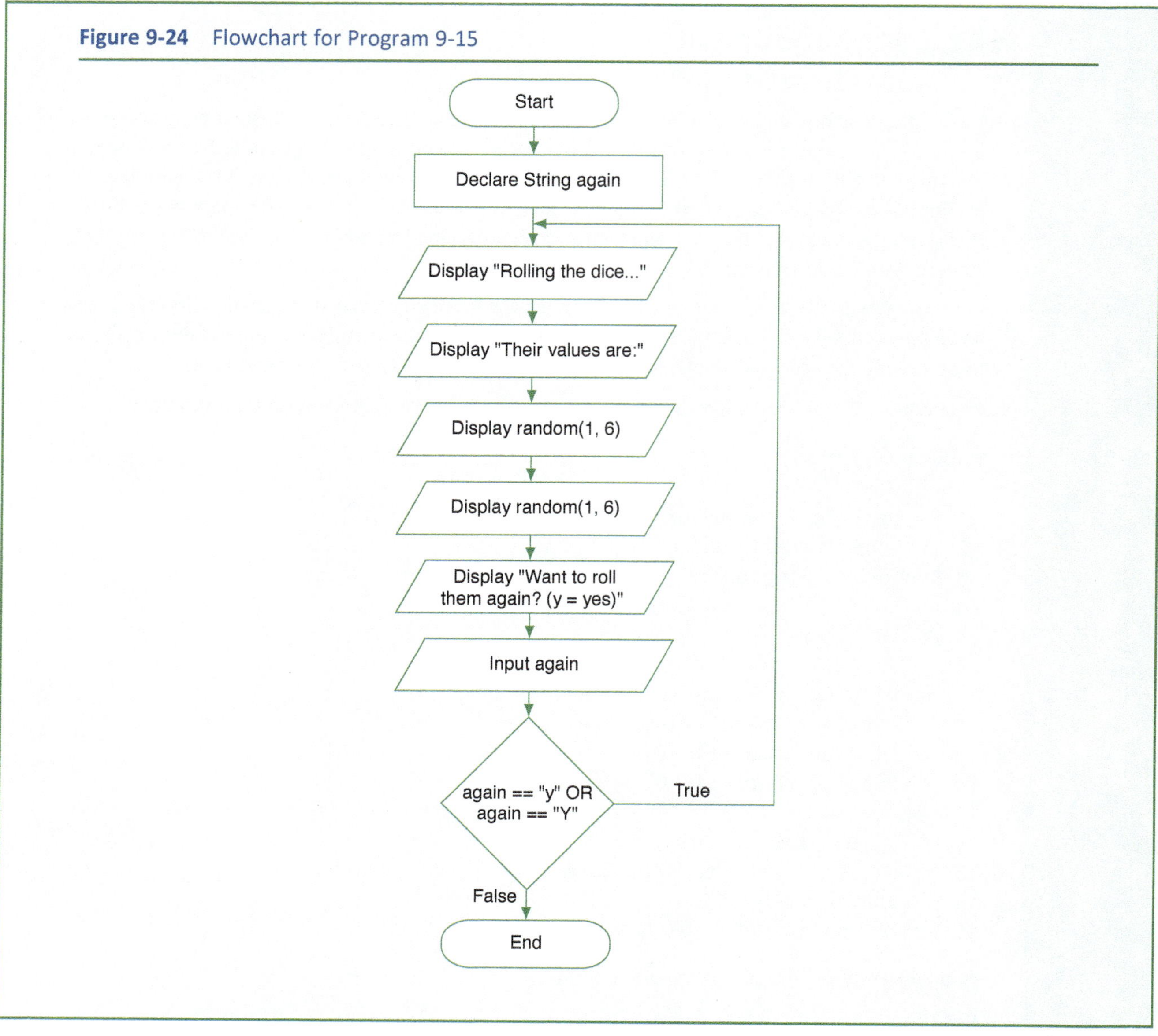

The `random` function returns an integer value, so you can write a call to the function anywhere that you can write an integer value. You have already seen examples where the function's return value is assigned to a variable and where the function's return value is sent to the `Display` statement. To further illustrate the point, here is a statement that uses the `random` function in a math expression:

```
Set x = random(1, 10) * 2
```

In this statement, a random number in the range of 1 through 10 is generated and then multiplied by 2. The result is assigned to the `x` variable. You can also test the return value of the function with an `If-Then` statement, as demonstrated in the following *In the Spotlight* section.

In the Spotlight:

Using Random Numbers to Represent Other Values

Dr. Kimura has asked you to write a program that simulates ten coin flips, one after the other. Each time the program simulates a coin flip, it should randomly display either "Heads" or "Tails."

You decide that you can simulate the flipping of a coin by randomly generating a number in the range of 1 through 2. You will design a decision structure that displays "Heads" if the random number is 1, or "Tails" otherwise.

On Your Own: Working alone or with a partner, write the algorithm steps, draw a flowchart, and write the pseudocode. Then, read on to see how you did. Remember, your solution does not have to be exactly the same as the one in the text in order to come up with the same result.

Program 9-16 shows the pseudocode for the program, and Figure 9-25 shows the flowchart.

Program 9-16:

```
// Declare a counter variable.
Declare Integer counter

// Constant for the number of flips.
Constant Integer NUM_FLIPS = 10

For counter = 1 To NUM_FLIPS
    // Simulate the coin flip.
    If random(1, 2) == 1 Then
        Display "Heads"
    Else
        Display "Tails"
    End If
End For
```

Program Output

```
Tails
Tails
Heads
Tails
Heads
Heads
Heads
Tails
Heads
Tails
```

Figure 9-25 Flowchart for Program 9-16

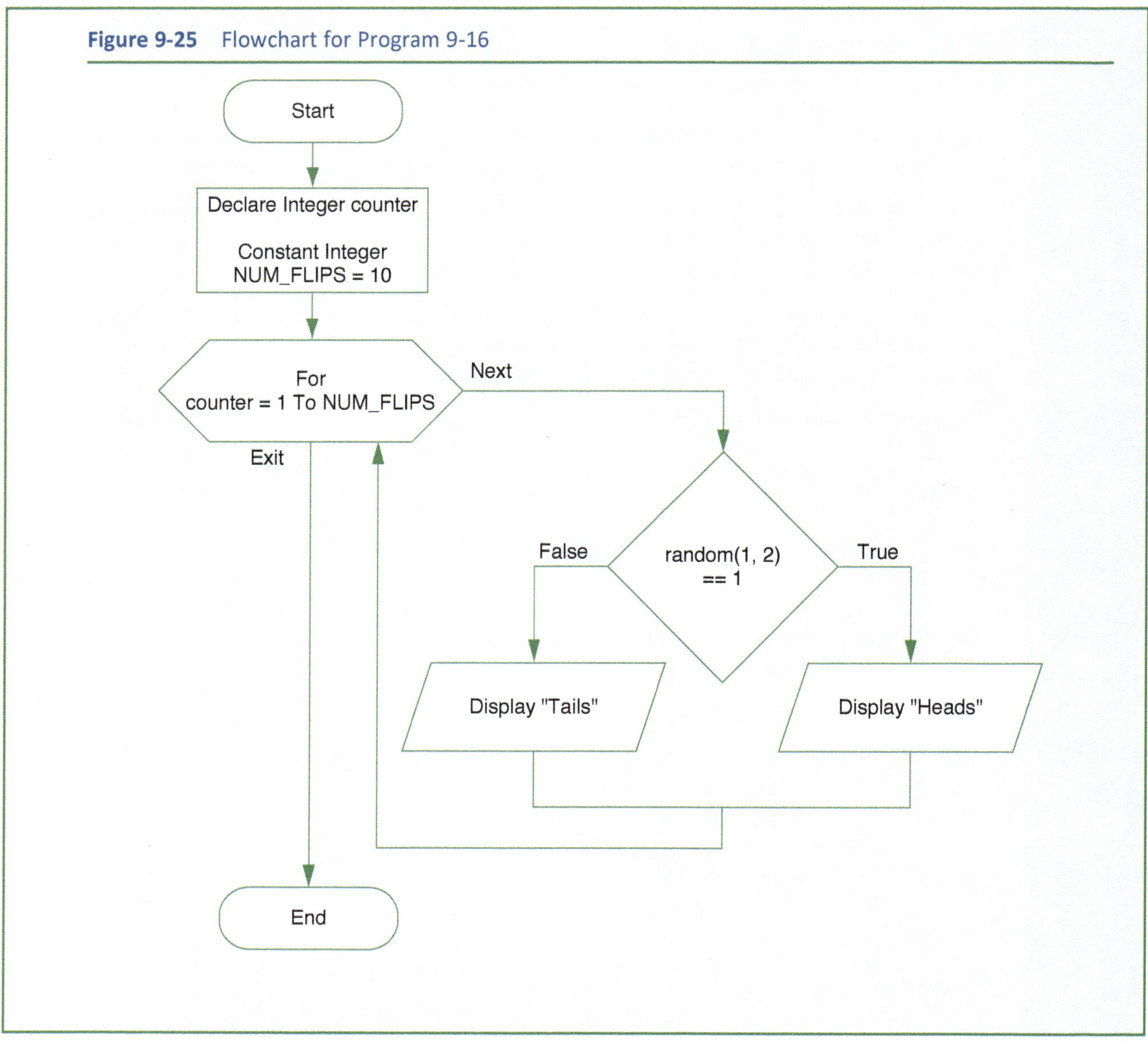

Checkpoint

9.21 How does a function differ from a module?

9.22 What is a library function?

9.23 Why are library functions like "black boxes"?

9.24 In pseudocode, what does the following statement do?

```
Set x = random(1, 100)
```

9.25 In pseudocode, what does the following statement do?

```
Display random(1, 20)
```

9.7 Writing Your Own Functions

Most programming languages allow you to write your own functions. When you write a function, you are essentially writing a module that can send a value back to the part of the program that called it.

VideoNote
Writing a Function

Recall that when you create a module you write its definition. Functions are defined in a manner similar to modules. The following are the important characteristics of a function definition:

- The first line of a function definition, the **function header**, specifies the data type of the value that is returned from the function, the name of the function, and any parameter variables used by the function to accept arguments.
- Following the function header is the **function body**, which is comprised of one or more statements that are executed when the function is called.
- One of the statements in the function body must be a `Return` statement. A `Return` statement specifies the value that is returned from the function when the function ends.

Here is the general format that we will use for writing functions in pseudocode:

```
Function DataType FunctionName(ParameterList)
   statement
   statement
   etc.
   Return value
End Function
```

A function must have a Return statement. This causes a value to be sent back to the part of the program that called the function.

The first line in this pseudocode, the function header, begins with the word Function and is followed by these items:

- `DataType` is the data type of the value that the function returns. For example, if the function returns an integer, the word `Integer` will appear here. If the function returns a real number, the word `Real` will appear here. Likewise, if the function returns a string, the word `String` will appear here.
- `FunctionName` is the name of the function. As with modules, you should give a function a name that describes what the function does. In most languages you follow the same rules for naming functions that you follow for naming modules and variables.
- An optional parameter list appears inside a set of parentheses. If the function does not accept arguments, then an empty set of parentheses will appear.

On the line after the function header, one or more statements will appear. These statements, the function's body, are performed any time the function is executed. One of the statements in the body must be a `Return` statement, which takes the following form:

```
Return value
```

The *value* that follows the word `Return` is the value that the function will send back to the part of the program that called the function. This can be any value, variable, or expression that has a value (such as a math expression). The value that is returned must be of the same data type as that specified in the function header. Otherwise, an error will occur.

The last line of the definition, after the body, reads `End` Function. This line marks the end of the function definition.

Here is an example of a function written in pseudocode:

```
Function Integer sum(Integer num1, Integer num2)
  Declare Integer result
  Set result = num1 + num2
  Return result
End Function
```

Figure 9-26 illustrates the various parts of the function header. Notice that the function returns an `Integer`, the function's name is `sum`, and the function has two `Integer` parameters, named `num1` and `num2`.

Figure 9-26 Parts of the function header

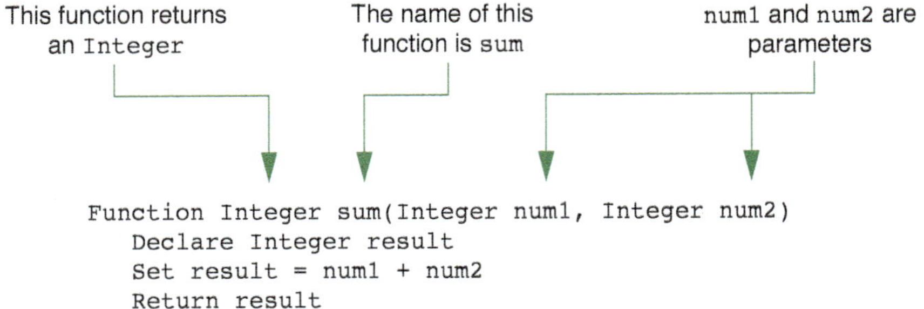

The purpose of this function is to accept two integer values as arguments and return their sum. Let's look at the body of the function to see how it works. The first statement, a variable declaration, declares a local `Integer` variable named result. The next statement assigns the value of `num1 + num2` to the `result` variable. Next, the `Return` statement executes, which causes the function to end execution and sends the value in the `result` variable back to the part of the program that called the function.

Program 9-17 shows a complete pseudocode program that uses the function.

Program 9-17:

```
Module main()
   // Local variables
   Declare Integer firstAge, secondAge, total

   // Get the user's age and the user's
   // best friend's age.
   Display "Enter your age."
   Input firstAge
   Display "Enter your best friend's age."
   Input secondAge

   // Get the sum of both ages.
   Set total = sum(firstAge, secondAge)

   // Display the sum.
   Display "Together you are ", total, " years old."
End Module
```

Program 9-17: *(continued)*

```
18
19 // The sum function accepts two Integer arguments and
20 // returns the sum of those arguments as an Integer.
21 Function Integer sum(Integer num1, Integer num2)
22     Declare Integer result
23     Set result = num1 + num2
24     Return result
25 End Function
```

Program Output (with Input Shown in Bold)

```
Enter your age.
22 [Enter]
Enter your best friend's age.
24 [Enter]
Together you are 46 years old
```

In the `main` module, the program gets two integer values from the user and stores them in the `firstAge` and `secondAge` variables. The statement in line 13 calls the `sum` function, passing `firstAge` and `secondAge` as arguments. The value that is returned from the `sum` function is assigned to the `total` variable. In this case, the function will return 46. Figure 9-27 shows how the arguments are passed into the function, and how a value is returned back from the function.

Figure 9-27 Arguments are passed to the `sum` function and a value is returned

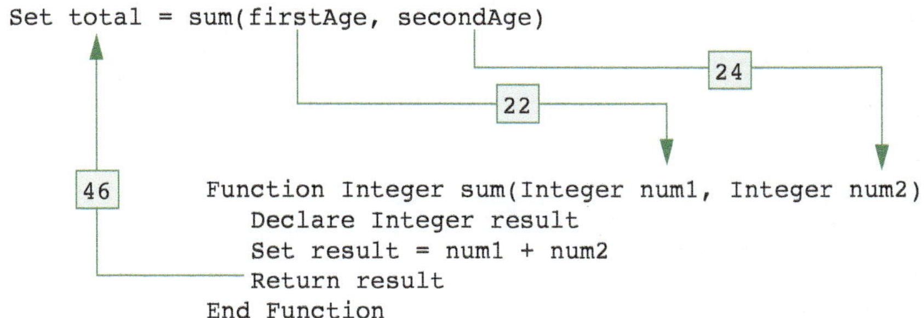

Flowcharting a Function

When creating a flowchart for a program that has functions, you draw a separate flowchart for each function. In a flowchart for a function, the starting terminal symbol usually shows the name of the function, along with any parameters that the function has. The ending terminal symbol reads *Return*, followed by the value or expression that is being returned. Figure 9-28 shows the flowchart for the `sum` function in Program 9-17.

Figure 9-28 Flowchart for the sum function

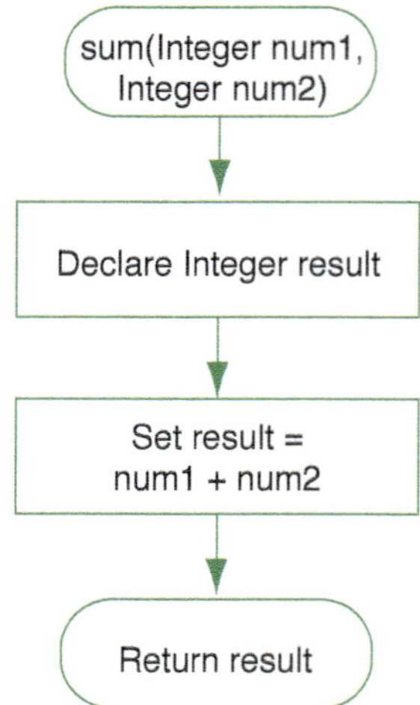

Making the Most of the Return Statement

Look again at the sum function presented in Program 9-17:

```
Function Integer sum(Integer num1, Integer num2)
  Declare Integer result
  Set result = num1 + num2
  Return result
End Function
```

Notice that three things happen inside this function: (1) a local variable, result, is declared, (2) the value of the expression `num1 + num2` is assigned to the `result` variable, and (3) the value of the `result` variable is returned.

Although this function does what it sets out to do, it can be simplified. Because the `Return` statement can return the value of an expression, you can eliminate the `result` variable and rewrite the function as:

```
Function Integer sum(Integer num1, Integer num2)
  Return num1 + num2
End Function
```

This version of the function does not store the value of `num1` + `num2` in a variable. Instead, it takes advantage of the fact that the `Return` statement can return the value of an expression. This version of the function does the same thing as the previous version, but in only one step.

NOTE: In most programming languages you can pass as many arguments into a function as you need, but you can return only one value from a function.

How to Use Functions

Most programming languages allow you to create both modules and functions. Functions provide many of the same benefits as modules: they simplify code, reduce duplication, enhance your ability to test code, increase the speed of development, and ease the facilitation of teamwork.

Because functions return a value, they can be useful in specific situations. For example, you can use a function to prompt the user for input, and then it can return the value entered by the user. Suppose you've been asked to design a program that calculates the sale price of an item in a retail business. To do that, the program would need to get the item's regular price from the user. Here is a function you could define for that purpose:

```
Function Real getRegularPrice()
   // Local variable to hold the price.
   Declare Real price

   // Get the regular price.
   Display "Enter the item's regular price."
   Input price

   // Return the regular price.
   Return price
End Function
```

Then, elsewhere in the program, you could call that function, as shown here:

```
   // Get the item's regular price.
   Set regularPrice = getRegularPrice()
```

When this statement executes, the `getRegularPrice` function is called, which gets a value from the user and returns it. That value is then assigned to the `regularPrice` variable.

You can also use functions to simplify complex mathematical expressions. For example, calculating the sale price of an item seems like it would be a simple task: you calculate the discount and subtract it from the regular price. In a program, however, a statement that performs this calculation is not that straightforward, as shown in the following example. (Assume `DISCOUNT_PERCENTAGE` is a global constant that is defined in the program, and it specifies the percentage of the discount.)

```
Set salePrice = regularPrice - (regularPrice * DISCOUNT_PERCENTAGE)
```

This statement isn't easy to understand because it performs so many steps: it calculates the discount amount, subtracts that value from regularPrice, and assigns the result to salePrice. You could simplify the statement by breaking out part of the math expression and placing it in a function. Here is a function named `discount` that accepts an item's price as an argument and returns the amount of the discount:

```
Function Real discount(Real price)
   Return price * DISCOUNT_PERCENTAGE
End Function
```

You could then call the function in your calculation:

```
Set salePrice = regularPrice - discount(regularPrice)
```

This statement is easier to read than the one previously shown, and it is clearer that the discount is being subtracted from the regular price. The pseudocode in Program 9-18 shows the complete sale price calculating program using the functions just described.

Program 9-18:

```
// Global constant for the discount percentage.
Constant Real DISCOUNT_PERCENTAGE = 0.20

// The main module is the program's starting point.
Module main()
   // Local variables to hold regular and sale prices.
   Declare Real regularPrice, salePrice

   // Get the item's regular price.
   Set regularPrice = getRegularPrice()

   // Calculate the sale price.
   Set salePrice = regularPrice - discount(regularPrice)

   // Display the sale price.
   Display "The sale price is $", salePrice
End Module

// The getRegularPrice function prompts the
// user to enter an item's regular price and
// returns that value as a Real.
Function Real getRegularPrice()
   // Local variable to hold the price.
   Declare Real price

   // Get the regular price.
   Display "Enter the item's regular price."
   Input price

   // Return the regular price.
   Return price
End Function

// The discount function accepts an item's price
// as an argument and returns the amount of the
// discount specified by DISCOUNT_PERCENTAGE.
Function Real discount(Real price)
   Return price * DISCOUNT_PERCENTAGE
End Function
```

Program Output (with Input Shown in Bold)

Enter the item's regular price.
100.00 [Enter]
The sale price is $80

Using IPO Charts with Functions

Recall from Chapter 5 that an IPO chart is a simple but effective tool for designing a program. IPO stands for *input*, *processing*, and *output*, and an *IPO chart* describes the input, processing, and output of a program. You can also create IPO charts for the individual functions in a program. The input column shows a description of the data that is passed to the function as arguments, the processing column shows a description of the process that the function performs, and the output column describes the data that is returned from the function. For example, Figure 9-29 shows IPO charts for the `getRegularPrice` and `discount` functions that you saw in Program 9-18.

Figure 9-29 IPO charts for the `getRegularPrice` and `discount` functions

IPO Chart for the `getRegularPrice` Function		
Input	Processing	Output
None	Prompts the user to enter an item's regular price	The item's regular price, as a `Real`

IPO Chart for the `discount` Function		
Input	Processing	Output
An item's regular price	Calculates an item's discount by multiplying the regular price by the global constant `DISCOUNT_PERCENTAGE`	The item's discount, as a `Real`

Notice that the IPO charts provide only brief descriptions of a function's input, processing, and output, but do not show the specific steps taken in a function. In many cases, however, IPO charts include sufficient information so that they can be used instead of a flowchart. The decision of whether to use an IPO chart, a flowchart, or both is often left to the programmer's personal preference.

Returning Strings

So far you've seen examples of functions that return numbers. Most programming languages also allow you to write functions that return strings. For example, the following pseudocode function prompts the user to enter their name, and then returns the string that the user entered.

```
Function String getName()
   // Local variable to hold the user's name.
   Declare String name
   // Get the user's name.
   Display "Enter your name."
   Input name
   // Return the name.
   Return name
End Function
```

Returning Boolean Values

Most languages also allow you to write **Boolean functions**, which return either `True` or `False`. You can use a Boolean function to test a condition, and then return either `True` or `False` to indicate whether the condition exists. Boolean functions are useful for simplifying complex conditions that are tested in decision and repetition structures.

For example, suppose you are designing a game that will ask the user to enter a number, and then determine whether that number is even or odd. The following pseudocode shows how you can make that determination. Assume `number` is an `Integer` variable containing the number entered by the user.

```
If number MOD 2 == 0 Then
   Display "The number is even."
Else
   Display "The number is odd."
End If
```

The meaning of the Boolean expression being tested by this `If-Then` statement isn't clear, so let's take a closer look at it:

```
number MOD 2 == 0
```

This expression uses the `MOD` operator. Recall that the `MOD` operator divides two integers and returns the remainder of the division. So this pseudocode is saying, "If the remainder of `number` divided by 2 is equal to 0, then display a message indicating the number is even, or else display a message indicating the number is odd."

Because dividing an even number by 2 will always give a remainder of 0, this logic will work. The pseudocode would be easier to understand, however, if you could somehow rewrite it to say, "If the number is even, then display a message indicating it is even, or else display a message indicating it is odd." As it turns out, this can be done with a Boolean function. In this example, you could design a Boolean function named `isEven` that accepts a number as an argument and returns `True` if the number is even, or `False` otherwise. The following is the pseudocode for such a function.

```
Function Boolean isEven(Integer number)
   // Local variable to hold True or False.
   Declare Boolean status
   // Determine whether number is even. If it is, set
   // status to True. Otherwise, set status to False.
   If number MOD 2 == 0 Then
      Set status = True
   Else
      Set status = False
   End If
   // Return the value in the status variable.
   Return status
End Function
```

Then you can rewrite the `If-Then` statement so it calls the `isEven` function to determine whether number is even.

```
If isEven(number) Then
   Display "The number is even."
Else
   Display "The number is odd."
End If
```

Not only is this logic easier to understand, but now you have a function that you can call in the program any time you need to test a number to determine whether it is even.

Checkpoint

9.26 What is the purpose of the Return statement in a function?

9.27 Look at the following pseudocode function definition:

```
Function Integer doSomething(Integer number)
  Return number * 2
End Function
```

a. What is the name of the function?

b. What type of data does the function return?

c. Given the function definition, what will the following statement display?

```
Display doSomething (10)
```

9.28 What is a Boolean function?

Chapter Review

Multiple Choice

1. A group of statements that exist within a program for the purpose of performing a specific task is a(n) __________.
   a. block
   b. parameter
   c. module
   d. expression

2. A benefit of using modules that helps to reduce the duplication of code within a program is __________.
   a. code reuse
   b. divide and conquer
   c. debugging
   d. facilitation of teamwork

3. The first line of a module definition is known as the __________.
   a. body
   b. introduction
   c. initialization
   d. header

4. You __________ the module to execute it.
   a. define
   b. call
   c. import
   d. export

5. A __________ point is the memory address of the location in the program that the computer will return to when a module ends.
   a. termination
   b. module definition
   c. return
   d. reference

6. A design technique that programmers use to break down an algorithm into modules is known as __________.
   a. top-down design
   b. code simplification
   c. code refactoring
   d. hierarchical subtasking

7. A __________ is a diagram that gives a visual representation of the relationships between modules in a program.
   a. flowchart
   b. module relationship chart
   c. symbol chart
   d. hierarchy chart

8. A __________ is a variable that is declared inside a module function.
   a. global variable
   b. local variable
   c. hidden variable
   d. none of the above; you cannot declare a variable inside a module

9. A(n) __________ is the part of a program in which a variable may be accessed.
   a. declaration space
   b. area of visibility
   c. scope
   d. mode

10. A(n) __________ is a piece of data that is sent into a module.
    a. argument
    b. parameter
    c. header
    d. packet

11. A(n) __________ is a special variable that receives a piece of data when a module is called.
    a. argument
    b. parameter
    c. header
    d. packet

12. A variable that is visible to every module in the program is a __________.
    a. local variable
    b. universal variable
    c. program-wide variable
    d. global variable

13. When possible, you should avoid using __________ variables in a program.
    a. local
    b. global
    c. reference
    d. parameter

14. This is a prewritten function that is built into a programming language.
    a. standard function
    b. library function
    c. custom function
    d. cafeteria function

15. This part of a function definition specifies the data type of the value that the function returns.
    a. header
    b. footer
    c. body
    d. Return statement

16. This part of a function definition is comprised of one or more statements that are executed when the function is called.
    a. header
    b. footer
    c. body
    d. Return statement

17. In pseudocode, this statement causes a function to end and sends a value back to the part of the program that called the function.
    a. End
    b. Send
    c. Exit
    d. Return

18. This is a design tool that describes the input, processing, and output of a function.
    a. hierarchy chart
    b. IPO chart
    c. datagram chart
    d. data processing chart

19. This type of function returns either True or False.
    a. Binary
    b. TrueFalse
    c. Boolean
    d. logical

True or False

1. The code for a library function must appear in a program in order for the program to call the library function.
2. Modules make it easier for programmers to work in teams.
3. Module names should be as short as possible.
4. Calling a module and defining a module mean the same thing.
5. A flowchart shows the hierarchical relationships between modules in a program.
6. A hierarchy chart does not show the steps that are taken inside a module.
7. A statement in one module can access a local variable in another module.
8. In most programming languages, you cannot have two variables with the same name in the same scope.
9. Programming languages typically require that arguments be of the same data type as the parameters that they are passed to.
10. Most languages do not allow you to write modules that accept multiple arguments.
11. Complex mathematical expressions can sometimes be simplified by breaking out part of the expression and putting it in a function.
12. In many languages it is an error to assign a real number to an integer variable.

Short Answer

1. How do modules help you to reuse code in a program?
2. Name and describe the two parts that a module definition has in most languages.
3. When a module is executing, what happens when the end of the module is reached?
4. What is a local variable? What statements are able to access a local variable?
5. In most languages, where does a local variable's scope begin and end?
6. What is the difference between a module and a function?
7. Why do global variables make a program difficult to debug?
8. What is a substring?

Algorithm Workbench

1. Design a module named `timesTen`. The module should accept an `Integer` argument. When the module is called, it should display the product of its argument multiplied times 10.

2. Examine the following pseudocode module header, and then write a statement that calls the module, passing 12 as an argument.

```
Module showValue(Integer quantity)
```

3. Look at the following pseudocode module header:

```
Module myModule(Integer a, Integer b, Integer c)
```

   Now look at the following call to `myModule`:

```
Call myModule(3, 2, 1)
```

   When this call executes, what value will be stored in a? What value will be stored in b? What value will be stored in c?

4. Assume that a pseudocode program contains the following module:

```
Module display(Integer arg1, Real arg2, String arg3)
   Display "Here are the values:"
   Display arg1, " ", arg2, " ", arg3
End Module
```

   Assume that the same program has a `main` module with the following variable declarations:

```
Declare Integer age
Declare Real income
Declare String name
```

   Write a statement that calls the `display` module and passes these variables to it.

5. Design a module named `getNumber`, which uses a reference parameter variable to accept an `Integer` argument. The module should prompt the user to enter a number and then store the input in the reference parameter variable.

6. As shown in this chapter, write a pseudocode statement that generates a random number in the range of 1 through 100 and assigns it to a variable named rand.

7. The following pseudocode statement calls a function named half, which returns a value that is half that of the argument. (Assume both the result and number variables are Real.) Write pseudocode for the function.

```
Set result = half(number)
```

8. A pseudocode program contains the following function definition:

```
Function Integer cube(Integer num)
   Return num * num * num
End Function
```

Write a statement that passes the value 4 to this function and assigns its return value to the variable result.

9. Design a pseudocode function named `timesTen` that accepts an Integer argument. When the function is called, it should return the value of its argument multiplied times 10.

10. Design a pseudocode function named `getFirstName` that asks the user to enter their first name, and returns it.

Debugging Exercises

1. Find the error in the following pseudocode.

```
Module main()
    Declare Real mileage
    Call getMileage()
    Display "You've driven a total of ", mileage, " miles."
End Module

Module getMileage()
    Display "Enter your vehicle's mileage."
    Input mileage
End Module
```

2. Find the error in the following pseudocode.

```
Module main()
    Call getServings()
End Module
Module getServings()
    Declare Real servings
    Display "How many servings are in the first bag of chips?"
    Input servings

    Declare Real servings
    Display "How many servings are in the second bag of chips?"
    Input servings
End Module
```

3. Find the potential error in the following pseudocode.

```
Module main()
    Call squareNumber(5)
End Module

Module squareNumber(Integer Ref number)
    Set number = number^2
    Display number
End Module
```

4. Find the error in the following pseudocode.

```
Module main()
    Call raiseToPower(2, 1.5)
End Module

Module raiseToPower(Real value, Integer power)
    Declare Real result
    Set result = value^power
    Display result
End Module
```

5. The programmer intends for this pseudocode to display three random numbers in the range of 1 through 7. According to the way we've been generating random numbers in this book, however, there appears to be an error. Can you find it?

```
// This program displays three random numbers
// in the range of 1 through 7.
Declare Integer count

// Display three random numbers.
For count = 1 To 3
     Display random(7, 1)
End For
```

6. Can you find the reason that the following pseudocode function does not return the value indicated in the comments?

```
// The calcDiscountPrice function accepts an item's price and
// the discount percentage as arguments. It uses those
// values to calculate and return the discounted price.
Function Real calcDiscountPrice(Real price, Real percentage)
    // Calculate the discount.
    Declare Real discount = price * percentage

    // Subtract the discount from the price.
    Declare Real discountPrice = price - discount

    // Return the discount price.
    Return discount

End Function
```

Programming Exercises

VideoNote Kilometer Converter

1. Kilometer Converter

Design a modular program that asks the user to enter a distance in kilometers, and then converts that distance to miles. The conversion formula is as follows:

$$Miles = Kilometers \times 0.6214$$

2. Inventory Shrinkage

In business, inventory shrinkage is the percentage of inventory that is lost to damage, theft, and miscalculations. The formula to calculate inventory shrinkage is:

$$IS = \left(\frac{RI - AI}{RI}\right) 100$$

where:

- *IS* is inventory shrinkage, which is the percentage of inventory that has been lost
- *RI* is the recorded inventory, which is the amount of inventory that should be on-hand
- *AI* is the actual inventory, which is the amount of inventory that is actually on-hand

Design a modular program that calculates a business's inventory shrinkage. The program should use modules to get the amounts of recorded inventory and actual inventory from the user, and then display the inventory shrinkage percentage.

3. Stadium Seating

There are three seating categories at a stadium. For a softball game, Class A seats cost $15, Class B seats cost $12, and Class C seats cost $9. Design a modular program that asks how many tickets for each class of seats were sold, and then displays the amount of income generated from ticket sales.

4. Paint Job Estimator

A painting company has determined that for every 115 square feet of wall space, one gallon of paint and eight hours of labor will be required. The company charges $20.00 per hour for labor. Design a modular program that asks the user to enter the square feet of wall space to be painted and the price of the paint per gallon. The program should display the following data:

- The number of gallons of paint required
- The hours of labor required
- The cost of the paint
- The labor charges
- The total cost of the paint job

5. Hot Dog Cookout Calculator

Assume that hot dogs come in packages of 10, and hot dog buns come in packages of 8. Design a modular program that calculates the number of packages of hot dogs and the number of packages of hot dog buns needed for a cookout, with the minimum amount of leftovers. The program should ask the user for the number of people attending the cookout, and the number of hot dogs each person will be given. The program should display the following:

- The minimum number of packages of hot dogs required
- The minimum number of packages of buns required

- The number of hot dogs that will be left over
- The number of buns that will be left over

6. Rectangle Area

The area of a rectangle is calculated according to the following formula:

$$Area = Width \times Length$$

Design a function that accepts a rectangle's width and length as arguments and returns the rectangle's area. Use the function in a program that prompts the user to enter the rectangle's width and length, and then displays the rectangle's area.

7. Feet to Inches

One foot equals 12 inches. Design a function named feetToInches that accepts a number of feet as an argument, and returns the number of inches in that many feet. Use the function in a program that prompts the user to enter a number of feet and then displays the number of inches in that many feet.

8. Math Quiz

Design a program that gives simple math quizzes. The program should display two random numbers that are to be added, such as:

```
  247
+ 129
```

The program should allow the student to enter the answer. If the answer is correct, a message of congratulations should be displayed. If the answer is incorrect, a message showing the correct answer should be displayed.

9. Odd/Even Counter

In this chapter you saw an example of how to design an algorithm that determines whether a number is even or odd (see *Returning Boolean Values* in Section 6.2). Design a program that generates 100 random numbers, and keeps a count of how many of those random numbers are even and how many are odd.

10. Guess the Number

Design a number guessing game program. The program should generate a random number and then ask the user to guess the number. Each time the user enters their guess, the program should indicate whether it was too high or too low. The game is over when the user correctly guesses the number. When the game ends, the program should display the number of guesses that the user made.

11. Rock, Paper, Scissors Game

Design a program that lets the user play the game of Rock, Paper, Scissors against the computer. The program should work as follows:

(1) When the program begins, a random number in the range of 1 through 3 is generated. If the number is 1, then the computer has chosen rock. If the number is 2, then the computer has chosen paper. If the number is 3, then the computer has chosen scissors. (Don't display the computer's choice yet.)

(2) The user enters their choice of "rock," "paper," or "scissors" at the keyboard.

(3) The computer's choice is displayed.

(4) The program should display a message indicating whether the user or the computer was the winner. A winner is selected according to the following rules:

- If one player chooses rock and the other player chooses scissors, then rock wins. (The rock smashes the scissors.)
- If one player chooses scissors and the other player chooses paper, then scissors wins. (Scissors cut paper.)
- If one player chooses paper and the other player chooses rock, then paper wins. (Paper wraps rock.)
- If both players make the same choice, the game must be played again to determine the winner.

5. ESP Game

Design a program that tests your ESP, or extrasensory perception. The program will randomly pick a color, and you will be asked to predict the program's selection before it is revealed. Design the program to randomly select one of the following words:

Red, Green, Blue, Orange, Yellow

To select a word, the program can generate a random number. For example, if the number is 0, the selected word is Red, if the number is 1, the selected word is Green, and so forth. Next, the program should ask the user to enter the color that the computer has selected. After the user has entered their guess, the program should display the name of the randomly selected color. The program should repeat this 10 times and then display the number of times the user correctly guessed the selected color.

Understanding Input Validation

TOPICS

10.1 Garbage In, Garbage Out

If a program reads bad data as input, it will produce bad data as output. Programs should be designed to reject bad data that is given as input.

One of the most famous sayings among computer programmers is "garbage in, garbage out." This saying, sometimes abbreviated as **GIGO,** refers to the fact that computers cannot tell the difference between good data and bad data. If a user provides bad data as input to a program, the program will process that bad data and, as a result, will produce bad data as output.

For example, look at the pseudocode for the payroll program in Program 10-1 and notice what happens in the sample run when the user gives bad data as input.

Program 10-1:

```
// Variables to hold the hours worked, the
// hourly pay rate, and the gross pay.
Declare Real hours, payRate, grossPay

// Get the number of hours worked.
Display "Enter the number of hours worked."
Input hours

// Get the hourly pay rate.
Display "Enter the hourly pay rate."
```

Program 10-1: *(continued)*

```
Input payRate

// Calculate the gross pay.
Set grossPay = hours * payRate

// Display the gross pay.
Display "The gross pay is", currencyFormat(grossPay)
```

Program Output (with Input Shown in Bold)

```
Enter the number of hours worked.
400 [Enter]
Enter the hourly pay rate.
20 [Enter]
The gross pay is $8,000.00
```

Did you spot the bad data that was provided as input? The person receiving the paycheck will be pleasantly surprised, because in the sample run the payroll clerk entered 400 as the number of hours worked. The clerk probably meant to enter 40, because there are not 400 hours in a week. The computer, however, is unaware of this fact, and the program processed the bad data just as if it were good data. Can you think of other types of input that can be given to this program that will result in bad output? One example is a negative number entered for the hours worked; another is an invalid hourly pay rate.

Sometimes stories are reported in the news about computer errors that mistakenly cause people to be charged thousands of dollars for small purchases or to receive large tax refunds that they were not entitled to. These "computer errors" are rarely caused by the computer, however; they are more commonly caused by software bugs or bad data that was read into a program as input.

The integrity of a program's output is only as good as the integrity of its input. For this reason, you should design your programs in such a way that bad input is never accepted. When input is given to a program, it should be inspected before it is processed. If the input is invalid, the program should discard it and prompt the user to enter the correct data. This process is known as **input validation**. This chapter discusses techniques that you can use to validate data before it is processed.

Checkpoint

10.1 What does the phrase "garbage in, garbage out" mean?

10.2 Give a general description of the input validation process.

10.3 At a prompt for how many days an employee worked in October, the user entered 34. Explain why this results in an error.

10.2 The Input Validation Loop

Input validation is commonly done with a loop that iterates as long as an input variable contains bad data.

VideoNote
The Input Validation Loop

Figure 10-1 shows a common technique for validating an item of input. In this technique, the input is read, and then a pretest loop is executed. If the input data is invalid, the body of the loop executes. The loop displays an error message so the user will know that the input was invalid, and then the loop reads the new input. The loop repeats as long as the input is invalid.

Figure 10-1 Logic containing an input validation loop

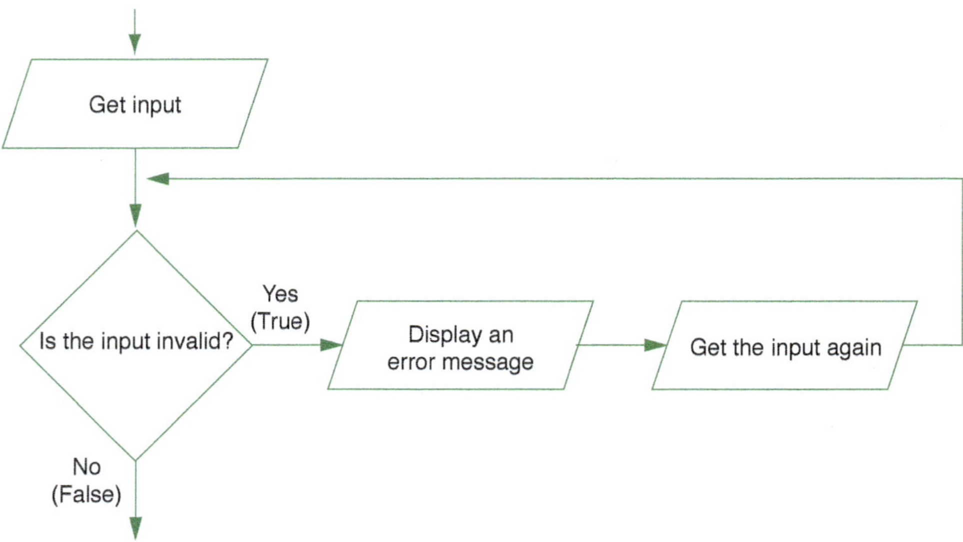

Notice that the flowchart in Figure 10-1 reads input in two places: first just before the loop and then inside the loop. The first input operation—just before the loop—is called a **priming read,** and its purpose is to get the first input value that will be tested by the validation loop. If that value is invalid, the loop will perform subsequent input operations.

Let's consider an example. Suppose you are designing a program that reads a test score and you want to make sure the user does not enter a value less than 0. The following pseudocode shows how you can use an input validation loop to reject any input value that is less than 0.

```
// Get a test score.
Display "Enter a test score."
Input score
// Make sure it is not less than 0.
While score < 0
   Display "ERROR: The score cannot be less than 0."
   Display "Enter the correct score."
   Input score
End While
```

This pseudocode first prompts the user to enter a test score (this is the priming read), and then the `While` loop executes. Recall that the `While` loop is a pretest loop, which means it tests the expression `score < 0` before performing an iteration. If the user entered a valid test score, this expression will be false and the loop will not iterate. If the test score is invalid, however, the expression will be true and the statements in the body of the loop will execute. The loop displays an error message and prompts the user to enter the correct test score. The loop will continue to iterate until the user enters a valid test score.

NOTE: An input validation loop, such as the one in Figure 7-1, is sometimes called an *error trap* or an *error handler*.

This pseudocode only rejects negative test scores. What if you also want to reject any test scores that are greater than 100? You can modify the input validation loop so it uses a compound Boolean expression, as shown next.

```
// Get a test score.
Display "Enter a test score."
Input score
// Validate the test score.
While score < 0 OR score > 100
  Display "ERROR: The score cannot be less than 0"
  Display "or greater than 100."
  Display "Enter the correct score."
  Input score
End While
```

The loop in this pseudocode determines whether `score` is less than 0 or greater than 100. If either is true, an error message is displayed and the user is prompted to enter a correct score.

NOTE: This pseudocode used the OR operator to determine whether `score` was outside the range. Think about what would happen if this Boolean expression used the AND operator instead:

```
score < 0 AND score > 100
```

This expression would never be true because it is impossible for a number to be less than 0 AND greater than 100!In the Spotlight:

In the Spotlight:

Designing an Input Validation Loop

Samantha has a program for calculating the retail price of an item in her import business. Samantha has encountered a problem when using the program, however. Some of the items that she sells have a wholesale cost of 50 cents, which she enters into the program as 0.50. Because the 0 key is next to the key for the negative sign, she sometimes accidentally enters a negative number. She has asked you to revise the program so it will not allow a negative number to be entered for the wholesale cost.

On Your Own: Working alone or with a partner, draw a flowchart and write the pseudocode. Then, read on to see how you did. Remember, your solution does not have to be exactly the same as the one in the text in order to come up with the same result.

You decide to add an input validation loop to the `showRetail` module that rejects any negative numbers that are entered into the `wholesale` variable. Program 10-2 shows the new pseudocode, with the new input validation code shown in lines 28 through 33.

Figure 10-2 shows a new flowchart for the `showRetail` module.

Program 10-2:

```
1  Module main()
2     // Local variable
3     Declare String doAnother
4
5     Do
6        // Calculate and display a retail price.
7        Call showRetail()
8
9        // Do this again?
10       Display "Do you have another item? (Enter y for yes.)"
11       Input doAnother
12    While doAnother == "y" OR doAnother == "Y"
13 End Module
14
15 // The showRetail module gets an item's wholesale cost
16 // from the user and displays its retail price.
17 Module showRetail()
18    // Local variables
19    Declare Real wholesale, retail
20
21    // Constant for the markup percentage
22    Constant Real MARKUP = 2.50
23
24    // Get the wholesale cost.
25    Display "Enter an item's wholesale cost."
26    Input wholesale
27
```

Program 10-2: *(continued)*

```
    // Validate the wholesale cost.
    While wholesale < 0
       Display "The cost cannot be negative. Please"
        Display "enter the correct wholesale cost."
       Input wholesale
    End While

    // Calculate the retail price.
    Set retail = wholesale * MARKUP

    // Display the retail price.
    Display "The retail price is $", retail
 End Module
```

Program Output (with Input Shown in Bold)

```
Enter an item's wholesale cost.
-0.50 [Enter]
The cost cannot be negative. Please
enter the correct wholesale cost.
0.50 [Enter]
The retail price is $1.25
Do you have another item? (Enter y for yes.)
n [Enter]
```

Figure 7-2 Flowchart for the `showRetail` module

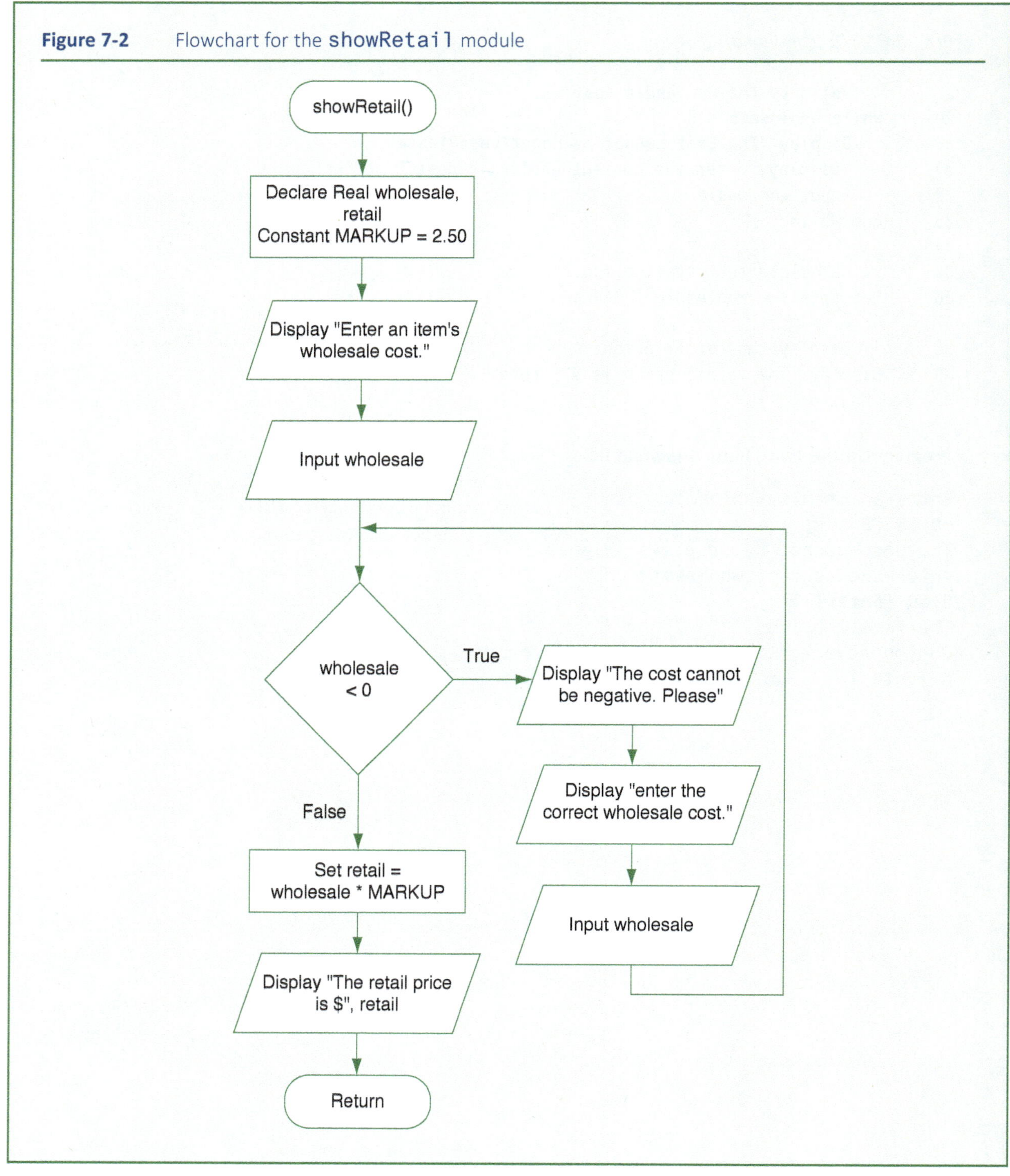

Using a Posttest Loop to Validate Input

You might be wondering whether you could use a posttest loop to validate input instead of using the priming read. For example, the pseudocode to get a test score and validate it could be written as follows with a `Do-While` loop.

```
Do
   Display "Enter a test score."
   Input score
While score < 0 OR score > 100
```

Although this logic will work, it does not display an error message when the user enters an invalid value—it simply repeats the original prompt each time the loop iterates. This might be confusing to the user, so it is usually better to have a priming read followed by a pretest validation loop.

Writing Validation Functions

The input validation examples shown so far have been simple and straightforward. You have seen how to write validation loops that reject both negative numbers and numbers that are outside of a range. However, input validation can sometimes be more complex than these examples.

For instance, suppose you are designing a program that prompts the user to enter a product model number and should only accept the values 100, 200, and 300. You could design the input algorithm as follows:

```
// Get the model number.
Display "Enter the model number."
Input model
While model != 100 AND model != 200 AND model != 300
   Display "The valid model numbers are 100, 200, and 300."
   Display "Enter a valid model number."
   Input model
End While
```

The validation loop uses a long compound Boolean expression that will iterate as long as `model` does not equal 100 AND `model` does not equal 200 AND `model` does not equal 300. Although this logic will work, you can simplify the validation loop by writing a Boolean function to test the `model` variable and then calling that function in the loop. For example, suppose you pass the `model` variable to a function you write named `isInvalid`. The function returns `True` if `model` is invalid, or `False` otherwise. You could rewrite the validation loop as follows:

```
// Get the model number.
Display "Enter the model number."
Input model
While isInvalid(model)
   Display "The valid model numbers are 100, 200, and 300."
   Display "Enter a valid model number."
   Input model
End While
```

This makes the loop easier to read. It is evident now that the loop iterates as long as `model` is invalid. The following pseudocode shows how you might design the `isInvalid` function. It accepts a model number as an argument, and if the argument is not 100 AND the argument is not 200 AND the argument is not 300, the function returns `True` to indicate that it is invalid. Otherwise, the function returns `False`.

```
Function Boolean isInvalid(Integer model)
   // A local variable to hold True or False.
   Declare Boolean status

   // If the model number is invalid, set status to True.
   // Otherwise, set status to False.
   If model != 100 AND model != 200 AND model != 300 Then
      Set status = True
   Else
      Set status = False
   End If
   // Return the test status.

   Return status
End Function
```

Validating String Input

In some programs you must validate string input. For example, suppose you are designing a program that asks a yes/no question, and you want to make sure that only the strings `"yes"` and `"no"` are accepted as valid input. The following pseudocode shows how this might be done.

```
// Get the answer to the question.
Display "Is your supervisor an effective leader?"
Input answer

// Validate the input.
While answer != "yes" AND answer != "no"
   Display "Please answer yes or no. Is your supervisor an"
   Display "effective leader?"
   Input answer
End While
```

This input validation loop rejects any input except the strings `"yes"` and `"no"`. This particular design might be too rigid, however; as it is written, the loop performs a case-sensitive comparison. This means that strings such as `"YES"`, `"NO"`, `"Yes"`, and `"NO"` will be rejected. To make the program more convenient for users, the program should accept `"yes"` and `"no"` written in any combination of upper- or lowercase letters. Recall from Chapter 6 that library functions such as `toUpper` and `toLower` can help make case-insensitive string comparisons. The following pseudocode shows an example using the `toLower` function.

```
// Get the answer to the question.
Display "Is your supervisor an effective leader?"
Input answer

// Validate the input.
```

```
While toLower(answer) != "yes" AND toLower(answer) != "no"
   Display "Please answer yes or no. Is your supervisor an"
   Display "effective leader?"
   Input answer
End While
```

Sometimes the length of a string plays a role in the string's validity. For example, you probably have online accounts for which you have set up passwords. Some systems require that passwords have a minimum number of characters. To set the length of a string, you use the `length` function. In the following pseudocode, the `length` function is used to make sure a password is at least six characters long.

```
// Get the new password.
Display "Enter your new password."
Input password
// Validate the length of the password.
While length(password) < 6
   Display "The password must be at least six"
   Display "characters long. Enter your new password."
   Input password
End While
```

Checkpoint

10.4 Describe the steps that are generally taken when an input validation loop is used to validate data.

10.5 What is a priming read? What is its purpose?

10.6 If the input that is read by the priming read is valid, how many times will the input validation loop iterate?

10.3 Defensive Programming

Input validation is part of the practice of defensive programming. Thorough input validation anticipates both obvious and unobvious errors.

Defensive programming is the practice of anticipating errors that can happen while a program is running, and designing the program to avoid those errors. All of the input validation algorithms examined in this chapter are examples of defensive programming.

Some types of input errors are obvious and easily handled. For example, you should make sure that negative numbers are not entered for items such as prices and test scores.

Some types of input errors are not so obvious, however. One example of such an error is reading **empty input,** which happens when an input operation attempts to read data, but there is no data to read. This occurs when an `Input` statement executes and the user simply presses the Enter key without typing a value. Although different programming languages handle the problem of empty input in different ways, there is often a way to determine whether an input operation failed to read data.

Another often overlooked type of error is the entry of the wrong type of data. This happens, for example, when a program attempts to read an integer but the user enters a real number or a string. Most programming languages provide library functions that you can use to avoid this type of error. Quite often you will find functions similar to the `isInteger` and `isReal` functions. To use these functions in an input validation algorithm, you typically follow these steps:

1. Read the input as a string.
2. Determine whether the string can be converted to the desired data type.
3. If the string can be converted, convert it and continue processing; otherwise, display an error message and attempt to read the data again.

Thorough input validation also requires that you check for accurate data. Even when the user provides the right type of data, it might not be accurate. Consider the following examples:

- When the user enters a U.S. address, the state abbreviation should be checked to make sure it is a two-character string and also a valid U.S. Postal Service abbreviation. For example, there is no U.S. state with the abbreviation NW. Similar validations can be performed on international addresses. For example, Canadian province abbreviations are two-character strings.
- When the user enters a U.S. address, the value entered as the ZIP code should be checked to verify that it is both in the correct format (a 5- or 9-digit number) and a valid U.S. Postal Service ZIP code. For example, 99999 is not currently a valid U.S. ZIP code. In addition, ZIP codes should be valid for the state that is entered. (Databases of valid ZIP codes are readily available for a small fee. Programmers usually purchase one of these and use it in the validation process.)
- Hourly wages and salary amounts should be checked to make sure they are numeric values and within the range of allowable wages established by the company.
- Dates should be checked for validity. For example, the date February 29 should be accepted only in leap years, and invalid dates such as February 30 should never be accepted.
- Time measurements should also be checked for validity. For example, there are 168 hours in a week, so a payroll program should verify that no value greater than 168 is entered for the number of hours worked in a week.
- Reasonableness should also be considered when validating data. Even though there are 168 hours in a week, it is improbable that any employee ever works 24 hours a day, 7 days a week. Dates should also be checked for reasonableness. For example, a birth date can't be in the future and a person, based on birth year, probably isn't 150 years old. When unreasonable data is entered, the program should at least ask the user to confirm that they intended to enter it.

Checkpoint

10.7 What is defensive programming?

10.8 Give an example of an obvious input error.

10.9 What is empty input and when might it occur?

?

Chapter Review

Multiple Choice

1. GIGO stands for ________.
   a. great input, great output
   b. garbage in, garbage out
   c. GIGahertz Output
   d. GIGabyte Operation

2. The integrity of a program's output is only as good as the integrity of the program's ________.
   a. compiler
   b. programming language
   c. input
   d. debugger

3. The input operation that appears just before a validation loop is known as the ________.
   a. prevalidation read
   b. primordial read
   c. initialization read
   d. priming read

4. Validation loops are also known as ________.
   a. error traps
   b. doomsday loops
   c. error avoidance loops
   d. defensive programming loops

5. The term *empty input* describes what happens when ________.
   a. the user presses the [Spacebar] and then the [Enter] key
   b. an input operation attempts to read data, but there is no data to read
   c. the user enters 0 when 0 is an invalid value
   d. the user enters any invalid data as input

True or False

1. The process of input validation works like this: When the user of a program enters invalid data, the program should ask the user, "Are you sure you meant to enter that?" If the user answers "yes," the program should accept the data.
2. The priming read appears inside the validation loop.
3. The approach of using a posttest validation loop shown in this chapter requires a priming read.

Short Answer

1. What does the phrase "garbage in, garbage out" mean?
2. Give a general description of the input validation process.
3. What is the purpose of the priming read?
4. In this chapter you saw how a posttest loop can be used in input validation, as an alternative to the priming read followed by a pretest loop. Why is it typically not best to use a posttest loop approach?

Algorithm Workbench

1. Design an algorithm that prompts the user to enter a positive nonzero number and validates the input.
2. Design an algorithm that prompts the user to enter a number in the range of 1 through 100 and validates the input.
3. Design an algorithm that prompts the user to enter "yes" or "no" and validates the input. (Use a case-insensitive comparison.)
4. Design an algorithm that prompts the user to enter a number that is greater than 99 and validates the input.
5. Design an algorithm that prompts the user to enter a secret word. The secret word should be at least 8 characters long. Validate the input.

Debugging Exercises

1. Why does the following pseudocode not perform as indicated in the comments?

```
// This program asks the user to enter a value
// between 1 and 10 and validates the input.
Declare Integer value

// Get a value from the user.
Display "Enter a value between 1 and 10."
Input value

// Make sure the value is between 1 and 10.
While value < 1 AND value > 10
   Display "ERROR: The value must be between 1 and 10."
   Display "Enter a value between 1 and 10."
   Input value
End While
```

2. Why does the following pseudocode not perform as indicated in the comments?

```
// This program gets a dollar amount from the user
// and validates the input.
Declare Real amount

// Get the amount from the user.
Display "Enter a dollar amount"
Input amount

// Make sure the amount is not less than zero. If it is,
// get a new amount from the user.
While amount < 0
   Display "ERROR: The dollar amount cannot be less than 0."
   Display "Enter a dollar amount."
End While
```

3. The following pseudocode works, but it performs a case-sensitive validation of the user's input. How could the algorithm be improved so the user does not have to pay attention to capitalization when entering a name?

```
// This program asks the user to enter a string
// and validates the input.
Declare String choice

// Get the user's response.
Display "Cast your vote for Chess Team Captain."
Display "Would you like to nominate Lisa or Tim?"
Input choice

// Validate the input.
While choice != "Lisa" AND choice != "Tim"
   Display "Please enter Lisa or Tim."
   Display "Cast your vote for Chess Team Captain."
   Display "Would you like to nominate Lisa or Tim?"
   Input response
End While
```

Programming Exercises

VideoNote
The Payroll Program with Input Validation Problem

1. **Payroll Program with Input Validation**

   Design a payroll program that prompts the user to enter an employee's hourly pay rate and the number of hours worked. Validate the user's input so that only pay rates in the range of $7.50 through $18.25 and hours in the range of 0 through 40 are accepted. The program should display the employee's gross pay.

2. **Theater Seating Revenue with Input Validation**

   A dramatic theater has three seating sections, and it charges the following prices for tickets in each section: section A seats cost $20 each, section B seats cost $15 each, and section C seats cost $10 each. The theater has 300 seats in section A, 500 seats in section B, and 200 seats in section C. Design a program that asks for the number of tickets sold in each section and then displays the amount of income generated from ticket sales. The program should validate the numbers that are entered for each section.

3. **Speeding Violation Calculator**

   Design a program that calculates and displays the number of miles per hour over the speed limit that a speeding driver was doing. The program should ask for the speed limit and the driver's speed. Validate the input as follows:

   - The speed limit should be at least 20, but not greater than 70.
   - The driver's speed should be at least the value entered for the speed limit (otherwise the driver was not speeding).

   Once correct data has been entered, the program should calculate and display the number of miles per hour over the speed limit that the driver was doing.

4. **Rock, Paper, Scissors Modification**

   Programming Exercise 11 in Chapter 9 asked you to design a program that plays the Rock, Paper, Scissors game. In the program, the user enters one of the three strings—`"rock"`, `"paper"`, or `"scissors"`—at the keyboard. Add input validation (with a case-insensitive comparison) to make sure the user enters one of those strings only.

Arrays

TOPICS

11.1 Array Basics

An array allows you to store a group of items of the same data type together in memory. Processing a large number of items in an array is usually easier than processing a large number of items stored in separate variables.

In the programs you have designed so far, you have used variables to store data in memory. In most programming languages, the simplest way to store a value in memory is to store it in a variable. Variables work well in many situations, but they have limitations. For example, they can hold only one value at a time. Consider the following pseudocode variable declaration:

```
Declare Integer number = 99
```

This pseudocode statement declares an `Integer` variable named `number`, initialized with the value 99. Consider what happens if the following statement appears later in the program:

```
Set number = 5
```

This statement assigns the value 5 to `number`, replacing the value 99 that was previously stored there. Because `number` is an ordinary variable, it can hold only one value at a time.

Because variables hold only a single value, they can be cumbersome in programs that process lists of data. For example, suppose you are asked to design a program that holds the names of 50 employees. Imagine declaring 50 variables to hold all of those names:

```
Declare String employee1
Declare String employee2
Declare String employee3
and so on . . .
Declare String employee50
```

Then, imagine designing the code to input all 50 names:

```
// Get the first employee name.
Display "Enter the name of employee 1."
Input employee1
// Get the second employee name.
Display "Enter the name of employee 2."
Input employee2
// Get the third employee name.
Display "Enter the name of employee 3."
Input employee3
and so on . . .
// Get the fiftieth employee name.
Display "Enter the name of employee 50."
Input employee50
```

As you can see, variables are not well-suited for storing and processing lists of data. Each variable is a separate item that must be declared and individually processed. Fortunately, most programming languages allow you to create an **array**, which is a complex data type specifically designed for storing and processing lists of data. Like a variable, an array is a named storage location in memory.

NOTE: In Python, you create lists, not arrays. See Chapter 17 for more about working with Python Lists.

Unlike a variable, an array can hold a group of values. All of the values in an array must be the same data type. You can have an array of `Integers`, an array of `Reals`, or an array of `Strings`, but you cannot store a mixture of data types in an array. The following example shows how we will declare an array in pseudocode:

```
Declare Integer units[10]
```

Notice that this statement looks like a regular `Integer` variable declaration except for the number inside the brackets. The number inside the brackets, called a **size declarator,** specifies the number of values that the array can hold. This pseudocode statement declares an array named `units` that can hold 10 integer values. In most programming languages, an array size declarator must be a nonnegative integer. Here is another example:

```
Declare Real salesAmounts[7]
```

This statement declares an array named `salesAmounts` that can hold 7 real numbers. The following pseudocode shows one more example. This statement declares an array that can hold 50 strings. The name of the array is `names`.

```
Declare String names[50]
```

In most languages, an array's size cannot be changed while the program is running. If you have written a program that uses an array and then find that you must change the array's size, you have to change the array's size declarator in the source code. Then you must recompile the program (or rerun the program if you are using an interpreted language) with the new size declarator. To make array sizes easier to maintain, many programmers prefer to use named constants as array size declarators. Here is an example:

```
Constant Integer SIZE = 10
Declare Integer units[SIZE]
```

Many array processing techniques require you to refer to the array's size. When you use a named constant as an array's size declarator, you can use the constant to refer to the size of the array in your algorithms. If you ever need to modify the program so the array is a different size, you need only to change the value of the named constant.

NOTE: In this book, we use brackets [ ] in an array declaration to enclose the size declarator. Some languages use parentheses instead.

Array Elements and Subscripts

The storage locations in an array are known as **elements.** In memory, an array's elements are usually located in consecutive memory locations. Each element in an array is assigned a unique number known as a **subscript.** (Subscripts are also known as **indexes.**) Subscripts are used to identify specific elements in an array. In most languages, the first element is assigned the subscript 0, the second element is assigned the subscript 1, and so forth. For example, suppose a pseudocode program has the following declarations:

```
Constant Integer SIZE = 5
Declare Integer numbers[SIZE]
```

As shown in Figure 11-1, the `numbers` array has five elements. The elements are assigned the subscripts 0 through 4. (Because subscript numbering starts at zero, the subscript of the last element in an array is one less than the total number of elements in the array.)

Figure 11-1 Array subscripts

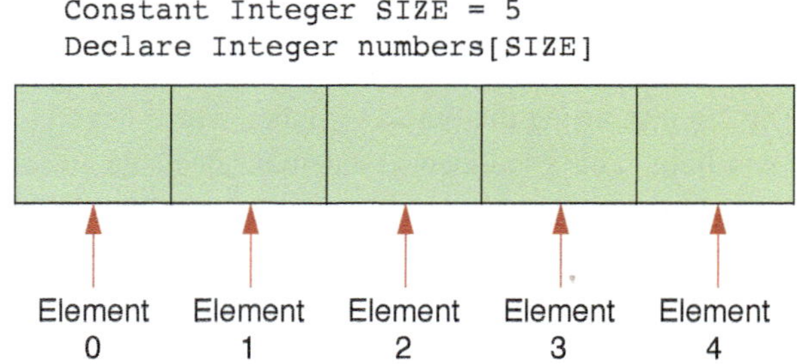

NOTE: In some languages, subscript numbering starts at 1. It is more common, however, for subscript numbering to start at 0, so that is the convention we follow in this book.

Assigning Values to Array Elements

You access the individual elements in an array by using their subscripts. For example, assuming `numbers` is the `Integer` array just described, the following pseudocode assigns the values to each of its five elements.

```
Set numbers[0] = 20
Set numbers[1] = 30
Set numbers[2] = 40
Set numbers[3] = 50
Set numbers[4] = 60
```

This pseudocode assigns the value 20 to element 0, the value 30 to element 1, and so forth. Figure 11-2 shows the contents of the array after these statements execute.

Figure 11-2 Values assigned to each element

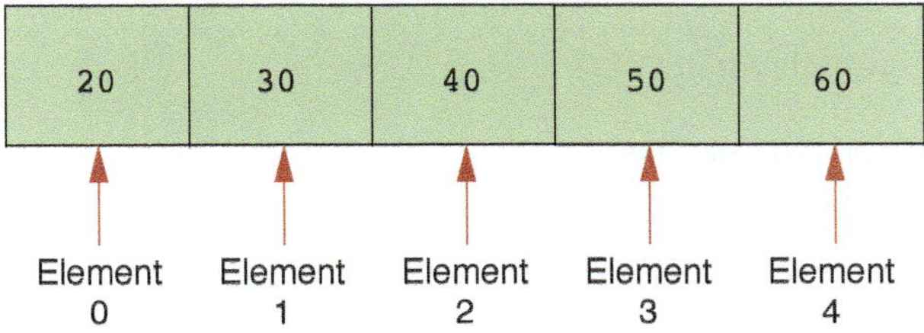

NOTE: The expression `numbers[0]` is spoken as "numbers sub zero."

Inputting and Outputting Array Contents

You can read values from the keyboard and store them in an array element just as you can a regular variable. You can also output the contents of an array element. The pseudocode in Program 11-1 shows an array being used to store and display values entered by the user.

Program 11-1:

```
// Create a constant for the number of employees.
Constant Integer SIZE = 3

// Declare an array to hold the number of hours
// worked by each employee.
Declare Integer hours[SIZE]

// Get the hours worked by employee 1.
Display "Enter the hours worked by employee 1."
```

Program 11-1: *(continued)*

```
10 Input hours[0]
11
12 // Get the hours worked by employee 2.
13 Display "Enter the hours worked by employee 2."
14 Input hours[1]
15
16 // Get the hours worked by employee 3.
17 Display "Enter the hours worked by employee 3."
18 Input hours[2]
19
20 // Display the values entered.
21 Display "The hours you entered are:"
22 Display hours[0]
23 Display hours[1]
24 Display hours[2]
```

Program Output (with Input Shown in Bold)

```
Enter the hours worked by employee 1.
40 [Enter]
Enter the hours worked by employee 2.
20 [Enter]
Enter the hours worked by employee 3.
15 [Enter]
The hours you entered are:
40
20
15
```

Let's take a closer look at the program. A named constant, `SIZE`, is declared in line 2 and initialized with the value 3. Then, an `Integer` array named `hours` is declared in line 6. The `SIZE` constant is used as the array size declarator, so the `hours` array will have 3 elements. The `Input` statements in lines 10, 14, and 18 read values from the keyboard and store those values in the elements of the `hours` array. Then, the `Display` statements in lines 22 through 24 output the values stored in each array element.

In the sample running of the program, the user entered the values 40, 20, and 15, which were stored in the `hours` array. Figure 11-3 shows the contents of the array after these values are stored in it.

Figure 11-3 Contents of the `hours` array

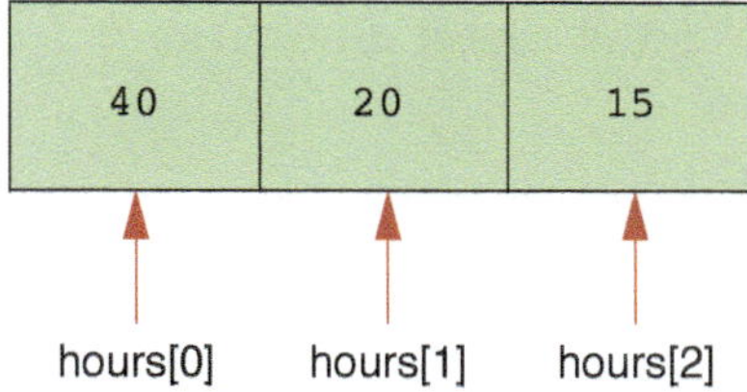

VideoNote
Using a Loop to Step Through an Array

Using a Loop to Step Through an Array

Most programming languages allow you to store a number in a variable and then use that variable as a subscript. This makes it possible to use a loop to step through an entire array, performing the same operation on each element. For example, look at the pseudocode in Program 11-2.

Program 11-2:

```
1  // Declare an Integer array with 10 elements.
2  Declare Integer series[10]
3
4  // Declare a variable to use in the loop.
5  Declare Integer index
6
7  // Set each array element to 100.
8  For index = 0 To 9
9     Set series[index] = 100
10 End For
```

In line 2, an `Integer` array named `series` is declared with 10 elements, and in line 5 an `Integer` variable named `index` is declared. The `index` variable is used as a counter in the `For` loop that appears in lines 8 through 10. In the loop, the `index` variable takes on the values 0 through 9. The first time the loop iterates, `index` is set to 0, so the statement in line 9 causes the array element `series[0]` to be set to 100. The second time the loop iterates, `index` is set to 1, so the array element `series[1]` is set to 100. This continues until the last loop iteration, in which `series[9]` is set to 100.

Let's look at another example. Program 11-1 could be simplified by using two `For` loops: one for inputting the values into the array and the other for displaying the contents of the array. This is shown in Program 11-3.

Program 11-3: 

```
// Create a constant for the size of the array.
Constant Integer SIZE = 3

```

Program 11-3: *(continue)*

```
4  // Declare an array to hold the number of hours
5  // worked by each employee.
6  Declare Integer hours[SIZE]
7
8  // Declare a variable to use in the loops.
9  Declare Integer index
10
11 // Get the hours for each employee.
12 For index = 0 To SIZE - 1
13    Display "Enter the hours worked by"
14    Display "employee number ", index + 1
15    Input hours[index]
16 End For
17
18 // Display the values entered.
19 Display "The hours you entered are:"
20 For index = 0 To SIZE - 1
21    Display hours[index]
22 End For
```

Program Output (with Input Shown in Bold)

```
Enter the hours worked by
employee number 1
40 [Enter]
Enter the hours worked by
employee number 2
20 [Enter]
Enter the hours worked by
employee number 3
15 [Enter]
The hours you entered are:
40
20
15
```

Let's take a closer look at the first `For` loop, which appears in lines 12 through 16. Here is the first line of the loop:

```
For index = 0 To SIZE - 1
```

This specifies that the `index` variable will be assigned the values 0 through 2 as the loop executes. Why did we use the expression `SIZE - 1` as the ending value for the `index` variable? Remember, the subscript of the last element in an array is one less than the size of the array. In this case, the subscript of the last element of the `hours` array is 2, which is the value of the expression `SIZE - 1`.

Notice that inside the loop, in line 15, the `index` variable is used as a subscript:

```
Input hours[index]
```

During the loop's first iteration, the index variable will be set to 0, so the user's input is stored in `hours[0]`. During the next iteration, the user's input is stored in `hours[1]`. Then, during the last iteration the user's input is stored in `hours[2]`. Notice that the loop correctly starts and ends the `index` variable with valid subscript values (0 through 2).

There is one last thing to point out about Program 11-3. This program reads the number of hours worked by three employees referred to as "employee number 1," "employee number 2," and "employee number 3." Here are the `Display` statements that appear inside the first `For` loop, in lines 13 and 14:

```
Display "Enter the hours worked by"
Display "employee number ", index + 1
```

Notice that the second `Display` statement uses the expression `index + 1` to display the employee number. What do you think would happen if we left out the `+ 1` part of the expression, and the statements were written like this?

```
Display "Enter the hours worked by"
Display "employee number ", index
```

Because the `index` variable is assigned the values 0, 1, and 2 as the loop runs, these statements would cause the program to refer to the employees as "employee number 0," "employee number 1," and "employee number 2." Most people find it unnatural to start with 0 when counting people or things, so we used the expression `index + 1` to start the employee numbers at 1.

Processing the Elements of an Array

Processing array elements is no different than processing other variables. In the previous programs you saw how you can assign values to array elements, store input in array elements, and display the contents of array elements. The following *In the Spotlight* section shows how array elements can be used in math expressions.

In the Spotlight:

Using Array Elements in a Math Expression

Megan owns a small neighborhood coffee shop, and she has six employees who work as baristas (coffee bartenders). All of the employees have the same hourly pay rate. Megan has asked you to design a program that will allow her to enter the number of hours worked by each employee and then display the amounts of all the employees' gross pay. You determine that the program should perform the following steps:

1. For each employee: get the number of hours worked and store it in an array element.
2. For each array element: use the value stored in the element to calculate an employee's gross pay. Display the amount of the gross pay.

On Your Own: Working alone or with a partner, write the algorithm steps, draw a flowchart, and write the pseudocode. Then, read on to see how you did. Remember, your solution does not have to be exactly the same as the one in the text in order to come up with the same result.

Program 11-4 shows pseudocode for the program, and Figure 11-4 shows a flowchart.

Program 11-4:

```
// Constant for the size of the array.
Constant Integer SIZE = 6

// Array to hold each employee's hours.
Declare Real hours[SIZE]

// Variable to hold the hourly pay rate.
Declare Real payRate

// Variable to hold a gross pay amount.
Declare Real grossPay

// Variable to use as a loop counter.
Declare Integer index

// Get each employee's hours worked.
For index = 0 To SIZE - 1
   Display "Enter the hours worked by"
   Display "employee ", index + 1, "."
   Input hours[index]
End For

// Get the hourly pay rate.
Display "Enter the hourly pay rate."
Input payRate

// Display each employee's gross pay.
Display "Here is each employee's gross pay."
For index = 0 To SIZE - 1
   Set grossPay = hours[index] * payRate
   Display "Employee ", index + 1, ": $",
           currencyFormat(grossPay)
End For
```

Program Output (with Input Shown in Bold)

Enter the hours worked by
employee 1
10 [Enter]
Enter the hours worked by
employee 2
20 [Enter]
Enter the hours worked by
employee 3
15 [Enter]

Program Output (with Input Shown in Bold) *(continued)*

```
Enter the hours worked by
employee 4
40 [Enter]
Enter the hours worked by
employee 5
20 [Enter]
Enter the hours worked by
employee 6
18 [Enter]
Enter the hourly pay rate.
12.75 [Enter]
Here is each employee's gross pay.
Employee 1: $127.50
Employee 2: $255.00
Employee 3: $191.25
Employee 4: $510.00
Employee 5: $255.00
Employee 6: $229.50
```

Figure 11-4 Flowchart for Program 11-4

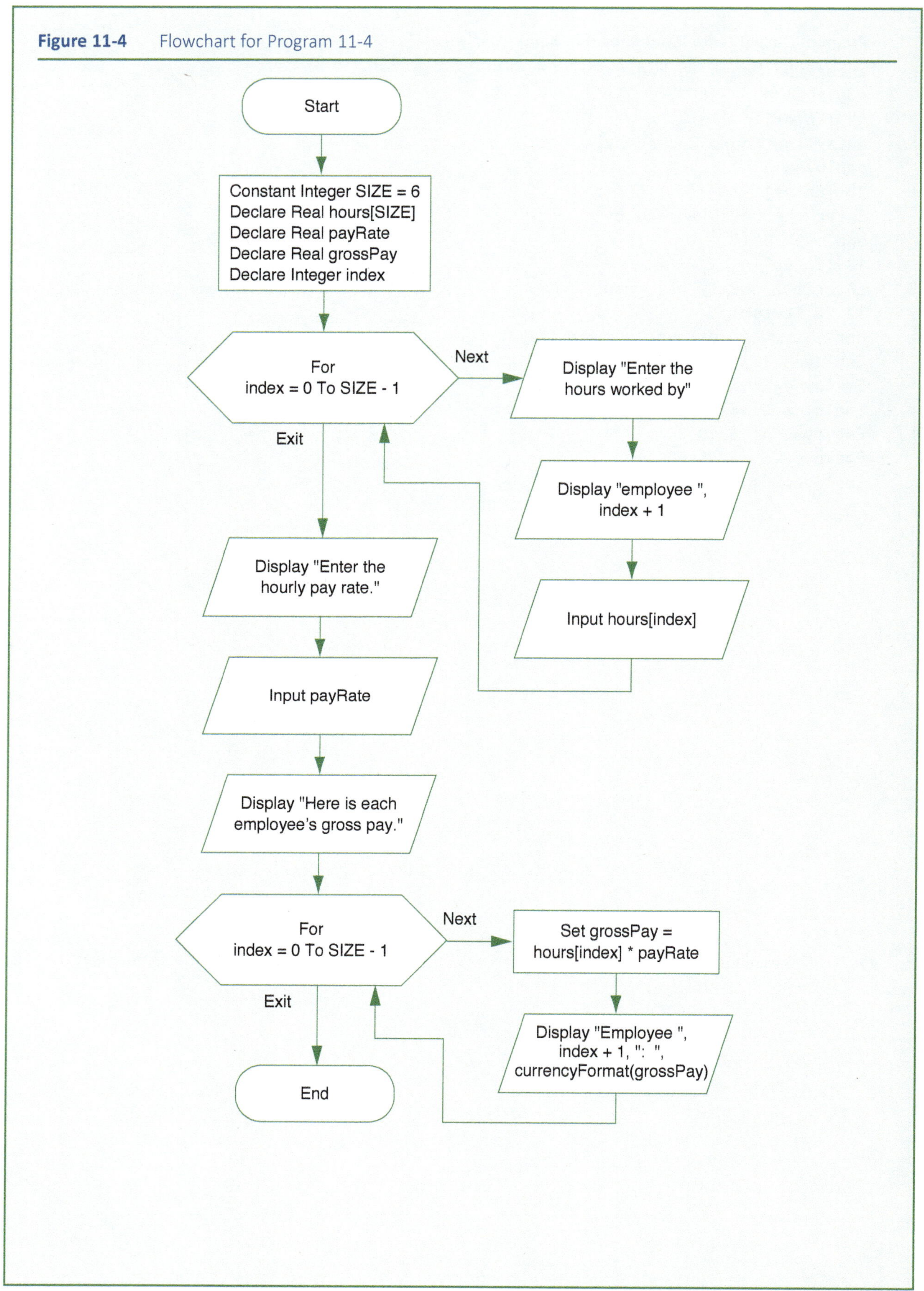

Suppose Megan's business increases and she has to hire two additional baristas. This would require you to change the program so it processes 8 employees instead of 6. Because you used a named constant for the array size, this is a simple modification— you just have to change the statement in line 2 to read:

```
Constant Integer SIZE = 8
```

Because the `SIZE` constant is used as the array size declarator in line 5, the size of the hours array will automatically become 8. Also, because you used the `SIZE` constant to control the loop iterations in lines 17 and 29, the loops will automatically iterate 8 times, once for each employee.

Imagine how much more difficult this modification would be if you had not used a named constant to specify the array size. You would have to change each individual statement in the program that refers to the array size. Not only would this require more work, but it would open the possibility for errors. If you overlooked only one of the statements that refer to the array size, a bug would occur.

TIP: Programs 11-1, 11-3, and 11-4 show how values can be read from the keyboard into array elements. When a large amount of data is stored in an array, it is usually read from another source, such as a file on the computer's disk drive.

Array Initialization

Most languages allow you to initialize an array with values when you declare it. In this book's pseudocode, we will initialize arrays in the following manner:

```
Constant Integer SIZE = 5
Declare Integer numbers[SIZE] = 10, 20, 30, 40, 50
```

The series of values separated with commas is called an **initialization list.** These values are stored in the array elements in the order they appear in the list. (The first value, 10, is stored in `numbers[0]`, the second value, 20, is stored in `numbers[1]`, and so forth.) Here is another example:

```
Constant Integer SIZE = 7
Declare String days[SIZE] = "Sunday", "Monday", "Tuesday",
                            "Wednesday", "Thursday", "Friday",
                            "Saturday"
```

This pseudocode declares `days` as an array of 7 `Strings`, and initializes `days[0]` with `"Sunday"`, `days[1]` with `"Monday"`, and so forth.

Array Bounds Checking

Most programming languages perform **array bounds checking,** which means they do not allow a program to use an invalid array subscript. For example, look at the following pseudocode:

```
// Create an array.
Constant Integer SIZE = 5
Declare Integer numbers[SIZE]
// ERROR! This statement uses an invalid subscript!
```

```
Set numbers[5] = 99
```

This pseudocode declares an array with 5 elements. The subscripts for the array's elements are 0 through 4. The last statement will cause an error in most languages because it attempts to assign a value in `numbers[5]`, a nonexistent element.

NOTE: Array bounds checking typically happens at runtime, which is while the program is running.

Watch for Off-by-One Errors

Because array subscripts start at 0 rather than 1, you have to be careful not to perform an off-by-one error. An **off-by-one error** occurs when a loop iterates one time too many or one time too few. For example, look at the following pseudocode:

```
// This code has an off-by-one error.
Constant Integer SIZE = 100;
Declare Integer numbers[SIZE]
Declare Integer index
For index = 1 To SIZE - 1
   Set numbers[index] = 0
End For
```

The intent of this pseudocode is to create an array of integers with 100 elements, and store the value 0 in each element. However, this code has an off-by-one error. The loop uses its counter variable, `index`, as a subscript with the `numbers` array. During the loop's execution, the `index` variable takes on the values 1 through 99, when it should take on the values 0 through 99. As a result, the first element, which is at subscript 0, is skipped.

Assuming `numbers` is the same array as previously declared, the following loop also performs an off-by-one error. This loop correctly starts with the subscript 0, but it iterates one too many times, ending with the subscript 100:

```
// ERROR!
For index = 0 To SIZE
   Set numbers[index] = 0
End For
```

Because the last subscript in this array is 99, this loop will cause a bounds-checking error.

Partially Filled Arrays

Sometimes you need to store a series of items in an array, but you do not know the number of items in the series. As a result, you do not know the exact number of elements needed for the array. One solution is to make the array large enough to hold the largest possible number of items. This can lead to another problem, however. If the actual number of items stored in the array is less than the number of elements, the array will be only partially filled. When you process a partially filled array, you must process only the elements that contain valid data items.

A partially filled array is normally used with an accompanying integer variable that holds the number of items that are actually stored in the array. If the array is empty, then 0 is stored in this variable because there are no items in the array. Each time an item is added to the array, the variable is incremented. When code steps through the array's elements, the value of this variable is used instead of the array's size to determine the maximum subscript. Program 11-5 shows a demonstration.

Program 11-5:

```
// Declare a constant for the array size.
Constant Integer SIZE = 100

// Declare an array to hold integer values.
Declare Integer values[SIZE]

// Declare an Integer variable to hold the number of items
// that are actually stored in the array.
Declare Integer count = 0

// Declare an Integer variable to hold the user's input.
Declare Integer number

// Declare a variable to step through the array.
Declare Integer index

// Prompt the user to enter a number. If the user enters the
// sentinel value - 1 we will stop accepting input.
Display "Enter a number or - 1 to quit."
Input number

// If the input is not - 1 and the array is not
// full, process the input.
While (number != - 1 AND count < SIZE)
   // Store the input in the array.
   Set values[count] = number

   // Increment count.
   count = count + 1

   // Prompt the user for the next number.
   Display "Enter a number or - 1 to quit."
   Input number
End While

// Display the values stored in the array.
Display "Here are the numbers you entered:"
For index = 0 To count - 1
   Display values[index]
End For
```

Program Output (with Input Shown in Bold) *(continued)*

```
Enter a number or - 1 to quit.
2 [Enter]
Enter a number or - 1 to quit.
4 [Enter]
Enter a number or - 1 to quit.
6 [Enter]
Enter a number or - 1 to quit.
- 1 [Enter]
Here are the numbers you entered:
2
4
6
```

Let's examine the pseudocode in detail. Line 2 declares a constant, `SIZE`, initialized with the value 100. Line 5 declares an `Integer` array named `values`, using `SIZE` as the size declarator. As a result, the `values` array will have 100 elements. Line 9 declares an `Integer` variable named `count`, which will hold the number of items that are stored in the `values` array. Notice that `count` is initialized with 0 because there are no values stored in the array. Line 12 declares an `Integer` variable named `number` that will hold values entered by the user, and line 15 declares an `Integer` variable named `index` that will be used in a loop to step through the array, displaying its elements.

Line 19 prompts the user to enter a number or −1 to quit. This program uses the value −1 as a sentinel value. When the user enters −1, the program will stop reading input. Line 20 reads the user's input and stores it in the `number` variable. A `While` loop begins in line 24. The loop iterates as long as `number` is not −1 and `count` is less than the size of the array. Inside the loop, in line 26 the `numbers` variable is assigned to `values[count]`, and in line 29 the `count` variable is incremented. (Each time a number is assigned to an array element, the `count` variable is incremented. As a result, the `count` variable will hold the number of items that are stored in the array.) Then, line 32 prompts the user to enter another number (or −1 to quit) and line 33 reads the user's input into the `number` variable. The loop then starts over.

When the user enters −1, or `count` reaches the size of the array, the `While` loop stops. The `For` loop that begins in line 38 displays all of the items that are stored in the array. Rather than stepping through all of the elements in the array, however, the loop steps through only the elements that contain values. Notice that the `index` variable's starting value is 0, and its ending value is `count - 1`. By setting the ending value to `count - 1` rather than `SIZE - 1`, the loop will stop when the element containing the last valid value has been displayed, not when the end of the array has been reached.

The For Each Loop

Several programming languages provide a specialized version of the `For` loop that is known as the `For Each` loop. The `For Each loop` can simplify array processing when your task is simply to step through an array, retrieving the value of each element. The `For Each` loop is typically used in the following general format:

```
For Each var In array
   statement
   statement
   statement
   etc.
End For
```

In the general format, *var* is the name of a variable and *array* is the name of an array. The loop will iterate once for every element in the array. Each time the loop iterates, it copies an array element to the *var* variable. For example, the first time the loop iterates, *var* will contain the value of *array*[0], the second time the loop iterates *var* will contain the value of *array*[1], and so forth. This continues until the loop has stepped through all of the elements in the array. For example, suppose we have the following declarations:

```
Constant Integer SIZE = 5
Declare Integer numbers[SIZE] = 5, 10, 15, 20, 25
Declare Integer num
```

The following `For Each` loop can be used to display all of the values stored in the `numbers` array:

```
For Each num In numbers
   Display num
End For
```

NOTE: The `For Each` loop is not available in all languages, so we will continue to use the regular `For` loop in our example programs.

Checkpoint

11.1 Can you store a mixture of data types in an array?

11.2 What is an array size declarator?

11.3 In most languages, can the size of an array be changed while the program is running?

11.4 What is an array element?

11.5 What is a subscript?

11.6 What is usually the first subscript in an array?

11.7 Look at the following pseudocode and answer questions a through d.

```
Constant Integer SIZE = 7
Declare Real numbers[SIZE]
```

a. What is the name of the array that is being declared?
b. What is the size of the array?
c. What data type are the array elements?
d. What is the subscript of the last element in the array?

11.8 What does "array bounds checking" mean?

11.9 What is an off-by-one error?

11.2 Sequentially Searching an Array

The sequential search algorithm is a simple technique for finding an item in an array. It steps through the array, beginning at the first element, and compares each element to the item being searched for. The search stops when the item is found or the end of the array is reached.

Programs commonly need to search for data that is stored in an array. Various techniques known as **search algorithms** have been developed to locate a specific item in a larger collection of data, such as an array. This section shows you how to use the simplest of all search algorithms—the sequential search. The **sequential search algorithm** uses a loop to sequentially step through an array, starting with the first element. It compares each element with the value being searched for and stops when the value is found or the end of the array is encountered. If the value being searched for is not in the array, the algorithm unsuccessfully searches to the end of the array.

Figure 11-5 shows the general logic of the sequential search algorithm. Here is a summary of the data items in the figure:

- `array` is the array being searched.
- `searchValue` is the value that the algorithm is searching for.
- `found` is a Boolean variable that is used as a flag. Setting `found` to `False` indicates that `searchValue` has not been found. Setting `found` to `True` indicates that `searchValue` has been found.
- `index` is an `Integer` variable used as a loop counter.

Figure 11-5 Sequential search logic

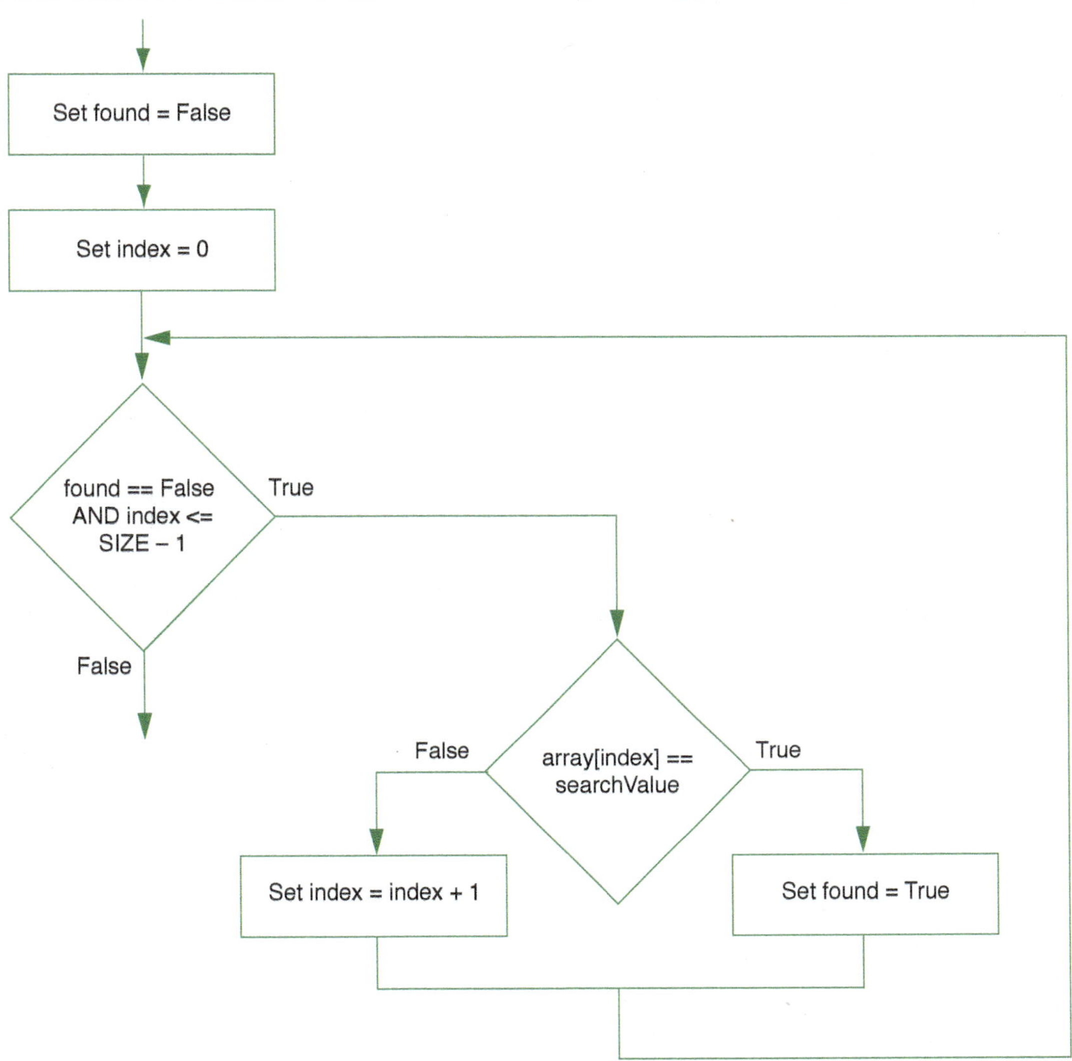

When the algorithm finishes, the `found` variable will be set to `True` if the `searchValue` was found in the array. When this is the case, the `index` variable will be set to the subscript of the element containing the `searchValue`. If the `searchValue` was not found in the array, `found` will be set to `False`. The following shows how you can express this logic in pseudocode:

```
Set found = False
Set index = 0
While found == False AND index <= SIZE - 1
   If array[index] == searchValue Then
      Set found = True
   Else
      Set index = index + 1
   End If
End While
```

The pseudocode in Program 11-6 demonstrates how to implement the sequential search in a program. This program has an array that holds test scores. It sequentially searches the array for a score of 100. If a score of 100 is found, the program displays the test number.

Program 11-6: 

```
// Constant for the array size.
Constant Integer SIZE = 10

// Declare an array to hold test scores.
Declare Integer scores[SIZE] = 87, 75, 98, 100, 82,
                               72, 88, 92, 60, 78

// Declare a Boolean variable to act as a flag.
Declare Boolean found

// Declare a variable to use as a loop counter.
Declare Integer index

// The flag must initially be set to False.
Set found = False

// Set the counter variable to 0.
Set index = 0

// Step through the array searching for a
// score equal to 100.
While found == False AND index <= SIZE - 1
   If scores[index] == 100 Then
      Set found = True
   Else
      Set index = index + 1
   End If
End While

// Display the search results.
If found Then
   Display "You earned 100 on test number ", index + 1
Else
   Display "You did not earn 100 on any test."
End If
```

Program Output

```
You earned 100 on test number 4
```

Searching a `String` Array

Program 11-6 demonstrates how to use the sequential search algorithm to find a specific number in an `Integer` array. As shown in Program 11-7, you can also use the algorithm to find a string in a `String` array.

Program 11-7: 

```
// Declare a constant for the array size.
Constant Integer SIZE = 6

// Declare a String array initialized with values.
Declare String names[SIZE] = "Ava Fischer", "Alex Prieto",
                             "Ingrid Olen", "Matt Hoyle",
                             "Rose Harrison", "Giovanni Ricci"

// Declare a variable to hold the search value.
Declare String searchValue

// Declare a Boolean variable to act as a flag.
Declare Boolean found

// Declare a counter variable for the array.
Declare Integer index

// The flag must initially be set to False.
Set found = False

// Set the counter variable to 0.
Set index = 0

// Get the string to search for.
Display "Enter a name to search for in the array."
Input searchValue

// Step through the array searching for
// the specified name.
While found == False AND index <= SIZE - 1
   If names[index] == searchValue Then
      Set found = True
   Else
      Set index = index + 1
   End If
End While

// Display the search results.
If found Then
   Display "That name was found at subscript ", index
Else
   Display "That name was not found in the array."
End If
```

Program Output (with Input Shown in Bold) *(continued)*

```
Enter a name to search for in the array.
Matt Hoyle [Enter]
That name was found at subscript 3.
```

Program Output (with Input Shown in Bold) *(continued)*

```
Enter a name to search for in the array.
Matt [Enter]
That name was not found in the array.
```

This program finds a string in the array only if the user types the complete string, exactly as it appears in the array. For example, in the first sample run the user enters "Matt Hoyle" as the search string and the program locates it at subscript 3. But, in the second sample run the user enters "Matt" and the program reports that the name was not found in the array. This is because the string "`Matt`" is not equal to the string "`Matt Hoyle`".

Often, programs must be designed to search for partial string matches. Most languages provide a library function that can determine whether a string partially matches another string. In pseudocode you can use the `contains` function to implement this. Recall from Chapter 6 that the contains function accepts two strings as arguments, and it returns True if the first string contains the second string; otherwise, the function returns False. The pseudocode in Program 11-8 shows how you can modify Program 11-7 to use the `contains` function. This version of the program will find strings in the array that partially match the string entered by the user.

Program 11-8:

```
// Declare a constant for the array size.
Constant Integer SIZE = 6

// Declare a String array initialized with values.
Declare String names[SIZE] = "Ava Fischer", "Alex Prieto",
                             "Ingrid Olen", "Matt Hoyle",
                             "Rose Harrison", "Giovanni Ricci"

// Declare a variable to hold the search value.
Declare String searchValue

// Declare a Boolean variable to act as a flag.
Declare Boolean found

// Declare a counter variable for the array.
Declare Integer index

// The flag must initially be set to False.
Set found = False

// Set the counter variable to 0.
Set index = 0

// Get the string to search for.
Display "Enter a name to search for in the array."
```

Program 11-8: *(continued)*

```
Input searchValue

// Step through the array searching for
// the specified name.
While found == False AND index <= SIZE - 1
   If contains(names[index], searchValue) Then
      Set found = True
   Else
      Set index = index + 1
   End If
End While

// Display the search results.
If found Then
   Display "That name matches the following element:"
   Display names[index]
Else
   Display "That name was not found in the array."
End If
```

Program Output (with Input Shown in Bold)

```
Enter a name to search for in the array.
Matt [Enter]
That name matches the following element:
Matt Hoyle
```

Checkpoint

11.10 What is a search algorithm?

11.11 Which array element does the sequential search algorithm first look at?

11.12 What does the loop do in the sequential search algorithm? What happens when the value being searched for is found?

11.13 How many elements does the sequential search algorithm look at in the case that the search value is not found in the array?

11.14 How do you look for a partial string match when searching an array of strings for a value?

11.3 Processing the Contents of an Array

There are many operations that you can perform on an array using a loop.

Totaling the Values in an Array

To calculate the total of the values in an array, you use a loop with an accumulator variable. The loop steps through the array, adding the value of each array element to the accumulator. Figure 11-6 shows the logic of the algorithm. In the algorithm `total` is an accumulator variable, `index` is a loop counter, and `array` is an array containing numeric values.

Figure 11-6 Algorithm for totaling the values in an array

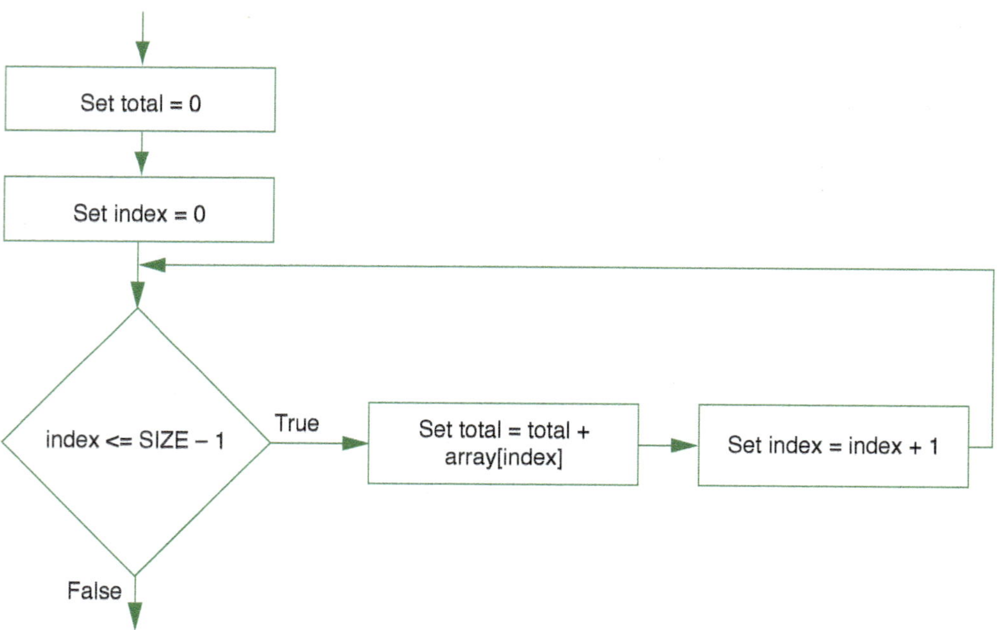

The pseudocode in Program 11-9 demonstrates the algorithm with an `Integer` array named `numbers`.

Program 11-9:

```
// Declare a constant for the array size.
Constant Integer SIZE = 5

// Declare an array initialized with values.
Declare Integer numbers[SIZE] = 2, 4, 6, 8, 10

// Declare and initialize an accumulator variable.
Declare Integer total = 0

// Declare a counter variable for the loop.
Declare Integer index
```

Program 11-9: *(continued)*

```

// Calculate the total of the array elements.
For index = 0 To SIZE - 1
    Set total = total + numbers[index]
End For

// Display the sum of the array elements.
Display "The sum of the array elements is ", total
```

Program Output

```
The sum of the array elements is 30
```

Averaging the Values in an Array

The first step in calculating the average of the values in an array is to get the total of the values. You saw how to do that with a loop in the preceding section. The second step is to divide the total by the number of elements in the array. The pseudocode in Program 11-10 demonstrates the algorithm.

Program 11-10:

```
// Declare a constant for the array size.
Constant Integer SIZE = 5

// Declare an array initialized with values.
Declare Real scores[SIZE] = 2.5, 8.3, 6.5, 4.0, 5.2

// Declare and initialize an accumulator variable.
Declare Real total = 0

// Declare a variable to hold the average.
Declare Real average

// Declare a counter variable for the loop.
Declare Integer index

// Calculate the total of the array elements.
For index = 0 To SIZE - 1
    Set total = total + numbers[index]
End For

// Calculate the average of the array elements.
 Set average = total / SIZE

// Display the average of the array elements.
Display "The average of the array elements is ", average
```

Program Output

```
The average of the array elements is 5.3
```

Finding the Highest Value in an Array

Some programming tasks require you to find the highest value in a set of data. Examples include programs that report the highest sales amount for a given time period, the highest test score in a set of test scores, the highest temperature for a given set of days, and so forth.

The algorithm for finding the highest value in an array works like this: You create a variable to hold the highest value (the following examples name this variable `highest`). Then, you assign the value at element 0 to the `highest` variable. Next, you use a loop to step through the rest of the array elements, beginning at element 1. Each time the loop iterates, it compares an array element to the `highest` variable. If the array element is greater than the `highest` variable, then the value in the array element is assigned to the `highest` variable. When the loop finishes, the `highest` variable will contain the highest value in the array. The flowchart in Figure 11-7 illustrates this logic. The pseudocode in Program 11-11 shows a simple demonstration of the algorithm.Figure 11-7 Flowchart for finding the highest value in an array

Program 11-11:

```
// Declare a constant for the array size.
Constant Integer SIZE = 5

// Declare an array initialized with values.
Declare Integer numbers[SIZE] = 8, 1, 12, 6, 2

// Declare a counter variable for the array.
Declare Integer index

// Declare a variable to hold the highest value.
Declare Integer highest

// Assign the first element to highest.
Set highest = numbers[0]

// Step through the rest of the array,
// beginning at element 1. When a value
// greater than highest is found, assign
// that value to highest.
For index = 1 To SIZE - 1
   If numbers[index] > highest Then
      Set highest = numbers[index]
   End If
End For

// Display the highest value.
Display "The highest value in the array is ", highest
```

Program Output

```
The highest value in the array is 12
```

Figure 11-7 Flowchart for finding the highest value in an array

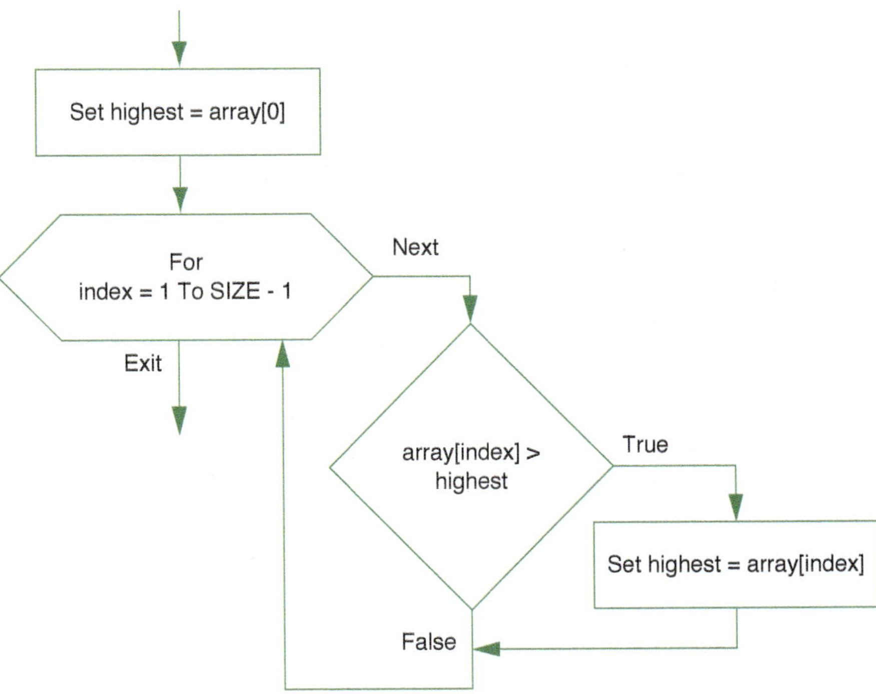

Finding the Lowest Value in an Array

In some programs you are more interested in finding the lowest value than the highest value in a set of data. For example, suppose you are designing a program that stores several players' golf scores in an array and you need to find the best score. In golf, the lower the score the better, so you would need an algorithm that finds the lowest value in the array.

The algorithm for finding the lowest value in an array is very similar to the algorithm for finding the highest score. It works like this: You create a variable to hold the lowest value (the following examples name this variable `lowest`). Then, you assign the value at element 0 to the `lowest` variable. Next, you use a loop to step through the rest of the array elements, beginning at element 1. Each time the loop iterates, it compares an array element to the `lowest` variable. If the array element is less than the `lowest` variable, then the value in the array element is assigned to the `lowest` variable. When the loop finishes, the `lowest` variable will contain the lowest value in the array. The flowchart in Figure 11-8 illustrates this logic. The pseudocode in Program 11-12 shows a simple demonstration of the algorithm.

Figure 11-8 Flowchart for finding the lowest value in an array

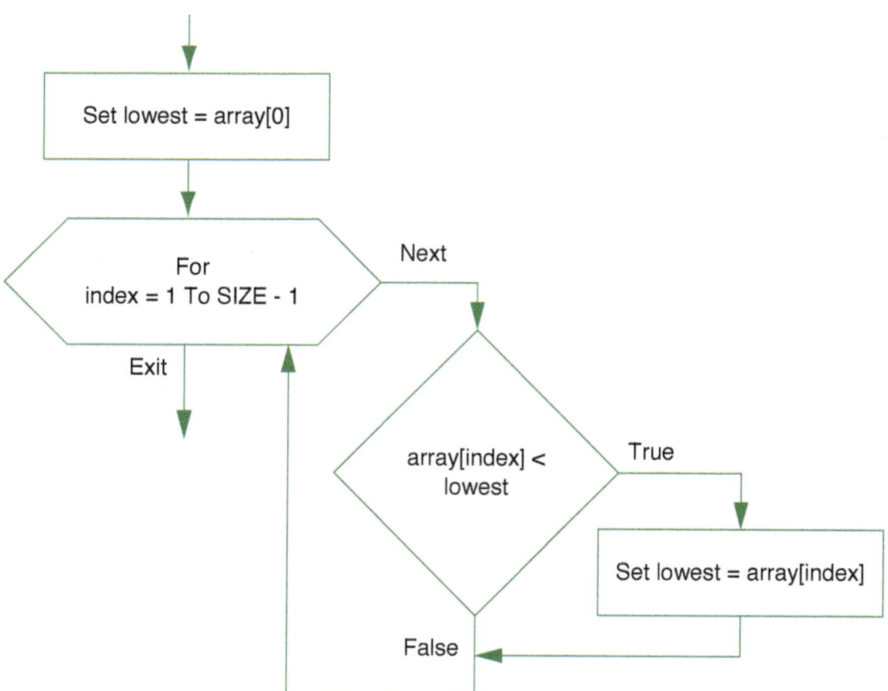

Program 11-12:

```
// Declare a constant for the array size.
Constant Integer SIZE = 5

// Declare an array initialized with values.
Declare Integer numbers[SIZE] = 8, 1, 12, 6, 2

// Declare a counter variable for the array.
Declare Integer index

// Declare a variable to hold the lowest value.
Declare Integer lowest

// Assign the first element to lowest.
Set lowest = numbers[0]

// Step through the rest of the array,
// beginning at element 1. When a value
// less than lowest is found, assign
// that value to lowest.
For index = 1 To SIZE - 1
   If numbers[index] < lowest Then
      Set lowest = numbers[index]
   End If
End For
```

Program 11-12: *(continue)*

```

// Display the lowest value.
Display "The lowest value in the array is ", lowest
```

Program Output

```
The lowest value in the array is 1
```

Copying an Array

In most programming languages, if you need to copy the contents of one array to another you have to assign the individual elements of the array that you are copying to the elements of the other array. Usually, this is best done with a loop. For example, look at the following pseudocode:

```
Constant Integer SIZE = 5
Declare Integer firstArray[SIZE] = 100, 200, 300, 400, 500
Declare Integer secondArray[SIZE]
```

Suppose you want to copy the values in `firstArray` to `secondArray`. The following pseudocode assigns each element of `firstArray` to the corresponding element in `secondArray`.

```
Declare Integer index
For index = 0 To SIZE - 1
   Set secondArray[index] = firstArray[index]
End For
```

Passing an Array as an Argument to a Module or a Function

Most languages allow you to pass an array as an argument to a module or a function. This gives you the ability to modularize many of the operations that you perform on an array. Passing an array as an argument typically requires that you pass two arguments: (1) the array itself, and (2) an integer that specifies the number of elements in the array. The pseudocode in Program 11-13 shows an example of a function that accepts an `Integer` array as an argument. The function returns the total of the array's elements.

Program 11-13: 

```
Module main()
   // A constant for the array size.
   Constant Integer SIZE = 5

   // An array initialized with values.
   Declare Integer numbers[SIZE] = 2, 4, 6, 8, 10

   // A variable to hold the sum of the elements.
   Declare Integer sum

   // Get the sum of the elements.
```

```
12     Set sum = getTotal(numbers, SIZE)
13
14     // Display the sum of the array elements.
15     Display "The sum of the array elements is ", sum
16  End Module
17
18  // The getTotal function accepts an Integer array and the
19  // array's size as arguments. It returns the total of the
20  // array elements.
21  Function Integer getTotal(Integer array[], Integer arraySize)
22     // Loop counter
23     Declare Integer index
24
25     // Accumulator, initialized to 0
26     Declare Integer total = 0
27
28     // Calculate the total of the array elements.
29     For index = 0 To arraySize - 1
30        Set total = total + array[index]
31     End For
32
33     // Return the total.
34     Return total
35  End Function
```

Program Output

```
The sum of the array elements is 30
```

In the `main` module, an `Integer` array is declared in line 6 and initialized with five values. In line 12, the following statement calls the `getTotal` function and assigns its return value to the `sum` variable:

```
Set sum = getTotal(numbers, SIZE)
```

This statement passes two arguments to the `getTotal` function: the `numbers` array and the value of the `SIZE` constant. Here is the first line of the `getTotal` function, which appears in line 21:

```
Function Integer getTotal(Integer array[], Integer arraySize)
```

Notice that the function has the following two parameters.

- `Integer array[]`—This parameter accepts an array of `Integers` as an argument.
- `Integer arraySize`—This parameter accepts an `Integer` that specifies the number of elements in the array.

When the function is called in line 12, it passes the `numbers` array into the `array` parameter, and the value of the `SIZE` constant into the `arraySize` parameter. This is shown in Figure 11-9. The function then calculates the total of the values in `array` and returns that value.

Figure 11-9 Passing arguments to the `getTotal` function

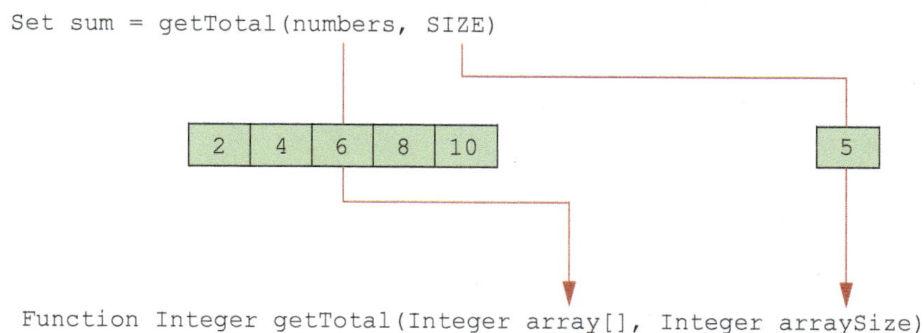

NOTE: In many of the most common programming languages (including Java, C++, and C#), arrays are *always* passed by reference. This is because it is inefficient to make a copy of an entire array each time it is passed as an argument to a module or function. In such languages, when you pass an array as an argument, the parameter variable in the module or function becomes a reference to the array. That means the module or function has access to the original data in the array (not a copy). When using one of these languages, take care that in modules and functions you do not unintentionally modify an array that has been passed as an argument.

Checkpoint

11.15 Briefly describe how you calculate the total of the values in an array.

11.16 Briefly describe how you get the average of the values in an array.

11.17 Describe the algorithm for finding the highest value in an array.

11.18 Describe the algorithm for finding the lowest value in an array.

11.19 How do you copy the contents of one array to another array?

11.4 Parallel Arrays

By using the same subscript, you can establish relationships between data stored in two or more arrays.

VideoNote
Parallel Arrays

Sometimes it is useful to store related data in two or more arrays. For example, assume you have designed a program with the following array declarations:

```
Constant Integer SIZE = 5
Declare String names[SIZE]
Declare String addresses[SIZE]
```

The names array stores the names of five people, and the `addresses` array stores the addresses of the same five people. The data for each person is stored in the same relative location in each array.

For instance, the first person's name is stored in `names[0]`, and that same person's address is stored in `addresses[0]`. Figure 11-10 illustrates this.

To access the data, you use the same subscript with both arrays. For example, the loop in the following pseudocode displays each person's name and address:

```
Declare Integer index
For index = 0 To SIZE - 1
   Display names[index]
   Display addresses[index]
End For
```

Figure 11-10 The `names` and `addresses` arrays

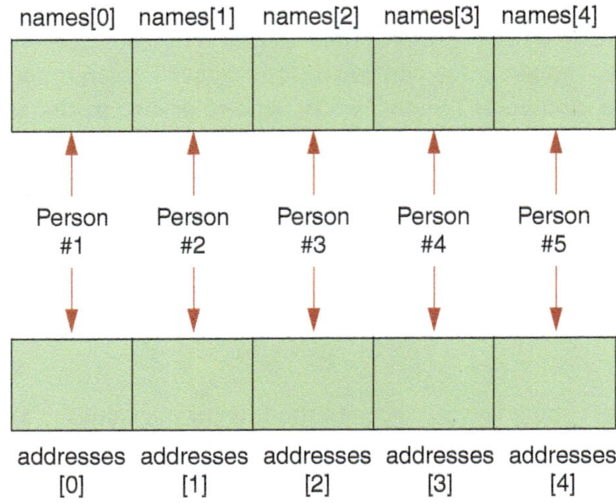

The `names` and `addresses` arrays are examples of parallel arrays. **Parallel arrays** are two or more arrays that hold related data, and the related elements in each array are accessed with a common subscript.

In the Spotlight:

Using Parallel Arrays

In this chapter's first *In the Spotlight* section (see Program 11-4), Megan asked you to design a program that allows her to enter the number of hours worked by each of her employees and then displays each employee's gross pay. As it is currently designed, the program refers to the employees as "employee 1," employee 2," and so on. Megan has asked you to modify the program so she can enter employees' names along with their hours, and then it should display each employee's name along with their gross pay.

On Your Own: Working alone or with a partner, write the algorithm steps, draw a flowchart, and write the pseudocode. Then, read on to see how you did. Remember, your solution does not have to be exactly the same as the one in the text in order to come up with the same result.

Currently, the program has an array named `hours` that holds each employee's hours worked. You decide to add a parallel array named `names` that will hold each employee's name. The first employee's data will appear in `names[0]` and in `hours[0]`, the second employee's data will appear in `names[1]` and in `hours[1]`, and so on.

Here is the updated algorithm:

1. For each employee:
   a. Get the employee's name and store it in the `names` array.
   b. Get the employee's number of hours worked and store it in the corresponding element of the `hours` array.
2. Step through each set of elements in the parallel arrays and display the employee's name and gross pay.

Program 11-14 shows the pseudocode for the revised program, and Figure 11-11 shows a flowchart.

Program 11-14:

```
// Constant for the array sizes.
Constant Integer SIZE = 6

// Array to hold each employee's name.
Declare String names[SIZE]

// Array to hold each employee's hours.
Declare Real hours[SIZE]

// Variable to hold the hourly pay rate.
Declare Real payRate

// Variable to hold a gross pay amount.
Declare Real grossPay

// Variable to use as a loop counter.
Declare Integer index

// Get each employee's data.
For index = 0 To SIZE - 1
    // Get an employee's name.
    Display "Enter the name of employee ", index + 1
    Input names[index]

    // Get the employee's hours.
    Display "Enter the hours worked by that employee."
    Input hours[index]
End For

// Get the hourly pay rate.
Display "Enter the hourly pay rate."
Input payRate

```

Program 11-14: *(continued)*

```
// Display each employee's gross pay.
Display "Here is each employee's gross pay."
For index = 0 To SIZE - 1
    Set grossPay = hours[index] * payRate
    Display names[index], ": ", currencyFormat(grossPay)
End For
```

Program Output (with Input Shown in Bold)

```
Enter the name of employee 1
Jamie Lynn [Enter]
Enter the hours worked by that employee.
10 [Enter]
Enter the name of employee 2
Courtney [Enter]
Enter the hours worked by that employee.
20 [Enter]
Enter the name of employee 3
Ashley [Enter]
Enter the hours worked by that employee.
15 [Enter]
Enter the name of employee 4
Brian [Enter]
Enter the hours worked by that employee.
40 [Enter]
Enter the name of employee 5
Jane [Enter]
Enter the hours worked by that employee.
20 [Enter]
Enter the name of employee 6
Ian [Enter]
Enter the hours worked by that employee.
18 [Enter]
Enter the hourly pay rate.
12.75 [Enter]
Here is each employee's gross pay.
Jamie Lynn: $127.50
Courtney: $255.00
Ashley: $191.25
Brian: $510.00
Jane: $255.00
Ian: $229.50
```

Figure 11-11 Flowchart for Program 11-14

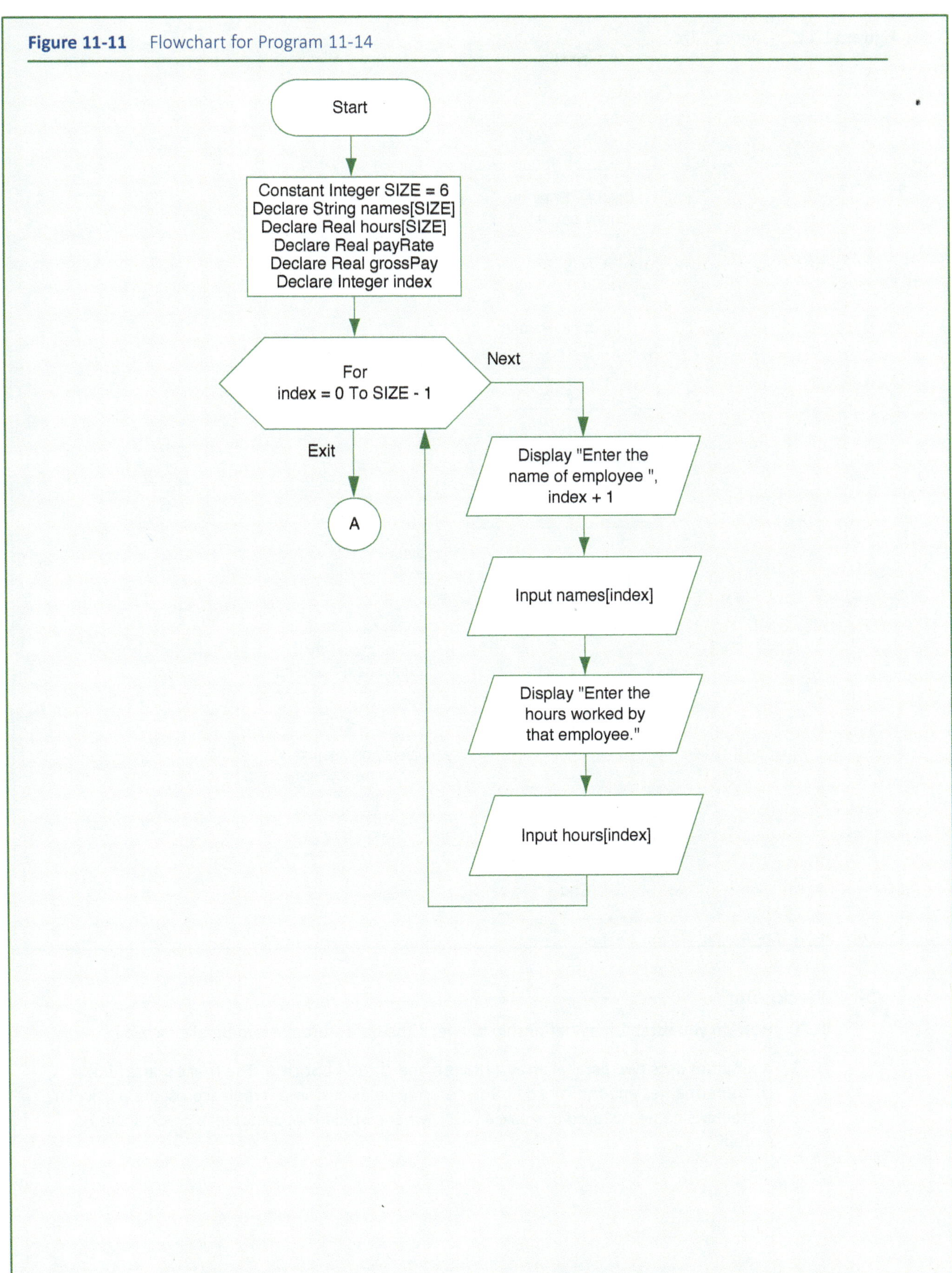

Figure 11-11 (continued)

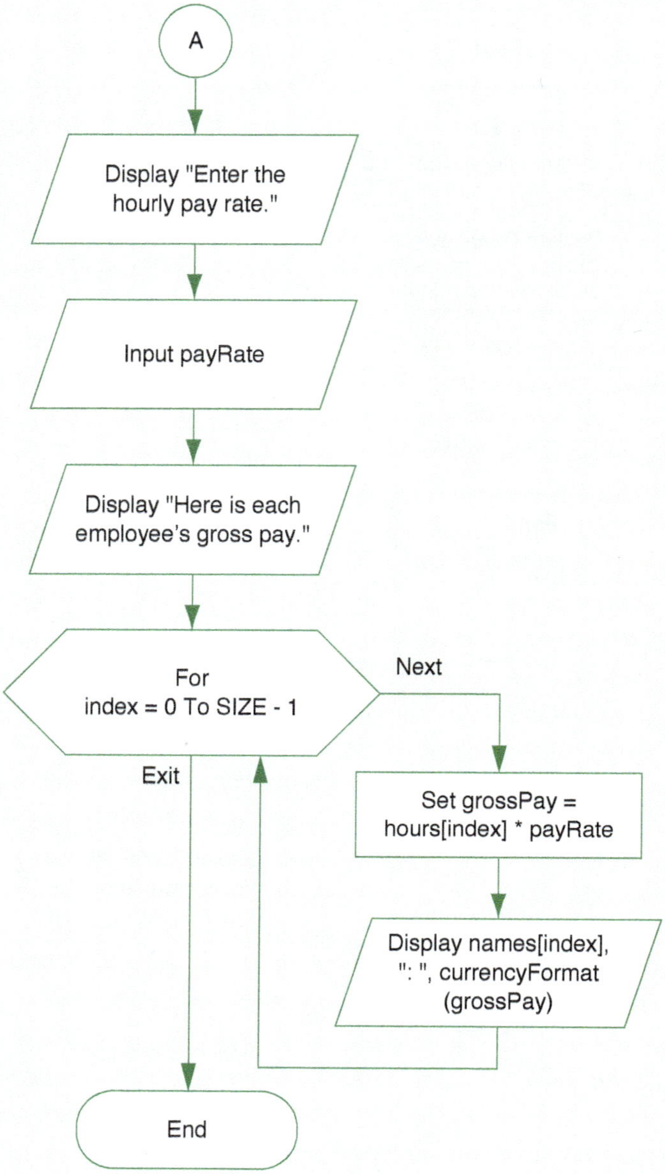

Checkpoint

11.20 How do you establish a relationship between the data stored in two parallel arrays?

11.21 A program uses two parallel arrays: `names` and `creditScore`. The `names` array holds customer names and the `creditScore` array holds customer credit scores. If a particular customer's name is stored in `names[82]`, where would that customer's credit score be stored?

Chapter Review

Multiple Choice

1. ____________ appears in an array declaration and specifies the number of elements in the array.
   a. subscript
   b. size declarator
   c. array name
   d. initialization value

2. To make programs easier to maintain, many programmers use ____________ to specify the size of an array.
   a. real numbers
   b. string expressions
   c. math expressions
   d. named constants

3. ____________ is an individual storage location in an array.
   a. element
   b. bin
   c. cubby hole
   d. size declarator

4. ____________ is a number that identifies a storage location in an array.
   a. element
   b. subscript
   c. size declarator
   d. identifier

5. ____________ is typically the first subscript in an array.
   a. − 1
   b. 1
   c. 0
   d. The size of the array minus one

6. ____________ is typically the last subscript in an array.
   a. − 1
   b. 99
   c. 0
   d. The size of the array minus one

7. ____________ uses a loop to step through each element of an array, starting with the first element, searching for a value.
   a. sequential search
   b. step-by-step search
   c. elemental search
   d. binary search

8. Many programming languages perform this, which means they do not allow a program to use an invalid array subscript.
   a. memory checking
   b. bounds checking
   c. type compatibility checking
   d. syntax checking

9. Term ____________ describes two or more arrays that hold related data, and the related elements in each array are accessed with a common subscript.
   a. synchronous arrays
   b. asynchronous arrays
   c. parallel arrays
   d. two-dimensional arrays

True or False

1. You can store a mixture of different data types in an array.

2. In most languages, an array's size cannot be changed while the program is running.

3. Array bounds checking typically occurs while a program is running.

4. You can do many things with arrays, but you cannot pass one as an argument to a module or a function.

Short Answer

1. What is an off-by-one error?

2. Look at the following pseudocode:

```
Constant Integer SIZE = 10
Declare Integer values[SIZE]
```

   a. How many elements does the array have?
   b. What is the subscript of the first element in the array?
   c. What is the subscript of the last element in the array?

3. Look at the following pseudocode:

```
Constant Integer SIZE = 3
Declare Integer numbers[SIZE] = 1, 2, 3
```

   a. What value is stored in `numbers[2]`?
   b. What value is stored in `numbers[0]`?

4. A program uses two parallel arrays named `customerNumbers` and `balances`. The `customerNumbers` array holds customer numbers and the `balances` array holds customer account balances. If a particular customer's customer number is stored in `customerNumbers[187]`, where would that customer's account balance be stored?

5. Look at the following pseudocode array declaration:

```
Declare Real sales[8][10]
```

   a. How many rows does the array have?
   b. How many columns does the array have?
   c. How many elements does the array have?
   d. Write a pseudocode statement that stores a number in the last column of the last row in the array.

Algorithm Workbench

1. Write a pseudocode declaration for a `String` array initialized with the following strings: "`Einstein`", "`Newton`", "`Copernicus`", and "`Kepler`".

2. Assume `names` is an `Integer` array with 20 elements. Design a `For` loop that displays each element of the array.

3. Assume the arrays `numberArray1` and `numberArray2` each have 100 elements. Design an algorithm that copies the values in `numberArray1` to `numberArray2`.

4. Draw a flowchart showing the general logic for totaling the values in an array.

5. Draw a flowchart showing the general logic for finding the highest value in an array.

6. Draw a flowchart showing the general logic for finding the lowest value in an array.

7. Assume the following declarations appear in a pseudocode program:

```
Constant Integer SIZE = 100
Declare Integer firstArray[SIZE]
Declare Integer secondArray[SIZE]
```

   Also, assume that values have been stored in each element of `firstArray`. Design an algorithm that copies the contents of `firstArray` to `secondArray`.

8. Design an algorithm for a function that accepts an `Integer` array as an argument and returns the total of the values in the array.

9. Write a pseudocode algorithm that uses the `For Each` loop to display all of the values in the following array:

```
Constant Integer SIZE = 10
Declare Integer values[SIZE] = 1, 2, 3, 4, 5, 6, 7, 8, 9, 10
```

Debugging Exercises

1. What is the error in the following pseudocode?

```
// This program uses an array to display five names.
Constant Integer SIZE = 5
Declare String names[SIZE] = "Meg", "Jack", "Steve",
                             "Bill", "Lisa"
Declare Integer index
For index = 0 To SIZE
   Display names[index]
End For
```

2. What is the error in the following pseudocode?

```
// This program displays the highest value in the array.
Declare Integer SIZE = 3
Declare Integer values[SIZE] = 1, 3, 4
Declare Integer index
Declare Integer highest

For index = 0 To SIZE - 1
   If values[index] > highest Then
      Set highest = values[index]
   End If
End For
Display "The highest number is ", highest
```

3. What is the error in the following pseudocode?

```
// The searchName function accepts a string containing the name
// to search for, an array of strings containing the names, and
// an integer specifying the size of the array. The function
// searches for the name in the array. If the name is found, the
// string containing the name is returned; otherwise a message
// indicating that the name was not found in the array is
// returned.
Function String searchName(String name, String names[],
                           Integer size)
   Declare Boolean found
   Declare Integer index
   Declare String result
```

```
        // Step through the array searching for the
        // specified name.
        While found == False AND index <= size - 1
           If contains(names[index], name) Then
              Set found = True
           Else
              Set index = index + 1
           End If
        End While
        // Determine the result.
        If found == True Then
           Set result = names[index]
        Else
           Set result = "That name was not found in the array."
        End If
        Return result
     End Function
```

Programming Exercises

VideoNote
The Total Sales Problem

1. **Total Sales**

   Design a program that asks the user to enter a store's sales for each day of the week. The amounts should be stored in an array. Use a loop to calculate the total sales for the week and display the result.

2. **Lottery Number Generator**

   Design a program that generates a 7-digit lottery number. The program should have an `Integer` array with 7 elements. Write a loop that steps through the array, randomly generating a number in the range of 0 through 9 for each element. (Use the `random` function that was discussed in Chapter 6.) Then write another loop that displays the contents of the array.

3. **Rainfall Statistics**

   Design a program that lets the user enter the total rainfall for each of 12 months into an array. The program should calculate and display the total rainfall for the year, the average monthly rainfall, and the months with the highest and lowest amounts.

4. **Number Analysis Program**

   Design a program that asks the user to enter a series of 20 numbers. The program should store the numbers in an array and then display the following data:

   - The lowest number in the array
   - The highest number in the array
   - The total of the numbers in the array
   - The average of the numbers in the array

5. **Charge Account Validation**

Design a program that asks the user to enter a charge account number. The program should determine whether the number is valid by comparing it to the following list of valid charge account numbers:

```
5658845  4520125  7895122  8777541  8451277  1302850
8080152  4562555  5552012  5050552  7825877  1250255
1005231  6545231  3852085  7576651  7881200  4581002
```

These numbers should be stored in an array. Use the sequential search algorithm to locate the number entered by the user. If the number is in the array, the program should display a message indicating the number is valid. If the number is not in the array, the program should display a message indicating the number is invalid.

6. **Days of Each Month**

Design a program that displays the number of days in each month. The program's output should be similar to this:

```
January has 31 days.
February has 28 days.
March has 31 days.
April has 30 days.
May has 31 days.
June has 30 days.
July has 31 days.
August has 31 days.
September has 30 days.
October has 31 days.
November has 30 days.
December has 31 days.
```

The program should have two parallel arrays: a 12-element `String` array that is initialized with the names of the months, and a 12-element `Integer` array that is initialized with the number of days in each month. To produce the output specified, use a loop to step through the arrays getting the name of a month and the number of days in that month.

7. **Phone Number Lookup**

Design a program that has two parallel arrays: a `String` array named `people` that is initialized with the names of seven of your friends, and a `String` array named `phoneNumbers` that is initialized with your friends' phone numbers. The program should allow the user to enter a person's name (or part of a person's name). It should then search for that person in the `people` array. If the person is found, it should get that person's phone number from the `phoneNumbers` array and display it. If the person is not found in the `people` array, the program should display a message indicating so.

8. **Driver's License Exam**

The local driver's license office has asked you to design a program that grades the written portion of the driver's license exam. The exam has 20 multiple choice questions. Here are the correct answers:

(1) B	(6) A	(11) B	(16) C
(2) D	(7) B	(12) C	(17) C
(3) A	(8) A	(13) D	(18) B
(4) A	(9) C	(14) A	(19) D
(5) C	(10) D	(15) D	(20) A

Your program should store these correct answers in an array. (Store each question's correct answer in an element of a `String` array.) The program should ask the user to enter the student's answers for each of the 20 questions, which should be stored in another array. After the student's answers have been entered, the program should display a message indicating whether the student passed or failed the exam. (A student must correctly answer 15 of the 20 questions to pass the exam.) It should then display the total number of correctly answered questions, the total number of incorrectly answered questions, and a list showing the question numbers of the incorrectly answered questions.

CHAPTER 12

Testing and Debugging Your Code

TOPICS

12.1 Types of Errors

KEY POINT

Programming errors can be categorized into three types: syntax errors, runtime errors, and logic errors.

Note In this chapter, examples are provided using Python-specific code.

Syntax Errors

Errors that are detected by the interpreter are called **syntax errors** or **compile errors**. Syntax errors result from errors in code construction, such as mistyping a keyword, omitting some necessary punctuation, or using an uppercase or lowercase character in the wrong place. For example, Python is a case-sensitive language. This means that it sees an uppercase character different than a lowercase character. For example, 'A' is not the same as 'a'. These errors are usually easy to detect because the information about the error displays in an error message when you try to run the program.

For example, try entering the following code in Python. When you run it, a syntax error displays.

```
1  # Add two numbers and assign to total.
2  total = 3 + 4
3  print(Total)
```

In most cases, you will be able to use the line number reported in the error message to identify and fix the error. A closer examination of your code reveals that 'total' was referenced using an uppercase 'T'. It should be changed to lowercase 't' to match the spelling of the variable declared in line 2. Try making the change and running the program. It should execute correctly.

Since a single error will often display many lines of compile errors, it is a good practice to fix errors from the top line and work downward. Fixing errors that occur earlier in the program may also fix additional errors that occur later.

Runtime Errors

Runtime errors are errors that cause a program to terminate abnormally. They occur while a program is running if the environment detects an operation that is impossible to carry out.

Input mistakes typically cause runtime errors. An **input error** occurs when the program is waiting for the user to enter a value, but the user enters a value that the program cannot handle. For example, if the program expects to read in a number, but instead the user enters a string, this causes a data type mismatch and a runtime error occurs.

Another example of a runtime error is **division by zero**. This happens when the divisor is zero for integer divisions. For instance, try entering and running the following program. It will result in a runtime error that causes the program to terminate abnormally.

```
# If the user inputs zero, a runtime error occurs.
total = 10
num = int(input("Enter a value: "))
total = total/num
print(total)
```

Logic Errors

Logic errors occur when a program does not perform the way it was intended to. Errors of this kind occur for many different reasons and can be harder to find than syntax and runtime errors. This is demonstrated in the following Python code, which is supposed to determine if a user is eligible to vote, based on being 18 years old. Can you find the logic error?

```
1 # An 18 year old is eligible to vote.
2 # This code causes a logic error printing "you cannot vote".
3 voting_age = 18
4 age = 18
5 if age > voting_age:
6   print("you can vote")
7 else:
8   print("you cannot vote")
```

This program will print "you cannot vote' when the age=18. This is wrong because we have stated that an 18 year old is eligible to vote. To get the correct result, you need to change line 5 operator from '>' to '>=' so that all ages greater than or equal to 18 will display a message "you can vote".

Finding Errors

In general, syntax errors are easy to find and easy to correct because the compiler gives error messages as to where the errors came from and why they are wrong. Runtime errors are not difficult to find, either, since the reasons and locations for the errors are displayed in a message on the console when the program aborts. Finding logic errors, on the other hand, can be very challenging. In the next section, you will learn the techniques of tracing programs and finding logic errors.

Checkpoint

12.1 What are syntax errors (compile errors), runtime errors, and logic errors?

12.2 Give examples of syntax errors, runtime errors, and logic errors.

12.3 If you forget to put a closing quotation mark on a string, what kind of error will be raised?

12.4 Suppose you write a program for computing the perimeter of a rectangle, and you mistakenly write your program so that it computes the area of a rectangle. What kind of error is this?

12.2 Handling Exceptions

An exception is an error that occurs while a program is running, causing the program to abruptly halt. You can use the try/except statement to gracefully handle exceptions.

An **exception** is an error that occurs while a program is running. In most cases, an exception causes a program to abruptly halt. For example, look at Program 12-1. This program gets two numbers from the user, then divides the first number by the second number. In the sample running of the program, however, a ZeroDivisionError exception occurred because the user entered 0 as the second number. Division by 0 causes an exception because it is mathematically impossible.

Program 12-1:

```
# This program divides a number by another number.

def main():
    # Get two numbers.
    num1 = int(input('Enter a number: '))
    num2 = int(input('Enter another number: '))

    # Divide num1 by num2 and display the result.
    result = num1 / num2
    print(f'{num1} divided by {num2} is {result}')

# Call the main function.
if __name__ == '__main__':
    main()
```

Program Output (with input shown in bold)

```
Enter a number: 10 (Enter)
Enter another number: 0 (Enter)
Traceback (most recent call last):
```

Program Output (with input shown in bold) *(continued)*

```
  File "C:\Python\division.py," line 13, in <module>
    main()
  File "C:\Python\division.py," line 9, in main
    result = num1 / num2
ZeroDivisionError: integer division or modulo by zero
```

The error message that is shown in the sample run is called a **traceback**. It gives information regarding the line number(s) that caused the exception. The last line of the error message shows the name of the exception (`ZeroDivisionError`) and a brief description of the error that caused the exception (`integer division or modulo by zero`). You use the information to solve the problem by fixing the code.

You can prevent many exceptions from being raised by carefully coding your program. For example, Program 12-2 shows how division by 0 can be prevented with a simple `if` statement. Rather than allowing the exception to be raised, the program tests the value of `num2`, and displays an error message if the value is 0. This is an example of gracefully avoiding an exception.

Program 12-2: 

```
# This program divides a number by another number.

def main():
    # Get two numbers.
    num1 = int(input('Enter a number: '))
    num2 = int(input('Enter another number: '))

    # If num2 is not 0, divide num1 by num2
    # and display the result.
    if num2 != 0:
        result = num1 / num2
        print(f'{num1} divided by {num2} is {result}')
    else:
        print('Cannot divide by zero.')

# Call the main function.
if __name__ == '__main__':
    main()
```

Program Output (with input shown in bold)

```
Enter a number: 10 [Enter]
Enter another number: 0 [Enter]
Cannot divide by zero.
```

Some exceptions cannot be avoided regardless of how carefully you write your program. For example, look at Program 12-3. This program calculates gross pay. It prompts the user to enter the number of hours worked and the hourly pay rate. It gets the user's gross pay by multiplying these two numbers and displays that value on the screen.

Program 12-3: 

```
1  # This program calculates gross pay.
2
3  def main():
4      # Get the number of hours worked.
5      hours = int(input('How many hours did you work? '))
6
7      # Get the hourly pay rate.
8      pay_rate = float(input('Enter your hourly pay rate: '))
9
10     # Calculate the gross pay.
11     gross_pay = hours * pay_rate
12
13     # Display the gross pay.
14     print(f'Gross pay: ${gross_pay:,.2f}')
15
16 # Call the main function.
17 if _ _name_ _ == '_ _main_ _':
18     main()
```

Program Output (with input shown in bold)

```
How many hours did you work? forty [Enter]
Traceback (most recent call last):
  File "C:\Users\Tony\Documents\Python\Source
Code\Chapter 06\gross_pay1.py", line 17, in <module>
    main()
  File "C:\Users\Tony\Documents\Python\Source
Code\Chapter 06\gross_pay1.py", line 5, in main
    hours = int(input('How many hours did you work? '))
ValueError: invalid literal for int() with base 10: 'forty'
```

Look at the Program Output. An exception occurred because the user entered the string `'forty'` instead of the number 40 when prompted for the number of hours worked. Because the string `'forty'` cannot be converted to an integer, the `int()` function raised an exception in line 5, and the program halted. Look carefully at the last line of the traceback message, and you will see that the name of the exception is `ValueError`, and its description is: `invalid literal for int() with base 10: 'forty'`.

Most modern programming languages, allows you to write code that responds to exceptions when they are raised and prevents the program from abruptly crashing. Such code is called an **exception handler.** In some languages, including Python and C++, an exception handler is written with the `try/except` statement. (In Java, you use a `try/catch`) There are several ways to write a `try/except` statement, but the following general format shows the simplest variation in Python:

```
try:
  statement
  statement
  etc.
except ExceptionName:
  statement
  statement
  etc.
```

First, the keyword `try` appears, followed by a colon. Next, a code block appears, which we will refer to as the **try suite**. The try suite is one or more statements that can potentially raise an exception.

After the try suite, an **except clause** appears. The `except` clause begins with the keyword `except`, optionally followed by the name of an exception and ending with a colon. Beginning on the next line is a block of statements that we will refer to as a **handler**.

When the `try/except` statement executes, the statements in the try suite begin to execute. The following describes what happens next:

- If a statement in the try suite raises an exception that is specified by the **ExceptionName** in an `except` clause, then the handler that immediately follows the `except` clause executes. Then, the program resumes execution with the statement immediately following the `try/except` statement.
- If a statement in the try suite raises an exception that is *not* specified by the `ExceptionName` in an `except` clause, then the program will halt with a traceback error message.
- If the statements in the try suite execute without raising an exception, then any `except` clauses and handlers in the statement are skipped, and the program resumes execution with the statement immediately following the `try/except` statement.

Program 12-4 shows how we can write a `try/except` statement to gracefully respond to a `ValueError` exception.

Program 12-4: 

```
# This program calculates gross pay.

def main():
    try:
        # Get the number of hours worked.
        hours = int(input('How many hours did you work? '))

        # Get the hourly pay rate.
        pay_rate = float(input('Enter your hourly pay rate: '))
```

Program 12-4: *(continued)*

```
10
11         # Calculate the gross pay.
12         gross_pay = hours * pay_rate
13
14         # Display the gross pay.
15         print(f'Gross pay: ${gross_pay:,.2f}')
16     except ValueError:
17         print('ERROR: Hours worked and hourly pay rate must')
18         print('be valid numbers.')
19
20 # Call the main function.
21 if _ _name_ _ == '_ _main_ _':
22     main()
```

Program Output (with input shown in bold)

```
How many hours did you work? forty [Enter]
ERROR: Hours worked and hourly pay rate must be valid numbers.
```

Let's look at what happened in the sample run. The statement in line 6 prompts the user to enter the number of hours worked, and the user enters the string `'forty'`. Because the string `'forty'` cannot be converted to an integer, the `int()` function raises a `ValueError` exception. As a result, the program jumps immediately out of the try suite to the `except ValueError` clause in line 16 and begins executing the handler block that begins in line 17. This is illustrated in Figure 12-3.

Figure 12-3 Handling an exception

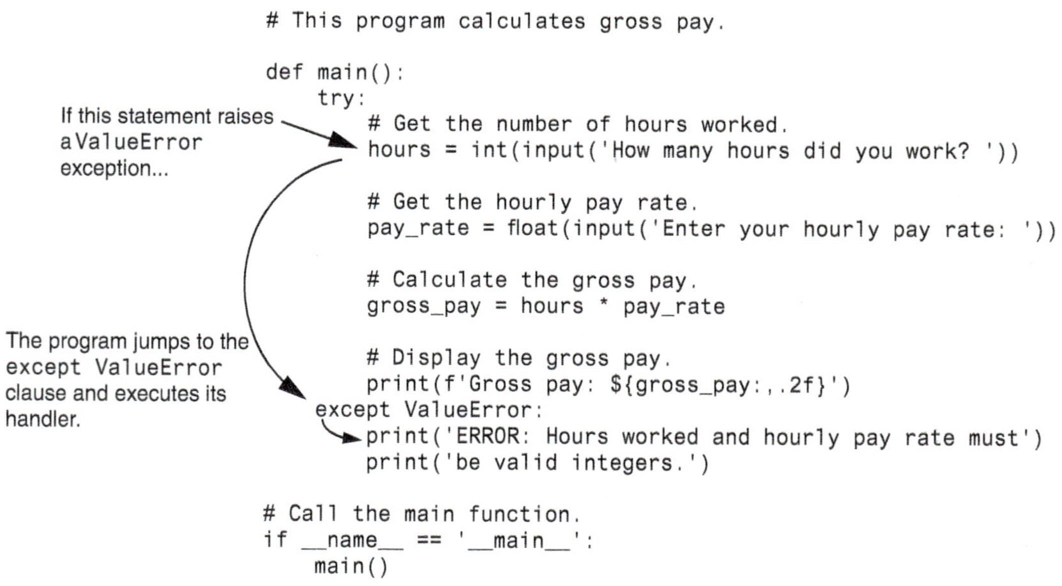

```
# This program calculates gross pay.

def main():
    try:
        # Get the number of hours worked.
        hours = int(input('How many hours did you work? '))

        # Get the hourly pay rate.
        pay_rate = float(input('Enter your hourly pay rate: '))

        # Calculate the gross pay.
        gross_pay = hours * pay_rate

        # Display the gross pay.
        print(f'Gross pay: ${gross_pay:,.2f}')
    except ValueError:
        print('ERROR: Hours worked and hourly pay rate must')
        print('be valid integers.')

# Call the main function.
if __name__ == '__main__':
    main()
```

Let's look at another example in Program 12-5. This program, which does not use exception handling, gets the name of a file from the user, then displays the contents of the file. The program works as long as the user enters the name of an existing file. An exception will be raised, however, if the file specified by the user does not exist. This is what happened in the sample run.

Program 12-5: 

```
1  # This program displays the contents
2  # of a file.
3
4  def main():
5      # Get the name of a file.
6      filename = input('Enter a filename: ')
7
8      # Open the file.
9      infile = open(filename, 'r')
10
11     # Read the file's contents.
12     contents = infile.read()
13
14     # Display the file's contents.
15     print(contents)
16
17     # Close the file.
18     infile.close()
19
20 # Call the main function.
21 if _ _name_ _ == '_ _main_ _':
22     main()
```

Program Output (with input shown in bold)

```
Enter a filename: bad_file.txt [Enter]
Traceback (most recent call last):
File "C:\Python\display_file.py," line 21, in <module>
main()
File "C:\Python\display_file.py," line 9, in main
infile = open(filename, 'r')
IOError: [Errno 2] No such file or directory: 'bad_file.txt'
```

The statement in line 9 raised the exception when it called the `open` function. Notice in the traceback error message that the name of the exception that occurred is `IOError`. This is an exception that is raised when a file I/O operation fails. You can see in the traceback message that the cause of the error was `No such file or directory: 'bad_file.txt'`.

Program 12-6 shows how we can modify Program 12-5 with a `try/except` statement that gracefully responds to an `IOError` exception. In the sample run, assume the file `bad_file.txt` does not exist.

Program 12-6: 

```
1  # This program displays the contents
2  # of a file.
3
4  def main():
5      # Get the name of a file.
6      filename = input('Enter a filename: ')
7
8      try:
9          # Open the file.
10         infile = open(filename, 'r')
11
12         # Read the file's contents.
13         contents = infile.read()
14
15         # Display the file's contents.
16         print(contents)
17
18         # Close the file.
19         infile.close()
20     except IOError:
21         print('An error occurred trying to read')
22         print('the file', filename)
23
24 # Call the main function.
25 if _ _name_ _ == '_ _main_ _':
26     main()
```

Program Output (with input shown in bold)

Enter a filename: **bad_file.txt** [Enter]
An error occurred trying to read the file bad_file.txt

Let's look at what happened in the sample run. When line 6 executed, the user entered `bad_file.txt`, which was assigned to the `filename` variable. Inside the try suite, line 10 attempts to open the file `bad_file.txt`. Because this file does not exist, the statement raises an `IOError` exception. When this happens, the program exits the try suite, skipping lines 11 through 19. Because the `except` clause in line 20 specifies the `IOError` exception, the program jumps to the handler that begins in line 21.

Handling Multiple Exceptions

In many cases, the code in a try suite will be capable of throwing more than one type of exception. In such a case, you need to write an `except` clause for each type of exception that you want to handle. For example, Program 12-7 reads the contents of a file named `sales_data.txt`. Each line in the file contains the sales amount for one month, and the file has several lines. Here are the contents of the file:

```
24987.62
26978.97
32589.45
31978.47
22781.76
29871.44
```

Program 12-7 reads all of the numbers from the file and adds them to an accumulator variable.

Program 12-7: 

```
# This program displays the total of the
# amounts in the sales_data.txt file.

def main():
    # Initialize an accumulator.
    total = 0.0

    try:
        # Open the sales_data.txt file.
        infile = open('sales_data.txt', 'r')

        # Read the values from the file and
        # accumulate them.
        for line in infile:
            amount = float(line)
            total += amount

        # Close the file.
        infile.close()

        # Print the total.
        print(f'{total:,.2f}')

    except IOError:
        print('An error occured trying to read the file.')

    except ValueError:
        print('Non-numeric data found in the file.')

    except:
        print('An error occured.')

# Call the main function.
if _ _name_ _ == '_ _main_ _':
    main()
```

The try suite contains code that can raise different types of exceptions. For example:

- The statement in line 10 can raise an `IOError` exception if the `sales_data.txt` file does not exist. The `for` loop in line 14 can also raise an `IOError` exception if it encounters a problem reading data from the file.
- The `float` function in line 15 can raise a `ValueError` exception if the `line` variable references a string that cannot be converted to a floating-point number (an alphabetic string, for example).

Notice the `try/except` statement has three `except` clauses:

- The `except` clause in line 24 specifies the `IOError` exception. Its handler in line 25 will execute if an `IOError` exception is raised.
- The `except` clause in line 27 specifies the `ValueError` exception. Its handler in line 28 will execute if a `ValueError` exception is raised.
- The `except` clause in line 30 does not list a specific exception. Its handler in line 31 will execute if an exception that is not handled by the other `except` clauses is raised.

If an exception occurs in the try suite, the interpreter examines each of the `except` clauses, in the `try/except` statement from top to bottom. When it finds an `except` clause that specifies a type that matches the type of exception that occurred, it branches to that `except` clause. If none of the `except` clauses specifies a type that matches the exception, the interpreter branches to the `except` clause in line 30.

Using One `except` Clause to Catch All Exceptions

The previous example demonstrated how multiple types of exceptions can be handled individually in a `try/except` statement. Sometimes you might want to write a `try/except` statement that simply catches any exception that is raised in the try suite and, regardless of the exception's type, responds the same way. You can accomplish that in a `try/except` statement by writing one `except` clause that does not specify a particular type of exception. Program 12-8 shows an example.

Program 12-8: 

```
# This program displays the total of the
# amounts in the sales_data.txt file.

def main():
    # Initialize an accumulator.
    total = 0.0

    try:
        # Open the sales_data.txt file.
        infile = open('sales_data.txt', 'r')

        # Read the values from the file and
        # accumulate them.
        for line in infile:
            amount = float(line)
            total += amount

```

Program 12-8: *(continued)*

```
18         # Close the file.
19         infile.close()
20
21         # Print the total.
22         print(f'{total:,.2f}')
23     except:
24         print('An error occurred.')
25
26 # Call the main function.
27 if __name__ == '__main__':
28     main()
```

Notice the `try/except` statement in this program has only one `except` clause, in line 23. The `except` clause does not specify an exception type, so any exception that occurs in the try suite (lines 9 through 22) causes the program to branch to line 23 and execute the statement in line 24.

Displaying an Exception's Default Error Message

When an exception is thrown, an object known as an **exception object** is created in memory. The exception object usually contains a default error message pertaining to the exception. (In fact, it is the same error message that you see displayed at the end of a traceback when an exception goes unhandled.) When you write an `except` clause, you can optionally assign the exception object to a variable, as shown here:

```
except ValueError as err:
```

This `except` clause catches `ValueError` exceptions. The expression that appears after the `except` clause specifies that we are assigning the exception object to the variable `err`. (There is nothing special about the name `err`. That is simply the name that we have chosen for the examples. You can use any name that you wish.) After doing this, you can pass the `err` variable to the `print` function in the exception handler to display the default error message for that type of error. Program 12-9 shows an example of how this is done.

Program 12-9: 

```
# This program calculates gross pay.

def main():
    try:
        # Get the number of hours worked.
        hours = int(input('How many hours did you work? '))

        # Get the hourly pay rate.
        pay_rate = float(input('Enter your hourly pay rate: '))

        # Calculate the gross pay.
        gross_pay = hours * pay_rate
```

Program 12-9: *(continued)*

```
13
14         # Display the gross pay.
15         print(f'Gross pay: ${gross_pay:,.2f}')
16     except ValueError as err:
17         print(err)
18
19 # Call the main function.
20 if __name__ == '__main__':
21     main()
```

Program Output (with input shown in bold)

```
How many hours did you work? forty [Enter]
invalid literal for int() with base 10: 'forty'
```

When a `ValueError` exception occurs inside the try suite (lines 5 through 15), the program branches to the `except` clause in line 16. The expression `ValueError as err` in line 16 causes the resulting exception object to be assigned to a variable named `err`. The statement in line 17 passes the `err` variable to the `print` function, which causes the exception's default error message to be displayed.

If you want to have just one `except` clause to catch all the exceptions that are raised in a try suite, you can specify `Exception` as the type. Program 12-10 shows an example.

Program 12-10: 

```
# This program displays the total of the
# amounts in the sales_data.txt file.

def main():
    # Initialize an accumulator.
    total = 0.0

    try:
        # Open the sales_data.txt file.
        infile = open('sales_data.txt', 'r')

        # Read the values from the file and
        # accumulate them.
        for line in infile:
            amount = float(line)
            total += amount

        # Close the file.
        infile.close()

        # Print the total.
        print(f'{total:,.2f}')
    except Exception as err:
```

Program 12-10: *(continued)*

```
        print(err)

# Call the main function.
if _ _name_ _ == '_ _main_ _':
    main()
```

The else Clause

The `try/except` statement may have an optional `else` clause, which appears after all the `except` clauses. Here is the general format of a `try/except` statement with an `else` clause:

```
try:
   statement
   statement
   etc.
except ExceptionName:
   statement
   statement
   etc.
else:
   statement
   statement
   etc.
```

The block of statements that appears after the `else` clause is known as the **else suite**. The statements in the else suite are executed after the statements in the try suite, only if no exceptions were raised. If an exception is raised, the else suite is skipped. Program 12-11 shows an example.

Program 12-11: 

```
# This program displays the total of the
# amounts in the sales_data.txt file.

def main():
    # Initialize an accumulator.
    total = 0.0

    try:
        # Open the sales_data.txt file.
        infile = open('sales_data.txt', 'r')

        # Read the values from the file and
        # accumulate them.
```

Program 12-11: *(continued)*

```
14         for line in infile:
15             amount = float(line)
16             total += amount
17 
18         # Close the file.
19         infile.close()
20     except Exception as err:
21         print(err)
22     else:
23         # Print the total.
24         print(f'{total:,.2f}')
25 
26 # Call the main function.
27 if _ _name_ _ == '_ _main_ _':
28     main()
```

In Program 12-11, the statement in line 24 is executed only if the statements in the try suite (lines 9 through 19) execute without raising an exception.

The `finally` Clause

The `try/except` statement may have an optional `finally` clause, which must appear after all the `except` clauses. Here is the general format of a `try/except` statement with a `finally` clause:

```
try:
    statement
    statement
    etc.
except ExceptionName:
    statement
    statement
    etc.
finally:
    statement
    statement
    etc.
```

The block of statements that appears after the `finally` clause is known as the **finally suite**. The statements in the finally suite are always executed after the try suite and any exception handlers have executed. The statements in the finally suite execute whether an exception occurs or not. The purpose of the finally suite is to perform cleanup operations, such as closing files or other resources. Any code that is written in the finally suite will always execute, even if the try suite raises an exception.

What If an Exception Is Not Handled?

Unless an exception is handled, it will cause the program to halt. There are two possible ways for a thrown exception to go unhandled. The first possibility is for the `try/except` statement to contain no `except` clauses specifying an exception of the right type. The second possibility is for the exception to be raised from outside a try suite. In either case, the exception will cause the program to halt.

In this section, you've seen examples of programs that can raise `ZeroDivisionError` exceptions, `IOError` exceptions, and `ValueError` exceptions. There are many different types of exceptions that can occur. When you are designing `try/except` statements, one way you can learn about the exceptions that you need to handle is to consult **reference materials**, such as the programming language documentation.

Reference materials, programming language documentation, and error messages, are all effective strategies you can use to identify and solve problems with your code. Another effective strategy is experimentation. You can run a program and deliberately perform actions that will cause errors. By watching the traceback error messages that are displayed, you will see the names of the exceptions that are raised. You can then write `except` clauses to handle these exceptions.

Checkpoint

12.8 Briefly describe what an exception is.

12.9 If an exception is raised and the program does not handle it with a try/except statement, what happens?

12.10 What type of exception does a program raise when it tries to open a nonexistent file?

12.11 What type of exception does a program raise when it uses the float function to convert a non-numeric string to a number?

12.3 Avoiding Common Errors

Avoiding common errors is the best way to develop clean code that executes properly.

Writing code to handle exceptions will help prevent your application from crashing. Additionally, you can implement standard coding practices that will reduce the number of runtime and logic errors. The three most effective practices for avoiding errors are:

- Being mindful of spelling.
- Using proper white spacing.
- Indenting your code in the right places.

While comments do not prevent errors, they help you find them. If you develop the habit of commenting your code now, it will be very helpful later as your project size grows. Likewise, using descriptive identifiers does not prevent errors, but may make it easier to avoid them or find them when they do occur.

Pay Attention to Style Conventions

Recall that programming style conventions are guidelines and best practices for how to enter and format code. Benefits of using conventions include making it easier to find errors.

Each language has its own set of conventions. For example, indenting in the right places is very important in Python. In other languages, indenting code is simply a way to make your code easier to read. In Python, it has a specific purpose. All lines of code with the same indentation are executed as a single block of code. Improper indentation can cause both syntax and logic errors. Can you figure out why the following code generates a syntax error?

```
1 # While count is less than 20.
2 # Print count.
3 # Print a final message when finished.
4 count = 0
5 while (count < 20):
6 print(count)
7  count = count + 3
8 print("finished")
```

If you enter and run the code, you will get an error message that there is an unexpected indent on line 6.

The following code generates a logic error. The message 'finished" is printed seven times rather than once. Can you figure out why?

```
1 # Loop while count is less than 20.
2 # Print count.
3 # Print a final message when finished.
4 count = 0
5 while (count < 20):
6  print(count)
7  count = count + 3
8  print("finished")
Output:
      0
      finished
      3
      finished
      6
      finished
      9
      finished
      12
      finished
      15
      finished
      18
      finished
```

Ending Conditional and Looping Statements

Forgetting to end conditional and looping statements with the correct punctuation is a common mistake. In some languages, including Java and C++, you use a semicolon. In Python, you use a colon. The following Python code generates a syntax error because the colon is missing at the end of line 2.

```
1 count = 0
2 while (count < 20)
3  print(count)
4  count = count + 3
5 print("finished")
```

Don't Forget to Place Begin and End Quotes Around a String

When you are troubleshooting errors, look for missing begin and end quotes around strings. The following Python code generates a syntax error because the end quote around the output string is missing from line 3.

```
1 count = 0
2 while (count < 20):
3       print("Your count value is:, count)
4       count = count + 3
5 print("finished")
```

Use the Correct Character Case

When coding in a case-sensitive language such as Python, Java, or C++, using the wrong character case creates a syntax error. Each programming language has its own set of rules about case sensitivity. It's a common mistake that even the best of software developers who program in multiple languages make. It's a bothersome mistake, but easy to fix!

In case-sensitive languages, keywords are all lowercase. The following Python code generates an error because the keyword `import` is capitalized in line 1.

```
1 Import turtle
2 turtle.forward(100)
3 turtle.right(90)
```

Watch for Lexical Errors

Lexical errors are simply misspellings and invalid characters that the interpreter does not recognize. The following code generates an error because an incorrect character was typed on line 2.

```
1 Import turtle
2 turtle,forward(100)
3 turtle.right(90)
```

Checkpoint

12.12 Correct each of the above code samples. Type in each code segment and run the code to test the results.

12.13 What is wrong with the following lines of Python code?

```
count = 0
while (count < 20):
  print(“Your count value is:, count")
  count = count + 3
print(“finished)
```

12.14 What is wrong with the following lines of Python code?

```
count = 0
while (Count < 20):
  print(“Your count value is:, count")
  count = count + 3
print(“finished")
```

12.15 Does adding comments to your code prevent errors? Explain your answer.

Chapter Review

Multiple Choice

1. What type of error occurs when you use the incorrect character?
   a. logic
   b. lexical
   c. exception
   d. variable

2. What type of error occurs when a program does not perform the way it was intended to?
   a. logic
   b. lexical
   c. exception
   d. input

3. What type of error occurs if the computer expects user input to be a number but the user enters a string?
   a. logic
   b. lexical
   c. runtime
   d. exception

4. In most cases, an exception causes a program to __________.
   a. run faster
   b. display the incorrect output
   c. abruptly halt
   d. request user input

5. What is a term for one or more statements that can potentially raise an exception?
   a. run handler
   b. except clause
   c. try suite
   d. else suite

6. What is created in memory when an exception is thrown?
   a. exception handler
   b. logic error
   c. exception statement
   d. exception object

7. The block of statements that appears after the finally clause in a try/except statement is called:
   a. try suite
   b. else suite
   c. finally suite
   d. except suite

True or False

1. Logic errors are easier to find than syntax errors.
2. Hand tracing is the process of translating a pseudocode program into machine language by hand.
3. Indentation does not matter in Python.
4. You must have a colon to end conditional and looping statements in Java.
5. In C++, you only need quotes to identify the beginning of a string.
6. Python is case-sensitive.

Short Answer

1. What happens when a computer encounters a runtime error while trying to execute a program?
2. Explain why syntax errors are usually easier to find than logic errors.
3. What is a traceback?
4. Explain how to use one except clause to catch all exceptions.
5. What are two ways a thrown exception might not be handled?

Debugging Exercises

1. If the following pseudocode were an actual program, why would it not display the output that the programmer expects?

```
Declare String favoriteFood
Display "What is the name of your favorite food?"
Input favoriteFood
Display "Your favorite food is "
Display "favoriteFood"
```

2. If the programmer translates the following pseudocode to an actual programming language, a syntax error is likely to occur. Can you find the error?

```
Declare String 1stPrize
Display "Enter the award for first prize."
Input 1stPrize
Display "The first prize winner will receive ", 1stPrize
```

3. The following code will not display the results expected by the programmer. Can you find the error?

```
Declare Real lowest, highest, average
Display "Enter the lowest score."
Input lowest
Display "Enter the highest score."
Input highest
Set average = low + high / 2
Display "The average is ", average, "."
```

4. Find the error in the following pseudocode.

```
Display "Enter the length of the room."
Input length
Declare Integer length
```

5. Find the error in the following pseudocode.

```
Declare Integer value1, value2, value3, sum
Set sum = value1 + value2 + value3
Display "Enter the first value."
Input value1
Display "Enter the second value."
Input value2
Display "Enter the third value."
Input value3
Display "The sum of numbers is ", sum
```

6. Find the error in the following pseudocode.

```
Declare Real pi
Set 3.14159265 = pi
Display "The value of pi is ", pi
```

7. Find the error in the following pseudocode.

```
Constant Real GRAVITY = 9.81
Display "Rates of acceleration of an object in free fall:"
Display "Earth: ", GRAVITY, " meters per second every second."
Set GRAVITY = 1.63
Display "Moon: ", GRAVITY, " meters per second every second."
```

Programming Exercises

1. **Wear a Sweater**

   Working alone or with a partner, brainstorm, design a sequential algorithm, and write a program that tells users to wear a sweater if the temperature is 50 degrees Fahrenheit or below. Write a version of the code using proper programming style so there are no errors, and write a version that has at least one error. Exchange the version of the code that includes errors with a classmate or other team. Analyze the other team's code. Use error messages and other effective strategies including reference materials and language documentation to identify and solve the problems in the code. Debug the code. Exchange code back, and compare your original error-free code with the code the other team debugged. Discuss how they are the same, and how they are different.

2. **Bedtime**

   Working alone or with a partner, brainstorm, design, and write a program that tells users to go to sleep if it is 10 p.m. or later. Write a version of the code using proper programming style so there are no errors, and write a version that has at least error. Exchange the version of the code that includes errors with a classmate or other team. Analyze the other team's code. Use error messages and other effective strategies including reference materials and language documentation to identify and solve the problems in the code. Debug the code. Exchange code back, and compare your original error-free code with the code the other team debugged. Discuss how they are the same, and how they are different.

3. **Handling Errors**

   Working alone or with a partner, brainstorm, design, and write a program that uses error handling techniques that you learned in this chapter to prevent common errors such as division by zero or data type mismatch. Exchange your code with a classmate or other team. Analyze the code. If necessary, use reference materials and language documentation to find information on any techniques you do not recognize. Write a paragraph explaining how the other team used error handling techniques to produce error-free code.

13 Getting Started with Object-Oriented Programming

TOPICS

13.1 Introducing Object-Oriented Programming

Object-oriented programming uses rules for creating and managing objects. Objects are created from abstract data types that encapsulate data and functions together.

There are primarily two methods of programming in use today: procedural and object-oriented. The earliest programming languages were procedural, meaning a program was made of one or more procedures. A **procedure** is simply a module or function that performs a specific task such as gathering input from the user, performing calculations, reading or writing files, displaying output, and so on. The programs that you have written so far have been procedural in nature.

Typically, procedures operate on data items that are separate from the procedures. In a procedural program, the data items are commonly passed from one procedure to another. As you might imagine, the focus of procedural programming is on the creation of procedures that operate on the program's data. The separation of data and the code that operates on the data can lead to problems, however, as the program becomes larger and more complex.

For example, suppose you are part of a programming team that has written an extensive customer database program. The program was initially designed so that a customer's name, address, and phone number were stored in three `String` variables. Your job was to design several modules that accept those three variables as arguments and perform operations on them.

The software has been operating successfully for some time, but your team has been asked to update it by adding several new features. During the revision process, the senior programmer informs you that the customer's name, address, and phone number will no longer be stored in variables. Instead, they will be stored in a `String` array. This means that you will have to modify all of the modules that you have designed so that they accept and work with a `String` array instead of the three variables. Making these extensive modifications not only is a great deal of work, but also opens the opportunity for errors to appear in your code.

Whereas **procedural programming** uses step-by-step instructions (procedures) to create modules and functions to tell a computer what to do, **object-oriented programming** (**OOP**) uses rules for creating and managing objects to tell a computer what to do. An **object** is a software entity that contains both data and procedures. The data contained in an object is known as the object's **fields**. An object's fields are simply variables, arrays, or other data structures that are stored in the object. The procedures that an object performs are known as **methods**. An object's methods are nothing more than modules or functions. The object is, conceptually, a self-contained unit that consists of data (fields) and procedures (methods). This is illustrated in Figure 13-1.

Figure 13-1 An object contains data and procedures

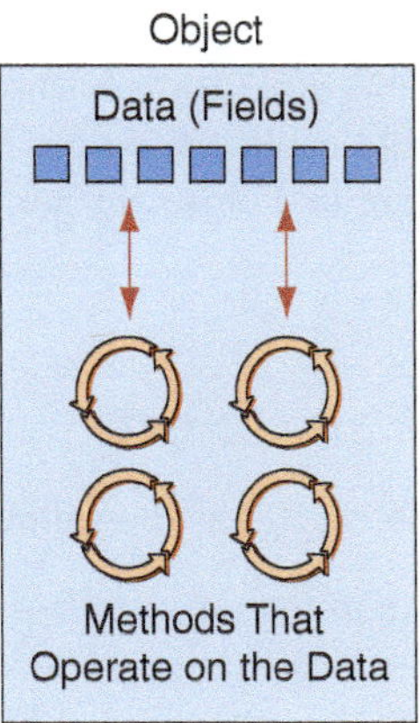

OOP addresses the problem of code/data separation through encapsulation and data hiding. **Encapsulation** refers to the combining of data and code into a single object. **Data hiding** refers to an object's ability to hide its data from code that is outside the object. Only the object's methods may then directly access and make changes to the object's data. An object typically hides its data, but allows outside code to access its methods. As shown in Figure 13-2, the object's methods provide programming statements outside the object with indirect access to the object's data.

Figure 13-2 Code outside the object interacts with the object's methods

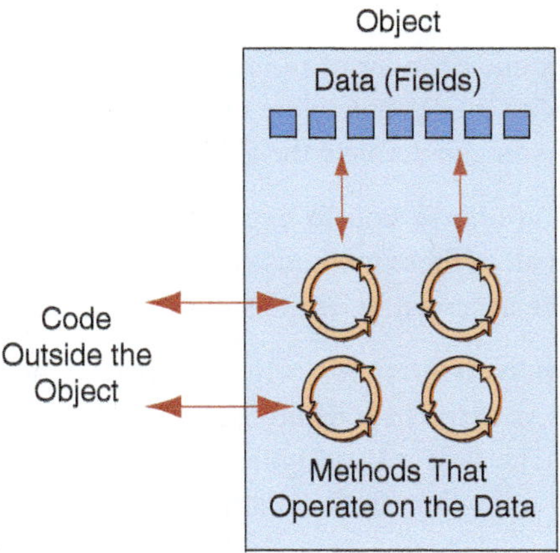

When an object's internal data is hidden from outside code and access to that data is restricted to the object's methods, the data is protected from accidental corruption. In addition, the programming code outside the object does not need to know about the format or internal structure of the object's data. The code only needs to interact with the object's methods. When a programmer changes the structure of an object's internal data, the object's methods are also modified so they may properly operate on the data. The way in which outside code interacts with the methods, however, does not change.

Object Reusability

In addition to solving the problems of code/data separation, the use of OOP has also been encouraged by the trend of **object reusability**. An object is not a stand-alone program, but is used by programs that need its service.

For example, Kamila is a programmer who has developed an object for rendering 3D images. She is a math whiz and knows a lot about computer graphics, so her object is coded to perform all of the necessary 3D mathematical operations and handle the computer's video hardware. Omar, who is writing a program for an architectural firm, needs his application to display 3D images of buildings. Because he is working under a tight deadline and does not possess a great deal of knowledge about computer graphics, he can use Kamila's object to perform the 3D rendering (for a small fee, of course!).

An Everyday Example of an Object

Think of your alarm clock as an object. It has the following fields:

- The current second (a value in the range of 0–59)
- The current minute (a value in the range of 0–59)
- The current hour (a value in the range of 1–12)
- The time the alarm is set for (a valid hour and minute)
- Whether the alarm is on or off ("on" or "off")

As you can see, the fields are merely data values that define the **state** that the alarm clock is currently in. You, the user of the alarm clock object, cannot directly manipulate these fields because they are **private**. To change a field's value, you must use one of the object's methods. The following are some of the alarm clock object's methods:

- `Set time`
- `Set alarm time`
- `Turn alarm on`
- `Turn alarm off`

Each method manipulates one or more of the fields. For example, the `Set time` method allows you to set the alarm clock's time. You activate the method by pressing a button on top of the clock. By using another button, you can activate the `Set alarm time` method.

In addition, another button allows you to execute the `Turn alarm on` and `Turn alarm off` methods. Notice that all of these methods can be activated by you, who are outside of the alarm clock. Methods that can be accessed by entities outside the object are known as **public methods**.

The alarm clock also has **private methods**, which are part of the object's private, internal workings. External entities (such as you, the user of the alarm clock) do not have direct access to the alarm clock's private methods. The object is designed to execute these methods automatically and hide the details from you. The following are the alarm clock object's private methods:

- `Increment the current second`
- `Increment the current minute`
- `Increment the current hour`
- `Sound alarm`

Every second, the `Increment the current second` method executes. This changes the value of the current second field. If the current second field is set to 59 when this method executes, the method is programmed to reset the current second to 0, and then cause the `Increment the current minute` method to execute. This method adds 1 to the current minute, unless it is set to 59. In that case, it resets the current minute to 0 and causes the `Increment the current hour` method to execute. Note that the `Increment the current minute` method compares the new time to the alarm time. If the two times match and the alarm is turned on, the `Sound alarm` method is executed.

Checkpoint

13.1 What is an object?

13.2 What is encapsulation?

13.3 Why is an object's internal data usually hidden from outside code?

13.4 What are public methods? What are private methods?

13.2 Classes

A class is code that specifies the fields and methods for a particular type of object.

VideoNote Classes and Objects

Now, let's discuss how objects are created in software. Before an object can be created, it must be designed by a programmer. The programmer determines the fields and methods that are necessary, and then creates a **class**. A class is code that specifies the fields and methods of a particular type of object.

Think of a class as a "blueprint" that objects may be created from. It serves a similar purpose as the blueprint for a house. The blueprint itself is not a house, but is a detailed description of a house. When we use the blueprint to build an actual house, we could say we are building an instance of the house described by the blueprint. If we so desire, we can build several identical houses from the same blueprint. Each house is a separate instance of the house described by the blueprint. This idea is illustrated in Figure 13-3.

Another way of thinking about the difference between a class and an object is to think of the difference between a cookie cutter and a cookie. While a cookie cutter itself is not a cookie, it describes a cookie. The cookie cutter can be used to make one cookie, or several cookies. Think of a class as a cookie cutter and the objects created from the class as cookies.

So, a class is not an object, but it can be a description of an object. When the program is running, it can use the class to create, in memory, as many objects of a specific type as needed. Each object that is created from a class is called an **instance** of the class.

Figure 14-3 A blueprint and houses built from the blueprint

Blueprint that describes a house

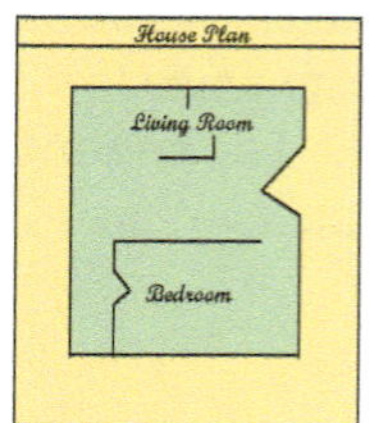

Instances of the house described by the blueprint

For example, Carmen is an entomologist (someone who studies insects) and she also enjoys writing computer programs. She designs a program to catalog different types of insects. As part of the program, she creates a class named `Insect`, which specifies fields and methods for holding and manipulating data common to all types of insects. The `Insect` class is not an object, but a specification that objects may be created from.

Next, she writes programming statements that create a `housefly` object, which is an instance of the `Insect` class. The `housefly` object is an entity that occupies computer memory and stores data about a housefly. It has the fields and methods specified by the `Insect` class. Then she writes programming statements that create a `mosquito` object. The `mosquito` object is also an instance of the `Insect` class. It has its own area in memory, and stores data about a mosquito. Although the `housefly` and `mosquito` objects are separate entities in the computer's memory, they were both created from the `Insect` class. This means that each of the objects has the fields and methods described by the `Insect` class. This is illustrated in Figure 13-4.

Figure 13-4 The `housefly` and `mosquito` objects are instances of the `Insect` class

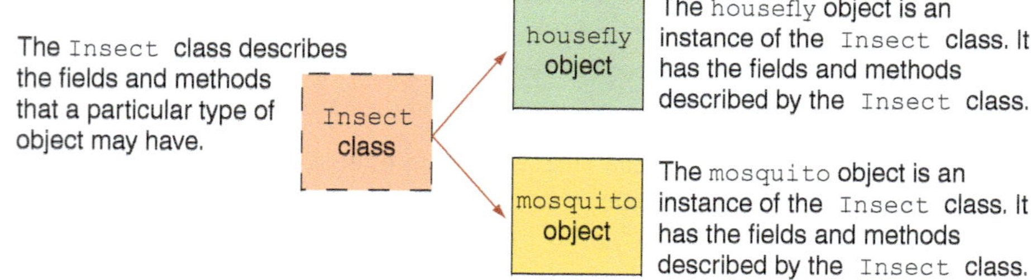

Creating a Class, Step by Step

The general format that we will use to write a class definition in pseudocode is as follows:

```
Class ClassName
        Field declarations and method definitions go here...
End Class
```

The first line starts with the word `Class`, followed by the name of the class. In most languages, you follow the same rules for naming variables as when naming classes. Next, you write the declarations for the class's fields and the definitions of the class's methods. (In general terms, the fields and methods that belong to a class are referred to as the class's **members**.) The words `End Class` appear at the end of the class definition.

Now we will demonstrate how a class is typically created in an object-oriented language. Because classes have several parts, we will not show the entire class all at once. Instead, we will put it together in a step-by-step fashion.

Suppose we are designing a program for Wireless Solutions, a business that sells cell phones and wireless service. The program will be used to keep track of the cell phones that the company has in inventory. The data that we need to keep for a cell phone is as follows:

- The name of the phone's manufacturer
- The phone's model number
- The phone's retail price

If we were designing a procedural program, we would simply use variables to hold this data. In this example, we are designing an object-oriented program, so we will create a class that represents a cell phone. The class will have fields to hold these items of data. The pseudocode in Class Listing 13-1 shows how we will start writing the class definition:

Class Listing 13-1:

```
1  Class CellPhone
2      // Field declarations
3      Private String manufacturer
4      Private String modelNumber
5      Private Real retailPrice
6
7      // This class is not finished!
8  End Class
```

First, notice that in line 1 we have named the class `CellPhone`. In this book, we will always begin class names with an uppercase letter. This is not required, but many programmers follow this practice because it helps distinguish class names from variable names.

Lines 3, 4, and 5 declare three fields. Line 3 declares a `String` field named `manufacturer`, line 4 declares a `String` field named `modelNumber`, and line 5 declares a `Real` field named `retailPrice`. Notice that each declaration begins with the word `Private`. When the word `Private` appears before a field declaration, it specifies that the field cannot be directly accessed by any statement outside the class. In most object-oriented programming languages, the word `Private` is known as an **access specifier**. It specifies how a class field or method can be accessed.

By using the `Private` access specifier, a class can hide its data from code outside the class. When a class's fields are hidden from outside code, the data is protected from accidental corruption. It is a common practice in object-oriented programming to make all of a class's fields private and to provide access to those fields only through methods. Next, we will add the following methods to the class, which will allow code outside the class to store values in the fields:

- `setManufacturer`: The `setManufacturer` method will be a module that stores a value in the `manufacturer` field.
- `setModelNumber`: The `setModelNumber` method will be a module that stores a value in the `modelNumber` field.
- `setRetailPrice`: The `setRetailPrice` method will be a module that stores a value in the `retailPrice` field.

The pseudocode in Class Listing 13-2 shows how the `CellPhone` class will appear with these methods added to it.

Class Listing 13-2:

```
1  Class CellPhone
2      // Field declarations
3      Private String manufacturer
4      Private String modelNumber
5      Private Real retailPrice
6
7      // Method definitions
8      Public Module setManufacturer(String manufact)
9         Set manufacturer = manufact
10     End Module
11
12     Public Module setModelNumber(String modNum)
13        Set modelNumber = modNum
14     End Module
15
16     Public Module setRetailPrice(Real retail)
17        Set retailPrice = retail
18     End Module
19
20     // This class is not finished!
21 End Class
```

The `setManufacturer` method appears in lines 8 through 10. This looks like a regular module definition, except that the word `Public` appears in the header. In most object-oriented languages, the word `Public` is an access specifier. When it is applied to a method, it specifies that the method can be called from statements outside the class.

The `setManufacturer` method has a `String` parameter named `manufact`. When the method is called, a string must be passed to it as an argument. In line 9, the value passed to the `manufact` parameter is assigned to the `manufacturer` field.

The `setModelNumber` method appears in lines 12 through 14. The method has a `String` parameter named `modNum`. When the method is called, a string must be passed to it as an argument. In line 13, the value passed to the `modNum` parameter is assigned to the `modelNumber` field.

The `setRetailPrice` method has a `Real` parameter named `retail`. When the method is called, a `Real` value must be passed to it as an argument. In line 17, the value passed to the `retail` parameter is assigned to the `retailPrice` field.

Because the `manufacturer`, `modelNumber`, and `retailPrice` fields are private, we wrote the `setManufacturer`, `setModelNumber`, and `setRetailPrice` methods to allow code outside the `CellPhone` class to store values in those fields. We must also write methods that allow code outside the class to get the values that are stored in these fields.

For this purpose we will write the `getManufacturer`, `getModelNumber`, and `getRetailPrice` methods. The `getManufacturer` method will return the value stored in the `manufacturer` field, the `getModelNumber` method will return the value stored in the `modelNumber` field, and the `getRetailPrice` method will return the value stored in the `retailPrice` field.

The pseudocode in Class Listing 13-3 shows how the `CellPhone` class will appear with these methods added to it. The new methods are shown in lines 20 through 30.

Class Listing 13-3: 

```
1   Class CellPhone
2      // Field declarations
3      Private String manufacturer
4      Private String modelNumber
5      Private Real retailPrice
6
7      // Method definitions
8      Public Module setManufacturer(String manufact)
9         Set manufacturer = manufact
10     End Module
11
12     Public Module setModelNumber(String modNum)
13        Set modelNumber = modNum
14     End Module
15
16     Public Module setRetailPrice(Real retail)
17        Set retailPrice = retail
18     End Module
19
20     Public Function String getManufacturer()
21        Return manufacturer
22     End Function
23
24     Public Function String getModelNumber()
25        Return modelNumber
26     End Function
27
28     Public Function Real getRetailPrice()
29        Return retailPrice
30     End Function
31  End Class
```

The `getManufacturer` method appears in lines 20 through 22. Notice that this method is written as a function instead of a module. When the method is called, the statement in line 21 returns the value stored in the `manufacturer` field.

The `getModelNumber` method in lines 24 through 26 and the `getRetailPrice` method in lines 28 through 30 are also functions. The `getModelNumber` method returns the value stored in the `modelNumber` field, and the `getRetailPrice` method returns the value stored in the `retailPrice` field.

The pseudocode in Class Listing 13-3 is a complete class, but it is not a program. It is a blueprint that objects may be created from. To demonstrate the class we must design a program that uses it to create an object, as shown in Program 13-1.

Program 13-1: 

```
1  Module main()
2     // Declare a variable that can reference
3     // a CellPhone object.
4     Declare CellPhone myPhone
5
6     // The following statement creates an object
7     // using the CellPhone class as its blueprint.
8     // The myPhone variable will reference the object.
9     Set myPhone = New CellPhone()
10
11    // Store values in the object's fields.
12    Call myPhone.setManufacturer("Motorola")
13    Call myPhone.setModelNumber("G200")
14    Call myPhone.setRetailPrice(399.99)
15
16    // Display the values stored in the fields.
17    Display "The manufacturer is ", myPhone.getManufacturer()
18    Display "The model number is ", myPhone.getModelNumber()
19    Display "The retail price is ", myPhone.getRetailPrice()
20 End Module
```

Program Output

```
The manufacturer is Motorola
The model number is G200
The retail price is 399.99
```

The statement in line 4 is a variable declaration. It declares a variable named `myPhone`. This statement looks like any other variable declaration that you have seen, except that the data type is the name of the `CellPhone` class. This is shown in Figure 13-5. When you declare a variable and specify the name of a class as the variable's data type, you are creating a class variable. A **class variable** is a special type of variable that can reference an object in the computer's memory, and work with that object. The `myPhone` variable that is declared in line 4 can be used to reference an object that is created from the `CellPhone` class.

Figure 13-5 Class variable declaration

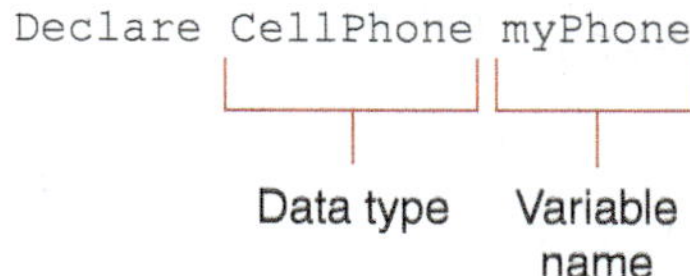

In many object-oriented languages, the act of declaring a class variable does not actually create an object in memory. It only creates a variable that can be used to work with an object. The next step is to create an object. This is done with the following assignment statement, which appears in line 9:

```
Set myPhone = New CellPhone()
```

Notice that on the right side of the = operator, the key word `New` appears. In many programming languages, the key word `New` creates an object in memory. The name of a class appears next (in this case it is `CellPhone`), followed by a set of parentheses. This specifies the class that should be used as a blueprint to create the object. Once the object is created, the = operator assigns the memory address of the object to the `myPhone` variable. The actions performed by this statement are shown in Figure 13-6.

> **NOTE: In some languages, such as C++, the act of declaring a class variable also creates an object in memory. In these languages, it is not necessary to use the** `New` **key word to create the object as we did in line 9 of Program 13-1.**

Figure 13-6 Creating an object and assigning its address to a class variable

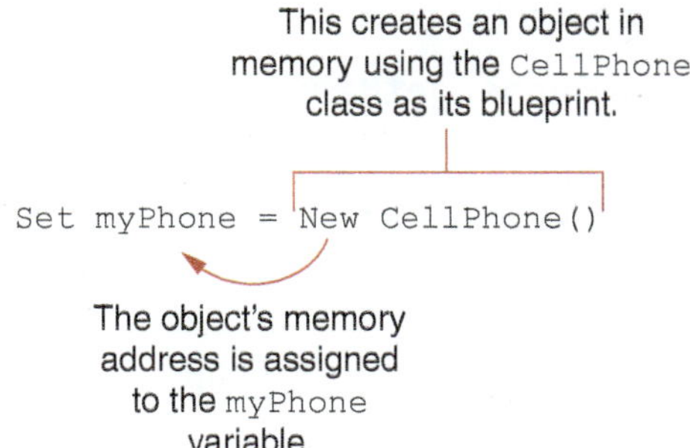

When a class variable is assigned the address of an object, it is said that the variable **references** the object. As shown in Figure 13-7, the `myPhone` variable will reference a `CellPhone` object after this statement executes.

Figure 13-7 The `myPhone` variable references a `CellPhone` object

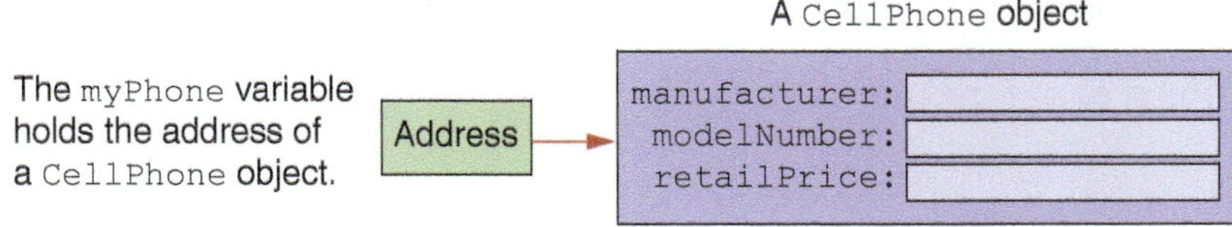

The following statement, which appears in line 12, is next:

```
Call myPhone.setManufacturer("Motorola")
```

This statement calls the `myPhone.setManufacturer` method. The expression `myPhone.setManufacturer` is written in **dot notation**. It's called dot notation because programmers refer to the period as a "dot." On the left side of the dot is the name of a class variable that references an object. On the right side of the dot is the name of the method we are calling. When this statement executes, it uses the object referenced by `myPhone` to call the `setManufacturer` method, passing the string `"Motorola"` as an argument. As a result, the string `"Motorola"` will be assigned to the object's `manufacturer` field.

Line 13 calls the `myPhone.setModelNumber` method, passing the string `"G200"` as an argument. After this statement executes, the string `"G200"` will be stored in the object's `modelNumber` field. Line 14 calls the `myPhone.setRetailPrice` method, passing 399.99 as an argument. This causes 399.99 to be assigned to the `retailPrice` field. Figure 13-8 shows the state of the object after the statements in lines 12 through 14 execute.

Figure 13-8 The state of the object referenced by `myPhone`

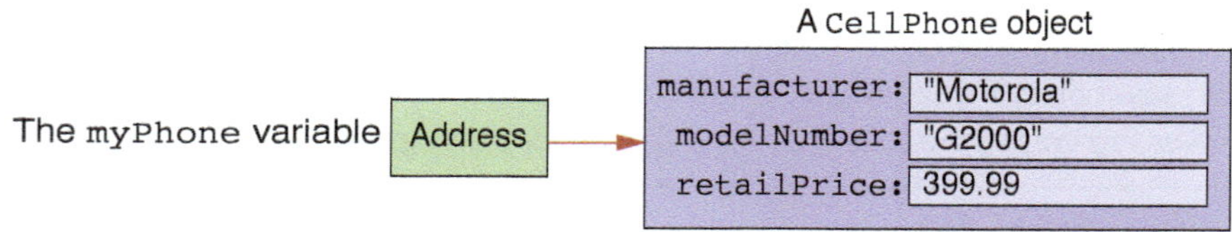

The statements in lines 17 through 19 display the values in the object's fields. Here is the statement in line 17:

```
Display "The manufacturer is ", myPhone.getManufacturer()
```

This statement calls the `myPhone.getManufacturer` method, which returns the string `"Motorola"`. The following message is displayed on the screen:

```
The manufacturer is Motorola
```

The following statement, in line 18, executes next:

```
Display "The model number is ", myPhone.getModelNumber()
```

This statement calls the `myPhone.getModelNumber` method, which returns the string `"G200"`. The following message is displayed on the screen:

```
The model number is G200
```

The following statement, in line 19, executes next:

```
Display "The retail price is ", myPhone.getRetailPrice()
```

This statement calls the `myPhone.getRetailPrice` method, which returns the value 399.99. The following message is displayed on the screen:

```
The retail price is 399.99
```

Accessor and Mutator Methods

As mentioned earlier, it is a common practice to make all of a class's fields private and to provide public methods for accessing and changing those fields. This ensures that the object owning those fields is in control of all changes being made to them.

A method that gets a value from a class's field but does not change it is known as an **accessor method**. A method that stores a value in a field or changes the value of a field in some other way is known as a **mutator method**. In the `CellPhone` class, the methods `getManufacturer`, `getModelNumber`, and `getRetailPrice` are accessors, and the methods `setManufacturer`, `setModelNumber`, and `getRetailPrice` are mutators.

> **NOTE: Mutator methods are sometimes called "setters" and accessor methods are sometimes called "getters."**

Constructors

A **constructor** is a method that is automatically called when an object is created. In most cases, a constructor is used to initialize an object's fields with starting values. These methods are called "constructors" because they help construct an object.

In many programming languages, a constructor has the same name as the class that the constructor is in. That is the convention followed in this book. For example, if we write a constructor in the `CellPhone` class, we will write a module named `CellPhone`. The pseudocode in Class Listing 13-4 shows a new version of the class with a constructor added to it. The constructor appears in lines 8 through 13.

> **NOTE: In Visual Basic, constructors are named** `New`.

Class Listing 13-4:

```
1  Class CellPhone
2     // Field declarations
3     Private String manufacturer
4     Private String modelNumber
5     Private Real retailPrice
6
7     // Constructor
8     Public Module CellPhone(String manufact,
9                             String modNum, Real retail)
10       Set manufacturer = manufact
11       Set modelNumber = modNum
12       Set retailPrice = retail
13    End Module
14
15     // Mutator methods
16     Public Module setManufacturer(String manufact)
17        Set manufacturer = manufact
18     End Module
```

Class Listing 13-4: *(continued)*

```
19
20     Public Module setModelNumber(String modNum)
21        Set modelNumber = modNum
22     End Module
23
24     Public Module setRetailPrice(String retail)
25        Set retailPrice = retail
26     End Module
27
28     // Accessor methods
29     Public Function String getManufacturer()
30        Return manufacturer
31     End Function
32
33     Public Function String getModelNumber()
34        Return modelNumber
35     End Function
36
37     Public Function Real getRetailPrice()
38        Return retailPrice
39     End Function
40  End Class
```

The constructor accepts three arguments, which are passed into the `manufact`, `modNum`, and `retail` parameters. In lines 10 through 12, these parameters are assigned to the `manufacturer`, `modelNumber`, and `retailPrice` fields.

The pseudocode in Program 13-2 creates a `CellPhone` object and uses the constructor to initialize the object's fields. In line 9, notice that after the class name, the values `"Motorola"`, `"G200"`, and `399.99` appear inside the parentheses. These arguments are passed to the `manufact`, `modelNum`, and `retail` parameters in the constructor. The code in the constructor then assigns those values to the `manufacturer`, `modelNumber`, and `retailPrice` fields.

Program 13-2: 

```
 1  Module main()
 2     // Declare a variable that can reference
 3     // a CellPhone object.
 4     Declare CellPhone myPhone
 5
 6     // The following statement creates a CellPhone
 7     // object and initializes its fields with the
 8     // values passed to the constructor.
 9     Set myPhone = New CellPhone("Motorola", "G200", 399.99)
10
11     // Display the values stored in the fields.
12     Display "The manufacturer is ", myPhone.getManufacturer()
13     Display "The model number is ", myPhone.getModelNumber()
```

Program 13-2: *(continued)*

```
    Display "The retail price is ", myPhone.getRetailPrice()
End Module
```

Program Output

```
The manufacturer is Motorola
The model number is G200
The retail price is 399.99
```

The pseudocode in Program 13-3 shows another example that uses the `CellPhone` class. This program prompts the user to enter the data for a cell phone and then creates an object containing that data.

Program 13-3:

```
Module main()
   // Variables to hold data entered by the user.
   Declare String manufacturer, model
   Declare Real retail

   // Declare a variable that can reference
   // a CellPhone object.
   Declare CellPhone phone

   // Get the data for a cell phone from the user.
   Display "Enter the phone's manufacturer."
   Input manufacturer
   Display "Enter the phone's model number."
   Input model
   Display "Enter the phone's retail price."
   Input retail

   // Create a CellPhone object initialized with the
   // data entered by the user.
   Set phone = New CellPhone(manufacturer, model, retail)

   // Display the values stored in the fields.
   Display "Here is the data you entered."
   Display "The manufacturer is ", myPhone.getManufacturer()
   Display "The model number is ", myPhone.getModelNumber()
   Display "The retail price is ", myPhone.getRetailPrice()
End Module
```

Program Output (with Input Shown in Bold)

```
Enter the phone's manufacturer.
Apple [Enter]
Enter the phone's model number.
iPhone 12 [Enter]
```

Program Output (with Input Shown in Bold) *(continued)*

```
Enter the phone's retail price.
599.99 [Enter]
Here is the data you entered.
The manufacturer is Apple
The model number is iPhone 12
The retail price is 599.99
```

Default Constructors

In most object-oriented languages, when an object is created its constructor is *always* called. But what if we do not write a constructor in the class that the object is created from? If you do not write a constructor in a class, most languages automatically provide one when the class is compiled. The constructor that is automatically provided is usually known as the **default constructor**. The actions performed by the default constructor vary from one language to another. Typically, the default constructor assigns default starting values to the object's fields.

Checkpoint

13.5 You hear someone make the following comment: "A blueprint is a design for a house. A carpenter can use the blueprint to build the house. If desired, the carpenter can build several identical houses from the same blueprint." Think of this as a metaphor for classes and objects. Does the blueprint represent a class, or does it represent an object?

13.6 In this chapter, we use the metaphor of a cookie cutter and cookies that are made from the cookie cutter to describe classes and objects. In this metaphor, are objects the cookie cutter, or the cookies?

13.7 What is an access specifier?

13.8 What access specifier is commonly used with a class's fields?

13.9 When a class variable is said to reference an object, what is actually stored in the class variable?

13.10 What does the New key word do?

13.11 What is an accessor? What is a mutator?

13.12 What is a constructor? When does a constructor execute?

13.13 What is a default constructor?

13.3 Using the Unified Modeling Language to Design Classes

The Unified Modeling Language (UML) is a standard way of drawing diagrams that describe object-oriented systems.

When designing a class, it is often helpful to draw a **Unified Modeling Language (UML)** diagram. UML is a visual language that provides a set of standard diagrams you use to graphically depict object-oriented systems.

Drawing a UML diagram is often the first step developing an object-oriented program design. Figure 13-9 shows the general layout of a UML diagram for a class. Notice that the diagram is a box that is divided into three sections. The top section is where you write the name of the class. The middle section holds a list of the class's fields. The bottom section holds a list of the class's methods.

Figure 13-9 General layout of a UML diagram for a class

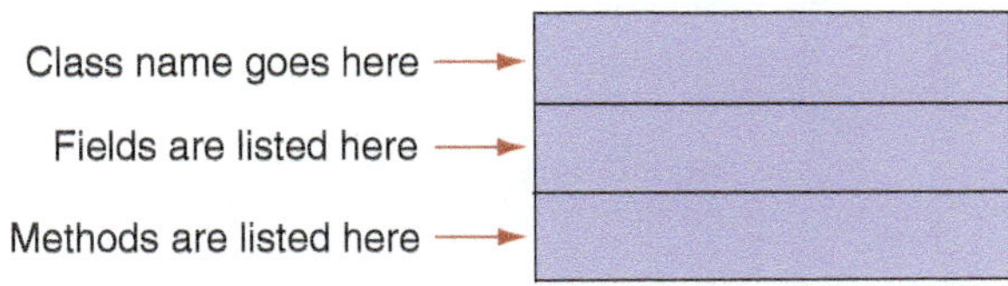

Following this layout, Figure 13-10 shows a simplified UML diagram for our `CellPhone` class.

Figure 13-10 Simplified UML diagram for the `CellPhone` class

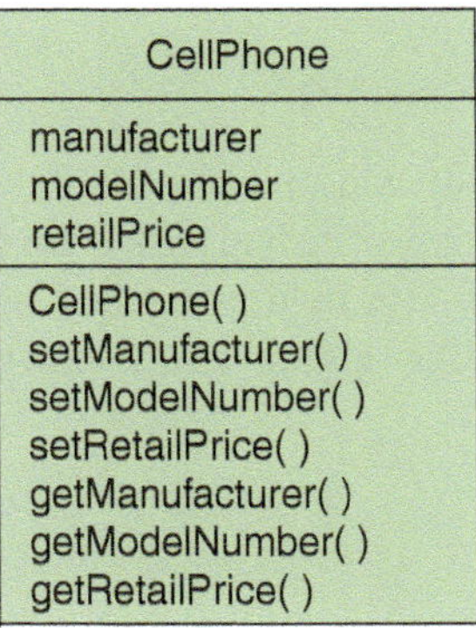

Data Type and Method Parameter Notation

The UML diagram in Figure 13-10 shows only basic information about the `CellPhone` class. It does not show details such as data types and the method's parameters. To indicate the data type of a field, place a colon followed by the name of the data type after the name of the field. For example, the `manufacturer` field in the `CellPhone` class is a `String`. It could be listed in the UML diagram as follows:

```
manufacturer : String
```

The return type of a method can be listed in the same manner. After the method's name, place a colon followed by the return type. The `CellPhone` class's `getRetailPrice` method returns a `Real`, so it could be listed in the UML diagram as follows:

```
getRetailPrice() : Real
```

Parameter variables and their data types may be listed inside a method's parentheses. For example, the `CellPhone` class's `setManufacturer` method has a `String` parameter named `manufact`, so it could be listed in the UML diagram as follows:

```
setManufacturer(manufact : String)
```

Figure 13-11 shows the UML diagram for the `CellPhone` class with data type and parameter notation added to it.

Figure 13-11 UML diagram for the `CellPhone` class with data type and parameter notation

CellPhone
manufacturer : String modelNumber : String retailPrice : Real
CellPhone(manufact : String, modelNum : String, retail : Real) setManufacturer(manufact : String) setModelNumber(modNum : String) setRetailPrice(retail : Real) getManufacturer( ) : String getModelNumber( ) : String getRetailPrice( ) : Real

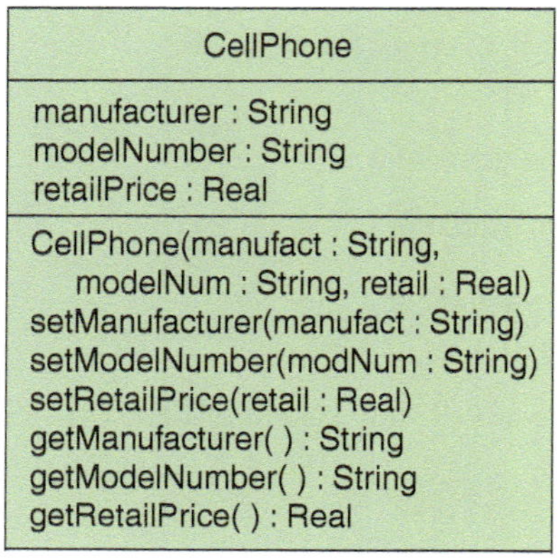

Access Specification Notation

The UML diagrams in Figures 13-10 and 13-11 list all of the fields and methods in the `CellPhone` class but do not indicate which are private and which are public. In a UML diagram, you have the option to place a `-` character before a field or method name to indicate that it is private, or a `+` character to indicate that it is public. Figure 13-12 shows the UML diagram modified to include this notation.

Figure 13-12 UML diagram for the `CellPhone` class with access specification notation

CellPhone
– manufacturer : String – modelNumber : String – retailPrice : Real
+ CellPhone(manufact : String, modelNum : String, retail : Real) + setManufacturer(manufact : String) + setModelNumber(modNum : String) + setRetailPrice(retail : Real) + getManufacturer( ) : String + getModelNumber( ) : String + getRetailPrice( ) : Real

Checkpoint

13.14 The typical UML diagram for a class has three sections. What appears in these three sections?

13.15 Suppose a class has a field named `description`. The field's data type is `String`. How would you indicate the field's data type in a UML diagram?

13.16 What symbols do you use in a UML diagram to indicate private and public access specification?

13.4 Finding the Classes in a Problem

One of the first steps when designing an object-oriented program is finding the classes that should be created.

So far, you have learned the basics of writing a class, creating an object from the class, and using the object to perform operations. Although this knowledge is necessary to create an object-oriented application, it is not the first step. The first step is to analyze the problem that you are trying to solve and determine the classes that you will need. In many cases, this means identifying the different types of real-world objects that are present in the problem, and then creating classes for those types of objects within your program.

Over the years, software professionals have developed numerous techniques for finding the classes in a given problem. One simple and popular technique involves the following steps:

1. Get a written description of the problem domain.
2. Identify all the nouns (including pronouns and noun phrases) in the description. Each of these is a potential class.
3. Refine the list to include only the classes that are relevant to the problem.

The following *In the Spotlight* section leads you through a simple process for finding the classes in a problem.

In the Spotlight:
Finding the Classes in a Problem

The owner of Joe's Automotive Shop has asked you to design a program that will print service quotes for customers. You decide to use an object-oriented approach to design the program.

Start by writing a problem domain. The **problem domain** is the set of real-world objects, parties, and major events related to a problem. If you understand the nature of the problem you are trying to solve, you can write a description of the problem domain yourself. If you do not thoroughly understand the nature of the problem, you should have an expert write the description for you.

A problem domain description should include any or all of the following:

- Physical objects, such as vehicles, machines, or products
- Roles played by people, such as manager, employee, customer, teacher, student, and so on
- The results of a business event, such as a customer order, or in this case a service quote
- Record-keeping items, such as customer histories and payroll records

Here is a description that was written by Joe, the owner of Joe's Automotive Shop:

> Joe's Automotive Shop services foreign cars, and specializes in servicing cars made by Mercedes, Porsche, and BMW. When a customer brings a car to the shop, the manager gets the customer's name, address, and telephone number. The manager then determines the make, model, and year of the car, and gives the customer a service quote. The service quote shows the estimated parts charges, estimated labor charges, sales tax, and total estimated charges.

The next step is to identify all of the nouns and noun phrases in the problem description. (If the description contains pronouns, include them, too.)

On Your Own: Can you identify the nouns (and pronouns) in Joe's description above? Working alone or with a partner, make a list of all that you find, without duplicates.

Here's another look at the previous problem domain description that was written by Joe. This time the nouns and noun phrases appear in bold.

> **Joe's Automotive Shop** services **foreign cars**, and specializes in servicing **cars** made by **Mercedes**, **Porsche**, and **BMW**. When a **customer** brings a **car** to the **shop**, the **manager** gets the **customer's name**, **address**, and **telephone number**. The **manager** then determines the **make**, **model**, and **year** of the **car**, and gives the **customer** a **service quote**. The **service quote** shows the **estimated parts charges**, **estimated labor charges**, **sales tax**, and **total estimated charges**.

Notice that some of the nouns are repeated. The following list shows all of the nouns without duplicates:

address
BMW
car
cars
customer
estimated labor charges
estimated parts charges
foreign cars
Joe's Automotive Shop
make
manager
Mercedes
model
name
Porsche
sales tax
service quote
shop
telephone number
total estimated charges
year

Next, refine the list of nouns. The nouns that appear in the problem description are merely candidates to become classes. It might not be necessary to make classes for all of them. The next step is to refine the list to include only the classes that are necessary to solve the particular problem at hand. We will look at the common reasons that a noun can be eliminated from the list of potential classes.

1. **Some of the nouns really mean the same thing.**

In this example, the following sets of nouns refer to the same thing:

- **cars** and **foreign cars**
- Both of these refer to the general concept of a car.
- **Joe's Automotive Shop** and **shop**
- Both of these refer to the company "Joe's Automotive Shop."

What would you eliminate? We can settle on a single class for each of these. In this example, we will arbitrarily eliminate **foreign cars** from the list, and use the word **cars**. Likewise, we will eliminate **Joe's Automotive Shop** from the list and use the word **shop**. The updated list of potential classes is as follows:

address
BMW
car
cars
customer
estimated labor charges
estimated parts charges
~~foreign cars~~
~~Joe's Automotive Shop~~
make
manager
Mercedes
model
name
Porsche
sales tax
service quote
shop
telephone number
total estimated charges
year

Because **cars** and **foreign cars** mean the same thing in this problem, we have eliminated **foreign cars**. Also, because **Joe's Automotive Shop** and **shop** mean the same thing, we have eliminated **Joe's Automotive Shop**.

2. **Some nouns might represent items that we do not need to be concerned with in order to solve the problem.**

A quick review of the problem description reminds us of what our application should do: print a service quote. In this example, we can eliminate two unnecessary classes from the list:

- We can cross **shop** off the list because our application only needs to be concerned with individual service quotes. It doesn't need to work with or determine any company-wide information. If the problem description asked us to keep a total of all the service quotes, then it would make sense to have a class for the shop.
- We will not need a class for the **manager** because the problem statement does not direct us to process any information about the manager. If there were multiple shop managers, and the problem description had asked us to record which manager generated each service quote, then it would make sense to have a class for the manager.

The updated list of potential classes at this point is as follows:

address
BMW
car
cars
customer
estimated labor charges
model
name
Porsche
sales tax
service quote
estimated parts charges
~~foreign cars~~
~~Joe's Automotive Shop~~
make
~~manager~~
Mercedes
~~shop~~
telephone number
total estimated charges
year

Our problem description does not direct us to process any information about the **shop**, or any information about the **manager**, so we have eliminated those from the list.

3. **Some of the nouns might represent objects, not classes.**

We can eliminate **Mercedes, Porsche**, and **BMW** as classes because, in this example, they all represent specific cars, and can be considered instances of the **cars** class. Also, we can eliminate the word **car** from the list. In the description, it refers to a specific car brought to the shop by a customer. Therefore, it would also represent an instance of the **cars** class. At this point the updated list of potential classes is as follows:

address
~~BMW~~
~~car~~
cars
customer
estimated labor charges
estimated parts charges
~~foreign cars~~
~~Joe's Automotive Shop~~
make
~~manager~~
~~Mercedes~~
model
name
~~Porsche~~
sales tax
service quote
~~shop~~
telephone number
total estimated charges
year

We have eliminated **Mercedes**, **Porsche**, **BMW**, and **car** because they are all instances of the **cars** class. That means that these nouns identify objects, not classes.

TIP: Some object-oriented designers note whether a noun is plural or singular. Sometimes a plural noun will indicate a class and a singular noun will indicate an object.

4. **Some of the nouns might represent simple values that can be stored in a regular variable and do not require a class.**

Remember, a class contains fields and methods. Fields are related items that are stored within an object of the class, and define the object's state. Methods are actions or behaviors that may be performed by an object of the class. If a noun represents a type of item that would not have any identifiable fields or methods, then it can probably be eliminated from the list. To help determine whether a noun represents an item that would have fields and methods, ask the following questions:

- Would you use a group of related values to represent the item's state?
- Are there any obvious actions to be performed by the item?

If the answers to both of these questions are no, then the noun probably represents a value that can be stored in a regular variable.

If we apply this test to each of the nouns that remain in our list, we can conclude that the following are probably not classes: **address**, **estimated labor charges**, **estimated parts charges**, **make**, **model**, **name**, **sales tax**, **telephone number**, **total estimated charges**, and **year**. These are all simple string or numeric values that can be stored in variables. The following is the updated list of potential classes:

~~address~~
~~BMW~~
~~car~~
cars
customer
~~estimated labor charges~~
~~estimated parts charges~~
~~foreign cars~~
~~Joe's Automotive Shop~~
~~make~~
~~manager~~
~~Mercedes~~
~~model~~
~~name~~
~~Porsche~~
~~sales tax~~
~~service quote~~
~~shop~~
~~telephone number~~
~~total estimated charges~~
~~year~~

We have eliminated **address, estimated labor charges, estimated parts charges, make, model, name, sales tax, telephone number, total estimated charges**, and **year** as classes because they represent simple values that can be stored in primitive variables.

As you can see from the list, we have eliminated everything except **cars**, **customer**, and **service quote**. This means that in our application, we will need classes to represent cars, customers, and service quotes. In the next section, we will write a `Car` class, a `Customer` class, and a `ServiceQuote` class.

13.5 Finding the Responsibilities of Classes in a Problem

After identifying classes in a problem, the next step is to determine the responsibilities of those classes.

To continue developing an object-oriented program, you must determine the **responsibilities** of each class. A class's responsibilities are as follows:

- The things that the class is responsible for knowing
- The actions that the class is responsible for doing

When you have identified the things that a class is responsible for knowing, then you have identified the values that will be stored in fields. Likewise, when you have identified the actions that a class is responsible for doing, you have identified its methods. It is often helpful to ask the questions "In this program, what must the class know? What must the class do?" The first place to look for the answers is in the description of the problem domain. Many of the things that a class must know and do will be mentioned. Some class responsibilities, however, might not be directly mentioned in the problem domain, so brainstorming is often required.

In the Spotlight:

Determining Class Responsibilities

In the previous *In the Spotlight* section, we examined the problem domain description for the Joe's Automotive Shop program. We also identified the classes that we will need, which are `Car`, `Customer`, and `ServiceQuote`. Now, we will determine those classes' responsibilities.

In this program, what must the `Customer` class know? The problem domain description directly mentions the following items:

- The customer's name
- The customer's address
- The customer's telephone number

These are all values that can be represented as strings and stored in the class's fields. The `Customer` class can potentially know many other things. One mistake that can be made at this point is to identify too many things that an object is responsible for knowing. In some programs, a `Customer` class might know the customer's email address. This particular problem domain does not mention that the customer's email address is used for any purpose, so we should not include it as a responsibility.

Now, let's identify the class's methods. In this program, what must the `Customer` class do? The following are the only obvious actions:

- Create an object of the `Customer` class
- Set and get the customer's name
- Set and get the customer's address
- Set and get the customer's telephone number

From this list, we can see that the `Customer` class will have a constructor, as well as accessor and mutator methods, for each of its fields.

On Your Own: Alone or with a partner, make a UML diagram for the Customer class and then write the pseudocode for its class definition.

Figure 13-13 shows a UML diagram for the `Customer` class. Class Listing 13-5 shows the pseudocode for a class definition.

Figure 13-13 UML diagram for the `Customer` class

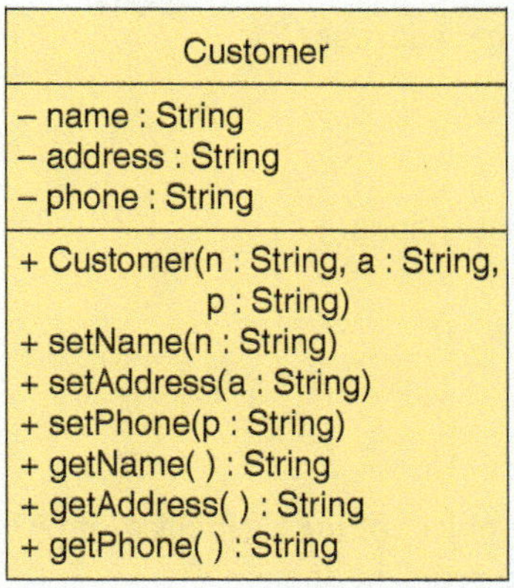

Customer
– name : String – address : String – phone : String
+ Customer(n : String, a : String, p : String) + setName(n : String) + setAddress(a : String) + setPhone(p : String) + getName( ) : String + getAddress( ) : String + getPhone( ) : String

Class Listing 13-5:

```
Class Customer
   // Fields
   Private String name
   Private String address
   Private String phone

   // Constructor
   Public Module Customer(String n, String a,
                          String p)
      Set name = n
      Set address = a
      Set phone = p
   End Module

   // Mutators
   Public Module setName(String n)
      Set name = n
   End Module

   Public Module setAddress(String a)
      Set address = a
   End Module

   Public Module setPhone(String p)
      Set phone = p
   End Module

   // Accessors
   Public Function String getName()
      Return name
   End Function

```

Class Listing 13-5: *(continued)*

```
    Public Function String getAddress()
       Return address
    End Function

    Public Function String getPhone()
       Return phone
    End Function
End Class
```

In this program, what must an object of the Car class know? The following items are all attributes of a car, and are mentioned in the problem domain:

- the car's make
- the car's model
- the car's year

Now let's identify the class's methods. In this program, what must the Car class do? Once again, the only obvious actions are the standard set of methods that we will find in most classes (constructors, accessors, and mutators). Specifically, the actions are as follows:

- create an object of the Car class
- set and get the car's make
- set and get the car's model
- set and get the car's year

On Your Own: Alone or with a partner, make a UML diagram for the Car class and then write the pseudocode for its class definition.

Figure 13-14 shows a UML diagram for the Car class, and Class Listing 13-6 shows the pseudocode for a class definition.

Figure 13-14 UML diagram for the Car classClass

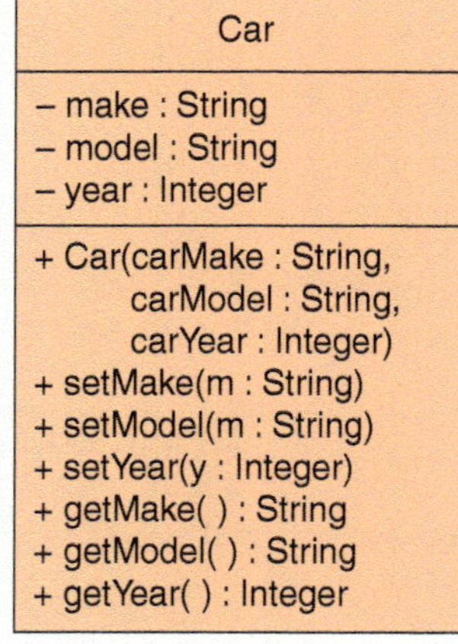

Class Listing 13-6:

```
Class Car
   // Fields
   Private String make
   Private String model
   Private Integer year

   // Constructor
   Public Module Car(String carMake,
           String carModel, Integer carYear)
      Set make = carMake
      Set model = carModel
      Set year = carYear
   End Module

   // Mutators
   Public Module setMake(String m)
      Set make = m
   End Module

   Public Module setModel(String m)
      Set model = m
   End Module

   Public Module setYear(Integer y)
      Set year = y
   End Module

   // Accessors
   Public Function String getMake()
      Return make
   End Function

   Public Function String getModel()
      Return model
   End Function

   Public Function Integer getYear()
      Return year
   End Function
End Class
```

In this program, what must an object of the `ServiceQuote` class know? The problem domain mentions the following items:

- the estimated parts charges
- the estimated labor charges
- the sales tax
- the total estimated charges

Careful thought and a little brainstorming will reveal that two of these items are the results of calculations: sales tax and total estimated charges. These items are dependent on the values of the estimated parts and labor charges. Instead of storing these values in fields, we will provide methods that calculate these values and return them. (In a moment we will explain why we take this approach.)

The other methods that we will need for this class are a constructor and the accessors and mutators for the estimated parts charges and estimated labor charges fields.

On Your Own: Alone or with a partner, make a UML diagram for the ServiceQuote class and then write the pseudocode for its class definition.

Figure 13-15 shows a UML diagram for the `ServiceQuote` class, and Class Listing 13-7 shows the pseudocode for a class definition.

Figure 13-15 UML diagram for the `ServiceQuote` class

ServiceQuote
– partsCharges : Real – laborCharges : Real
+ ServiceQuote(pc : Real, lc : Real) + setPartsCharges(pc : Real) + setLaborCharges(lc : Real) + getPartsCharges( ) : Real + getLaborCharges( ) : Real + getSalesTax(taxRate : Real) : Real + getTotalCharges( ) : Real

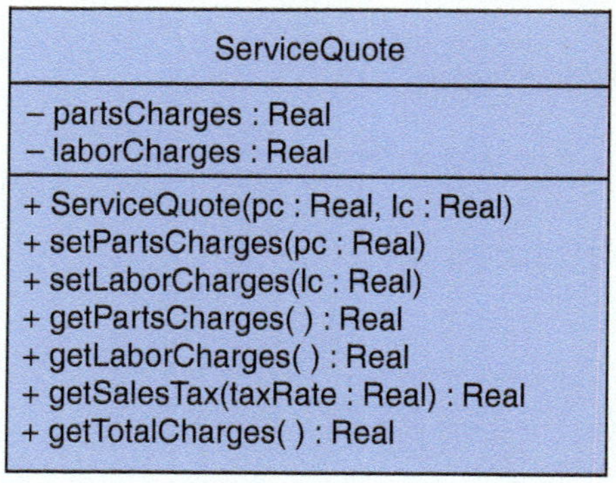

Class Listing 13-7:

```
Class ServiceQuote
   // Fields
   Private Real partsCharges
   Private Real laborCharges

   // Constructor
   Public Module ServiceQuote(Real pc, Real lc)
      Set partsCharges = pc
      Set laborCharges = lc
   End Module

   // Mutators
   Public Module setPartsCharges(Real pc)
      Set partsCharges = pc
   End Module

   Public Module setLaborCharges(Real lc)
      Set laborCharges = lc
   End Module

   // Accessors
   Public Function Real getPartsCharges()
```

Class Listing 13-7: *(continued)*

```
23          Return partsCharges
24       End Function
25
26       Public Function Real getLaborCharges()
27          Return laborCharges
28       End Function
29
30       Public Function Real getSalesTax(Real taxRate)
31          // Sales tax is charged only on parts.
32          Return partsCharges * taxRate
33       End Function
34
35       Public Function Real getTotalCharges(Real taxRate)
36          Return partsCharges + laborCharges + getSalesTax(taxRate)
37       End Function
38    End Class
```

First, notice that the `getSalesTax` method, in lines 30 through 33, accepts a `Real` argument for the tax rate. The method returns the amount of sales tax in line 32, which is the result of a calculation.

The `getTotalCharges` method, in lines 35 through 37, returns the total charges estimate. The value that is returned by this method is the result of a calculation. The value that is returned in line 36 is the result of the expression `partsCharges + laborCharges + getSalesTax(taxRate)`. Notice that this expression calls one of the object's own methods: `getSalesTax`.

Avoiding Stale Data

In the `ServiceQuote` class, the `getPartsCharges` and `getLaborCharges` methods return the values stored in fields, but the `getSalesTax` and `getTotalCharges` methods return the results of calculations. You might be wondering why the sales tax and the total charges are not stored in fields, like the parts charges and labor charges. These values are not stored in fields because they could potentially become **stale**. When the value of an item is dependent on other data and that item is not updated when the other data is changed, it is said that the item has become stale. If the sales tax and total charges were stored in fields, the values of those fields would become incorrect as soon as the `partsCharges` or `laborCharges` field changed.

When designing a class, you should take care not to store in a field any calculated data that can potentially become stale. Instead, provide a method that returns the result of the calculation.

Checkpoint

13.17 What is a problem domain description?

13.18 What technique was described in this section for finding the classes in a particular problem?

13.19 What are classes' responsibilities?

13.20 What causes an item of data to become stale?

13.6 Inheritance

Inheritance allows a new class to extend an existing class. The new class inherits the members of the class it extends.

Generalization and Specialization

In the real world, you can find many objects that are specialized versions of other more general objects. For example, the term *insect* describes a very general type of creature with numerous characteristics. Because grasshoppers and bumblebees are insects, they have all the general characteristics of an insect. In addition, they have special characteristics of their own. For example, the grasshopper has its jumping ability, and the bumblebee has its stinger. Grasshoppers and bumblebees are specialized versions of an insect. This is illustrated in Figure 13-16.

Figure 13-16 Bumblebees and grasshoppers are specialized versions of an insect

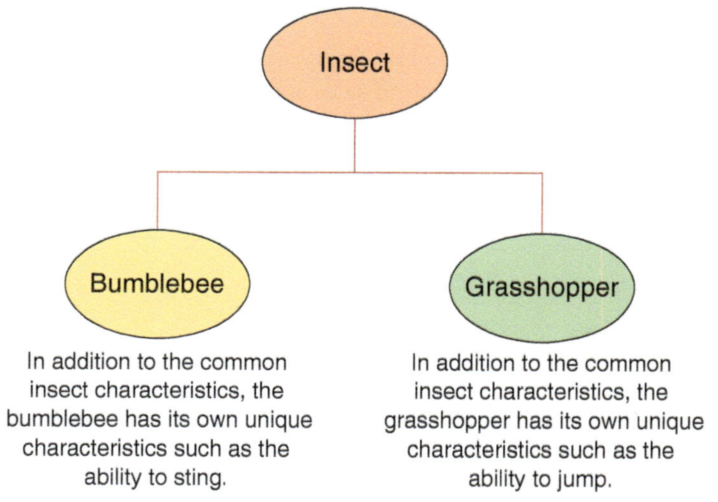

Inheritance and the "Is a" Relationship

When one object is a specialized version of another object, there is an "is a" relationship between them. For example, a grasshopper is an insect. Here are a few other examples of the "is a" relationship:

- A poodle is a dog.
- A car is a vehicle.
- A flower is a plant.
- A rectangle is a shape.
- A football player is an athlete.

When an "is a" relationship exists between objects, it means that the specialized object has all of the characteristics of the general object, plus additional characteristics that make it special. In object-oriented programming, inheritance is used to create an "is a" relationship among classes.

This allows you to extend the capabilities of a class by creating another class that is a specialized version of it.

Inheritance involves a superclass and a subclass. The **superclass** is the general class and the **subclass** is the specialized class. You can think of the subclass as an extended version of the superclass. The subclass inherits fields and methods from the superclass without any of them having to be rewritten. Furthermore, new fields and methods may be added to the subclass, and that is what makes it a specialized version of the superclass.

NOTE: Superclasses are also called *base classes,* and subclasses are also called *derived classes.* Either set of terms is correct. For consistency, this text will use the terms *superclass* and *subclass*.

Let's look at an example of how inheritance can be used. Most teachers assign various graded activities for their students to complete. A graded activity can be given a numeric score such as 70, 85, 90, and so on, and a letter grade such as A, B, C, D, or F. Figure 13-17 shows a UML diagram for the `GradedActivity` class, which is designed to hold the numeric score of a graded activity. The `setScore` method sets a numeric score, and the `getScore` method returns the numeric score. The `getGrade` method returns the letter grade that corresponds to the numeric score. Class Listing 13-8 shows the pseudocode for the class. The pseudocode in Program 13-4 demonstrates how the class works.

Figure 13-17 UML diagram for the `GradedActivity` class

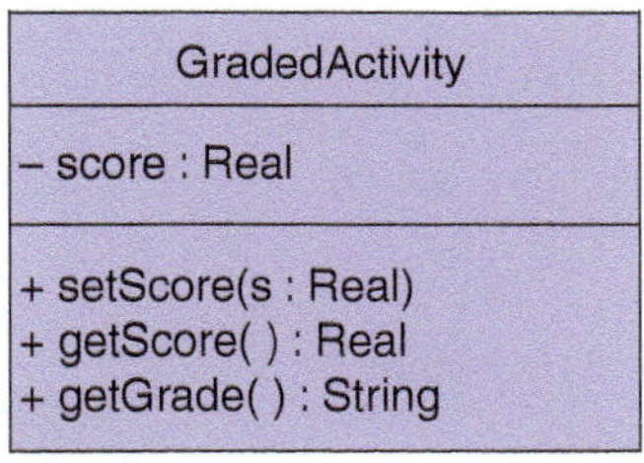

Class Listing 13-8:

```
Class GradedActivity
   // The score field holds a numeric score.
   Private Real score

   // Mutator
   Public Module setScore(Real s)
      Set score = s
   End Module

   // Accessor
   Public Function Real getScore()
      Return score
   End Function

   // getGrade method
   Public Function String getGrade()
```

Class Listing 13-8: *(continued)*

```
      // Local variable to hold a grade.
      Declare String grade

      // Determine the grade.
      If score >= 90 Then
         Set grade = "A"
      Else If score >= 80 Then
         Set grade = "B"
      Else If score >= 70 Then
         Set grade = "C"
      Else If score >= 60 Then
         Set grade = "D"
      Else
         Set grade = "F"
      End If

      // Return the grade.
      Return grade
   End Function

End Class
```

Program 13-4:

```
Module main()
   // A variable to hold a test score.
   Declare Real testScore

   // A class variable to reference a
   // GradedActivity object.
   Declare GradedActivity test

   // Create a GradedActivity object.
   Set test = New GradedActivity()

   // Get a test score from the user.
   Display "Enter a numeric test score."
   Input testScore

   // Store the test score in the object.
   test.setScore(testScore)

   // Display the grade for the object.
   Display "The grade for that test is ",
            test.getGrade()
End Module
```

Program Output (with Input Shown in Bold) *(continued)*

```
Enter a numeric test score.
89 [Enter]
The grade for that test is B
```

Program Output (with Input Shown in Bold)

```
Enter a numeric test score.
75 [Enter]
The grade for that test is C
```

The GradedActivity class represents the general characteristics of a student's graded activity. Many different types of graded activities exist, however, such as quizzes, midterm exams, final exams, lab reports, essays, and so on. Because the numeric scores might be determined differently for each of these graded activities, we can create subclasses to handle each one. For example, we could create a FinalExam class that would be a subclass of the GradedActivity class. Figure 13-18 shows the UML diagram for such a class, and Class Listing 13-9 shows its definition in pseudocode. The class has fields for the number of questions on the exam (numQuestions), the number of points each question is worth (pointsEach), and the number of questions missed by the student (numMissed).

Figure 13-18 UML diagram for the FinalExam classClass

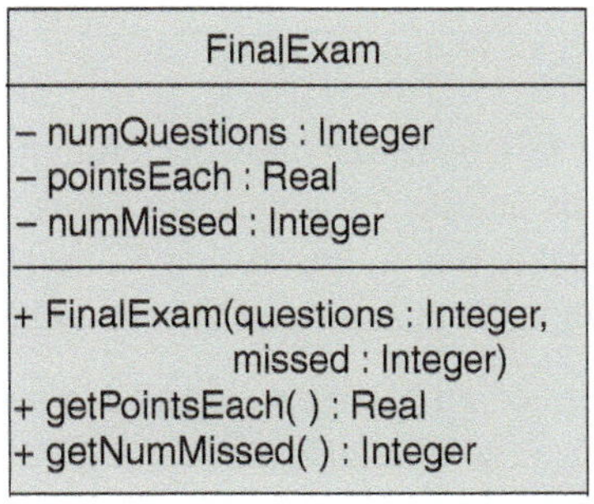

FinalExam
– numQuestions : Integer – pointsEach : Real – numMissed : Integer
+ FinalExam(questions : Integer, missed : Integer) + getPointsEach( ) : Real + getNumMissed( ) : Integer

Class Listing 13-9:

```
Class FinalExam Extends GradedActivity
   // Fields
   Private Integer numQuestions
   Private Real pointsEach
   Private Integer numMissed

   // The constructor sets the number of
   // questions on the exam and the number
   // of questions missed.
   Public Module FinalExam(Integer questions,
                           Integer missed)
      // Local variable to hold the numeric score.
      Declare Real numericScore

      // Set the numQuestions and numMissed fields.
```

Class Listing 13-9: *(continued)*

```
        Set numQuestions = questions
        Set numMissed = missed

        // Calculate the points for each question
        // and the numeric score for this exam.
        Set pointsEach = 100.0 / questions
        Set numericScore = 100.0 - (missed * pointsEach)

        // Call the inherited setScore method to
        // set the numeric score.
        Call setScore(numericScore)
    End Module

    // Accessors
    Public Function Real getPointsEach()
        Return pointsEach
    End Function

    Public Function Integer getNumMissed()
        Return numMissed
    End Function
End Class
```

Notice that the first line of the `FinalExam` class declaration uses the `Extends` key word, which indicates that this class extends another class (a superclass). The name of the superclass is listed after the word `extends`. So, this line indicates that `FinalExam` is the name of the class being declared and `GradedActivity` is the name of the superclass it extends.

If we want to express the relationship between the two classes, we can say that a `FinalExam` is a `GradedActivity`. Because the `FinalExam` class extends the `GradedActivity` class, it inherits all of the public members of the `GradedActivity` class. Here is a list of the members of the `FinalExam` class:

Fields:

`numQuestions`	Declared in the `FinalExam` class
`pointsEach`	Declared in the `FinalExam` class
`numMissed`	Declared in the `FinalExam` class

Methods:

`Constructor`	Declared in the `FinalExam` class
`getPointsEach`	Declared in the `FinalExam` class
`getNumMissed`	Declared in the `FinalExam` class
`setScore`	Inherited from the `GradedActivity` class
`getScore`	Inherited from the `GradedActivity` class
`getGrade`	Inherited from the `GradedActivity` class

Notice that the `GradedActivity` class's `score` field is not listed among the members of the `FinalExam` class. That is because the `score` field is private. In most languages, private members of the superclass cannot be accessed by the subclass, so technically speaking, they are not inherited. When an object of the subclass is created, the private members of the superclass exist in memory, but only methods in the superclass can access them. They are truly private to the superclass.

To see how inheritance works in this example, let's take a closer look at the `FinalExam` constructor in lines 10 through 27. The constructor accepts two arguments: the number of test questions on the exam, and the number of questions missed by the student. In lines 16 and 17 these values are assigned to the `numQuestions` and `numMissed` fields. Then, in lines 21 and 22, the number of points for each question and the numeric test score are calculated. In line 26, the last statement in the constructor reads as follows:

```
Call setScore(numericScore)
```

This is a call to the `setScore` method, which is inherited from the `GradedActivity` class. Although the `FinalExam` constructor cannot directly access the `score` field (because it is declared private in the `GradedActivity` class), it can call the `setScore` method to store a value in the `score` field.

The pseudocode in Program 13-5 demonstrates the `FinalExam` class.

Program 13-5: 

```
Module main()
   // Variables to hold user input.
   Declare Integer questions, missed

   // Class variable to reference a FinalExam object.
   Declare FinalExam exam

   // Prompt the user for the number of questions
   // on the exam.
   Display "Enter the number of questions on the exam."
   Input questions

   // Prompt the user for the number of questions
   // missed by the student.
   Display "Enter the number of questions that the ",
           "student missed."
   Input missed

   // Create a FinalExam object.
   Set exam = New FinalExam(questions, missed)

   // Display the test results.
   Display "Each question on the exam counts ",
           exam.getPointsEach(), " points."
   Display "The exam score is ", exam.getScore()
   Display "The exam grade is ", exam.getGrade()
End Module
```

Program Output (with Input Shown in Bold) *(continued)*

```
Enter the number of questions on the exam.
20 [Enter]
Enter the number of questions that the student missed.
3 [Enter]
Each question on the exam counts 5 points.
The exam score is 85
The exam grade is B
```

In line 20, the following statement creates an instance of the `FinalExam` class and assigns its address to the `exam` variable:

```
Set exam = New FinalExam(questions, missed)
```

When a `FinalExam` object is created in memory, not only does it have the members declared in the `FinalExam` class, but also it has the non-private members declared in the `GradedActivity` class. Notice in lines 25 and 26, shown here, that two public methods of the `GradedActivity` class, `getScore` and `getGrade`, are directly called with the `exam` object:

```
Display "The exam score is ", exam.getScore()
Display "The exam grade is ", exam.getGrade()
```

When a subclass extends a superclass, the public members of the superclass become public members of the subclass. In this program, the `getScore` and `getGrade` methods can be called with the `exam` object because they are public members of the object's superclass.

Inheritance in UML Diagrams

You show inheritance in a UML diagram by connecting two classes with a line that has an open arrowhead at one end. The arrowhead points to the superclass. Figure 13-19 is a UML diagram showing the relationship between the `GradedActivity` and `FinalExam` classes.

Figure 13-19 UML diagram showing inheritance

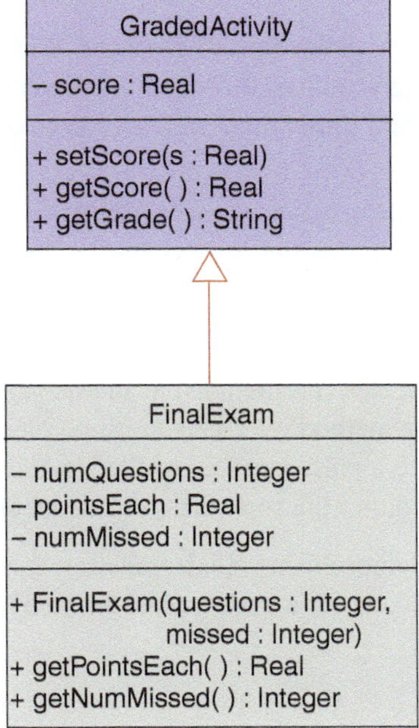

Inheritance Does Not Work in Reverse

In an inheritance relationship, the subclass inherits members from the superclass, not the other way around. This means it is not possible for a superclass to call a subclass's methods. For example, if we create a `GradedActivity` object, it cannot call the `getPointsEach` and the `getNumMissed` methods because they are members of the `FinalExam` class.

Checkpoint

13.21 In this section, we discussed superclasses and subclasses. Which is the general class and which is the specialized class?

13.22 What does it mean to say there is an "is a" relationship between two objects?

13.23 What does a subclass inherit from its superclass?

13.24 Look at the following pseudocode; which is the first line of a class definition? What is the name of the superclass? What is the name of the subclass?

```
Class Canary Extends Bird
```

13.7 Polymorphism

Polymorphism allows you to create methods with the same name in different classes (that are related through inheritance) and gives you the ability to call the correct method depending on the type of object that is used to call it.

The term **polymorphism** refers to an object's ability to take different forms. It is a powerful feature of object-oriented programming. In this section, we will look at two essential ingredients of polymorphic behavior:

1. The ability to define a method in a superclass, and then define a method with the same name in a subclass. When a subclass method has the same name as a superclass method, it is often said that the subclass method overrides the superclass method.
2. The ability to declare a class variable of the superclass type, and then use that variable to reference objects of either the superclass or the subclass types.

The best way to describe polymorphism is to demonstrate it, so let's look at a simple example. Class Listing 13-10 shows pseudocode for a class named `Animal`.

Class Listing 13-10:

```
Class Animal
   // showSpecies method
   Public Module showSpecies()
      Display "I'm just a regular animal."
   End Module

   // makeSound method
   Public Module makeSound()
      Display "Grrrrr"
   End Module
End Class
```

The class has two methods: `showSpecies` and `makeSound`. Here is an example of pseudocode that creates an instance of the class and calls the methods:

```
Declare Animal myAnimal
Set myAnimal = New Animal()
Call myAnimal.showSpecies()
Call myAnimal.makeSound()
```

If this were actual code, it would display the following:

```
I'm just a regular animal.
Grrrrr
```

Next, look at Class Listing 13-11, which shows the pseudocode for the `Dog` class. The `Dog` class is a subclass of the `Animal` class.

Class Listing 13-11: 

```
Class Dog Extends Animal
   // showSpecies method
   Public Module showSpecies()
      Display “I'm a dog."
   End Module

   // makeSound method
   Public Module makeSound()
      Display “Woof! Woof!"
   End Module
End Class
```

Even though the Dog class inherits the showSpecies and makeSound methods that are in the Animal class, those methods are not adequate for the Dog class. So, the Dog class has its own showSpecies and makeSound methods, which display messages that are more appropriate for a dog. We say that the showSpecies and makeSound methods in the Dog class override the showSpecies and makeSound methods in the Animal class. Here is an example of pseudocode that creates an instance of the Dog class and calls the methods:

```
Declare Dog myDog
Set myDog = New Dog()
Call myDog.showSpecies()
Call myDog.makeSound()
```

If this were actual code, it would display the following:

```
I'm a dog.
Woof! Woof!
```

Class Listing 13-12 shows pseudocode for the Cat class, which is also a subclass of the Animal class.

Class Listing 13-12: 

```
Class Cat Extends Animal
   // showSpecies method
   Public Module showSpecies()
      Display “I'm a cat."
   End Module

   // makeSound method
   Public Module makeSound()
      Display “Meow"
   End Module
End Class
```

The Cat class also has methods named showSpecies and makeSound. Here is an example of pseudocode that creates an instance of the Cat class and calls the methods:

```
Declare Cat myCat
Set myCat = New Cat()
Call myCat.showSpecies()
Call myCat.makeSound()
```

If this were actual code, it would display the following:

```
I'm a cat.
Meow
```

Because of the "is a" relationship between a superclass and a subclass, an object of the Dog class is not just a Dog object. It is also an Animal object. (A dog is an animal.) Because of this relationship, we can use an Animal class variable to reference a Dog object. For example, look at the following pseudocode:

```
Declare Animal myAnimal
Set myAnimal = New Dog()
Call myAnimal.showSpecies()
Call myAnimal.makeSound()
```

The first statement declares myAnimal as an Animal variable. The second statement creates a Dog object and stores the object's address in the myAnimal variable. In most object-oriented languages this type of assignment is perfectly legal because a Dog object is also an Animal object. The third and fourth statements use the myAnimal object to call the showSpecies and makeSound methods. If this pseudocode were actual code, it would display the following in most programming languages:

```
I'm a dog.
Woof! Woof!
```

Similarly, we can use an Animal variable to reference a Cat object, as shown here:

```
Declare Animal myAnimal
Set myAnimal = New Cat()
Call myAnimal.showSpecies()
Call myAnimal.makeSound()
```

If this pseudocode were actual code, it would display the following in most programming languages:

```
I'm a cat.
Meow
```

This aspect of polymorphism gives us a great deal of flexibility when designing programs. For example, look at the following module:

```
Module showAnimalInfo(Animal creature)
   Call creature.showSpecies()
   Call creature.makeSound()
End Module
```

This module displays information about an animal. Because it has an Animal variable as its parameter, you can pass an Animal object to the module when you call it. The module then calls the object's showSpecies method and makeSound method.

The `showAnimalInfo` module works with an `Animal` object, but what if you also need modules that display information about `Dog` objects and `Cat` objects? Do you need to write additional modules for each of these types? Because of polymorphism, the answer is *no*. In addition to `Animal` objects, you can also pass `Dog` objects or `Cat` objects as arguments to the `showAnimalInfo` module previously shown. The pseudocode in Program 13-6 demonstrates this.

Program 13-6: 

```
Module main()
   // Declare three class variables.
   Declare Animal myAnimal
   Declare Dog myDog
   Declare Cat myCat

   // Create an Animal object, a Dog object,
   // and a Cat object.
   Set myAnimal = New Animal()
   Set myDog = New Dog()
   Set myCat = New Cat()

   // Show info about an animal.
   Display "Here is info about an animal."
   showAnimalInfo(myAnimal)
   Display

   // Show info about a dog.
   Display "Here is info about a dog."
   showAnimalInfo(myDog)
   Display

   // Show info about a cat.
   Display "Here is info about a cat."
   showAnimalInfo(myCat)
End Module

// The showAnimalInfo module accepts an Animal
// object as an argument and displays information
// about it.
Module showAnimalInfo(Animal creature)
   Call creature.showSpecies()
   Call creature.makeSound()
End Module
```

Program Output

```
Here is info about an animal.
I'm just a regular animal.
Grrrrr
Here is info about a dog.
I'm a dog.
Woof! Woof!
Here is info about a cat.
I'm a cat.
Meow
```

Although these examples are very simple, polymorphism has many practical uses. For example, a university's software processes a lot of data about students, so it might use a `Student` class. One of the methods in the `Student` class might be called `getFees`. This method would return the amount of a typical student's fees for a semester.

In addition, the software might have a `BiologyStudent` class as a subclass of the `Student` class (because a biology student is a student). Because of additional lab charges, a biology student's fees are usually more than those of the typical student. So, the `BiologyStudent` class would have its own `getFees` method that returns the fees for a biology student.

Checkpoint

14.25 Look at the following pseudocode class definitions:

```
Class Vegetable
   Public Module message()
      Display "I'm a vegetable."
   End Module
End Class

Class Potato Extends Vegetable
   Public Module message()
      Display "I'm a potato."
   End Module
End Class
```

Given these class definitions, what will the following pseudocode display?

```
Declare Vegetable v
Declare Potato p
Set v = New Potato()
Set p = New Potato()
Call v.message()
Call p.message()
```

Chapter Review

Multiple Choice

1. A(n) __________ programming practice is centered on creating modules and functions that are separate from the data that they work on.
   a. modular
   b. procedural
   c. functional
   d. object-oriented

2. A(n) __________ programming practice is centered on creating objects.
   a. object-centric
   b. objective
   c. procedural
   d. object-oriented

3. A(n) __________ is a member of a class that holds data.
   a. method
   b. instance
   c. field
   d. constructor

4. The __________ specifies how a class's field or method may be accessed by code outside the class.
   a. field declaration
   b. New key word
   c. access specifier
   d. constructor

5. A class's fields are commonly declared with the __________ access specifier.
   a. `Private`
   b. `Public`
   c. `ReadOnly`
   d. `Hidden`

6. A __________ variable is a special type of variable that can reference an object in the computer's memory.
   a. memory
   b. procedural
   c. class
   d. dynamic

7. In many programming languages, the __________ key word creates an object in memory.
   a. `Create`
   b. `New`
   c. `Instantiate`
   d. `Declare`

8. A(n) __________ method gets a value from a class's field but does not change it.
   a. retriever
   b. constructor
   c. mutator
   d. accessor

9. A(n) __________ method stores a value in a field or changes the value of a field in some other way.
   a. modifier
   b. constructor
   c. mutator
   d. accessor

10. A(n) __________ method is automatically called when an object is created.
    a. accessor
    b. constructor
    c. setter
    d. mutator

11. A set of standard diagrams for graphically depicting object-oriented systems is provided by __________.
    a. the Unified Modeling Language
    b. flowcharts
    c. pseudocode
    d. the Object Hierarchy System

12. When the value of an item is dependent on other data, and that item is not updated when the other data is changed, we say that the value has become __________.
    a. bitter
    b. stale
    c. asynchronous
    d. moldy

13. A class's responsibilities are __________.
    a. objects created from the class
    b. things the class knows
    c. actions the class performs
    d. both b and c

14. In an inheritance relationship, the __________ is the general class.
    a. subclass
    b. superclass
    c. prototype class
    d. child class

15. In an inheritance relationship, the __________ is the specialized class.
    a. superclass
    b. prototype class
    c. subclass
    d. parent class

16. The __________ characteristic of object-oriented programming allows a superclass variable to reference a subclass object.
    a. polymorphism
    b. inheritance
    c. generalization
    d. specialization

True or False

1. Procedural programming uses rules for creating and managing objects.
2. Object reusability has been a factor in the increased use of object-oriented programming.
3. It is a common practice in object-oriented programming to make all of a class's fields public.
4. One way to find the classes needed for an object-oriented program is to identify all of the verbs in a description of the problem domain.
5. The superclass inherits fields and methods from the subclass.
6. Polymorphism allows a class variable of the superclass type to reference objects of either the superclass or the subclass types.

Short Answer

1. What is encapsulation?
2. Why is an object's internal data usually hidden from outside code?
3. What is the difference between a class and an instance of a class?
4. In many programming languages, what does the `New` key word do?
5. The following pseudocode statement calls an object's method. What is the name of the method? What is the name of the variable that references the object?

```
Call wallet.getDollar()
```

6. What is stale data?
7. What does a subclass inherit from its superclass?
8. Look at the following pseudocode, which is the first line of a class definition. What is the name of the superclass? What is the name of the subclass?

```
Class Tiger Extends Felis
```

Algorithm Workbench

1. Suppose `myCar` is the name of a class variable that references an object, and `go` is the name of a method. (The `go` method does not take any arguments.) Write a pseudocode statement that uses the `myCar` variable to call the method.

2. Look at this partial class definition, and then follow the subsequent instructions:

```
Class Book
   Private String title
   Private String author
   Private String publisher
   Private Integer copiesSold
End Class
```

   a. Write a constructor for this class. The constructor should accept an argument for each of the fields.
   b. Write accessor and mutator methods for each field.
   c. Draw a UML diagram for the class, including the methods you have written.

3. Look at the following description of a problem domain:

   The bank offers the following types of accounts to its customers: savings accounts, checking accounts, and money market accounts. Customers are allowed to deposit money into an account (thereby increasing its balance), withdraw money from an account (thereby decreasing its balance), and earn interest on the account. Each account has an interest rate.

   Assume that you are writing a program that will calculate the amount of interest earned for a bank account.

   a. Identify the potential classes in this problem domain.
   b. Refine the list to include only the necessary class or classes for this problem.
   c. Identify the responsibilities of the class or classes.

4. In pseudocode, write the first line of the definition for a `Poodle` class. The class should extend the `Dog` class.

5. Look at the following pseudocode class definitions:

```
Class Plant
   Public Module message()
      Display "I'm a plant."
   End Module
End Class
Class Tree Extends Plant
   Public Module message()
      Display "I'm a tree."
   End Module
End Class
Given these class definitions, what will the following pseudocode
display?
Declare Plant p
Set p = New Tree()
Call p.message()
```

Programming Exercises

VideoNote
The Pet Class Problem

1. **Pet Class**

Design a class named Pet, which should have the following fields:

- name: The name field holds the name of a pet.
- type: The type field holds the type of animal that a pet is. Example values are "Dog", "Cat", and "Bird".
- age: The age field holds the pet's age.

The Pet class should also have the following methods:

- setName: The setName method stores a value in the name field.
- setType: The setType method stores a value in the type field.
- setAge: The setAge method stores a value in the age field.
- getName: The getName method returns the value of the name field.
- getType: The getType method returns the value of the type field.
- getAge: The getAge method returns the value of the age field.

Once you have designed the class, design a program that creates an object of the class and prompts the user to enter the name, type, and age of his or her pet. This data should be stored in the object. Use the object's accessor methods to retrieve the pet's name, type, and age and display this data on the screen.

2. **Car Class**

Design a class named Car that has the following fields:

- yearModel: The yearModel field is an Integer that holds the car's year model.
- make: The make field references a String that holds the make of the car.
- speed: The speed field is an Integer that holds the car's current speed.

In addition, the class should have the following constructor and other methods:

- **Constructor:** The constructor should accept the car's year model and make as arguments. These values should be assigned to the object's `yearModel` and `make` fields. The constructor should also assign 0 to the `speed` field.
- **Accessors:** Design appropriate accessor methods to get the values stored in an object's `yearModel`, `make`, and `speed` fields.
- `accelerate`: The `accelerate` method should add 5 to the `speed` field each time it is called.
- `brake`: The `brake` method should subtract 5 from the `speed` field each time it is called.

Next, design a program that creates a `Car` object, and then calls the `accelerate` method five times. After each call to the `accelerate` method, get the current speed of the car and display it. Then call the `brake` method five times. After each call to the `brake` method, get the current speed of the car and display it.

3. **`Personal Information` Class**

Design a class that holds the following personal data: name, address, age, and phone number. Write appropriate accessor and mutator methods. Also, design a program that creates three instances of the class. One instance should hold your information, and the other two should hold your friends' or family members' information.

4. **`Essay` Class**

Design an `Essay` class that extends the `GradedActivity` class presented in this chapter. The `Essay` class should determine the grade a student receives for an essay. The student's essay score can be up to 100 and is determined in the following manner:

- Grammar: up to 30 points
- Spelling: up to 20 points
- Correct length: up to 20 points
- Content: up to 30 points

Once you have designed the class, design a program that prompts the user to enter the number of points that a student has earned for grammar, spelling, length, and content. Create an `Essay` object and store this data in the object. Use the object's methods to get the student's overall score and grade, and display this data on the screen.

CHAPTER 14

Getting Started with GUI Applications

TOPICS

14.1 What is a Graphical User Interface?

A graphical user interface allows the user to interact with the operating system and other programs using graphical elements such as icons, buttons, and dialog boxes.

VideoNote
Graphical User Interfaces

A computer's **user interface** is the part of the computer that the user interacts with. One part of the user interface consists of hardware devices, such as the keyboard and the video display. Another part of the user interface lies in the way that the computer's operating system accepts commands from the user.

For many years, the only way that the user could interact with an operating system was through a **command line interface**, such as the one shown in Figure 14-1. A command line interface typically displays a prompt, and the user types a command, which is then executed.

Figure 14-1 A command line interface

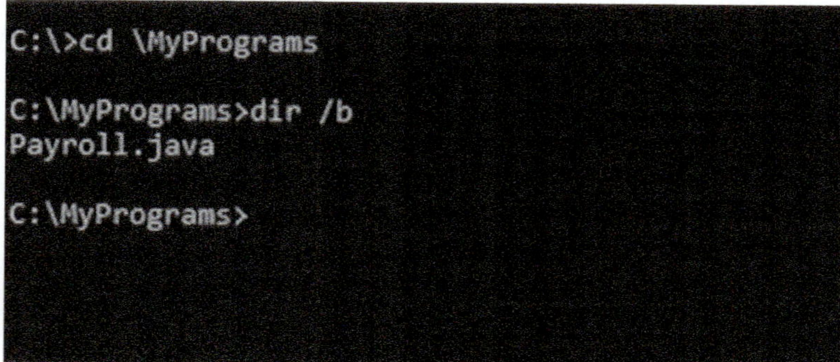

Microsoft Corporation

Many computer users, especially beginners, find command line interfaces difficult to use. This is because there are many commands to be learned, and each command has its own syntax, much like a programming statement. If a command isn't entered correctly, it will not work.

In the 1980s, a new type of interface known as a graphical user interface came into use in commercial operating systems. A **graphical user interface (GUI)** (pronounced "gooey") allows the user to interact with the operating system through graphical elements on the screen. GUIs also popularized the use of the mouse as an input device. Instead of requiring the user to type commands on the keyboard, GUIs allow the user to point at graphical elements and click the mouse button to activate them.

Much of the interaction with a GUI is done through **dialog boxes**, which are small windows that display information and allow the user to perform actions. Figure 14-2 shows an example of a dialog box that allows the user to change their internet settings in the Windows operating system. Instead of typing cryptic commands, the user interacts with graphical elements such as icons, buttons, and slider bars.

Figure 14-2 A dialog box

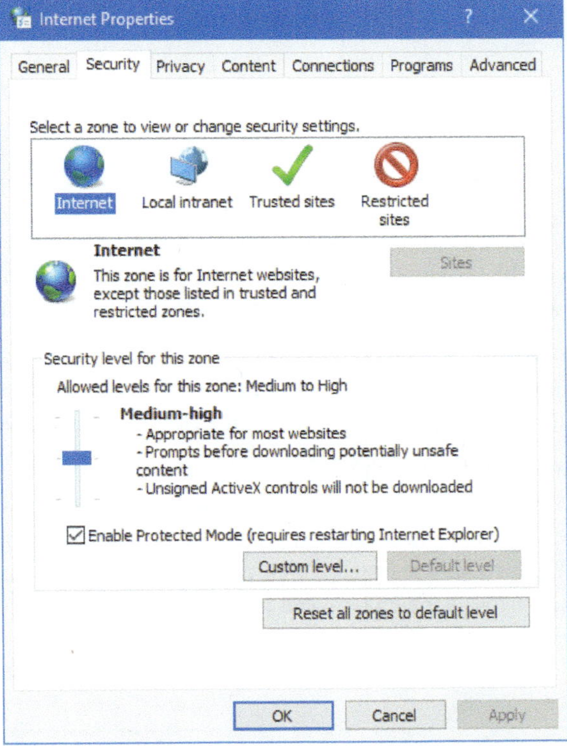

Microsoft Corporation

If you are developing software in an operating system that uses a GUI, such as Windows, macOS, or Linux, you can also use the GUI in the programs that you write. This allows you to incorporate standard GUI elements such as dialog boxes with icons, buttons, and so on into your programs.

GUI Programs Are Event-Driven

In a text-based environment, such as a command line interface, programs determine the order in which things happen. For example, consider a program that calculates the area of a rectangle. First, the program prompts the user to enter the rectangle's width. The user enters the width and then the program prompts the user to enter the rectangle's length. The user enters the length and then the program calculates the area. The user has no choice but to enter the data in the order that it is requested.

In a GUI environment, however, the user determines the order in which things happen. For example, Figure 14-3 shows a GUI program that calculates the area of a rectangle. The user can enter the length and the width in any order. If a mistake is made, the user can delete the data that was entered and retype it. To calculate the area, the user clicks the *Calculate Area* button and the program performs the calculation. Because GUI programs must respond to the actions of the user, it is said that they are **event-driven**. The user causes events to take place, such as the clicking of a button, and the program must respond to the events.

Figure 14-3 A GUI program

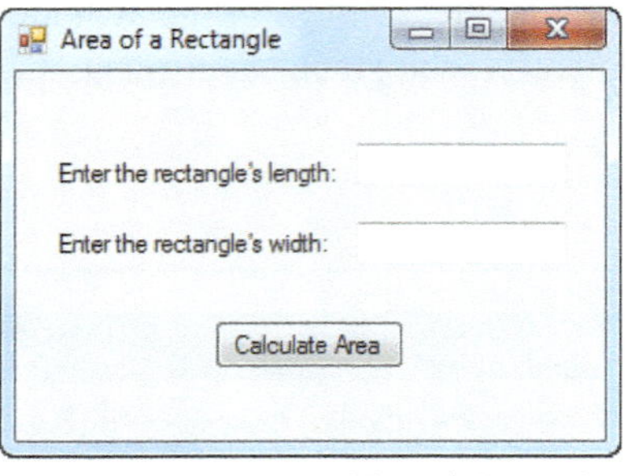

Microsoft Corporation

Creating a GUI Program

Many of the steps involved in creating a GUI program are the same as those that you have used to create text-based programs throughout this course. For example, you must understand the task that the program is to perform and determine the steps that must be taken to perform the task.

In addition, you must design the on-screen GUI elements that make up each window in the program's user interface. You must also determine how the program will flow from one window to the next as the user interacts with it. Some programmers find it helpful to draw a **user interface flow diagram**.

Figure 14-4 shows an example of such a diagram. Each box represents a window that is displayed by the program. If actions performed in one window can cause another window to open, then an arrow appears between the two windows in the diagram. In the diagram, notice that an arrow points away from Window 1 to Window 2. This means that actions in Window 1 can cause Window 2 to open. When a double-headed arrow appears between two windows, then either window can open the other.

Figure 14-4 A user interface flow diagram

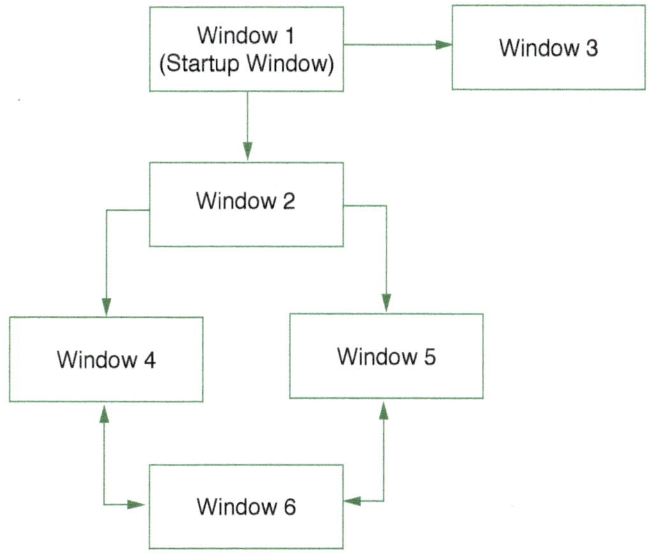

Checkpoint

14.1 What is a user interface?

14.2 How does a command line interface work?

14.3 When the user runs a program in a text-based environment, such as the command line, what determines the order in which things happen?

14.4 What is an event-driven program?

14.5 What is a user interface flow diagram?

14.2 Designing the User Interface for a GUI Program

When creating a GUI program you must design the program's windows and all of the graphical components that appear in them.

A GUI program's user interface consists of one or more windows that appear on the screen when the program is running. While creating a GUI program, one of your tasks is to design the windows and all of the graphical elements that appear in them. It is good practice to use generally accepted design standards for spacing, fonts, and color schemes to create functional user interfaces. These standards help make sure screens can be read by all users, no matter whether the screens are static, like a message or output display, or interactive, like a dialog box with input links or text fields.

Most languages have **integrated development environments (IDEs)** that allow you to construct a program's windows and its graphical elements visually without writing a single line of code. For example, Microsoft Visual Studio allows you to create GUI programs using the Visual Basic, C++, and C# programming languages.

The Java language does not come with an IDE, but Oracle provides a free IDE called NetBeans. You can download NetBeans for free from www.netbeans.org/downloads. Be sure to download the Java SE version.

Python does not have GUI programming features built into the language itself. However, it comes with a module named Tkinter that allows you to create simple GUI programs. The name "Tkinter" is short for "Tk interface." It is named this because it provides a way for Python programmers to use a GUI library named Tk. Many other programming languages use the Tk library as well. Python does include IDLE, a programming IDE, and you can use other IDEs, such as Replit.

C++ does not have GUI programming features built into the language itself. However, there are many third-party libraries and programming tools available that you can use to write GUI applications in C++. For example, Microsoft Visual C++ is very popular. You can use the Microsoft Visual Studio IDE to develop Visual C++ applications. Some free IDEs you can use for C++ include Visual Studio Code and Eclipse.

Most IDEs display a window editor that allows you to create windows, and a "toolbox" that displays all of the items that you can place in a window. You construct a window by dragging the desired items from the toolbox to the window editor. This is shown in Figures 14-5 and 14-6. The screen in Figure 14-5 is from Visual Basic, and the screen in Figure 14-6 is from NetBeans. As you visually construct the user interface in the window editor, the IDE automatically generates the code needed to display it.

Figure 14-5 Visually constructing a window in Visual Basic

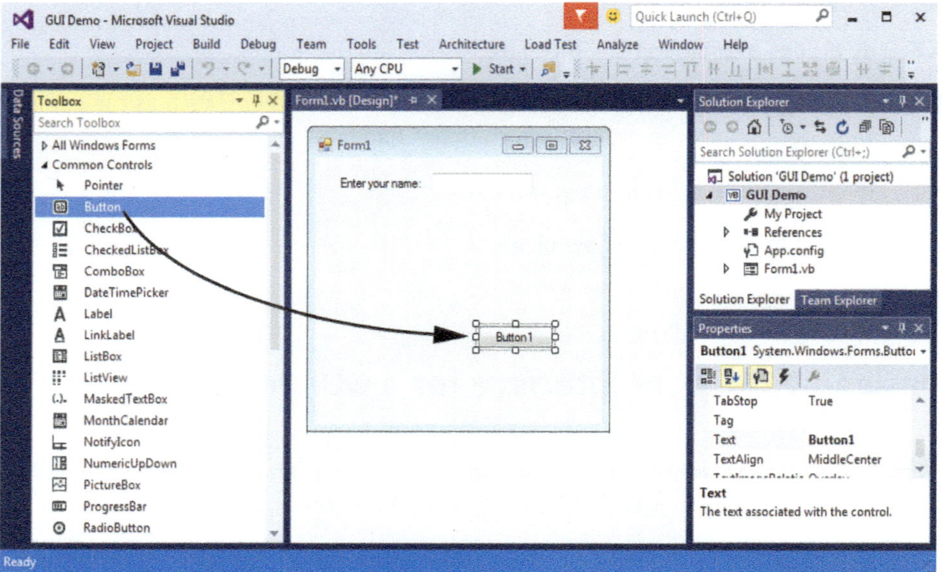

Microsoft Corporation

Figure 14-6 Visually constructing a window in NetBeans

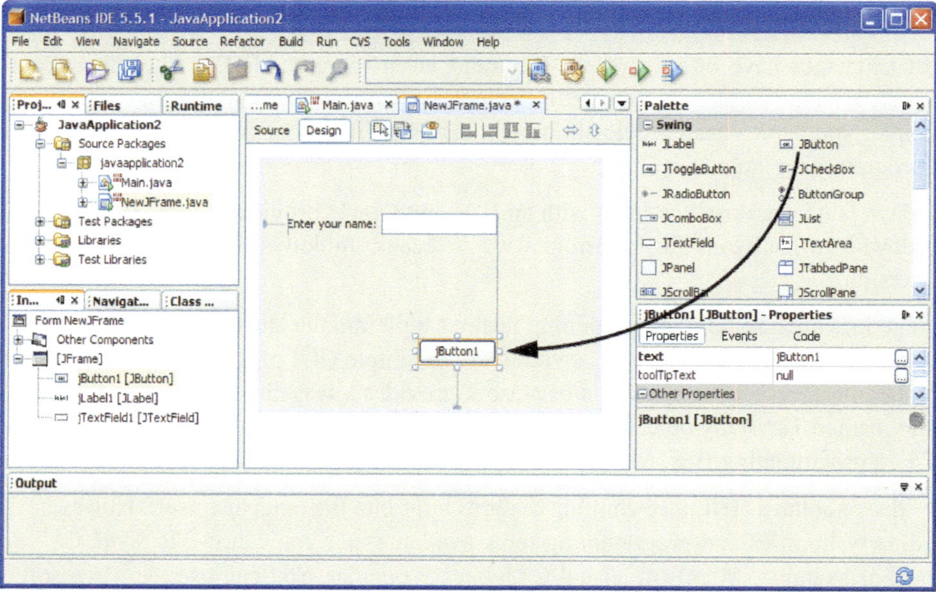

Microsoft Corporation

Components

The items that appear in a program's graphical user interface are known as **components**. Some of the common GUI components are buttons, labels, text boxes, check boxes, and radio buttons. Figure 14-7 shows an example of a window with a variety of components. Table 14-1 describes the components that appear in the window.

Figure 14-7 Various components in a GUI window

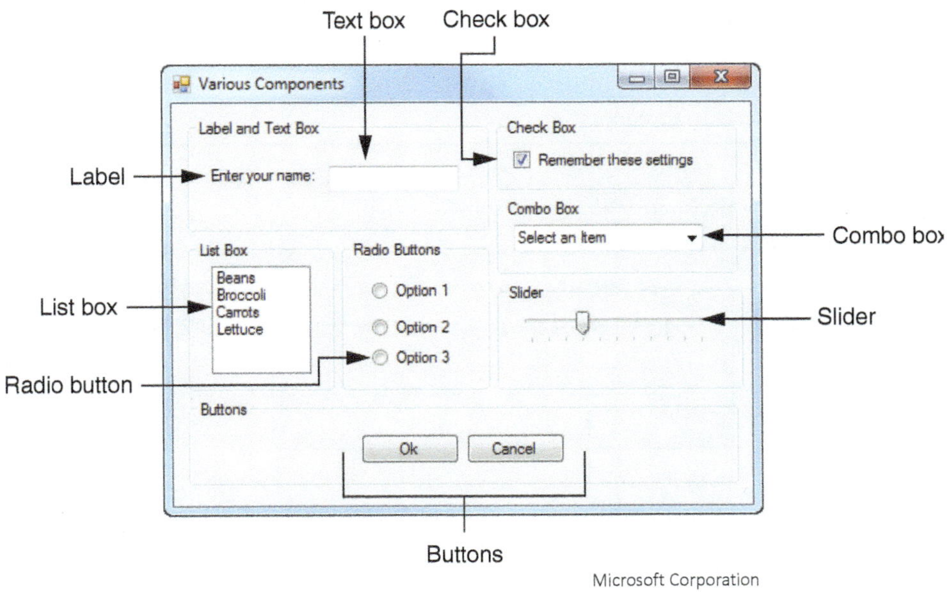

Microsoft Corporation

Table 14-1 Common GUI components

Component	Description
Button	A component that causes an action to occur when it is clicked
Label	An area that can display text
Text box	An area in which the user may type a single line of input from the keyboard
Check box	A component that has a box that may be checked or unchecked
Radio button	A component that can be either selected or deselected; usually appears in groups and allows the user to select one of several options
Combo box	A component (combination of a list and a text box) that displays a drop-down list of items from which the user may select; provides a text box in which the user may type input
List box	A list from which the user may select an item
Slider	A component that allows the user to select a value by moving a slider along a track

NOTE: GUI components are also known as *controls* and *widgets*.

Component Names

In most IDEs, you must assign unique names to the components that you place in a window. A component's name identifies the component in the program, in the same way that a variable's name identifies the variable. For example, Figure 14-8 shows a window from a program that calculates gross pay.

The figure also shows the names that the programmer assigned to each component in the window. Notice that each component's name describes the component's purpose in the program. For example, the text box that the user enters the number of hours worked into is named `hoursTextBox`, and the button that calculates the gross pay is named `calcButton`. Additionally, in most programming languages, the rules for naming components are the same as the rules for naming variables.

Figure 14-8 Components and their names

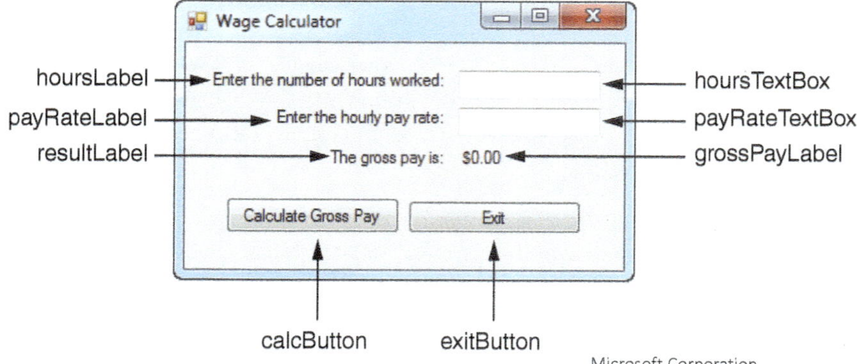

Microsoft Corporation

NOTE: In most IDEs, if you look at the code that is generated to display a window, you will see that each component in the window is an object, and the name that you have assigned to the component is used as the name of the object.

Properties

Most GUI components have a set of **properties** that determines how the component appears on the screen. Typically, components have properties that specify the component's color, size, and position. Like variables, properties can be set to values. When you set a property to a value, it changes some aspect of the component that it belongs to.

Let's look at an example from Visual Basic. Suppose you have placed a button in a window and you want to display the text "Show Result" on the button. In Visual Basic, the `Text` property controls the text that is displayed on a component, so you change the value of the button's `Text` property to "Show Result." This causes the text "Show Result" to be displayed on the button, as shown in Figure 14-9.

Figure 14-9 A button with its `Text` property set to "Show Result"

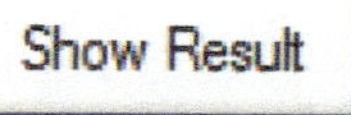

Most components in Visual Basic also have a property named `BackColor` that specifies the component's color, and another property named `ForeColor` that specifies the color of any text that is displayed on the component. For example, if you want to change the color of the text that is displayed on a button to blue, you set its `ForeColor` property to the value `Blue`.

Most IDEs allow you to set a component's properties while you are constructing the window. Typically, IDEs provide a **property window** that displays all of a component's properties, and allows you to change the properties to the desired values.

Constructing a Window—A Summary

Now that you have an idea of how GUI windows are created in an IDE, let's look at a simple set of steps that you can follow to construct a window.

1. **Sketch the window.**
   You should draw a sketch of the window before you start constructing it in the IDE. By doing this you will determine the components that are needed. At this point, it is often helpful to make a list of the necessary components.
2. **Create the necessary components and name them.**
   After sketching the window and determining the components you will need, you can start constructing it in the IDE. As you place each component in the window, you should assign it a unique and meaningful name.
3. **Set the components' properties to the desired values.**
   A component's properties control its visual characteristics, such as color, size, position, and any text that is displayed on the component. To get the visual appearance that you want, set each component's properties to the desired values. In most IDEs, you will use a property window to set the starting values for the properties of each component.

In the Spotlight:
Designing a Window

Kathryn teaches a science class. She has a program that her students can use to calculate the average of three test scores. The program prompts the student to enter each score, and then it displays the average. She has asked you to design a GUI program that performs a similar operation. She would like the program to have three text boxes that the test scores can be entered into, and a button that causes the average to be displayed when clicked.

On Your Own: Working alone or with a partner, plan and develop a GUI window that meets Kathryn's needs. Start by sketching the window and making a list of the components you will need. Then, use an IDE to create the window. Your instructor may tell you which IDE to use, or you may select one, such as Replit. When you finish, read on to see how closely your solution matches the one here.

Figure 14-10 shows a sketch of the window. The sketch also shows the type of each component. (The numbers that appear in the sketch will help us when we make a list of all the components.)

Figure 14-10 A sketch of the window

By examining the sketch we can make a list of all the components that we need. As we make the list, we will include a brief description of each component and a name that we will assign to each component when we construct it.

Component Number in the Sketch	Component Type	Description	Name
1	Label	Instructs the user to enter the score for test 1.	`test1Label`
2	Label	Instructs the user to enter the score for test 2.	`test2Label`
3	Label	Instructs the user to enter the score for test 3.	`test3Label`
4	Label	Identifies the average, which will be displayed next to this label.	`resultLabel`
5	Text box	This is where the user will enter the score for test 1.	`test1TextBox`
6	Text box	This is where the user will enter the score for test 2.	`test2TextBox`
7	Text box	This is where the user will enter the score for test 3.	`test3TextBox`
8	Label	The program will display the average test score in this label.	`averageLabel`
9	Button	When this button is clicked, the program will calculate the average test score and display it in the `averageLabel` component.	`calcButton`
10	Button	When this button is clicked the program will end.	`exitButton`

Now that we have a sketch of the window and a list of the components we will need, we can use our IDE to construct it. As we place the components, we will set the appropriate properties to make the components look the way we want them to. Assuming we are constructing the window in Visual Basic, we will set the following properties:

- The `test1Label` component's `Text` property will be set to "Enter the score for test 1:"
- The `test2Label` component's `Text` property will be set to "Enter the score for test 2:"
- The `test3Label` component's `Text` property will be set to "Enter the score for test 3:"
- The `resultLabel` component's `Text` property will be set to "Average"
- The `calcButton` component's `Text` property will be set to "Calculate Average"
- The `exitButton` component's `Text` property will be set to "Exit"
- The `averageLabel` component's `BorderStyle` property will be set to `FixedSingle`. This will cause a thin border to appear around the label, as shown in the sketch.

TIP: Although the properties listed here are specific to Visual Basic, other languages have similar properties. The names, however, may be different.

Figure 14-11 shows an example of how the window will appear. The figure shows the name of each component.

Figure 14-11 The completed window

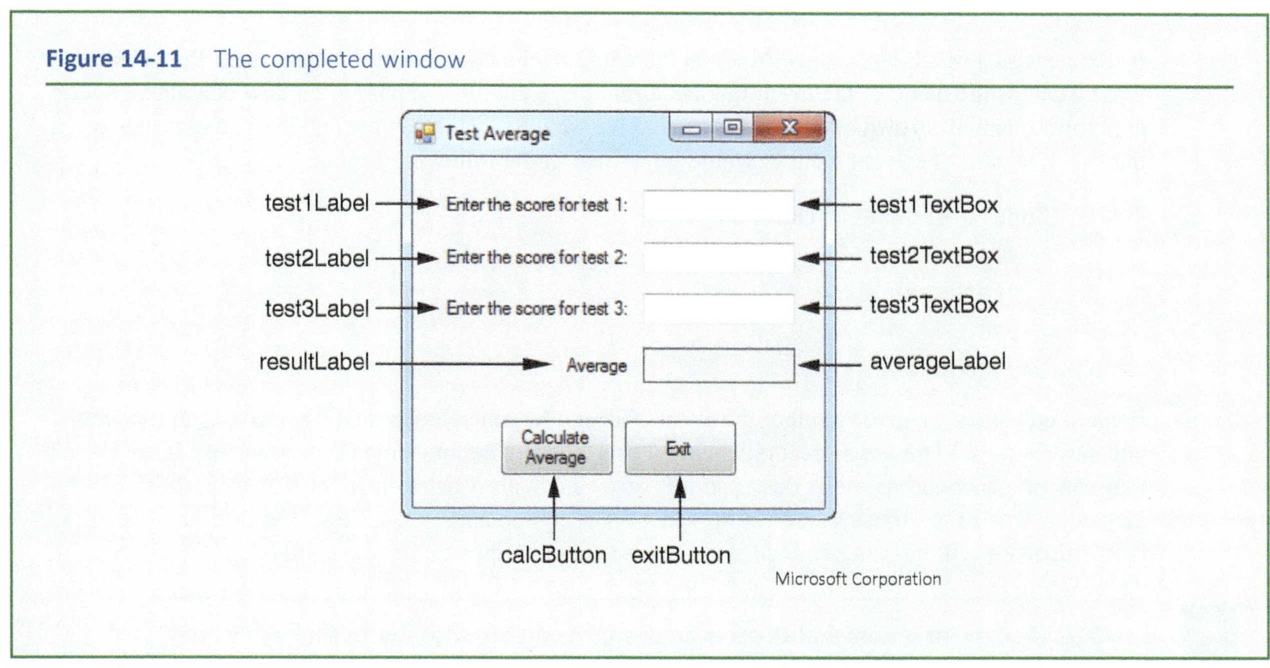

Checkpoint

14.6 Why was GUI programming complex and time consuming in the early days of GUI technology?

14.7 In an IDE that allows you to visually construct a window, how do you place an item such as a button in the window?

14.8 In the context of a GUI, what is a component?

14.9 Why must components be assigned names?

14.10 What do a component's properties do?

14.3 Writing Event Handlers

If you want a GUI program to perform an action when an event occurs, you must write code, known as an event handler, which responds to that event.

After you create a GUI program's user interface, you can write the code that responds to events. As previously mentioned, an **event** is an action that takes place within a program, such as the clicking of a button. Part of writing a GUI application is creating event handlers. An **event handler** is a module that automatically executes when a specific event occurs. If you want a program to perform an operation when a particular event occurs, you must create an event handler that responds when that event takes place. In pseudocode, our event handlers will be written in the following general format:

```
Module ComponentName_EventName()
  The statements that appear here
  are executed when the event occurs.
End Module
```

In the general format, *ComponentName* is the name of the component that generated the event, and *EventName* is the name of the event that occurred. For example, suppose a window contains a button component named `showResultButton`, and we want to write an event handler that executes when the user clicks it. The event handler would be written in the following format:

```
Module showResultButton_Click()
  statement
  statement
  etc.
End Module
```

Predefined names are given to all of the events that can be generated in a GUI system. In this example, you saw that a `Click` event occurs when the user clicks a component. There are many other events that can be generated as well. For example, an event with a name such as `MouseEnter` will be generated when the mouse cursor is moved over a component, and an event with a name such as `MouseLeave` will be generated when the mouse cursor is moved off of a component.

NOTE: If an event occurs and there is no event handler to respond to that event, the event is ignored.

Let's look at an example of how we can write an event handler in pseudocode. Previously in this chapter, you saw a GUI window for a program that calculates an employee's gross pay. For your convenience the window is shown again, in Figure 14-12. The figure also shows the names of the components.

Figure 14-12 A GUI window

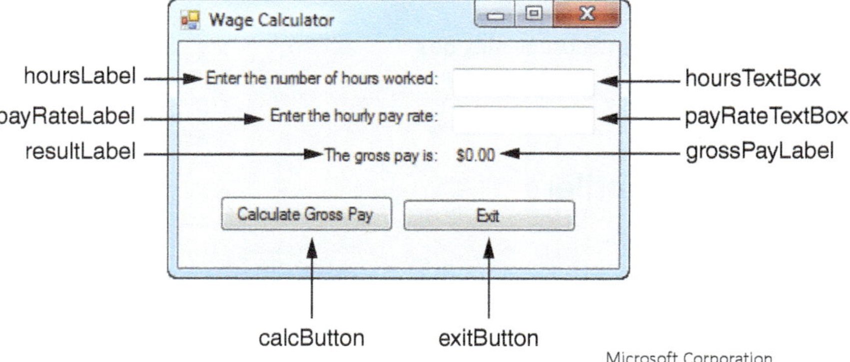

Microsoft Corporation

When this program runs, there are two possible events that we want it to respond to: the user clicking the `calcButton` component and the user clicking the `exitButton` component. If the user clicks the `calcButton` component, we want the program to calculate the gross pay and display it in the `grossPayLabel` component. If the user clicks the `exitButton` component, we want the program to end.

To handle the event that occurs when the user clicks the `calcButton`, we would write the following event handler in pseudocode, as shown in Program 14-1.

Program 14-1:

```
1  Module calcButton_Click()
2     // Local variables to hold the hours worked, the
3     // pay rate, and the gross pay.
4     Declare Real hours, payRate, grossPay
5
6     // Get the number of hours worked from the
7     // hoursTextBox component.
8     Set hours = stringToReal(hoursTextBox.Text)
9
10    // Get the pay rate from the payRateTextBox
11    // component.
12    Set payRate = stringToReal(payRateTextBox.Text)
13
14    // Calculate the gross pay.
15    Set grossPay = hours * payRate
16
17    // Display the gross pay in the grossPayLabel
18    // component.
19    Set grossPayLabel.Text = realToString(grossPay)
20 End Module
```

Let's take a closer look at each statement in this event handler.

- Line 4 declares three local variables: `hours`, `payRate`, and `grossPay`.
- Line 8 gets the value that has been typed into the `hoursTextBox` component and assigns it to the `hours` variable. A lot of things are happening in this line, so it deserves a thorough explanation.

When the user types a value into a text box component, the value is stored in the component's `Text` property. In pseudocode, we use dot notation to refer to a component's `Text` property. For example, to refer to the `hoursTextBox` component's `Text` property, we write `hoursTextBox.Text`.

In many languages, you cannot assign the value of a component's `Text` property directly to a numeric variable. For example, if line 8 were written as follows, an error would occur:

```
Set hours = hoursTextBox.Text
```

This logic will cause an error because the `Text` property holds strings, and strings cannot be assigned to numeric variables. So, we need to convert the value in the `Text` property to a real number. This can be done with the `stringToReal` function, as follows:

```
Set hours = stringToReal(hoursTextBox.Text)
```

- Line 12 gets the value that has been typed into the `payRateTextBox` component, converts it to a real number, and assigns it to the `payRate` variable.
- Line 15 multiplies `hours` by `payRate` and assigns the result to the `grossPay` variable.
- Line 19 displays the gross pay. It does this by assigning the value of the `grossPay` variable to the `grossPayLabel` component's `Text` property. Notice that a function, `realToString`, is used to convert the `grossPay` variable to a string. This is necessary because in many languages an error will occur if we try to assign a `Real` number directly to a `Text` property. When we assign a value to a label component's `Text` property, that value will be displayed in the label.

To handle the event that occurs when the user clicks the `exitButton`, we would write the following event handler:

```
Module exitButton_Click()
   Close
End Module
```

This event hander executes the `Close` statement. In pseudocode, the `Close` statement causes the window that is currently open to close. If the current window is the only one open, closing it causes the program to end.

The `Init` Module

Quite often, you need to perform some actions when a GUI application starts executing. For example, you might need to display some initial data in one or more Label components. In our pseudocode, you can perform these actions in the `Init` module. If a GUI application has an `Init` module, it executes automatically when the application begins running. For example, we might want to add the following `Init` module to the Wage Calculator program:

```
Module Init()
   Set grossPayLabel.Text = "$0.00"
End Module
```

This module initializes the `grossPayLabel` component's `Text` property with the string `"$0.00"`. As a result, the label will display $0.00 when the application starts running.

In the Spotlight:
Designing an Event Handler

In the previous *In the Spotlight* section, we designed the window shown in Figure 14-13 for Kathryn's test score averaging program.

Figure 14-13 The window for the test score averaging program

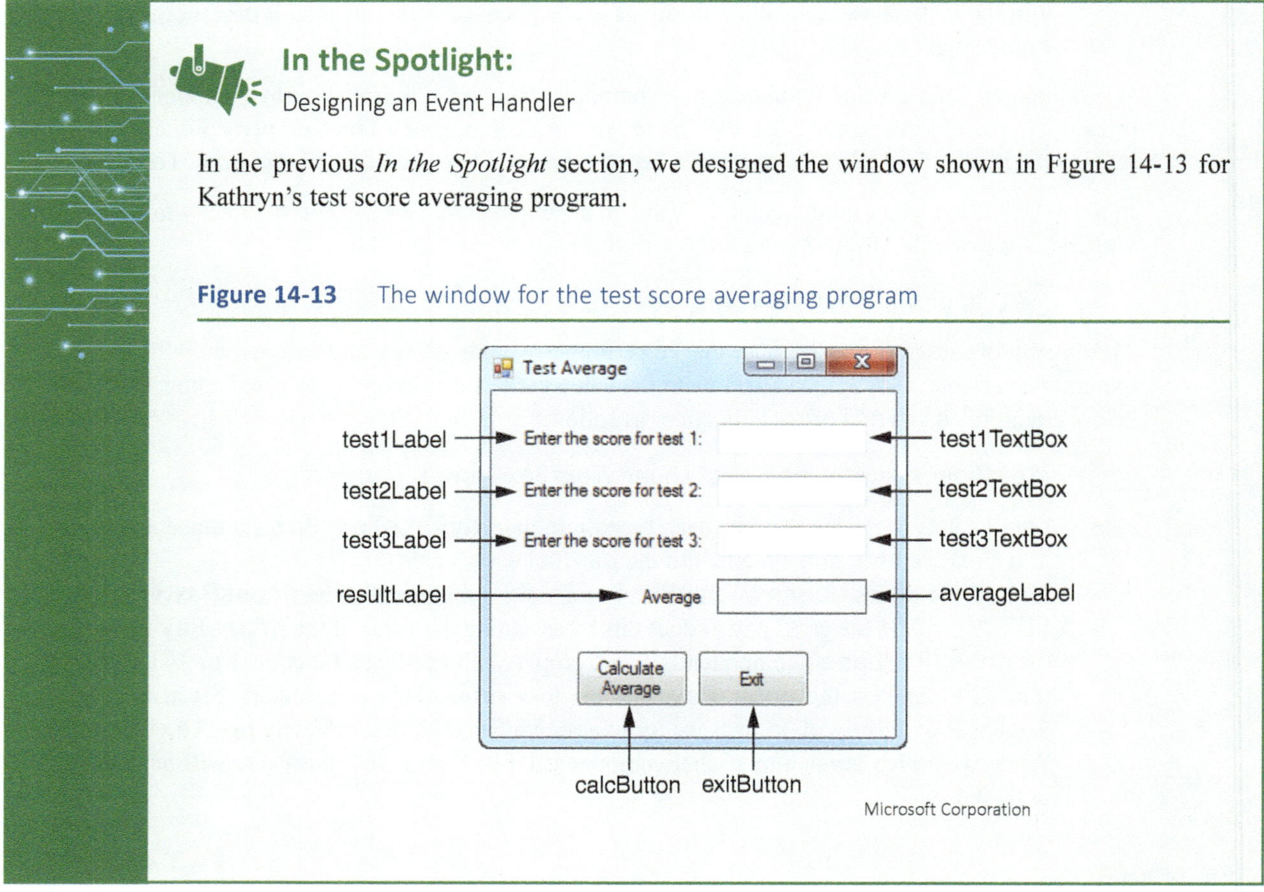

On Your Own: Working alone or with a partner, write the pseudocode to show both event handlers and an Init module that will display an initial value in the averageLabel component. You may want to use your IDE to actually create te event handlers and test them. When you have finished, read on to see how your code compares with Program 14-2.

Now, we will design the program's event handlers. When the user clicks the `calcButton` component, the program should calculate the average of the three test scores and display it in the `averageLabel` component. When the user clicks the `exitButton` component, the program should end. The pseudocode in Program 14-2 shows both event handlers, as well as an `Init` module that displays an initial value in the `averageLabel` component.

Program 14-2:

```
1 Module Init()
2    Set averageLabel.Text = "0"
3 End Module
4
5 Module calcButton_Click()
6    // Declare local variables to hold the test
7    // scores and the average.
8    Declare Real test1, test2, test3, average
9
10   // Get the first test score.
11   Set test1 = stringToReal(test1TextBox.Text)
12
13   // Get the second test score.
14   Set test2 = stringToReal(test2TextBox.Text)
15
16   // Get the third test score.
17   Set test3 = stringToReal(test3TextBox.Text)
18
19   // Calculate the average test score.
20   Set average = (test1 + test2 + test3) / 3
21
22   // Display the average test score in the
23   // averageLabel component.
24   Set averageLabel.Text = realToString(average)
25 End Module
26
27 Module exitButton_Click()
28    Close
29 End Module
```

The `Init` Module initializes the `averageLabel` component's `Text` property with the value "0". This causes 0 to be initially displayed in the label. Here is a description of each statement in the `calcButton_Click` module:

- Line 8 declares local variables to hold the three test scores and the average of the test scores.
- Line 11 gets the value that has been entered into the `test1TextBox` component, converts it to a real number, and stores it in the `test1` variable.

- Line 14 gets the value that has been entered into the `test2TextBox` component, converts it to a real number, and stores it in the `test2` variable.
- Line 17 gets the value that has been entered into the `test3TextBox` component, converts it to a real number, and stores it in the `test3` variable.
- Line 20 calculates the average of the three test scores and stores the result in the `average` variable.
- Line 24 converts the value in the `average` variable to a string and stores it in the `averageLabel` component's `Text` property. Doing this displays the value in the label component.

The `exitButton_Click` module executes the `Close` statement to close the window and subsequently end the program.

Figure 14-14 shows an example of how the program's window will appear after the user has entered values into the text boxes and clicked the `calcButton` component.

Figure 14-14 The window with an average displayed

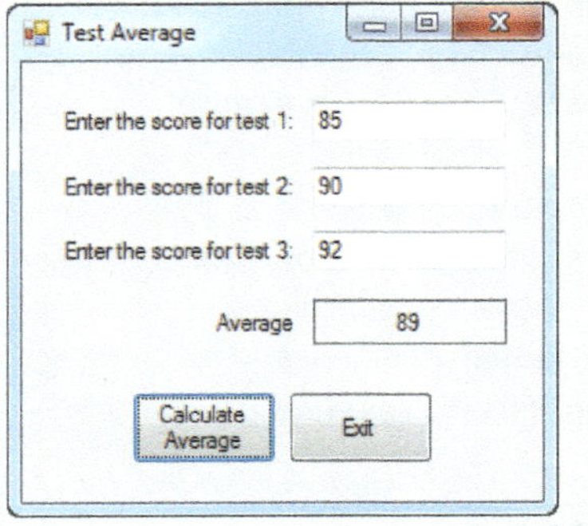

Microsoft Corporation

Checkpoint

14.11 What is an event?

14.12 What is an event handler?

14.13 Look at the following pseudocode and then answer the questions that follow it:

```
Module showValuesButton_Click()
   statement
   statement
   etc.
End Module
```

a. What event does this module respond to?

b. What is the name of the component that generates the event?

14.14 We introduced a module named `Init` in our pseudocode. What is the purpose of this module? When does it execute?

14.4 Designing Apps for Mobile Devices

Smaller screen size and special hardware capabilities typically require special consideration from developers creating mobile applications.

GUIs are used in applications, or **apps**, that are developed for mobile devices such as smartphones and tablets. The physical screens on mobile devices are much smaller than those used with desktop and laptop computers. As a result, the GUI for a mobile app is usually designed differently than the GUI for an application that is intended for a desktop or laptop computer. Also, mobile users typically interact with apps via a touchscreen, not a mouse and a physical keyboard.

These are important considerations that programmers must keep in mind when developing apps for mobile devices. Here are a few guidelines that mobile developers must follow:

- **Present less information at once**—Mobile apps must present less information per screen than traditional applications that are viewed on desktop and laptop computers. The content that will easily fit in one window in a desktop application must sometimes be separated into multiple screens in a mobile app.
- **Use larger font sizes for easier reading**—To reduce eye strain and make mobile screens easier to read, a larger font size is typically required.
- **Arrange components in a way that works for the smaller screen size**—Quite often, the user of a mobile device must scroll the screens in an app to see all their content. Because of this, the more important and the most often used components should be placed near the top of the screen.
- **Use components that work well with touchscreens**—Mobile apps need to use GUI components that work well in a touch environment, and are arranged in such a way that the user can easily interact with them. For example, you might discover that on a touchscreen it is difficult to select buttons that are placed near the edges of the screen. You might also discover that list boxes work better than combo boxes in a touch environment.

Using the Unique Hardware Capabilities of Mobile Devices

Mobile devices typically have capabilities that are not available on laptop and desktop computers. For example, smartphones can typically do the following:

- make and receive phone calls
- send and receive text messages
- determine the device's location
- detect the device's physical orientation in 3D space
- determine when the device is moving

These capabilities are possible because of specialized hardware components that most mobile devices are equipped with. A program, or app, that is running on a mobile device can interact with these hardware components. The program can obtain data from the components and, in many cases, cause the components to perform actions. In this section, we will look at some pseudocode and flowchart algorithms that interact with the specialized hardware components that are typically found in mobile devices.

NOTE: In our pseudocode, we will use generic programming techniques for interacting with a simulated mobile device. When you start learning to program for a specific type of mobile device, the syntax will be different. Much of the logic, however, will be the same.

Making Phone Calls

A smartphone's most fundamental hardware component is the one that makes and receives phone calls. In our algorithms, we will refer to this component as the PhoneCall component. Our PhoneCall component has a method named `makeCall` that makes a call to a specified phone number. (Recall that a method is a module or function that an object can execute.) Here is an example of how we call the `makeCall` method:

```
PhoneCall.makeCall("919-555-1212")
```

This statement causes the device to make a phone call to the phone number 919-555-1212. Note that the phone number is a string, and it is passed as an argument to the method.

NOTE: The PhoneCall component is a *non-visual component*. This means it does not visually appear in the app's GUI, like a Button or a Label. Non-visual components are objects that you cannot see in a GUI, but provide special capabilities to your programs.

Let's look at the design for a very simple app that uses this method. Figure 14-15 shows a simulated smartphone displaying the app's GUI. The app's GUI has a Button component named `callButton`, and another Button component named `exitButton`. When the user presses the `callButton` component, the app dials a predefined phone number and initiates a phone call. When the user presses the `exitButton` component, the app closes. Program 14-3 shows the pseudocode for the app's event handlers.

Figure 14-15 Screen for the Call Home Mobile App

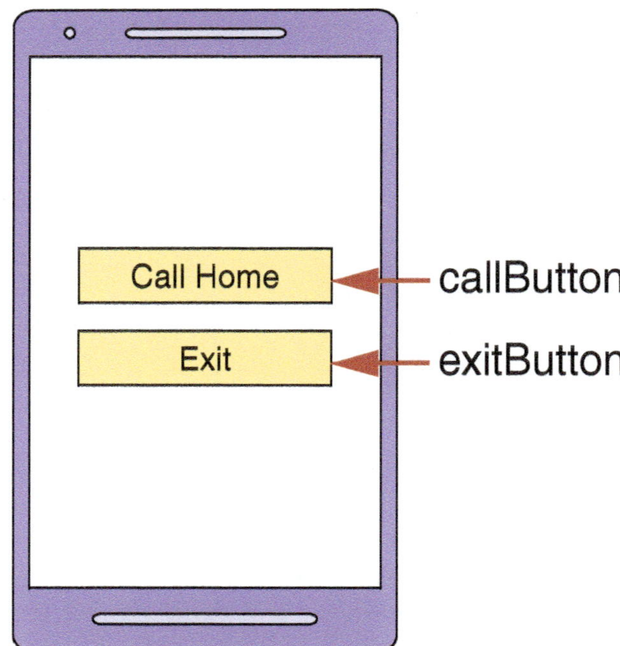

Program 14-3:

```
1 Module callButton_Click()
2    PhoneCall.makeCall("919-555-1212")
3 End Module
4
5 Module exitButton_Click()
6    Close
7 End Module
```

In the `callButton_Click` module, the statement in line 2 calls the PhoneCall component's `makeCall` method, passing the string "919-555-1212" as an argument. This causes the device to dial the specified phone number. In the `exitButton_Click` module, the `Close` statement in line 6 causes the app to end execution.

Sending Text Messages

Another important smartphone component is the one that sends and receives text messages. In our algorithms, we will refer to this component as the `TextMessage` component. Like the `PhoneCall` component, our `TextMessage` component is a non-visual component. The `TextMessage` component has a method named `sendText` that sends a text message to a specified phone number. Here is an example of how we call the `sendText` method:

```
Declare String phoneNumber = "919-555-1212"
Declare String message = "What time are you coming over?"
TextMessage.sendText(phoneNumber, message)
```

Notice that we pass two string arguments to the `sendText` method: the first is the phone number that the message will be sent to, and the second is the text that you want to send. This statement causes the device to send the text message *What time are you coming over?* to the phone number 919-555-1212.

Let's look at the design for a simple app that uses this method. Figure 15-16 shows the app's GUI on a simulated mobile smartphone screen. It has a Button component named `sendButton`, and another Button component named `exitButton`. When the user presses the `sendButton` component, the app sends a text message to a predefined phone number. When the user presses the `exitButton` component, the app closes. Program 14-4 shows the pseudocode for the app's event handlers.

Program 14-4:

```
Module sendButton_Click()
   Declare String phoneNumber = "919-555-1212"
   Declare String message = "I'm on my way home."
   TextMessage.sendText(phoneNumber, message)
End Module

Module exitButton_Click()
   Close
End Module
```

Figure 14-16 Screen for the Send Text Mobile App

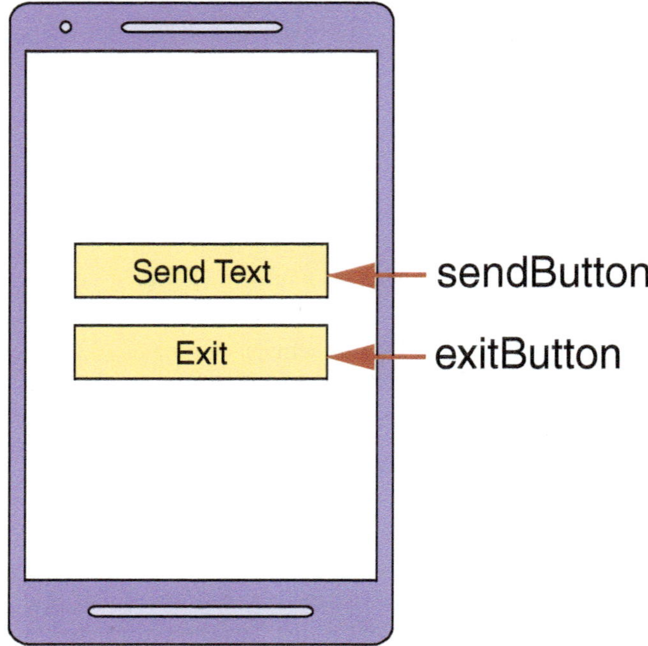

In the `sendButton_Click` module, the statement in line 2 declares a `String` variable named `phoneNumber`, initialized with "`919-555-1212`". Line 3 declares a `String` variable named `message`, initialized with "`I'm on my way home.`" Line 4 calls the TextMessage component's `sendText` method, passing the `phoneNumber` and `message` variables as arguments. This causes the device to send the text message *I'm on my way home* to the phone number 919-555-1212. In the `exitButton_Click` module, the `Close` statement in line 8 causes the app to end execution.

Receiving Phone Calls

In pseudocode, the PhoneCall component in our simulated mobile device generates an `IncomingCall` event when the device receives an incoming phone call. If you want your app to perform an action when the device receives an incoming phone call, you have to write an event handler in the following general format:

```
Module PhoneCall_IncomingCall()
    statement
    statement
    etc.
End Module
```

The statements that appear inside the `PhoneCall_IncomingCall` module will be executed each time the device receives an incoming phone call.

The PhoneCall component also has a property named `IncomingNumber` that holds the phone number, as a string, of the last incoming call. The following code shows an example of how to get the phone number from this property:

```
Declare String phoneNumber
phoneNumber = PhoneCall.IncomingNumber
```

After this code executes, the `phoneNumber` variable will hold the phone number of the last incoming phone call.

Let's look at an example app design that responds to an incoming phone call. Suppose you are going to be away from your smartphone for a while, and each time the phone receives a call, you want it to automatically send a text message to the caller indicating that you are away from your phone. Figure 14-17 shows the app's GUI on a simulated smartphone screen. It has one Button component, named `exitButton`. Program 14-5 shows the pseudocode for the app's event handlers.

Figure 14-17 Screen for the Call Auto Responder Mobile App

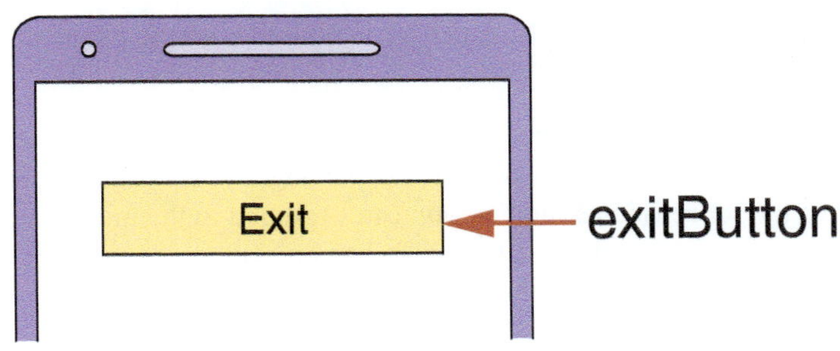

Program 14-5:

```
Module PhoneCall_IncomingCall()
    Declare String phoneNumber
    Declare String message = "I'll call you back later."

    phoneNumber = PhoneCall.IncomingNumber
    TextMessage.sendText(phoneNumber, message)
End Module

Module exitButton_Click()
    Close
End Module
```

In a nutshell, we can describe the app like this: When the app runs, it waits for incoming phone calls. When an incoming phone call occurs, it sends the caller a text message saying *I'll call you back later.* To close the app, the user presses the Exit button.

Receiving Text Messages

In pseudocode, the TextMessage component in our simulated mobile device generates an `IncomingText` event when the device receives an incoming text message. If you want your app to perform an action when the device receives an incoming text message, you have to write an event handler in the following general format:

```
Module TextMessage_IncomingText()
    statement
    statement
```

```
        etc.
    End Module
```

The statements that appear inside the `TextMessage_IncomingText` module will be executed each time the device receives an incoming text message.

The TextMessage component also has a property named `IncomingNumber` that holds the phone number, as a string, of the device that sent the last incoming text message. The following code shows an example of how to get the phone number from this property:

```
Declare String phoneNumber
phoneNumber = TextMessage.IncomingNumber
```

After this code executes, the `phoneNumber` variable will hold the phone number of the device that sent the last incoming text message.

Let's look at an example app design that responds to an incoming text message. Suppose you are driving, and each time the phone receives a text message, you want it to automatically send a text message back to the sender indicating that you can't respond to the message. Figure 14-18 shows the app's GUI on a simulated smartphone screen. It has one Button component, named `exitButton`. Program 14-6 shows the pseudocode for the app's event handlers.

Figure 14-18 Screen for the Text Auto Responder Mobile App

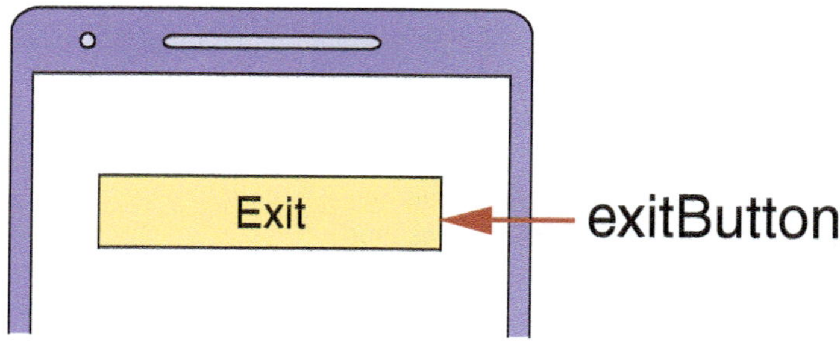

Program 14-6:

```
Module TextMessage_IncomingMessage()
    Declare String phoneNumber
    Declare String message = "I'm driving, so I'll reply later."

    phoneNumber = TextMessage.IncomingNumber
    TextMessage.sendText(phoneNumber, message)
End Module

Module exitButton_Click()
    Close
End Module
```

When the app runs, it waits for incoming text messages. When text message arrives, the app sends back a text message saying *I'm driving, so I'll reply later.* When the user is finished using the app, the Exit button can be pressed to close it.

Detecting the Device's Location

Most mobile devices are equipped with a location sensor. A **location sensor** is a component that can determine the device's latitude, longitude, and nearest street address. In our pseudocode, we will refer to this component as the Location component. Our Location component has the following three methods that we can use to get the device's location:

- `getLatitude()`—returns the device's latitude as a `Real` number
- `getLongitude()`—returns the device's longitude as a `Real` number
- `getAddress()`—returns a string containing the street address that is nearest to the device

Our Location component also generates a `LocationChanged` event each time the device's location changes. If you want your app to perform an action when the device's location changes, you have to write an event handler in the following general format:

```
Module Location_LocationChanged()
    statement
    statement
    etc.
End Module
```

The statements that appear inside the `Location_LocationChanged` module will be executed each time the device's location changes.

Let's look at an example app design that uses the location sensor. The app's GUI is shown in Figure 14-19, on a simulated smartphone screen. When the app starts, it displays the device's current latitude, longitude, and nearest street address in Label components. Each time the device's location changes, the app gets the new latitude, longitude, and street address, and updates the Label components with the new information. Program 14-7 shows the app's pseudocode.

Figure 14-19 Screen for the Get Location Mobile App

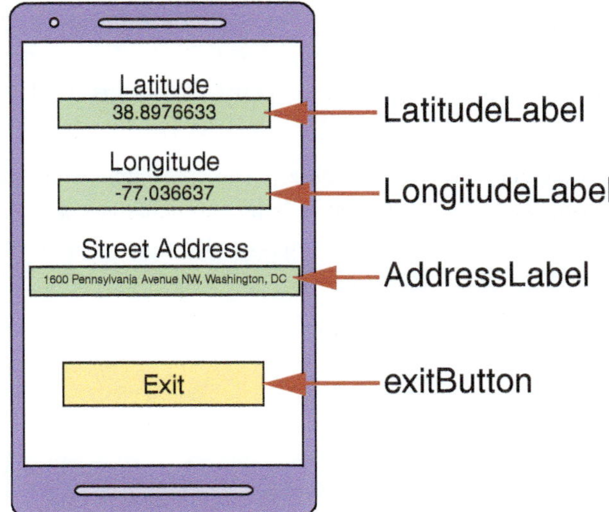

Program 14-7:

```
1 Module Init()
2    // Initialize the Labels with the device's
3    // current location.
4    LatitudeLabel.Text = realToString(Location.getLatitude())
5    LongitudeLabel.Text = realToString(Location.getLongitude())
6    AddressLabel.Text = Location.getAddress()
7 End Module
8
9 Module Location_LocationChanged()
10    // Update the Labels when the device's
11    // location changes.
12    LatitudeLabel.Text = realToString(Location.getLatitude())
13    LongitudeLabel.Text = realToString(Location.getLongitude())
14    AddressLabel.Text = Location.getAddress()
15 End Module
16
17 Module exitButton_Click()
18    Close
19 End Module
```

Let's take a closer look at the pseudocode. The `Init` module, shown in lines 1 through 7, executes when the app starts. It performs the following steps to display the device's initial location:

- Line 4 gets the device's current latitude, converts it to a string, and assigns the string to the `LatitudeLabel` component's `Text` property. Doing this displays the latitude in the Label component.
- Line 5 gets the device's current longitude, converts it to a string, and assigns the string to the `LongitudeLabel` component's `Text` property. Doing this displays the longitude in the Label component.
- Line 6 gets the street address nearest to the device's current location and assigns it to the `AddressLabel` component's `Text` property. Doing this displays the address in the Label component.

The `Location_LocationChanged` module is shown in lines 9 through 15. This module is an event handler that executes each time the device's location changes. The code in lines 12 through 14 get the device's latitude, longitude, and nearest street address, and displays this new information in the Label components.

The `exitButton_Clicked` module, shown in lines 17 through 19, closes the app when the user clicks the *Exit* button.

Checkpoint

14.15 Do mobile devices allow you to show more information on a screen than a desktop computer, or less?

14.16 Do mobile device screens typically require a larger font or a smaller font compared to desktop screens?

14.17 Name at least three unique capabilities that mobile devices usually have, compared to desktop computers.

14.18 What is a non-visual component? Give two examples that we discussed in this section.

14.19 Suppose you are writing pseudocode for an app that performs an action each time the smartphone receives an incoming call. How does the app know that a call is coming in?

14.20 Suppose you are writing pseudocode for an app that performs an action each time the smartphone receives an incoming text message. How does the app know that a message is coming in?

14.21 Suppose you are writing pseudocode for a mobile app that performs an action each time the device's location changes. How does the app know that the device's location has changed?

Chapter Review

Multiple Choice

1. The __________ is the part of a computer with which the user interacts.
   a. central processing unit
   b. user interface
   c. control system
   d. interactivity system
2. Before GUIs became popular, the __________ interface was the most commonly used.
   a. command line
   b. remote terminal
   c. sensory
   d. event-driven
3. A __________ is a small window that displays information and allows the user to perform actions.
   a. menu
   b. confirmation window
   c. startup screen
   d. dialog box
4. A type of program that is typically event-driven is the __________ program.
   a. command line
   b. text-based
   c. GUI
   d. procedural
5. An item that appears in a program's graphical user interface is known as a __________.
   a. gadget
   b. component
   c. tool
   d. graphic object
6. By specifying characteristics such as color, size, and location, __________ determine how a GUI element appears on the screen.
   a. properties
   b. attributes
   c. methods
   d. event handlers
7. An __________ is an action that takes place within a program, such as the clicking of a button.
   a. event handler
   b. anomaly
   c. event
   d. exception

8. A(n) __________ is a module that automatically executes when a specific event occurs.
   a. event handler
   b. auto module
   c. startup module
   d. exception

9. In our pseudocode, the __________ module executes automatically when the GUI application starts executing.
   a. `StartUp`
   b. `Init`
   c. `Auto`
   d. `Main`

10. The __________ component that we discussed in this chapter is an example of a non-visual component.
   a. Button
   b. Label
   c. TextMessage
   d. Text box

True or False

1. Many computer users, especially beginners, find command line interfaces difficult to use.
2. Writing a GUI program today is complex and time consuming because you have to write all of the code that constructs the program's windows without seeing it on the screen.
3. A component's `Text` property typically holds string values.
4. Predefined names are given to all of the events that can be generated in a GUI system.
5. A user interface flow diagram shows how a GUI program flows from one window to the next as the user interacts with it.
6. In our pseudocode, the `Init` module automatically executes when the application starts.
7. When developing GUIs for mobile devices and desktop computers, you typically use a smaller font with the mobile device than with the desktop computer.

Short Answer

1. When a program runs in a text-based environment, such as a command line interface, what determines the order in which things happen?
2. What determines how a component appears on the screen?
3. Describe how you typically change the color of a component.
4. Why must components be assigned names?
5. What happens if an event occurs and there is no event handler to respond to the event?
6. What is a non-visual component? Give an example of a non-visual component that we discussed in this chapter.

Algorithm Workbench

1. Design an event handler that will execute when the `showNameButton` component is clicked. The event handler should perform the following:
   - Store your first name in a label component named `firstNameLabel`.
   - Store your middle name in a label component named `middleNameLabel`.
   - Store your last name in a label component named `lastNameLabel`.

   (Remember, to store a value in a label component, you must store the value in the component's `Text` property.)

2. Design an event handler that will execute when the `calcAvailableCreditButton` component is clicked. The event handler should perform the following:
   - Declare the following `Real` variables: `maxCredit`, `usedCredit`, and `availableCredit`.
   - Get a value from a text box named `maxCreditTextBox` and assign it to the `maxCredit` variable.
   - Get a value from a text box named `usedCreditTextBox` and assign it to the `usedCredit` variable.
   - Subtract the value in `usedCredit` from `maxCredit` and assign the result to `availableCredit`.
   - Store the value in the `availableCredit` variable in a label component named `availableCreditLabel`.

3. The GUI for a mobile app has a Label component named `phoneNumberLabel`. Write an event handler that executes when the device receives an incoming phone call. The event handler should display the phone number of the incoming call in the `phoneNumberLabel` component.

4. The GUI for a mobile app has a Label component named `addressLabel`. Write an `Init` module that gets the street address nearest to the device and displays it in the `addressLabel` component.

Programming Exercises

VideoNote The Name and Address Problem

1. **Name and Address**

   Design a GUI program that displays your name and address when a button is clicked. Use generally-accepted design standards for spacing, fonts, and color schemes. The program's window should appear as the sketch on the left side of Figure 14-20 when it runs. When the user clicks the **Show Info** button, the program should display your name and address, as shown in the sketch on the right side of the figure.

Figure 14-20 Name and address program

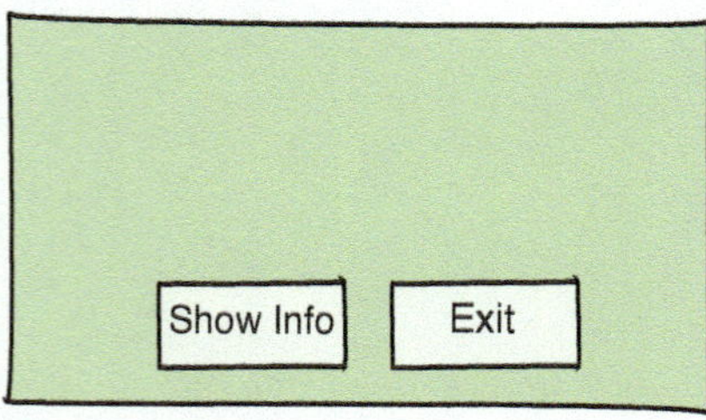

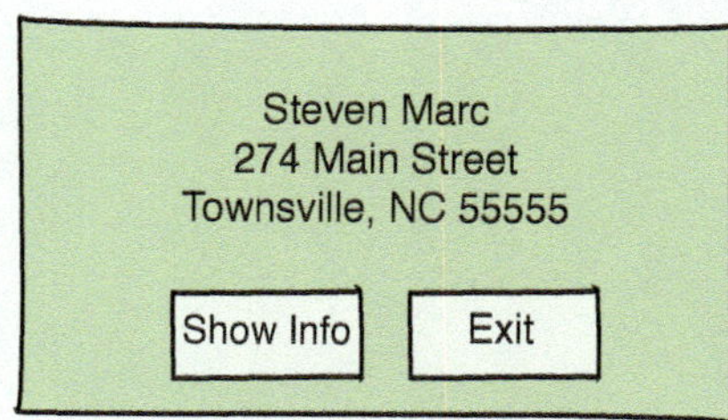

2. **Latin Translator**

Look at the following list of Latin words and their meanings:

Latin	English
autem	up
descendit	down
medium	center

Design a GUI program that translates the Latin words to English. The window should have three buttons, one for each Latin word. When the user clicks a button, the program displays the English translation in a label component. Use generally-accepted design standards for spacing, fonts, and color schemes.

3. **Miles-per-Gallon Calculator**

Design a GUI program that calculates a car's gas mileage. The program's window should have text boxes that let the user enter the number of gallons of gas the car holds, and the number of miles it can be driven on a full tank. When a *Calculate MPG* button is clicked, the program should display the number of miles that the car may be driven per gallon of gas. Use the following formula to calculate miles-per-gallon:

$$MPG = \frac{Miles}{Gallons}$$

4. **Celsius to Fahrenheit**

Design a GUI program that converts Celsius temperatures to Fahrenheit temperatures. The user should be able to enter a Celsius temperature, click a button, and then see the equivalent Fahrenheit temperature. Use the following formula to make the conversion:

$$F = \frac{9}{5}C + 32$$

F is the Fahrenheit temperature and C is the Celsius temperature.

5. **Property Tax**

A county collects property taxes on the assessment value of property, which is 60 percent of the property's actual value. If an acre of land is valued at $10,000, its assessment value is $6,000. The property tax is then $0.64 for each $100 of the assessment value. The tax for the acre assessed at $6,000 will be $38.40. Design a GUI program that displays the assessment value and property tax when a user enters the actual value of a property.

6. **Location Texting Mobile App**

Sometimes it is helpful to update another person with your current location via a text message. Design a mobile app that does the following:

- Allows the user to enter the phone number of the person that you wish to send the text message to.
- Provides a button that sends a text message to the last specified phone number. The text message should contain the street address nearest the mobile device.

Note that the user should not have to enter a phone number each time the text message is sent. When the text message is sent, it should go to the last phone number that was specified. If the user attempts to send a text message before a phone number is entered, the app should display an error message.

7. **Track Your Route**

   Design a mobile app that will write the device's latitude and longitude to a file each time the device's location changes. Use generally-accepted design standards for spacing, fonts, and color schemes.

CHAPTER 15 Preparing for a Career in Computer Science

TOPICS

15.1 Exploring Computer Science Careers

Careers in computer science involve designing and developing computers and computer programs.

The Information Technology Career Cluster

A career is a chosen field of work in which you try to advance over time by gaining responsibility and earning more money. The career you choose has a major impact on the kind of life you will lead. It determines the type of training and education you will need. It might impact where you live and the type of lifestyle you achieve.

The U.S. Department of Education organizes careers into 16 clusters, or groups. Career clusters help you sort career possibilities so you can pursue one that suits your interests and abilities. Information Technology is one of the career clusters. People with careers in information technology design, develop, support, and manage hardware, software, multimedia and systems integration services.

Within each of the 16 career clusters are related job, industry, and occupation types called pathways. Each pathway offers a variety of careers you might choose. The pathways in Information Technology include:

- Information Support and Services
- Network Systems
- Programming and Software Development
- Web and Digital Communications

People interested in computer science careers usually choose the programming and software development pathway. Careers in this pathway involve the design, development, implementation, and maintenance of computer systems and software. When you complete a course of study in the programming and software development pathway, you learn how to research, design, develop, and test operating systems-level software, compilers, and network distribution software. You also learn about creating, modifying, and testing the codes, forms, and scripts that allow computer applications to run. You can go on to use your skills in a wide range of industries such as medical, industrial, military, communications, aerospace, business, scientific, and general computer applications.

People who find satisfaction working in programming and software development take pride in designing, creating, and seeing projects through to completion. Some personal qualities that are helpful for success in computer science careers include:

- Independent
- Organized
- Analytical

Programming and software development professionals must have effective communication skills, a strong sense of self, and the ability to analyze and solve problems. Developing these qualities and skills will help you succeed in a computer science career.

Careers in Computer Science

Every industry that uses computer technology needs computer science professionals. Entry-level positions generally require a bachelor's degree. A master's degree may be required for advancement. According to the U.S. Bureau of Labor Statistics (BLS), in 2021, the median annual salary for computer programmers was about $93,000. The median annual salary for computer and information research scientists was about $131,500.

Knowledge of computer science can help you succeed in many careers. Even if you do not work as a programmer or computer scientist, the logic and problem-solving skills you learn in this course of study are highly valued by employers in many industries and will make you a strong candidate for other positions.

Some careers in computer science include:

- Computer programmer
- Computer system analyst
- Health informatics specialist
- Software developer
- Game designer
- Applications software developer
- Software application specialist
- Computer and information research scientist

Checkpoint

15.1 What is a career?

15.2 What pathway do people interested in computer science careers choose?

15.3 What are three personal qualities that are helpful for success in computer science careers?

15.4 What was the median annual income for a computer programmer in 2021?

15.2 Academic Planning for a Computer Science Career

There are many things you can do while in school to prepare for a computer science career.

How Education Affects Employment

Can you name one thing you can do to increase the amount of money you will earn in your lifetime? How about graduating from high school? Even better, graduating from college! (Figure 15-1.)

Figure 15-1 Employers prefer to hire graduates

Blend Images/Shutterstock

Graduates are more likely to be hired than non-graduates. They earn more money, are healthier, and live better lifestyles. Completing your education is one of the best things you can do for yourself and your career. Academic planning can help you reach that goal.

School also provides an opportunity to prepare for a career. Core subjects such as reading, writing, and math are vital for the career-search process. Science, social studies, music, art, technology, family and consumer sciences, and sports all help you gain knowledge and build skills you will need to succeed at work, such as teamwork, leadership, and problem-solving. School clubs and organizations also help you build skills for future success.

Education teaches you skills and information you need to get and keep a job. Most companies will not hire an employee who has not graduated from high school. Some will not hire an employee who has not graduated from college or university. If a company does hire non-graduates, it usually pays them less than it pays graduates.

Employers assume that graduates have certain characteristics that dropouts don't have. If a graduate and a dropout apply for the same job, the employer thinks that the graduate:

- Knows how to read and write.
- Understands basic math.
- Can communicate with others.

- Knows how to solve problems.
- Has a good work ethic.
- Has a positive attitude.
- Is self-disciplined.
- Is motivated to succeed.

Developing Communications Skills

Almost every employer wants workers who can read, write, and speak effectively. As a computer programmer, you will be called on to read and write documentation as well as emails and text messages with co-workers. You may have to explain your work to teammates and clients, and listen to others explain project goals. In all these situations, you will be expected to demonstrate the use of relevant topics and content, technical concepts, and vocabulary, and to use correct grammar, punctuation, and terminology.

In school, there are many opportunities to develop communications skills. Language Arts classes help you organize written information, understand the things you read, and speak out loud in front of an audience. Clubs and organizations also help you build communications skills. You can join the debate team to learn how to argue politely and effectively. You can write for the school newspaper or website. You can perform with the drama club.

Building Math Skills

Basic math skills such as addition, subtraction, multiplication, and division are vital for success in all careers. For example, you may need basic math to prepare budgets and invoices. You may use time-based mathematics to calculate the number of hours you worked and how much you should be paid. In a computer science career, you will have to apply mathematics knowledge and skill when you write code. You will need an understanding of algorithms to design a program. While in school, you can develop the necessary math skills by taking classes in algebra and geometry. Statistics also provides a good foundation for programming and software development. Other useful math skills include advanced algebra, calculus, trigonometry, and the ability to read and create charts and graphs.

Study Strategies for Success in School

People who do well in school usually work very hard. They know how to use study strategies—careful plans and methods—that improve their ability to remember new things. You can make study strategies part of your academic plan.

- **General strategies.** Sit near the front of the class so you pay attention; take notes; set a daily study goal, such as completing your homework.
- **Strategies for memory.** Study your notes soon after class; make flash cards with a key idea on one side and a definition or explanation on the other side.
- **Strategies for listening and note-taking.** Listen for clues that the speaker is giving a key point; underline or star the main points; use abbreviations for commonly used words.
- **Strategies for planning and organization.** Keep a calendar, schedule, or to-do list; write assignments and due dates in an assignment notebook and on a calendar; prioritize your responsibilities and tasks; break a large project into smaller steps, and set a deadline for each step.
- **Strategies for tests.** Ask your teacher what the test will cover and what type of questions it will include; don't wait until the night before to study—study a little bit each evening in the days leading up to the test; read test directions carefully; check your answers; skip questions you are unsure of and go back to them after you have completed the others.

Setting Goals for Postsecondary Education

Is a high school diploma enough education to land you the career of your choice? If not, you will want to start thinking about postsecondary education, or school after high school. For most people, postsecondary education means college or university, but it can also include military training and apprenticeships.

Many careers require a minimum of an associate's degree (two years after high school) and many require a bachelor's degree (four years after high school). Most computer science careers require a Bachelor of Science (BS) degree in a field such as computer science, information technology, or informatics.

Planning for postsecondary education involves:

- Selecting a school or program
- Making sure you have the necessary qualifications
- Applying for admission
- Obtaining financial aid

Goal-setting skills can help you manage the process from start to finish. They can help you stay focused on the educational objectives that you need to achieve your career goals.

Researching Universities

You can find information about different postsecondary opportunities online, in your school guidance center, and at the library. For example, you can look up a university's computer science program on the school's website. You should be able to find a Contact page where you can request information via email or regular mail.

When considering a postsecondary college or university, it is helpful to compare the computer science programs offered at multiple schools. Some things to consider include:

- What are the requirements for acceptance into the program?
- What are the requirements for completing a degree?
- How many years will it take to complete a degree?
- What courses or specialties are offered?
- What percent of students who start the program graduate?
- What percent of students who graduate are hired for a computer science career?

As you research the programs, ask yourself the following:

- **Where is the school located?** Will I live at home or on campus? Is it in a city or a small town?
- **How many students are there?** Will I be more comfortable in a small school or a large school?
- **How much does it cost?** What is the annual **tuition**—cost of education? How much is room and board—the cost of a dorm room and meals? Are there additional fees?
- **Am I qualified for admission?** Does my grade point average meet the school standards? Are my admissions scores high enough? Do I have the right extracurricular activities?

Things You Need to Apply to College or University

A college application form asks for information about yourself and your family. Most have space for listing your extracurricular activities and for a personal essay that tells the college about you, your goals, and your abilities. In addition to the application form, you will also need:

- **An official transcript,** which is a record of the courses you took in high school and the grades you earned.

- **An official score report,** which gives the results of the standard college entrance exam, such as the Scholastic Aptitude Test (SAT) or American College Test (ACT). Some states have their own entrance exams for state universities and colleges.
- **Recommendations,** which are forms that you ask one teacher and one counselor to fill out, describing your qualities as a student and a person.
- **Financial aid forms,** which provide information about your ability to pay tuition.

Nondegree Certificates

An alternative to a degree program at a college or university is a **nondegree certificate**. These certificate programs allow you to learn skills that may help advance your career without attending a college or university. For example, you might be able to earn a certificate for completing a course to learn a particular programming tool, such as C++ or Java. When you complete the program, you are awarded a certificate that shows you are qualified for work that requires those skills. You may complete certification programs before applying for a job or while you work to stay up-to-date on new developments in the field.

Some computer science-related certificate programs are sponsored by businesses that develop and sell programming platforms and other related products. For example, Microsoft offers certifications to software developers who use Microsoft products. Other certificate programs are run by educational institutions or professional organizations.

To earn a certificate, you will have to enroll in a training program, which can cost up to $5,000. You will also have to pay to take the exam, which may add up to $500 to your costs.

In most cases, a certificate alone will not guarantee you will be hired. However, when you combine it with other academic and career skills, a certificate may help you stand out from other job candidates and to advance once you are hired.

Checkpoint

15.5 True or false: A high school dropout usually earns as much money as a high school graduate.

15.6 In high school, what classes can help you develop math skills?

15.7 What are three things you can compare when considering computer science programs at colleges and universities?

15.8 What is a computer science-related certificate?

15.3 Developing Employability Skills

Employability means having and using skills and abilities to get hired and stay hired.

Career-Ready Practices

You might graduate from college with a bachelor's degree in computer science, but if employers think you are unfriendly, or if they question your confidence, they are unlikely to hire you. Attitude and confidence are part of employability. **Employability** means having and using your life skills and abilities to get hired and stay hired. It is more than just meeting the qualifications for a position. It also means knowing how to:

- Present your positive qualities to an employer.
- Communicate effectively with employers, co-workers, and customers.
- Meet your responsibilities at work.

Having employability skills will give you an advantage when you are ready to apply and interview for a position, no matter what career you choose. Use the following list of career-ready practices as a guide for the types of skills employers look for when hiring and promoting employees:

- Act as a responsible and contributing citizen and employee.
- Apply appropriate academic and technical skills.
- Attend to personal health and financial well-being.
- Communicate clearly and effectively and with reason.
- Consider the environmental, social, and economic impacts of decisions.
- Demonstrate creativity and innovation.
- Employ valid and reliable research strategies.
- Utilize critical thinking to make sense of problems and persevere in solving them.
- Model integrity, ethical leadership, and effective management.
- Plan education and career paths so they align to personal goals.
- Use technology to enhance productivity.
- Work productively in teams while using cultural global competence.

Employability skills can generally be placed into two groups: **hard skills** and **transferable skills**. Employers often look for people with hard skills to fill specific jobs. For example, a mobile app developer looks to hire people skilled at designing and developing software for mobile devices.

Transferable skills can be used on almost any job. They are called transferable skills because you can transfer them from one situation or career to another. They include:

- Problem-solving.
- Time management.
- Professionalism.
- Critical-thinking.
- Effective communication.
- Cooperation.

Solving Problems

Any barrier or obstacle between you and a goal is a **problem**. Problems pop up all the time. Mostly, we come up with a solution without thinking too hard. Knowing how to solve problems at work is a valuable skill. Employers like to hire problem-solvers. Clients and co-workers respect problem-solvers. Programming and software development are based on problem-solving strategies.

One way to solve a problem is to use a process, or **algorithm**, to figure out the best **solution**:

1. Describe the problem. This includes identifying the problem, its purpose, and its goals.
2. Consider all possible solutions for overcoming the problem.
3. Identify the consequences of each solution.
4. Select the best solution.
5. Make and implement a plan of action.
6. Evaluate the solution, process, and outcome.

Planning and Time Management Skills

Planning and time management are critical skills for succeeding at work. **Time management** means organizing your schedule so you have time to complete tasks and meet your responsibilities. To achieve your career goals, you will have to manage your time effectively and **prioritize** tasks—decide which tasks must be completed first.

Time management techniques include figuring out exactly how you currently spend your time, creating a schedule, making to-do lists, and ranking list items in order of importance.

- **You can create a time log to figure out how you are currently spending your time.** Simply track how much time you spend each day on specific tasks. The log will help you identify how you can use your time more effectively.
- **Scheduling helps you plan ahead because you know when you will do something and you can be ready for it.** You can schedule by any time period, but the most useful are by month, week, and day. For example, a monthly schedule can help you plan a project. You can schedule the time you need to meet with your team, conduct research, and complete your work. If you don't have a schedule, you might find yourself in the stressful situation of trying to complete the whole project in just a few days.
- **Making a to-do list every morning can help you plan your time for that day.** Prioritize the items on the list by ranking them in order of importance so you know what you should do first. If something doesn't get done, put it at the top of the to-do list for the next day.

You can make use of technology tools to automate some of your time management tasks and increase your **productivity**, which is the amount of work you accomplish. Computer applications can help you organize and meet your responsibilities, as shown in Figure 15-2.

Figure 15-2 Creating a schedule

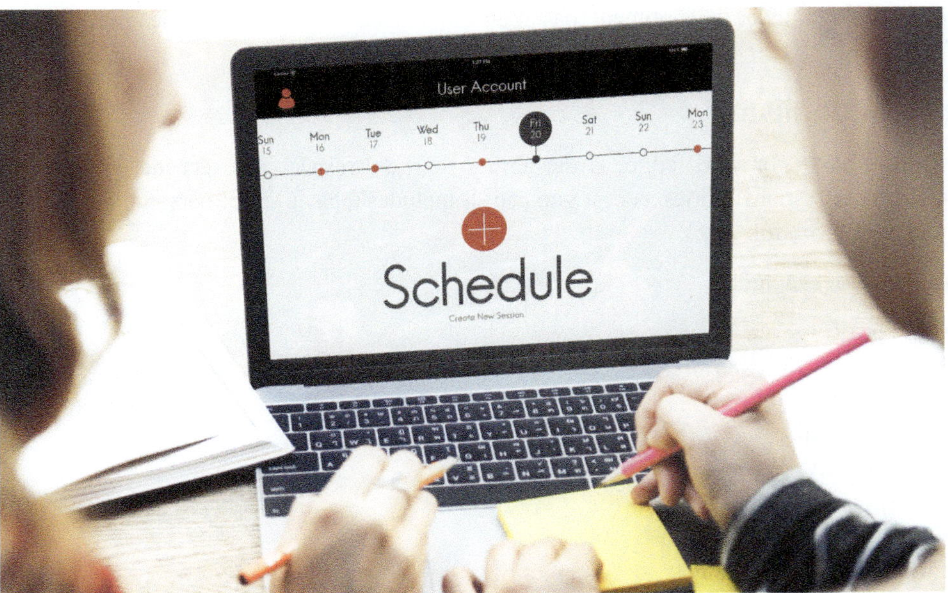

Rawpixel.com/Shutterstock

Make use of the calendar app on your computer or mobile device. You can enter schedules, phone calls, and appointments. Use the tasks list feature to record and prioritize the things you need to accomplish. Set the app to display a message or make a sound to remind you of deadlines. Apps can also help you complete the tasks on your to-do list. The more skilled you are at using applications, the faster and more efficient you will be at completing everyday tasks. Some applications such as Microsoft Excel even include templates for tracking projects or creating a to-do list or schedule.

Project Management

Employers value employees who know how to use project management skills to make sure work is completed on time. **Project management** is a process used to take a project from conception to completion. It helps you design and implement procedures to track trends, set timelines, and evaluate progress for continual improvement. There are four basic parts to the project management process:

1. **Identifying measurable objectives.** An **objective** is a short-term goal used to keep a project on track for completion. A measurable objective can be evaluated by specific standards.
2. **Identifying deliverables.** A **deliverable** is a product, or segment of a product, that can be provided to an employer, client, or the public.
3. **Setting a schedule.** The schedule should include a timeline with a final deadline, as well as milestones for achieving each objective. This helps you prioritize your tasks.
4. **Developing supporting plans.** Supporting plans usually specify things like how to allocate resources such as funds and technology, how to identify and manage risk, and develop methods for communication.

Many companies have project management software for scheduling, organizing, coordinating, and tracking project tasks. You can find basic project management templates in programs such as Microsoft Excel. There are also specific tools for project management, such as a **Gantt chart**, which is a horizontal bar chart developed by Henry L. Gantt in 1917, that shows a graphical illustration of a schedule, and a **PERT chart** (Program Evaluation Review Technique), developed by the U.S. Navy in the 1950s, which shows project tasks, the order in which they must be completed, and the time requirements.

These applications help you and your clients evaluate a project's success by tracking both the process and the product under development, based on established criteria, such as deadlines.

Professionalism

Professionalism, or work ethic, is the ability to show respect to everyone around you while you perform your responsibilities as best you can. It includes a basic set of personal qualities that make an employee successful.

These qualities include:

- Integrity
- Courtesy
- Honesty
- Dependability
- Punctuality
- Responsibility
- Cooperativeness
- Positivity
- Open-mindedness
- Flexibility

Professionalism also means you demonstrate positive work behaviors, such as regular attendance. A professional also maintains a clean and safe work environment, performs tasks effectively, shows initiative, and takes pride in their work accomplishments. These behaviors lead to advancement at work, in school, and in everyday life.

Employers and co-workers expect you to honor and respect time in the workplace. You can expect the same thing from them. That means:

- Showing up on time.
- Showing up every day—except vacations and holidays.
- Leaving for lunch and breaks at the scheduled time—not before—and returning promptly—not late.
- Staying until the end of the work day.
- Meeting your deadlines, which means completing all work before it is due.
- Taking care of personal business on your own time, not during work hours.

Respecting time at work shows that you respect your co-workers. It demonstrates to your supervisor that you take your responsibilities seriously. It is one way you prove you are ready for new challenges, such as those that might come from a promotion.

In the Spotlight:

Professional Appearance

Dress standards vary depending on the career that you choose. For example, you wouldn't expect a boom operator to be wearing a suit and tie, and you wouldn't want a business manager to be wearing grease-covered clothing. However, good grooming habits are required in all professions. The following are recommendations for maintaining a well-groomed, professional appearance:

- Wear clothes that are clean, neat, and in good repair.
- Wear clean and appropriate shoes.
- Keep your hair neat and clean.
- Brush your teeth at least twice a day.
- Floss daily.
- Use mouthwash or breath mints.
- Bathe daily.
- Use unscented deodorant.
- Keep makeup light and neutral.
- Keep jewelry to a minimum.
- Do not use perfume or cologne.
- Keep nails clean.

Thinking Critically

Critical thinking can help you evaluate your options in many situations. You can use it when you are making decisions, setting goals, and solving problems, both individually and when you are working with a team. When you think critically, you are honest, rational, and open-minded about your options. You consider all possibilities before rushing to judgment.

- Being honest means acknowledging selfish feelings and preexisting opinions.
- Being rational means relying on reason and thought instead of on emotion or impulse.
- Being open-minded means being willing to evaluate all possible options—even those that are unpopular.

You can think critically about a lot of things, not just decisions and problems. You don't have to believe everything you hear or read. You can question a news report, look deeper into the meaning of a magazine article, or investigate the truth behind a rumor.

When you think critically, you consider all possible options and other points of view. You look objectively at information. **Objective** means fairly, without emotion or prejudice. Then, you use your values, standards, and ethics to interpret the information subjectively. **Subjective** means affected by existing opinions, feelings, and beliefs. Looking at things both objectively and subjectively can help you make choices that are right for you.

Checkpoint

15.9 What is the first step in the problem-solving process?

15.10 What is productivity?

15.11 What is project management?

15.12 What are three qualities of professionalism?

15.4 Developing Communication Skills

Employers hire employees who know how to communicate effectively with clients, co-workers, and managers.

Effective Communication

Communicating is how people connect with others. Communication prevents misunderstandings. It gives you a way to share ideas. It even makes it easier for you to appreciate and respect other people's opinions.

At its most basic, communication is an exchange between a sender and a receiver. The sender transmits the message with a specific intent. The receiver interprets the message and responds.

- **Effective communication** is when the receiver and the sender understand each other.
- **Ineffective communication** is when the receiver and the communicators don't understand each other, whether they're aware of the confusion or not.

You can communicate effectively by using a six-step process:

1. **Be clear.** The receiver is more likely to get your message if you deliver it in a way they can understand. Speak slowly. Consider who you are talking to. You probably use different language when you talk to a client than when you talk to a friend.
2. **Be personal.** Use the other person's name or title so there's no doubt who you are talking to. Use an **"I" statement**—a statement that starts with the word "I"—to frame the statement in terms of you and your goals. An "I" statement indicates that you are taking responsibility for your thoughts and feelings. It helps the receiver understand your point of view and respond to you.
3. **Be positive.** Phrase your message in positive terms. Say what you want, not what you don't want. For example, say, "I want to start shooting at 9:30," instead of saying, "I don't want to start later than 9:30."

4. **Get to the point.** Follow the "I" statement with an explanation of the message you are sending. Explain how or why you feel a certain way, or how or why you think a certain thing. For example, say, "I want to start shooting at 9:30. I think that will give us enough time to get everything done without having to rush."
5. **Listen to the response.** Pay attention and use active listening techniques to make sure you hear the response.
6. **Think before you respond.** Make sure you understand the message. Repeat it, if necessary, and ask questions for clarification. Use critical thinking to make sure you are not letting emotions and preconceived ideas get in the way.

Ways to Communicate

Verbal communication is the exchange of messages by speaking or writing. For most of us, verbal communication is the most common way we stay in touch with other people in our lives. We talk face to face or on the phone. We send text messages, emails, and instant messages. We write blogs, tweet, pass notes, and send cards.

Talking is usually a very effective form of verbal communication. When you speak clearly and use language the receiver understands, they almost always gets the message the way you intend it.

Clear, concise writing is also an effective form of verbal communication, whether it is in a letter, report, email, or text message. However, sometimes the context can be lost through writing, because the receiver cannot hear the sender's tone of voice or see the sender's facial expression.

Nonverbal communication helps put words into context. This form of communication includes visual messages that the receiver can see, such as a smile when you are talking. It also includes physical messages, such as a pat on the back. During a conversation, the tone of your voice and the language you use combine to provide context for the words.

Reading and writing are also verbal communication. Effective writing is simple, clear, and to the point. It is free from spelling and grammatical errors. Effective writing usually uses the active voice rather than the passive voice. In the active voice, the subject takes action. In the passive voice, the subject is acted upon. For example, "She threw the ball." is in the active voice; "The ball was thrown by her." is in the passive voice.

When you write, you lose some of the context, which can make the communication less effective. Exchanging written messages doesn't take place face to face. It might be across great distances. When the receiver can't hear your voice, they might misinterpret the message.

There are different ways to read, depending on what you are reading. Passive reading is the kind of reading you do for entertainment, such as when you read a magazine or a comic book. In this kind of reading, you are just taking in information or following the plot. When you read critically, you take time to really think about what is written and why. Critical reading happens when you are actively engaging the subject as you read.

Critical reading is essential for success. Here are three steps you can use to be sure you are reading critically:

1. Determine the best reading strategy for the text. This means that you need to figure out whether to skim the text, read closely for detail, or read for meaning or critical analysis.
2. As you read, stop and think about what is being said and try to put it in your own words, or rephrase it from your own point of view.
3. Take notes while you are reading to make sure you understand and remember the main points.

Technical Reading and Writing

Technical communication explains technical or specialized information to people who may or may not be familiar with them. Its purpose is to convey very specific information, without extra words or language. In computer science, you will use **technical writing** to communicate your ideas and explain your work to a variety of people, including clients and co-workers. When you write technical information, keep your audience in mind. Be direct and to the point, use the simplest language possible, and define all terms that readers may not know.

Effective technical writing is:

- Clear
- Concise
- Complete
- Logical
- Sequential

Technical reading is a process that uses specific strategies to help you understand technical writing. These include:

- Skimming the document before reading to determine the information it is intended to convey.
- Noting or highlighting headings so you understand how the document is organized.
- Reviewing terminology at the start to make sure you know the meanings.
- Reading to identify key points in each sentence or paragraph.
- Writing an outline or summary to reinforce your understanding. This may include creating a concept map or other diagram that helps you visualize and remember the information.
- Rereading the information.
- Discussing the information with someone else who has read it.

Active Listening

Active listening is an important part of effective communication. When you are an active listener, you mindfully pay attention to the speaker and make sure you hear and understand the message.

Use these skills to be an active listener:

- Show interest using eye contact and positive nonverbal messages.
- Let the other person finish speaking before you respond.
- Ignore distractions such as cell phones and other people.
- Set your predetermined opinions and emotions aside.
- Repeat the message that you hear out loud, to make sure you received it correctly.

Active listening is a sign of respect. It shows you are willing to communicate and that you care about the speaker and the message. When you listen actively, the other person is more likely to listen when you speak, too.

Communicating at Work

Just as you use different types of verbal communication when speaking to your friends and your parents, you use different types of verbal communication when speaking to people with whom you relate on the job, such as your manager, your co-workers, your clients, and your **subordinates**—the people you supervise.

- **Your manager has a higher position in the company than you do and has control over your job.** When communicating with a manager, you usually use a formal style of verbal communication. You show deference—courteous regard or respect—by using their title and refraining from jokes or casual remarks you might use with a friend. You must also recognize that your manager has the final say on most matters, and so you must know when to agree with their decisions, even if you disagree with them personally.
- **Your co-workers, or colleagues, have the same rank in the company that you do.** This does not mean that you should joke around with them as you do with your friends. It also does not mean you should use the same style of verbal communication you would use with your manager. You can speak to them more casually.
- **Your clients are the source of your business.** When communicating with clients, remember the old saying, "The customer is always right." This means that in order to be successful, you must respect your clients and speak with them positively.
- **If you supervise others in the company, you communicate with them using the respect that is due to any worker.** You can also use an assertive or positive style of verbal communication, so that they know exactly what is expected of them.

Not only is what you say important, but so is how you say it. In addition to the different ways you can verbally communicate with others in the workplace, you can use different tones to make your meaning clear. These include:

- **Assertive speech,** which includes action verbs such as "should," "does," and "will."
- **Aggressive speech,** which you should avoid in the workplace, since it can lead to arguments or hurt feelings. An example of aggressive speech would be, "You better help me now!"
- **Passive speech,** which is usually best to use when you also want to show respect or deference. Examples of passive speech include words such as "can," "might," and "could."

Constructive Criticism

Criticism is an analysis and judgement of the positive and negative aspects of something, such as a product, design, work of art, or project. **Constructive criticism** is when the judgement is delivered as positive feedback that you can use to improve your work. Seeking and responding to feedback from peers, educations, and professionals is an important part of communication and collaboration. It can help you evaluate problem solutions so you can achieve a successful outcome.

Use these communication skills to seek and respond to feedback such as constructive criticism:

- When you offer constructive criticism, it is important that you deliver your message in a positive, friendly way so the recipient recognizes the value in your advice.
- When you receive constructive criticism, it is important that you listen carefully and consider the message as it is intended—to provide positive feedback to help you improve.

Checkpoint

15.13 What is effective communication?

15.14 What is nonverbal communication?

15.15 What are five qualities of effective technical writing?

15.16 What is one strategy you can use for effective technical reading?

15.5 Developing Teamwork and Leadership

Most computer science careers rely on teamwork and leadership to meet project goals.

A **team** is a group of two or more people who work together to achieve a common goal. When you are part of a team, you have access to all the knowledge, experience, and abilities of your teammates. Together, you can have more ideas, achieve more goals, and solve more problems.

A successful team relationship depends on all team members working together. They depend on and trust one another. If one team member does not do their share, the entire team suffers. The challenges of a team relationship come from having different people working together. Even if everyone agrees on a common goal, they may not agree on how to achieve that goal.

Most computer science projects require teamwork. For example, programmers may work with a partner, or with a group of other programmers, usually under the direction of a team leader or project manager. (Figure 15-3). Depending on the size and scope of the project, the team may also include an analyst, senior developer, junior developer, and client/subject matter expert. But, no matter who is on the team and what the team is doing, the interactions between team members will be most productive if the members of the team:

- Listen to each other.
- Respect each other's opinions.
- Recognize each other's skills and abilities.
- Share the work load.
- Share responsibility.

Figure 15-3 Programmers usually work with a team

Jacob Lund/Shutterstock

Developing Leadership Characteristics

Even when all members of a team have an equal role in making decisions and solving problems, it is important to have a **leader**. A leader is a type of manager who knows how to use available resources to help others achieve their goals.

Leaders exhibit positive qualities that other people respect, such as self-confidence, honesty, effective listening and speaking skills, decisiveness, respect for others, and open-mindedness. They are organized and supportive of the other team members. Being the leader does not mean you are always right. A strong leader considers the ideas and opinions of the other team members. An effective leader keeps the team on track and focused on achieving its goals.

Although you might have heard that someone is a "born leader," that's not usually the case. Becoming a leader takes time and patience. Leaders have to prove that they can make decisions, set goals, and solve problems. You can develop leadership characteristics by recognizing and modeling positive leadership qualities.

One way to do this is by participating in student leadership and professional development opportunities. For example, you can join clubs and activities such as your school newspaper, yearbook, drama club, or audio-visual club, and volunteer for leadership roles. You might also join a career technical student organization (CTSO) such as SkillsUSA. CTSOs offers members a range of individual and group programs, activities, and competitions designed to build professional skills as well as leadership qualities.

Qualities of an Effective Team Member

While a strong leader is important to the success of a team, team members must also be committed to the group's success. An effective team member helps teammates if they need help, does not blame teammates for problems or mistakes, and offers ideas and suggestions instead of criticism. Effective team members use critical-thinking skills and interpersonal skills to identify and solve problems, overcome conflict, and achieve their goals.

You are a good team member if you are:

- Open-minded
- Willing to compromise
- Cooperative
- Friendly
- Trustworthy

Checkpoint

15.17 What is a team?

15.18 What is a leader?

15.19 What are three qualities of a good team member?

15.6 Career Search Basics

Career search documents are your first chance to make a positive impression on a potential employer.

Career Search Documents

As part of a search for a career in computer science, you will need to prepare and organize the materials neccessary for a job search. Every job search requires the following:

- A resume, which is a written summary of your work-related skills, experience, and education. It introduces you to the prospective employer by presenting a snapshot of your qualifications. It should be brief, direct, true, and accurate with no typographical, grammatical, or spelling errors. A good resume attracts the interest of the reader so they want to learn more about you.
- A cover letter, or letter of interest, which is a letter of introduction that you send with a resume.
- A list of references that includes the names and contact information of people who know you and your qualifications and who are willing to speak about you to potential employers.
- A thank-you letter that you send to the employer after an interview to show your interest in the position.
- A portfolio, which is a collection of your best work that you can show a potential employer.

Cover Letter

A **cover letter** is a strong and succinct way to introduce yourself to a potential client or employer. It also helps convince employers to review your resume by focusing attention on specific resume information, such as credentials, skills, or specific projects in your portfolio. The letter should be concise and well-written, with no grammar or spelling mistakes. The cover letter is your first point of contact, so craft one that makes an excellent impression.

Resume

A **resume**, as shown in Figure 15-4, summarizes your training and experience. It is absolutely necessary when searching for a computer science position. Employers often have to sort through large numbers of resumes, so make yours informative, easy to read, concise, and very specific to the posted position.

Most resumes are first assessed by automated filtering systems that use algorithms to quickly scan hundreds of documents to find a match. That means they look for key terms that indicate the applicant meets the requirements the company is looking for. Make sure you include key terms relevant to the specific job you are seeking. Even when the resume is read by a human, that human is likely to skim the document looking for the same key terms.

In addition to relevant key terms, a resume should list your education, related experience, certificates you have earned, and skills. For a programming resume, you should list specific projects relevant to the job. Make sure to include the coding language and software you used and what you did specifically as a team member or leader on the project. You can even link the projects to your portfolio so employers can actually see the work.

Figure 15-4 A resume is necessary to apply for a job

Andrea De Martin/123rf.com

Here are some general best practice guidelines for a professional resume:

- Include a list of schools you attended, with dates and degrees you have earned.
- Include your work history, including internships and volunteer work. Emphasize jobs where you gained relevant experience, summarizing your responsibilities and skills with bullet lists.
- List all licenses and certifications you have earned.
- List relevant work samples, and/or provide links to an online portfolio where employers can view digital versions of your work.
- Use key words specific to the job requirements and qualifications. For example, if a job posting mentions experience with Python, make sure you include "experience with Python" on your resume.
- Make it easy to read. Leave space between lines so it is not crowded or overloaded.
- Use one easy-to-read font, and apply different font styles and sizes for emphasis.
- Emphasize and organize your text with bullet points.
- Use proper spelling, punctuation, grammar, technical terms.
- Keep it to one page, if possible—two pages at the most. (If you use two pages, be sure to put your name in the header or footer on page 2, in case it becomes separated from page 1.)
- If you are printing the document, use plain white paper.

Portfolio

A **portfolio** is your opportunity to show a potential employer what you are capable of. As a high school student, you might keep a portfolio that includes examples of your work from core subjects, along with a transcript of grades and awards you have won. As you begin looking for a computer science career, you will need to develop a portfolio of projects that show off your coding and other programming-related skills.

A **coding portfolio** provides concrete proof that you have the skills you claim on your resume. For example, having the key term "Python" on your resume might get you an interview, but a project that shows you really know how to use Python will get you a job.

If you have the skills, you can create your own portfolio website. Otherwise, there are many online sites where you can create a portfolio. Some sites specialize in portfolios for computer science careers, such as GitHub Pages for coders and Itch.io for game developers.

The portfolio should include information similar to your resume that explains your academic and word-related qualifications. But, the highlight should be the projects. Include at least four, and no more than ten.

Before you include a project in your portfolio, check it to make sure it is quality work. Clean up and improve the code, and add comments that will explain the work to the potential employer.

Filling out a Job Application

A **job application** is a standard form you will fill out when you apply for a job, as shown in Figure 15-5. You might fill it out in person when you visit a potential employer, or you might fill it out online. It requires a lot of the same information that you put on your resume, such as your contact information, as well as details about your education and work experience. It may ask for your Social Security number.

Figure 15-5 A typical job application form

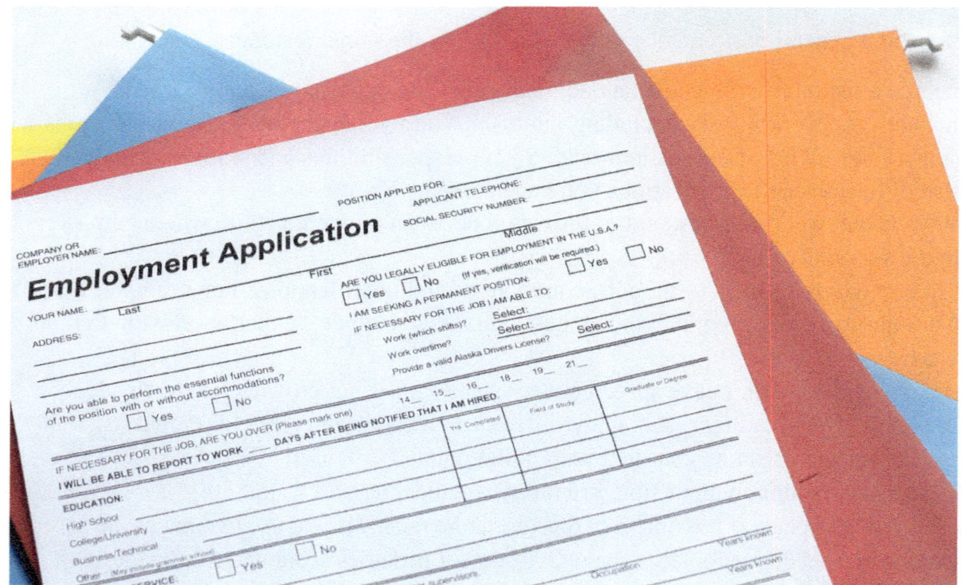

zwola fasola/Shutterstock

Filling out an application form may seem simple, but a lot of people make mistakes or forget important information. A messy or incomplete job application will not make a positive impression on the employer.

- Read the form before you start filling it out.
- Follow all instructions.
- Be truthful and accurate.
- Write neatly.
- Enter N/A for not applicable if there is a question that does not apply to you.
- Check your spelling and grammar.
- If you make a mistake, ask for a new form and start again.

You might find it helpful to bring a personal information card with you when you apply for a job. A personal information card is an index card on which you write the information you might need, such as your Social Security number and the contact information for your past employers.

Checkpoint

15.20 Why is it important to include relevant key terms on a resume?

15.21 True or False: You do not need a portfolio when searching for a computer science career.

15.22 How many projects should you include in a coding portfolio?

15.7 Conducting a Job Search

Finding career opportunities is hard work.

Finding Career Opportunities

The first step in applying for a job is finding out what jobs are available. How can you find opportunities that meet your needs and fit your strengths? You can use **job search resources**—tools designed to help you find **job leads**—to identify opportunities for employment.

You can use a variety of resources to identify available jobs. You will probably need to use more than one of the following resources.

- Networking is using your existing connections with people (friends, family, etc) to find job opportunities.
- Online resources let you access information and job listings on the internet.
- Career counselors help you identify jobs that match your skills, interests, and abilities.
- Employment agencies work to match employers with employees.
- Job fairs provide an opportunity to introduce yourself to many different employers.

Knowing how to make the most out of available job search resources is critical for finding a job.

What Is Networking?

Some studies show that nearly 80 percent of all job openings are never advertised. How can you find out about a job if it isn't advertised? Network! **Networking** in a job search means sharing information about yourself and your career goals with personal contacts—people you know already, or new people you meet in any area of your life. Hopefully, one of the contacts works for a company that is hiring, or knows someone at a company that is hiring. The contact recommends you for the position. Employers like to hire people who come with a recommendation from someone they know and trust.

How Do I Network?

The first step in networking is to tell everyone you know that you are looking for work. Be specific about your career goals. Tell your family, friends, classmates, and teachers. If you volunteer, tell the people at the volunteer organization. If you are a member of a club or organization, tell the other members. Stay in touch with your contacts through regular calls, texts, or email. Set up a networking file to keep track of each contact. Set up the file using index cards or a computer program. In the file, include:

- The name, occupation, mailing address, phone number, and email address of each contact.
- A reminder of how you know the contact. Are they a personal friend? Did you meet through someone else? Did you meet through a club or organization?
- Notes about each time you communicate with the contact. The first time you call a contact, explain who you are and why you are calling.

Do not ask for a job. Instead, ask for:

- Job leads.
- Information about occupations and companies, such as what trends are affecting a certain industry.
- Introductions to people who might become part of your network.

Remember to give the contact your phone number and email address so they can reach you. Always be polite, speak clearly, and say thank you.

Using Online Resources

The internet is the primary means for finding career prospects and job leads. Most companies post jobs online. You can even use the internet to make contacts for networking. Some of the more effective online resources include:

- Company websites. You can learn a lot about a company from its website, including what they do, the backgrounds of the people who work there, and who to contact in each department. Most sites also have a page listing job openings, with information to help you identify the duties and tasks for each job, and how to apply. Even if there are no openings for someone with your skills and abilities, you can contact the human resources department to try to set up an **informational interview**.
- Government sites. Like corporations, government agencies list information and job openings. There are also government websites that provide job listings.
- Industry sites. Many industries and industry associations have websites that list job opportunities. This is particularly true for graphic and web design jobs.
- Social networking sites. You can use social networking to meet contacts and learn about jobs. There are groups for people in certain careers, or who work for specific companies. Employers join these sites, as well. They look for potential employees based on the personal profile you create.

Using a Career Center

A career center is an excellent place to start a job search. Your school might have a career center that you can use free of charge. Career centers have job listings, research resources, and counselors who will help you identify jobs that match your skills and interests. They can also introduce you to former students who are now employed—giving you more opportunities for networking.

Employment offices are similar to career centers. Some are sponsored by the state or local government. They provide job search resources and assistance free of charge.

Private employment agencies charge a fee to match employees with employers. Sometimes you pay the fee, and sometimes the employer pays the fee. Sometimes you pay even if you don't find a job. They all have different policies, so be sure to ask before you sign a contract.

Managing Your Job Search Resources

Keeping your job search resources organized will help you follow up every possibility. When you are actively looking for work at many companies, it is easy to forget who you spoke to and even what you spoke about. An employer might not look favorably on someone who repeats the same conversation, or cannot remember who referred them in the first place.

- Keep a to-do list of tasks you want to accomplish each day, such as people you want to contact, resumes you have to send out, and thank you notes to write. Cross off each item you complete, and add new items as they come up.
- Contact some people in your network every day. Make brief phone calls, or send brief email messages to let them know you are looking for work, and to ask for assistance finding job opportunities.
- Follow up on all leads. Keep a record of the people you contact, including phone numbers, email addresses, and mailing addresses. Include the dates and times, the method of communication, and the result. Did they invite you in for an interview? Did they refer you to someone else?
- Get in the habit of using various media to report on your findings to someone who supports your job search.

Set up computer folders for storing document files that relate to your job search. Use the folders to keep track of information you send to each contact or potential employer, and the response you get back. The folder might include copies of the cover letter and work samples (in PDF format, perhaps) that you sent. It might also include notes you took during a phone call or interview, a brochure about the company, and copies of emails you received.

Internship Opportunities

Despite your best job search efforts, as a student or new graduate you might not have the computer science experience an employer is looking for. An **internship** is one way you can work while you build experience and develop skills. An internship is a position in a company in which you learn while you work. For example, an intern in a software development department might participate in team meetings, learn a new programming language, write code, and test software.

You can find internship opportunities the same way you find job opportunities. Use networking, online resources, career counselors, and job fairs. Some companies have formal internship programs that they post on their websites. If not, contact managers or human resources and ask if the company has internship positions, and if you can meet or speak to someone about them.

Most internships do not pay a salary, or pay very little. But, you earn valuable experience. If the intern demonstrates that they can learn and do the work, at the end of the internship they may receive a job offer.

Preparing for a Job Interview

If an employer thinks you have the qualifications for the job, you will be invited for a job interview. A job interview is a meeting between a job seeker and a potential employer—the interviewer. A preliminary interview may be by phone or video conference, but almost all employers will expect a face-to-face meeting at some point. The interview is an opportunity for you and the interviewer to ask questions and decide if the position is right for you.

A job interview is stressful. You are trying to make a good impression. You want to look and sound your best. You want the interviewer to like you and to respect you. You can rehearse how you will act or respond to questions during the interview, to boost your confidence.

Working with a partner is probably the best way to practice. You can take turns being the interviewer and the job seeker. If you are alone, practice in front of a mirror. If possible, record your practice so you can watch yourself.

- Be truthful.
- Pronounce your words in a strong, clear voice.
- Keep your answers brief and to the point.
- Use positive nonverbal communication, such as eye contact, relaxed arms, and good posture.
- Dress as you would for an actual interview.
- Avoid fidgeting or playing with your hair.
- Ask someone to critique your interviewing skills and use their comments to improve your technique.

After the interview, you should write a thank-you note. A thank-you note reminds the interviewer that you are serious about wanting the job. You use a thank-you note to restate your interest in the job and your qualifications and to thank the interviewer for spending time with you. Refer to something specific that you discussed during the interview. Address the note to the person who interviewed you. It may be acceptable to send a thank-you note by email, but mailing an actual printed letter will make a positive impression.

Comparing Job Opportunities

What happens if you are offered a job? A job offer is good news. But, before you accept the offer, make sure you have the information you need to make the best decision. You should evaluate and compare every opportunity to make sure the position is right for you. Some points to consider include:

- What are the responsibilities?
- What is the salary?
- What is the work environment?
- Are there benefits, such as health insurance and vacation time?
- When does the job start, and, for a contract or project-based position, when does it end?
- What are the hours?

When you have all the information you need, use the decision-making process to decide whether to accept the position or not. If you accept the offer, thank the employer and ask when and where you should report to work. You may have to sign a formal letter of acceptance, sign a contract, or write a letter of intent, which states that you are accepting the position.

If you reject the offer, you should still write a letter of intent, thanking the employer and stating that you are not accepting the position.

Checkpoint

15.23 What is networking?

15.24 What is an example of an online job search resource?

15.25 How can you practice for a job interview?

15.8 Ethics in Computer Science Careers

Ethical behavior is a responsibility for all computer science professionals.

Work Ethics

Recall that ethics are a set of beliefs about what is right and what is wrong. **Work ethics** are beliefs and behaviors about what is right and wrong in a work environment. Ethical behavior includes treating people with respect and also following the law. For example, taking credit for someone else's ideas is not ethical, and taking home office supplies is not ethical—it's stealing.

Ethical employees make ethical decisions, which means they consider how their decisions will impact others, including their employer. Ethical employees respect confidentiality. They do not share client information or sensitive company content with unauthorized individuals. Employers value employees who behave ethically at work. It shows that you are honest and respectful, so others will trust and respect you in return.

Behaving ethically at work also means following the company rules, regulations, and processes. Usually, when you start a new job, you are given an employee handbook. An employee handbook describes company policies and procedures, such as the process for requesting vacation time, and the different benefits that are available. It should also list all rules and policies that you are expected to obey. These might include:

- Maintaining confidentiality of information.
- Respecting copyrights and patents.
- Respecting co-workers' and customers' rights.

Ethics extends beyond the actions and behaviors of individual workers. It also applies to companies and organizations as a whole. A company that ignores the safety of workers, or hides information customers need to make an informed purchasing decision, is not behaving ethically. Sometimes an employee becomes aware that the employer is behaving in an unethical manner. In that case, the employee might be faced with a difficult decision about how to proceed. Options include speaking up in order to try to change the behavior or resigning. In some cases, it may include contacting the police or other law-enforcement agency to report illegal activity.

Legal and Ethical Responsibilities in Computer Science

Computer science professionals, including computer programmers, have many legal and ethical responsibilities. Some are the same as in any industry, such as treating co-workers and clients with respect, obeying all laws and regulations, and calling attention to negligent, illegal, unethical, abusive, or dangerous business practices. Some, however, are unique to computer science.

One of the most significant legal and ethical responsibilities for computer science worker is to stop **software piracy**, which is the act of enabling access to software illegally. This is an area in which computer science workers may be tempted to violate laws and policies for personal gain, but should also recognize the harm it does to their profession.

Another legal and ethical responsibility is to protect **proprietary information**. Computer science workers may have access to a company's trade secrets and other confidential information, such as copyrighted code. Proprietary information includes business information that is generally not available to the public, that has some degree of uniqueness, and that requires cost or effort to develop.

Many companies require employees to sign a **non-disclosure agreement (NDA)** that prohibits them from sharing proprietary information. However, there may be temptations for an employee to break that agreement. They may leave and start working at a competitor, or even be offered money to share the information.

Many computer science workers also have access to employee and client personal information. It is imperative that they follow all security protocols to maintain an individual's right to privacy. **Identity theft** and **fraud** are serious crimes. Computer science workers may be responsible for protecting systems from security breaches which could compromise personal data.

To help computer science professionals recognize and adhere to their legal and ethical responsibilities, some professional associations have developed their own codes of ethics and professional conduct. Both the International Association of Computer Science and Information Technology (IACSIT) and the Association for Computing Machinery (ACM) have their own codes of conduct. These codes include standards such as the following:

- Not misrepresenting or withholding information concerning the capabilities of equipment, software, or systems.
- Not using or taking credit for the work of others without specific acknowledgement and authorization.
- Protecting the privacy and confidentiality of all information.
- Not exploiting the weakness of a computer system for personal gain or personal satisfaction.

Equitable Access to Technology

The **digital divide** refers to the educational and economic divide that exists between people who have access to technology and those who do not. There are different causes for lack of access. It may be geographic—rural areas may not have reliable internet service. It may be physical—websites and programs may not use **accessible color schemes** or **alternate text** for images. Or it may even be content driven—input questions and images may display unintentional bias toward specific groups of people.

As a computer science professional, you may be in a position to influence the impact of technology on society. For example, if you are part of a team developing a database for collecting user input, you can identify and avoid prompts that may show bias. If you are designing a website, you can make sure to use accessible colors and images that reflect all of society.

In fact, your legal and ethical responsibilities include abiding by accessible technology laws and standards. For example,the Americans with Disabilities Act requires equal access to technology for all. The World Wide Web Consortium's Web Content Accessibility Guidelines provide guidance on designing websites that can be used by all.

Checkpoint

15.26 Why is taking credit for someone else's work unethical?

15.27 What is software piracy?

15.28 Why might a company have employees sign a non-disclosure agreement?

15.29 What is the digital divide?

15.30 What is accessible technology?

Chapter Review

Multiple Choice

1. What pathway do people interested in computer science usually choose?
   a. Information Support and Services
   b. Network Systems
   c. Programming and Software Development
   d. Web and Digital Communications

2. What quality will help you succeed in a computer science career?
   a. effective communication skills
   b. strong sense of self
   c. ability to analyze and solve problems
   d. all of the above

3. Which of the following is a career in computer science?
   a. game designer
   b. photojournalist
   c. emergency medical technician
   d. architect

4. When comparing computer science programs offered at universities, what should you consider?
   a. quality of food in the dining hall
   b. percent of graduates who get computer science jobs
   c. record of the football team
   d. school colors

5. Colleges and universities require you to submit a record of the courses you took in high school and the grades you earned, called a __________.
   a. certificate
   b. resume
   c. transcript
   d. recommendation

6. Companies such as Microsoft offer _____________ to software developers who use Microsoft products.
   a. bonuses
   b. jobs
   c. free computers
   d. certificates

7. Having and using your life skills and abilities to get hired and stay hired is called __________.
   a. hireability
   b. employability
   c. responsibility
   d. manageability

8. Any barrier between you and a goal is a __________.
   a. solution
   b. product
   c. problem
   d. algorithm

9. When you ____________ tasks, you decide which ones must be completed first.
   a. prioritize
   b. manage
   c. schedule
   d. identify

10. The amount of work you accomplish is one way to determine your ____________.
    a. productivity
    b. project management
    c. problem-solving
    d. critical-thinking

11. The process used to take a project from conception to completion is called project ____________
    a. productivity
    b. management
    c. solving
    d. responsibility

12. A horizontal bar chart that shows a graphical illustration of a schedule is called a ____________
    a. ORG chart
    b. PERT chart
    c. Gantt chart
    d. Venn chart

13. Which of the following demonstrates that you respect time at work?
    a. showing up on time
    b. returning late from lunch
    c. leaving early
    d. missing deadlines

14. ____________________ thinking can help you evaluate your options in many situations.
    a. quick
    b. critical
    c. emergency
    d. emotional

15. ____________________ communication is when the receiver interprets the message the way the sender intended.
    a. verbal
    b. nonverbal
    c. effective
    d. ineffective

16. Computer scientists use __________________ writing to explain their work to a variety of people.
    a. scientific
    b. technical
    c. complicated
    d. simplified

17. Most computer science projects require co-workers to work together in a __________.
    a. conference room
    b. online chat room
    c. team
    d. pod

18. A _______ is a type of manager who knows how to use available resources to help others achieve their goals.
    a. leader
    b. programmer
    c. executive
    d. teammate

19. On your resume, make sure you include ___________ relevant to the specific job you are seeking.
    a. a. pictures
    b. b. key terms
    c. c. code
    d. d. locations

20. A coding ___________ provides concrete proof that you have the skills you claim on your resume.
    a. diagram
    b. project
    c. letter
    d. portfolio

21. The act of enabling access to software illegally is called ___________.
    a. software theft
    b. software secrets
    c. software piracy
    d. software larceny

22. A(n) ______________ agreement prohibits employees from sharing proprietary information.
    a. non-disclosure
    b. disclosure
    c. non-discussion
    d. piracy

True or False

1. Careers in the programming and software development pathway involve the design, development, implementation, and maintenance of computer systems and software.
2. Computer system analyst is not a career in the field of computer science.
3. You can look up a university's computer science program online to learn about the requirements for acceptance.
4. You must attend a four-year university program to earn a nondegree certificate in computer science.
5. Time management is a transferable skill.
6. Coding is a transferable skill.
7. You can use an algorithm to solve a problem.
8. Scheduling is a good tool for time management.
9. The four basic parts to the project management process are identifying measureable objectives, identifying deliverables, setting a schedule, and developing supporting plans.
10. Critical thinking helps you rush to judgment.
11. Effective technical writing should be clear and concise.
12. Technical reading is just another way of saying reading technical documents.
13. You should include only one project in a coding portfolio.
14. It is ethical for a computer science professional to share information about clients and co-workers.

Short Answer

1. What are skills you study and develop careers in the programming and software development pathway?
2. Why do high school graduates earn more money than non-graduates?
3. What are four things to consider when you are comparing university computer science programs?
4. How can earning a certificate help you advance in a computer science career?
5. Explain how a schedule can help you with planning and time management.
6. How can you avoid ineffective communication?
7. What is a benefit of working in a team?
8. Why is it important to include key terms on a resume?
9. Examine and explain the importance of a portfolio for someone trying to start a career as a computer science professional.
10. How can you behave ethically at work?
11. How can computing technologies perpetuate inequalities and help to bring about equity in society?

Exercises

1. With your teacher's permission, research programs in computer science at two different universities. You may do this on the internet, in a library, or by contacting the universities directly. Use technical reading strategies to make sure you understand the information you find. Use critical thinking to evaluate the information, and only use content that is valid and accurate. Record and cite all source information. When your research is complete, write a paragraph comparing the two programs and explaining which you would choose and why. Read your paragraph to a partner or to the class.

2. Alone, with a partner, or with a small group, and with your teacher's permission, use the internet or other resources to investigate and explore careers in computer science. Employee effective technical reading strategies to make sure you understand the information you find. Use critical thinking to evaluate the information, and only use content that is valid and accurate. Record and cite all source information. When your research is complete, make a three-column chart. In one column, identify at least three jobs available in the programming and software development pathway. In the second column, identify the type of business or industry in which someone in that position might work. In the third column, identify the job duties and tasks. Select one of the careers and employ effective technical writing skills to write a fact sheet explaining the career, including information about job duties and tasks. Report your research in a presentation, on a published web page, or in a printed paragraph.

3. Using the information on one of the careers you researched in exercise 2, create an online job posting for the position. Then, create a cover letter and resume for someone applying for that career. Exchange documents with a classmate. Provide constructive criticism to your classmate, and use the feedback you receive to improve your documents. Create a portfolio that includes the cover letter and resume. Write a paragraph examining the role of resumes and portfolios for computer science professionals.

4. Use the techniques described in this chapter to investigate and identify companies or organizations that hire computer science professionals. Explore the career and internship opportunities by contacting at least two of the companies. Locate or request information about the education and experience they look for when hiring. Ask if they have internship programs and if you could meet with someone for an informational interview. Report what you learn to a partner or to the class.

5. Alone, with a partner, or with a small group, and with your teacher's permission, use the internet to research certificates in the computer science field. Employ effective technical reading strategies to make sure you understand the information you find. Use critical thinking to evaluate the information, and only use content that is valid and accurate. Record and cite all source information. When your research is complete, create a presentation examining the role of certification in computer science professions and explaining why earning certificates can be an important part of a career in computer science. Deliver your presentation to another group or to the class.

6. Working in small teams, plan a presentation about legal and ethical responsibilities in relation to the field of computer science. Demonstrate problem-solving, planning, and time-management skills such as project management to organize the project. You may want to use a project management template in a program such as Excel. Take turns so each team member has the opportunity to demonstrate team leadership skills and function effectively as a team member.. With your teacher's permission, use the internet to research the topic using effective technical reading skills. Use critical thinking to evaluate the information that you find online, and only use content that is valid and accurate. Record and cite all source information. When your research is complete, compile the information into a presentation that communicates your understanding of legal and ethical responsibilities in relation to the field of computer science. Employ effective writing skills to develop a script to accompany the slides. Take turns employing effective verbal and nonverbal communications skills to read the script out loud and deliver the presentation.

CHAPTER 16

Digital Citzenship

TOPICS

16.1 Responsible Use of Technology

A responsible user of technology respects the legal rights of individuals and corporations.

Using Software and Other Assets Legally

Software is a **digital asset**, which means it is stored digitally and has value. Other digital assets include documents and media files, such as videos and images. Some digital assets are available to use and share for free, but most require a subscription or purchase. Table 16-1 lists types of legal software. (The categories apply to most digital assets.)

Table 16.1 Categories of Software

Commercial software	Copyrighted software, also called proprietary software. The company or individual that developed the software owns the copyright. This means it is illegal for others to sell it, give it away, or even share it. When you buy commercial software, you are paying for the right to use the software, not necessarily for the right to the software's code. Software where the user doesn't gain access to the program's code is also called closed-source software.
Open-source software	A program, like proprietary software, and you may have to pay for it. Unlike proprietary software, it makes the source code available to the public. The idea is that the software will improve and benefit from the innovations of users, who troubleshoot weak points and expand features.
Public domain software	Software that the developers or authors allow others to use, copy, share, and even alter for free.

Shareware	Copyrighted software that you can use on a try-before-you-buy basis. If you decide to keep it, you must pay a fee.
Freeware	Copyrighted software that the copyright owner gives away for free on the condition that users do not resell it.

Proprietary, copyrighted software comes with a software license, which allows the buyer to use and install the program and sometimes entitles the buyer to receive free or reduced-cost support and updates. A **software license** is a legally-binding agreement between the software producer and the user. It specifies the terms of use and defines the rights of both the software producer and the user.

Individuals might buy a single-user license for one copy of the program or a single-seat license to install the program on a single device. Organizations such as schools or businesses usually buy a volume or site license, which lets them install on multiple systems or a network for multiple users. Network licensing generally costs less per user and allows users to share resources.

Copyright

Federal laws that involve **copyright** protect individuals and companies from the theft or misuse of their **intellectual property**, such as creative, literary, or artistic work. This includes software code.

Copyright exists as soon as a work is created, but the creator can register it with the U.S. Copyright Office. It is a crime to copy this kind of work without the permission of the person who owns the copyright to it. Penalties include paying a large fine and possibly jail time.

Copyright laws protect software developers from the misuse of their intellectual property by others. Someone who pretends that another person's work is their own has broken the law by committing copyright infringement. They have stolen another person's work. If you copy someone else's code and try to pass it off as your own or use it in your own product, you are breaking the law. If you want to use content or other copyrighted digital assets created by someone else, such as software code, you must obtain permission from the copyright holder.

Plagiarism

If you do not cite your sources, you are guilty of **plagiarism**, which is the unauthorized use of another person's ideas or creative work without giving that person credit. Plagiarism is equivalent to stealing another person's work and passing it off as your own. The consequences of plagiarism can be quite significant. If you plagiarize work in school, you may have to redo the assignment or lose credit altogether. Your school may also take disciplinarian actions, like detention. In the professional world, the consequences of plagiarism are even more significant. A professional who plagiarizes work suffers a loss to their reputation and may face legal ramifications, such as a lawsuit. They may be liable for fines and other punishments.

To avoid plagiarism, you just need to properly cite your source. You should insert a citation when you quote, summarize, or paraphrase someone else, use someone else's idea, or reference someone else's work. In a works cited section or footnote, tell the reader the source of your credited information.

Software Piracy

People who copy copyrighted software to install on other computers, give away, or sell are guilty of violating federal copyright laws and stealing. This is called **software piracy**. Violating a copyright and pirating software are both morally wrong and illegal. These activities discourage the authors of good software from writing new and better programs because they may not get paid for their work. Pirated software cannot be registered, so users do not get the support services they may need.

Cite Your Source

If you want to use content created by someone else, make sure that you identify the source or owner of the content. If you use information you find on the internet in your work, you must give credit to the source. You do this by inserting a reference to the source called a **citation**, in a footnote, endnote, or bibliography. A proper citation gives credit to the source, and provides the tools a reader needs to locate the source on their own. Some websites have features that automatically generate citation information for you.

Fair Use Doctrine and Creative Commons

If the content or digital asset is protected by copyright, you must have permission from the copyright holder to use the work. However, part of copyright law called the **Fair Use Doctrine** allows you to use a limited amount of copyrighted material without permission for educational purposes. For example, you can quote a few lines of a song or a passage from a book.

Similarly, an author may issue a **creative commons license** allowing others to use the work. The owner may set limitations on the usage, such as allowing students or teachers unlimited use but restricting commercial use. Some software developers create open-source software, which means they make the source code for their programs available to the public so users can change the way it works.

Trademarks and Patents

Some intellectual property is protected by a trademark or patent. A **trademark** is a symbol that indicates that a brand or brand name is legally protected and cannot be used by other businesses. A **patent** is the exclusive right to make, use, or sell a device or process. Many types of inventions can be patented. Using trademarked or patented property without permission is called infringement. The penalty is usually a large fine and a court order to stop.

Other Tools for Protecting Intellectual Property

Owners of intellectual property might also enter into an **intellectual property agreement.** This is a legal contract between or among various parties to buy and sell intellectual property rights. For example, if you create a program that you have agreed to sell to a specified buyer for a specified purpose, an intellectual property agreement with the buyer will ensure that it's used as intended.

Many business owners ask employees to sign **nondisclosure agreements**. With this type of agreement, employees are legally restricted from sharing certain types of information, even if they leave the company. These types of agreements are common in the computer science industry. Many software development companies require their programmers to sign nondisclosure agreements to bar them from sharing or reusing proprietary computer code outside of the company.

Checkpoint

16.1 What is a software license?

16.2 What is the difference between digital assets that are available as open source, freeware, or public domain?

16.3 What is software piracy?

16.2 Evaluating Information for Accuracy and Validity

Critical thinking is your best tool for assessing whether information is true and accurate.

Whether you're doing schoolwork, working for an employer, or pursuing your own interests, it is important to use critical thinking to evaluate printed, spoken, and digital information for accuracy before you believe it or incorporate it into your work.

Consider news. Before the internet, most news was covered by professional news organizations. With the internet's easy access and global reach, anyone can post articles online or upload photos and videos. These people may give accurate reports of world events and fact-check the news in newspapers. However, they can also make things up or support others who spread information that may be based on rumors or lies. In addition, electronic media itself can be manipulated to affect the reliability of information. For example, software makes it easy to alter images and even video.

When evaluating information, consider these criteria:

- **Author.** The author should be identified. If you can't locate this information, there may be a reason the author chooses to remain anonymous, or the work may be used without permission. If you do locate a name, conduct a search to find out more about the person or organization responsible for the content.
- **Purpose.** Evaluate whether the information is objective or designed for a purpose. Objective information is balanced and fair. Information designed for a purpose is presented to achieve the desired result, such as promoting a particular viewpoint, misleading, or supporting preconceived assumptions. An **assumption** is something that is accepted as being true even if there is no factual proof. Many people try to twist information or use it out of context in order to influence thinking. This type of misleading information is called **propaganda**. Always evaluate the content to determine if it is presented in a balanced, factual manner and supported by facts, or if it is biased or argumentative.
- **Content validity.** Does the author indicate the sources of the work? Do those sources appear to be respected, valid, and authoritative? Run a search on the references or other sources to see what you can learn. Determine if the information given is fact or just opinion. Also check for spelling and grammatical errors, which can indicate that the creator is not a professional.
- **Relevancy.** Evaluate the work to make sure it is relevant to your purpose before you choose to believe it or use it. Online, most search engines list results in the order of hits received. Thus, search engines sometimes place popular sites before relevant sites. Don't be fooled into thinking that a page is relevant simply because it appears at the top of a list of results. Also, commercial search engines allow advertising and sponsored links, which are paid for by companies hoping to get your business. Don't assume the first link on a results page is the best. It might just be for the company that pays the most.

Checkpoint

16.4 Why is it important for an online article or website to provide information about the author?

16.5 What is an assumption?

16.6 What is propaganda?

16.3 Digital Etiquette

Each of us has a responsibility to be aware of the social and ethical ramifications of using technology, and to always treat other people and organizations as we want them to treat us.

Acceptable Use Policies

Organizations, including schools and businesses, have a right to expect people to follow certain rules when using their technology. These rules may address the ethical and legal use of computers, other devices, and networks.

Most organizations have an **acceptable use policy (AUP).** These policies spell out certain rules of behavior and explain the consequences of breaking those rules. An AUP may include the following ethical and legal guidelines:

- Do not visit websites that contain content that does not meet community standards.
- Do not use language that is profane, abusive, or impolite.
- Do not copy copyrighted material.
- Do not physically damage equipment.
- Do not access restricted information.
- Do not open suspicious links.
- Do not forward spam email.
- Do respect the privacy of other people.

Schools and businesses may restrict the content that users can access from internal computers. For example, they may censor, or block, specific sites that they determine are inappropriate.

They may also use a filter to block access to sites. Disabling the filters or otherwise accessing blocked sites is considered breaking the AUP and may result in punishment.

People who do not follow these rules may face consequences. They might lose privileges or be fired or suspended from school activities. Very serious violations, such as using the system to threaten or bully someone or to access and distribute confidential information, may require police involvement.

Social and Ethical Challenges of Technology

Technology provides many tools for communicating and interacting with others. In addition, advancements in technology may open the door to social and ethical challenges. For example, how will we communicate and interact with others in virtual and augmented reality environments? How will we use devices equipped with artificial intelligence?

As an ethical user of technology, you have a responsibility to use netiquette at all times. For example, email, social networking, and other forms of digital communication sometimes feel anonymous, which might make you think you do not have to be polite and respectful. When the time comes to meet with a team or with friends in a virtual situation, you must still behave as you would when meeting in the real world.

Some ways to practice **netiquette** in digital communication include:

- When writing, use correct spelling. Proofread before sending to make sure there are no errors. Also, using all capital letters is considered to be shouting. Be sure to use proper capitalization.
- Don't forward or send unwanted messages or information or spam.
- Don't flame, or insult, anyone, even as a joke. Using technology can result in a message being misinterpreted. A joke might be taken seriously, even when if you said it out loud it might be considered funny.
- Don't be a cyberbully. Using technology to hurt, scare, intimidate, or otherwise bully others is a crime.
- Don't make false statements that might hurt someone's reputation. It's called libel, or slander, and it's illegal.
- Send emails only to people who really need to see a message.
- Avoid transmitting extremely large files.
- Do not use impolite or rude language
- Do not pretend to be someone else.
- Do not use someone else's work without citing the source.
- Do not share files illegally.
- Do not share inappropriate pictures online.
- Don't meet in person with strangers who you've met online, especially if you have no way to verify the person is who they say they are.
- Do not download software or apps from unknown or untrusted sources.

In a company setting, netiquette might include rules for cyber safety and security, some of which may be mandated by your company's policy or even by law. These might include things such as:

- Following company policies or legal standards with regard to security, storing, and disposing of client information and records.
- Using spam filters as directed by company policy, and disposing of any suspicious communication. Note that in some industries, companies are required by law to keep backups of email and private messages for a period of years, so keep your communication clean and ethical.
- Following company rules and procedures about what software and apps you can install on company devices.
- Following strong password practices. A secure password should have at least 8 characters, including a mix of upper- and lowercased letters, and numbers and symbols. Store passwords in a secure location, and follow company policies for changing passwords when needed.
- Backing up work files and other information as required by company policy.

Impact of Technology on Society

As a computer-science professional, you will benefit from understanding the historical impact of computing on society as well as how computing-related advancements can impact society. This information can help you make informed decisions about your contributions to the field.

Computing technology has had many positive impacts on the way people and communities live and thrive. For example, in the past, automated systems have taken on repetitive tasks, such as assembly line work, which lets people take on more challenging and better paying jobs.

Other ways computing technology has positively impacted society is in the transfer of information. We can use the internet to quickly find information about any topic, and share documents, photos, and videos with others. Computing technology has made communication fast and easy. You can reach others through text or voice immediately at any time of day or night, almost anywhere in the world. Other areas where computing and computing-related advancements provide benefits to society include medicine, research, and education.

However, there can also be negative impacts on society from computing and computing-related advancements. For example, the internet of things lets us turn on lights or unlock doors using an app; video doorbells record people passing by a home. While convenient, these digital tools can impact person privacy. Some other negative impacts include the spread of misinformation and cybercrime, which can affect businesses, organizations, and individuals.

Checkpoint

16.7 Give three examples of rules that might be part of an acceptable use policy.

16.8 What advances in technology might pose social or ethical challenges?

16.9 What is netiquette?

16.10 Give at least two examples of how computing impacts society.

16.11 Give at least two examples of how computing-related advancements impact society.

16.4 Cybercrime Awareness

Cybercriminals use many attack methods to infiltrate personal and corporate systems. It is your responsibility to be aware of these methods to protect your data and the data of your employer and clients.

The internet has opened the door to new kinds of crime and new ways of carrying out traditional crimes. **Computer crime** is any act that violates state or federal laws and involves using a computer. The term **cybercrime** often refers specifically to crimes carried out by means of the internet. Many cybercrimes are based on the ability of people to tap illegally into computer networks. They may create a **virus**, **worm**, or **Trojan horse** program to infiltrate computers and damage or delete data, unless you use strong virus prevention techniques. Or, they may use a variety of other criminal techniques.

More and more often, cybercriminals are trying to access corporate computer systems by targeting employees. As a computer science professional, you may have access to your company's most sensitive information. You may also have a responsibility for the security of the system. You must be aware of how criminals try to attack so you do not fall for their schemes and so you can warn others of the risks.

Cybercrime Tactics

Some intruders pretend to be network administrators. They call network users and ask for their passwords, claiming that the passwords are needed to solve a problem in the system. Users with access to the most data will likely be the target. With a password, the criminals have access to data stored on the network. They may be able to alter files or programs (Figure 16-1) or download data. They also may change user passwords to ones that only they know, so the real users cannot log in.

Figure 16-1 Once hackers gain access, they can alter files or programs

Andrey_Popov/Shutterstock

Another method of gaining access is to use programs that try many different passwords until one works. This is called **scanning**, or probing. Networks can be blocked from scanners by limiting the number of failed attempts to log onto the system. After three password failures, for instance, the network can refuse access.

A program called a **superzapper** allows authorized users to access a network in an emergency situation by skipping security measures. In the hands of an intruder, a superzapper opens the possibility of damage to the system.

Some intruders **spoof**, or use a false Internet Protocol (IP) or email address to gain access. Intruders assume the IP address of a trusted source to enter a secure network and distribute emails containing **viruses**.

Phishing criminals try to lure victims into giving them usernames, passwords, bank account numbers, or credit card details, usually by sending an email that looks like it comes from an official and legitimate source. For example, in a typical phishing scam, a thief sends an email message that looks as if it is from your bank, asking you to verify or update your account information. The thief captures the information you enter and can then steal from your account. An employee who clicks a link in a phishing message while using a company device opens the entire system to the criminal.

Some criminals may use **packet sniffers.** A packet sniffer is a program that examines data streams on networks to try to find information, such as passwords and credit card numbers.

A **time bomb** is a program that sits on a system until a certain event or set of circumstances activates the program. For example, an employee could create a time bomb designed to activate on a certain date after they resign from the company. Although a time bomb is not necessarily a virus, these malicious programs are often categorized or described as viruses.

Some employees may create a **trap door**, or a secret way into the system. Once they quit working for the employer, they can use this to access the system and damage it. Not all trap doors are viruses, but some viruses are trap doors. Many Trojan horse programs, for example, act as trap doors.

Some criminals use advertisements and email messages to scam you into sending them money or gift cards. For example, they might claim you have won a lottery, and if you pay a tax or fee, they will send you the winnings.

A common criminal tactic is to use **social engineering** to trick you into clicking a link that will install a virus or capture your personal information. Social engineering is not technical. It relies on human nature and manipulation to convince someone to do something. A common social engineering hack would be a phishing scheme that sends an official-looking email notifying you about a problem with your bank account. When you click a link, you are sent to a fake bank website.

When a cybercriminal pretends to be someone else online, it is called **catfishing**. The criminal tries to trick the victim into revealing personal information or sending money.

Strong Passwords

Many computer crimes start when an unauthorized user hacks, or gains unauthorized entry, into a computer network. This often happens when the intruder learns the password to access the victim's computer and the network.

Too often, computer users choose passwords that are easy for them to remember, such as birthdates, names of pets, names of celebrities, and names of family members. Unfortunately, these passwords are also easy for intruders to guess. Surprisingly, the most common passwords used are "password" and "123456," both of which are extremely weak.

Always use a **strong password**. Don't use things like family names, nicknames, or birth dates. Random passwords are often the strongest, like S3nD3v?. Use a combination of at least six upper- and lowercase letters, numbers, and symbols. Often the site will let you know if your password is strong enough. Some sites require you to use a passphrase, which is similar to a password but is longer and includes a string of words, not just characters.

Other tips for a strong password or **passphrase** include:

- Change your password or passphrase every few months. Some sites may require this.
- Do not keep a record of your passwords or passphrases on your computer or on a piece of paper near your computer.
- Never give out your passwords or passphrases to anyone.
- Never type a password or passphrase while someone is watching

Most websites now offer **multifactor authentication**, which adds a second or even third layer of security to password access. Multifactor authentication requires you to use two or more verification factors to access a resource. It can be used for devices, like a smartphone, tablet, or computer, or for access to an online account or private network.

For example, instead of just entering a password, you might also have to enter a biometric identifier, such as a fingerprint or face scan, a code that you receive via text or email on a different, verified device, or the answer to a security question.

Protecting Data

In addition to strong passwords, one of the simplest and most important methods of protecting data and privacy, and keeping your computer running efficiently is to detect and prevent viruses. Be sure to install and use an **antivirus program** or **antimalware program**. These programs detect, quarantine, and remove viruses, spyware, and malware. These programs continually monitor your system for dangerous files so they can prevent them from getting into your system in the first place. Once they detect a virus, they block it. If they find a virus, they delete it or quarantine it so it can do no harm.

Simply installing an antivirus program is not enough to protect your data and computer. New viruses are created every day. Software publishers update their antivirus programs to defeat each new attack, and you must make sure you keep the program on your computer up-to-date. The easiest way to do this is to set your antivirus program to update automatically using an internet connection.

To help block unauthorized users from accessing your computer through a network, you can install and activate a **firewall**. A firewall is a program that restricts unauthorized network access to your computer. Most operating systems come with a firewall, and so do many antivirus programs.

In the Spotlight:
Securing Device Data

Imagine you are taking a picture of a sunset over a lake, and your phone slips out of your hands. You watch as it sinks to the bottom. Or, you put it down in the driveway and someone backs a car over it. What happens to your files, contacts, pictures, and videos?

Losing a device does not have to be a disaster as long as you have backed up your data. Backing up is simply creating a copy of the data that is stored separately in an off-site or remote location away from the original. You can back up data manually or use a program that performs the backup automatically on a set schedule. You can restore the data to a new device from the backup.

Now, think about what happens to your data when you trade in the device for a new one. Is your old data still stored on the old device? Who might have access to it? Deleting a file will not keep it secure. Hackers can easily find deleted files.

To make sure information is not left on a device, you must reformat or wipe the drive, which destroys all files. You can clear a smartphone or tablet by resetting it to its factory configuration or using the Erase All command, then removing the SIM card, if there is one. Before you do, however, make sure you back up your contacts, photos, and any other information you want to keep so you can install it on your new device.

Checkpoint

16.12 Why might cybercriminals want to target computer science professionals?

16.13 What is phishing?

16.14 Give an example of social engineering as a criminal tactic.

16.15 Explain how to create a strong password.

16.16 What does an antivirus program do?

16.5 Digital Privacy

Using technology responsibly protects personal and corporate privacy.

Many people share personal information about themselves, their habits, and their finances. Sometimes, however, such information is gathered without a person's knowledge or approval. Personal information can be used for criminal activity such as identity fraud, phishing, and catfishing. The more you understand about how personal information is collected and shared, the better prepared you will be to protect your digital privacy and security.

Some businesses gather information from public records kept by the government. They may also access information that people volunteer about themselves. These are some ways businesses collect information:

- **Website registration.** Many websites require visitors to fill out registration forms.
- **Online purchases.** Some websites gather information about people who buy their goods or services.
- **Browsing.** A **cookie** is a small file that is saved to your storage device when you visit a website. Cookies give websites a way of storing information about you, so it is available when you return. Cookies are meant to make your web experience more pleasurable by personalizing what you see. However, they can also be used for **navigation tracking** and gathering data on your browsing and shopping habits without your consent.
- **Warranty registration.** To take advantage of a product warranty, you usually must register with the manufacturer. Some warranty registrations ask for a lot of personal information.
- **Sweepstakes entries.** Many people fill out sweepstakes entry forms hoping to win a prize. In doing so, they provide important personal information.
- **Social networking sites.** These sites gather information about their users from their profiles and posts, including where they live, what they like, and which products they use.
- **Search engines and messaging services.** Some of these sites collect data about users and their online search history to learn what interests them so they can target users with pop-up ads and recommendations.

Companies that gather personal information often sell it to other organizations, such as marketing companies, whose job is to sell products and services. As a result, marketing companies have access to enormous quantities of data about people. This information is stored in large computerized databases, which can be hacked, giving criminals access to your data without your knowledge.

Expectations of Privacy

Everything you post online or send by email is on record. Employees of a company have no right to privacy for any digital communication, stored files, or browsing history when they use their employer's computer system. Although the employer may not say so, every message might be read, every browser history checked, and every social media post analyzed by someone authorized to alert management if anything seems amiss. Even if you think you have deleted the file, you should assume the company has retained a backup.

Employees may face serious consequences if they disclose inside information to competitors, threaten or harass other employees, or spend company time and resources on personal business or entertainment. The best way to ensure privacy at work is to avoid using company systems for anything that is not related to your work.

You also need to make sure not to infringe or interfere with the privacy and rights of others. Do not share personal information about others online, via texts, or in emails. As an employee, you must never post or share confidential or private information about your company, coworkers, or managers.

In addition, you should expect potential employers will look for you online. A simple search will let them see a history of what you have posted on almost every internet site. These are strong reasons why you should always be respectful and polite online and never post items that may be embarrassing to you in the future.

Protecting Your Personal Information

You can protect your privacy by being careful to whom you give personal information about yourself. You can also select privacy settings on websites and social networks that limit who can access your personal information or view your posts.

Some basic actions you can take immediately to protect your privacy include:

- **Clear your browser history,** especially when accessing the internet from a public location, such as an airport or café (Figure 16-2).
- **Delete** bookmarks for sites that may store personal data.
- **Select settings on social networks** to only share your personal information with friends.
- **Set your status to invisible** so other people do not know you are online.

Figure 16-2 Accessing the internet from a public location puts your information at risk

Иван Река/123rf.com

Following are some additional steps you can take for even more privacy and security.

Use a **virtual private network (VPN)**. A VPN uses encryption technology to make a public network, like the internet, more secure. Most companies provide VPNs for employees to access the company network. You can also use a VPN service for personal internet access.

Set your browser to reject cookies or warn you about them. Better yet, surf from sites that protect your identity. Anonymizer, Firefox Focus, and IDZap are examples of sites offering this service. Duck Duck Go is an example of an anonymous browser. Browsing anonymously can keep websites and browsers from tracking your history and may protect your personal information. These tools automatically delete your browsing history and default to high security levels.

Be careful of websites that require you to register. Do not fill out a registration form unless the site clearly says that the data will not be shared with other people without your permission. You can also sign up for a free email account from a website such as Outlook.com or Gmail. Use that address when you register at websites or participate in other public internet spaces. This will protect you from receiving unwanted mail, or spam, at your primary email address.

Privacy Laws

In 2022, the U.S. Congress moved forward the American Data Privacy and Protection Act. If it takes affect, it will restrict consumer data collection, and the use and transfer of that consumer data. Through 2022, however, there has been no single U.S. law governing data privacy. Consumer protection is achieved using a patchwork of laws, including:

- **Electronic Communications Privacy Act,** which protects some wire, oral, and electronic communications from unauthorized interception, access, use, and disclosure.
- **Computer Fraud & Abuse Act,** which protects against unauthorized access of a computer to defraud, get anything of value, transmit harmful items, or traffic in computer passwords.
- **Children's Online Privacy Protection Act** which requires verifiable parental consent before some websites and other digital platforms can collect, use, or share personal information from children under the age of 13.

Some states do have data privacy laws. These include California, Colorado, Virginia, Utah, and Connecticut. Among other things, these laws provide consumers with the right to access and delete personal information and to opt-out of the sale of personal information.

Checkpoint

16.17 What are three ways businesses collect personal information?

16.18 How do websites use cookies?

16.19 Write a paragraph discussing privacy laws.

Chapter Review

Multiple Choice

1. What type of software is free to use, copy, share, and alter?
   a. public domain
   b. shareware
   c. freeware
   d. commercial
2. What type of software license lets you install a program for one user?
   a. site license
   b. network license
   c. single-user license
   d. volume license
3. If you do not cite your sources, you are guilty of ________.
   a. piracy
   b. plagiarism
   c. libel
   d. infringement
4. If you copy and sell software you do not own, you are guilty of ________.
   a. piracy
   b. plagiarism
   c. libel
   d. infringement
5. What is a clue that information online might not be accurate and valid?
   a. author is listed
   b. information is objective
   c. common words are misspelled
   d. sources can be verified
6. AUP stands for _________.
   a. authentic user program
   b. acceptable user problem
   c. authentic update program
   d. acceptable use policy
7. Which of the following is not a good netiquette practice?
   a. proofreading before sending
   b. pretending to be someone else
   c. never forwarding spam
   d. being polite

8. Trying different passwords until one works is called ___________.
   a. zapping
   b. spoofing
   c. phishing
   d. scanning

9. What security tool is similar to a password but includes a string of words?
   a. passphrase
   b. face scan
   c. fingerprint
   d. strongpass

10. What security tool requires you to use a password and a biometric identifier to access a resource?
   a. passphrase
   b. multifactor authentication
   c. access code
   d. firewall

True or False

1. Copyright protection does not cover software code.
2. The source code for open-source software is available to the public.
3. It is legal to use proprietary software without a license.
4. Software piracy is illegal.
5. Propaganda is balanced and fair.
6. Most organizations approve of people using their systems to access questionable websites.
7. One rule of netiquette is to never share files illegally.
8. Catfishing is when someone pretends to be someone else online.
9. A strong password should be easy to remember.
10. Antivirus software is not important for system privacy and security.

Short Answer

1. Explain intellectual property. Give at least three examples.
2. How does copyright law protect software developers?
3. What are three ways to evaluate information for accuracy and validity?
4. How might a technology such as virtual reality affect social interactions?
5. Explain the importance of keeping antivirus protection up-to-date.
6. Explain three ways to protect privacy online.
7. Explain how sharing information online can lead to cybercrime.
8. Discuss an example of the impact of computing on society.
9. Discuss an example of the impact of computing-related advancements on society.
10. Analyze and explain how electronic media can affect the reliability of information.

Exercises

1. With a partner or small group, review rules your school district may have for technology use as part of its acceptable use policy. Categorize policies based on appropriate use, vandalism or destruction, and consequences of violations. As a class, debate the benefits and drawbacks of items in the policy, such as censorship and filtering.

2. With a partner or small group, write a list of cyber safety and security rules and procedures you might be asked to follow as a computer science professional.

3. With a partner or small group, investigate digital privacy and copyright laws. When using technology, follow your school's AUP while demonstrating proper digital etiquette, ethical acquisition and use of digital information, and responsible use of software. Assess all sources for accuracy and validity, and record all sources of information. Write a summary explaining what you have learned about digital privacy and copyright laws, citing all sources. Discuss your findings about digital privacy and copyright laws with another group or with the class.

4. With a partner or small group, investigate online privacy and information sharing. When using technology, follow your school's AUP while demonstrating proper digital etiquette, ethical acquisition and use of digital information, and responsible use of software. Assess all sources for accuracy and validity, and record all sources of information. Write a summary explaining what you have learned about online privacy and information sharing, citing all sources. Discuss your findings about privacy and information sharing with another group or with the class.

5. With a partner or small group, investigate software and other digital assets licensing and piracy. When using technology, follow your school's AUP while demonstrating proper digital etiquette, ethical acquisition and use of digital information, and responsible use of software. Assess all sources for accuracy and validity, and record all sources of information. Make a chart comparing digital asset sharing options such as open source, freeware, and public domain, citing all sources. Discuss your findings with another group or with the class.

6. With a partner or small group, make a presentation explaining computer privacy and security. You should include information explaining the value of strong passwords, passphrases, and other methods of authentication for safely accessing resources, as well as why virus detection and prevention is a valuable too for protecting privacy and security. Use the internet and other resources to investigate the topic. When using technology, follow your school's AUP while demonstrating proper digital etiquette, ethical acquisition and use of digital information, and responsible use of software. Assess all sources for accuracy and validity, and record all sources of information. Create the presentation about the topic citing all sources, and discuss it with another group or with the class.

7. With a partner or small group, investigate computing and computing-related advancements in technology. Use your research to write a report or news article, or to create a website. In your work, discuss and give examples of how computing and computing-related advancements impact society. When using technology, follow your school's AUP while demonstrating proper digital etiquette, ethical acquisition and use of digital information, and responsible use of software. Assess all sources for accuracy and validity, and record all sources of information. When you have enough information, write the report or article or create the website, citing all sources. Share it with another group or with the class.

Focus on Python

Topics

17.1 Input, Output, and Processing Standards

You can apply the basic input, output, and processing knowledge you have learned so far to create programs in Python.

Displaying Screen Output in Python

Recall that Python is a high-level programming language. Its intuitive syntax makes it suitable for many types of applications. See Appendix E for information on installing Python, and Appendix F for information on using the Python IDLE intergated development learning environment.

To display output on the computer's screen in Python, you use the `print` function. Here is an example of a statement that uses the `print` function to display the message *Hello world.*

```
print('Hello world')
```

To use the `print` function, you type the word `print`, followed by a set of parentheses. Inside the parentheses, you type an **argument**, which is the data that you want displayed on the screen. In this example, the argument is `'Hello world'`. The quote marks will not be displayed when the statement executes, however. The quote marks simply specify the beginning and the end of the text that we wish to display. Program 17-1 shows an example of a complete program that displays output on the screen.

NOTE:. The line numbers are NOT part of the program! Don't type the line numbers when you are entering program code. The line numbers are shown for reference purposes only.

Program 17-1:

```
print(‘My major is Computer Science.')
print(‘I plan to be a software developer.')
print(‘Programming is fun!')
```

Program Output

```
My major is Computer Science.
I plan to be a software developer.
Programming is fun!
```

In Python, you can enclose string literals in a set of single-quote marks (‘) or a set of double-quote marks ("). The string literals in Program 17-2 are enclosed in single-quote marks, but the program could also be written as shown here:

```
print("My major is Computer Science.")
print("I plan to be a software developer.")
print("Programming is fun!")
```

Python Variables

You do not declare variables in Python. Instead, you use an **assignment statement** to create a variable. Here is an example of an assignment statement:

```
age = 25
```

After this statement executes, a variable named `age` will be created and it will be assigned the integer value 25. Here is another example:

```
title = ‘Vice President'
```

After this statement executes, a variable named `title` will be created and it will be assigned the string `‘Vice President'`.

Variable Names in Python

You may choose your own variable names in Python, as long as you do not use any of the Python keywords. (See Appendix D for a for a complete list of Python keywords.) Additionally, you must follow these rules when naming variables in Python:

- A variable name cannot contain spaces.
- The first character must be one of the letters a through z, A through Z, or an underscore character (_).
- After the first character you may use the letters a through z or A through Z, the digits 0 through 9, or underscores.
- Uppercase and lowercase characters are distinct, or case-sensitive.. This means the variable name `ItemsOrdered` is not the same as `itemsordered`.

Displaying Multiple Items with the print Function in Python

You can pass multiple arguments to the print function, and Python will print each argument's value on the screen, separated by a space. Program 17-2 shows an example.

Program 17-2:

```
1 room = 503
2 print('I am staying in room number', room)
```

Program Output

```
I am staying in room number 503
```

The statement in line 1 creates a variable named `room`, and assigns it the integer value 503. The statement in line 2 displays two items: a string literal followed by the value of the `room` variable. Notice that Python automatically displayed a space between these two items.

Reading Input from the Keyboard in Python

You can use Python's built-in `input` function to read input from the keyboard. The `input` function reads a piece of data that has been entered at the keyboard and returns that piece of data, as a string, back to the program. You normally use the `input` function in an assignment statement that follows this general format:

```
variable = input(prompt)
```

In the general format, `prompt` is a string that is displayed on the screen. The string's purpose is to instruct the user to enter a value. `variable` is the name of a variable that will reference the data that was entered on the keyboard. Here is an example of a statement that uses the `input` function to read data from the keyboard:

```
name = input('What is your name? ')
```

When this statement executes, the following things happen:

- The string `'What is your name? '` is displayed on the screen.
- The program pauses and waits for the user to type something on the keyboard, and then press the Enter key.
- When the Enter key is pressed, the data that was typed is returned as a string, and assigned to the `name` variable.

Program 17-3 shows a complete program that uses the `input` function to read two strings as input from the keyboard.

Program 17-3:

```
first_name = input('Enter your first name: ')
last_name = input('Enter your last name: ')
print('Hello', first_name, last_name)
```

Program Output (with Input Shown in Bold)

```
Enter your first name:  Vinny [Enter]
Enter your last name:  Brown [Enter]
Hello Vinny Brown
```

Reading Numbers with the input Function in Python

The `input` function always returns the user's input as a string, even if the user enters numeric data. For example, suppose you call the `input` function and the user types the number 72 and pressed the Enter key. The value that is returned from the `input` function is the string `'72'`. This can be a problem if you want to use the value in a math operation. Math operations can be performed only on numeric values, not strings.

Fortunately, Python has built-in functions that you can use to convert a string to a data numeric type. Table 17-1 summarizes two of these functions.

Table 17-1 Python Data Conversion Functions

Function	Description
int(*item*)	You pass an argument to the int() function and it returns the argument's value converted to an integer.
float(*item*)	You pass an argument to the float() function and it returns the argument's value converted to a floating-point number.

For example, the following code gets an integer and a floating-point number from the user:

```
hours = int(input('How many hours did you work? '))
pay_rate = float(input('What is your hourly pay rate? '))
```

Performing Calculations in Python

The Python arithmetic operators are listed in Table 17-2.

Table 17-2 Python Arithmetic Operators

Symbol	Operator
+	Addition
–	Subtraction
*	Multiplication
/	Division
%	Modulus
**	Exponent

Here are some examples of Python statements that use an arithmetic operator to calculate a value, and assign that value to a variable:

```
total = price + tax
sale = price - discount
population = population * 2
half = number / 2
leftOver = 17 % 3
result = 4**2
```

Program 17-4 shows an example program that performs mathematical calculations.

Program 17-4:

```
original_price = float(input("Enter the item's original price: "))
discount = original_price * 0.2
sale_price = original_price - discount
print('The sale price is', sale_price)
```

Program Output (With Input Shown in Bold)

```
Enter the item's original price:  100.00 [Enter]
The sale price is 80.0
```

In Python, the order of operations and the use of parentheses as grouping symbols work as described in Chapter 6.

Operations that are enclosed in parentheses are performed first. When two operators share an operand, the operator with the higher precedence is applied first. The precedence of the math operators, from highest to lowest, are:

1. Exponentiation
2. Multiplication, division, and remainder
3. Addition and subtraction

When two operators with the same precedence share an operand, the operators execute from left to right.

NOTE: See Chapter 6 for more on using math operators in calculations.

Comments in Python

To write a line comment in Python, you simply place the # symbol where you want the comment to begin. The Python interpreter ignores everything from that point to the end of the line. Here is an example:

```
# This program calculates an employee's gross pay.
```

Checkpoint

17.1 What should you type in Python to display the text "Goodnight." on screen?

17.2 In Python, what do you do instead of declaring a variable?

17.3 What character do you type at the beginning of a line comment in Python?

17.2 Boolean Logic and Decision Structures

You can apply your knowledge of boolean logic and conditional statements to create decision structures in Python.

Relational Operators in Python

Python's relational operators, shown in Table 17-3, are the same as those used in our pseudocode programs earlier in this course. (See Chapter 7 for more on using relational operators.)

Table 17-3 Relational operators

Operator	Meaning
>	Greater than
<	Less than
>=	Greater than or equal to
<=	Less than or equal to
==	Equal to
!=	Not equal to

The `if` Statement in Python

Here is the general format of the `if` statement in Python:

```
if BooleanExpression:
    statement
    statement
    etc.
```

For simplicity, we will refer to the first line as the if *clause*. The `if` clause begins with the word `if`, followed by a Boolean expression. A colon appears after the Boolean expression. Beginning at the next line is a block of statements. All of the statements in a block must be consistently indented. This indentation is required because the Python interpreter uses it to tell where the block begins and ends.

When the `if` statement executes, the Boolean expression is tested. If the Boolean expression is true, the statements that appear in the block following the `if` clause are executed. If the Boolean expression is false, the statements in the block are skipped.

The `if-else` Statement (Python's Dual Alternative Decision Structure)

You use the `if-else` statement in Python to create a dual alternative decision structure. This is the format of the `if-else` statement:

```
if BooleanExpression:
    statement
    statement
    etc.
```

```
else:
    statement
    statement
    etc.
```

When this statement executes, the Boolean expression is tested. If it is true, the block of indented statements following the `if` clause is executed, and then control of the program jumps to the statement that follows the `if-else` statement. If the Boolean expression is false, the block of indented statements following the `else` clause is executed, and then control of the program jumps to the statement that follows the `if-else` statement.

Comparing Strings in Python

The relational operators can be used to compare strings, as shown here:

```
name1 = 'Mary'
name2 = 'Mark'
if name1 == name2:
    print('The names are the same.')
else:
    print('The names are NOT the same.')
```

The `==` operator compares `name1` and `name2` to determine whether they are equal. Because the strings `'Mary'` and `'Mark'` are not equal, the `else` clause will display the message `'The names are NOT the same.'`

Let's look at another example. Assume the `month` variable references a string. The following code uses the `!=` operator to determine whether the value referenced by `month` is not equal to `'October'`.

```
if month != 'October':
    print('This is the wrong time for Octoberfest!')
```

Logical Operators in Python

Table 17-4 shows Python's logical operators, (See Chapter 7 for more on using logical operators.)

Table 17-4 Python's logical operators

Operator	Meaning
and	Logical AND
or	Logical OR
not	Logical NOT

For example, the following `if` statement checks the value of `x` to determine if it is in the range of 20 through 40:

```
if x >= 20 and x <= 40:
    print(x, 'is in the acceptable range.')
```

The Boolean expression in the `if` statement will be true only when `x` is greater than or equal to 20 *AND* less than or equal to 40. The value in `x` must be within the range of 20 through 40 for this expression to be true. The following statement determines whether `x` is outside the range of 20 through 40:

```
if x < 20 or x > 40:
    print(x, 'is outside the acceptable range.')
```

Here is an `if` statement using the `not` operator:

```
if not (temperature > 100):
    print('This is below the maximum temperature.')
```

First, the expression `(temperature > 100)` is tested and a value of either true or false is the result. Then the `not` operator is applied to that value. If the expression `(temperature > 100)` is true, the `not` operator returns false. If the expression `(temperature > 100)` is false, the `not` operator returns true. The previous code is equivalent to asking: "Is the temperature not greater than 100?"

Boolean Variables in Python

The `bool` data type allows you to create variables that may reference one of two possible values: `True` or `False`. (For more on Boolean variables, see Chapter 7.) Here are examples of how we assign values to a `bool` variable:

```
hungry = True
sleepy = False
```

Boolean variables are most commonly used as flags that signals when some condition exists in the program. When the flag variable is set to `False`, it indicates the condition does not exist. When the flag variable is set to `True`, it means the condition does exist.

For example, suppose a salesperson has a quota of $50,000. Assuming sales references the amount that the salesperson has sold, the following code determines whether the quota has been met:

```
if sales >= 50000.0:
    sales_quota_met = True
else:
    sales_quota_met = False
```

Checkpoint

17.4 What relational operator means Less than or equal to in Python?

17.5 What character do you enter at the end of a Boolean expression in Python?

17.6 What is Python's dual alternative decision structure?

17.7 What are Python's logical operators?

17.3 Loop Statements

You can apply the basic knowledge you have learned so far about loop statements to create programs in Python.

The while Loop in Python

In Python, the `while` loop is written in the following general format:

```
while condition:
      statement
      statement
      etc.
```

The `while` clause begins with the word `while`, followed by a Boolean *condition* that will be evaluated as either true or false. A colon appears after the *condition.* Beginning at the next line is a block of statements. All of the statements in a block must be consistently indented. This indentation is required because the Python interpreter uses it to tell where the block begins and ends.

When the `while` loop executes, the *condition* is tested. If the *condition* is true, the statements that appear in the block following the `while` clause are executed, and then the loop starts over. If the *condition* is false, the program exits the loop. The following code shows an example of a `while` loop that prints "Hello" five times:

```
count = 0
while count < 5:
   print('Hello')
   count = count + 1
```

NOTE: See Chapter 8 for more on using loops. Note that Python does not provide loops that are equivalent to the `Do-While` or `Do-Until` loops.

The for Loop in Python

In Python, the `for` statement is designed to work with a sequence of data items. When the statement executes, it iterates once for each item in the sequence. We will use the `for` statement in the following general format:

```
for variable in [value1, value2, etc.]:
    statement
    statement
    etc.
```

In the `for` clause, *variable* is the name of a variable. Inside the brackets, a sequence of values appears, with a comma separating each value. (In Python, a comma-separated sequence of data items that are enclosed in a set of brackets is called a *list*.) Beginning at the next line is a block of statements that is executed each time the loop iterates.

The `for` statement executes in the following manner: The *variable* is assigned the first value in the list, and then the statements that appear in the block are executed. Then, *variable* is assigned the next value in the list, and the statements in the block are executed again. This continues until *variable* has been assigned the last value in the list. The following code shows a simple example that uses a `for` loop to display the numbers 1 through 5:

```
for num in [1, 2, 3, 4, 5]:
    print(num)
```

Using the range Function with the for Loop in Python

Python provides a built-in function named `range` that simplifies the process of writing a count-controlled `for` loop. Here is an example of a `for` loop that uses the `range` function:

```
for num in range(5):
    print(num)
```

Notice that instead of using a list of values, we call to the `range` function passing 5 as an argument. In this statement the `range` function will generate a list of integers in the range of 0 up to (but not including) 5. This code works the same as the following:

```
for num in [0, 1, 2, 3, 4]:
    print(num)
```

As you can see, the list contains five numbers, so the loop will iterate five times. The following code uses the `range` function with a `for` loop to display *Hello world* five times:

```
for x in range(5):
    print('Hello world!')
```

If you pass one argument to the `range` function, as previously demonstrated, that argument is used as the ending limit of the list. If you pass two arguments to the `range` function, the first argument is used as the starting value of the list and the second argument is used as the ending limit. Here is an example:

```
for num in range(1, 5):
    print(num)
```

This code will display the following:

```
1
2
3
4
```

By default, the `range` function produces a list of numbers that increase by 1 for each successive number in the list. If you pass a third argument to the `range` function, that argument is used as *step value*. Instead of increasing by 1, each successive number in the list will increase by the step value. The following code shows an example:

```
for num in range(1, 12, 2):
    print(num)
```

This code will display the following:

```
1
3
5
7
9
11
```

Checkpoint

17.8 When writing a loop statement in Python, why must the statements in a block be consistently indented?

17.9 When a for statement executes in Python, how many times does it iterate for each item in the sequence?

17.10 What is Python's built-in function for simplifying the process of writing a count-controlled loop?

17.4 Functions

In Python, you use functions instead of modules to break a program into small, manageable units.

Defining and Calling a Function in Python

To create a function you write its **definition**. Here is the general format of a function definition in Python:

```
def function_name():
    statement
    statement
    etc.
```

The first line is known as the **function header**. It marks the beginning of the function definition. The function header begins with the key word `def`, followed by the name of the function, followed by a set of parentheses, followed by a colon.

Beginning at the next line is a set of statements known as a block. A **block** is simply a set of statements that belong together as a group. These statements are performed any time the function is executed. Notice in the general format that all the statements in the block are indented. This indentation is required because the Python interpreter uses it to tell where the block begins and ends. Here is an example of a function definition:

```
def message():
    print('I am Arthur,')
    print('King of the Britons.')
```

This code defines a function named `message`. The `message` function contains a block with two statements. Executing the function will cause these statements to execute.

NOTE: For more on modules and functions, see Chapter 9.

Calling a Function in Python

A function definition specifies what a function does, but it does not cause the function to execute. To execute a function, you must *call* it. This is how we would call the `message` function:

```
message()
```

When a function is called, the interpreter jumps to that function and executes the statements in its block. Then, when the end of the block is reached, the interpreter jumps back to the part of the program that called the function, and the program resumes execution at that point. When this happens, we say that the function *returns*. Program 17-5 shows an example.

Program 17-5:

```
1  def message():
2      print('I am Arthur,')
3      print('King of the Britons.')
4
5  message()
```

Program Output

```
I am Arthur,
King of the Britons.
```

When the Python interpreter reads the `def` statement in line 1, a function named `message` is created in memory, containing the block of statements in lines 2 and 3. (A function definition creates a function, but it does not cause the function to execute.) Next, the interpreter executes the statement in line 5, which is a function call. This causes the `message` function to execute, which prints the two lines of output.

Indentation in Python

In Python, each line in a block must be indented. As shown in Figure 17-1, the last indented line after a function header is the last line in the function's block.

Figure 17-1 All of the statements in a Python block are indented

The last indented line is the last line in the block.

```
def greeting():
    print('Good morning!')
    print('Today we will learn about functions.')

print('I will call the greeting function.')
greeting()
```

These statements are not in the block.

When you indent the lines in a block, make sure each line begins with the same number of spaces. Otherwise an error will occur.

Local Variables in Python

Anytime you assign a value to a variable inside a function, you create a **local variable**. A local variable belongs to the function in which it is created, and only statements inside that function can access the variable. A local variable's scope is the function in which the variable is created.

Passing Arguments to Functions in Python

If you want a Python function to receive arguments when it is called, you must equip the function with one or more parameter variables. Here is an example of a function that has a parameter variable:

```
def double_number(value):
    result = value * 2
    print(result)
```

Look at the function header and notice the word `value` that appears inside the parentheses. This is the name of a parameter variable. This variable will be assigned the value of an argument when the function is called. Program 17-6 demonstrates the function in a program.

Program 17-6: 

```
1   # Define the main function.
2   def main():
3       double_number(4)
4
5   # Define the double_number function.
6   def double_number(value):
7       result = value * 2
8       print(result)
9
10  # Call the main function.
11  main()
```

Program Output

```
8
```

When this program runs, the `main` function is called in line 11. Inside the `main` function, line 3 calls the `double_number` function passing the value 4 as an argument.

The `double_number` function is defined in lines 6 through 8. The function has a parameter variable named `value`. In line 7, a local variable named `result` is assigned the value of the math expression `value * 2`. In line 8, the value of the `result` variable is displayed.

Passing Multiple Arguments in Python

Often it is useful to pass more than one argument to a function. When you define a function, you must have a parameter variable for each argument that you want passed into the function. Here is an example:

```
def show_sum(num1, num2):
    result = num1 + num2
    print(result)
```

Notice that two parameter variable names, `num1` and `num2`, appear inside the parentheses in the function header, separated by a comma. Here is an example of how we might call the function:

```
show_sum(12, 45)
```

This statement calls the `show_sum` function and passes two arguments: 12 and 45. These arguments are passed *by position* to the corresponding parameter variables in the function. In other words, the first argument is passed to the first parameter variable, and the second argument is passed to the second parameter variable. So, this statement causes 12 to be assigned to the `num1` parameter and 45 to be assigned to the `num2` parameter.

Making Changes to Parameters in Python

When an argument is passed to a function in Python, the function's parameter variable will be assigned the argument's value. However, any changes that are made to the parameter variable will not affect the argument. To demonstrate this look at Program 17-7.

Program 17-7: 

```
1   def main():
2       value = 99
3       print('The value is', value)
4       change_me(value)
5       print('Back in main the value is', value)
6
7   def change_me(arg):
8       print('I am changing the value.')
9       arg = 0
10      print('Now the value is', arg)
11
12  main()
```

Program Output

```
The value is 99
I am changing the value.
Now the value is 0
Back in main the value is 99
```

The `main` function creates a local variable named `value` in line 2, assigned the value 99. The statement in line 3 displays *The value is 99*. The `value` variable is then passed as an argument to the `change_me` function in line 4. This means that in the `change_me` function the `arg` parameter will also be assigned the value 99. When the statement in line 9 executes, however, the `arg` parameter is assigned a new value, 0. At this point in the program's execution, the `value` variable will still be assigned the value 99, and the `arg` parameter will be assigned the value 0.

Global Variables in Python

In Python, when a variable is created by an assignment statement that is written outside all the functions in a program file, the variable is global. A **global variable** can be accessed by any statement in the program file, including the statements in any function. For example, look at Program 17-8.

Program 17-8:

```
1   # Create a global variable.
2   my_value = 10
3
4   # The show_value function prints
5   # the value of the global variable.
6   def show_value():
7       print(my_value)
8
9   # Call the show_value function.
10  show_value()
```

Program Output

```
10
```

The assignment statement in line 2 creates a variable named `my_value`. Because this statement is outside any function, it is global. When the `show_value` function executes, the statement in line 7 prints the value referenced by `my_value`.

An additional step is required if you want a statement in a function to assign a value to a global variable. In the function, you must declare the global variable, as shown in Program 17-9.

Program 17-9:

```
# Create a global variable.
number = 0

def main():
    global number
    number = int(input('Enter a number: '))
    show_number()

def show_number():
    print('The number you entered is', number)

# Call the main function.
main()
```

Program Output

```
Enter a number:  22 [Enter]
The number you entered is 22
```

The assignment statement in line 2 creates a global variable named `number`. Notice that inside the `main` function, line 5 uses the `global` key word to declare the `number` variable. This statement tells the interpreter that the `main` function intends to assign a value to the global `number` variable. That's just what happens in line 6. The value entered by the user is assigned to `number`.

Global Constants in Python

The Python language does not allow you to create true global constants, but you can simulate them with global variables. If you do not declare a global variable with the `global` key word inside a function, then you cannot change the variable's assignment.

Generating Random Integers in Python

Python provides several library functions for working with random numbers. To use any of these functions, you first need to write this `import` statement at the top of your program:

```
import random
```

The first random-number generating function that we will discuss is `random.randint`. The following statement shows an example of how you might call the `random.randint` function.

```
number = random.randint(1, 100)
```

The part of the statement that reads `random.randint(1, 100)` is a call to the function. Notice that two arguments appear inside the parentheses: 1 and 100. These arguments tell the function to give an integer random number in the range of 1 through 100. (The values 1 and 100 are included in the range.) When the function is called, it will generate a random number in the range of 1 through 100 and then *return* that number. The number that is returned will be assigned to the `number` variable.

Writing Your Own Value-Returning Functions in Python

In Python, you write a value-returning function in the same way that you write a simple function, with one exception: a value-returning function must have a `return` statement. Here is the general format of a value-returning function definition in Python:

```
def function_name():
    statement
    statement
    etc.
    return expression
```

One of the statements in the function must be a `return` statement, which takes the following form:

```
return expression
```

The value of the *expression* that follows the key word `return` will be sent back to the part of the program that called the function. This can be any value, variable, or expression that has a value (such as a math expression). Here is a simple example of a value-returning function:

```
def sum(num1, num2):
    result = num1 + num2
    return result
```

The purpose of this function is to accept two integer values as arguments and return their sum. The first statement in the function's block assigns the value of `num1 + num2` to the `result` variable. Next, the `return` statement executes, which causes the function to end execution and sends the value of the `result` variable back to the part of the program that called the function. The following statement shows how we might call the `sum` function:

```
total = sum(2, 3)
```

After this code executes, the value assigned to the `total` variable will be 5.

Returning a String from a Python Function

So far you've seen examples of functions that return numbers. You can also write functions that return strings. For example, the following function prompts the user to enter their name, and then returns the string that the user entered.

```
def get_name():
    # Get the user's name.
    name = input('Enter your name: ')

    # Return the name.
    return name
```

Returning a Boolean Value from a Python Function

Python allows you to write Boolean functions, which return either `True` or `False`. For example, the following function accepts a number as an argument, and returns `True` if the argument is an even number. Otherwise, it returns `False`.

```
def is_even(number):
    # Determine whether number is even. If it is,
    # set status to true. Otherwise, set status
    # to false.
    if (number % 2) == 0:
        status = True
    else:
        status = False

    # Return the value of the status variable.
    return status
```

The following code gets a number from the user, and then calls the function to determine whether the number is even or odd:

```
value = int(input('Enter a number: '))
if is_even(value):
    print('The number is even.')
else:
    print('The number is odd.')
```

Checkpoint

17.11 What is the term for the first line of a function in Python?

17.12 What happens when you call a function in Python?

17.13 What is a local variable in Python?

17.14 What is a global variable in Python?

17.15 What are the two possible results returned by a Boolean function in Python?

17.5 Input Validation

Input validation can be an important security tool because it only allows user input that meets the specified requirements.

Program 17-10 is an example of how to use an input validation loop in Python to validate that the user does not enter a negative value.

NOTE: For more on input validation, see Chapter 10.

Program 7-10:

```
# This program calculates retail prices.

# MARK_UP is used as a global constant for
# the markup up percentage.
MARK_UP = 2.5

# The main function
def main():
    # Variable to control the loop.
    another = 'y'

    # Process one or more items.
    while another == 'y' or another == 'Y':
        # Display an item's retail price.
        show_retail()

        # Do this again?
        another = input('Do you have another item? ' +
                        '(Enter y for yes): ')

# The show_retail function gets an item's wholesale
# cost and displays the item's retail price.
def show_retail():
    # Get the item's wholesale cost.
    wholesale = float(input("Enter the item's wholesale cost: "))
```

Program 7-10: *(continued)*

```
26
27     # Validate the wholesale cost.
28     while wholesale < 0:
29         print('ERROR: the cost cannot be negative.')
30         wholesale = float(input('Enter the correct wholesale cost: '))
31
32     # Calculate the retail price.
33     retail = wholesale * MARK_UP
34
35     # Display the retail price.
36     print('The retail price is $', format(retail, '.2f'))
37
38 # Call the main function.
39 main()
```

Program Output

```
Enter the item's wholesale cost: -.50 [Enter]
ERROR: The cost cannot be negative.
Enter the correct wholesale cost: 0.50 [Enter]
The retail price is $ 1.25.
Do you have another item? (Enter y for yes): n [Enter]
```

Checkpoint

17.16 In Program 17-10, on what line does the validation loop start?

17.17 What happens in Program 17-10 if the user enters a negative number?

17.6 Lists

In Python, you create lists instead of arrays to store multiple items.

In Python, a **list** is similar to an array, but provides many more capabilities than a traditional array. A list is an object that contains multiple data items. Each item that is stored in a list is called an **element**. Here is a statement that creates a list of integers:

```
even_numbers = [2, 4, 6, 8, 10]
```

The items that are enclosed in brackets and separated by commas are the values of the list elements. The following is another example:

```
names = ['Molly', 'Steven', 'Will', 'Alicia', 'Adriana']
```

This statement creates a list of 5 strings.

You can use the `print` function to display an entire list, as shown here:

```
numbers = [5, 10, 15, 20]
```

```
print(numbers)
```

When the `print` function is called in the second statement, it will display the elements of the list like this:

```
[5, 10, 15, 20]
```

NOTE: For more on arrays, see Chapter 11.

List Elements and Subscripts in Python

You access each element of a list with a subscript. The first element's subscript is 0, the second element's subscript is 1, and so forth. The last element's subscript is the array size minus 1. For example, the following code creates a list named numbers, with three elements that are all set to the value 0. It then assigns different values to each element. The subscripts for the elements are 0, 1, and 2.

```
numbers = [0, 0, 0]
numbers[0] = 10
numbers[1] = 20
numbers[2] = 30
```

Using the len Function with Lists in Python

An error will occur if you use an invalid index with a list. For example, look at the following code:

```
# This code will cause an error.
my_list = [10, 20, 30, 40]
index = 0
while index < 5:
    print(my_list[index])
    index += 1
```

The last time that this loop iterates, the `index` variable will be assigned the value 4, which is an invalid index for the list. As a result, the statement that calls the `print` function will cause an error.

You can use the `len` function to get the length of a list in Python. When you pass a list as an argument, the `len` function returns the number of elements in the list. The previously shown code, which causes an error, can be modified as follows to prevent the error:

```
my_list = [10, 20, 30, 40]
index = 0
while index < len(my_list):
    print(my_list[index])
    index += 1
```

Iterating Over a List with the for Loop in Python

In Python, you can easily iterate over the contents of a list with the `for` loop, as shown here:

```
numbers = [99, 100, 101, 102]
for n in numbers:
    print(n)
```

The `for` statement executes in the following manner: The variable `n` is assigned a copy of the first value in the list, and then the statements that appear in the block are executed. Then, the variable `n` is assigned a copy of the next value in the list, and the statements in the block are executed again. This continues until the variable has been assigned the last value in the list. If we run this code, it will print:

```
99
100
101
102
```

Keep in mind that as the `for` loop executes, the `n` variable is assigned a copy of the list elements, and any changes made to the `n` variable do not affect the list. To demonstrate, look at the following:

```
1  numbers = [99, 100, 101, 102]
2  for n in my_list:
3      n = 0
4
5  print(my_list)
```

The statement in line 3 merely reassigns the `n` variable to a different value (0). It does not change the list element that `n` referred to before the statement executed. When this code executes, the statement in line 5 will print:

```
99
100
101
102
```

Passing a List as an Argument to a Function in Python

When passing a list as an argument to a function in Python, it is not necessary to pass a separate argument indicating the list's size. This is because Python provides the `len` function that reports the list's size. The following code shows a function that has been written to accept a list as an argument:

```
def set_to_zero(numbers):
    index = 0
    while index < len(numbers):
        numbers[index] = 0
        index = index + 1
```

The function's parameter, `numbers`, is used to refer to a list. When you call this function and pass a list as an argument, the loop sets each element to 0. Here is an example of a code that calls the function:

```
my_list = [1, 2, 3, 4, 5]
set_to_zero(my_list)
print(my_list)
```

The last statement will print:

```
0
0
0
0
0
```

Two-Dimensional Lists in Python

In Python, you can create a list of lists, which acts much like a two-dimensional array. Here is an example:

```
numbers = [ [1, 2, 3], [10, 20, 30] ]
```

This creates a list named `numbers`, with two elements. The first element is the following list:

```
[1, 2, 3]
```

The second element is the following list:

```
[10, 20, 30]
```

The following statement prints the contents of `numbers[0]`, which is the first element:

```
print(numbers[0])
```

If we execute this statement, the following be displayed:

```
[1, 2, 3]
```

The following statement prints the contents of `numbers[1]`, which is the second element:

```
print(numbers[1])
```

If we execute this statement, the following be displayed:

```
[10, 20, 30]
```

Rows and Columns

We normally think of two-dimensional arrays as having rows and columns. We can use this metaphor with two-dimensional lists as well. For example, let's say the following two-dimensional list contains sets of test scores:

```
scores = [ [70, 80, 90],
           [80, 60, 75],
           [85, 75, 95] ]
```

By declaring the list this way (with each list that is an element shown on a separate line) it's easy to see how we can think of the list as a set of rows and columns.

When processing the data in a two-dimensional list, we use two subscripts: one for the row and another for the column. In the `scores` list, the elements in row 0 are referenced as follows:

```
scores[0][0]
scores[0][1]
scores[0][2]
```

The elements in row 1 are as follows:

```
scores[1][0]
scores[1][1]
scores[1][2]
```

And the elements in row 2 are as follows:

```
scores[2][0]
scores[2][1]
scores[2][2]
```

To access one of the elements in a two-dimensional list, you use both subscripts. For example, the following statement prints the number in `scores[0][2]`:

```
print(scores[0][2])
```

And the following statement assigns the number 95 to `scores[2][1]`:

```
scores[2][1] = 95
```

Programs that process two-dimensional lists can do so with nested loops. For example, the following code displays all the elements in the `scores` list:

```
NUM_ROWS = 3
NUM_COLS = 3

row = 0
while row < NUM_ROWS:
    col = 0
    while col < NUM_COLS:
        print(scores[row][col])
        col = col + 1
    row = row + 1
```

And the following code prompts the user to enter a score, once for each element in the list:

```
NUM_ROWS = 3
NUM_COLS = 3

row = 0
while row < NUM_ROWS:
    col = 0
    while col < NUM_COLS:
        scores[row][col] = int(input('Enter a score: '))
        col = col + 1
    row = row + 1
```

Checkpoint

17.18 What is a list in Python?

17.19 What is each item stored in a list called?

17.20 Why do you not have to pass a separate argument indicating a list's size in Python?

17.7 Classes and Objects

You can apply the basic knowledge you have learned so far for object-oriented programming with Python.

Class Declarations in Python

In Python, a **class** is like an outline or template for creating a new object. Here is the general format of a class declaration in Python:

```
class ClassName:
    Method definitions go here...
```

The first line of a class declaration begins with the keyword `class`, followed by the name of the class, followed by a colon. The class's method definitions follow this line. Method definitions are written much like regular function definitions. Because they belong to the class, method definitions must be indented.

NOTE: For more on object-oriented programming and classes, see Chapter 13.

One difference that you will notice between Python class declarations and the pseudocode class declarations in the text is that there are no field declarations in a Python class. This is because an object's fields are created by assignment statements that appear inside the class's methods.

Another difference that you will notice is the absence of access specifiers such as `Private` and `Public`. In Python, we hide a field or method by starting its name with two underscores. This is similar to making the field or method private.

The Python program shown in Program 17-11 contains a `CellPhone` class. It also has a `main` method to demonstrate the class.

Program 17-11:

```
class CellPhone:
    def set_manufacturer(self, manufact):
        self.__manufacturer = manufact

    def set_model_number(self, model):
        self.__model_number = model

    def set_retail_price(self, retail):
        self.__retail_price = retail

    def get_manufacturer(self):
        return self.__manufacturer

    def get_model_number(self):
        return self.__model_number

    def get_retail_price(self):
```

Program 7-11: *(continued)*

```
18         return self.__retail_price
19
20 def main():
21     # Create a CellPhone object. The phone
22     # variable will reference the object.
23     phone = CellPhone()
24
25     # Store values in the object's fields.
26     phone.set_manufacturer("Motorola")
27     phone.set_model_number("G200")
28     phone.set_retail_price(399.99)
29
30     # Display the values stored in the fields.
31     print('The manufacturer is', phone.get_manufacturer())
32     print('The model number is', phone.get_model_number())
33     print('The retail price is', phone.get_retail_price())
34
35 # Call the main function.
36 main()
```

Program Output

```
The manufacturer is Motorola
The model number is G200
The retail price is 399.99
```

Notice that each of the methods has a parameter named `self`. The `self` parameter is required in every method that a class has. A method operates on a specific object's data attributes. When a method executes, it must have a way of knowing which object's data attributes it is supposed to operate on. That's where the `self` parameter comes in. When a method is called, Python automatically makes its `self` parameter reference the specific object that the method is supposed to operate on.

Now let's look at the `set_maufacturer` method in lines 2 through 3. Notice that in addition to the `self` parameter, it also has a parameter named `manufact`. The statement in line 3 assigns `manufact` to `self.__manufacturer`. What is `self.__manufacturer`? Let's analyze it:

- `self` refers to a specific `CellPhone` object in memory.
- `__manufacturer` is the name of a field. The two underscores at the beginning of the field name make it private to code outside the `CellPhone` class.

So, the statement in line 3 assigns the value of the `manufact` parameter to a `CellPhone` object's `__manufacturer` field.

The `set_model_number` method, in lines 5 through 6 is similar. It has a `model` parameter that is assigned to the object's `__model_number` field.

The `set_retial_price` method, in lines 8 through 9 is also similar. It has a `retail` parameter that is assigned to the object's `__retail_price` field.

The `get_manufacturer` method, in lines 11 through 12, returns the value of the object's `__manufacturer` field. The `get_model_number` method, in lines 14 through 15, returns the value of the object's `model_number` field. The `get_retail_price` method, in lines 17 through 18, returns the object's `__retail_price` field.

Inside the main function, line 23 creates an instance of the CellPhone class in memory and assigns it to the phone variable. We say that the object is referenced by the phone variable. (Notice that Python does not require the New keyword, as discussed earlier in this chaptertext.) Lines 26 through 28 call the object's set_manufacturer, set_model_number, and set_retail_price methods, passing arguments to each.

Recall that in the CellPhone class, the set_manufacturer, set_model_number, and set_retail_price methods each have two parameters. However, when we call these methods in lines 26 through 28, we pass only one argument. The first parameter in each of these methods is the self parameter. When you call a method, you do not pass an argument for the self parameter because Python automatically passes a reference to the calling object into the method's first parameter. As a result, the self parameter will automatically reference the object that the method is to operate on. This means that:

- In line 26, the argument "Motorola" is being passed into the set_manufacturer method's manufact parameter.
- In line 27 the argument "G200" is being passed into the set_model_number method's model parameter.
- In line 28 the 399.99 argument is being passed into the set_retail_price method's retail parameter.

Lines 31 through 33 call the print function to display the values of the object's fields.

Constructors in Python

In Python, classes can have a method named __init__ which is automatically executed when an instance of the class is created in memory. The __init__ method is commonly known as an **initializer method** because it initializes the object's data attributes. (The name of the method starts with two underscore characters, followed by the word init, followed by two more underscore characters.)

Program 17-12 shows a version of the CellPhone class that has an __init__ method.

Program 17-12:

```
class CellPhone:
    def __init__(self, manufact, model, retail):
        self.__manufacturer = manufact
        self.__model_number = model
        self.__retail_price = retail

    def set_manufacturer(self, manufact):
        self.__manufacturer = manufact

    def set_model_number(self, model):
        self.__model_number = model

    def set_retail_price(self, retail):
        self.__retail_price = retail

    def get_manufacturer(self):
        return self.__manufacturer

    def get_model_number(self):
        return self.__model_number
```

Program 17-12: *(continued)*

```
21
22     def get_retail_price(self):
23         return self.__retail_price
24
25 def main():
26     # Create a CellPhone object and initialize its
27     # fields with values passed to the __init__ method.
28     phone = CellPhone("Motorola", "G200", 399.99)
29
30     # Display the values stored in the fields.
31     print('The manufacturer is', phone.get_manufacturer())
32     print('The model number is', phone.get_model_number())
33     print('The retail price is', phone.get_retail_price())
34
35 # Call the main function.
36 main()
```

Program Output

```
The manufacturer is Motorola
The model number is G200
The retail price is 399.99
```

The statement in line 28 creates a `CellPhone` object in memory and assigns it to the `phone` variable. Notice that the values "Motorola," "G200," and 399.99 appear inside the parentheses after the class name. These values are passed as arguments to the class's `__init__` method.

Inheritance in Python

Suppose we want to declare two classes: `ClassA` and `ClassB`. Furthermore, we want `ClassB` to be a subclass of `ClassA`. The general format of the declarations in Python is:

```
class ClassA:
        Field and method declarations

class ClassB(ClassA):
        Field and method declarations
```

Notice that in the class header for `ClassB`, we wrote `ClassA` inside parentheses. This indicates that `ClassB` extends `ClassA`. So, `ClassA` is the superclass, and `ClassB` is the subclass. `ClassB` inherits all of `ClassA`'s public members.

Polymorphism in Python

Program 17-13 presents a polymorphism demonstration that uses the `Animal` class as a superclass, and the `Dog` class and `Cat` class as subclasses of `Animal`.

Program 17-13:

```
class Animal:
    def show_species(self):
        print('I am just a regular animal.')

    def make_sound(self):
        print('Grrrrrr')

class Dog(Animal):
    def show_species(self):
        print('I am a dog.')

    def make_sound(self):
        print('Woof! Woof!')

class Cat(Animal):
    def show_species(self):
        print('I am a cat.')

    def make_sound(self):
        print('Meow')

# Here is the main function.

def main():
    # Create an animal object, a Dog object, and
    # a Cat object.
    my_animal = Animal()
    my_dog = Dog()
    my_cat = Cat()

    # Show info about an animal.
    print('Here is info about an animal.')
    show_animal_info(my_animal)
    print()

    # Show info about a dog.
    print('Here is info about a dog.')
    show_animal_info(my_dog)
    print()

    # Show info about a cat.
    print('Here is info about a cat.')
    show_animal_info(my_cat)

# The show_animal_info function accepts an Animal
# object as an argument and displays information
# about it.

def show_animal_info(creature):
    creature.show_species()
    creature.make_sound()
```

Program 17-13: *(continued)*

```

# Call the main function.
main()
```

Program Output

```
Here is info about an animal.
I am just a regular animal.
Grrrrrrr

Here is info about a dog.
I am a dog.
Woof! Woof!

Here is info about a cat.
I am a cat.
Meow
```

Using Third-Party Modules in Python

The Python standard library provides classes and functions that your programs can use to perform basic operations, as well as many advanced tasks. There are operations, however, that the standard library cannot perform. When you need to do something that is beyond the scope of the standard library, you have two choices: write the code yourself, or use code that someone else has already written.

In Python, a module is a file containing code that you can import into another file. Fortunately, there are thousands of Python modules, written by independent programmers, that provide capabilities that the standard Python library does not offer. These are known as **third-party modules**. A large collection of third-party modules exists at the website pypi. python.org, which is known as the *Python Package Index*, or *PyPI*.

The modules that are available at PyPI are organized as packages. A **package** is simply a collection of one or more related modules. The easiest way to download and install a package is with the pip utility. The pip utility is a program that is part of the standard Python installation, beginning with Python 3.4. To install a package on a Windows system with the pip utility, you must open a command prompt window, and type a command following this format:

```
pip install package_name
```

`package_name` is the name of a package that you want to download and install. If you are running a Mac or a Linux system, use the pip3 command instead of the pip command. In addition, you will need superuser privileges to execute the pip3 command on a Mac or Linux system, so you will have to prefix the command with sudo, as shown here:

```
sudo pip3 install package_name
```

Once you enter the command, the pip utility will start downloading and installing the package. Depending on the size of the package, it may take a few minutes to complete the installation process. Once the process is finished, you can typically verify that the package was correctly installed by starting IDLE and entering the command

```
>>> import package_name
```

where package_name is the name of the package that you installed. If you do not see an error message, you can assume the package was successfully installed.

Checkpoint

17.21 What is a class in Python?

17.22 Why are there no field declarations in a Python class?

17.23 How do you make a field or method private in Python?

17.24 What is a module in Python?

17.8 Animating Lines and Shapes withTurtle Graphics

The Python turtle graphics system simulates a "turtle" that obeys commands to draw simple graphics.

VideoNote Introduction to Turtle Graphics

Python has a **turtle graphics** system that simulates a robotic turtle. The system displays a small cursor (the turtle) on the screen. You can use Python statements to move the turtle around the screen to draw lines and shapes. In this way, you can create basic animations.

The first step in using Python's turtle graphics system is to write the following statement:

```
import turtle
```

This statement is necessary because the turtle graphics system is not built into the Python interpreter. Instead, it is stored in a file known as the turtle module. The import turtle statement loads the turtle module into memory so the Python interpreter can use it.

If you are writing a Python program that uses turtle graphics, you will write the `import` statement at the top of the program. If you want to experiment with turtle graphics in interactive mode, you can type the statement into the Python shell, as shown here:

```
>>> import turtle
>>>
```

NOTE: Some online development environments provide a program template that automatically imports in the Turtle library. As an example, if you are using replit.com, you should choose the Python (with Turtle) template when you create your program.

Drawing Lines

The Python turtle is initially positioned in the center of a graphics window that serves as its canvas. In interactive mode, you can enter the `turtle.showturtle()` command to display the turtle in its window. Here is an example session that imports the `turtle` module, and then shows the turtle:

```
>>> import turtle
>>> turtle.showturtle()
```

This causes a graphics window similar to the one shown in Figure 17-2 to appear. Notice the turtle doesn't look like a turtle at all. Instead, it looks like an arrowhead (➤). This is important, because it points in the direction that the turtle is currently facing. If we instruct the turtle to move forward, it will move in the direction that the arrowhead is pointing.

Let's try it out. You can use the `turtle.forward(n)` command to move the turtle forward *n* pixels. (Just type the desired number of pixels in place of *n*.) For example, the command `turtle.forward(200)` moves the turtle forward 200 pixels. Here is an example of a complete session in the Python shell:

```
>>> import turtle
>>> turtle.forward(200)
>>>
```

Figure 17-3 shows the output of this interactive session. Notice a line was drawn by turtle as it moved forward.

Figure 17-2 The turtle's graphics window

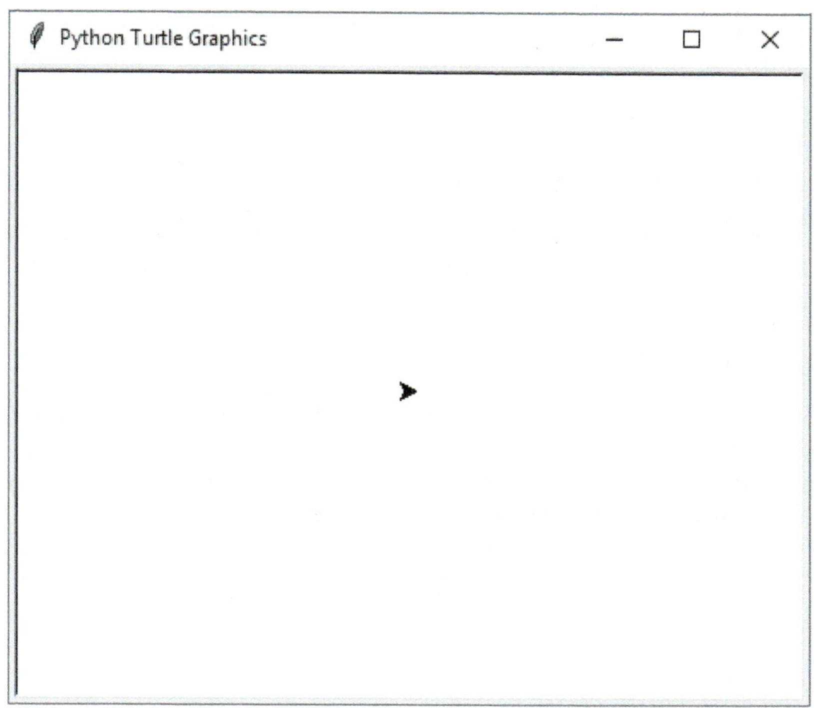

Python Software Foundation

Figure 17-3 The turtle moving forward 200 pixels

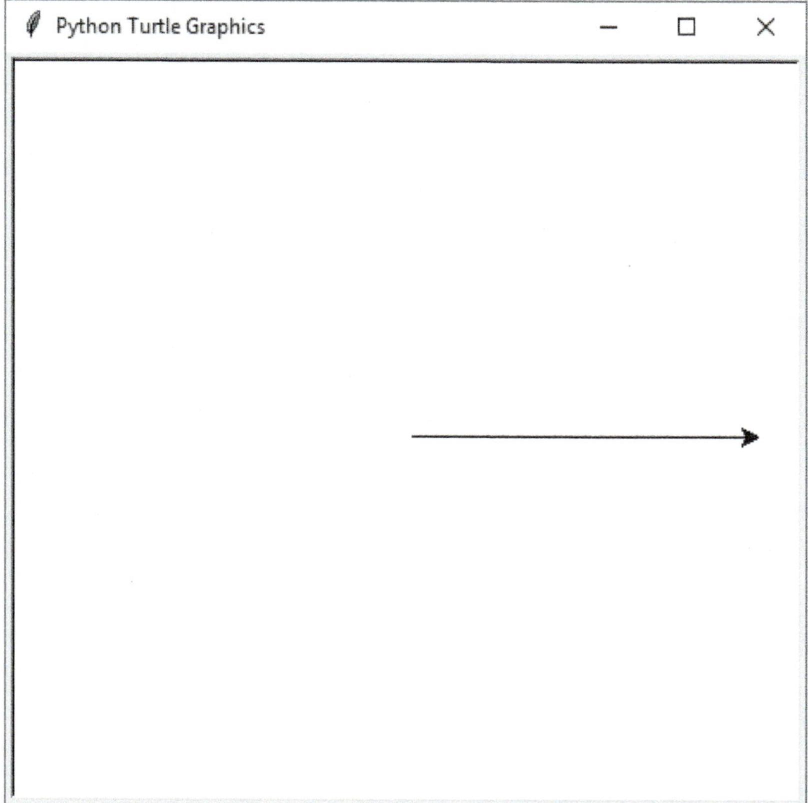

Python Software Foundation

Changing Line Direction

When the turtle first appears, its default heading is 0 degrees (east). This is shown in Figure 17-4.

You can turn the turtle so it faces a different direction by using either the `turtle.right(`*`angle`*`)` command, or the `turtle.left(`*`angle`*`)` command. The `turtle.right(`*`angle`*`)` command turns the turtle right by *`angle`* degrees, and the `turtle.left(`*`angle`*`)` command turns the turtle left by *`angle`* degrees. Here is an example session that uses the `turtle.right(`*`angle`*`)` command:

```
>>> import turtle
>>> turtle.forward(200)
>>> turtle.right(90)
>>> turtle.forward(200)
>>>
```

This session first moves the turtle forward 200 pixels. Then it turns the turtle right by 90 degrees (the turtle will be pointing down). Then it moves the turtle forward by 200 pixels. The session's output is shown in Figure 17-5.

Here is an example session that uses the `turtle.left(`*`angle`*`)` command:

```
>>> import turtle
>>> turtle.forward(100)
>>> turtle.left(120)
>>> turtle.forward(150)
>>>
```

Figure 17-4 The turtle's heading

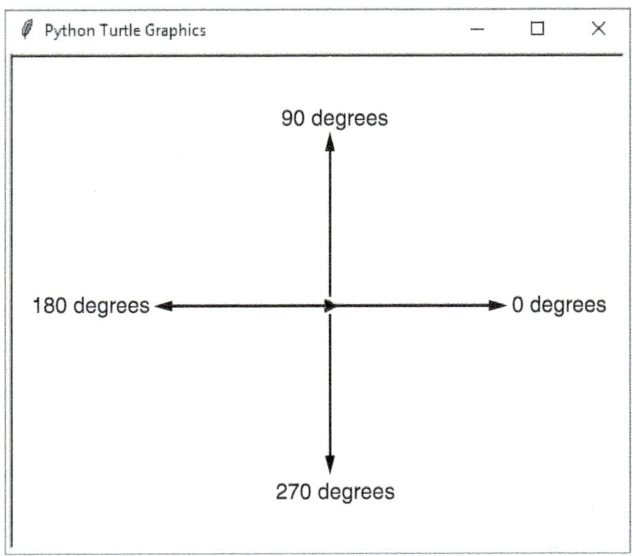

Python Software Foundation

Figure 17-5 The turtle turns right

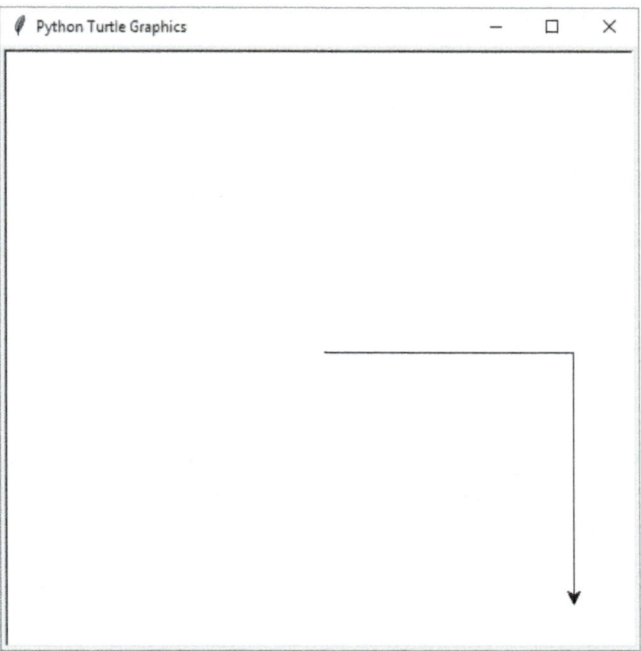

Python Software Foundation

This session first moves the turtle forward 100 pixels. Then it turns the turtle left by 120 degrees (the turtle will be pointing in a northwestern direction). Then it moves the turtle forward by 150 pixels. The session's output is shown in Figure 17-6.

Figure 17-6 The turtle turns left

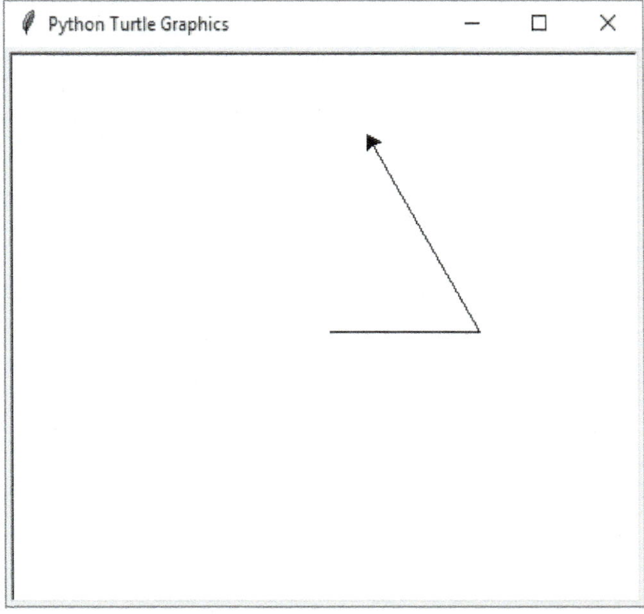

Python Software Foundation

Keep in mind that the `turtle.right` and `turtle.left` commands turn the turtle **by** a specified angle. For example, the turtle's current heading is 90 degrees (due north). If you enter the command `turtle.left(20)`, then the turtle will be turned left by 20 degrees. This means the turtle's heading will be 110 degrees. For another example, look at the following interactive session:

```
>>> import turtle
>>> turtle.forward(50)
>>> turtle.left(45)
>>> turtle.forward(50)
>>> turtle.left(45)
>>> turtle.forward(50)
>>> turtle.left(45)
>>> turtle.forward(50)
>>>
```

Figure 17-7 shows the session's output. At the beginning of this session, the turtle's heading is 0 degrees. In the third line, the turtle is turned left by 45 degrees. In the fifth line, the turtle is turned left again by an additional 45 degrees. In the seventh line, the turtle is once again turned left by 45 degrees. After all of these 45 degree turns, the turtle's heading will finally be 135 degrees.

Figure 17-7 Turning the turtle by 45 degree angles

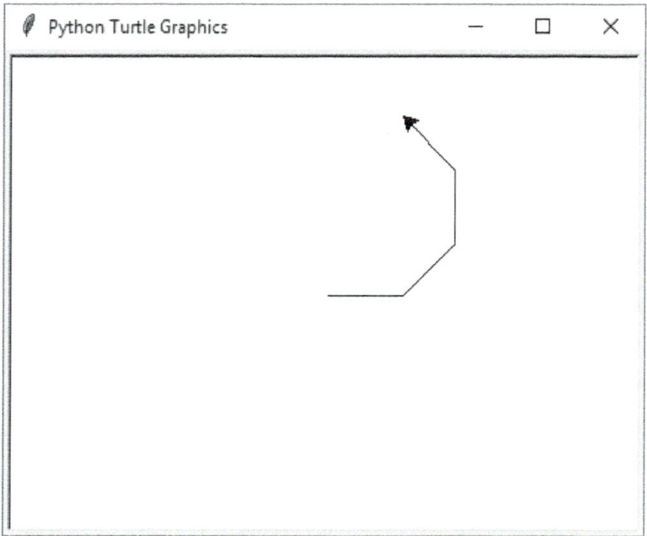

Python Software Foundation

Setting the Turtle's Heading to a Specific Angle

You can use the `turtle.setheading(angle)` command to set the turtle's heading to a specific angle. Simply specify the desired angle as the *angle* **argument**. The following interactive session shows an example:

```
>>> import turtle
>>> turtle.forward(50)
>>> turtle.setheading(90)
>>> turtle.forward(100)
>>> turtle.setheading(180)
>>> turtle.forward(50)
>>> turtle.setheading(270)
>>> turtle.forward(100)
>>>
```

As usual, the turtle's initial heading is 0 degrees. In the third line, the turtle's heading is set to 90 degrees. Then, in the fifth line, the turtle's heading is set to 180 degrees. Then, in the seventh line, the turtle's heading is set to 270 degrees. The session's output is shown in Figure 17-8.

Figure 17-8 Setting the turtle's heading

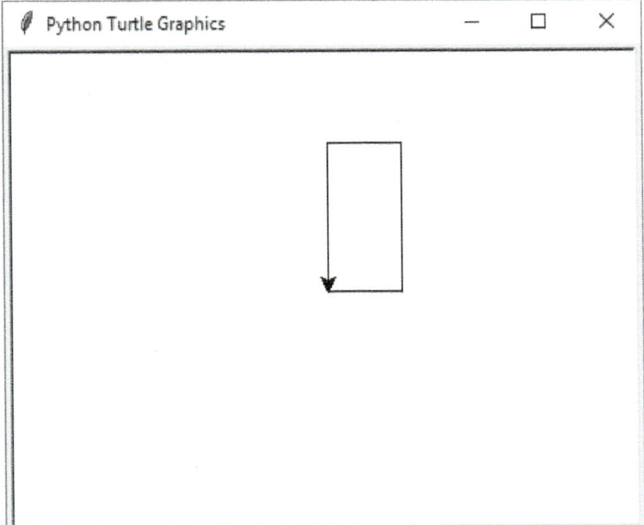

Python Software Foundation

Getting the Turtle's Current Heading

In an interactive session, you can use the `turtle.heading()` command to display the turtle's current heading. Here is an example:

```
>>> import turtle
>>> turtle.heading()
0.0
>>> turtle.setheading(180)
>>> turtle.heading()
180.0
>>>
```

Moving the Pen Up and Down

The original robotic turtle sat on a large sheet of paper, and had a pen that could be raised and lowered. When the pen was down, it was in contact with the paper and would draw a line as the turtle moved. When the pen was up, it was not touching the paper, so the turtle could move without drawing a line.

In Python, you can use the `turtle.penup()` command to "raise the pen," and the `turtle.pendown()` command to "lower the pen." When the pen is up, you can move the turtle without drawing a line. When the pen is down, the turtle leaves a line when it is moved. (By default, the pen is down.) The following session shows an example. The session's output is shown in Figure 17-9.

```
>>> import turtle
>>> turtle.forward(50)
>>> turtle.penup()
>>> turtle.forward(25)
>>> turtle.pendown()
>>> turtle.forward(50)
>>> turtle.penup()
>>> turtle.forward(25)
>>>
```

Figure 17-9 Raising and lowering the pen

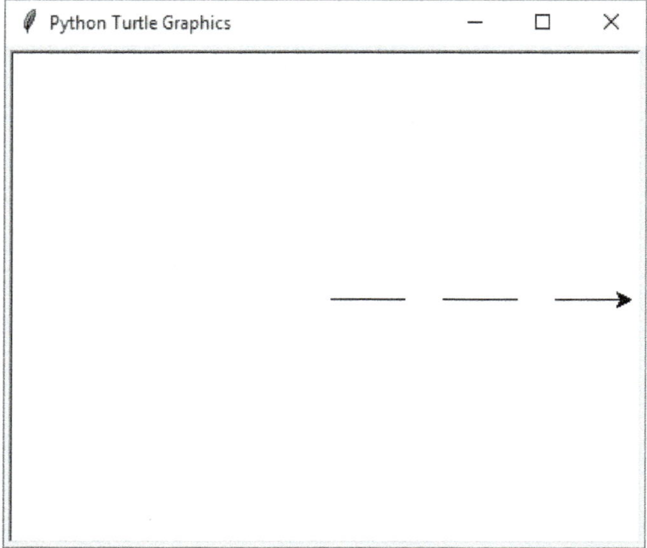

Python Software Foundation

Drawing Circles and Dots

You can use the `turtle.circle(radius)` command to make the turtle draw a circle with a radius of *radius* pixels. For example, the command `turtle.circle(100)` causes the turtle to draw a circle with a radius of 100 pixels. The following interactive session displays the output shown in Figure 17-10:

```
>>> import turtle
>>> turtle.circle(100)
>>>
```

You can use the `turtle.dot()` command to make the turtle draw a simple dot. For example, the following interactive session produces the output shown in Figure 17-11:

```
>>> import turtle
>>> turtle.dot()
>>> turtle.forward(50)
>>> turtle.dot()
>>> turtle.forward(50)
>>> turtle.dot()
>>> turtle.forward(50)
>>>
```

Changing the Pen Size

You can use the `turtle.pensize(width)` command to change the width of the turtle's pen, in pixels. The *width* argument is an integer specifying the pen's width. For example, the following interactive session sets the pen's width to 5 pixels, then draws a circle:

```
>>> import turtle
>>> turtle.pensize(5)
>>> turtle.circle(100)
>>>
```

Figure 17-10 A circle

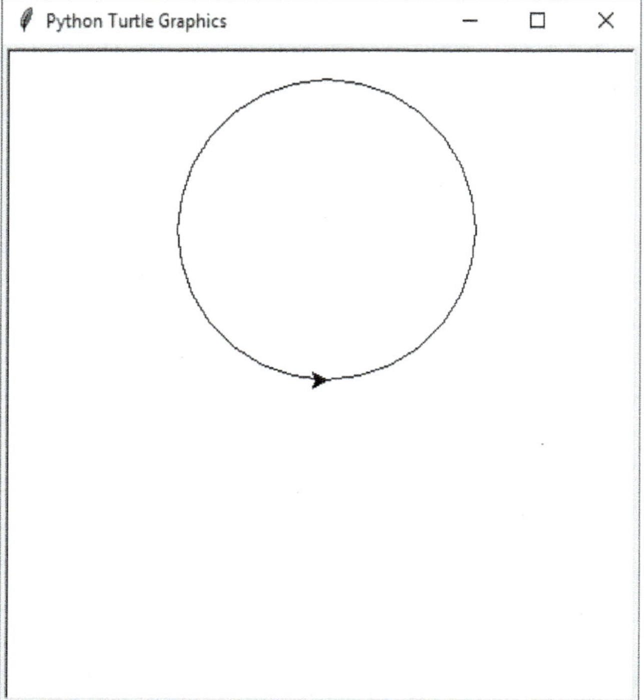

Python Software Foundation

Figure 17-11 Drawing dots

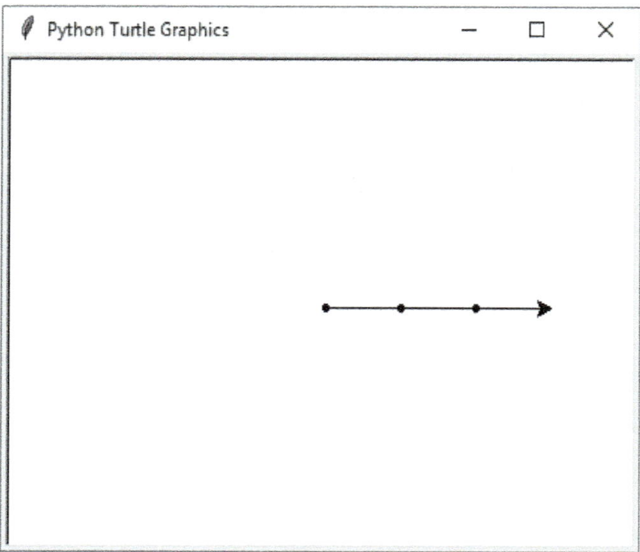

Python Software Foundation

Changing the Drawing Color

You can use the `turtle.pencolor(color)` command to change the turtle's drawing color. The *color* argument is the name of a color, as a string. For example, the following interactive session changes the drawing color to red, then draws a circle:

```
>>> import turtle
>>> turtle.pencolor('red')
>>> turtle.circle(100)
>>>
```

There are numerous predefined color names that you can use with the `turtle.pencolor` command, and Appendix D shows the complete list. Some of the more common colors are `'red'`, `'green'`, `'blue'`, `'yellow'`, and `'cyan'`.

Changing the Background Color

You can use the `turtle.bgcolor(color)` command to change the background color of the turtle's graphics window. The *color* argument is the name of a color, as a **string**, or sequence of characters. For example, the following interactive session changes the background color to gray, changes the drawing color to red, then draws a circle:

```
>>> import turtle
>>> turtle.bgcolor('gray')
>>> turtle.pencolor('red')
>>> turtle.circle(100)
>>>
```

See Appendix D for a complete list of predefined color names.

Resetting the Screen

There are three commands that you can use to reset the turtle's graphics window: `turtle.reset()`, `turtle.clear()`, and `turtle.clearscreen()`. Here is a summary of the commands:

- The `turtle.reset()` command erases all drawings that currently appear in the graphics window, resets the drawing color to black, and resets the turtle to its original position in the center of the screen. This command does not reset the graphics window's background color.
- The `turtle.clear()` command simply erases all drawings that currently appear in the graphics window. It does not change the turtle's position, the drawing color, or the graphics window's background color.
- The `turtle.clearscreen()` command erases all drawings that currently appear in the graphics window, resets the drawing color to black, reset the graphics window's background color to white, and resets the turtle to its original position in the center of the graphics window.

Specifying the Size of the Graphics Window

You can use the `turtle.setup(width, height)` command to specify a size for the graphics window. The *width* and *height* arguments are the width and height, in pixels. For example, the following interactive session creates a graphics window that is 640 pixels wide and 480 pixels high:

```
>>> import turtle
>>> turtle.setup(640, 480)
>>>
```

Moving the Turtle to a Specific Location

A **Cartesian coordinate system** is used to identify the position of each pixel in the turtle's graphics window, as illustrated in Figure 17-12. Each pixel has an X coordinate and a Y coordinate. The X coordinate identifies the pixel's horizontal position, and the Y coordinate identifies its vertical position. Here are the important things to know:

- The pixel in the center of the graphics window is at the position (0, 0), which means that its X coordinate is 0 and its Y coordinate is 0.
- The X coordinates increase in value as we move toward the right side of the window, and they decrease in value as we move toward the left side of the window.
- The Y coordinates increase in value as we move toward the top of the window, and decrease in value as we move toward the bottom of the window.
- Pixels that are located to the right of the center point have positive X coordinates, and pixels that are located to the left of the center point have negative X coordinates.
- Pixels that are located above the center point have positive Y coordinates, and pixels that are located below the center point have negative Y coordinates.

Figure 17-12 Cartesian coordinate system

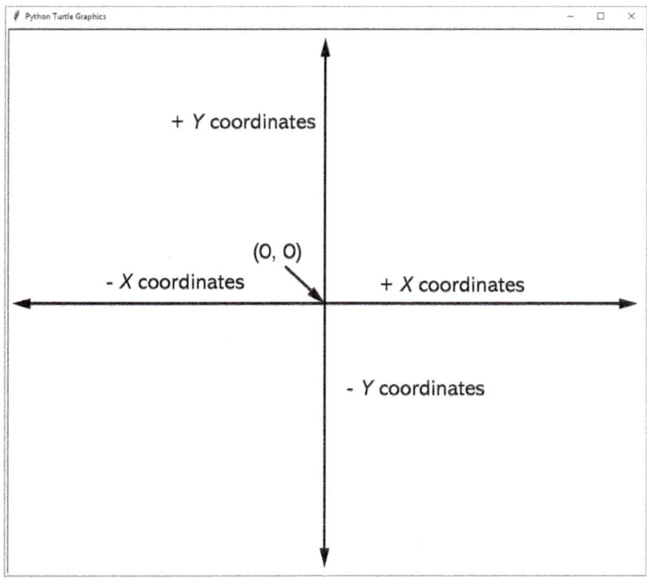

Python Software Foundation

You can use the `turtle.goto(x, y)` command to move the turtle from its current location to a specific position in the graphics window. The *x* and *y* arguments are the coordinates of the position to which to move the turtle. If the turtle's pen is down, a line will be drawn as the turtle moves. For example, the following interactive session draws the lines shown in Figure 17-13:

```
>>> import turtle
>>> turtle.goto(0, 100)
>>> turtle.goto(-100, 0)
>>> turtle.goto(0, 0)
>>>
```

Figure 17-13 Moving the turtle

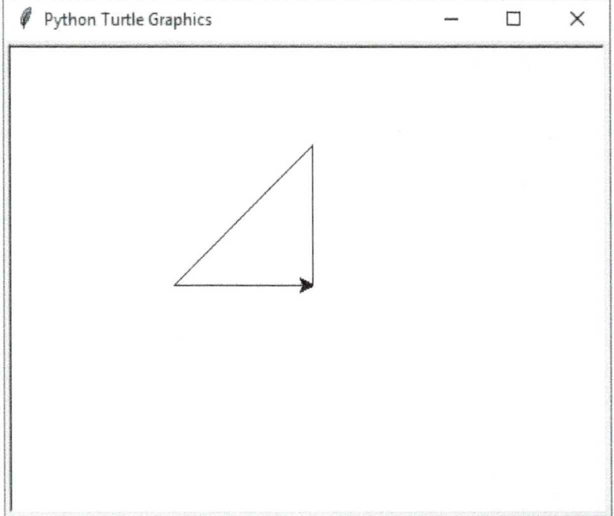

Python Software Foundation

Getting the Turtle's Current Position

In an interactive session, you can use the `turtle.pos()` command to display the turtle's current position. Here is an example:

```
>>> import turtle
>>> turtle.goto(100, 150)
>>> turtle.pos()
(100.00, 150.00)
>>>
```

You can also use the `turtle.xcor()` command to display the turtle's **X** coordinate, and the `turtle.ycor()` command to display the turtle's **Y** coordinate. Here is an example:

```
>>> import turtle
>>> turtle.goto(100, 150)
>>> turtle.xcor()
100
>>> turtle.ycor()
150
>>>
```

Controlling the Turtle's Animation Speed

You can use the `turtle.speed(speed)` command to change the speed at which the turtle moves. The *speed* argument is a number in the range of 0 through 10. If you specify 0, then the turtle will make all of its moves instantly (animation is disabled). For example, the following interactive session disables the turtle's animation, then draws a circle. As a result, the circle will be instantly drawn:

```
>>> import turtle
>>> turtle.speed(0)
>>> turtle.circle(100)
>>>
```

If you specify a *speed* value in the range of 1 through 10, then 1 is the slowest speed, and 10 is the fastest speed. The following interactive session sets the animation speed to 1 (the slowest speed) then draws a circle:

```
>>> import turtle
>>> turtle.speed(1)
>>> turtle.circle(100)
>>>
```

You can get the current animation speed with the `turtle.speed()` command (do not specify a *speed* argument). Here is an example:

```
>>> import turtle
>>> turtle.speed()
3
>>>
```

Hiding the Turtle

If you don't want the turtle to be displayed, you can use the `turtle.hideturtle()` command to hide it. This command does not change the way graphics are drawn, it simply hides the turtle icon. When you want to display the turtle again, use the `turtle.showturtle()` command.

Displaying Text in the Graphics Window

You can use the `turtle.write(text)` command to display text in the graphics window. The *text* argument is a string that you want to display. When the string is displayed, the lower-left corner of the first character will be positioned at the turtle's X and Y coordinates. The following interactive session demonstrates this. The session's output is shown in Figure 17-14.

```
>>> import turtle
>>> turtle.write('Hello World')
>>>
```

Figure 17-14 Text displayed in the graphics window

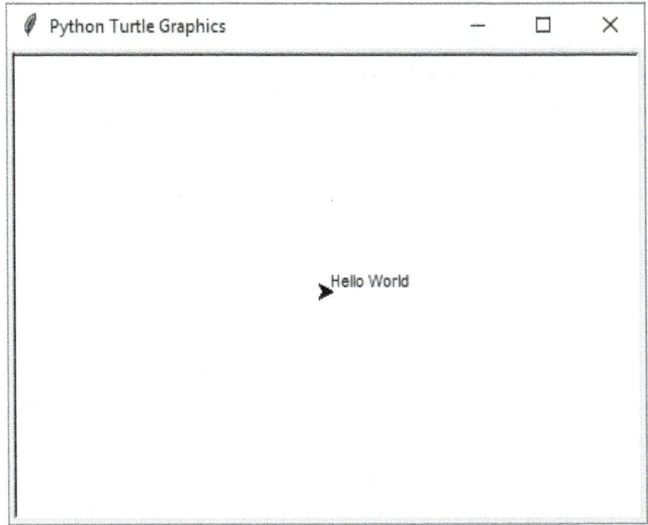

Python Software Foundation

The following interactive session shows another example in which the turtle is moved to specific locations to display text. The session's output is shown in Figure 17-15.

```
>>> import turtle
>>> turtle.setup(300, 300)
>>> turtle.penup()
>>> turtle.hideturtle()
>>> turtle.goto(-120, 120)
>>> turtle.write("Top Left")
>>> turtle.goto(70, -120)
>>> turtle.write("Bottom Right")
>>>
```

Filling Shapes

To fill a shape with a color, you use the `turtle.begin_fill()` command before drawing the shape, then you use the `turtle.end_fill()` command after the shape is drawn. When the `turtle.end_fill()` command executes, the shape will be filled with the current fill color. The following interactive session demonstrates this. The session's output is shown in Figure 17-16.

```
>>> import turtle
>>> turtle.hideturtle()
>>> turtle.begin_fill()
>>> turtle.circle(100)
>>> turtle.end_fill()
>>>
```

Figure 17-15 Text displayed at specific locations in the graphics window

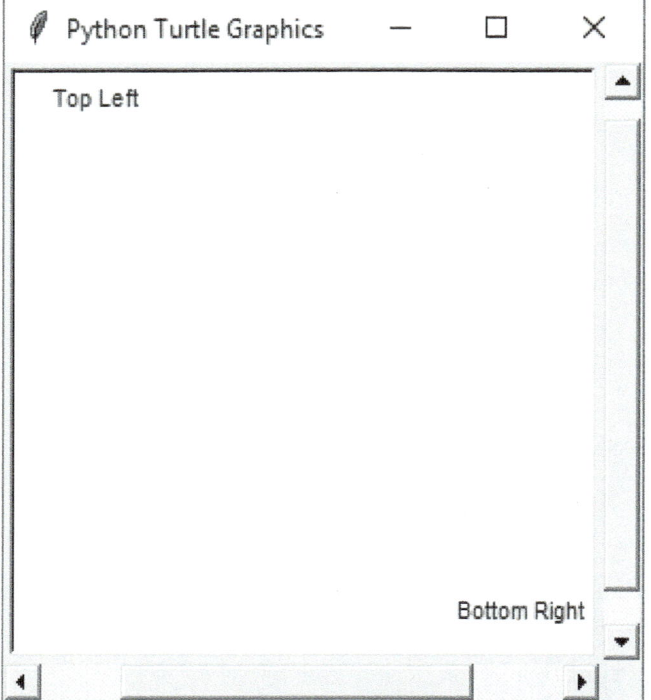

Python Software Foundation

Figure 17-16 A filled circle

Python Software Foundation

The circle that is drawn in Figure 17-16 is filled with black, which is the default color. You can change the fill color with the `turtle.fillcolor(color)` command. The *`color`* argument is the name of a color, as a string. For example, the following interactive session changes the drawing color to red, then draws a circle:

```
>>> import turtle
>>> turtle.hideturtle()
>>> turtle.fillcolor('red')
>>> turtle.begin_fill()
>>> turtle.circle(100)
>>> turtle.end_fill()
>>>
```

There are numerous predefined color names that you can use with the `turtle.fillcolor` command, and Appendix D shows the complete list. Some of the more common colors are `'red'`, `'green'`, `'blue'`, `'yellow'`, and `'cyan'`.

The following interactive session demonstrates how to draw a square that is filled with the color blue. The session's output is shown in Figure 17-17.

```
>>> import turtle
>>> turtle.hideturtle()
>>> turtle.fillcolor('blue')
>>> turtle.begin_fill()
>>> turtle.forward(100)
>>> turtle.left(90)
>>> turtle.forward(100)
>>> turtle.left(90)
>>> turtle.forward(100)
>>> turtle.left(90)
>>> turtle.forward(100)
>>> turtle.end_fill()
>>>
```

Figure 17-17 A square filled with the color blue

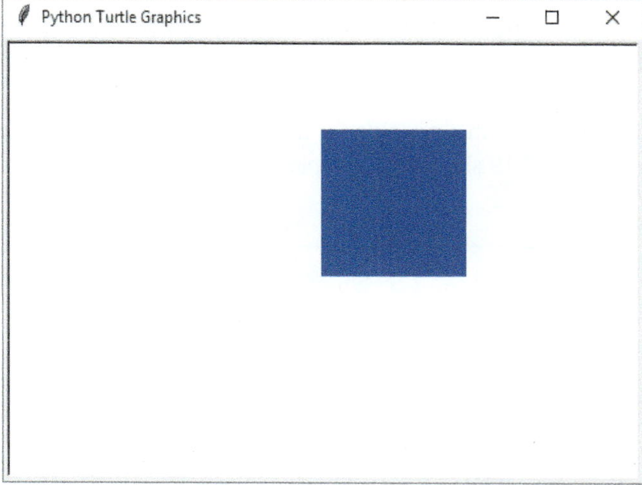

Python Software Foundation

If you fill a shape that is not enclosed, the shape will be filled as if you had drawn a line connecting the starting point with the ending point. For example, the following interactive session draws two lines. The first is from (0, 0) to (120, 120), and the second is from (120, 120) to (200, −100). When the `turtle.end_fill()` command executes, the shape is filled as if there were a line from (0, 0) to (200, −120). Figure 17-18 shows the session's output.

```
>>> import turtle
>>> turtle.hideturtle()
>>> turtle.begin_fill()
>>> turtle.goto(120, 120)
>>> turtle.goto(200, -100)
>>> turtle.end_fill()
>>>
```

Figure 17-18 Shape filled

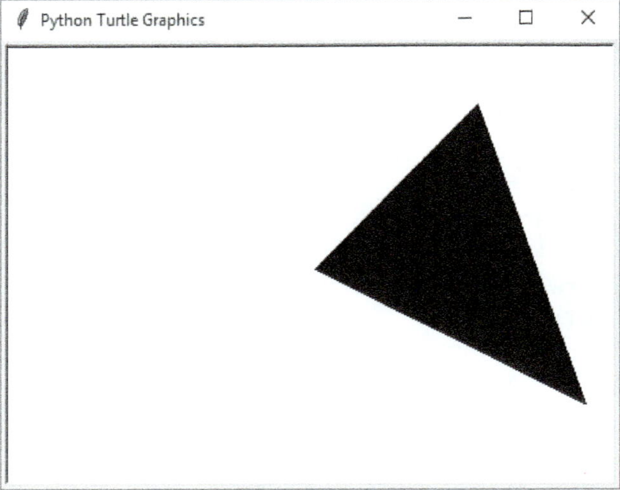

Python Software Foundation

Getting User Input with a Dialog Box

You can use the `turtle.numinput` command to get numeric input from the user and assign it to a **variable**. The `turtle.numinput` command displays a small graphical window known as a **dialog box**. The dialog box provides an area for the user to type input, as well as an OK button and a Cancel button. A dialog box that prompts for user input is a common feature of a **graphical user interface (GUI)**. Figure 17-19 shows an example.

Figure 17-19 A dialog box

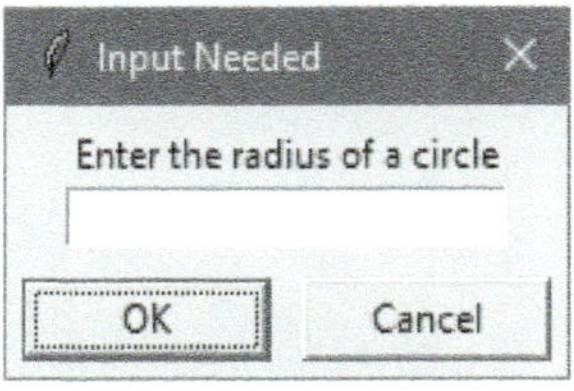

Python Software Foundation

Here is the general format of a statement that uses the `turtle.numinput` command:

```
variable = turtle.numinput(title, prompt)
```

In the general format, *`variable`* is the name of a variable that will be assigned the value that the user enters. The *`title`* argument is a string that is displayed in the dialog box's title bar (the bar at the top of the window), and the *`prompt`* argument is a string that is displayed inside the dialog box. The purpose of the *`prompt`* string is to instruct the user to enter some data. When the user clicks the OK button, the command returns the number (as a floating-point value) that the user entered into the dialog box. The number is then assigned to *`variable`*.

In addition to the *`title`* and *`prompt`* arguments, there are three optional arguments that you can use with the `turtle.numinput` command, as shown in the following general format:

```
variable = turtle.numinput(title, prompt, default=x, minval=y,
maxval=z)
```

- The `default=`*`x`* argument specifies that you want the default value `x` displayed in the input box. This makes it easy for the user to simply click the OK button and accept the default value.
- The `minval=`*`y`* argument specifies that you want to reject any number entered by the user that is less than `y`. If the user enters a number less than `y`, an error message will be displayed and the dialog box will remain open.
- The `maxval=`*`z`* argument specifies that you want to reject any number entered by the user that is greater than `z`. If the user enters a number greater than `z`, an error message will be displayed and the dialog box will remain open.

Here is an example of a statement that uses all the optional arguments:

```
num = turtle.numinput('Input Needed', 'Enter a value in the range 1-10',
                      default=5, minval=1, maxval=10)
```

This statement specifies a default value of 5, a minimum value of 1, and a maximum value of 10. Figure 17-20 shows the dialog box displayed by this statement. If the user enters a value less than 1 and clicks OK, the system will display a message similar to the one shown on the left in Figure 17-20. If the user enters a value greater than 10 and clicks OK, the system will display a message similar to the one shown on the right in Figure 17-21.

Figure 17-20 Dialog box with a default value displayed

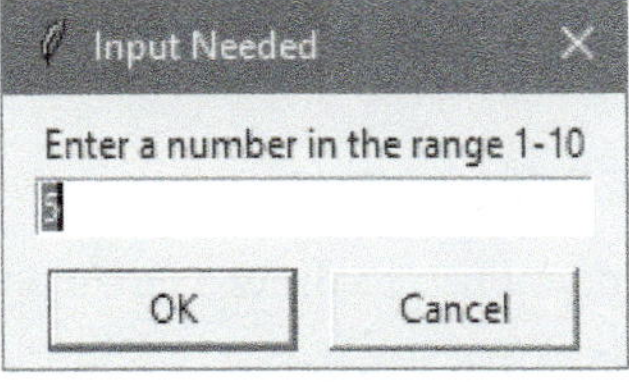

Python Software Foundation

Figure 17-21 Error messages for input out of range

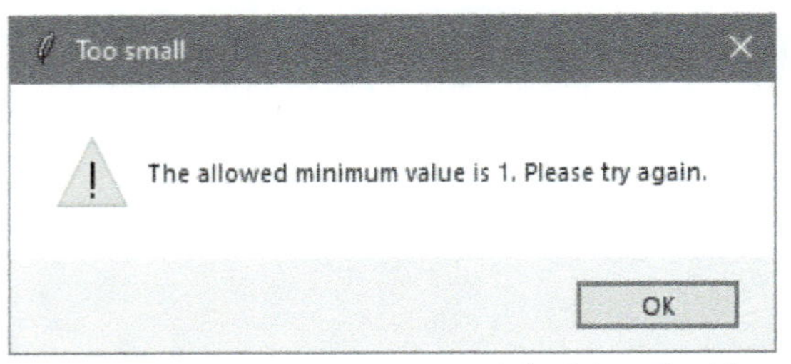

Python Software Foundation

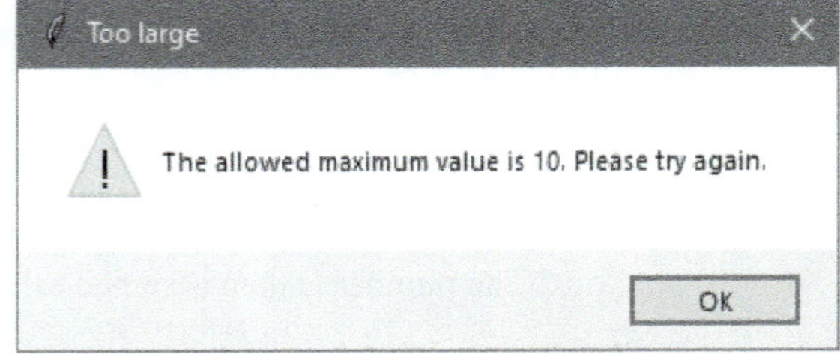

Python Software Foundation

Getting String Input with the `turtle.textinput` Command

You can also use the `turtle.textinput` command to get string input from the user. Here is the general format of a statement that uses the `turtle.textinput` command:

```
variable = turtle.textinput(title, prompt)
```

The `turtle.textinput` command works like the `turtle.numinput` command, except the `turtle.textinput` command returns the user's input as a string. The following interactive session demonstrates.

```
>>> import turtle
>>> name = turtle.textinput('Input Needed', 'Enter your name')
>>> print(name)
Jess Klaus
>>>
```

NOTE: If you are running a Python turtle graphics program from an environment other that IDLE (for example, at the command line), you may notice the graphics window disappears as soon as your program ends. To prevent the window from closing after the program ends, you will need to add the turtle.done() statement to the very end of your turtle graphics programs.

Checkpoint

17.25 Explain how turtle graphics lets you create animations.

17.26 How do you move the turtle forward?

17.27 What command would you use to draw a circle with a radius of 100 pixels?

17.28 What command would you use to change the turtle's pen size to 8 pixels?

17.29 What command would you use to change the turtle's drawing color to blue?

17.30 What command would you use to set the size of the turtle's graphics window to 500 pixels wide by 200 pixels high?

Chapter Review

Multiple Choice

1. What function do you use to display output on the computer's screen in Python?
   a. a. output
   b. b. print
   c. c. display
   d. d. screen

2. What is the argument in the Python statement:
   ```
   print('Enter your name.')
   ```
   a. a. print
   b. b. Enter
   c. c. ()
   d. d. Enter your name.

3. In Python, what do you use in place of declaring a variable?
   a. a. variable statement
   b. b. variable assignment
   c. c. assignment statement
   d. d. assignment variable

4. Which of the following is NOT a valid option for the first character of a variable name in Python?
   a. a. D
   b. b. v
   c. c. _
   d. d. !

5. What function do you use to read input from the keyboard in Python?
   a. a. input
   b. b. key
   c. c. prompt
   d. d. read

6. What Python function returns an argument's value converted to a floating-point number?
   a. a. int
   b. b. num
   c. c. float
   d. d. val

7. What Python function returns an argument's value converted to an integer?
   a. a. int
   b. b. num
   c. c. float
   d. d. val

8. What is the symbol for the Modulus arithmetic operator in Python?
   a. a. +
   b. b. %
   c. c. *
   d. d. /

9. What is the symbol for the Exponent arithmetic operator in Python?
   a. a. +
   b. b. %
   c. c. **
   d. d. /

10. What symbol do you place at the beginning of a line comment in Python?
   a. a. //
   b. b. *
   c. c. ?
   d. d. #

True or False

1. In Python, you can enclose string literals in single-quote marks or double-quote marks.
2. You do not declare variables in Python.
3. A variable name in Python must include at least one space.
4. Python does not support passing multiple arguments to the print function.
5. You cannot convert a string to a numeric data type in Python.
6. In Python, mathematical operations that are enclosed in parentheses are performed first.

Short Answer

1. Explain and demonstrate how to use quote marks in a print function in Python.
2. Explain and demonstrate how to use the print function in Python to display 'Welcome to class, students!' on the screen.
3. What happens when the following assignment statement executes?
   ```
   date = 15
   ```
4. Explain why the variable names YearSales and Yearsales are not the same.
5. Explain and demonstrate how to enter a line comment in Python.
6. What is the purpose of third-party modules in Python?

Algorithmic Workbench

1. Write a Python statement that assigns the sum of 10 and 14 to the variable total.
2. Write a Python statement that subtracts the variable down_payment from the variable total and assigns the result to the variable due.
3. Write a Python statement that multiplies the variable subtotal by 0.15 and assigns the result to the variable total.
4. Design a Python program that generates five random numbers.

Programming Exercises

1. Alone, with a partner, or with a team, write a Python program that displays the name, email address, and mailing address of your school on the screen.
2. Alone or with a partner, write a Python program that prompts the user to enter the name, email address, and mailing address of your school and then displays it on the screen.
3. Alone or with a partner, brainstorm a programmed story or game that includes displaying a student's daily schedule on the screen. Consider the input you will need, and how you want it to display. Design the program using tools such as algorithms, flowcharts, and pseudocode. Then, write the code in Python. Share your program with others in the class and improve it based on feedback.
4. Alone, or with a partner write the code to command the turtle to draw a circle with a radius determined by user input.
5. Alone, with a partner, or with a team, brainstorm an animation you can create using turtle graphics. Design the program using an algorithm, flowchart, and pseudocode. Then, use turtle graphics or the IDE of your choice to create the program and test it. Share the program with others in the class, and improve it based on their feedback.

Chapter 18 Focus on Java

Topics

18.1 Input, Output, and Processing Standards

You can apply the basic input, output, and processing knowledge you have learned so far to create programs in Java.

Setting Up a Java Program

Recall that Java is a high-level programming language used for many business applications. When you start a new Java program, you must first write a **class declaration** to contain your Java code. You can think of a class declaration as a container for Java code. Here is an example:

```
public class Simple
{

}
```

The first line of the class declaration is called the **class header**. In this example, the class header reads:

```
public class Simple
```

The words `public` and `class` are keywords in the Java language, and the word `Simple` is the name of the class. Notice that the words `public` and `class` are written in all lowercase letters. In Java, all keywords are written in lowercase letters. If you mistakenly write an uppercase letter in a keyword, an error will occur when you compile the program.

The class name, which in this case is `Simple`, does not have to be written in all lowercase letters because it is not a keyword in the Java language. This is just a word that the programmer uses as the name of the class. Notice that the first character of the class name is written in uppercase. It is not required, but it is a standard practice in Java to write the first character of a class name in uppercase. Java programmers do this so class names are more easily distinguishable from the names of other items in a program.

Another important thing to remember about the class name is that it must be the same as the name of the file that the class is stored in. For example, if you create a class named `Simple` (as shown previously), that class declaration will be stored in a file named `Simple.java`. (All Java source code files must be named with the `.java` extension.)

Notice that a set of curly braces follows the class header. Curly braces are meant to enclose things, and these curly braces will enclose all the code that will be written inside the class. So, the next step is to write some code inside the curly braces.

Inside the class's curly braces you must write the definition of a method named `main`. A **method** is another type of container that holds code. (Using methods is covered in section 18.4.) When a Java program executes, it automatically begins running the code in Java that is inside the `main` method. Here is how our `Simple` class will appear after we have added the `main` method declaration:

```
public class Simple
{
   public static void main(String[] args)
   {

   }
}
```

The first line of the method definition, which is called the **method header**, begins with the words `public static void main` and so forth. At this point, don't be concerned about the meaning of any of these words. Just remember that you have to write the method header *exactly* as it is shown. Notice that a set of curly braces follow the method header. All of the code that you will write inside the method must be written inside these curly braces.

Displaying Screen Output in Java

To display text on the screen in Java, you use the following statements:

- `System.out.println()`
- `System.out.print()`

First, let's look at the `System.out.println()` statement. The purpose of this statement is to display a line of output. Notice that the statement ends with a set of parentheses. The text that you want to display is written as a string inside the parentheses. Program 18-1 shows an example.

NOTE: The line numbers are NOT part of the program! Don't type the line numbers when you are entering program code. The line numbers are shown for reference purposes only.

Program 18-1:

```
public class Output
{
   public static void main(String[] args)
   {
      System.out.println("My major is Computer Science.");
```

Program 18-1: *(continued)*

```
6        System.out.println("I plan to be a software developer.");
7        System.out.println("Programming is fun!");
8     }
9 }
```

Program Output

```
My major is Computer Science.
I plan to be a software developer.
Programming is fun!
```

The statements that appear in lines 5 through 7 end with a semicolon. Just as a period marks the end of a sentence in English, a semicolon marks the end of a statement in Java. You'll notice that some lines of code in the program do not end with a semicolon, however. For example, class headers and method headers do not end with a semicolon because they are not considered statements. Also, the curly braces are not followed by a semicolon because they are not considered statements.

Notice that the output of the `System.out.println()` statements appears on separate lines. When the `System.out.println()` statement displays output, it advances the output cursor (the location where the next item of output will appear) to the next line. That means the `System.out.println()` statement displays its output, and then the next thing that is displayed will appear on the following line.

The `System.out.print()` statement displays output, but it does not advance the output cursor to the next line. Program 18-2 shows an example.

Program 18-2:

```
1 public class Output2
2 {
3    public static void main(String[] args)
4    {
5       System.out.print("Programming");
6       System.out.print("is");
7       System.out.print("fun.");
8    }
9 }
```

Program Output

```
Programmingisfun.
```

Notice in the program output that all the words are jammed together into one long series of characters. If you want spaces to appear between the words, you have to explicitly display them. Program 18-3 shows how we have to insert spaces into the strings that we are displaying, if we want the words to be separated on the screen. Notice that in line 5, we have inserted a space in the string, after the letter `g`, and in line 6, we have inserted a space in the string after the letter `s`.

Program 18-3:

```
public class Output3
{
   public static void main(String[] args)
   {
      System.out.print("Programming ");
      System.out.print("is ");
      System.out.print("fun.");
   }
}
```

Program Output

```
Programming is fun.
```

Variables in Java

In Java, variables must be declared before they can be used in a program. A variable declaration statement is written in the following general format:

```
DataType VariableName;
```

In the general format, *`DataType`* is the name of a Java data type, and *`VariableName`* is the name of the variable that you are declaring. The declaration statement ends with a semicolon. For example, the keyword `int` is the name of the integer data type in Java, so the following statement declares a variable named `number`.

```
int number;
```

Table 18-1 lists Java data types and describes the type of data that each can hold. Recall that a data type specifies the type of data stored in a variable, and how it will be used.

Table 18-1 Java Data Types

Data Type	What It Can Hold
`byte`	Integers in the range of – 128 to + 127
`short`	Integers in the range of – 32,768 to + 32,767
`int`	Integers in the range of – 2,147,483,648 to + 2,147,483,647
`long`	Integers in the range of – 9,223,372,036,854,775,808 to + 9,223,372,036,854,775,807
`float`	Floating-point numbers in the range of $\pm 3.4 \times 10^{-38}$ to $\pm 3.4 \times 10^{38}$, with 7 digits of accuracy
`double`	Floating-point numbers in the range of $\pm 1.7 \times 10^{-308}$ to $\pm 1.7 \times 10^{308}$, with 15 digits of accuracy
`String`	Strings of text

NOTE: String is not actually a data type in Java, it is a class. In this course, we use it as a data type.

Here are some other examples of Java variable declarations:

```
int speed;
double distance;
String name;
```

Several variables of the same data type can be declared with the same declaration statement. For example, the following statement declares three `int` variables named `width`, `height`, and `length`.

```
int width, height, length;
```

You can also initialize variables with starting values when you declare them. The following statement declares an `int` variable named `hours`, initialized with the starting value 40:

```
int hours = 40;
```

Variable Names in Java

You may choose your own variable names (and class names) in Java, as long as you do not use any of the Java keywords. The keywords make up the core of the language and each has a specific purpose. See Appendix D for a list of Java keywords.

The following are some specific rules that you must follow when naming variables in Java:

- The first character must be one of the letters a–z, A–Z, an underscore (_), or a dollar sign ($).
- After the first character, you may use the letters a–z or A–Z, the digits 0–9, underscores (_), or dollar signs ($).
- Uppercase and lowercase characters are distinct. This means `itemsOrdered` is not the same as `itemsordered`.
- Variable names cannot include spaces.

Program 18-4 shows an example with three variable declarations. Line 5 declares a `String` variable named `name`, initialized with the string "Alex Prieto." Line 6 declares an `int` variable named `hours` initialized with the value 40. Line 7 declares a `double` variable named `pay`, initialized with the value 852.99. Notice that in lines 9 through 11, we use `System.out.println` to display the contents of each variable.

Program 18-4:

```
1 public class VariableDemo
2 {
3    public static void main(String[] args)
4    {
5       String name = "Alex Prieto";
6       int hours = 40;
7       double pay = 852.99;
8
9       System.out.println(name);
10      System.out.println(hours);
11      System.out.println(pay);
```

Program 18-4: *(continued)*

```
    }
}
```

Program Output

```
Alex Prieto
40
852.99
```

Reading Keyboard Input in Java

To read keyboard input in Java, you have to create a type of object in memory known as a `Scanner` object. You can then use the `Scanner` object to read values from the keyboard, and assign those values to variables. Program 18-5 shows an example of how this is done. Let's take a closer look at the code:

- Line 1 has the following statement: `import java.util.Scanner;` This statement is necessary to tell the Java compiler that we are going to create a `Scanner` object in the program.
- Line 7 creates a `Scanner` object and gives it the name `keyboard`.
- Line 8 declares an `int` variable named `age`.
- Line 10 displays the string "`What is your age?`"
- Line 11 reads an integer value from the keyboard and assigns that value to the `age` variable.
- Line 12 displays the string "`Here is the value that you entered:`"
- Line 13 displays the value of the `age` variable.

Program 18-5: 

```
1 import java.util.Scanner;
2
3 public class GetAge
4 {
5    public static void main(String[] args)
6    {
7       Scanner keyboard = new Scanner(System.in);
8       int age;
9
10      System.out.println("What is your age?");
11      age = keyboard.nextInt();
12      System.out.println("Here is the value that you entered:");
13      System.out.println(age);
14   }
15 }
```

Program Output (with Input Shown in Bold)

What is your age?
24 [Enter]
Here is the value that you entered:
24

Notice that in line 11, we used the expression `keyboard.nextInt()` to read an integer from the keyboard. If we wanted to read a `double` from the keyboard, we would use the expression `keyboard.nextDouble()`. Moreover, if we want to read a string from the keyboard, we would use the expression `keyboard.nextLine()`.

Program 18-6 shows how a `Scanner` object can be used to read not only integers, but also `double`s and strings:

- Line 7 creates a `Scanner` object and gives it the name `keyboard`.
- Line 8 declares a `String` variable named `name`, line 9 declares a `double` variable named `payRate`, and line 10 declares an `int` variable named `hours`.
- Line 13 uses the expression `keyboard.nextLine()` to read a string from the keyboard, and assigns the string to the `name` variable.
- Line 16 uses the expression `keyboard.nextDouble()` to read a `double` from the keyboard, and assigns it to the `payRate` variable.
- Line 19 uses the expression `keyboard.nextInt()` to read an integer from the keyboard, and assigns it to the `hours` variable.

Program 18-6:

```
 1 import java.util.Scanner;
 2
 3 public class GetInput
 4 {
 5    public static void main(String[] args)
 6    {
 7       Scanner keyboard = new Scanner(System.in);
 8       String name;
 9       double payRate;
10       int hours;
11
12       System.out.print(“Enter your name: ”);
13       name = keyboard.nextLine();
14
15       System.out.print(“Enter your hourly pay rate: ”);
16       payRate = keyboard.nextDouble();
17
18       System.out.print(“Enter the number of hours worked: ”);
19       hours = keyboard.nextInt();
20
21       System.out.println(“Here are the values that you entered:”);
22       System.out.println(name);
23       System.out.println(payRate);
24       System.out.println(hours);
25    }
26 }
```

Program Output (with Input Shown in Bold)

Enter your name: **Rosa Lopez [Enter]**
Enter your hourly pay rate: **55.25 [Enter]**
Enter the number of hours worked: **40 [Enter]**
Here are the values that you entered:
Rosa Lopez
55.25
40

Displaying Multiple Items with the + Operator in Java

When the + operator is used with strings, it is known as the **string concatenation operator**. To **concatenate** means to append, or join together so the string concatenation operator appends one string to another. For example, look at the following statement:

```
System.out.println("This is " + "one string.");
```

This statement will display:

```
This is one string.
```

The + operator produces a string that is the combination of the two strings used as its operands. You can also use the + operator to concatenate the contents of a variable to a string. The following code shows an example:

```
number = 5;
System.out.println("The value is " + number);
```

The second line uses the + operator to concatenate the contents of the `number` variable with the string `"The value is "`. Although `number` is not a string, the + operator converts its value to a string and then concatenates that value with the first string. The output that will be displayed is:

```
The value is 5
```

Performing Calculations in Java

The Java arithmetic operators are listed in Table 18-2. See Chapter 6 for more on performing math calculations.

The order of operations and the use of parentheses as grouping symbols work as described in Chapter 6. Operations that are enclosed in parentheses are performed first. When two operators share an operand, the operator with the higher precedence is applied first. The precedence of the math operators, from highest to lowest, are:

1. Exponentiation

    1. 2. Multiplication, division, and remainder
    2. 3. Addition and subtraction

When two operators with the same precedence share an operand, the operators execute from left to right.

Table 18-2 Java Arithmetic Operators

Symbol	Operator
+	Addition
–	Subtraction
*	Multiplication
/	Division
%	Modulus

Here are some examples of Java statements that use an arithmetic operator to calculate a value, and assign that value to a variable:

```
total = price + tax;
sale = price - discount;
population = population * 2;
half = number / 2;
leftOver = 17 % 3;
```

Java does not have an exponent operator, but it does provide a method named Math.pow for this purpose. Here is an example of how the Math.pow method is used:

```
result = Math.pow(4.0, 2.0);
```

The method takes two double arguments (the numbers shown inside the parentheses). It raises the first argument to the power of the second argument, and returns the result as a double. In this example, 4.0 is raised to the power of 2.0. This statement is equivalent to the following algebraic statement:

$$result = 4^2$$

Named Constants in Java

You create named constants in Java using the final keyword in a variable declaration. The word final is written just before the data type. Here is an example:

```
final double INTEREST_RATE = 0.069;
```

This statement looks just like a regular variable declaration except that the word final appears before the data type, and the variable name is written in all uppercase letters. It is not required that the variable name appear in all uppercase letters, but many programmers prefer to write them this way so they are easily distinguishable from regular variable names.

Documenting a Java Program with Comments

To write a line comment in Java, you simply place two forward slashes (//) where you want the comment to begin. The compiler ignores everything from that point to the end of the line. Here is an example:

```
// This program calculates an employee's gross pay.
```

Multiline comments, or block comments, start with /* (a forward slash followed by an asterisk) and end with */ (an asterisk followed by a forward slash). Everything between these markers is ignored. Here is an example:

```
/*
     This program calculates an employee's gross pay
     including any overtime wages the employee has worked.
```

Checkpoint

18.1 What is the purpose of a class declaration in Java?

18.2 What happens if you write an uppercase letter in a Java keyword?

18.3 What is a method header in Java?

18.4 What should you type in Java to display the text "Goodnight." on screen?

18.5 What is a Scanner object in Java?

18.2 Boolean Logic and Decision Structures

You can apply your knowledge of boolean logic and conditional statements to create decision structures in Java.

Relational Operators in Java

Java's relational operators are shown in Table 18-3. For more on relational operators, see Chapter 7.

Table 18-3 Relational operators

Operator	Meaning
>	Greater than
<	Less than
>=	Greater than or equal to
<=	Less than or equal to
==	Equal to
!=	Not equal to

The `if` Statement in Java

Here is the general format of the `if` statement in Java:

```
if (BooleanExpression)
{
    statement;
    statement;
    etc;
}
```

When the `if` statement executes, it evaluates the Boolean expression. If the expression is true, the statements inside the curly braces are executed. If the Boolean expression is false, the statements inside the curly braces are skipped.

If you are writing an `if` statement that has only one conditionally executed statement, you do not have to enclose the conditionally executed statement inside curly braces. Such an `if` statement can be written in the following general format:

```
if (BooleanExpression)
    statement;
```

When an `if` statement written in this format executes, the Boolean expression is tested. If it is true, the one statement that appears on the next line will be executed. If the Boolean expression is false, however, that one statement is skipped.

The `if-else` Statement in Java

You use the `if-else` statement in Java to create a dual alternative decision structure. This is the format of the `if-else` statement:

```
if (BooleanExpression)
{
    statement;
    statement;
    etc;
}
else
{
    statement;
    statement;
    etc;
}
```

The `if-else` statement tests a Boolean expression. If the expression is true, the block of statements following the `if` clause is executed, and then control of the program jumps to the statement that follows the `if-else` statement. If the Boolean expression is false, the block of statements following the `else` clause is executed, and then control of the program jumps to the statement that follows the `if-else` statement.

If either set of conditionally executed statements contains only one statement, the curly braces are not required. For example, the following general format shows only one statement following the `if` clause and only one statement following the `else` clause:

```
if (BooleanExpression)
    statement;
else
    statement;
```

Comparing Strings in Java

In Java, you do not use the relational operators to compare strings. To determine whether `string1` is equal to `string2`, you use the following notation:

```
string1.equals(string2)
```

This is an expression that returns true if `string1` is equal to `string2`. Otherwise, it returns false. Here is an example:

```
String password = "Prospero";
if (password.equals("prospero"))
   System.out.println("Password accepted.");
else
   System.out.println("Sorry, that is not the correct password.");
```

You can also determine whether *`string1`* is less-than, equal-to, or greater-than *`string2`* using the following notation:

```
string1.compareTo(string2)
```

This expression returns an integer value that can be used in the following manner:

- If the expression's value is negative, then *string1* is less than *string2*.
- If the expression's value is 0, then *string1* and *string2* are equal.
- If the expression's value is positive, then *string1* is greater than *string2*.

For example, assume that `name1` and `name2` are `String` variables. The following `if` statement compares the strings:

```
if (name1.compareTo(name2) == 0)
   System.out.println("The names are the same.");
```

Also, the following statement compares `name1` to the string literal "Joe":

```
if (name1.compareTo("Joe") == 0)
   System.out.println("The names are the same.");
```

The `switch` Statement (Java's Case Structure)

In Java, case structures are written as `switch` statements. Here is the general format of the `switch` statement:

```
switch (testExpression)  ←  This is a variable or an expression.
{
  case value_1:
     statement        }
     statement        }  These statements are executed if the
     etc.             }  testExpression is equal to value_1.
     break;
  case value_2:
     statement        }
     statement        }  These statements are executed if the
     etc.             }  testExpression is equal to value_2.
     break;
Insert as many case sections as necessary
  case value_N:
     statement        }
     statement        }  These statements are executed if the
     etc.             }  testExpression is equal to value_N.
     break;
default:
     statement        }  These statements are executed if the
     statement        }  testExpression is not equal to any of
     etc.             }  the values listed ° the Case statements.
}                     ←  This is the end of the switch statement.
```

Consider this code as an example:

```
switch (month)
{
  case 1:
     System.out.println("January");
     break;
  case 2:
```

```
            System.out.println("February");
            break;
        case 3:
            System.out.println("March");
            break;
        default:
            System.out.println("Error: Invalid month");
    }
```

In this example, the *testExpression* is the `month` variable. If the value in the `month` variable is 1, the program will branch to the `case 1:` section and execute the `System.out.println("January")` statement that immediately follows it. If the value in the `month` variable is 2, the program will branch to the `case 2:` section and execute the `System.out.println("February")` statement that immediately follows it. If the value in the `month` variable is 3, the program will branch to the `case 3:` section and execute the `System.out.println("March")` statement that immediately follows it. If the value in the `month` variable is not 1, 2, or 3, the program will branch to the `default:` section and execute the `System.out.println("Error: Invalid month")` statement that immediately follows it.

Here are some important points to remember about the `switch` statement in Java:

- The *testExpression* must be a value or expression of one of these types: `char`, `byte`, `short`, `int`, or `String`.
- The value that follows a `case` statement must be a literal or a named constant of one of these types: `char`, `byte`, `short`, `int`, or `String`.
- The `break` statement that appears at the end of a `case` section is optional, but in most situations, you will need it. If the program executes a `case` section that does not end with a `break` statement, it will continue executing the code in the very next `case` section.
- The `default` section is optional, but in most situations, you should have one. The `default` section is executed when the *testExpression* does not match any of the `case` values.
- Because the `default` section appears at the end of the switch statement, it does not need a `break` statement.

Logical Operators in Java

Java's logical operators look different than the ones introduced in Chapter 7, but they work in the same manner. Table 18-4 shows Java's logical operators.

Table 18-4 Java's logical operators

Operator	Meaning
&&	Logical AND
||	Logical OR
!	Logical NOT

For example, the following `if` statement checks the value in `x` to determine if it is in the range of 20 through 40:

```
if (x >= 20 && x <= 40)
```

```
    System.out.println(x + " is in the acceptable range.");
```

The Boolean expression in the `if` statement will be true only when `x` is greater than or equal to 20 AND less than or equal to 40. The value in `x` must be within the range of 20 through 40 for this expression to be true. The following statement determines whether `x` is outside the range of 20 through 40:

```
if (x < 20 || x > 40)
    System.out.println(x + " is outside the acceptable range.");
```

Here is an `if` statement using the ! operator:

```
if (!(temperature > 100))
    System.out.println("This is below the maximum temperature.");
```

First, the expression `(temperature > 100)` is tested and a value of either true or false is the result. Then the ! operator is applied to that value. If the expression `(temperature > 100)` is true, the ! operator returns false. If the expression `(temperature > 100)` is false, the ! operator returns true. The previous code is equivalent to asking: "Is the temperature not greater than 100?"

Boolean Variables in Java

In Java, you use the `boolean` data type to create Boolean variables. A `boolean` variable can hold one of two possible values: `true` or `false`. Here is an example of a `boolean` variable declaration:

```
boolean highScore;
```

The variable might be used to signal that a high score has been achieved by the following code:

```
if (average > 95)
    highScore = true;
```

Later, the same program might use code similar to the following to test the `highScore` variable, in order to determine whether a high score has been achieved:

```
if (highScore)
    System.out.println("That's a high score!");
```

Checkpoint

18.6 Explain when you have to enclose a conditionally executed statement inside curly braces.

18.7 What statement do you use in Java to create a dual alternative decision structure?

18.8 How do you compare strings in Java?

18.9 What symbols are used for Java's logical operators?

18.3 Loop Statements

You can apply the basic knowledge you have learned so far about loop statements to create programs in Java.

Incrementing and Decrementing Variables in Java

Recall that to increment a variable means to increase its value and to decrement a variable means to decrease its value. Incrementing and decrementing is so common in programs that Java provides a set of simple unary operators designed just for incrementing and decrementing variables. The increment operator is `++` and the decrement operator is `--`. In Java, these operators are used often in certain types of loops.

The following statement uses the `++` operator to add 1 to `num`:

```
num++;
```

After this statement executes, the value of `num` will increased by 1. The following statement uses the `--` operator to subtract 1 from `num`:

```
num--;
```

In these examples, we have written the `++` and `--` operators after their operands (or, on the right side of their operands). This is called **postfix mode**. The operators can also be written before (or, on the left side) of their operands, which is called **prefix mode**. Here are examples:

```
++num;
--num;
```

When you write a simple statement to increment or decrement a variable, such as the ones shown here, it doesn't matter if you use prefix mode or postfix mode. The operators do the same thing in either mode. However, if you write statements that mix these operators with other operators or with other operations, there is a difference in the way the two modes work. Such complex code can be difficult to understand and debug. In this book, we use the increment and decrement operators only in ways that are straightforward and easy to understand, such as the statements previously shown.

NOTE: For more on loops, see Chapter 8.

The `while` Loop in Java

In Java, the `while` loop is written in the following general format:

```
while (BooleanExpression)
{
     statement;
     statement;
     etc;
}
```

When the `while` loop executes, the Boolean expression is tested. If the Boolean expression is true, the statements that appear inside the curly braces are executed, and then the loop starts over. If the Boolean expression is false, the loop ends and the program resumes execution at the statement immediately following the loop.

If you are writing a `while` loop that has only one statement in its body, you do not have to enclose the statement inside curly braces. Such a loop can be written in the following general format:

```
while (BooleanExpression)
    statement;
```

When a `while` loop written in this format executes, the Boolean expression is tested. If it is true, the one statement that appears on the next line will be executed, and then the loop starts over. If the Boolean expression is false, however, the loop ends.

The following code shows an example of a `while` loop that prints "Hello" five times:

```
int count = 0;
while (count < 5)
{
   System.out.println("Hello");
   count++;
}
```

The `do-while` Loop in Java

Here is the general format of the `do-while` loop:

```
do
{
      statement;
      statement;
      etc;
} while (BooleanExpression);
```

As with the `while` loop, the braces are optional if there is only one statement in the body of the loop. This is the general format of the `do-while` loop with only one conditionally executed statement:

```
do
      statement;
while (BooleanExpression);
```

Notice that a semicolon appears at the very end of the `do-while` statement. This semicolon is required, and leaving it out is a common error.

The following code shows an example of a `do-while` loop that prints "Hello" five times:

```
int count = 0;
do
{

   System.out.println("Hello");
   count++;
} while (count < 5);
```

NOTE: Java does not provide a loop that is equivalent to the `Do-Until` loop.

The `for` Loop in Java

The `for` loop is specifically designed to initialize, test, and increment a counter variable. Here is the general format of the `for` loop:

```
for (InitializationExpression;  TestExpression;  IncrementExpression)
{
      statement;
      statement;
      etc.
}
```

The statements that appear inside the curly braces are executed each time the loop iterates. The curly braces are optional if the body of the loop contains only one statement, as shown in the following general format:

```
for (InitializationExpression;  TestExpression;  IncrementExpression)
      statement;
```

The first line of the `for` loop is the **loop header**. After the keyword `for`, there are three expressions inside the parentheses, separated by semicolons. (Notice there is not a semicolon after the third expression.)

The first expression is the **initialization expression**. It is normally used to initialize a counter variable to its starting value. This is the first action performed by the loop, and it is only done once. The second expression is the **test expression**. This is a Boolean expression that controls the execution of the loop. As long as this expression is true, the body of the `for` loop will repeat. The `for` loop is a pretest loop, so it evaluates the test expression before each iteration. The third expression is the **increment expression**. It executes at the end of each iteration. Typically, this is a statement that increments the loop's counter variable.

Here is an example of a simple `for` loop that prints "Hello" five times:

```
for (count = 1; count <= 5; count++)
{
    System.out.println("Hello");
}
```

In this loop, the initialization expression is `count = 1`, the test expression is `count <= 5`, and the increment expression is `count++`. The body of the loop has one statement, which is the call to `System.out.println`. This is a summary of what happens when this loop executes:

1. The initialization expression `count = 1` is executed. This assigns 1 to the `count` variable.
2. The expression `count <= 5` is tested. If the expression is true, continue with step 3. Otherwise, the loop is finished.
3. The statement `System.out.println("Hello");` is executed.
4. The increment expression `count++` is executed. This adds 1 to the `count` variable.
5. Go back to step 2.

Checkpoint

18.10 What is the increment operator in Java?

18.11 What is the decrement operator in Java?

18.12 In Java, when can you omit curly braces around a statement in a loop?

18.13 What symbol must appear at the end of a `do-while` statement?

18.4 Methods

In Java, you use methods to break a program into small, manageable units.

In Java, modules are called **methods**. To create a method, you must write its **definition**, which consists of two general parts: a header and a body. The **method header** is the line that appears at the beginning of a method definition. It lists several things about the method, including the method's name. The **method body** is a collection of statements that are performed when the method is executed. These statements are enclosed inside a set of curly braces.

NOTE: For more on modules, see Chapter 9.

Recall that every complete Java program must have a `main` method. Java programs can have other methods as well. Here is an example of a simple method that displays a message on the screen:

```
public static void showMessage()
{
    System.out.println("Hello world");
}
```

For now, the headers for all of the Java methods that you will write will begin with the keywords `public static void`. Following this you write the name of the method, and a set of parentheses. Remember that a method header never ends with a semicolon!

Calling a Method in Java

When a method is called, the program branches to that method and executes the statements in its body. Here is an example of a method call statement that calls the `showMessage` method we previously examined:

```
showMessage();
```

The statement is simply the name of the method followed by a set of parentheses. Because it is a complete statement, it is terminated with a semicolon.

Local Variables

Variables that are declared inside a method are known as **local variables**. They are called *local* because they are local to the method in which they are declared. Statements outside a method cannot access that method's local variables.

Passing Arguments to Methods

If you want to be able to pass an argument into a method, you must declare a parameter variable in that method's header. The parameter variable will receive the argument that is passed when the method is called. Here is the definition of a method that uses a parameter:

```
public static void displayValue(int num)
{
    System.out.println("The value is " + num);
}
```

Notice the integer variable declaration that appears inside the parentheses (`int num`). This is the declaration of a parameter variable, which enables the `displayValue` method to accept an integer value as an argument. Here is an example of a call to the `displayValue` method, passing 5 as an argument:

```
displayValue(5);
```

This statement executes the `displayValue` method. The argument that is listed inside the parentheses is assigned to the method's parameter variable, `num`.

Passing Multiple Arguments

Often it is useful to pass more than one argument to a method. When you define a method, you must declare a parameter variable for each argument that you want passed into the method. The parameter declarations are separated by commas. Here is an example:

```
public static void showSum(int num1, int num2)
{
   int result;
   result = num1 + num2;
   System.out.println(result);
}
```

Here is an example of how we might call the method:

```
showSum(12, 45);
```

This statement calls the `showSum` method and passes two arguments: 12 and 45. These arguments are **passed by position** to the corresponding parameter variables in the function. In other words, the first argument is passed to the first parameter variable, and the second argument is passed to the second parameter variable. So, this statement causes 12 to be assigned to the `num1` parameter and 45 to be assigned to the `num2` parameter.

Arguments Are Passed by Value in Java

In Java, all arguments of the built-in data types are **passed by value**, which means that only a copy of an argument's value is passed into a parameter variable. A method's parameter variables are separate and distinct from the arguments that are listed inside the parentheses of a method call. If a parameter variable is changed inside a method, it has no effect on the original argument.

Global Constants

In Java, variables and constants cannot be declared outside of a class. If you declare a variable or constant inside a class, but outside of all the class's methods, that variable or constant is known as a **class field**, and will be available to all the methods within the class. Program 18-7 demonstrates how to declare such a constant. Notice that in line 3, we have declared a constant named `VALUE`. The declaration is inside the class, but it is not inside any of the methods. As a result, the constant is available to all the methods in the class. Also, notice that the declaration begins with the keywords `public static`. At this point, you do not need to be too concerned about why these keywords are required, except that this makes the constant available to all `public static` methods.

Program 18-7: 

```
1  public class FieldTest
2  {
3     public static final int VALUE = 10;
4
5     public static void main(String[] args)
6     {
7        // Statements here have access to
8        // the VALUE constant.
9     }
10
11    public static void method2()
12    {
13       // Statements here have access to
14       // the VALUE constant.
15    }
16
17    public static void method3()
18    {
19       // Statements here have access to
20       // the VALUE constant.
21    }
22 }
```

Generating Random Integers in Java

To generate random numbers in Java you create a type of object in memory known as a `Random` object. You can then use the `Random` object to generate random numbers. First, you write the following statement at the top of your program:

```
import java.util.Random;
```

Then, at the point where you wish to create the `Random` object you write a statement like this:

```
Random randomNumbers = new Random();
```

This statement creates a `Random` object in memory and gives it the name `randomNumbers`. (You can give the object any name that you wish. We simply chose `randomNumbers` for this one.) Once you've created a `Random` object, you can use it to call a value-returning method named `nextInt`, which returns a random integer number. A `Random` object's `nextInt` method is similar to the `random` library function that is discussed in your textbook. The following code snippet shows an example of how to use it:

```
int number;
number = randomNumbers.nextInt(10);
```

In this example, we are passing the argument 10 to the `randomNumbers.nextInt` method. This causes the method to return a random integer in the range of 0 through 9. The argument that we pass to the method is the upper limit of the range, but is not included in the range. In the code snippet, we are assigning the random number to the `number` variable. Here is an example of how we would generate a random number in the range of 1 through 100:

```
int number;
number = randomNumbers.nextInt(100) + 1;
```

In this example, we are passing the argument 100 to the `randomNumbers.nextInt` method. This generates a random integer in the range of 0 through 99. Then we add 1 to that number, thus causing it to be in the range of 1 through 100, and assigning the result to the `number` variable.

Writing Your Own Value-Returning Methods in Java

When you are writing a value-returning method, you must decide what type of value the method will return. This is because, instead of specifying `void` in the method header, you must specify the data type of the return value. A value-returning method will use `int`, `double`, `String`, `boolean`, or any other valid data type in its header. Here is an example of a method that returns an `int` value:

```
public static int sum(int num1, int num2)
{
    int result;
    result = num1 + num2;
    return result;
}
```

The name of this method is `sum`. Notice in the method header that instead of the word `void` we have specified `int` as the return type. This code defines a method named `sum` that accepts two `int` arguments. The arguments are passed into the parameter variables `num1` and `num2`. Inside the method, a local variable, `result`, is declared. The parameter variables `num1` and `num2` are added, and their sum is assigned to the `result` variable. The last statement in the method is:

```
return result;
```

You must have a `return` statement in a value-returning method. It causes the method to end execution and it returns a value to the statement that called the method. In a value-returning method, the general format of the `return` statement is as follows:

```
return Expression;
```

Expression is the value to be returned. It can be any expression that has a value, such as a variable, literal, or mathematical expression. In this case, the `sum` method returns the value of the `result` variable. The following code snippet shows how we might call the `sum` method:

```
int total;
total = sum(2, 3);
```

After this code executes, the value of the `total` variable will be 5.

Returning a String from a Java Method

The following code shows an example of how a method can return string. Notice that the method header specifies `String` as the return type. This method accepts two string arguments (a person's first name and last name). It combines those two strings into a string that contains the person's full name. The full name is then returned.

```
public static String fullName(String firstName, String lastName)
{
   String name;

   name = firstName + " " + lastName;
   return name;
}
```

The following code snippet shows how we might call the method:

```
String customerName;
customerName = fullName("John", "Martin");
```

After this code executes, the value of the `custerName` variable will be "John Martin".

Returning a `boolean` Value from a Java Method

Methods can also return `boolean` values. The following method accepts an argument and returns `true` if the argument is within the range of 1 through 100, or `false` otherwise:

```
public static boolean isValid(int number)
{
    boolean status;

    if (number >= 1 && number <= 100)
       status = true;
    else
       status = false;
    return status;
}
```

The following code shows an `if-else` statement that uses a call to the method:

```
int value = 20;

if (isValid(value))
   System.out.println("The value is within range.");
else
   System.out.println("The value is out of range.");
```

When this code executes, the message "The value is within range." will be displayed.

Checkpoint

18.14 What is the term for the first line of a method in Java?

18.15 What happens when you call a method in Java?

18.16 What is a local variable in Java?

18.17 What is a class field in Java?

18.5 Input Validation

Input validation can be an important security tool because it only allows user input that meets the specified requirements.

Program 18-8 is an example of how to use an input validation loop to validate that the user does not enter a negative value. For more on input validation, see Chapter 10.

Program 18-8:

```
import java.util.Scanner;

public class InputValidation
{
   public static void main(String[] args)
   {
      // Create a Scanner object for keyboard input.
      Scanner keyboard = new Scanner(System.in);

      // Local variable
      String doAnother;

      do
      {
         // Calculate and display a retail price.
         showRetail();

         // Do this again?
```

Program 18-8: *(continued)*

```
19          System.out.print(“Do you have another item? (Enter y for yes): ");
20          doAnother = keyboard.next();
21       } while (doAnother.equals(“y") || doAnother.equals(“Y"));
22    }
23
24    // The showRetail module gets an item's wholesale cost
25    // from the user and displays its retail price.
26    public static void showRetail()
27    {
28       // Create a Scanner object for keyboard input.
29       Scanner keyboard = new Scanner(System.in);
30
31       // Local variables
32       double wholesale, retail;
33
34       // Constant for the markup percentage
35       final double MARKUP = 2.5;
36
37       // Get the wholesale cost.
38       System.out.print(“Enter an item's wholesale cost: ");
39       wholesale = keyboard.nextDouble();
40
41       // Validate the wholesale cost.
42       while (wholesale < 0)
43       {
44          System.out.println(“The cost cannot be negative. Please");
45          System.out.print(“enter the correct wholesale cost: ");
46          wholesale = keyboard.nextDouble();
47       }
48
49       // Calculate the retail price.
50       retail = wholesale * MARKUP;
51
52       // Display the retail price.
53       System.out.println(“The retail price is $" + retail);
54    }
55 }
```

Program Output

```
Enter an item's wholesale cost: -1 [Enter]
The cost cannot be negative. Please
enter the correct wholesale cost: 1.50 [Enter]
The retail price is $3.75
Do you have another item? (Enter y for yes): n [Enter]
```

Checkpoint

18.18 In Program 18-8, on what line does the validation loop start?

18.19 What happens in Program 18-8 if the user enters a negative number?

18.6 Arrays

Use arrays in Java to store multiple items of the same type.

Java Array Declarations

Here is an example of an array declaration in Java:

```
int[] numbers = new int[6];
```

This statement declares `numbers` as an `int` array. The size declarator specifies that the array has 6 elements. Recall that it is a good practice to use a named constant for the size declarator, as shown here:

```
final int SIZE = 6;
int[] numbers = new int[SIZE];
```

Here is another example:

```
final int SIZE = 200;
double[] temperatures = new double[SIZE];
```

This code snippet declares `temperatures` as an array of 200 `double`s. Here is one more:

```
final int SIZE = 10;
String[] names = new String[SIZE];
```

This declares `names` as an array of 10 `String`s.

NOTE: For more on Arrays, see Chapter 11.

Array Elements and Subscripts in Java

You access each element of an array with a subscript. Recall that an element is an item stored in an array. The first element's subscript is 0, the second element's subscript is 1, and so forth. The last element's subscript is the array size minus 1. For example, the following code declares an `int` array with three elements, and then assigns values to each element. The subscripts for the elements are 0, 1, and 2.

```
final int SIZE = 3;
int[] numbers = new int[SIZE];
numbers[0] = 10;
numbers[1] = 20;
numbers[2] = 30;
```

Initializing an Array in Java

You can initialize an array with values when you declare it. Here is an example:

```
int[] days = {31, 28, 31, 30, 31, 30, 31, 31, 30, 31, 30, 31};
```

This statement declares days as an array of `int`s, and stores initial values in the array. The series of values inside the braces and separated with commas is called an initialization list. These values are stored in the array elements in the order they appear in the list. (The first value, 31, is stored in `days[0]`, the second value, 28, is stored in `days[1]`, and so forth.) Note that you do not use the `new` keyword when you use an initialization list. Java automatically creates the array and stores the values in the initialization list in it.

The Java compiler determines the size of the array by the number of items in the initialization list. Because there are 12 items in the example statement's initialization list, the array will have 12 elements.

The `length` Attribute

Each array in Java has an attribute named `length`. The value of the attribute is the number of elements in the array. For example, consider the array created by the following statement:

```
double[] temperatures = new double[25];
```

Because the `temperatures` array has 25 elements, the following statement would assign 25 to the variable `size`:

```
size = temperatures.length;
```

The `length` attribute can be useful when processing the entire contents of an array. For example, the following loop steps through an array and displays the contents of each element. The array's `length` attribute is used in the test expression as the upper limit for the loop control variable:

```
for (int i = 0; i < temperatures.length; i++)
   System.out.println(temperatures[i]);
```

Be careful not to cause an off-by-one error when using the `length` attribute as the upper limit of a subscript. The `length` attribute contains the number of elements in an array. The largest subscript in an array is `length - 1`.

Passing an Array as an Argument to a Method in Java

When passing an array as an argument to a method in Java, it is not necessary to pass a separate argument indicating the array's size. This is because arrays in Java have the `length` attribute that reports the array's size. The following code shows a method that has been written to accept an array as an argument:

```
public static void showArray(int[] array)
{
   for (int i = 0; i < array.length; i++)
      System.out.print(array[i] + " ");
}
```

Notice that the parameter variable, `array`, is declared as an `int` array. When we call this method we must pass an `int` array to it as an argument. Assuming that `numbers` is the name of an `int` array, here is an example of a method call that passes the `numbers` array as an argument to the `showArray` method:

```
showArray(numbers);
```

Two-Dimensional Arrays in Java

Here is an example declaration of a two-dimensional array with three rows and four columns:

```
double[][] scores = new double[3][4];
```

The two sets of brackets in the data type indicate that the scores variable will reference a two-dimensional array. The numbers 3 and 4 are size declarators. The first size declarator specifies the number of rows, and the second size declarator specifies the number of columns. Notice that each size declarator is enclosed in its own set of brackets.

When processing the data in a two-dimensional array, each element has two subscripts: one for its row and another for its column. In the `scores` array, the elements in row 0 are referenced as follows:

```
scores[0][0]
scores[0][1]
scores[0][2]
scores[0][3]
```

The elements in row 1 are as follows:

```
scores[1][0]
scores[1][1]
scores[1][2]
scores[1][3]
```

And the elements in row 2 are as follows:

```
scores[2][0]
scores[2][1]
scores[2][2]
scores[2][3]
```

To access one of the elements in a two-dimensional array, you must use both subscripts. For example, the following statement stores the number 95 in `scores[2][1]`:

```
scores[2][1] = 95;
```

Programs that process two-dimensional arrays can do so with nested loops. For example, the following code prompts the user to enter a score, once for each element in the array:

```
final int ROWS = 3;
final int COLS = 4;
double[][] scores = new double[ROWS][COLS];
for (int row = 0; row < ROWS; row++)
{
   for (int col = 0; col < COLS; col++)
   {
      System.out.print("Enter a score: ");
      scores[row][col] = keyboard.nextDouble();
   }
}
```

And the following code displays all the elements in the `scores` array:

```
for (int row = 0; row < ROWS; row++)
{
   for (int col = 0; col < COLS; col++)
   {
      System.out.println(scores[row][col]);
   }
}
```

Arrays with Three or More Dimensions in Java

Java allows you to create arrays with virtually any number of dimensions. Here is an example of a three-dimensional array declaration:

```
double[][][] seats = new double[3][5][8];
```

This array can be thought of as three sets of five rows, with each row containing eight elements. The array might be used to store the prices of seats in an auditorium, where there are eight seats in a row, five rows in a section, and a total of three sections.

Checkpoint

18.20 What should you use for a size declarator in a Java array statement?

18.21 When can you initialize a Java array with values?

18.22 What is the length attribute in a Java array?

18.23 Why do you not have to pass a separate argument indicating an array's size in Java?

18.7 Classes and Objects

You can apply the basic knowledge you have learned so far for object-oriented programming with Java.

NOTE: For more on classes and object-oriented programming, see Chapter 13.

Class Declarations in Java

Class Listing 18-1 shows a `CellPhone` Class in Java. Notice that each of the field declarations (lines 4 through 6) begin with the keyword `private`. This is an access specifier that makes the fields private to the class. No code outside the class can directly access private class fields. Also, notice that each of the method headers begin with the `public` access specifier. This makes the methods public, which means that code outside the class can call the methods.

Class Listing 18-1:

```
public class CellPhone
{
   // Field declarations
   private String manufacturer;
   private String modelNumber;
   private double retailPrice;

   // Method Definitions
   public void setManufacturer(String manufact)
   {
      manufacturer = manufact;
   }

   public void setModelNumber(String modNum)
   {
      modelNumber = modNum;
   }

   public void setRetailPrice(double retail)
   {
      retailPrice = retail;
   }

   public String getManufacturer()
   {
      return manufacturer;
   }

   public String getModelNumber()
   {
      return modelNumber;
   }

   public double getRetailPrice()
   {
      return retailPrice;
   }
}
```

Notice that none of the field and method declarations contain the `static` keyword. All of the fields and methods in this class are **non-static**. A non-static class field belongs to a specific object. For example, the `CellPhone` class has three fields: `manufacturer`, `modelNumber`, and `retailPrice`. Because these fields are non-static, they do not actually exist in memory until an instance of the `CellPhone` class is created. When an instance of the `CellPhone` class is created, its fields are created. Because non-static fields belong to a specific instance of the class, they are commonly referred to as **instance fields**.

Now let's discuss the difference between static and non-static methods. Static methods, such as the `main` method that you have written in every program so far, are general purpose methods that can simply be called in the program. They are defined in a class, but you do not have to create an instance of the class in order to use them. Non-static methods, however, are intended to work on an instance of the class in which they are defined. For this reason, non-static methods are usually referred to as **instance methods**. To call an instance method, an instance of the class in which the method is declared must exist.

For example, all of the methods that are declared in the `CellPhone` class are instance methods. They are meant to operate on the data that belongs to an instance of the `CellPhone` class. Before we can call any of the `CellPhone` class's methods, we must create an instance of the `CellPhone` class (in other words, we must create a `CellPhone` object). Then, we can call the `setManufacturer` method to set the manufacturer for that object. We can call the `setModelNumber` method to set the model number for that object. And, we can call the `setRetailPrice` method to set the retail price for that object. Likewise, we can call the `getManufacturer`, `getModelNumber`, and `getRetail` methods to get the manufacturer, model number, and retail price for that object.

The following code demonstrates how to create an instance of the `CellPhone` class, and use the class's methods to store data in the object:

```
// Declare a CellPhone reference variable.
CellPhone myPhone;

// Create a CellPhone object.
myPhone = new CellPhone();

// Store values in the object's fields.
myPhone.setManufacturer("Motorola");
myPhone.setModelNumber("G200");
myPhone.setRetailPrice(399.99);

// Display the values stored in the object's fields.
System.out.println(myPhone.getManufacturer());
System.out.println(myPhone.getModelNumber());
System.out.println(myPhone.getRetailPrice());
```

Constructors in Java

A class constructor in Java is a method that has the same name as the class. Class Listing 18-2 is a version of the `CellPhone` class that has a constructor. The constructor appears in lines 9 through 14.

Class Listing 18-2:

```
1 public class CellPhone
2 {
3    // Field declarations
4    private String manufacturer;
5    private String modelNumber;
6    private double retailPrice;
7
8    // Constructor
9    public CellPhone(String manufact, String modNum, double retail)
10   {
```

Class Listing 18-2: *(continued)*

```
        manufacturer = manufact;
        modelNumber = modNum;
        retailPrice = retail;
    }

    // Mutator methods
    public void setManufacturer(String manufact)
    {
        manufacturer = manufact;
    }

    public void setModelNumber(String modNum)
    {
        modelNumber = modNum;
    }

    public void setRetailPrice(double retail)
    {
        retailPrice = retail;
    }

    // Accessor methods
    public String getManufacturer()
    {
        return manufacturer;
    }

    public String getModelNumber()
    {
        return modelNumber;
    }

    public double getRetailPrice()
    {
        return retailPrice;
    }
}
```

The following code demonstrates how to create an instance of the class, passing arguments to the constructor. This code creates an instance of the `CellPhone` class, passing the arguments `"Motorola"`, `"G200"`, and `399.99` to the constructor:

```
CellPhone myPhone;
myPhone = new CellPhone("Motorola", "G200", 399.99);
```

Inheritance in Java

In Java, you use the `extends` keyword to indicate that a class is a subclass of another class. For example, look at the following class declarations:

```
public class ClassA
{
    Field and method declarations
}

public class ClassB extends ClassA
{
    Field and method declarations
}
```

The header for `ClassB` indicates that `ClassB` extends `ClassA`. So, `ClassA` is the superclass, and `ClassB` is the subclass. `ClassB` inherits all of `ClassA`'s public members.

Polymorphism in Java

Class Listing 18-3 presents Java code that demonstrates polymorphism by using the `Animal` class as a superclass.

Class Listing 18-3: 

```
public class Animal
{
   // showSpecies method
   public void showSpecies()
   {
      System.out.println("I'm just a regular animal.");
   }

   // makeSound method
   public void makeSound()
   {
      System.out.println("Grrrrrr");
   }
}
```

Class Listing 18-4 shows the Java code for the `Dog` class, which extends the `Animal` class.

Class Listing 18-4: 

```
public class Dog extends Animal
{
   // showSpecies method
   public void showSpecies()
   {
      System.out.println("I'm a dog.");
```

Class Listing 18-4: *(continued)*

```
    }

    // makeSound method
    public void makeSound()
    {
        System.out.println("Woof! Woof!");
    }
}
```

Class Listing 18-5 shows the `Cat` class, which also extends the `Animal` class.

Class Listing 18-5:

```
public class Cat extends Animal
{
    // showSpecies method
    public void showSpecies()
    {
        System.out.println("I'm a cat.");
    }

    // makeSound method
    public void makeSound()
    {
        System.out.println("Meow");
    }
}
```

Program 18-9, shown here, demonstrates the polymorphic behavior of these classes.

Program 18-9:

```
public class PolymorphismDemo
{
    public static void main(String[] args)
    {
        // Declare three class variables.
        Animal myAnimal;
        Dog myDog;
        Cat myCat;

        // Create an Animal object, a Dog object,
        // and a Cat object.
        myAnimal = new Animal();
        myDog = new Dog();
        myCat = new Cat();

```

Program 18-9: *(contined)*

```
      // Show info about an animal.
      System.out.println("Here is info about an animal.");
      showAnimalInfo(myAnimal);
      System.out.println();

      // Show info about a dog.
      System.out.println("Here is info about a dog.");
      showAnimalInfo(myDog);
      System.out.println();

      // Show info about a cat.
      System.out.println("Here is info about a cat.");
      showAnimalInfo(myCat);
   }

   // The showAnimalInfo method accepts an Animal
   // object as an argument and displays information
   // about it.
   public static void showAnimalInfo(Animal creature)
   {
      creature.showSpecies();
      creature.makeSound();
   }
}
```

Program Output

```
Here is info about an animal.
I'm just a regular animal.
Grrrrrr

Here is info about a dog.
I'm a dog.
Woof! Woof!

Here is info about a cat.
I'm a cat.
Meow
```

Checkpoint

18.24 What is the purpose of the keyword "private" in a Java class declaration?

18.25 What is another term for a non-static class field?

18.26 What is a class constructor in Java?

18.27 What is the Java keyword to indicate that a class is a subclass of another class?

Chapter Review

Multiple Choice

1. What do you write to contain your Java code?
   a. class header
   b. class footer
   c. class declaration
   d. class container
2. What character do you use to end a statement in Java?
   a. #
   b. ;
   c. :
   d. }
3. What Java data type do you use for integers in the range of –128 to +127?
   a. byte
   b. short
   c. int
   d. long
4. What Java data type do you use for integers in the range of –32,768 to +32,767?
   a. byte
   b. short
   c. int
   d. long
5. What type of object do you have to create in memory to read keyboard input in Java?
   a. Memory
   b. Key
   c. Input
   d. Scanner
6. What is the Java relational operator for Not equal to?
   a. ==
   b. >=
   c. <=
   d. !=
7. What is the Java logical operator for Logical AND?
   a. ??
   b. !!
   c. &&
   d. **

8. What loop is designed to initialize, test, and increment a counter variable in Java?
   a. for
   b. while
   c. do while
   d. for now
9. What is the term for a module in Java?
   a. module
   b. function
   c. method
   d. class
10. What is the term for each item in an array in Java?
   a. header
   b. class
   c. string
   d. element

True or False

1. In Java, a class name must be the same as the name of the file that the class is stored in.
2. In Java, you can include upper- and lower-case letters in a keyword.
3. In Java, you use the relational operators to compare strings
4. Java does not provide a `Do-Until` loop.
5. In Java, create a `Random` object in memory to generate random numbers.
6. Java methods do not allow you to return a string.
7. It is good practice to use a named constant for the size declarator in a Java array statement.
8. Java allows you to create arrays with up to four dimensions.

Short Answer

1. Explain the difference between using curly braces and parentheses in Java.
2. Explain and demonstrate in Java code how to display 'Welcome to class, students!' on the screen.
3. Explain the purpose of following Java statement:

   ```
   num++;
   ```
4. What is a Java array?
5. What is the value of the length attribute in a Java array?
6. Explain the difference between a static and a non-static method in Java.

Algorithmic Workbench

1. Write a Java statement that assigns the sum of 10 and 14 to the variable `total`.
2. Write a Java statement that subtracts the variable `down_payment` from the variable `total` and assigns the result to the variable `due`.
3. Write a Java statement that multiplies the variable `subtotal` by 0.15 and assigns the result to the variable `total`.
4. Design a Java program that generates five random numbers.

Programming Exercises

1. Alone or with a partner, write a Java program that displays the name, email address, and mailing address of your school on the screen.
2. Alone or with a partner, write a Java program that prompts the user to enter the name, email address, and mailing address of your school and then displays it on the screen.
3. Alone, with a partner, or with a team, brainstorm a programmed story or game that includes displaying a student's daily schedule on the screen. Consider the input you will need, and how you want it to display. Design the program using tools such as alogorithms, flowcharts, and pseudocode. Then, write the program in Java. Share your program with others in the class and improve it based on feedback.

Chapter 19 Focus on C++

Topics

19.1 Input, Output, and Processing Standards

You can apply the basic input, output, and processing knowledge you have learned so far to create programs in C++.

The Parts of a C++ Program

Recall that C++ is a high-level programming language often used to create operating systems, graphical user interfaces, and functionality for embedded devices. The typical C++ program contains the following code:

```
#include <iostream>
using namespace std;

int main()
{

    return 0;
}
```

You can think of this as a skeleton program. As it is, it does absolutely nothing. However, you can add additional code to this program to make it perform an operation. When you write your first C++ programs, you will write other statements inside the curly braces, as shown in Figure 19-1.

Semicolons in C++

In C++, a complete programming statement ends with a semicolon. Just as a period marks the end of a sentence in English, a semicolon marks the end of a statement in C++. You'll notice that some lines of code in our example programs do not end with a semicolon, however. That's because not every line of code is a statement.

Figure 19-1 The Skeleton C++ Program

```
#include <iostream>
using namespace std;

int main()
{
                    ← You will write other C++
                      statements in this area.
    return 0;
}
```

Displaying Screen Output in C++

To display output on the screen in C++, you write a `cout` statement (pronounced *see out*). A `cout` statement begins with the word `cout`, followed by the << operator, followed by an item of data that is to be displayed. The statement ends with a semicolon. Program 19-1 demonstrates.

Program 19-1:

```
1 #include <iostream>
2 using namespace std;
3
4 int main()
5 {
6    cout << "Hello world";
7    return 0;
8 }
```

Program Output

```
Hello world
```

The << operator is known as the **stream insertion operator**. It always appears on the left side of the item of data that you want to display. Notice that in line 6, the << operator appears to the left of the string "`Hello world`". When the program runs, *Hello world* is displayed.

You can display multiple items with a single `cout` statement, as long as a << operator appears to the left of each item. Program 19-2 shows an example. In line 6, three items of data are being displayed: the string "`Programming `", the string "`is `", and the string "`fun.`". Notice that the << operator appears to the left of each item.

Program 19-2:

```
#include <iostream>
using namespace std;

int main()
{
   cout << “Programming “ << “is “ << “fun.”;
   return 0;
}
```

Program Output

```
Programming is fun.
```

When you display output with `cout`, the output is displayed as one continuous line on the screen, for example, look at Program 19-3. Even though the program has three `cout` statements, its output appears on one line.

Program 19-3:

```
#include <iostream>
using namespace std;

int main()
{
   cout << “Programming “;
   cout << “is “;
   cout << “fun.”;
   return 0;
}
```

Program Output

```
Programming is fun.
```

The output comes out as one long line because the `cout` statement does not start a new line unless told to do so. You can use the `endl` manipulator to instruct `cout` to start a new line. Program 19-4 shows an example.

Program 19-4:

```
#include <iostream>
using namespace std;

int main()
{
   cout << “Programming” << endl;
   cout << “is” << endl;
   cout << “fun.” << endl;
   return 0;
}
```

Program 19-4: *(continued)*

Program Output

```
Programming
is
fun.
```

Variables in C++

In C++, variables must be declared before they can be used in a program. A variable declaration statement is written in the following general format:

```
DataType VariableName;
```

In the general format, `DataType` is the name of a C++ data type, and `VariableName` is the name of the variable that you are declaring. The declaration statement ends with a semicolon. For example, the keyword `int` is the name of the integer data type in C++, so the following statement declares a variable named `number`.

```
int number;
```

Table 19-1 lists some of the C++ data types and describes the type of data that each can hold.

NOTE: To use the string data type, you must write the directive #include <string> at the top of your program. To be correct, string is not a data type in C++, it is a class. We use it as a data type in this course.

Here are some other examples of variable declarations:

```
int speed;
double distance;
String name;
```

Several variables of the same data type can be declared with the same declaration statement. For example, the following statement declares three `int` variables named `width`, `height`, and `length`.

```
int width, height, length;
```

Table 19-1 C++ Data Types

Data Type	What It Can Hold
`short`	Integers in the range of − 32,768 to + 32,767
`int`	Integers in the range of − 2,147,483,648 to + 2,147,483,647
`long`	Integers in the range of − 2,147,483,648 to + 2,147,483,647
`float`	Floating-point numbers in the range of $\pm 3.4 \times 10^{-38}$ to $\pm 3.4 \times 10^{38}$, with 7 digits of accuracy
`double`	Floating-point numbers in the range of $\pm 1.7 \times 10^{-308}$ to $\pm 1.7 \times 10^{308}$, with 15 digits of accuracy
`char`	Can store integers in the range of − 128 to + 127. Typically used to store characters.

Data Type	What It Can Hold
string	Strings of text
bool	Stores the values true or false

You can also initialize variables with starting values when you declare them. The following statement declares an int variable named hours, initialized with the starting value 40:

```
int hours = 40;
```

Variable Names in C++

You may choose your own variable names in C++, as long as you do not use any of the C++ keywords. (See Appendix D for a list of C++ keywords.) The keywords make up the core of the language and each has a specific purpose. The following are some additional rules that must be followed when naming variables:

- The first character must be one of the letters a–z, A–Z, or an underscore (_).
- After the first character, you may use the letters a–z or A–Z, the digits 0–9, underscores (_).
- Uppercase and lowercase characters are distinct. This means itemsOrdered is not the same as itemsordered.
- Variable names cannot include spaces.

Program 19-5 shows an example with three variable declarations. Notice that, because we are using a string variable, we have the #include <string> directive in line 2. Line 7 declares a string variable named name, initialized with the string "Alex Prieto." Line 8 declares an int variable named hours initialized with the value 40. Line 9 declares a double variable named pay, initialized with the value 852.99. Notice that in lines 11 through 13, we use cout to display the contents of each variable.

Program 19-5:

```
1 #include <iostream>
2 #include <string>
3 using namespace std;
4
5 int main()
6 {
7     string name = "Alex Prieto";
8     int hours = 40;
9     double pay = 852.99;
10
11    cout << name << endl;
12    cout << hours << endl;
13    cout << pay << endl;
14    return 0;
15 }
```

Program Output

```
Alex Prieto
40
852.99
```

Reading Keyboard Input in C++

To read keyboard input in C++, you write a `cin` statement (pronounced *see in*). A `cin` statement begins with the word `cin`, followed by the >> operator, followed by the name of a variable. The statement ends with a semicolon. When the statement executes, the program will wait for the user to enter input at the keyboard, and press the Enter key. When the user presses Enter, the input will be assigned to the variable that is listed after the >> operator. Program 19-6 demonstrates.

Program 19-6:

```
#include <iostream>
using namespace std;

int main()
{
   int age;

   cout << "What is your age?" << endl;
   cin >> age;
   cout << "Here is the value that you entered:" << endl;
   cout << age;
   return 0;
}
```

Program Output (with Input Shown in Bold)

```
What is your age?
24 [Enter]
Here is the value that you entered:
24
```

The program shown in Program 19-7 uses `cin` statements to read a string, an integer, and a `double`.

Program 19-7:

```
#include <iostream>
#include <string>
using namespace std;

int main()
{
   string name;
   double payRate;
   int hours;


   cout << "Enter your first name." << endl;
   cin >> name;
   cout << "Enter your hourly pay rate." << endl;
   cin >> payRate;
   cout << "Enter the number of hours worked." << endl;
   cin >> hours;

   cout << "Here are the values that you entered:" << endl;
```

Program 19-7: *(continued)*

```
   cout << name << endl;
   cout << payRate << endl;
   cout << hours << endl;
   return 0;
}
```

Program Output (with Input Shown in Bold)

```
Enter your first name.
Connie [Enter]
Enter your hourly pay rate.
55.25 [Enter]
Enter the number of hours worked.
40 [Enter]
Here are the values that you entered:
Connie
55.25
40
```

Special Case: Reading String Input Containing Spaces

A `cin` statement can read one-word string input, as previously shown in Program 19-7, but it does not behave as you would expect when the user's input is a string containing multiple words, separated by spaces. If you want to read a string that contains multiple words, you must use the `getline` function. The `getline` function reads an entire line of input, including embedded spaces, and stores it in a `string` variable. The `getline` function looks like the following, where `inputLine` is the name of the `string` variable receiving the input.

```
getline(cin, inputLine);
```

Program 19-8 shows an example of how the `getline` function is used.

Program 19-8:

```
// This program demonstrates using the getline function
// to read input into a string variable.
#include <iostream>
#include <string>
using namespace std;

int main()
{
   string name;
   string city;

   cout << "Please enter your name." << endl;
   getline(cin, name);

   cout << "Enter the city you live in." << endl;
   getline(cin, city);
```

Program 19-8: *(continued)*

```

    cout << "Hello, " << name << endl;
    cout << "You live in " << city << endl;
    return 0;
}
```

Program Output (with Input Shown in Bold)

```
Please enter your name.
Kiran Sharma [Enter]
Enter the city you live in.
New York City [Enter]
Hello, Kiran Sharma
You live in New York City
```

Performing Calculations in C++

The C++ arithmetic operators are listed in Table 19-2.

The order of operations and the use of parentheses as grouping symbols work as described in Chapter 6. Operations that are enclosed in parentheses are performed first. When two operators share an operand, the operator with the higher precedence is applied first. The precedence of the math operators, from highest to lowest, are:

1. Exponentiation
2. Multiplication, division, and remainder
3. Addition and subtraction

When two operators with the same precedence share an operand, the operators execute from left to right.

Table 19-2 C++ Arithmetic Operators

Symbol	Operator
+	Addition
–	Subtraction
*	Multiplication
/	Division
%	Modulus

Here are some examples of C++ statements that use an arithmetic operator to calculate a value, and assign that value to a variable:

```
total = price + tax;
sale = price - discount;
population = population * 2;
half = number / 2;
leftOver = 17 % 3;
```

C++ does not have an exponent operator, but it does provide a function named pow for this purpose. Here is an example of how the pow function is used:

```
result = pow(4.0, 2.0);
```

The function takes two double arguments (the numbers shown inside the parentheses). It raises the first argument to the power of the second argument, and returns the result as a double. In this example, 4.0 is raised to the power of 2.0. This statement is equivalent to the following algebraic statement:

$$result = 4^2$$

Named Constants in C++

You create named constants in C++ using the const keyword in a variable declaration. The word const is written just before the data type. Here is an example:

```
const double INTEREST_RATE = 0.069;
```

NOTE: It is not required that a const variable name appear in all uppercase letters, but many programmers prefer to write them this way so they are easily distinguishable from regular variable names.

An initialization value must be given when declaring a variable with the const modifier, or an error will result when the program is compiled. A compiler error will also result if there are any statements in the program that attempt to change the value of a const variable.

Documenting a Program with Comments in C++

To write a line comment in C++, you simply place two forward slashes (//) where you want the comment to begin. The compiler ignores everything from that point to the end of the line. Here is an example:

```
// This program calculates an employee's gross pay.
```

Multiline comments, or block comments, start with /* (a forward slash followed by an asterisk) and end with */ (an asterisk followed by a forward slash). Everything between these markers is ignored. Here is an example:

```
/*
    This program calculates an employee's gross pay
    including any overtime wages the employee has worked.
*/
```

Checkpoint

19.1 What character ends a complete programming statement in C++?

19.2 What statement to you use to display output on the screen in C++?

19.3 What character do you enter to the left of data you want to display in C++?

19.2 Boolean Logic and Decision Structures

You can apply your knowledge of boolean logic and conditional statements to create decision structures in C++.

Relational Operators in C++

C++'s relational operators, shown in Table 19-3. For more on relational operators, see Chapter 7.

Table 19-3 Relational operators

Operator	Meaning
>	Greater than
<	Less than
>=	Greater than or equal to
<=	Less than or equal to
==	Equal to
!=	Not equal to

The `if` Statement in C++

Here is the general format of the `if` statement in C++:

```
if (BooleanExpression)
{
    statement;
    statement;
    etc;
}
```

When the `if` statement executes, it evaluates the Boolean expression. If the expression is true, the statements inside the curly braces are executed. If the Boolean expression is false, the statements inside the curly braces are skipped.

If you are writing an `if` statement that has only one conditionally executed statement, you do not have to enclose the conditionally executed statement inside curly braces. Such an `if` statement can be written in the following general format:

```
if (BooleanExpression)
    statement;
```

When an `if` statement written in this format executes, the Boolean expression is tested. If it is true, the one statement that appears on the next line will be executed. If the Boolean expression is false, however, that one statement is skipped.

The `if-else` Statement in C++

You use the `if-else` statement in C++ to create a dual alternative decision structure. This is the format of the `if-else` statement:

```
if (BooleanExpression)
{
    statement;
    statement;
    etc;
}
else
{
    statement;
    statement;
    etc;
}
```

The `if-else` statement tests a Boolean expression. If the expression is true, the block of statements following the `if` clause is executed, and then control of the program jumps to the statement that follows the `if-else` statement. If the Boolean expression is false, the block of statements following the `else` clause is executed, and then control of the program jumps to the statement that follows the `if-else` statement.

If either set of conditionally executed statements contains only one statement, the curly braces are not required. For example, the following general format shows only one statement following the `if` clause and only one statement following the `else` clause:

```
if (BooleanExpression)
    statement;
else
    statement;
```

The `switch` Statement (C++'s Case Structure)

In C++, case structures are written as `switch` statements. Here is the general format of the `switch` statement:

```
switch (testExpression)      ← This is an integer variable or an expression.
{
case value_1:
    statement
    statement      } These statements are executed if the
    etc.           } testExpression is equal to value_1.
    break;
case value_2:
    statement
    statement      } These statements are executed if the
    etc.           } testExpression is equal to value_2.
    break;
Insert as many case sections as necessary.
```

```
    case value_N:
        statement          } These statements are executed if the
        statement          } testExpression is equal to value_N.
        etc.
        break;
    default:
        statement          } These statements are executed if the
        statement          } testExpression is not equal to any of the
        etc.               } values listed after the Case statements.
}                 <------  This is the end of the switch statement.
```

When the `switch` statement executes, it compares the value of the *testExpression* with the values that follow each of the `case` statements (from top to bottom). When it finds a `case` value that matches the *testExpression*'s value, the program branches to the `case` statement. The statements that follow the `case` statement are executed, until a `break` statement is encountered. At that point, program jumps out of the `switch` statement. If the *testExpression* does not match any of the `case` values, the program branches to the `default` statement and executes the statements that immediately following it.

Consider this code as an example:

```
switch (month)
{
   case 1:
     cout << "January" << endl;
     break;
   case 2:
     cout << "February" << endl;
     break;
   case 3:
     cout << "March" << endl;
     break;
   default:
     cout << "Error: Invalid month" << endl;
}
```

Here are some important points to remember about the `switch` statement in C++:

- The *testExpression* must be a value or expression of one of the integer data types (including `char`).
- The value that follows a `case` statement must be a literal or a named constant of one of the integer data types (including `char`).
- The `break` statement that appears at the end of a `case` section is optional, but in most situations, you will need it. If the program executes a `case` section that does not end with a `break` statement, it will continue executing the code in the very next `case` section.
- The `default` section is optional, but in most situations, you should have one. The `default` section is executed when the *testExpression* does not match any of the `case` values.
- Because the `default` section appears at the end of the `switch` statement, it does not need a `break` statement.

Logical Operators in C++

C++'s logical operators look different than the ones used in this chapter's pseudocode, but they work in the same manner. Table 19-4 shows C++'s logical operators. See Chapter 7 for more on logical operators.

Table 19-4 C++'s logical operators

Operator	Meaning
&&	Logical AND
||	Logical OR
!	Logical NOT

For example, the following `if` statement checks the value in `x` to determine if it is in the range of 20 through 40:

```
if (x >= 20 && x <= 40)
   cout << x << " is in the acceptable range." << endl;
```

The Boolean expression in the `if` statement will be true only when `x` is greater than or equal to 20 AND less than or equal to 40. The value in `x` must be within the range of 20 through 40 for this expression to be true. The following statement determines whether `x` is outside the range of 20 through 40:

```
if (x < 20 || x > 40)
   cout << x << " is outside the acceptable range." << endl;
```

Here is an `if` statement using the ! operator:

```
if (!(temperature > 100))
   cout << "This is below the maximum temperature." << endl;
```

First, the expression `(temperature > 100)` is tested and a value of either true or false is the result. Then the ! operator is applied to that value. If the expression `(temperature > 100)` is true, the ! operator returns false. If the expression `(temperature > 100)` is false, the ! operator returns true. The previous code is equivalent to asking: "Is the temperature not greater than 100?"

`bool` Variables in C++

In C++, you use the `bool` data type to create Boolean variables. A `boolean` variable can hold one of two possible values: `true` or `false`. See Chapter 7 for more on Boolean variables. Here is an example of a `bool` variable declaration:

```
bool highScore;
```

Boolean variables are commonly used as flags that signal when some condition exists in the program. When the flag variable is set to false, it indicates the condition does not yet exist. When the flag variable is set to true, it means the condition does exist.

For example, suppose a test grading program has a `bool` variable named `highScore`. The variable might be used to signal that a high score has been achieved by the following code:

```
if (average > 95)
   highScore = true;
```

Checkpoint

19.4 In C++, w do you have to enclose a conditionally executed statement inside curly braces?

19.5 What statement do you use in C++ to create a dual alternative decision structure?

19.6 What symbols are used for C++'s logical operators?

19.7 In C++, what data type do you use to create Boolean variables?

19.3 Loop Statements

You can apply the basic knowledge you have learned so far about loop statements to create programs in C++.

Incrementing and Decrementing Variables in C++

Recall that to increment a variable means to increase its value and to decrement a variable means to decrease its value. Incrementing and decrementing is so common in programs that C++ provides a set of simple unary operators designed just for incrementing and decrementing variables. The increment operator is `++` and the decrement operator is `--`. In C++, these operators are used often in certain types of loops.

The following statement uses the `++` operator to add 1 to `num`:

```
num++;
```

After this statement executes, the value of `num` will increased by 1. The following statement uses the `--` operator to subtract 1 from `num`:

```
num--;
```

In these examples, we have written the `++` and `--` operators after their operands (or, on the right side of their operands). This is called **postfix mode**. The operators can also be written before (or, on the left side) of their operands, which is called **prefix mode**. Here are examples:

```
++num;
--num;
```

When you write a simple statement to increment or decrement a variable, such as the ones shown here, it doesn't matter if you use prefix mode or postfix mode. The operators do the same thing in either mode. However, if you write statements that mix these operators with other operators or with other operations, there is a difference in the way the two modes work. Such complex code can be difficult to understand and debug. In this book, we use the increment and decrement operators only in ways that are straightforward and easy to understand, such as the statements previously shown.

NOTE: For more on loops, see Chapter 8.

The `while` Loop in C++

In C++, the `while` loop is written in the following general format:

```
while (BooleanExpression)
{
      statement;
      statement;
      etc;
}
```

When the `while` loop executes, the Boolean expression is tested. If the Boolean expression is true, the statements that appear inside the curly braces are executed, and then the loop starts over. If the Boolean expression is false, the loop ends and the program resumes execution at the statement immediately following the loop.

If you are writing a `while` loop that has only one statement in its body, you do not have to enclose the statement inside curly braces. Such a loop can be written in the following general format:

```
while (BooleanExpression)
      statement;
```

When a `while` loop written in this format executes, the Boolean expression is tested. If it is true, the one statement that appears on the next line will be executed, and then the loop starts over. If the Boolean expression is false, however, the loop ends.

The following code shows an example of a `while` loop that prints *Hello* five times:

```
int count = 0;
while (count < 5)
{
   cout << "Hello" << endl;
   count++;
}
```

The `do-while` Loop in C++

Here is the general format of the `do-while` loop:

```
do
{
     statement;
     statement;
     etc;
} while (BooleanExpression);
```

As with the `while` loop, the braces are optional if there is only one statement in the body of the loop. This is the general format of the `do-while` loop with only one conditionally executed statement:

```
do
     statement;
while (BooleanExpression);
```

Notice that a semicolon appears at the very end of the `do-while` statement. This semicolon is required, and leaving it out is a common error.

The following code shows an example of a `do-while` loop that prints *Hello* five times:

```
int count = 0;
do
{
   cout << "Hello" << endl;
   count++;
} while (count < 5);
```

NOTE: C++ does not provide a loop that is equivalent to the `Do-Until` loop.

The `for` Loop in C++

The `for` loop is specifically designed to initialize, test, and increment a counter variable. Here is the general format of the `for` loop:

```
for (InitializationExpression;  TestExpression;  IncrementExpression)
{
      statement;
      statement;
      etc.
}
```

The statements that appear inside the curly braces are executed each time the loop iterates. The curly braces are optional if the body of the loop contains only one statement, as shown in the following general format:

```
for (InitializationExpression;  TestExpression;  IncrementExpression)
      statement;
```

The first line of the `for` loop is the **loop header**. After the keyword `for`, there are three expressions inside the parentheses, separated by semicolons. (Notice there is not a semicolon after the third expression.)

The first expression is the **initialization expression**. It is normally used to initialize a counter variable to its starting value. This is the first action performed by the loop, and it is only done once. The second expression is the **test expression**. This is a Boolean expression that controls the execution of the loop. As long as this expression is true, the body of the `for` loop will repeat. The `for` loop is a pretest loop, so it evaluates the test expression before each iteration. The third expression is the **increment expression**. It executes at the end of each iteration. Typically, this is a statement that increments the loop's counter variable.

Here is an example of a simple `for` loop that prints "Hello" five times:

```
for (count = 1; count <= 5; count++)
{
    cout << "Hello" << endl;
}
```

In this loop, the initialization expression is `count = 1`, the test expression is `count <= 5`, and the increment expression is `count++`. The body of the loop has one statement. This is a summary of what happens when this loop executes:

1. The initialization expression `count = 1` is executed. This assigns 1 to the `count` variable.
2. The expression `count <= 5` is tested. If the expression is true, continue with step 3. Otherwise, the loop is finished.
3. The statement `cout << "Hello" << endl;` is executed.
4. The increment expression `count++` is executed. This adds 1 to the `count` variable.
5. Go back to step 2.

Checkpoint

19.8 What is the decrement operator in C++?

19.9 What mode is being used when the increment operator is written after its operands?

19.10 What symbol must appear at the end of a `do-while` statement in C++?

19.11 In C++, when are curly braces optional in the body of a loop?

19.4 Functions

In C++, you use functions instead of modules to break a program into small, manageable units.

Defining and Calling a Function in C++

To create a function in C++, you write its **definition**. Here is the general format of a function definition:

```
void showMessage()
{
    cout << "Hello world" << endl;
}
```

For now, the headers for all the C++ functions that you will write will begin with the keyword `void`. Following this you write the name of the function, and a set of parentheses. Remember that a function header never ends with a semicolon!

NOTE: For more on functions, see Chapter 9.

Calling a Function

A function executes when it is called. The `main` function is automatically called when a program starts, but other functions are executed by function call statements. When a function is called, the program branches to that function and executes the statements in its body. Here is an example of a function call statement that calls the `showMessage` function we previously examined:

```
showMessage();
```

The statement is simply the name of the function followed by a set of parentheses. Because it is a complete statement, it is terminated with a semicolon. Program 19-9 shows a C++ program that demonstrates the `showMessage` function.

Program 19-9:

```
1  #include <iostream>
2  using namespace std;
3
4  void showMessage();
5
6  int main()
7  {
8     cout << "I have a message for you." << endl;
9     showMessage();
10    cout << "That's all, folks!" << endl;
11    return 0;
12 }
13
14 void showMessage()
15 {
16    cout << "Hello world" << endl;
17 }
```

Program Output

```
I have a message for you.
Hello world
That's all, folks!
```

The program has two functions: `main` and `showMessage`. The `main` function appears in lines 6 through 12, and the `showMessage` function appears in lines 14 through 17. When the program runs, the `main` function executes. The statement in line 8 displays "I have a message for you." Then the statement in line 9 calls the `showMessage` function. This causes the program to branch to the `showMessage` function and execute the statement that appears in line 16. This displays "Hello world". The program then branches back to the `main` function and resumes execution at line 10. This displays "That's all, folks!"

Notice the statement that appears in line 4:

```
void showMessage();
```

This line of code is a function prototype. A **function prototype** is a statement that declares the existence of a function, but does not define the function. It is merely a way of telling the compiler that a particular function exists in the program, and its definition appears at a later point. Without this statement, an error would occur when the program is compiled.

Local Variables in C++

Variables that are declared inside a function are known as **local variables**. They are called *local* because they are local to the function in which they are declared. Statements outside a function cannot access that function's local variables. Because a function's local variables are hidden from other functions, the other functions may have their own local variables with the same name.

Passing Arguments to Functions in C++

If you want to be able to pass an argument into a C++ function, you must declare a parameter variable in that function's header. The parameter variable will receive the argument that is passed when the function is called. Here is the definition of a function that uses a parameter:

```
void displayValue(int num)
{
    cout << "The value is " << num << endl;
}
```

Notice the integer variable declaration that appears inside the parentheses (`int num`). This is the declaration of a parameter variable, which enables the `displayValue` function to accept an integer value as an argument. Here is an example of a call to the `displayValue` function, passing 5 as an argument:

```
displayValue(5);
```

This statement executes the `displayValue` function. The argument that is listed inside the parentheses is copied into the function's parameter variable, `num`.

Passing Multiple Arguments in C++

Often it is useful to pass more than one argument to a function. When you define a function, you must declare a parameter variable for each argument that you want passed into the method. The parameter declarations are separated by commas. Here is an example:

```
void showSum(int num1, int num2)
{
   int result;
   result = num1 + num2;
   cout << result << endl;
}
```

Here is an example of how we might call the method:

```
showSum(12, 45);
```

This statement calls the `showSum` method and passes two arguments: 12 and 45. These arguments are **passed by position** to the corresponding parameter variables in the function. In other words, the first argument is passed to the first parameter variable, and the second argument is passed to the second parameter variable. So, this statement causes 12 to be assigned to the `num1` parameter and 45 to be assigned to the `num2` parameter.

Passing Arguments by Reference in C++

When an argument is **passed by reference**, it means that the function has access to the argument and makes changes to it. C++ provides a special type of variable called a **reference variable** that, when used as a function parameter, allows access to the original argument.

A reference variable is an alias for another variable. Any changes made to the reference variable are actually performed on the variable for which it is an alias. Using a reference variable as a parameter, a function may change a variable that is defined in another function.

Reference variables are declared like regular variables, except you place an ampersand (&) in front of the name. For example, look at the `setToZero` function shown here:

```
void setToZero(int &num)
{
    num = 0;
}
```

The `setToZero` function sets its parameter variable to 0, which also sets the original variable that was passed as an argument to 0.

Global Variables and Global Constants in C++

To declare a global variable or constant in a C++ program, you write the declaration outside of all functions, and above the definitions of the functions. As a result, all the functions in the program have access to the variable or constant.

Recall that global variables may make programs difficult to debug. Global constants are permissible, however, because statements in the program cannot change their value. Program 19-10 demonstrates how to declare such a constant. Notice that in line 9, we have declared a constant named `INTEREST_RATE`. The declaration is not inside any of the functions, and is written above all function definitions. As a result, the constant is available to all the functions in the program.

Program 19-10:

```
1  #include <iostream>
2  using namespace std;
3
4  // Function prototypes
5  void function2();
6  void function3();
7
8  // Global constant
9  const double INTEREST_RATE = 0.05;
10
11 int main()
12 {
13    // Statements here have access to
14    // the INTEREST_RATE constant.
15    return 0;
16 }
17
18 void function2()
19 {
20    // Statements here have access to
21    // the INTEREST_RATE constant.
22 }
23
24 void function3()
25 {
26    // Statements here have access to
27    // the INTEREST_RATE constant.
28 }
```

Generating Random Integers in C++

The C++ library provides a value-returning function named `rand()` that returns a random number. (The `rand()` function requires the directive `#include <cstdlib>`). The random number that is returned from the `rand()` function is an `int`. Here is an example of its usage:

```
y = rand();
```

After this statement executes, the variable `y` will contain a random number. In actuality, the numbers produced by `rand()`are pseudorandom. The function uses an algorithm that produces the same sequence of numbers each time the program is repeated on the same system. For example, suppose the following statements are executed:

```
cout << rand() << endl;
cout << rand() << endl;
cout << rand() << endl;
```

The three numbers displayed will appear to be random, but each time the program runs, the same three values will be generated. In order to randomize the results of `rand()`, the `srand()` function must be used. The `srand()` function accepts an `unsigned int` argument, which acts as a seed value for the algorithm. By specifying different seed values, `rand()` will generate different sequences of random numbers.

A common practice for getting unique seed values is to call the `time()` function, which is part of the C++ standard library. The `time()` function returns the number of seconds that have elapsed since midnight, January 1, 1970. The `time()` function requires the directive `#include <ctime>`. When you call the `time()` function, you pass 0 as an argument. The following code snippet shows an example:

```
// Get the system time.
unsigned seed = time(0);

// Seed the random number generator.
srand(seed);

// Display a random number.
cout << rand() << endl;
```

If you wish to limit the range of the random number, use the following formula:

```
y = 1 + rand() % maxRange;
```

The `maxRange` value is the upper limit of the range. For example, if you wish to generate a random number in the range of 1 through 100, use the following statement:

```
y = 1 + rand() % 100;
```

This is how the statement works: Look at the following expression:

```
rand() % 100
```

Assuming `rand()` returns 37894, the value of the expression above is 94. That is because 37894 divided by 100 is 378 with a remainder of 94. (The modulus operator returns the remainder.) But, what if `rand()` returns a number that is evenly divisible by 100, such as 500? The expression above will return a 0. If we want a number in the range 1–100, we must add 1 to the result. That is why we use the expression `1 + rand() % 100`.

Writing Your Own Value-Returning Functions in C++

When you are writing a value-returning function in C++, you must decide what type of value the function will return. This is because, instead of specifying `void` in the function header, you must specify the data type of the value that will be returned. A value-returning function will use `int`, `double`, `string`, `bool`, or any other valid data type in its header. Here is an example of a function that returns an `int` value:

```
int sum(int num1, int num2)
{
    int result;
    result = num1 + num2;
    return result;
}
```

The name of this function is `sum`. Notice in the function header that instead of the word `void` we have specified `int` as the return type. This code defines a function named `sum` that accepts two `int` arguments. The arguments are passed into the parameter variables `num1` and `num2`. Inside the function, a local variable, `result`, is declared. The parameter variables `num1` and `num2` are added, and their sum is assigned to the `result` variable. The last statement in the function is as follows:

```
return result;
```

You must have a `return` statement in a value-returning function. It causes the function to end execution and it returns a value to the statement that called the function. In a value-returning function, the general format of the return statement is as follows:

```
return Expression;
```

Expression is the value to be returned. It can be any expression that has a value, such as a variable, literal, or mathematical expression. In this case, the `sum` function returns the value of the `result` variable. The following code snippet shows how we might call the `sum` function:

```
int total;
total = sum(2, 3);
```

After this code executes, the value of the `total` variable will be 5.

Returning a String from a C++ Function

The following code shows an example of how a function can return string. Notice that the function header specifies `string` as the return type. This function accepts two string arguments (a person's first name and last name). It combines those two strings into a string that contains the person's full name. The full name is then returned.

```
string fullName(string firstName, string lastName)
{
    string name;
```

```
        name = firstName + " " + lastName;
        return name;
    }
```

The following code snippet shows how we might call the function:

```
    string customerName;
    customerName = fullName("John", "Martin");
```

After this code executes, the value of the `customerName` variable will be "John Martin".

Returning a `bool` Value from a C++ Function

Functions can also return `bool` values. The following function accepts an argument and returns `true` if the argument is within the range of 1 through 100, or `false` otherwise:

```
bool isValid(int number)
{
    bool status;

    if (number >= 1 && number <= 100)
       status = true;
    else
       status = false;

    return status;
}
```

The following code shows an `if-else` statement that uses a call to the function:

```
int value = 20;

if (isValid(value))
   cout << "The value is within range." << endl;
else
   cout << "The value is out of range." << endl;
```

When this code executes, the message "The value is within range." will be displayed.

Checkpoint

19.12 What character must you never put at the end of a function header in C++?

19.13 What happens when you call a function in C++?

19.14 What is a function prototype?

19.5 Input Validation

Input validation can be an important security tool because it only allows user input that meets the specified requirements.

Program 19-11 is an example of how to use an input validation loop in C++ to validate that the user does not enter a negative value. For more on input validation, see Chapter 10.

Program 19-11:

```
#include <iostream>
#include <string>
using namespace std;

// Function prototype
void showRetail();

int main()
{
   // Local variable
   string doAnother;

   do
   {
      // Calculate and display a retail price.
      showRetail();

      // Do this again?
      cout << “Do you have another item? (Enter y for yes.)" << endl;
      cin >> doAnother;
   } while (doAnother == “y" || doAnother == “Y");

   return 0;
}

// The showRetail function gets an item's wholesale cost
// from the user and displays its retail price.
void showRetail()
{
   // Local variables
   double wholesale, retail;

   // Constant for the markup percentage
   const double MARKUP = 2.5;

   // Get the wholesale cost.
   cout << “Enter an item's wholesale cost." << endl;
   cin >> wholesale;

   // Validate the wholesale cost.
   while (wholesale < 0)
   {
      cout << “The cost cannot be negative. Please" << endl;
```

Program 19-11: *(continued)*

```
44         cout << "enter the correct wholesale cost." << endl;
45         cin >> wholesale;
46      }
47
48      // Calculate the retail price.
49      retail = wholesale * MARKUP;
50
51      // Display the retail price.
52      cout << "The retail price is $" << retail << endl;
53 }
```

Program Output

```
Enter an item's wholesale cost.
-1 [Enter]
The cost cannot be negative. Please
enter the correct wholesale cost.
1.50 [Enter]
The retail price is $3.75
Do you have another item? (Enter y for yes.)
n [Enter]
```

Checkpoint

19.15 In Program 19-11, on what line does the validation loop start?

19.16 What happens in Program 19-11 if the user enters a negative number?

19.6 Arrays

Use arrays in C++ to store multiple items of the same type.

C++ Array Declarations

Here is an example of an array declaration in C++:

```
int numbers[6];
```

This statement declares `numbers` as an `int` array. The size declarator specifies that the array has 6 elements. Recall that it is a good practice to use a named constant for the size declarator, as shown here:

```
const int SIZE = 6;
int numbers[SIZE];
```

Here is another example:

```
const int SIZE = 200;
double temperatures[SIZE];
```

This code snippet declares `temperatures` as an array of 200 `double`s. Here is one more:

```
const int SIZE = 10;
string names[SIZE];
```

This declares `names` as an array of 10 `string`s.

NOTE: For more on arrays, see Chapter 11.

Array Elements and Subscripts in C++

You access each element of an array with a subscript. Recall that an element is an item stored in an array. The first element's subscript is 0, the second element's subscript is 1, and so forth. The last element's subscript is the array size minus 1. For example, the following code declares an `int` array with three elements, and then assigns values to each element. The subscripts for the elements are 0, 1, and 2.

```
const int SIZE = 3;
int numbers[SIZE];
numbers[0] = 10;
numbers[1] = 20;
numbers[2] = 30;
```

Initializing an Array in C++

You can initialize an array with values when you declare it. Here is an example:

```
const int SIZE = 12;
int days[SIZE] = {31, 28, 31, 30, 31, 30, 31, 31, 30, 31, 30, 31};
```

This statement declares `days` as an array of `int`s, and stores initial values in the array. The series of values inside the braces and separated with commas is called an **initialization list**. These values are stored in the array elements in the order they appear in the list. (The first value, 31, is stored in `days[0]`, the second value, 28, is stored in `days[1]`, and so forth.)

When initializing an array, it is not necessary to specify a size declarator. The C++ compiler will determine the size of the array by counting the number of items in the initialization list. For example, the previous declaration could be written like this:

```
int days[] = {31, 28, 31, 30, 31, 30, 31, 31, 30, 31, 30, 31};
```

Passing an Array as an Argument to a Function in C++

When passing an array as an argument to a function in C++, you should also pass a separate `int` argument indicating the array's size. The following code shows a function that has been written to accept an array as an argument:

```
void showArray(int array[], int size)
```

```
{
   for (int i = 0; i < size; i++)
      cout << array[i] << " ";
}
```

Notice that the parameter variable, `array`, is declared as an `int` array, without a size declarator. When we call this function we must pass an `int` array to it as an argument. Let's assume that `numbers` is the name of an `int` array, and `SIZE` is a constant that specifies the size of the array. Here is a statement that calls the `showArray` function, passing the `numbers` array and `SIZE` as arguments:

```
showArray(numbers, SIZE);
```

Two-Dimensional Arrays in C++

Here is an example declaration of a two-dimensional array with three rows and four columns:

```
double scores[3][4];
```

The two sets of brackets in the data type indicate that the scores variable will reference a two-dimensional array. The numbers 3 and 4 are size declarators. The first size declarator specifies the number of rows, and the second size declarator specifies the number of columns. Notice that each size declarator is enclosed in its own set of brackets.

When processing the data in a two-dimensional array, each element has two subscripts: one for its row and another for its column. In the `scores` array, the elements in row 0 are referenced as follows:

```
scores[0][0]
scores[0][1]
scores[0][2]
scores[0][3]
```

The elements in row 1 are as follows:

```
scores[1][0]
scores[1][1]
scores[1][2]
scores[1][3]
```

And the elements in row 2 are as follows:

```
scores[2][0]
scores[2][1]
scores[2][2]
scores[2][3]
```

To access one of the elements in a two-dimensional array, you must use both subscripts. For example, the following statement stores the number 95 in `scores[2][1]`:

```
scores[2][1] = 95;
```

Programs that process two-dimensional arrays can do so with nested loops. For example, the following code prompts the user to enter a score, once for each element in the array:

```
const int ROWS = 3;
```

```
const int COLS = 4;
double scores[ROWS][COLS];
for (int row = 0; row < ROWS; row++)
{
   for (int col = 0; col < COLS; col++)
   {
      cout << "Enter a score." << endl;
      cin >> scores[row][col];
   }
}
```

And the following code displays all the elements in the `scores` array:

```
for (int row = 0; row < ROWS; row++)
{
   for (int col = 0; col < COLS; col++)
   {
      cout << scores[row][col] << endl;
   }
}
```

Arrays with Three or More Dimensions in C++

C++ allows you to create arrays with virtually any number of dimensions. Here is an example of a three-dimensional array declaration:

```
double seats[3][5][8];
```

This array can be thought of as three sets of five rows, with each row containing eight elements. The array might be used to store the prices of seats in an auditorium, where there are eight seats in a row, five rows in a section, and a total of three sections.

Checkpoint

19.17 What should you use for a size declarator in a C++ array statement?

19.18 What is the subscript of the first element in a C++ array?

19.19 In a C++ array, what is the term for a series of values inside the braces and separated with commas?

19.7 Classes and Objects

You can apply the basic knowledge you have learned so far for object-oriented programming with C++.

NOTE: For more on classes and object-oriented programming, see Chapter 13.

Class Declarations in C++

Here is the general format of a class declaration in C++:

```
class ClassName
{
    Field declarations and member function definitions go here...
};
```

Notice that a class declaration in C++ ends with a semicolon.

Program 19-12 shows a `CellPhone` class in C++. Notice that line 3 reads `private:`, and line 9 reads `public:`. These are **access specifiers**, and they control how class fields and member functions can be accessed by code outside the class. All the field declarations that appear after the `private:` access specifier in line 3 are private. They can be accessed only by code inside the class. All of the member functions that appear after the `public:` access specifier in line 9 are public, and can be called by code outside the class.

Program 19-12 also has a `main` function to demonstrate the class.

Program 19-12:

```
 1 #include <iostream>
 2 #include <string>
 3 using namespace std;
 4
 5 class CellPhone
 6 {
 7 private:
 8    // Field declarations
 9    string manufacturer;
10    string modelNumber;
11    double retailPrice;
12
13 public:
14    // Member functions
15    void setManufacturer(string manufact)
16    {
17       manufacturer = manufact;
18    }
19
20    void setModelNumber(string modNum)
21    {
22       modelNumber = modNum;
```

Program 19-12: *(continued)*

```
   }

   void setRetailPrice(double retail)
   {
      retailPrice = retail;
   }

   string getManufacturer()
   {
      return manufacturer;
   }

   string getModelNumber()
   {
      return modelNumber;
   }

   double getRetailPrice()
   {
      return retailPrice;
   }
};

int main()
{
   // Declare a variable that can reference
   // a CellPhone object.
   CellPhone myPhone;

   // Store values in the object's fields.
   myPhone.setManufacturer("Motorola");
   myPhone.setModelNumber("G200");
   myPhone.setRetailPrice(399.99);

   // Display the values stored in the fields.
   cout << "The manufacturer is "
        << myPhone.getManufacturer() << endl;
   cout << "The model number is "
        << myPhone.getModelNumber() << endl;
   cout << "The retail price is "
        << myPhone.getRetailPrice() << endl;

   return 0;
}
```

Program Output

```
The manufacturer is Motorola
The model number is G200
The retail price is 399.99
```

Inside the `main` function, line 50 creates an instance of the `CellPhone` class in memory and assigns it to the `myPhone` variable. We say that the object is referenced by the `myPhone` variable. (Notice that C++ does not require the `New` keyword.) Lines 53 through 55 call the object's `setManufacturer`, `setModelNumber`, and `setRetailPrice` member functions, passing arguments to each.

Constructors in C++

A **class constructor** in C++ is a member function that has the same name as the class. Program 19-13 shows a version of the `CellPhone` class that has a constructor. The constructor appears in lines 9 through 14.

Program 19-13:

```
 1 #include <iostream>
 2 #include <string>
 3 using namespace std;
 4
 5 class CellPhone
 6 {
 7 private:
 8    // Field declarations
 9    string manufacturer;
10    string modelNumber;
11    double retailPrice;
12
13 public:
14    // Constructor
15    CellPhone(string manufact, string modNum, double retail)
16    {
17       manufacturer = manufact;
18       modelNumber = modNum;
19       retailPrice = retail;
20    }
21
22    // Member functions
23    void setManufacturer(string manufact)
24    {
25       manufacturer = manufact;
26    }
27
28    void setModelNumber(string modNum)
29    {
30       modelNumber = modNum;
31    }
32
33    void setRetailPrice(double retail)
34    {
35       retailPrice = retail;
36    }
37
38    string getManufacturer()
39    {
40       return manufacturer;
```

Program 19-13: *(continued)*

```
   }

   string getModelNumber()
   {
      return modelNumber;
   }

   double getRetailPrice()
   {
      return retailPrice;
   }
};

int main()
{
   // Create a CellPhone object and initialize its
   // fields with values passed to the constructor.
   CellPhone myPhone("Motorola", "G200", 399.99);

   // Display the values stored in the fields.
   cout << "The manufacturer is "
        << myPhone.getManufacturer() << endl;
   cout << "The model number is "
        << myPhone.getModelNumber() << endl;
   cout << "The retail price is "
        << myPhone.getRetailPrice() << endl;

   return 0;
}
```

Program Output

```
The manufacturer is Motorola
The model number is G200
The retail price is 399.99
```

Inheritance in C++

Suppose we want to declare two classes: `ClassA` and `ClassB`. Furthermore, we want `ClassB` to be a subclass of `ClassA`. The general format of the declarations in C++ is:

```
class ClassA
{
    Member declarations
};

class ClassB : public ClassA
{
```

```
        Member declarations
    };
```

Notice that the header for `ClassB` ends with the following clause:

```
    : public ClassA
```

This specifies that the `ClassB` class extends the `ClassA` class. So, `ClassA` is the superclass, and `ClassB` is the subclass. `ClassB` inherits all of `ClassA`'s public members.

Polymorphism in C++

Program 19-14 presents C++ code that demonstrates polymorphism by using the Animal class as a superclass and the Dog class and the Cat class as subclasses of Animal.

Notice that the keyword `virtual` appears in the function headers for the `showSpecies` and `makeSound` functions (lines 9, 15, 25, 31, 40, and 46). The `virtual` keyword tells the compiler to expect the function to be redefined in a subclass.

Also, notice that in line 82, the `showAnimalInfo` function accepts an `Animal` object by reference. In C++, polymorphic behavior is possible only when an object is passed by reference.

Program 19-14:

```
 1 #include <iostream>
 2 #include <string>
 3 using namespace std;
 4
 5  class Animal
 6 {
 7 public:
 8    // showSpecies function
 9    virtual void showSpecies()
10    {
11       cout << "I'm just a regular animal." << endl;
12    }
13
14    // makeSound function
15    virtual void makeSound()
16    {
17       cout << "Grrrrrr" << endl;
18    }
19 };
20
21 class Dog : public Animal
22 {
23 public:
24    // showSpecies function
25    virtual void showSpecies()
26    {
27       cout << "I'm a dog." << endl;
28    }
29
30    // makeSound function
31    virtual void makeSound()
```

Program 19-14: *(continued)*

```
   {
      cout << "Woof! Woof!" << endl;
   }
};

class Cat : public Animal
{
   // showSpecies function
   virtual void showSpecies()
   {
      cout << "I'm a cat." << endl;
   }

   // makeSound function
   virtual void makeSound()
   {
      cout << "Meow" << endl;
   }
};

// Function prototype
void showAnimalInfo(Animal &creature);

int main()
{
   // Declare three class variables.
   Animal myAnimal;
   Dog myDog;
   Cat myCat;

   // Show info about an animal.
   cout << "Here is info about an animal." << endl;
   showAnimalInfo(myAnimal);
   cout << endl;

   // Show info about a dog.
   cout << "Here is info about a dog." << endl;
   showAnimalInfo(myDog);
   cout << endl;

   // Show info about a cat.
   cout << "Here is info about a cat." << endl;
   showAnimalInfo(myCat);

   return 0;
}

// The showAnimalInfo function accepts an Animal
// object as an argument and displays information
// about it.
void showAnimalInfo(Animal &creature)
{
```

Program 19-14: *(continued)*

```
    creature.showSpecies();
    creature.makeSound();
}
```

Program Output

```
Here is info about an animal.
I am just a regular animal.
Grrrrrrr

Here is info about a dog.
I am a dog.
Woof! Woof!

Here is info about a cat.
I am a cat.
Meow
```

Checkpoint

19.20 What is the purpose of the access specifier "private" in a C++ class declaration?

19.21 What is a class constructor in C++?

19.22 What is the C++ keyword that tells the compiler to expect the function to be redefined in a subclass?

Chapter Review

Multiple Choice

1. Inside what symbols do you write C++ statements?
   a. [ ]
   b. ( )
   c. < >
   d. { }

2. What character do you use to end a statement in C++?
   a. #
   b. ;
   c. :
   d. }

3. What is the correct C++ statement to display the output: *Enter your name.* on the screen?
   a. cout << "Enter your name."
   b. print << "Enter your name."
   c. output << "Enter your name."
   d. display << "Enter your name."

4. What manipulator instructs `cout` to start a new line?
   a. line1
   b. new1
   c. start1
   d. end1

5. What C++ data type stores the values true or false?
   a. byte
   b. short
   c. bool
   d. float

6. What function must you use if you want C++ to read a string that contains multiple words?
   a. getline
   b. newline
   c. include
   d. inputline

7. What is the C++ relational operator for Less than or equal to?
   a. ==
   b. >=
   c. <=
   d. !=

8. What is the C++ logical operator for Logical AND?
   a. ??
   b. !!
   c. &&
   d. **

9. What loop is designed to initialize, test, and increment a counter variable in C++?
   a. for
   b. while
   c. do while
   d. for now

10. What function is automatically called when a C++ program starts?
    a. set
    b. start
    c. show
    d. main

True or False

1. In C++, the << operator always appears on the right side of the item of data that you want to display.
2. C++ does not differentiate between upper- and lower-case characters.
3. C++ does not have an exponent operator.
4. C++ does not provide a `Do-Until` loop.
5. C++ functions do not allow you to return a string.
6. It is good practice to use a named constant for the size declarator in a C++ array statement.
7. C++ allows you to create arrays with any number of dimensions.

Short Answer

8. What is the difference between a `cout` statement and a `cin` statement in C++?
9. Explain the purpose of the `pow` function in C++.
10. What is the difference between starting a comment with // or /* in C++?
11. Explain the purpose of following C++ statement:
    ```
    num--;
    ```
12. Explain the use of a reference variable in C++.
13. Explain why input validation can be an important security tool.

Algorithmic Workbench

14. Write a C++ statement that assigns the sum of 10 and 14 to the variable `total`.
15. Write a C++ statement that subtracts the variable `down_payment` from the variable `total` and assigns the result to the variable `due`.
16. Write a C++ statement that multiplies the variable `subtotal` by 0.15 and assigns the result to the variable `total`.
17. Design a C++ program that generates five random numbers.

Programming Exercises

1. Alone or with a partner, write a C++ program that displays the name, email address, and mailing address of your school on the screen.
2. Alone or with a partner, write a C++ program that prompts the user to enter the name, email address, and mailing address of your school and then displays it on the screen.
3. Alone, with a partner, or a team brainstorm a programmed story or game that includes displaying a student's daily schedule on the screen. Consider the input you will need, and how you want it to display. Design the program using tools such as algorithms, flowcharts, and pseudocode. Then, write the program in C++. Share your program with others in the class and improve it based on feedback.

ASCII Character Set with Decimal and Binary Codes

Character	Decimal Code	Binary Code
!	33	100001
"	34	100010
#	35	100011
$	36	100100
%	37	100101
&	38	100110
'	39	100111
(	40	101000
)	41	101001
*	42	101010
+	43	101011
,	44	101100
-	45	101101
.	46	101110
/	47	101111
0	48	110000
1	49	110001
2	50	110010
3	51	110011
4	52	110100
5	53	110101
6	54	110110
7	55	110111
8	56	111000
9	57	111001
:	58	111010
;	59	111011
<	60	111100
=	61	111101
>	62	111110
?	63	111111
@	64	1000000

(continued)

Character	Decimal Code	Binary Code
A	65	1000001
B	66	1000010
C	67	1000011
D	68	1000100
E	69	1000101
F	70	1000110
G	71	1000111
H	72	1001000
I	73	1001001
J	74	1001010
K	75	1001011
L	76	1001100
M	77	1001101
N	78	1001110
O	79	1001111
P	80	1010000
Q	81	1010001
R	82	1010010
S	83	1010011
T	84	1010100
U	85	1010101
V	86	1010110
W	87	1010111
X	88	1011000
Y	89	1011001
Z	90	1011010
[	91	1011011
\	92	1011100
]	93	1011101
^	94	1011110
_	95	1011111
`	96	1100000

Character	Decimal Code	Binary Code
a	97	1100001
b	98	1100010
c	99	1100011
d	100	1100100
e	101	1100101
f	102	1100110
g	103	1100111
h	104	1101000
i	105	1101001
j	106	1101010
k	107	1101011
l	108	1101100
m	109	1101101
n	110	1101110
o	111	1101111
p	112	1110000
q	113	1110001
r	114	1110010
s	115	1110011
t	116	1110100
u	117	1110101
v	118	1110110
w	119	1110111
x	120	1111000
y	121	1111001
z	122	1111010
{	123	1111011
|	124	1111100
}	125	1111101
~	126	1111110
DEL	127	1111111

APPENDIX

B Flowchart Symbols

These are the flowchart symbols used in this text.

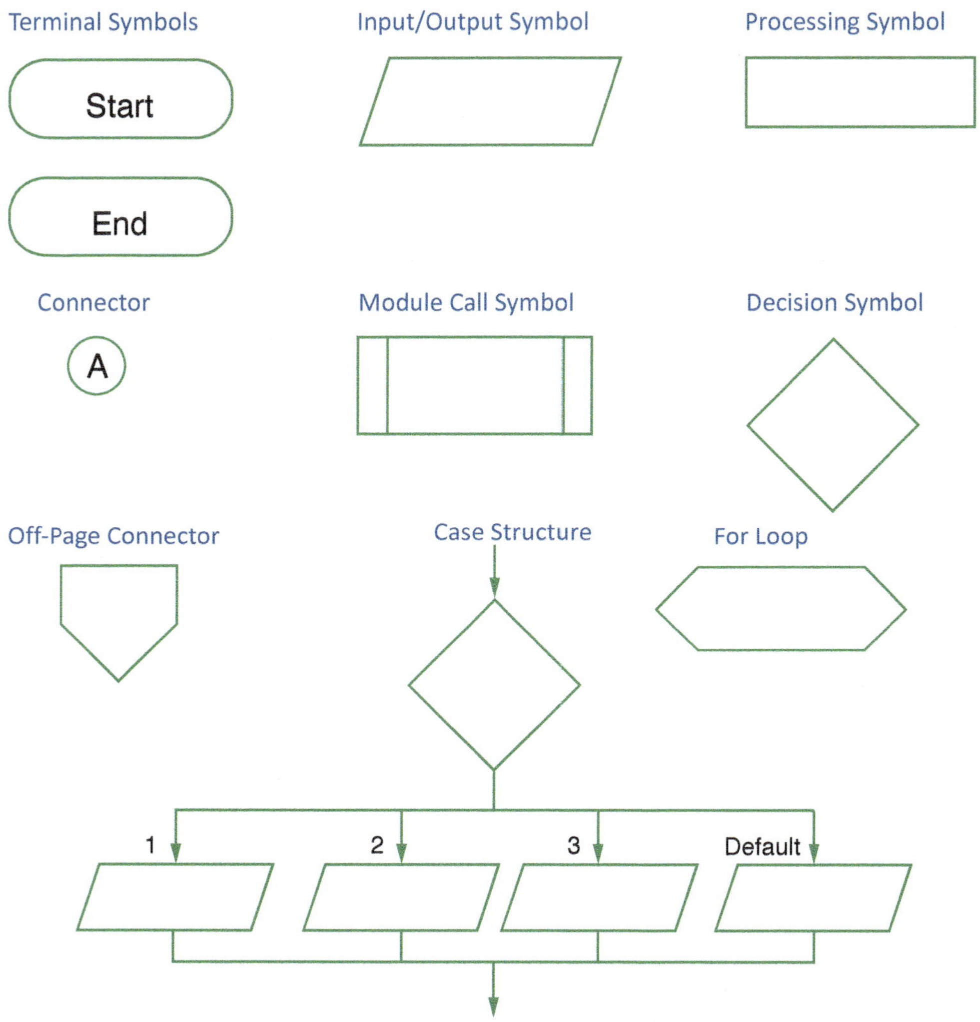

Terminal Symbols

Start

End

Input/Output Symbol

Processing Symbol

Connector

A

Module Call Symbol

Decision Symbol

Off-Page Connector

Case Structure

1

2

3

Default

For Loop

APPENDIX

C Pseudocode Reference

This appendix serves as a quick reference for the pseudocode that is used in this text. This reference concisely covers the text's statements and operators. It does not cover the library functions.

Data Types	Description
`Integer`	Used for variables that will store whole numbers
`Real`	Used for variables that will store numbers with a fractional part
`String`	Used for variables that will store strings
`Character`	Used for variables that will store a single character

Variables

To declare a variable, you use the `Declare` statement. Here is the general format:

```
Declare DataType VariableName
```

In the general format, *DataType* is the variable's data type and *VariableName* is the variable's name. Here are some examples:

```
Declare Integer distance
Declare Real grossPay
Declare String name
Declare Character letter
```

You can optionally initialize a variable with a starting value when you declare it. Here is an example:

```
Declare Real price = 49.95
```

Named Constants

You create a named constant by using the `Constant` statement instead of the `Declare` statement. Here is the general format:

```
Constant DataType Name = Value
```

In the general format, *DataType* is the constant's data type, *Name* is the constant's name, and *Value* is the constant's value. Here is an example:

```
Constant Real INTEREST_RATE = 0.072
```

Arrays

Here is the general format of an array declaration:

```
Declare DataType ArrayName[Size]
```

In the general format, *DataType* is the array's data type, *ArrayName* is the array's name, and *Size* is the number of elements in the array. Here is an example:

```
Declare Integer units[10]
```

This statement declares an array of `Integer` values. The array's name is `units`, and it has 10 elements.

Two-Dimensional Arrays

Here is the general format of a two-dimensional array declaration:

```
Declare DataType ArrayName[Rows][Cols]
```

In the general format, *DataType* is the array's data type, *ArrayName* is the array's name, *Rows* is the number of rows in the array, and *Cols* is the number of columns. Here is an example:

```
Declare Integer values[10][20]
```

This statement declares an array of `Integer` values. The array's name is `values`, and it has 10 rows and 20 columns.

Displaying Output

To display output you use the `Display` statement. The `Display` statement displays a line of output on the screen. Here is the general format to use when you are displaying one item of data:

```
Display Item
```

To display multiple items, you separate the items with commas, as shown in the following general format:

```
Display Item, Item, Item . . .
```

Here are some examples:

```
Display "Hello world"
Display grossPay
Display "My name is ", name
```

You can use the word `Tab` to indent screen output to the next tab position. Here is an example:

```
Display amount1, Tab, amount2, Tab, amount3
```

Reading Input

You use the `Input` statement to read keyboard input. Here is the general format:

```
Input VariableName
```

In the general format, *VariableName* is the name of the variable that will receive the input. Here is an example:

```
Input hours
```

Comments

In this text, we begin a comment with two forward slashes. Everything appearing on the line after the slashes is a comment. Here is an example:

```
// Get the number of hours worked.
```

Math Operators

Symbol	Operator	Description
+	Addition	Adds two numbers
–	Subtraction	Subtracts one number from another
*	Multiplication	Multiplies one number by another
/	Division	Divides one number by another and gives the quotient
MOD	Modulus	Divides one number by another and gives the remainder
^	Exponent	Raises a number to a power

Relational Operators

Operator	Meaning
>	Greater than
<	Less than
>=	Greater than or equal to
<=	Less than or equal to
==	Equal to
!=	Not equal to

Logical Operators

Operator	Meaning
AND	The AND operator connects two Boolean expressions into one compound expression. Both subexpressions must be true for the compound expression to be true.
OR	The OR operator connects two Boolean expressions into one compound expression. One or both subexpressions must be true for the compound expression to be true. It is only necessary for one of the subexpressions to be true, and it does not matter which.
NOT	The NOT operator is a unary operator, meaning it works with only one operand. The operand must be a Boolean expression. The NOT operator reverses the truth of its operand. If it is applied to an expression that is true, the operator returns false. If it is applied to an expression that is false, the operator returns true.

The If-Then Statement

General format:

```
If condition Then
   statement   }
   statement   }  These statements are conditionally executed.
   etc.        }
End If
```

In the general format, the *condition* is a Boolean expression. If the expression is true, the statements appearing between the `If` clause and the End `If` clause are executed. Otherwise, the statements are skipped. Here is an example:

```
If sales > 50000 Then
   Set bonus = 500.0
   Set commissionRate = 0.12
   Display "You've met your sales quota!"
End If
```

The If-Then-Else Statement

General format:

```
If condition Then
   statement   }
   statement   }  These statements are executed if the condition is true.
   etc.        }
Else
   statement   }
   statement   }  These statements are executed if the condition is false..
   etc.        }
End If
```

In the general format, the *condition* is a Boolean expression. If the expression is true, the statements appearing between the `If` clause and the `Else` clause are executed. Otherwise, the statements between the `Else` clause and the End `If` clause are executed. Here is an example:

```
If temperature < 40 Then
   Display "A little cold, isn't it?"
Else
   Display "Nice weather we're having."
End If
```

The Select Case Statement

General format:

```
Select testExpression  <--  This is a variable or an expression.
   Case value_1:
      statement   }  These statements are executed if the
      statement   }  testExpression is equal to value_1.
      etc.        }
```

```
Case value_2:
   statement
   statement
   etc.
```

These statements are executed if the *testExpression* is equal to *value_2*.

```
Insert as many Case sections as necessary

Case value_N:
   statement
   statement
   etc.
```

These statements are executed if the *testExpression* is equal to *value_N*.

```
Default:
   statement
   statement
   etc.
```

These statements are executed if the *testExpression* is not equal to any of the values listed after the Case statements.

```
End Select
```

This is the end of the structure.

The first line of the structure starts with the word `Select`, followed by a *testExpression*. Inside the structure there is one or more blocks of statements that begin with a `Case` statement. Notice that the word `Case` is followed by a value.

When the `Select Case` statement executes, it compares the value of the *testExpression* with the values that follow each of the `Case` statements (from top to bottom). When it finds a `Case` value that matches the *testExpression's* value, the program branches to the `Case` statement. The statements that immediately follow the `Case` statement are executed, and then the program jumps out of the structure. If the *testExpression* does not match any of the `Case` values, the program branches to the `Default` statement and executes the statements that immediately follow it. Here is an example:

```
Select month
   Case 1:
      Display "January"
   Case 2:
      Display "February"
   Case 3:
      Display "March"
   Default:
      Display "Error: Invalid month"
End Select
```

The `While` Loop

General format:

```
While condition
      statement
      statement
      etc.
End While
```

These statements are the body of the loop. They are repeated while the condition is true.

In the general format, the *condition* is a Boolean expression, and the statements that appear on the lines between the `While` and the `End While` clauses are the body of the loop. When the loop executes, the *condition* is tested. If it is true, the statements that appear in the body of the loop are executed, and then the loop starts over. If the *condition* is false, the program exits the loop. The following pseudocode shows an example:

```
Set count = 0
While count < 10
   Display count
   Set count = count + 1
End While
```

The Do-While Loop

General format:

```
Do
  statement
  statement
  etc.
While condition
```

These statements are the body of the loop. They are always performed once, and then repeated while the condition is true.

In the general format, the statements that appear in the lines between the Do and the While clauses are the body of the loop. The *condition* that appears after the While clause is a Boolean expression. When the loop executes, the statements in the body of the loop are executed, and then the *condition* is tested. If the *condition* is true, the loop starts over and the statements in the body are executed again. If the condition is false, however, the program exits the loop. Here is an example:

```
Set count = 10
Do
   Display count
   Set count = count - 1
While count > 0
```

The Do-Until Loop

General format:

```
Do
  statement
  statement
  etc.
Until condition
```

These statements are the body of the loop. They are always performed once, and then repeated until the condition is true.

In the general format, the statements that appear in the lines between the Do and the Until clauses are the body of the loop. The *condition* that appears after the While clause is a Boolean expression. When the loop executes, the statements in the body of the loop are executed, and then the *condition* is tested. If the *condition* is true, the program exits the loop. If the *condition* is false, the loop starts over and the statements in the body are executed again. Here is an example:

```
Set count = 10
Do
   Display count
   Set count = count - 1
Until count == 0
```

The For Loop

General format:

```
For counterVariable = startingValue To maxValue
    statement
    statement
    statement
    etc.
End For
```

These statements are the body of the loop.

In the general format, *counterVariable* is the name of a variable that is used as a counter, *startingValue* is the value that the counter will be initially set to, and *maxValue* is the maximum value that the counter can contain. When the loop executes, the following actions are performed:

1. The *counterVariable* is set to the *startingValue*.
2. The *counterVariable* is compared to the *maxValue*. If the *counterVariable* is greater than *maxValue*, the loop stops. Otherwise:
   a. The statements that appear in the body of the loop are executed.
   b. The *counterVariable* is incremented.
   c. The loop starts over again at step 2.

Here is an example:

```
For counter = 1 To 10
   Display "Hello world"
End For
```

The For Each Loop

General format:

```
For Each var In array
    statement
    statement
    statement
    etc.
End For
```

In the general format, *var* is the name of a variable and *array* is the name of an array. The loop will iterate once for every element in the *array*. Each time the loop iterates, it copies an array element to the *var* variable. For example, the first time the loop iterates, *var* will contain the value of *array*[0], the second time the loop iterates *var* will contain the value of *array*[1], and so forth. This continues until the loop has stepped through all of the elements in the array. The following pseudocode shows an example:

```
Constant Integer SIZE = 5
Declare Integer numbers[SIZE] = 5, 10, 15, 20, 25
Declare Integer num
For Each num In numbers
   Display num
End For
```

Defining a Module

To create a module you write its definition, which has two parts: a header and a body. The header indicates the starting point of the module, and the body is a list of statements that belong to the module. Here is the general format used in this text to write a module definition in pseudocode:

```
Module name()
  statement    }
  statement    }  These statements are the body of the module.
  etc.         }
End Module
```

Calling a Module

To call a module you use the `Call` statement. Here is the general format:

```
Call ModuleName()
```

In the general format, *`ModuleName`* is the name of the module being called. In the following example, a module named `showMessage` is being called:

```
Call showMessage()
```

Parameter Variables

If you want a module or function to receive arguments when it is called, you must equip the module or function with one or more parameter variables. Parameter variables are declared inside the parentheses of the module definition. Here is an example of a pseudocode module that has an `Integer` parameter variable:

```
Module doubleNumber(Integer value)
  Declare Integer result
  Set result = value * 2
  Display result
End Module
```

When this module is called, an `Integer` argument will be passed to it by value. To pass an argument by reference, the word `Ref` is used in the parameter variable declaration, and shown here:

```
Module setToZero(Integer Ref value)
 value = 0
End Module
```

Defining a Function

A function definition is similar to a module definition. Here is the general format:

```
Function DataType FunctionName(ParameterList)
  statement
  statement
  etc.

  Return value  <----  A function must have a Return statement. This causes a
                       value to be sent back to the part of the program that called
End Function           the function.
```

The first line is the function header. It begins with the word `Function`, followed by these items:

`DataType` is the data type of the value that the function returns.

`FunctionName` is the name of the function.

An optional parameter list appears inside a set of parentheses. If the function does not accept arguments, then an empty set of parentheses will appear.

Beginning at the line after the function header, one or more statements will appear. These statements are the function's body, and are performed any time the function is executed. One of the statements in the body must be a `Return` statement, which takes the following form:

```
Return value
```

The *`value`* that follows the word `Return` is the value that the function will send back to the part of the program that called the function. Here is an example:

```
Function Integer sum(Integer num1, Integer num2)
  Declare Integer result
  Set result = num1 + num2
  Return result
End Function
```

Defining a Class

General format:

```
Class ClassName
  Field declarations and method definitions go here . . .
End Class
```

The first line starts with the word `Class`, followed by the name of the class. Next you write the declarations for the class's fields and the definitions of the class's methods. The words `End Class` appear at the end of the class definition. Here is the `CellPhone` example that is shown in Chapter 13:

```
Class CellPhone
   // Field declarations
   Private String manufacturer
   Private String modelNumber
   Private Real retailPrice

   // Method definitions
   Public Module setManufacturer(String manufact)
      Set manufacturer = manufact
   End Module

   Public Module setModelNumber(String modNum)
      Set modelNumber = modNum
   End Module

   Public Module setRetailPrice(Real retail)
      Set retailPrice = retail
   End Module

   Public Function String getManufacturer()
      Return manufacturer
   End Function

   Public Function String getModelNumber()
      Return modelNumber
   End Function

   Public Function Real getRetailPrice()
      Return retailPrice
   End Function
End Class
```

Creating an Instance of a Class

To create an instance of a class (in other words, an object), you declare a variable to reference the object, and then you use the New operator to create the instance. Here is an example that creates an instance of the CellPhone class previously shown:

```
Declare CellPhone myPhone
Set myPhone = New CellPhone()
```

The first statement declares a variable named myPhone. The second statement creates an instance of the CellPhone class and assigns its memory address to the myPhone variable.

The Init Module in a GUI Application

If a GUI application has an Init module, it executes automatically when the application begins running. The Init module is written in the following general format:

```
Module Init()
   The statements that appear here are executed
   when the application begins running.
End Module
```

GUI Components

Several GUI components are listed in Table 15-1. However, our examples use the following components:

- **Button**—A component that causes an action to occur when it is clicked. The Button component has a Text property that specifies the text that is displayed on the Button.
- **Label**—An area that can display text. The Label component has a Text property that specifies the text that is displayed on the Label.
- **Text box**—An area in which the user may type a single line of input from the keyboard. The Text box component has a Text property that holds the input that the user entered into the component.

Mobile Device Components

The following components are discussed in Chapter 14 as being specific to mobile devices:

- **PhoneCall**—A non-visual component that is responsible for making and receiving phone calls.
- **TextMessage**—A non-visual component that is responsible for sending and receiving text messages.
- **Location**—A non-visual component that can determine the device's latitude, longitude, and nearest street address.

Making a Phone Call on a Mobile Device

To make a phone call on a mobile device, we call the PhoneCall component's makeCall method. The makeCall method takes a string argument that contains the phone number to call. Here is an example:

```
PhoneCall.makeCall("919-555-1212")
```

Sending a Text Message from a Mobile Device

To send a text message from a mobile device, we call the TextMessage component's `sendText` method. The `sendText` method takes two arguments: (1) a string that contains the phone number to send the message to, and (2) a string containing the message. Here is the general format:

```
TextMessage.sendText(PhoneNumber, Message)
```

Getting a Mobile Device's Current Location

The Location component has the following methods that we can use to get the device's location:

- **`getLatitude()`**—returns the device's latitude as a `Real` number
- **`getLongitude()`**—returns the device's longitude as a `Real` number
- **`getAddress()`**—returns a string containing the street address that is nearest to the device

Handling GUI Events

Our pseudocode event handlers are written in the following general format:

```
Module ComponentName_EventName()
   The statements that appear here
   are executed when the event occurs.
End Module
```

In the general format, *`ComponentName`* is the name of the component that generated the event, and *`EventName`* is the name of the event that occurred. The GUI events that we discussed in this text are:

- **`Click`**—an event that occurs when a Button component is clicked
- **`IncomingCall`**—an event that occurs in a smartphone when the device receives an incoming phone call
- **`Incoming_Text`**—an event that occurs in a smartphone when the device receives an incoming text message
- **`LocationChanged`**—an event that occurs in a mobile device when the device's location changes

For example, suppose a GUI application has a Button component named `calculateButton`. The `Click` event handler for the component would be written in the following general format:

```
Module calculateButton_Click()
   The statements that appear here
   are executed when the event occurs.
End Module
```

In a mobile app, the *`IncomingCall`* event handler would be written in the following general format:

```
Module PhoneCall_IncomingCall ()
   The statements that appear here
   are executed when the event occurs.
End Module
```

Appendix D Keywords for Python, C++, and Java

Python Keywords

Table D-1 lists the keywords that are reserved and cannot be used as a variable name, function name, or an identifier in a Python program.

NOTE: The list of keywords may change based on the current version of Python. You can display the list of keywords for the version of Python you are using by entering the following at the prompt:

```
>>> import keyword
>>> print(keyword.kwlist)
```

Table D-1 Python Keywords

and	else	not
as	except	or
assert	False	pass
async	finally	raise
await	for	return
break	from	try
class	in	True
continue	is	while
def	lambda	with
del	nonlocal	yield
elif	None	

C++ Keywords

Table D-2 lists the keywords that are reserved and cannot be used as a variable name, function name, or as an identifier in a C++ program

Table D-2 C++ Keywords

asm	double	new	switch
auto	else	operator	template
break	enum	private	this
case	extern	protected	throw
catch	float	public	try
char	for	register	typedef
class	friend	return	union
const	goto	short	unsigned
continue	if	signed	virtual
default	inline	sizeof	void
delete	int	static	volatile
do	long	struct	while

Java Keywords

Table D-3 lists keywords that are reserved and cannot be used as identifiers in the Java programming language.

Table D-3 Java Keywords

abstract	continue	for	new	switch
assert	default	goto	package	synchronized
boolean	do	if	private	this
break	double	implements	protected	throw
byte	else	import	public	throws
case	enum	instanceof	return	transient
catch	extends	int	short	try
char	final	interface	static	void
class	finally	long	strictfp	volatile
const	float	native	super	while

APPENDIX

E Installing Python or OpenJDK

Downloading Python

To run Python programs, you will need to install Python 3.6 or a later version. You can download the latest version of Python from www.python.org/downloads. This appendix discusses installing Python for Windows. Python is also available for Mac OS, Linux, and several other platforms. Links to download versions of Python for these systems are shown on the Python download site at www.python.org/downloads.

TIP: Keep in mind that there are two *families* of Python that you can download: Python 3.*x* and Python 2.*x*. The programs in this text work only with the Python 3.*x* family.

Installing Python 3.x For Windows

When you visit the Python download site at www.python.org/downloads, you should download the latest version of Python 3.*x* that is available. At the time this text was written, Python 3.10.6 was the latest version. Downloading puts the .exe file into your downloads folder.

Once you have downloaded the Python program, you should install it and set it up for use. Click the down arrow on the program name and select Open, or locate the program in your Downloads folder and double-click it.

If Windows prompts you with a message such as “Do you want to allow this app to make changes to your device?” or “The app you’re trying to install isn’t a Microsoft-verified app.” click *Yes* or *Install* anyway to proceed. It is highly recommended that you check both options at the bottom of the screen: *Install launcher for all users*, and *Add Python 3.x to PATH*. Once you have done that, click *Install Now*. When the installation has finished, you will see the message “Setup was successful.” Select the Close button to exit the installer. To launch Python, type py in the Windows search box and select the Python 3.x app.

Installing OpenJDK

To use the Java programming language you need to install OpenJDK, which is the free, open source version of the JDK Standard Edition. OpenJDK can be downloaded from this website:

```
https://jdk.java.net/
```

On that website you should see a link to download the latest “ready for use” version of the JDK. New versions of the JDK are released twice per year. Select the option for your operating system to download the program files.

Installing OpenJDK for Windows

When you select the option for installing on a Windows system, a zip file with a name similar to OpenJDK downloads. Follow these steps to install it:

1. Create a folder named `Java` in the root folder of drive `C:`. The folder's path will be `C:\Java`. This will be the location where you will install the OpenJDK files. Your instructor may tell you to use different location.
2. Open the `Downloads` folder (or the location where you downloaded the OpenJDK `zip` file.). Right-click on the `zip` file and select *Extract All…* In the window that appears next, keep the default destination, and make sure that the *Show extracted files when complete box is checked.*
3. The `zip` file's contents will now be extracted to a folder with a name such as `openjdk-16.0.2_windows-x64_bin`. Inside this folder you will see another folder with a name such as `jdk-16.0.2`. Move this folder to the `Java` folder that you created in step 1. You have installed the OpenJDK files to this folder.

Installing OpenJDK for macOS

When you select the option for installing on a macOS system, a compressed file with a name similar to OpenJDK downloads. Follow these steps to install it:

1. Open the Terminal app.
2. Change your current directory to the `Downloads` directory.
3. Move the OpenJDK compressed file that you downloaded to the `/Library/Java/JavaVirtualMachines` directory.
4. Change your current directory to the `/Library/Java/JavaVirtualMachines` directory.
5. Extract the contents of the OpenJDK compressed file.
6. Remove the compressed file.
7. Display a directory listing to see the contents of the current directory. You should see a directory with a name similar to this: `jdk-16.0.2.jdk`. You have installed the OpenJDK files to this folder.

Installing NetBeans for Java

NetBeans is a popular integrated development environment (IDE) for the Java programming language. To download and install NetBeans, follow these steps:

1. Go to https://netbeans.apache.org/
2. Select the *Find out more* link to go to the download page for the latest release of NetBeans.
3. Select the link for the type of system you are using.
4. Select the link for the recommended mirror site. This downloads an .exe file.
5. Once the file is downloaded, execute it. The program will ask you to select various options, such as the installation location, components to install, etc. If you are unsure of the answer to any of these questions, keep the default response that is provided. When the program is finished, NetBeans will be installed on your system.

APPENDIX

F Introduction to IDLE

VideoNote
Introduction to IDLE

IDLE is an integrated development environment that combines several development tools into one program, including the following:

- A Python shell running in interactive mode. You can type Python statements at the shell prompt and immediately execute them. You can also run complete Python programs.
- A text editor that color codes Python keywords and other parts of programs.
- A "check module" tool that checks a Python program for syntax errors without running the program.
- Search tools that allow you to find text in one or more files.
- Text formatting tools that help you maintain consistent indentation levels in a Python program.
- A debugger that allows you to single-step through a Python program and watch the values of variables change as each statement executes.
- Several other advanced tools for developers.

The IDLE software is bundled with Python. When you install the Python interpreter, IDLE is automatically installed, as well. This appendix provides a quick introduction to IDLE and describes the basic steps of creating, saving, and executing a Python program.

Starting IDLE and Using the Python Shell

After Python is installed on your system, a Python program group will appear in your Start menu's program list. One of the items in the program group will be titled *IDLE (Python GUI)*. Click this item to start IDLE, and you will see the Python Shell window shown in Figure F-1. Inside this window, the Python interpreter is running in interactive mode, and at the top of the window is a menu bar that provides access to all of IDLE's tools.

Figure F-1 IDLE shell window

IDLE Shell 3.10.6

File Edit Shell Debug Options Window Help

```
Python 3.10.6 (tags/v3.10.6:9c7b4bd, Aug  1 2022, 21:53:49) [MSC v.1932 64 bit (
AMD64)] on win32
Type "help", "copyright", "credits" or "license()" for more information.
>>>
```

Ln: 3 Col: 0

Python Software Foundation

The >>> prompt indicates that the interpreter is waiting for you to type a Python statement. When you type a statement at the >>> prompt and press the Enter key, the statement is immediately executed. For example, Figure F-2 shows the Python Shell window after three statements have been entered and executed.

Figure F-2 Statements executed by the Python interpreter

```
IDLE Shell 3.10.6
File Edit Shell Debug Options Window Help
   Python 3.10.6 (tags/v3.10.6:9c7b4bd, Aug  1 2022, 21:53:49) [MSC v.1932 64 bit (
   AMD64)] on win32
   Type "help", "copyright", "credits" or "license()" for more information.
>>> name = 'Holly'
>>> favorite_food = 'spaghetti'
>>> print('My name is', name, 'and I like', favorite_food)
   My name is Holly and I like spaghetti
>>>
                                                                  Ln: 7 Col: 0
```

Python Software Foundation

When you type the beginning of a multiline statement, such as an `if` statement or a loop, each subsequent line is automatically indented. Pressing the Enter key on an empty line indicates the end of the multiline statement and causes the interpreter to execute it. Figure F-3 shows the Python Shell window after a `for` loop has been entered and executed.

Figure F-3 A multiline statement executed by the Python interpreter

```
IDLE Shell 3.10.6
File Edit Shell Debug Options Window Help
   Python 3.10.6 (tags/v3.10.6:9c7b4bd, Aug  1 2022, 21:53:49) [MSC v.1932 64 bit (A
   MD64)] on win32
   Type "help", "copyright", "credits" or "license()" for more information.
>>> for x in range(10):
...     print(x, end='')
...
...
   0123456789
>>>
                                                                  Ln: 8 Col: 0
```

Python Software Foundation

Writing a Python Program in the IDLE Editor

To write a new Python program in IDLE, you open a new editing window. Select File on the menu bar, then select New File on the dropdown menu. (Alternatively, you can press Ctrl+N.) This opens a text-editing window like the one shown in Figure F-4.

Figure F-4 A text editing window

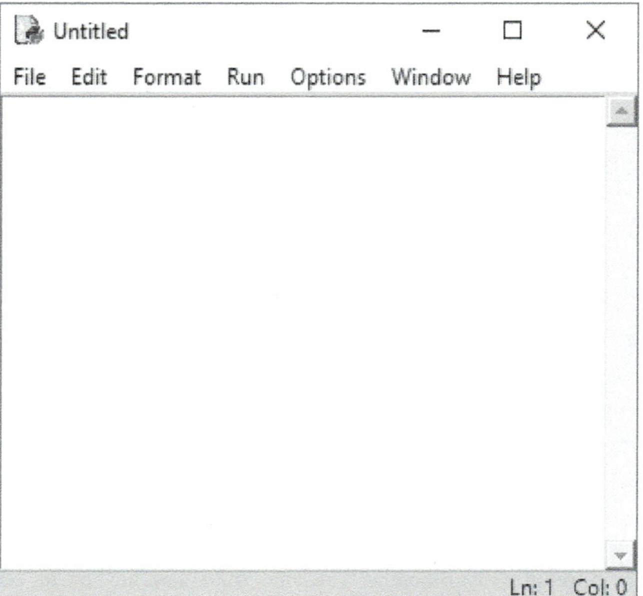

Python Software Foundation

To open a program that already exists, select File on the menu bar, then select Open. Browse to the file's location and select it, and it will open in an editor window.

Color Coding

Code that is typed into the editor window, as well as in the Python Shell window, is colorized as follows:

- Python keywords are displayed in orange.
- Comments are displayed in red.
- String literals are displayed in green.
- Defined names, such as the names of functions and classes, are displayed in blue.
- Built-in functions are displayed in purple.

TIP: You can change IDLE's color settings by clicking Options on the menu bar, then clicking Configure IDLE. Select the Highlighting tab at the top of the dialog box, and you can specify colors for each element of a Python program.

Automatic Indentation

The IDLE editor has features that help you to maintain consistent indentation in your Python programs. Perhaps the most helpful of these features is automatic indentation. The editor automatically indents after a function header, the first line of a loop, or any line ending with a colon (for example, an if clause).

For example, suppose you are typing the code shown in Figure F-5. After you press the Enter key at the end of the line marked ①, the editor will automatically indent the lines that you type next. Then, after you press the Enter key at the end of the line marked②, the editor indents again. Pressing the Backspace key at the beginning of an indented line cancels one level of indentation.

Figure F-5 Lines that cause automatic indentation

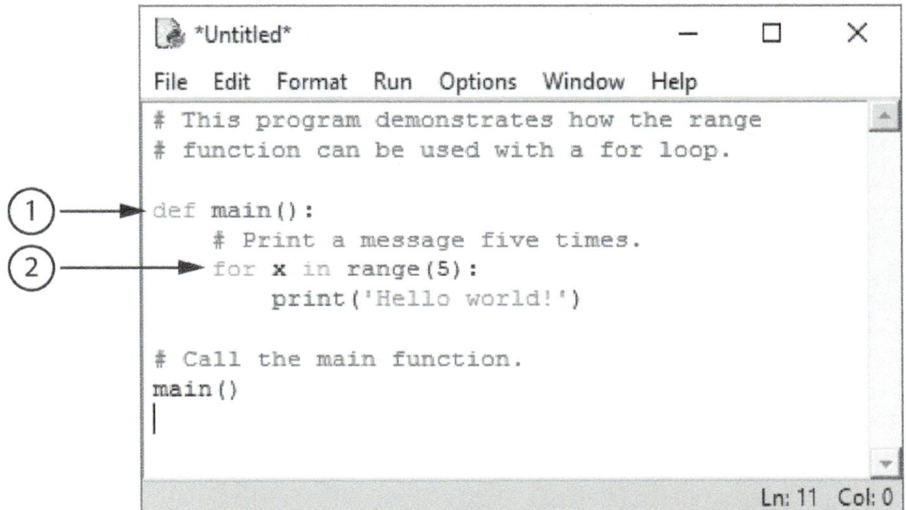

Python Software Foundation

By default, IDLE indents four spaces for each level of indentation. It is possible to change the number of spaces by clicking Options on the menu bar, then clicking Configure IDLE. Make sure Fonts/Tabs is selected at the top of the dialog box, and you will see a slider bar that allows you to change the number of spaces used for indentation width. However, because four spaces is the standard width for indentation in Python, it is recommended that you keep this setting.

Saving a Program

In the editor window, you can save the current program by selecting any of these operations from the File menu:

- Save
- Save As
- Save Copy As

The Save and Save As operations work just as they do in any Windows application. The Save Copy As operation works like Save As, but it leaves the original program in the editor window.

Running a Program

Once you have typed a program into the editor, you can run it by pressing the F5 key or by choosing Run on the editor window's menu bar, then choosing Run Module. If the program has not been saved since the last modification was made, you will see the dialog box shown in Figure F-6. Click OK to save the program. When the program runs, you will see its output displayed in IDLE's Python Shell window, as shown in Figure F-7.

Figure F-6 Save confirmation dialog box

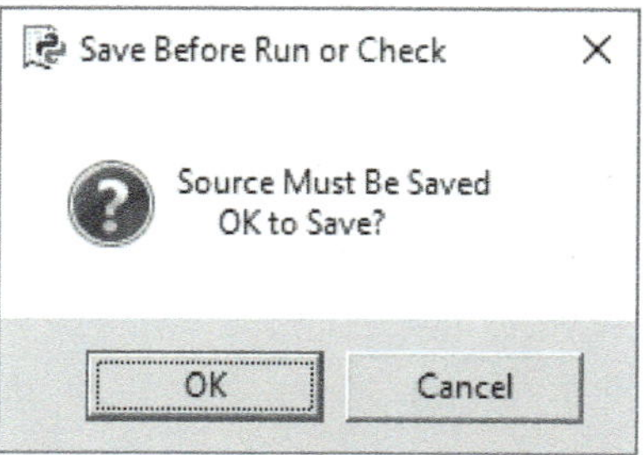

Python Software Foundation

Figure F-7 Output displayed in the Python Shell window

```
IDLE Shell 3.10.6
File Edit Shell Debug Options Window Help
    Python 3.10.6 (tags/v3.10.6:9c7b4bd, Aug  1 2022, 21:53:49) [MSC v.1932 64 bit
    (AMD64)] on win32
    Type "help", "copyright", "credits" or "license()" for more information.
>>>
    =========== RESTART: \\WORK\Users\Public\CS1_Figures\simple_loop4.py =========
    ==
    Hello world!
    Hello world!
    Hello world!
    Hello world!
    Hello world!
>>>
                                                                    Ln: 10 Col: 0
```

Python Software Foundation

If a program contains a syntax error, you will see the dialog box shown in Figure F-8 when you run the program. After you click the OK button, the editor will highlight the location of the error in the code. If you want to check the syntax of a program without trying to run it, you can click Run on the menu bar, then click Check Module. Any syntax errors that are found will be reported.

Figure F-8 Dialog box reporting a syntax error

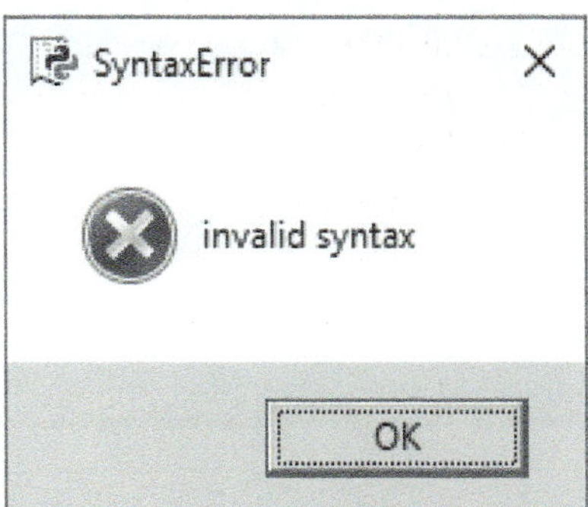

Python Software Foundation

Other Resources

This appendix has provided an overview for using IDLE to create, save, and execute programs. IDLE provides many more advanced features. To read about additional capabilities, see the official IDLE documentation at www.python.org/idle

APPENDIX

G Common Colors, Tags, and Properties for HTML5 and CSS

Commonly Used HTML5 Tags

Tag	Purpose	Commonly Used Attributes
<!-- -->	Comment	
<a>	Anchor tag: configures hyperlinks	accesskey, class, href, id, name, rel, style, tabindex, target, title
<abbr>	Configures an abbreviation	class, id, style
<address>	Configures contact information	class, id, style
<area>	Configures an area in an image map	accesskey, alt, class, href, hreflang, id, media, rel, shape, style, tabindex, target, type
<article>	Configures an independent section of a document as an article	class, id, style
<aside>	Configures tangential content	class, id, style
<audio>	Configures an audio control native to the browser	autoplay, class, controls, id, loop, preload, src, style, title
<b>	Configures bold text with no implied importance	class, id, style
<bdi>	Configures text used in bi-directional text formatting (bi-directional isolation)	class, id, style
<bdo>	Specifies a bi-directional override	class, id, style
<blockquote>	Configures a long quotation	class, id, style
<body>	Configures the body section	class, id, style
 	Configures a line break	class, id, style
<button>	Configures a button	accesskey, autofocus, class, disabled, format, formaction, formenctype, formmethod, formtarget, formnovalidate, id, name, type, style, value
<canvas>	Configures dynamic graphics	class, height, id, style, title, width
<caption>	Configures a caption for a table	class, id, style
<cite>	Configures the title of a cited work	class, height, id, style, title

Tag	Purpose	Commonly Used Attributes
<code>	Configures a fragment of computer code	class, id, style
<col>	Configures a table column	class, id, span, style
<colgroup>	Configures a group of one or more columns in a table	class, id, span, style
<command>	Configures an area to represent commands	class, id, style, type
<datalist>	Configures a control that contains one or more option elements	class, id, style
<dd>	Configures a description area in a description list	class, id, style
<del>	Configures deleted text (with strikethrough)	cite, class, datetime, id, style
<details>	Configures a control to provide additional information to the user on demand	class, id, open, style
<dfn>	Configures the definition of a term	class, id, style
<dialog>	Configures an interactive component such as a dialog box	class, id, open, style
<div>	Configures a generic section or division in a document	class, id, style
<dl>	Configures a description list (formerly called a definition list)	class, id, style
<dt>	Configures a term in a description list	class, id, style
<em>	Configures emphasized text (usually displays in italics)	class, id, style
<embed>	Plug-in integration (such as Adobe Flash Player)	class, id, height, src, style, type, width
<fieldset>	Configures a grouping of form elements with a border	class, id, style
<figcaption>	Configures a caption for a figure	class, id, style
<figure>	Configures a figure	class, id, style*(Continued)*(*Continued*)
<footer>	Configures a footer area	class, id, style
<form>	Configures a form	accept-charset, action, autocomplete, class, enctype, id, method, name, novalidate, style, target
<h1>...<h6>	Configures headings	class, id, style
<head>	Configures the head section	
<header>	Configures a header area	class, id, style

Tag	Purpose	Commonly Used Attributes
<hr>	Configures a horizontal line; indicates a thematic break in HTML5	class, id, style
<html>	Configures the root element of a web page document	lang, manifest
<i>	Configures italic text	class, id, style
<iframe>	Configures an inline frame	allow, allowfullscreen, class, height, id, loading, name, sandbox, src, style, width
<img>	Configures an image	alt, class, height, id, ismap, longdesc, name, sizes, src, srcset, style, usemap, width, loading
<input>	Configures an input control; such as a text box, email text box, URL text box, search text box, telephone number text box, scrolling text box, submit button, reset button, password box, calendar control, slider control, spinner control, color picker control, or hidden field form control	accept, accesskey, autocomplete, autofocus, capture, class, checked, disabled, form, id, list, max, maxlength, min, multiple, name, pattern, placeholder, readonly, required, size, step, style, tabindex, type, value
<ins>	Configures text that has been inserted with an underline	cite, class, datetime, id, style
<kbd>	Configures a representation of user input	class, id, style
<label>	Configures a label for a form control	class, for, form, id, style
<legend>	Configures a caption for a fieldset element	class, id, style
<li>	Configures a list item in an unordered or ordered list	class, id, style, value
<link>	Associates a web page document with an external resource	class, href, hreflang, id, rel, media, sizes, style, type
<main>	Configures the main content area of a web page	class, id, style
<map>	Configures an image map	class, id, name, style
<mark>	Configures text as marked (or highlighted) for easy reference	class, id, style
<menu>	Configures a list of commands	class, id, label, style, type
<meta>	Configures meta data	charset, content, http-equiv, name
<meter>	Configures visual gauge of a value	class, id, high, low, max, min, optimum, style, value
<nav>	Configures an area with navigation hyperlinks	class, id, style

Tag		Commonly Used Attributes
<noscript>	Configures content for browsers that do not support client-side scripting	
<object>	Configures a generic embedded object	classid, codebase, data, form, height, name, id, style, title, tabindex, type, width
<ol>	Configures an ordered list	class, id, reversed, start, style, type
<optgroup>	Configures a group of related options in a select list	class, disabled, id, label, style
<option>	Configures an option in a select list	class, disabled, id, selected, style, value
<output>	Configures result of processing in a form	class, for, form, id, style
<p>	Configures a paragraph	class, id, style
<param>	Configures a parameter for plug-ins	name, value
<picture>	Configures images for responsive display with media queries	class, id, style
<pre>	Configures preformatted text	class, id, style
<progress>	Configures a visual progress indicator	class, id, max, style, value
<q>	Configures quoted text	cite, class, id, style
<rp>	Configures a ruby parentheses	class, id, style
<rt>	Configures ruby text component of a ruby annotation	class, id, style
<ruby>	Configures a ruby annotation	class, id, style
<samp>	Configures sample output from a computer program or system	class, id, style
<script>	Configures a client-side script (typically JavaScript)	async, charset, defer, src, type
<section>	Configures a section of a document	class, id, style
<select>	Configures a select list form control	class, disabled, form, id, multiple, name, size, style, tabindex
<small>	Configures a disclaimer in small text size	class, id, style
<source>	Configures a media file and MIME type	class, id, media, sizes, src, srcset, style, type
<span>	Configures a generic section of a document with inline display	class, id, style

Tag	Purpose	Commonly Used Attributes
<strong>	Configures text with strong importance (typically displayed as bold)	class, id, style
<style>	Configures embedded styles in a web page document	media, scoped, type
<sub>	Configures subscript text	class, id, style
<summary>	Configures text as a summary, caption, or legend for a details control	class, id, style
<sup>	Configures superscript text	class, id, style
<table>	Configures a table	class, id, style, border (obsolete in HTML5)
<tbody>	Configures the body section of a table	class, id, style
<td>	Configures a table data cell in a table	class, colspan, id, headers, rowspan
<textarea>	Configures a scrolling text box form control	accesskey, autofocus, class, cols, disabled, id, maxlength, name, placeholder, readonly, required, rows, style, tabindex, wrap
<tfoot>	Configures the footer section of a table	class, id, style
<th>	Configures a table header cell in a table	class, colspan, id, headers, rowspan, scope, style
<thead>	Configures the head section of a table	class, id, style
<time>	Configures a date and/or time	class, datetime, id, pubdate, style
<title>	Configures the title of a web page document	
<tr>	Configures a row in a table	class, id, style
<track>	Configures a subtitle or caption track for media	class, default, id, kind, label, src, srclang, style
<u>	Configures text displayed with an underline	class, id, style
<ul>	Configures an unordered list	class, id, style
<var>	Configures text as a variable or placeholder text	class, id, style
<video>	Configures a video control native to the browser	autoplay, class, controls, height, id, loop, poster, preload, src, style, width
<wbr>	Configures a line-break opportunity	class, id, style

Commonly Used CSS Properties

Property	Description
align-items	Configures the extra space along the cross-axis of a flex container Value: flex-start, flex-end, center, baseline, or stretch
background	Shorthand to configure all the background properties of an element Value: background-color, background-image, background-repeat, background-position
background-attachment	Configures a background image as fixed-in-place or scrolling Value: scroll (default) or fixed
background-clip	Configures the area to display the background Value: border-box, padding-box, or content-box
background-color	Configures the background color of an element Value: Valid color value
background-image	Configures a background image for an element Value: url (*file name or path to the image*), none (default) Optional CSS3 functions: linear-gradient() and radial-gradient()
background-origin	Configures the background positioning area Value: padding-box, border-box, or content-box
background-position	Configures the position of a background image Value: Two percentages, pixel values, or position values (left, top, center, bottom, right)
background-repeat	Configures how the background image will be repeated Value: repeat (default), repeat-y, repeat-x, or no-repeat
background-size	Configures the size of the background images Value: Numeric value (px, em, rem, vh, and vw), percentage, contain, cover
border	Shorthand to configure the border of an element Value: border-width, border-style, border-color
border-bottom	Configures the bottom border of an element Value: border-width, border-style, border-color
border-collapse	Configures the display of borders in a table Value: separate (default) or collapse
border-color	Configures the border color of an element Value: Valid color value

Property	Description
border-image	Configures an image in the border of an element See https://www.w3.org/TR/css3-background/#the-border-image
border-left	Configures the left border of an element Value: border-width, border-style, border-color
border-radius	Configures rounded corners Value: One or two numeric values (px or em) or percentages that configure horizontal and vertical radius of the corner. If one value is provided, it applies to both horizontal and vertical radius. Related properties: border-top-left-radius, border-top-right-radius, border-bottom-left-radius, and border-bottom-right-radius
border-right	Configures the right border of an element Value: border-width, border-style, border-color
border-spacing	Configures the space between table cells in a table Value: Numeric value (px or em)
border-style	Configures the style of the borders around an element Value: none (default), inset, outset, double, groove, ridge, solid, dashed, or dotted
border-top	Configures the top border of an element Value: border-width, border-style, border-color
border-width	Configures the width of an element's border Value: Numeric pixel value (such as 1 px), thin, medium, or thick
bottom	Configures the offset position from the bottom of a containing element Value: Numeric value (px or em), percentage, or auto (default)
box-shadow	Configures a drop shadow on an element Value: Three or four numerical values (px or em) to indicate horizontal offset, vertical offset, blur radius, (optional) spread distance, and a valid color value. Use the inset keyword to configure an inner shadow.
box-sizing	Alters the default CSS box model that calculates widths and heights of elements Value: content-box (default), padding-box, or border-box
caption-side	Configures the placement of a table caption Value: top (default) or bottom
clear	Configures the display of an element in relation to floating elements Value: none (default), left, right, or both
color	Configures the color of text within an element Value: Valid color value
column-gap	Configures empty space or gutters between grid columns Value: Numeric length or percentage

Property	Description
display	Configures how and if an element will display Value: inline, inline-block, none, block, flex, grid, inline-flex, list-item, table, table-row, or table-cell
flex	Configures the size of each flex item proportionate to the whole Value: Numeric integer value, auto, flex-grow, flex-shrink, or flex-basis
flex-basis	Configures the initial dimension along the main axis of a flex item Value: auto (default), content, or a positive numeric value
flex-direction	Configures the direction of flex items Value: row, column, row-reverse, or column-reverse
flex-flow	Shorthand to configure direction and wrap of a flex container Value: flex-direction and flex-wrap
flex-grow	Determines the growth of a flex item relative to other items in the flex container Value: 0 (default) or a positive numeric value
flex-shrink	Configures the shrinkage of a flex item relative to others in the flex container Value: 1 (default) or another positive numeric value
flex-wrap	Configures whether flex items are displayed on multiple lines Value: nowrap (default), wrap, or wrap-reverse
float	Configures the horizontal placement (left or right) of an element Value: none (default), left, or right
font	Shorthand to configure the font properties of an element Value: font-style, font-variant, font-weight, font-size/line-height, font-family
font-family	Configures the font typeface of text Value: List of valid font names or generic font family names
font-size	Configures the font size of text Value: Numeric value (px, pt, em), percentage value, xx-small, x-small, small, medium (default), large, x-large, xx-large, smaller, or larger
font-stretch	Configures a normal, condensed, or expanded face from a font family Value: normal, wider, narrower, condensed, semi-condensed, expanded, or ultra-expanded
font-style	Configures the font style of text Value: normal (default), italic, or oblique
font-variant	Configures whether text is displayed in small-caps font Value: normal (default) or small-caps

Property	Description
font-weight	Configures the weight (boldness) of text Value: normal (default), bold, bolder, lighter, 100, 200, 300, 400, 500, 600, 700, 800, or 900
gap	Shorthand to configure empty space or gutters between grid tracks Value: row-gap and column-gap
grid-area	Associates a grid item with a named area of the grid Value: Name of a grid area
grid-column	Configures one or more columns in the grid for an item or area Value: See https://www.w3.org/TR/css-grid-1/#typedef-grid-row-start-grid-line
grid-column-gap	Configures empty space or gutters between grid columns Value: Numeric length or percentage
grid-gap	Shorthand to configure empty space or gutters between grid tracks Value: grid-row-gap and grid-column-gap
grid-row	Configures one or more rows in a grid for an item or area Value: See https://www.w3.org/TR/css-grid-1/#typedef-grid-row-start-grid-line
grid-row-gap	Configures empty space or gutters between grid rows Value: Numeric length or percentage
grid-template	Shorthand property that combines the grid-template-areas, grid-template-rows, and grid-template-columns properties Value: A series of strings for each row that indicate placement of named grid areas; the last row describes the columns widths See https://www.w3.org/TR/css-grid-1/#propdef-grid-template
grid-template-areas	Visually indicates the placement of the named grid areas on the grid Value: A series of strings for each row that indicate placement of named grid areas See https://www.w3.org/TR/css-grid-1/#grid-template-areas-property
grid-template-columns	Specifies how much space to reserve for each column in the grid Value: Numeric pixels, percentage, auto, and flex factor units; See https://www.w3.org/TR/css-grid-1/#propdef-grid-template-columns
grid-template-rows	Specifies how much space to reserve for each row in the grid Value: Numeric pixels, percentage, auto, and flex factor units; see https://www.w3.org/TR/css-grid-1/#propdef-grid-template-columns
height	Configures the height of an element Value: Numeric value (px, em, rem, vh, vmin, and vmax), percentage, or auto (default)
justify-content	Configures how the browser should display any extra space Value: center, space-between, space-around, flex-start (default), or flex-end

Property	Description
left	Configures the offset position from the left of a containing element Value: Numeric value (px or em), percentage, or auto (default)
letter-spacing	Configures the space between text characters Value: Numeric value (px or em) or normal (default)
line-height	Configures the line height of text Value: Numeric value (px or em), percentage, multiplier numeric value, or normal (default)
list-style	Shorthand to configure the properties of a list list-style-type, list-style-position, list-style-image
list-style-image	Configures an image as a list marker Value: url (*file name or path to the image*) or none (default)
list-style-position	Configures the position of the list markers Value: inside or outside (default)
list-style-type	Configures the type of list marker displayed Value: none, circle, disc (default), square, decimal, decimal-leading-zero, Georgian, lower-alpha, lower-roman, upper-alpha, or upper-roman
margin	Shorthand to configure the margin of an element Value: One to four numeric values (px or em), percentages, auto or 0
margin-bottom	Configures the bottom margin of an element Value: Numeric value (px or em), percentage, auto or 0
margin-left	Configures the left margin of an element Value: Numeric value (px or em), percentage, auto or 0
margin-right	Configures the right margin of an element Value: Numeric value (px or em), percentage, auto or 0
margin-top	Configures the top margin of an element Value: Numeric value (px or em), percentage, auto or 0
max-height	Configures the maximum height of an element Value: Numeric value (px, em, rem, and vh), percentage, none (default), max-content, min-content, fit-content, or fill-available
max-width	Configures the maximum width of an element Value: Numeric value (px, em, rem, and vw), percentage, or none (default), max-content, min-content, fit-content, or fill-available
min-height	Configures the minimum height of an element Value: Numeric value (px, em, rem, and vh), percentage, max-content, min-content, fit-content, fill-available, or auto
min-width	Configures the minimum width of an element Value: Numeric value (px, em, rem, and vw), or percentage, max-content, min-content, fit-content, or fill-available

Property	Description
opacity	Configures the transparency of an element Value: Numeric value between 1 (fully opaque) and 0 (completely transparent)
order	Configures the display of flex items and grid items in a different order than coded Value: Numeric integer
outline	Shorthand to configure an outline of an element Value: outline-width, outline-style, outline-color
outline-color	Configures the outline color of an element Value: Valid color value
outline-style	Configures the style of the outline around an element Value: none (default), inset, outset, double, groove, ridge, solid, dashed, or dotted
outline-width	Configures the width of an element's outline Value: Numeric pixel value (such as 1 px), thin, medium, or thick
overflow	Configures how content should display if it is too large for the area allocated Value: visible (default), hidden, auto, or scroll
padding	Shorthand to configure the padding of an element Value: One to four numeric values (px or em), percentages, or 0
padding-bottom	Configures the bottom padding of an element Value: Numeric value (px or em), percentage, or 0
padding-left	Configures the left padding of an element Value: Numeric value (px or em), percentage, or 0
padding-right	Configures the right padding of an element Value: Numeric value (px or em), percentage, or 0
padding-top	Configures the top padding of an element Value: Numeric value (px or em), percentage, or 0
page-break-after	Configures the page break after an element Value: auto (default), always, avoid, left, or right
page-break-before	Configures the page break before an element Value: auto (default), always, avoid, left, or right
page-break-inside	Configures the page break inside an element Value: auto (default) or avoid
position	Configures the type of positioning used to display an element Value: static (default), absolute, fixed, relative, or sticky
right	Configures the offset position from the right of a containing element Value: Numeric value (px or em), percentage, or auto (default)
row-gap	Configures empty space or gutters between grid rows Value: Numeric length or percentage

Property	Description
vertical-align	Configures the vertical alignment of an element Value: Numeric value (px or em), percentage, baseline (default), sub, super, top, text-top, middle, bottom, or text-bottom
visibility	Configures the visibility of an element Value: visible (default), hidden, or collapse
white-space	Configures white space inside an element Value: normal (default), nowrap, pre, pre-line, or pre-wrap
width	Configures the width of an element Value: Numeric value (px, em, rem, vw, vmin, and vmax), percentage, or auto (default)
word-spacing	Configures the space between words within text Value: Numeric value (px or em) or auto (default)
z-index	Configures the stacking order of an element Value: A numeric value or auto (default)

Web Safe Color Palette

Web safe colors look the most similar on various computer platforms and computer monitors. Back in the day of eight-bit color, it was crucial to use web safe colors. Since most modern video drivers support millions of colors, the use of web safe colors is now optional. The hexadecimal and decimal RGB values are shown for each color in the palette above.

GLOSSARY

G Glossary

A

absolute hyperlink
A hyperlink that specifies the entire path to a resource, including the protocol.

access specifier
A word in a declaration that identifies how a class field or method can be accessed.

acceptable use policy (AUP)
A policy—published by a school district, business, or other organization—that identifies rules of behavior that must be followed by anyone using that organization's telecommunications equipment, computers, network, or internet connection.

accessible color scheme
Colors that can be read and understood by everyone in accordance with the American with Disabilities Act (ADA).

accessor method
Accessor methods provide a safe way for code outside a class to retrieve the values of attributes, without exposing the attributes in a way that they could be changed by the code outside the method.

accumulator
A variable used to accumulate the total of the numbers.

active listening
A strategy for effective communication in which the listener pays attention to the speaker in order to hear and understand the message.

aggressive speech
Argumentative language that can lead to misunderstanding and resentment.

algorithm
A sequence of instructions. In programming, the specific steps the computer must follow in order to solve a problem or complete a task.

algorithmic solutions
Straight-forward solutions that can be solved using an algorithm or problem-solving approach.

alignment designators
A symbol used in programming to specify the horizontal alignment for a value.

alternate text
Text that is rendered by a web page or other digital document in place of an image or other element that cannot be rendered or viewed. Sometimes called Alt text.

American Standard Code for Information Interchange (ASCII)
A system that uses 128 numeric codes to represent English letters, punctuation marks, and other characters.

antimalware program
A software utility that detects, quarantines, and removes computer viruses, spyware, and other malware.

antivirus program
A software utility that detects, quarantines, and removes computer viruses.

app
An abbreviation for the term application, usually used for programs developed specifically for smartphones, tablet computers, and other handheld devices.

application software
A program or group of programs designed to perform specific tasks, such as create documents, store data, or edit graphics.

argument
A value sent to a function, subroutine or program.

array
A data structure consistence of a sequence of elements.

array bounds checking
A feature in most programming languages that blocks a program from using an invalid array subscript.

artificial intelligence
A branch of computer science that works to develop computers that can mimic human tasks such as heuristic problem solving and decision making.

ASCII
The acronym for American Standard Code for Information Interchange.

assembler
A program that converts low-level code into machine language.

assembly language
A low-level programming language that provides machine instructions using language that people can understand.

assertive speech
Strong, positive language that supports effective communication.

assignment operator
An operator, such as an equal sign (=), that you use to assign a value to a variable.

assignment statement
A statement that creates a variable and assigns it to a piece of data.

assistive technologies
Any item or service that helps people with disabilities use technology.

assumption
Something that is accepted as being true even if there is no factual proof.

attributes
Values that modify or refine the characteristics of coded elements.

augmented assignment operators
A set of operators designed to assign a value to common programming operations.

automated accessibility testing
A tool that evaluates a website to determine if it meets accessibility requirements.

B

binary
A format that has only two possible values: 0 and 1.

binary digit (bit)
The basic unit of data in computing that holds one of two possible values: 0 or 1.

binary numbering system
A base 2 numbering system in which all numeric values are written as sequences of 0s and 1s.

bit
The basic unit of data in computing that holds one of two possible values: 0 or 1.

black box
A term used to describe some library functions or other mechanisms that accept input, perform an unseen operation using the input, and produce output.

block
A set of statements that belong together as a group.

block comments
Comment that take up several lines and are used when lengthy explanations are required.

block display The rendered text within an HTML heading element.

body element
The HTML element that contains the body section.

body section
The HTML tags, text, images, and other objects that display as a web page.

Boolean data type
A data type that can hold one of two possible values.

Boolean expressions
Expressions that are tested by an if statement.

Boolean functions
Functions used to test a condition, then return either True or False to indicate whether the condition exists.

branching
A term for moving to the next step in a problem or algorithm based on whether certain conditions are true or false.

by position
A term that describes the way arguments are passed to corresponding variables in a function; the first argument is passed to the first variable, the second argument is passed to the second variable, and so on.

byte
A unit of computer memory size usually consisting of eight bits.

C

call
To execute a function.

calling
When a program executes a function.

camelCase
A method of naming variables that uses a lowercase letter as the first character and an uppercase letter to start all other words within the variable name.

cascading style sheets (CSS)
A cross-platform, standards-based language that provides the tools for applying consistent formatting instructions to web pages.

case-insensitive
Treating upper- and lower-case characters as being the same.

case-sensitive
Treating upper- and lower-case characters as different.

Cartesian coordinate system
A system used to locate the position of a point in two dimensions by referencing the x- and y- axes.

catfishing
When a cybercriminal pretends to be someone else online.

central processing unit (CPU)
The piece of computer hardware that processes and compares data, and completes arithmetic and logical operations.

character
A data type for text.

citation
A reference to a source that gives credit to the source and provides the tools a reader needs to locate the source on their own.

class
Code that specifies the data attributes and methods of a particular type of object.

class constructor
A C++ member function that has the same name as the class.

class declaration
A container for Java code that must be written when you start a new Java program.

class header
The first line of a class declaration.

class definition
A set of statements that define a class's methods and data attributes.

class variable
A variable that can reference an object in the computer's memory.

clause
An incomplete fragment of a statement.

closing tag
The code used to mark the end of an HTML container. Also called an end tag.

cloud storage
Data that is stored and accessed on a remote internet server instead of on a local storage device. Sometimes called online storage.

code
The set of instructions written in a programming language.

code reuse
Reusing code written in one program in a different program, to perform the same task.

codec
An algorithm used to compress and decompress media, such as audio or video.

coding portfolio
An online resume that includes examples of coding programs.

comments
Short notes placed in different parts of a program, explaining how those parts of the program work.

commercial software
Copyrighted software that must be purchased before it can be used.

compile errors
Errors that are detected by the interpreter.

compiler
A program that translates a high-level language program into a separate machine language program.

components
The parts of a computer system.

compound Boolean expressions
Boolean expressions that use more than one logical operator.

computer crime
Any act that violates state or federal laws and involves using a computer.

computer science
The study of computers and computing.

concatenate
To join two things together.

concatenation
The operation of joining two things together.

condition
A statement that can be evaluated as being either true or false.

conditionally executed
A term that described how a statement will be performed only when a certain condition is true.

condition-controlled loop
A loop that uses a true/false condition to control the number of times that it repeats.

connector symbol
A small circle with a letter or number in it, used to connect parts of a flowchart.

constructive criticism
Feedback that is delivered in a positive way, and includes advice for how to make improvements or solve problems.

constructor
A method that is automatically called when an object is created.

container
When working with media in HTML, the container is the file type designated by the file extension.

contributor
A person who actively participants in a learning event by making suggestions and completing tasks.

control structure
A logical design that controls the order in which a set of statements execute.

cookie
A small file that is saved to your storage device when you visit a website.

copyright
The legal right to control the use of creative, literary, or artistic work, including software code.

count-controlled loop
A loop that repeats a specific number of times.

counter
A variable that stores the number of iterations performed by a count-controlled loop. Also called a counter variable.

counter variable
A variable that stores the number of iterations performed by a count-controlled loop. Also called a counter.

cover letter
A letter of introduction that you send with a resume.

creative commons license
A license that lets copyright holders make some of their work available for public use while letting them retain copyright for other parts of the work.

critical thinking
When you think critically, you are honest, rational, and open-minded about your options.

criticism
An analysis and judgement of the positive and negative aspects of something, such as a product, design, work of art, or project.

customer
The person, group, or organization that hires you to write a program.

cybercrime
Crimes carried out by means of the internet.

D

data attributes
Variables that reference data.

data hiding
An object's ability to hide its data attributes from code that is outside the object. Only the object's methods may directly access and make changes to the object's data attributes.

data type
The type of value a variable can store.

date
A data type for coding dates.

debug
The process of finding and correcting errors in a program.

decision structure
A logical design that controls the order in which a set of statements execute. Also called a selection structure.

declaration
A means of specifying the variables (or properties, in HTML) that will be used in a program.

decrement
To decrease a value.

default constructor
The constructor that is assigned automatically and assigns default starting values to an object's fields.

defensive programming
The practice of anticipating and avoiding programming errors.

definiteness
A property of an algorithm that specifies the sequence of operations for transforming input into output.

definition
The code you write to create a function and other elements.

deliverable
A product or segment of a product that can be provided to an employer, client, or the public.

desk checking
A debugging exercise in which you step through each of the program's statements one by one. Also called hand tracing.

development environment
The software and hardware tools that a programmer uses to create, modify, and test code.

dialog box
An area onscreen where a program prompts a user for input.

dictionaries
In Python, objects that store elements as key-value pairs.

digital
Anything that uses binary numbers.

digital asset
An item that is stored digitally and that has value.

digital data
Data that is stored in binary format.

digital device
Any device that works with binary data.

directory
A computer's filing system.

disk drive
A secondary storage device.

divide and conquer
A method of work in which a large task is divided into several smaller tasks that are more easily performed.

division by zero
A runtime error that occurs when the divisor is zero for integer divisions.

DOCTYPE
The document type definition statement usually placed on the first line of an HTML document.

document type definition (DTD)
The statement that identifies the version of HTML used in a document.

domain name
The phrase that identifies an internet protocol (IP) address.

domain name redirection
A service that forwards visitors to a single domain name location.

dot notation
A way of writing statements using dots (periods) to separate the name of a class variable referencing an object from the name of the method being called.

dual alternative decision structure
A decision structure that has two possible paths of execution— one path is taken if a condition is true and the other path is taken if the condition is false.

E

effective communication
Communication in which all participants understand the message.

effectiveness
A property of an algorithm that indicates that the steps can be accomplished without additional input.

element
An item that is stored in a list or array.

else suite
A block of statements that appears after an else clause.

em unit
A unit of measurement that is the width of a square block of type (typically the uppercase M) for a particular font and type size.

embedded styles
Formatting rules defined in the head section of a web page that apply to the entire web page.

employability
Having and using your life skills and abilities to be hired and stay hired.

empty input
An error that occurs when no data is entered for an input operation.

encapsulation
Combining data and code into a single object.

end symbol
In a flowchart, the terminal symbol that marks the program's ending point.

end tag
The code used to mark the end of an HTML container. Also called a closing tag.

end-line comment
A comment that appears at the end of a line of code.

escape character
A special character inside a string literal that is preceded by a backslash (\); when the string literal is printed, the escape characters are treated as a special command embedded in the string.

event
An action that affects program processing, such as a user action.

event handler
A module that executes when a specific event occurs.

event-driven
Any program action that responds to an event.

exception
An unexpected error that occurs while a program is running, causing the program to halt.

exception handler
Code that responds to exceptions when they are raised, and prevents the program from abruptly crashing.

exception object
An object created in memory when an exception is thrown that usually contains a default error message pertaining to the exception.

executing
When a computer is performing the tasks that a program tells it to do.

expression
A statement that represents a value or calls a procedure.

external documentation
Documentation designed for the user, such as a reference guide or tutorials.

external style sheet
A text file for storing style code, that is linked to a web page.

external styles
Style codes stored in a text file that is linked to web a page.

F

Fair Use Doctrine
The use of copyrighted material in a review, in research, in schoolwork, or in a professional publication, which does not necessarily require permission from the material's owner.

fetch-decode-execute cycle
The process in which a CPU executes the instructions in a program by reading an instruction (fetch), determining which operation to perform (decode), and performing the operation (execute).

fields
Variables, arrays, or other data structures that are stored in an object in object-oriented programming.

file extension
A short series of letters that indicate the application used to create the file and the file format, or file type.

file format
Standards that are used to write data to a disk so that the data can be read and used by a program.

file name
A series of characters that gives each file in a folder a unique name.

File Transfer Protocol (FTP)
A communications standard that enables computers to exchange files and folders over the internet.

file type
The format that identifies the application that can open a file, usually identified by the file extension.

finally suite
A block of statements that appears after a finally clause.

finiteness
A property of an algorithm that specifies when the algorithm will end.

firewall
A program that restricts unauthorized network access to a computer system.

flag
A variable that signals when some condition exists in the program.

flash drives
Inexpensive, reliable, and small storage devices that use flash memory and a USB connection.

flash memory
Storage medium that has no moving parts and stores data in electronic cells.

float
A data type for real numbers that include a fractional part.

floating-point notation
An encoding scheme computers use to store real numbers in memory.

flowchart
A graphical representation of an algorithm or other step-by-step process.

font
A set of characters that have the same style.

format specifier
A specifier that causes a placeholder's value to be formatted when it is displayed.

formatted string literal
A type of string literal that allows you to format values in a variety of ways.

fraud
A crime in which deception is used for financial or personal gain.

freeware
Copyrighted software that the copyright owner gives away for free on the condition that users do not resell it.

f-string
A type of string literal that allows you to format values in a variety of ways.

function
A piece of prewritten code that performs an operation.

function body
The section of a function definition comprised of the statements that are executed when the function is called.

function header
The first line of a function definition.

function prototype
In C++ (and some other languages), a statement that declares the existence of a function, but does not define the function, so the compiler knows that the function exists.

G

Gantt chart
A horizontal bar chart developed by Henry L. Gantt in 1917 that shows a graphical illustration of a schedule.

garbage collection
A process the Python interpreter uses to automatically remove a value from memory when that value is no longer referenced by a variable.

garbage in, garbage out (GIGO)
A saying used to indicate that computer output is only as good as the input provided.

global constant
A global name that references a value that cannot be changed.

global variable
A variable that can be accessed by any statement in a program file, including the statements in any function.

goal
Something you are trying to achieve.

graphical user interface (GUI)
An interface that accepts user input through graphical elements on the screen, such as windows, buttons, icons, and menus.

greatest common divisor (GCD)
The largest number that can divide two (or more) integers.

H

hand tracing
A debugging exercise in which you step through each of the program's statements one by one. Also called desk checking

handler
Code designed to focus on a specific type of data or task, such as an event handler or an exception handler.

hard skills
Skills used for a specific job that do not transfer to other jobs.

hardware
The physical parts of a computer.

head element
HTML code that defines the head section for a web page.

head section
In HTML, the section within the HTML element that describes the web page document.

heading elements
In HTML, the tags used to define six levels of headings for a web page.

heuristic solutions
Solutions that cannot be reached through a direct set of steps, like an algorithm, but require critical thinking or experience.

hexadecimal color values
Six-digit codes used to define color using red, green, and blue. The first two digits represent the intensity of red, the second two are green, and the last two are blue.

hierarchical
Multilevel organization, usually arranged in order of rank.

hierarchy chart
A chart used to illustrate a hierarchical relationship. Also called a hierarchy chart. Also called a structure chart.

high-level language
A programming language that uses words that are easy to understand, allowing the creation of complex programs without large numbers of low-level instructions.

horizontal rule element
HTML code for displaying a horizontal line on a web page.

Hypertext Markup Language (HTML)
The code that describes the format, layout, and structure of a document for publication on the web.

HTML element
Coding near the top of a document that specifies that the document is formatted using HTML.

HTML validation
A system for checking HTML code to make sure it does not contain syntax errors.

hyperlink
HTML code that formats content on a web page as a link to a destination location; when the link is activated, the destination is displayed.

I

identity theft
The fraudulent use of a person's personal information.

IDLE
The integrated development learning environment included with Python.

if statement
A single alternative decision structure that executes the statement following the if clause if the condition is true.

if-else statement
A dual alternative decision structure that executes the statement following the if clause if the condition is true and the statement following the else clause if the condition is false.

image link
A graphic on a web page that is formatted as a hyperlink.

immutable
Unchangeable.

import
In Python, a keyword used to make code from one module available in another module.

imported styles
CSS styles that are imported from one style sheet into another style sheet.

increment
To increase a value.

increment expression
In a For loop, a statement that executes at the end of each iteration and increments a loop's counter variable.

index
In Python, an operator that refers to an element by its position within the list.

ineffective communication
Communication in which participants to not understand the message as it is intended.

infinite loop
A loop that continues to repeat until the program is interrupted.

informational interview
An interview at a company or organization to learn about career opportunities.

initiator
A person who starts a learning event, such as a discussion or activity.

initialization
Assigning a value to a variable in the declaration statement.

initialization expression
In a For loop, a statement that executes once at the start in order to set the counter to its starting value.

initialization list
A series of values, separated by commas, used to initialize an array.

initializer method
A method that initializes an object's data attributes.

inline styles
CSS styles that are coded in the body of the web page as an attribute of an HTML tag.

input
Data the computer collects from people and from other devices.

input device
A computer component, or peripheral device, that collects data and sends it to the computer.

input error
An error that occurs when a user enters an invalid value.

input symbols
The symbol used in a flowchart to identify when input is received; usually a parallelogram.

input validation
A process a program can follow to reject invalid input and accept valid input.

instance
In object-oriented programming, an object created based on an existing class.

instance attributes
In object-oriented programming, attributes that belong to a specific instance.

instance fields
Non-static fields that belong to a specific instance of a class.

instance methods
A non-static method intended to work on an instance of the class in which it is defined.

instruction set
The entire set of instructions that a CPU can execute.

integer
A data type for whole numbers.

integer division
A behavior of many programming languages in which an integer divided by an integer results in an integer. This can lead to errors if the programmer expects the result to be a data type other than integer.

integrated development environment
A single program that provides all of the tools necessary to write, execute, and test a program.

intellectual property
Creative, literary, or artistic work.

intellectual property agreement
A legal contract between or among various parties for the purchase and sale of intellectual property rights.

interactive mode
One of two operating modes, in which the Python interpreter waits for the programmer to type Python statements.

internal documentation
Comments written for human readers in a program's code that are ignored by the compiler or interpreter.

internship
A position in a company in which you learn while you work.

interpreter
A program that translates and executes the instructions in a high-level language program.

IPO chart
A chart that programmers use to describe the input, processing, and output of a function.

"I" statement
A strategy for effective communication in which the speaker presents information from their point of view.

iterable
An object that holds a series of values that can be iterated over and over.

iteration
The execution of the body of a loop.

iterative
A description of a repetitive process.

J

JavaScript
An object-based client-side scripting language that can be interpreted by a web browser.

job application
A standard form filled out when applying for a job.

job leads
Opportunities for employment.

job search resources
Resources that help identify job leads, including networking, online resources, career counselors, employment agencies, and job fairs.

K

keyword
Reserved words that have special meaning to the interpreter, and therefore cannot be used as an identifier, such as a variable name.

keyword argument
In Python, an argument written in accordance with syntax to specify which parameter variable an argument should be passed to.

knowledge base
A store of information or data a person or system can draw on.

L

leader
A type of manager who knows how to use available resources to help others achieve their goals.

learner
A person who is working to learn a new subject or skill.

learning community
A group of students, educators, and professionals who work together and support each other to achieve academic goals.

lexical error
An error that occurs due to a typing mistake such as a misspelling or invalid character that the interpreter does not recognize.

library
A collection of functions that have already been written and are available for use.

library functions
Functions stored in a library.

line break element
HTML code that causes the browser to advance content to the next line.

line comments
Comments that occupy a single line, and explain a short section of the program.

line continuation character
A character used to break a statement into multiple lines. In Python, it is a backslash (\).

list
In Python, a mutable comma-separated sequence of data items that are enclosed in a set of brackets.

local variable
A variable that can be used only within the function in which it is created.

location sensor
A component in a device that can determine the device's latitude, longitude, and nearest street address.

logic error
A mistake that does not prevent the program from running, but causes it to produce incorrect results.

logical operators
Operators used to create complex Boolean expressions.

loop
A repetition structure used to make the computer repeat code as many times as necessary.

loop header
The first line of a loop.

loosely-typed language
A flexible language that allows you to store data in variables without explicitly declaring the data type of the variable.

low-level language
A programming language that uses instructions that a computer can recognize without a compiler or interpreter.

M

machine language
Code that consists of binary or hexadecimal instructions.

magic number
An unexplained value that appears in a program's code.

main memory
The primary memory where the computer stores a program and the program's data while that program is running.

main module
A module required by many programming languages; it is the program's starting point and usually calls other modules.

mainline logic
The overall logic of a program.

maintenance
Periodic program modifications to correct logic errors, improve performance, and provide a better experience for the user.

manual accessibility testing
The process of examining web pages to make sure they meet all accessibility requirements.

markup language
A programming language that tells software that retrieves and renders web content how to display and manage a web document.

math expression
A mathematical statement that has at least two terms containing numbers or variables, or both, connected by an operator that performs a calculation and returns a value.

math operator
A symbol that identifies the mathematical operation you want to perform.

members
Fields and methods that belong to a class.

memory sticks
A type of inexpensive, reliable, and small USB secondary storage device.

mentor
A person who supports, encourages, and teaches someone with less experience.

meta element
HTML code in the head section that describes a characteristic of a web page, such as the character encoding.

metadata
Data about other data.

method
A function that belongs to an object and performs some operation on that object.

method body
A collection of statements that are performed when the method is executed.

method header
The line that appears at the beginning of a method definition.

microprocessors
The integrated circuits that perform all the functions of a central processing unit.

MIME type
The multipurpose internet mail extensions that identify a media file's file format.

mixed-type expression
An expression that uses operands of different data types.

mnemonics
In programming, short words used in place of binary numbers.

modularized program
A program that has been written with each task in its own function.

module definition
The code that defines the header (starting point) and body (statements that will execute) of a module.

modules
In Python, files that hold related functions, stored in the library, and copied to your computer when you install Python.

modulus operator
A mathematical operator that performs division, but instead of returning the quotient, it returns the remainder. In Python, it is the % symbol.

multifactor authentication
Two or more verification factors required to access a resource such as a website, account, or device.

multiline string
A string on more than one line.

mutable
Changeable.

mutator method
In Python, a method that stores a value in a data attribute or changes the value of a data attribute in some other way.

N

named constant
A name that represents a special value.

navigation tracking
A technique websites and browsers use to gather data on your browsing and shopping habits.

negative space
Empty space above and below a block of text.

nested decision structure
A decision structure with a sequence structure inside it.

nested function
A function that you define inside another function.

nested loop
A loop inside another loop.

netiquette
Rules for acceptable online behavior.

networking
Sharing information about yourself and your career goals with personal contacts that might be able to help you identify career opportunities.

newline character
A command that instructs the computer to start a new line of output.

non-branching
A problem that is strictly sequential and therefore does not require condition evaluation in order to go through the steps to a solution.

nondegree certificate
A certificate program that allows you to learn skills that may help advance your career without attending a college or university.

non-disclosure agreement (NDA)
A contract that prohibits the signee from sharing proprietary information.

non-iterative
A process where you put in the effort of designing up-front, so when you finally create and test the algorithm, it works as intended.

non-static
A type of class field that belongs to a particular object.

nonverbal communication
Communication that consists of visual and physical messages that the receiver can see, such as a smile.

nonvolatile memory
Memory that stores data permanently, even when the power to the computer is off.

numeric
A data type for numbers or amounts used in calculations.

numeric literal
A number that is written into a program's code.

O

object
A software entity that contains both data and procedures.

object code
Source code translated by a compiler into binary form so it can be read and acted on by a computer.

object reusability
A practice in object-oriented programming in which objects are reused in any program where they are needed.

objective
A short-term goal used to keep a project on track for completion. Also, a way of evaluating information fairly, without emotion or prejudice.

object-oriented programming (OOP)
A method of programming that provides rules for creating and managing objects.

off-by-one error
An error that occurs when a loop iterates one time too many or one time too few.

off-page connector symbol
In a flowchart, a "home plate" shape with a page number inside it indicating where to find the previous or next part of the flowchart.

online storage
Data that is stored and accessed on a remote internet server instead of on a local storage device. Sometimes called cloud storage.

opening tag
The code used to mark the start of an HTML container. Also called a start tag.

open-source software
A program that you may have to pay for, but for which the source code is available to the public.

operands
Values on the right and left of a mathematical operator.

operating system
The software instructions that control the internal operations of a computer's hardware.

operator
In programming, an object that can manipulate a value or other operator.

order of operations
The order in which mathematical calculations are performed.

ordered list
A list that is organized in a specific order.

output
Any data the computer produces for people or for other devices.

output device
Any piece of computer hardware that shows the result of computer processing.

output symbols.
The symbol used in a flowchart to identify when output is presented; usually a parallelogram.

P

package
A collection of one or more related modules.

packet sniffers
Programs that examine data streams on networks to try to find information, such as passwords and credit card numbers.

paragraph element
HTML code that groups sentences and sections of text together into a paragraph format.

parallel arrays
Two or more arrays that hold related data which is accessed using a common subscript.

parameter
A special variable that is assigned the value of an argument when a function is called. Also called a parameter variable.

parameter list
In Python, multiple parameter variable names separated by commas, that appear inside parentheses in a function header.

parameter variable
A special variable that is assigned the value of an argument when a function is called. Also called a parameter.

parameter_name
In Python, the name of a parameter variable.

passed by position
When arguments are passed to the corresponding parameter variables in a function, based on position.

passed by reference
When passing an argument, the function has access to the argument and makes changes to it.

passed by type
When arguments are passed to parameter variables based on corresponding type.

pass by value
A form of argument passing where a function cannot change the value of an argument that was passed to it.

passive speech
Deferential language that shows respect for others without stating individual opinions or needs.

passphrase
A security tool similar to a password that uses a string of words, not just characters.

patent
The exclusive right to make, use, or sell a device or process.

path
A string of characters used to identify the specific location of a folder or file within the directory system.

peripheral
Input, output, and storage devices that can be connected to a computer.

PERT chart
A project management tool developed by U.S. Navy in the 1950s, which shows project tasks, the order in which they must be completed, and the time requirements. Stands for Program Evaluation Review Technique.

phishing
A scheme in which criminals try to lure victims into giving them user names, passwords, bank account numbers, or credit card details, usually by sending an email that looks like it comes from an official and legitimate source.

picture element
The basic logical unit in digital graphics, which are combined to form a complete image, video, text, or any visible thing on a computer display. Abbreviated as pixel.

pixel
The basic logical unit in digital graphics, which are combined to form a complete image, video, text, or any visible thing on a computer display. Abbreviation for picture element.

plagiarism
The unauthorized use of another person's ideas or creative work without giving that person credit.

polymorphism
In object-oriented programming, the ability of an object to take different forms.

portfolio
A collection of information and documents that demonstrate your academic and career skills and achievements.

postfix mode
When increment and decrement operators are written after (to the right of) their operands.

posttest loop
A loop that tests its condition after an iteration is performed.

precedence
Priority in terms of importance or order.

prefix mode
When increment and decrement operators are written before (to the left of) their operands.

pretest loop
A loop that tests its condition before an iteration is performed.

primary memory
The main memory where the computer stores a program and the program's data while that program is running. Also called main memory or primary storage.

priming read
In an input validation loop, the first input operation designed to get the first input value that will be tested by the validation loop.

primitive
A designation meaning common or basic used for certain variables or data types, such as integer or float.

prioritize
Decide which tasks must be completed first.

private
In object-oriented programming, data attributes that can only be accessed by an object's methods.

private methods
In object-oriented programming, methods which can only be accessed in the class in which they are declared.

problem
Any barrier or obstacle between you and a goal.

problem domain
A set of real-world objects, parties, and major events related to a problem.

procedural programming
A method of programming that uses step-by-step instructions to tell a computer what to do.

procedure
A function that performs a specific task.

processing
The action of a computer executing the instructions in a program.

processing symbol
The symbol used in a flowchart to identify when the program is performing a process on data; usually a parallelogram.

productivity
A measurement of the amount of work accomplished.

professionalism
The ability to show respect to everyone around you while you perform your responsibilities to the best of your ability.

program
A set of instructions that a computer follows to perform a task.

program development cycle
The process of creating a computer program including designing, writing, testing, and correcting errors.

programmer
A person with the training and skills necessary to design, create, and test computer programs.

programming language
A set of instructions and rules used to create software programs.

programming style
Conventions used to keep code organized and easier to read.

programs
Algorithms customized to do a specific task.

project management
A process used to take a project from conception to completion.

prompt
A message that instructs the user to enter input.

propaganda
Misleading information.

property
A value that modifies the way an element functions or appears.

property window
In a GUI, an area on-screen that displays all the properties associated with a specific component.

proprietary information
Legally protected information such as copyrighted code, that is generally not available to the public, that has some degree of uniqueness, and that requires cost or effort to develop.

protocol
The rules that define how data is transmitted and formatted between computers.

pseudocode
An informal language that has no syntax rules and is used to design programs not meant to be compiled or executed.

pseudorandom numbers
Numbers that appear random but are really produced from a starting set that is repeated over and over.

public domain software
Software that the developers or authors allow others to use, copy, share, and even alter for free.

public methods
Methods that can be accessed by entities outside the object.

Python interpreter
A program that can read Python programming statements and execute them.

Python program
A computer program written in Python and saved in a file with a .py extension.

Python script
A collection of commands in a file designed to be executed like a Python program.

Python shell
The Python interpreter running in interactive mode.

Q

query processor
A program that creates an ordered list of pages that hit on keywords in a search query.

R

random-access memory (RAM)
Type of volatile primary memory that stores data and instructions while the computer is working.

read-only memory (ROM)
Type of nonvolatile primary memory that stores instructions for starting the computer.

real number
A number that includes a fractional part.

reference materials
Documentation, guides, tutorials, knowledge bases, and other sources of information that users can access to learn about a program.

references
When a variable represents a value stored in the computer's memory.

relational operator
An operator that determines whether a specific relationship exists between two values.

relative hyperlink
A hyperlink destination that is defined relative to the page currently being displayed.

remainder operator
The operator that performs division, but instead of returning the quotient, it returns the remainder. In Python, it is called the modulus operator.

repetition operator
An operator that makes multiple copies of a list and joins them all together.

repetition structure
A structure in which code for a sequence is repeated as many time as necessary.

reserved words
Words that have special meaning to the interpreter, and therefore cannot be used as an identifier, such as a variable name. Also called keywords.

responsibilities
Things others expect you to do or to accomplish. In Python, the things a class is responsible for knowing (data attributes) and the actions the class is responsible for doing (methods).

resume
A written summary of your work-related skills, experience, and education.

return
When, at the end of a block in a function, the interpreter jumps back to the part of the program that called the function and the program resumes execution from that point.

return point
A location stored in memory that a program returns to after executing the statements in a module.

root directory
A main storage location.

running
When a computer is performing the tasks that a program tells it to do.

running total
A total that accumulates as each number in the series is read.

runtime errors
Errors that cause a program to terminate abnormally.

S

scanning
A method hackers use to gain access to a system by trying many different passwords until one works.

scope
In programming, the part of a program in which a variable may be accessed.

script mode
In Python, the mode in which the interpreter reads the contents of a file that contains Python statements.

search algorithm
A process for locating a specific item in a larger collection of data.

search engine optimization (SEO)
The process of designing web pages for optimal ranking by search engines.

secondary memory
Memory that can hold data for long periods of time, even when there is not power to the computer. Also called secondary storage.

secondary storage
Secondary memory.

Section 508 of the Rehabilitation Act
A section of Federal law that requires electronic and information technology to be accessible to people with disabilities.

Secure Sockets Layer (SSL)
A protocol that allows data to be exchanged privately over public networks.

secondary memory
Memory that can hold data for long periods of time, even when there is no power to the computer. Also knows as secondary storage.

seed value
A value used to initialize a formula that generates random numbers. Also called a random seed.

selection structure
A logical design that controls the order in which a set of statements execute. Also called a decision structure.

selector
The part of each CSS style rule that tells the browser what HTML elements to select so the rule can be applied to them.

self-contained tag
In HTML, a tag with no closing tag. Also called a stand-alone tag.

sentinel
A special value that marks the end of a list of items.

sequence
An ordered set of logical steps. In Python, a sequence is a collection of items in a set order.

sequence structure
A set of statements that execute in the order in which they appear.

sequential search algorithm
A search algorithm that uses a loop to step through an array from beginning to end, stopping when it finds a match.

serializing
In Python, converting an object to a stream of bytes that can be saved to a file for later retrieval.

server
A computer that manages data and programs used on a network.

shareware
Copyrighted software that you can use for free on a try-before-you-buy basis. If you decide to keep it, you must pay a fee.

short-circuit evaluation
A technique used with Boolean operators in which evaluation is stopped as soon as the first condition which satisfies or negates the expression is found.

single alternative decision structure
A decision structure that provides only one alternative path of execution.

size declarator
A declaration that specifies the number of values that an array can hold.

slice
A span of items that are taken from a sequence.

social engineering
A tactic used to try to influence and change societal behaviors. In cybercrime, it is used to trick people into clicking a link that will install a virus or capture your personal information.

software
A set of instructions that a computer follows to perform a task.

software developer
A person with the training and skills necessary to design, create, and test computer programs.

software development applications
Programs used to develop software.

software development tools
Programs and hardware that programmers use to create, modify, and test software.

software license
A legally binding agreement between a software producer and a user that specifies the terms of use and defines the rights of both parties.

software piracy
The act of enabling illegal access to software.

software requirement
A single task that the program must perform to satisfy the customer.

solid-state drives
A disk drive that stores data in solid-state memory. It has no moving parts and operates faster than a traditional disk drive.

solution
Actions for overcoming a challenge or problem.

source code
The software instructions that tell a computer what to do, written by a programmer in a high-level language.

spoof
To use a false Internet Protocol (IP) or email address to gain access to a device or account.

stale
A description of an item that is not updated when another item on which the first item's value depends is changed.

stand-alone tag
In HTML, a tag with no closing tag. Also called a self-contained tag.

standard library
A collection of prewritten commonly-used functions.

start symbol
In a flowchart, the terminal symbol that marks the program's starting point.

start tag
The code used to mark the start of an HTML container. Also called an opening tag.

state
In object-oriented programming, the characteristics or properties of an object.

statements
The individual instructions, consisting of keywords, operators, punctuation and other allowable programming elements, used to write a program in a high-level programming language.

step amount
The amount by which a counter variable is incremented in a For loop.

storage
Memory or a device where data and programs are kept so they can be used again in the future.

stream insertion operator
In C++, the << operator is used with a count statement to display data.

string
A sequence of characters that is used as data.

string concatenation operator
In Java, when the + operator is used with strings to append one string to another.

string literal
A string that appears in the actual code of a program.

strong password
A password that combines random characters and symbols and is difficult for others to guess.

strongly-typed language
A programming language that requires programmers to explicitly declare the type of data that will be stored in a variable.

structure
The logical design that controls the order in which a set of statements in a program executes.

structure chart
A chart used to illustrate a hierarchical relationship. Also called a hierarchy chart.

style conventions
Recommended guidelines and best practices for writing code.

subclass
In object-oriented programming, a specialized version of a class that inherits fields and methods from the superclass but can be customized.

subjective
A way of evaluating information while influenced by existing opinions, feelings, and beliefs.

subordinates
People you supervise.

subroutine
A named block of code.

subscript
A unique number assigned to each element in an array. Also called an index.

substring
A string that appears within other strings.

subtasks
Smaller tasks broken out of larger tasks to make a problem or project easier to complete.

superclass
In object-oriented programming, a general class from which a subclass can inherit fields and methods.

superzapper
A program that allows authorized users to access a network in an emergency situation by skipping security measures.

syntax
A set of rules that must be strictly followed when writing a program.

syntax error
A coding mistake, such as a misspelled keyword, a missing punctuation character, or the incorrect use of an operator that is detected by the interpreter.

system software
Programs that control and manage the basic operations of a computer.

T

tag
In HTML, code used for formatting web pages.

target variable
In Python, the variable that is used in the for clause that is the target of an assignment at the beginning of each loop iteration.

technical reading
A process that uses specific strategies such as highlighting and reviewing terminology to help readers understand technical writing.

technical writing
A process that uses specific writing strategies to convey technical information to a variety of people.

test expression
In a For loop, a Boolean expression that repeats the body of the loop as long as the expression is true.

terminal symbols
The ovals, which appear at the top (starting point) and bottom (ending point) of the flowchart.

third-party modules
Python modules written by independent programmers that can be downloaded to provide capabilities that the standard Python library does not offer.

time bomb
A program that sits on a computer or network system until a certain event or set of circumstances activates it.

time management
The process of organizing a schedule to allow time to complete tasks and meet responsibilities.

tokenizing
The process of breaking a string into tokens.

top-down design
A technique for breaking down an algorithm into functions.

traceback
An error message that provides information about an exception error, such as the line number where the error occurred.

trademark
A symbol that indicates that a brand or brand name is legally protected and cannot be used by other businesses.

transcript
A record of the courses a student takes in high school and the grade earned in each course.

transferable skills
Skills such as problem solving and critical thinking that can be used in many careers and situations.

Transport Layer Security (TLS)
A protocol that allows encrypted, secure communication between a web browser and a web server.

trap door
A system vulnerability that is well-hidden and provides access to a computer or network.

Trojan horse
A program designed to infiltrate a computer or network and damage or delete data.

traverse
A method of iterating over a set of data, such as a list or array, in order to locate individual elements in the set.

truncate
To shorten by cutting off the end; in programming it means to remove characters from the right end of some data types, such as digits from a float or characters from a string.

try suite
One or more statements that can potentially raise an exception.

tuple
In Python, an immutable comma-separated sequence of data items.

turtle graphics
A method for creating vector graphics using a cursor (called a turtle) on a canvas, included with Python.

two's complement
An encoding scheme computers use to store negative numbers in memory.

typography
The style or arrangement of text.

U

Unicode
An extensive encoding scheme that is compatible with ASCII, but can also represent characters and symbols for many languages.

Unified Modeling Language (UML)
A standard language for modeling real-world objects when designing object-oriented programs.

uninitialized variable
A variable that has been declared, but has not been initialized or assigned a value.

unordered list
A list that can be displayed in any order.

usability
A measure of how easy, efficient, and pleasant it is for a person to use technology.

USB drive
A small storage device that uses flash memory and connects to the computer through a USB port.

user interface
A means for users to control, operate, or interact with technology.

user interface flow diagram
A chart that illustrates the relationship, or flow, between elements of a user interface.

utility program
A program that performs a specialized task that enhances the computer's operation or safeguards data.

V

value-returning function
A function that executes the statements that it contains then returns a value back to the statement that called it.

variable
A name that represents a value in the computer's memory.

variable declaration
A statement that specifies a variable's name and data type.

verbal communication
The exchange of messages by speaking or writing.

virtual private network (VPN)
A network that uses encryption technology to make a public network, like the internet, more secure.

virus
A program designed to infiltrate computers and damage or delete data.

void function
A function that executes the statements it contains and then terminates.

volatile
A type of memory that is used only for temporary storage while a program is running.

W

Web Content Accessibility Guidelines (WCAG 2.1)
A set of standards for ensuring that web pages are accessible to all users.

web host provider
A company that provides a storage location for website files to make them available on the internet.

white space
Blank space used as an element of design in graphics or on a web page.

whitespacing
Leaving blank lines in code in order to make the code easier to read.

widget
A small program or component, written in a language such as JavaScript, that can be embedded as an element on a web page.

wireframe
A diagram used to illustrate the components of a web page.

work ethics
Beliefs and behaviors about what is right and wrong in a work environment.

worm
A program designed to infiltrate computers and damage or delete data.

wrap around
When an integer is too large or too small to fit within the range specified for the data type.

WYSIWYG
Sophisticated web page authoring tools that automatically apply HTML code. An acronym for "What You See Is What You Get."

I Index